TRUE TALES OF THE WEST

CASTLE

TABLE OF CONTENTS

1

The Last War for the Cattle Range

Arthur Chapman

THE LAST WAR FOR THE CATTLE RANGE

By ARTHUR CHAPMAN

EVER since the first herd of cattle began to find sustenance on the plains of the Far West, white men have been fighting among themselves for possession of the range. It was only yesterday that the settler who dared fence in a water hole, or to stake out a homestead on any choice feeding-ground, did so at his peril. If the story of all the range wars and duels and assassinations could be written, it would be shown that the long struggle for the great stretches of plain, from the Rio Grande to the Canadian line, has cost the country more of its best fighting blood than the Spanish-American war. Cowboys, sheep-herders and ranchmen have been the victims. The ranchmen have died fighting for land they deemed theirs by right; the others have given their lives rather than see a coveted bit of public grazing fatten an enemy's stock.

The Wyoming cattle war of 1892 makes one of the most dramatic pages of frontier history. To this day it is called the Rustler War because of the widespread impression at the time that the fight was between the virtuous owners of cattle on one side and an organized community of cattle thieves, or "rustlers" on the other. But never was anything more misnamed. To be sure there were cattle rustlers in Northern Wyoming, and there is no doubt that they had become exceptionally bold. But it is doubtful if, outside of Wall Street, there has ever been a more lawless business than the old-time cattle business, since the world began. When the great cattle trails were opened, some cattle owners started with a small herd at one end of a trail and arrived at the other with thousands of strange beeves that had been "picked up" on the way. Some of these men became cattle kings, and built grand houses, in which they were always uncomfortable, and even went to the Legislature or to Congress. Beside them the rustler, who stole a few paltry head of cattle, must always remain a rather pitiable figure.

Considering the Wyoming cattle war from an unprejudiced view-point, it appears that the rustler merely figured as an excuse. The main object of the cattle owners who invaded Northern Wyoming with a half-hundred professional man-killers seems to have been to drive out the small ranchers. Some of the men who had taken up homesteads in the heart of the cattle country were to be killed, and life was to be made so miserable for the others that they would take down their fences and decamp, and the threatened disintegration of the great cattle herds would be postponed indefinitely. Had this plan been successfully carried out in Johnson County, no doubt it would have been made effective in other parts of the West where the settler was getting too strong a foothold. The cowboy would have been living his picturesque life on the open range to-day, but the growth of the agricultural West would have been set back a generation.

For several months prior to the spring of 1892 the country was regaled with stories about the wholesale depredations of cattle rustlers in Northern Wyoming, and in Johnson County in particular. The cattle of many big outfits had long thrived on the Johnson County range, which swept eastward from the base of the Big Horn mountains. It was claimed that the rustlers had effected an organization, and virtually ruled the county, so that it was impossible to secure a conviction for stealing cattle, even when the thief confessed his guilt. There is no doubt that bold work in rustling had been carried on, but the cattlemen made the mistake of confounding the innocent with the guilty. Their live-stock inspectors found many stolen cattle shipped to Eastern markets, and these, under the laws of the state, were confiscated and sold to the highest bidder, the money being held to await proof of brand ownership. Thousands of dollars of this fund were never claimed.

But instead of fighting the rustlers in the

3

"Arapahoe" Brown, who led the settlers in the siege of the T. A. ranch.

open, the cattlemen took to methods that were calculated to stir a community to righteous indignation. A series of assassinations began, and, while the perpetrators were never caught, the inference that the stock interests were concerned was too plain to be disregarded. The first lynchings took place in the summer of 1889, when "Jim" Averill, a small rancher in the Sweetwater country, and his neighbor, "Cattle Kate" (Ella Watson), were accused of rustling. Ten men rode up to their ranches and hanged the man and the woman. Nothing ever came of the indictments which were found against several men for complicity in the affair. In 1891 "Tom" Waggoner, who was accused of rustling horses, was hanged near Newcastle, Wyoming. Later in the same year an attempt was made to lynch "Nate" Champion and Ross Gilbertson, two alleged rustlers, on the Powder River in Johnson

County. The men were asleep in their bunk, when the door was swung open and several men fired upon them. Champion, who showed his bravery a few months later when he met his fate at the hands of invading cattlemen, sprang from the bed and emptied his revolver at his assailants, who fled in terror. A bloody tarpaulin was found near the cabin, and it is believed that Champion killed one of the would-be lynchers.

In November, 1891, two men who had been "blackballed" as rustlers, were assassinated. One was "Ranger" Jones, who was killed while crossing Muddy Creek, fifteen miles south of Buffalo, the county seat of Johnson County. Jones was shot three times by somebody in ambush. Two days later J. A. Tisdale, while on his way to his home, sixty miles from Buffalo, was also shot from ambush, only a few miles from the spot where "Ranger" Jones met his fate. Whether theirs was the responsibility or not, these deeds of violence did not aid the cause of the stock owners. The bitterness against the cattlemen increased, and certain stockmen, as they afterward claimed, were compelled to leave Johnson County under cover of darkness and on fast horses, while their herds fell prey to the rustlers.

Cheyenne was the headquarters of the cattle owners, and here a wholesale plan of extermination was arranged. A small army of determined men was to be raised, Johnson County was to be invaded, and the leading rustlers were to be killed. Such was the statement of one of the leaders of the invasion, made to a Denver newspaper reporter, after the whole wretched affair had ended. The "small army" materialized into about fifty men, mostly Texans, who had been induced to come along with the understanding that they were to get big pay for having a gunpowder lark. These Texans were cowboys who were never averse to unsheathing a gun, be their quarrel just or unjust. On April 6, 1892, this command, fully equipped with tents, provisions, medicine chest, etc., and each man armed with a rifle and a brace of revolvers, left Cheyenne by rail for Casper, which was reached about daylight the next morning. From Casper the command began the march to Buffalo, about one hundred miles across the brown Wyoming hills.

Before reaching Powder River, some fifty miles south of Buffalo, word was brought to the invaders that there were rustlers at the K. C. ranch. This ranch was on Powder River, at the foothills of the Big Horn mountains. It was claimed that the Powder River country was notorious for the number of rustlers it sheltered, so the invaders supposed that many "blackballed" men could be killed at this ranch. It happened, however, that most of the K. C. cowboys were on round-up work, and only "Nate" Champion, "Nick" Ray and two trappers who had stayed over night, were in the cabin. The invaders surrounded the place and, when a man stepped out of the house after a bucket of water, he was quietly captured. Then another man came out, and he, too, was captured. Nick Ray then stepped out of the door, and he was fired upon, falling a few feet from the cabin, mortally wounded. Champion rushed from the house, caught up Ray, and carried the wounded man inside amid a hail of bullets. He then barred the doors and windows and began one of the most remarkable sieges in the history of the West.

The invaders kept up a constant fire on the cabin all day long. Champion's reputation as a dead shot was so well known, however, that the assailants kept carefully under cover. Champion fired methodically from loopholes on every side of the house, but found time to take good care of his dying comrade, and also to write a memorandum of affairs of the day. This memorandum, which was found on Champion's body after the fight was over, stamps the man as one of the bravest and coolestheaded men in the history of Cattle Land. The diary, which was roughly scrawled in pencil, read as follows:

"Me and Nick was getting breakfast when the attack took place. Two men were here with us—Bill Jones and another man. The old man went after water and did not come back. His friend went out to see what was the matter and he did not come back. Nick started out and I told him to look out, that I thought there was someone at the stable and would not let them come back. Nick is shot, but not dead yet. He is awful sick. I must go and wait on him. It is now about two hours since the first shot. Nick is still alive. They are shooting and are all around the house. Boys, there is bullets coming in like hail. Them fellows is in such shape I can't get at them. They are shooting from the stable and river, and back of the house. Nick is dead, he died about 9 o'clock. I see a smoke down at the stable. I think they have fired it. I don't think they intend to let me get away this time.

"It is now about noon. There is someone at the stable yet. They are throwing a rope out at the door and drawing it back. I guess it is to draw me out. I wish that duck would get out further so I could get a shot at him. Boys, I don't know what they have done with them two fellows that staid here last night. Boys, I feel pretty lonesome just now. I wish there was someone here with me so we could watch all sides at once. They may fool around here until I get a good shot before they leave.

"It is about 3 o'clock now. There was a man in a buckboard and one on horseback just passed. They fired on them as they went by. I don't know if they killed them or not. I seen lots of men come out on horses on the other side of the river and take after them. I shot at the men in the stable just now. Don't know if I got any or not. I must go and look out again. It don't look as if there is much show of my getting away. I see twelve or fifteen men. One looks like (here a name was scratched out). I don't know whether it is or not. I hope they did not catch them fellows that ran over the bridge toward Smith's. They are shooting at the house now. If I had a pair of glasses I believe I would know some of those men. They are coming back. I've got to look out.

"Well, they have just got through shelling the house like hail. I heard them splitting wood. I guess they are going to fire the house to-night. I think I will make a break when night comes, if I am alive. Shooting again. I think they will fire the house this time. It's not night yet. The house is all fired. Good bye, boys, if I never see you again.

"NATHAN D. CHAMPION."

In the final entry, about firing the house, Champion referred to the action of the invaders in rolling a wagon, loaded with blazing pitch, pine wood and hay, to the side of the cabin. Soon the building was in flames and Champion, with a rifle in his hand and a revolver in his belt, ran out of the house toward a gulch to the south. He ran directly toward two of the best shots among the invaders, and, blinded by smoke, saw his enemies too late. A bullet shattered the arm that bore the Winchester, and, before Champion could draw his revolver, another bullet had found his heart. As he lay at the mouth of the gulch, where he had sought safety, a card was pinned to Champion's breast, reading: "Cattle thieves beware!" His personal effects were not touched and his diary was left intact, save for the scratching out of the name of one of the invaders. Then, elated at having killed the "bravest man in Johnson County," as one of their own number afterward termed Champion, and leaving Ray's body to be consumed in the burning cabin, the invaders continued their march toward Buffalo.

But the alarm had been spread, and the invasion was no longer a triumphal procession. In Champion's diary reference is made to two men, one on horseback and one in a wagon, who came past the cabin and who were fired upon and pursued by the invaders, but who escaped to the north. They were "Jack" Flagg and his son, the former being the owner of the J. F. brand—a brand that was to the eyes of a big stockowner what a red rag is to the eyes of a bull. Flagg was a schoolteacher and was also one of the leaders of the alleged rustlers. His escape carried consternation to the raiders, for they knew Flagg would lose no time in arousing the whole country-side. A forced march was made, but, about daybreak the next morning, after the party had traveled fifty miles toward Buffalo in a roundabout way, information was brought that a large party of cowboys and settlers had left the county seat to head off the invaders. Plans were changed, and about noon the command arrived at the T. A. ranch, on Crazy Woman Creek, twelve miles south of Buffalo. Here the invaders turned in and fortified the place. The house, stable and ice-house all being built of stout logs, formed natural forts. Breastworks of logs were built on either side of the house, loopholes were cut in all the buildings, and earthworks were thrown up. The place was practically impregnable against a rifle attack, and the only thing that worried the invaders was the capture of their two supply wagons containing provisions, powder and other supplies.

Hardly had the invading party completed its defenses, when the T. A. ranch was completely surrounded by angry residents of Johnson County, who had heard of the killing of Champion and Ray, and who were bent on vengeance. Cowboys, settlers, and citizens of Buffalo flocked to the scene, each man armed with rifle and revolvers. Dust-covered men kept arriving, some of them having ridden two hundred miles, all eager to fight the cattlemen and their "Hessians from Texas." Soon there were nearly four hundred men surrounding the ranch, every besieger being a trained and fearless fighter. There were some notorious rustlers in the party, and a few cowboys who were in the fight "just for the fun of the thing," but most of the men who surrounded the ranch were settlers who considered they were doing their duty in repelling an unlawful and unwarranted invasion. Thus, almost in a twinkling, had the situation of the invaders changed. The rosy picture of a triumphal march through a terror-stricken community faded away, and the men behind the stout logs of the T. A. ranch began to wonder how they were to get out of their predicament. One of their men, a Texan named Dudley, had been thrown from a bucking horse just before the arrival of the invaders at the ranch, and his revolver was discharged, the bullet breaking the man's leg. Dudley suffered tortures during the siege, and died later, at Fort McKinney.

The besiegers were soon under the direction of one of those natural military geniuses that always seem to arise in case of necessity on the frontier. A stalwart settler, "Arapahoe" Brown, one of the most picturesque characters Wyoming has ever known, was tacitly recognized as commander of the besieging forces. Brown, who was sometime afterward murdered by two of his own cowboys, was not only a man who dearly loved a fight but he was a strategist as well. The ranch buildings lay in a hollow, the top of the surrounding hills being four hundred yards away. On the ridge Brown had rifle pits dug, and from these pits a constant fire was kept up. In order to prevent a possible dash, the horses of the invaders were killed in the corral. At night a fresh party of besiegers took the places of those who had been firing during the day, and vigilance was never relaxed.

"Arapahoe" Brown soon realized that there were only two ways to dislodge the invaders—by direct assault or by cannon. The first would prove too costly, as the cattlemen could simply mow down any attacking party before the stout doors of the ranch buildings could be forced. Brown, who was a blacksmith by trade, built a clumsy cannon out of gaspipe. At the first fire the thing exploded, and only the extreme caution of those who fired it prevented serious results to the besiegers. Then Brown built what he called a "go-devil." The running gears of the captured supply wagons were placed side by side, and to the rear of the wagons was lashed a breastwork of logs over six feet high. There was room behind the breastwork for forty men, while five more could propel the strange device forward. The breastwork was provided with portholes, and it was Brown's plan to move it to the log fort and destroy that stronghold by giant powder. Then the ranch buildings would be likewise destroyed and the invaders forced out in the open. While this "go-devil" was being built, some daring cowboys rode to Fort McKinney, fifteen miles away, where a garrison of United States troops was stationed, and actually tried to take a cannon from the fort under the very nose of the commandant.

For two days the siege had kept up, a constant fire being maintained on both sides. Such was the terrible earnestness of both parties that the cattlemen did not think of asking for quarter, and the besiegers did not send in a request for surrender. It was to be a battle to the death, unless ended by outside interference. This interference came when least expected. Word of the plight of the invaders had been sent to Cheyenne from Buffalo, and soon Acting Governor Amos W. Barber was in telegraphic communication with President Harrison, urging that soldiers be sent from Fort McKinney to rescue the cattlemen. Early in the morning of April 13th, the third day of the siege, Colonel J. J. Van Horn received orders to go to the rescue. The Colonel acted so promptly that he ar-

Barn on T. A. ranch, which was stoutly defended by the invaders.

rived on the scene with three troops of cavalry soon after sun-up. "Arapahoe" Brown's "go-devil" was just ready to move, sheltering a storming party, and in another hour much blood would have been spilled, as the first bomb thrown from this strange device would have forced the cattlemen into the open, even as their blazing load of pitch-pine blocks had forced brave "Nate" Champion to run to his death.

Major Frank Walcott, who was in command of the invaders, demanded the protection of Col. Van Horn, intimating that he would rather fight to the death than surrender to Sheriff Angus. It was proved, however, that he need have had no fear of violence at the hands of the besiegers in case of his surrender to them. One of the invaders had secreted himself in the loft of the ranch house, and at dark made his way

Buffalo, Wyo., when it was the headquarters of the rustlers in the Wyoming cattle war.

Corrals and Bunk House at T. A. ranch, where the invaders were besieged by settlers.

to the road. Here he took the wrong turn and walked toward Buffalo, being arrested by Sheriff Angus and put in jail. The prisoner looked for nothing short of lynching, but he was accorded good treatment. Governor Barber ordered that the man be turned over to Colonel Van Horn, and that officer asked Sheriff Angus if three troops of cavalry would be enough to take the invader safely away from the jail. The sheriff answered that if the military man wanted trouble he should send all the troops at his disposal, but if he wanted the prisoner, without any trouble, he should detail only one man. Accordingly a sergeant, in an open wagon, was sent for the prisoner. The funeral of Champion and Ray had just been held and Buffalo was filled with armed friends of the two murdered men. When the sergeant reached the jail he found two hundred cowboys and settlers lined up on either side of the door. Through this pathway of grim, silent men, he marched his trembling prisoner to the wagon and drove away to the fort, not a hand being raised to stay his progress. A better illustration of the self control of this community of alleged lawless "rustlers" could not have been given.

After remaining at Fort McKinney a few days the prisoners were ordered to Fort Russell, near Cheyenne. Through a blinding blizzard the invaders were escorted to Fort Fetterman and thence by rail to Cheyenne, no demonstration being made against them, though the air was full of rumors of intended ambushes.

The invaders were kept under a loose sort of surveillance until August, when their trial was begun. Great difficulty was experienced in getting a jury, and finally the men were released on their own recognizance, to appear for trial in January, at which time, on the ground of Johnson County's inability to pay the costs, the cases against them were dropped. By that time all Wyoming was glad to be relieved of a suit that was certain to prove long and costly and with little chance of justice being secured on either side.

It is impossible to find any justification for the acts of the cattlemen, even if Johnson County had been such a headquarters for rustlers as they claimed. One can travel the whole length of Johnson County to-day and fail to find a man who will say that "Nate" Champion was a rustler. I have talked with settlers who knew Champion—men whose sympathies lay with neither the cattle nor the rustler interests —and they unite in declaring that the man who made such a wonderful defense at the K. C. ranch was above suspicion. He held positions of trust with one of the largest cattle outfits in Johnson County, but he was never accused of any dealing that was not "square." It is safe to assume that no mere rustler would have shown Champion's wonderful nerve. A cattle thief is a coward, as a rule, and the man who wrote a diary when surrounded by enemies who were thirsting for his blood was anything but cowardly.

The long list of assassinations in Northern Wyoming must also tell against the cattle interests. Nor did this form of "clearing the range" cease when the Johnson County war was ended. It was not many months ago that Tom Horn, a stock detective, was hanged at Cheyenne for foolishly confessing that he had killed several persons—one of them a mere boy— obnoxious to the cattle interests in whose pay he was. In nearly every case the method of assassination was about the same as in the Johnson County cases, the victim being shot from ambush. Horn was known to have been in Northern Wyoming at the time of the outbreak of the cattle war, under the name of Tom Hale. Many people in Johnson County now believe that he was the man who killed Jones and Tisdale, although another employee of the cattle interests was at the time accused of the work.

But the cattlemen made a fatal mistake when they assumed that either assassination or invasion would "clean out" the range of settlers. Civilization was pressing from all sides. It was the dusk of the gods for the cattle kings, who had known a power that was too great to last in a non-feudal age. But it was hard to convince the men who had made easy fortunes that the twilight of their supremacy had come. They were sure they could restore the golden times when the old 76, the Cross-H, the Bar-C and other outfits were in their glory, and when their bunk-houses were filled with the sinewy men who neither knew nor cared for anything but the cow-man's work and the cow-man's primitive pleasures.

Nor can the excuse of wholesale cattle rustling cover the stock interests' crimes of assassination and invasion. One stock owner, at the time of the Johnson County war, gave out an interview in which he estimated that 10,000 head of cattle had been rustled from the range. But if this were a fact, the stockmen had none but themselves to blame. They made every state law, and saw that each was made in their own favor. Even the estray law, of which so much is made as proof against the rustlers, was unfair to the hated small stockman, honest though he may have been. This small stockman's cattle might be seized as rustled stock, and the proceeds of their sale turned into the state fund, waiting for proof of ownership. But it was impossible for a small stock raiser to go to the expense of traveling to Cheyenne and starting legal proceedings to prove that he owned the few head of stock that had been taken from him.

To-day the transformation in Cattle Land is complete. Ranches dot Powder River and Crazy Woman Creek, and men are being hired because they know more about irrigation than they know about cow-punching. I have seen cattle and sheep feeding together on the little open range that remains, for the sheep man is also playing no small part in the changing of conditions. One can travel by stage from Buffalo to Kaycee (that being the name of the town that has sprung up on the site of "Nate" Champion's heroic defense), and between wire fences all the way. Everywhere one is reminded of the fact that the sudden ending of the last war for the range spelled oblivion for the cow-man, and that the pitiless utilitarianism of an advancing civilization has smothered another of the West's flickering embers of romance.

2

The Story of Montana

C.P. Connolly

ROAD-AGENT ROCK
A favorite haunt of the robbers

THE STORY OF MONTANA

BY

C. P. CONNOLLY

ILLUSTRATED WITH PHOTOGRAPHS FROM THE COLLECTION OF THE
MONTANA HISTORICAL SOCIETY

THIS is the first of a series of articles which will tell fully and accurately the story of the personal and political feuds, the legal and business wars which have kept the State of Montana in turmoil from the beginning of the rivalry between Marcus Daly and William A. Clark, in the early '90's, up to the compromise of the legal and commercial differences between the Amalgamated Copper Company and F. A. Heinze, in the early part of the present year. Of the motives and interests which lay behind this long fight, of the powerful and picturesque personalities who have led it, of the intrigue and plot which were always beneath the surface ; the public has never had any knowledge — the only information has been fragmentary accounts of the more sensational incidents.

C. P. Connolly, the author of these articles, is an attorney, and has been a resident of Montana for over twenty years. He is an important figure in the public life of the State, and saw from behind the scenes the making of the history that he tells. For one term he was prosecuting attorney of Silver Bow County, in which the city of Butte is located. His narrative has been written without bias, with impartiality and fairness as the first consideration and with rigid adherence to documentary records.

The present chapter deals with the beginnings of the State — history so recent that all of it is within the memory of men still living. It tells the story of the first clash between lawlessness and the forces of order.

The second chapter will deal with the arrival in Montana of Marcus Daly and William A. Clark, and the beginnings of the personal, commercial, and political rivalry which convulsed the State until the day of Daly's death. This chapter will also cover the famous Montana capital fight and Clark's early attempts to reach the United States Senate.

The next chapters will tell in detail the story of the purchase of the Montana legislature of 1899 with sums that aggregated over a million dollars.

Succeeding instalments will narrate the attempt to bribe the Montana Supreme Court with an amount "to reach a half a million if necessary," in order to prevent the disbarment of Clark's chief counsel, John B. Wellcome, on charges of bribing members of the previous legislature : — and will relate how Judge Hunt, former Governor of Porto Rico and classmate of Secretary Taft, was approached with a bribe of $100,000. The rejection of Clark by the Senate investigating committee at Washington ; the cross-examination of witnesses by Chairman William E. Chandler, and the consternation and horror of Senator Hoar at the corruption unearthed before that body, are described in detail. The ruse by which the Governor of Montana was lured beyond the borders of the State in order to let the Lieutenant-Governor appoint Clark United States Senator, and thus outwit the Senate, is told in full.

The final chapters deal with the entry of F. Augustus Heinze into Montana politics and mining, and the long struggle between him and the Amalgamated Copper Company to control corruptly the Courts of the State — EDITOR.

I

THE REIGN OF LAWLESSNESS AND ITS OVERTHROW BY THE VIGILANTES—THE BEGINNINGS OF LAW AND ORDER IN MONTANA

ONTANA is a State that stretches across plain and mountain for eight hundred miles east and west, nearly as great a distance as that between New York and Chicago. It is about four hundred miles in width. There is more than one county in the State out of which an area as large as the New England states might be carved and still leave room for a space larger than Manhattan Island. The eastern half is level and is devoted to ranching, cattle-raising, and sheep-raising. The western half is mountainous, thick with timber and studded with picturesque lakes and occasional glaciers. The climate, especially in the western half, is tempered by what the early Indians called the " Chinook" wind, which rises from the Japan current or Pacific Gulf Stream, and thaws ice and snow in a few short hours. In the winter of 1886–1887 the writer saw two feet of snow dissolved into running water in the streets of Helena by one of these winds in less than two hours, not a flake of snow remaining. In summer one is compelled to sleep under blankets indoors at night. In eastern Montana, near the Dakota line, and in the north, adjoining the Canadian line, the winters are often long and chill, but are redeemed by the rays of a never-lapsing sun. In southwestern Montana the farmer plows in February. The summer evenings are long and incomparably entrancing — the twilight often lasting in the mountains till near ten o'clock — and in the late sunsets there is a suggestion of distant climes. This broad expanse of fruitful plain and mountain prodigal with treasure, to-day the home of a prosperous and populous commonwealth, was, up to 1860, utterly uninhabited save by savage Indians and an occasional solitary white trapper or missionary.

Out of the southwestern part of what is now Montana there came one day in the early '60's the wild rumor of gold — of all rumors the one which flies the fastest and fastens itself most grippingly upon the yearnings and imagination of men. It soon reached Denver and flew furiously on to the eastward. Responding to this rumor, there flowed back upon that wide, crude highway which linked the border settlements of the Middle West with the golden sands of California, an untamable flood, the human outflow of the newly-settled states which had drawn their population from every disaffected corner of the globe. Men kissed their wives and

EXECUTIVE OFFICE AND LEGISLATIVE HALL AT BANNACK IN THE '60'S

children good-by and struck the trail for gold.

They followed the wide wagon-ways of the Mormons of '46 and the Californians of '49. It was a motley throng that toiled, with their prairie-schooners, over that wide expanse of prairie between St. Joe and St. Louis on the east and the Rocky Mountains on the west — a section of country which Webster, in the Senate, had declared was an arid region, unfitted for human habitation and frigid with the blight of perennial winter. They herded together in the early stages of the overland journey, but later struggled desperately for place in the fierce, primeval race for nature's loot. There were those in that throng who had drunk the cup of prosperity and the dregs of adversity. There were doctors of divinity, doctors of medicine, lawyers, gamblers, speculators — and here and there some noble, self-sacrificing woman and her children. Buoyed up by the hope of quickly-acquired wealth — that chimerical dream which has lured and duped the world in all ages — they pursued the treacherous journey across a plain that seemed boundless. Picket-men were chosen for constant guard against the attacks of Indians, and shallow graves were dug along the way for those who succumbed to

disease or were slain by savages. The throng, made up of the best and worst of human elements, was united against every common enemy.

The destination of this exodus was Alder Gulch, " Bill " Fairweather's discovery, in the southwestern part of Montana. Ten thousand people rushed into that gulch within ninety days after the discovery of the gold-beds. Out of Alder Gulch was taken, in pans, gold aggregating one hundred millions of dollars. It yielded a greater amount of gold, perhaps, than any other one field on our continent. A city was founded and called Virginia City.*

The population of Alder Gulch soon became a law unto itself. The millions that were taken out of the placer-beds and hidden in cabins and out-of-the-way corners until the owners seized the first favorable opportunity to depart for the States, aroused the cupidity of the criminal element. Half the people of Alder Gulch were working day and night to gather the gold that would take them back to the affluent enjoyment of the fruits of hardship and hazard; the other half gambled, and whiled away the time in

* It must not be confounded with Virginia City, Nevada, the home of the great Comstock silver lode which made millionaires of Mackay, Flood, Fair, and O'Brien.

idleness until the harvest of toil was gathered ; and then swept down, vulture-like, upon the treasure.

Out of these conditions came the imperative call for some kind of provisional government. In all this heterogeneous collection of fortune-seekers, no man was certain of the good faith of his neighbor. They had come from all parts of the earth and had here looked into the faces of each other for the first time.

The Rise of the Road-Agents

Each day brought forth some new and astounding revelation of the strength of the road-agents, who were masquerading in every walk of this rude, unfashioned life, prating loudly of their desire for order, and lamenting the violence which they themselves produced.

Between the towns in the Gulch — Nevada City, Virginia City, and the other settlements — and Bannack, 80 miles away, a

shots who maintained their skill by daily practice in actual conflicts. So common were these clashes that once, when two desperadoes had come together in a combination barber shop and saloon and had literally shot each other to pieces, the barber continued his operations on the face of his customer during the whistle and whang of the bullets without so much as a change of countenance. Henry Plummer, the sheriff, entrusted with the protection of the community, became the secret leader of these predatory bands of road-agents. He was a man of education and influence—a New Englander. As sheriff, he was likely to know when each man who had made his "stake" proposed to depart with his treasure, and by what route he intended to leave. Through him this information was promptly disseminated among the outlaws. The sheriff, piloting the unsuspecting victims, with their treasure, through dangerous mountain passes, gave the signal

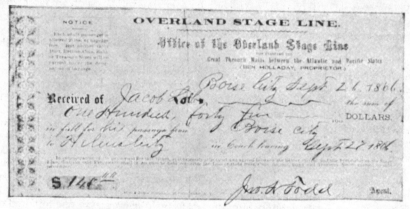

Ticket showing clause exempting stage line from liability for loss of gold-dust and money

constant correspondence was kept up by the road-agents. They had their captains, lieutenants, secretaries, and mail-carriers. The roads, everywhere, were under the constant surveillance of the freebooters. Horses, men, and coaches were marked by some secret sign, and troopers posted with speed at all hours of the day and night to convey intelligence of the contemplated operations of the gang. The usual arms carried by the road-agents were a brace of revolvers, a large-bore, double-barreled shot-gun, cut short in the barrel, and a bowie-knife. They were all well-mounted on fleet, well-trained horses, lifted from the settlements, in their forays. The members of the league were capital

which brought about the little party a troop of highwaymen who, after securing the gold-dust, often resorted to massacre to conceal evidence or prevent possible betrayal.

The Supremacy of the Lawless

The organization of the lawless antedated by many months the organization of law. For law was a thing without substance, among these people. The trained lawyer practises his profession through its forms and technicalities, and these the free, untrammeled, irresponsible spirit of this crude community would not tolerate. Gold was, for each, the all-alluring dream. It lay beneath their feet in exhaustless store, and they thought of nothing but possessing it. Far off to the southwest, in California, the first faint light of a permanent civilization had begun to glow, but no refraction of its ray reached this band of daring adventurers, who had broken all ties and thrown themselves into these twilighted hills, two thousand miles from the regions of men, where no law had been known save the tribal customs of wild Indians. To the far eastward, beyond the gateway of that broad, lonely, savage-haunted, seemingly endless highway over which they had come, the country was writhing in the throes of war. This derelict community, marooned among these distant hills, forgotten by a nation tense with the strain of civil conflict, was face to face with the primal problems of government.

The first case ever tried in Montana was a mining suit. Both parties to the suit claimed a certain piece of mining ground. The community had elected a president, Dr. William L. Steele, afterwards Mayor of Helena, and now a resident of that city. The regularly-elected judge of the community was a witness in the case and, according to the unwritten law, the case had to be tried before the president. It was winter time, but the case was tried in the open air on the foot-slopes of the mountains. The occasional balmy winters of that portion of Montana were a revelation to the gold-seekers then, as they are to the visitor to-day. During the trial, the plaintiff moved among the jury and the spectators with a box of cheap cigars, treating the crowd, while the defendant, not to be outdone in hospitality, went around with a bottle of what was known as "Valley Tan" whisky, a product of the Mormon settlements to the south, in the region of Salt Lake.

Dr. Steele had appointed Charlie Forbes clerk of the court. While the case was going on, two men — Hayes Lyons and "Buck" Stinson — stepped up and whispered something to Forbes. Forbes replied in an audible tone, "We'll kill him." He rose, and the three walked out to the edge of the crowd. They called to a man named Dillingham to step out from among the spectators. Dillingham stepped out to where Forbes and his companions stood, and was instantly shot dead. Forbes had fired the shot. Dr. Steele immediately ordered the arrest of the three men. Jack Gallagher, a deputy sheriff, who afterwards

proved to be one of the oath-bound gang of road-agents, was waiting on the court in his official capacity. He passed out from the crowd and placed the three men under arrest, taking their pistols from them. Dexterously exchanging his own pistol for that of Forbes, he held up the three weapons, which were found to be fully loaded. The court stood adjourned, and the civil suit was afterwards compromised.

The explanation of this tragic by-play to the first rude lawsuit in the camp as this:

A man named Dodge had accumulated considerable wealth in the placer diggings, and was about to return to the States. Plummer, the sheriff and the chief of the road-agents, had issued orders to Dillingham, Forbes, Lyons, and Stinson to ascertain the hour of his departure, to follow, and overtake, and rob him — instructions which meant the murder of Dodge. Dillingham, who said he had joined the gang for the purpose of informing on them later, disclosed the plot to Dodge. As time passed on, and Dodg failed to leave, Hayes Lyons met him one day and casually remarked: "I thought you were going to the States." "So I was," said the artless Dodge, "but I was told that you and Charlie Forbes and Buck Stinson were going to rob me." "Who told you that?" inquired Lyons. "Dillingham told me," was the response. This was the information that Lyons and Stinson had whispered to Forbes at the trial, and in the presence of the assembled general court, the clerk of the court shot Dillingham dead.

The First Rude Courts of the Frontier

They tried Forbes, Stinson, and Lyons by the only possible method — a miners' meeting. Some were in favor of a trial by twelve men, but others opposed this, knowing that the jury would be drawn by the road-agent sheriff — for there were those who knew that Plummer was the leader of the road-agents, though they dared not voice this conviction either in secret or in public. A *viva voce* vote was taken, but this proving indecisive, two wagons were drawn up, with a space between, and those in favor of a jury of twelve passed through and were counted, while those in favor of a jury of the entire populace followed, and were counted in turn. The vote in favor of the popular jury prevailed. Three judges were appointed, of whom Dr. Steele, the president of the community, was chief. E. R. Cutler, a blacksmith, was appointed

MAIN STREET, HELENA, IN THE EARLY '70'S

public prosecutor, the accused selecting their own counsel. The judge's bench was a wagon. Forbes, the actual guilty one, was acquitted, the other two were convicted. Forbes was saved because of his good looks and education, and by the deputy sheriff's subterfuge in producing the fully-loaded pistol which was sworn to be the pistol Forbes had at the time of the shooting. His trial came last, and many of the miners, weary of the long delays, had departed when the final question of Forbes's guilt or innocence was put. His masterly forensic appeal in his own behalf, still a tradition in the mountains, was no small element in his acquittal. Forbes laughed jovially, afterwards, at the gullibility of the men who acquitted him.

A committee was appointed to dig the graves of Stinson and Lyons. The deputy sheriff took the prisoners in a wagon to the place of execution. Most of the crowd remained where they were, but the friends of the doomed men followed the officers and culprits. When the party arrived at the gallows, it was decided to submit again to the crowd — now composed of the friends of the condemned — the question of hanging or not hanging. Before this motion was put, another motion was made, that Stinson and Lyons be given a horse and banished.

This was carried in a loud affirmative, by the friends of the men, and before any one could protest, the two rejoicing bandits were lifted upon the horse and told to fly.

Dr. Steele had left the open-air meeting over which he had presided and was on his way to his cabin, some distance down the road, when he heard behind him the clatter of hoofs. Looking up, he encountered the radiant faces of Stinson and Lyons, whose bodies he supposed were at that moment swinging from the limb of a pine. As they flew past him, they shouted a good-natured but defiant good-by.

John X. Biedler was digging away at their graves for two hours after the men left. When he found that Stinson and Lyons had got away, he put up a sign on the graves; "These graves to let; apply to X. Biedler." This bit of jocularity afterwards nearly cost Biedler his life. Sometime after the organization of the Vigilantes, Biedler stopped over night at a roadhouse on his way to Alder Gulch. He had hardly taken up his quarters when five road-agents, among them Stinson and Lyons, appeared at the house, having followed him with the intention of killing him. Their purpose was to kill every man who had had anything to do with the trial. One of these men said to Biedler: "You are the man who helped dig my grave.

"Yes," said Biedler, "and, by the way, you have never paid me for that yet." This was such an apt reply that the outlaws laughed, and one of them proposed to treat. An insult was offered in order to provoke a reply from Biedler, but it was parried in such a humorous way, that drinks were again proposed. The object of the road-agents was to provoke Biedler if possible and then kill him, but whether provoked or not, to kill him anyway. Biedler parried every thrust. In the nick of time, a committee of twelve Vigilantes walked in and called

agile in his movements. His manners were those of a gentleman, and he was intelligent, and even brilliant in conversation.

A man named Cleveland aspired to leadership of the road-agents. He got into a quarrel with Plummer one day in a saloon, while some of the members of the band were discussing affairs of business. Plummer suddenly sprang to his feet, exclaiming as he did so, "I am tired of this," and fired at Cleveland and struck him. Cleveland fell on his knees. He pleaded with Plummer not to shoot while he was down. "No,"

MAIN STREET, VIRGINIA CITY, AFTER ALDER GULCH HAD BEEN "PANNED"

"Hands up." The locks of twelve shotguns clicked, and the outlaws threw up their hands.

Henry Plummer, the ruling spirit among the road-agents, was probably the most skilful marksman of his time in the western country. He always pretended to give his adversary the advantage in drawing a weapon, knowing that his superior dexterity in the use of his Derringer would more than counterbalance any advantage his opponent might have. He was about five feet ten inches in height, and a very handsome man. When not in liquor, he was quiet and modest in demeanor, and was always dignified but

said Plummer. "Get up." Cleveland rose, only to receive another shot just below the eye, and fell dead to the floor.

Dr. Glick, brother of a later governor of Kansas, was surgeon for the road-agents. He was probably the best surgeon in the mountains. The road-agents would blindfold Glick and take him to the particular rendezvous where the injured member of the band happened to be. After the first of these visits, Plummer and Glick started on the return to town. While crossing a plateau, Plummer suddenly turned and thrust his revolver in Glick's face "Now you know," he said, "that these are my men. I am their chief. If you ever breathe a word of what you have seen, I'll murder you.'' And Plummer meant it.

Glick lived with the feeling that the gaping barrels of a hundred rifles were always leveled at his breast. He knew that disclosures by any confederate of the gang might at any time involve him in the general suspicion. He wanted to leave the country. He gave out to the road-agents that he wished to take a course of lectures in the East. "Stay right where you are. We have use for you here," was the comforting response.

On one occasion when Dr. Glick was performing a very delicate operation on Plummer, Bill Hunter, another of the outlaws, entered the room. "If Plummer dies from this operation,'' said Hunter, "I'll shoot the top of your head off.'' Glick performed the operation without the tremor of a muscle, though he did not expect it to be successful, and lay in hiding all one night with a horse ready saddled, awaiting word of the turn in Plummer's condition.

Former Governor Samuel T. Hauser, of Montana, now a resident of Helena, was one of the early pioneers who suspected Plummer's real character. Contemplating a trip from Bannack to Salt Lake with a large amount of treasure, he entered the stage-coach at Virginia City and immediately recognized Plummer among the passengers. Hauser took this to mean that Plummer had become aware of his intended trip, and had planned with the members of his band the robbery of the coach. His suspicions were strengthened by the fact that at Bannack Plummer had presented him with a woolen scarf, telling him he would find it useful on the cold nights during the trip. Hauser concluded that this was the badge by which the robbers would be able to pick him out from the other passengers. During the afternoon of the day of Hauser's departure it had been reported in Bannack that some new mining discoveries had been made at a point down the road, and Plummer, who affected some knowledge of mining matters, had been requested to go out and examine the discoveries. It was an excuse for his passage on the stage-coach and was a ruse that had been resorted to before.

In the presence of the other passengers Hauser made the remark to Plummer that he had a large amount of treasure which he was desirous of safely delivering at Salt Lake, and he desired Plummer, as sheriff of the community, to take charge of his treasure and guard it during the journey past the dangerous places on the road. As he spoke he passed the treasure over to Plummer. Plummer guessed Hauser's suspicions. The stage was not molested, the robbers failing to get their usual signal, and Hauser arrived at Salt Lake in due time with his treasure.

The principal amusements of the rougher element of the population were the stag-dances, a rough kind of dance in which only the men indulged, though in the more populous settlements gaily attired females were to be found, the belles of these boisterous carousals. Good women there were none, or so few that the sudden appearance of a good woman anywhere in the settlements produced visible signs of instant and profound respect. The miners would doff their hats and manifest their joy by rounds of huzzahs, making room for her as though the touch of their rough attire might soil her garments.

The discovery up to the fall of 1863 of no less than 110 bodies of victims of the road-agents had finally aroused the feelings of the law-abiding citizens to a pitch of frenzy. They felt that the mysterious disappearance of many other men whom they had known, was to be traced to the bandits. Scores of miners who had set out with large sums of money for various places had never been heard of and had never reached their destination. Murders occurred daily, almost hourly. Had there been the most perfect system of legal procedure, time would not have permitted of the orderly trials of offenders, so frequent were the crimes. Alder Gulch continued to disgorge its treasure in a steady stream, and the very excess of its bounty excited the most selfish passions of men. The heart of a man possessed with the thirst for gold is like the country where gold is produced — it is wild and barren, and the flowers wither.

It must not be supposed that during these long months of sickening dread and doubt attempts had not been made to organize justice. Rude courts were established and the guilt or innocence of offenders submitted to regularly chosen juries, but the swaggering outlaws would boldly force their way through the lines of spectators and into the presence of the qualified twelve men, announcing their determination to avenge upon every one connected with the case, any verdict other than acquittal. Witnesses and jurors, under these circumstances, were afraid for their lives, and justice had miscarried until the outlaws, seeing the blanch of fear everywhere, were supreme. In the early stages of this reign of terror some of the road-agents had been tried, found guilty, and condemned to death by unanimous vote, but as in the case of the murderers of Dillingham, between conviction and punishment motions to reconsider had intervened, and the vacillating mob, through fear or relenting doubt, had revoked the action of the previous hour.

The trial of two worthies known as Moore and Reeves will serve as a pertinent illustration. They had been guilty of the most atrocious and cold-blooded murders, the crime for which they were tried being particularly revolting and wanton. During the course of the trial, shots were fired and knives drawn, and the court was turned into a scene of wild disorder and indiscriminate violence. They were tried by a jury of twelve, and while the witnesses were giving their evidence the road-agents paraded in front of the jury-box, swearing vengeance upon every man who voted for a verdict of guilty. Some of these jurors had families in the States, and felt that to return a verdict of guilty would be signing their own death warrants. The verdict was acquittal, but that did not save them. Within six months, more than half of the men who participated in the trial of these desperadoes, whether as witnesses, jurors, judge, or officers, were assassinated by the road-agents. Under such circumstances, it was impossible to get men to act, individually or collectively, in any movement looking to the overthrow of the road-agents' power.

Another case ended more amusingly. A rough named Burch was on trial for his life. His counsel, foreseeing an adverse verdict, moved that Burch's life be spared on condition that he leave the diggings in fifteen minutes. The motion was carried. Some one gave Burch a mule. Thinking the crowd might reconsider, Burch vaulted onto the mule and looking quizzically at his jurors, exclaimed: "Fifteen minutes! Gentlemen, if this mule don't buck, five will do."—and disappeared down the road, amid the laughter of the crowd.

One day in November of 1863, into Nevada City, two miles below Virginia City, came a wagon containing the body of a murdered miner. It had been found in the bushes near Wisconsin Creek, several miles distant, and had been badly mutilated by birds and beasts. The body was recognized as that of Nicholas Tbalt, who had gone down to Wisconsin Creek after some mules. It bore the marks of a rope around the throat. The body had evidently been dragged to the place of concealment while the victim was still alive. The hands grasped fragments of sod and sage-brush. There was a bullet wound in the head.

The exhibition of this mangled corpse through the main streets of Nevada City and Virginia City aroused the populace to unusual frenzy. The time had come when the miners, callous to bloodshed, stood dumb with rage and impotence. They felt that they had remained too long indifferent to the roaming spirit of assassination which shot men down for luck or sport. A dozen men started out to find the murderer, or murderers, and returned at dusk to Nevada City with three men under arrest. One of the three had confessed, and there was ample corroborative proof against the others. One of these prisoners was George Ives, a leader among the freebooters. He was about twenty-seven years of age, tall, lithe, and handsome. He had bright eyes, an intelligent face, and like many of the leaders of the road-agents — he was next to Plummer in command — had apparently been a man of refinement. He had all the elements of leadership.

Ives had a habit, when he needed money, of riding his horse into a store or saloon, throwing his purse upon the bar or counter, and telling the proprietor to fill it with gold-dust. He would frequently amuse himself by breaking the lamps or the mirrors with a ball from his pistol, while waiting for his purse to be filled. He once learned that some member of Plummer's band had threatened to divulge some of its secrets. Ives met this man the next day on the public road, and shot him dead as he sat on his horse.

Ives and his companions, after their arrest for the murder of Nicholas Tbalt, laughed and joked coarsely over the prospect of an early acquittal. In settling upon the mode of trial, the miners finally determined that the men should be tried in the presence of the entire body of citizens, which reserved to itself the ultimate decision. A jury of twenty-four men was appointed to listen closely to the evidence, and to select for final appeal to the crowd, such questions as could not be unanimously agreed upon by the twenty-four during the course of the trials. Delays would thus be avoided.

"Long John," one of the accomplices, turned State's evidence. He swore that when Ives told Tbalt he was going to kill him, the young German asked for time to pray. Ives told him to kneel down, and then shot him through the head just as he had begun his prayer. In addition to the evidence, there was a general suspicion against Ives. It was believed that, next to Plummer, he was the most dangerous marauder on the road ; yet men were by no means sure that he would be convicted and punished. Ives was prepossessing in appearance ; he had friends in that crowd whose courage was instant and unflinching ; he was brave himself beyond any man's questioning ; he was rich with the booty of the road and the wealth of murdered miners ; his manners were affable and free — and such men have friends even beneath the church spires of civilization.

A wagon was drawn up and backed against a log cabin that faced the street. The crowd gathered around the out-of-door fires that tempered the atmosphere of the late December day. As usual, the Judge and attorneys of this primitive court occupied the wagon-box. The prisoners were seated in front of this rude temple of justice, and as the night drew on, the guards, flanked and surrounded by the impassive crowd, could be recognized by the flicker of the blazing fires. Beyond was the wavering line of desperadoes and their sympathizers.

The Coming of a Leader for the Law-Abiding

Upon that scene, in those wild hills, far removed from the arm of the law as we know it, there arose the figure of one of the intrepid heroes of that time. Col. Wilbur F. Sanders, since known as the " Vigilante" United States Senator from Montana, for whom one of Montana's counties has been named, was a lawyer and a new-comer, a comparative stranger to every one. But he was more than a mere lawyer. He was a man with the courage of a lion. Of Lincolnian height and features, he made a conspicuous figure in any gathering. Subsequent events always found him — often single-handed — championing the right against the lawlessness of Montana's wealth and power. Colonel Sanders had been approached to defend Ives and his companions, but this retainer he refused. Then he was asked to prosecute the men, and he consented.

In former public tribunals, judges, jurors, witnesses and mob alike had been overawed by threats of assassination. It was the firm belief of the miners that any one active in securing the conviction of Ives and his companions would be marked for death. All that the road-agents sought was to get the responsibility for the conviction of one of their number narrowed down from the crowd at large to any five or ten men, and then dispose of them separately.

But the courageous bearing of this new-comer dispelled the fears of judges, jurors and witnesses. He had the learning of the schools — and that alone commanded respect in that mixed assembly — and the eloquence that afterwards served well in defending the state against a more insidious fo.m of lawlessness. He looked witnesses in the face with unflinching courage. After the evidence for and against Ives was in, he stood in the open air, towering above the surrounding multitude, looking into the ugly bores of robber guns leveled from the outer fringe of the crowd, and moved for the conviction of the idolized leader of the road-agents. The courage of this man carried the day, the spell of the road-agents was broken, and the mob voted "guilty." No greater combination of physical and moral courage was ever witnessed on the frontier. But it did not end there. Many supposed that the proceedings, according to precedent, had come to a conclusion, and that the court would adjourn until the next day, it being already dark. Sanders again mounted the wagon, and, calming the tumult, stated that Ives had been declared a murderer and robber by the people there assembled and moved "That George Ives be *forthwith* hanged by the neck until he is dead." Again the mob, awed by the eloquence, the heroism and the sternness of this new-comer, voted in the affirmative — and before the crowd had time to recover, before the friends of Ives could rally their wavering forces, Ives had paid the penalty of his fragrant crimes.

To a place not more than ten yards from where he sat during the trial, Ives was led to execution. He had repeatedly declared he would never die in his boots, and he asked one of the guards for a pair of moccasins, which were given him, but he got chilled, and requested that his boots might be put on again, and he died in them. He was led to the scaffold fifty-eight minutes from the time his doom was fixed. Every excuse for delay had been resorted to by his friends, in the hope of rescue at the hands of Plummer and his men from Bannack and Virginia City. The surrounding roofs of the rough mountain homes were covered with spectators. Revolvers could be seen flashing in the moonlight, but the guards stood firm, prepared to beat back the friends of the road-agents. When all was ready, the word was given, and the large dry-goods box on which Ives stood was shattered from under him. The road-agents stampeded from the scene in wild affright. Some claimed that Plummer was present, but that, overawed by the determination of the mob, he kept in the background. Others denied that he was there. The trial and punishment of Ives's companions followed in quick succession. An hour or two after the exciting scenes attending the execution of Ives, Colonel Sanders sat quietly reading in the store of John A. Creighton, now a wealthy citizen of Omaha, and the endower of Creighton College at that place. Guards had been offered to protect Sanders's person, but he had refused to accept their services. Harvey Meade, with revolver cocked, walked up to Sanders and began abusing him in road-agent vernacular. Sanders dropped his hand into his coat pocket, in which lay a Derringer, and quietly observed: "Harvey, I should feel hurt if some men said this, but from such a dog as you, it is not worth noticing." Meade walked off. He said afterwards he had intended to kill Sanders, but that there was something about the man's manner that cooled his ardor.

For over forty years Wilbur F. Sanders remained a commanding figure in the history of Montana. In later years, when men were still shot down in the public streets, Sanders was engaged as counsel in the trial of a case in Deer Lodge. After one of those philippics for which he was noted, directed against one of the witnesses for the opposing side, Sanders was informed as he left the court room that the target of his vituperative

eloquence was waiting for him. "Did he say he would shoot?" asked Colonel Sanders of his informant, Andy O'Connell. "Not only said so," was the reply, "but he *will* shoot as sure as your name is Sanders." "Oh, no," said Sanders; "the man that says he will shoot, never shoots"— and Sanders walked out in front of the court straight up to the waiting "terror," who slunk away before the glance of his fearless eye.

Sanders was a man of wit as well as courage. Some years before his death, which took place in July, 1905, he was present at a Populist Convention in Helena, and being called on by the chairman, in a moment of weakness, for a speech, Sanders, who was a Republican, launched into a political argument against the heresies of Populism. Instantly there was a wild uproar in the hall, supplemented by cries of "Put him out." One speaker rose and interrupting Sanders said that the Populists had hired the hall and the lights and should be protected from insult. "I know," said Sanders, "but I am furnishing the heat."

The Organization of the Vigilantes

Two or three nights after the execution of Ives, it was decided to form a Vigilance Committee. The way had been paved by the courage of Sanders and by the fear which clutched at the hearts of the road-agents. Public sentiment had changed from terror to unfaltering decision — the wind had veered. Several resolute men, including Colonel Sanders, met in the back room of a store owned by John Kinna and J. A. Nye on Jackson Street, opposite the aristocratic saloon and gambling place known in those days as "No. 10," and then and there organized a Committee of Vigilance. Mr. Paris S. Pfouts was elected president, Colonel Sanders official prosecutor, and Captain James Williams executive officer. The candles were then extinguished, and standing about the room in a circle, with hands uplifted, the assembled company took this oath:

"We, the undersigned, uniting ourselves together for the laudable purpose of arresting thieves and murderers and recovering stolen property, do pledge ourselves on our sacred honor, each to all other and solemnly swear that we will reveal no secrets, violate no laws of right, and never desert each other or our standard of justice, so help us God."

Bill for coffin and interment of the Road-Agent Chief

Among the by-laws adopted by the Vigilantes was this Draconian provision:

"The only punishment that shall be inflicted by this committee is death."

While the Vigilantes were perfecting their plans, renewed impetus was given to the movement by one of the most atrocious crimes ever perpetrated in the history of the road-agents. This was the murder and robbery of Lloyd Magruder and his companions. Magruder was one of the most popular men in the settlements. He had been a merchant at Lewiston, Idaho, and the Independent Democratic candidate for Congress. He combined in his character so many good and noble traits that he was generally esteemed and admired.

In the summer of 1863 Magruder arrived in Virginia City with a large pack-train laden with merchandise. He opened a store and disposed of his goods, realizing some $30,000. He was about to return to Lewiston, accompanied by Charles Allen, Horace and Robert Chalmers, two young brothers, and a man named Phillips. These men likewise had treasure, and united for safety. James Romaine, "Doc" Howard. William Page and "Chris" Lowry were employed by them as helpers and stock tenders. Whisperings that Magruder and his party would be murdered reached the ears of more than one citizen, but terror sealed their lips.

The party traveled without accident to a camp near the Bitter Root range, the present dividing line between Montana and Idaho. This was the spot selected by the helpers and stock-tenders for the treacherous murder. At an afternoon consultation, they fixed upon the hour of ten that night for concerted attack on the party. A guard was stationed that evening, Magruder and Lowry being on watch. Promptly at ten, while Magruder was leaning over, lighting his pipe from the flame of the guard-fire and while all the other victims of the plot were asleep, Lowry crushed Magruder's skull with an ax. Howard and Romaine murdered the two Chalmers boys and Allen and Phillips while they slept. The work was so well done that only Phillips cried out, and a second blow silenced him.

The bodies were wrapped in a tent-cloth and rolled over a mountain precipice, where the winter's snow was expected to hide all evidence of the crime. All the horses except eight were taken into a cañon off the trail and shot. The camp equipment was burned. The murderers wore moccasins, so that if an early discovery should be made, the crime might be imputed to Indians.

After the capture of the murderers, Page, who had taken no active part in the crime, turned State's evidence, and the others were executed in Idaho after trial and conviction in regularly established courts.

This crime excited intense indignation, and whatever opposition there had been among the miners to the organization of the Vigilantes gave way before the necessity for self-preservation.

The Vigilance Committee set to work in orderly and determined fashion. The first men hanged were "Red" Yager and a companion named Brown. Their place of execution was the Stinkingwater Valley. Yager confessed and put the committee in possession of the names of the prominent leaders among the road-agents. He told them that Plummer was the chief of the band. The password of the confederates was "Innocent." Each wore a necktie tied in a sailor's knot for the better identification of one another. Death was the penalty for all traitors, and for any outsider who came into possession of, and revealed, the secrets of the band.

A lantern and some stools were brought from a house near the spot where Yager and Brown were captured, and the party, crossing a creek behind Loraine's ranch, made for some neighboring trees which loomed in outline through the night shadows. On the road to the gallows Yager was cool and collected. Brown sobbed and cried for mercy. The stools, one placed upon the other, flew from under Brown first. Yager, without a sign of trepidation, saw his companion drop. He asked to shake hands with his executioners, and begged that they would follow the road-agents until they were completely exterminated. "You are on a good undertaking," said he. "No country was ever cursed with a more bloodthirsty or desperate pack of villains than this, and I know them all." His voice was as calm and steady as though he were conversing with old friends.

The road-agents were hanged in pairs, or in large numbers, as they were apprehended.

Henry Plummer was undressing at his house when he was taken. He was seized the moment his door was opened in answer to a knock. His favorite pistol lay near by, but it was secured by one of the committee before Plummer could reach for it.

On the road to the gallows Plummer heard the voice and recognized the person of the leader of the Vigilantes. He had been the companion and close friend of every man among his captors. He went to the leader and begged for his life.

"It is useless for you to plead for your life," said the leader. "That affair is settled and cannot be altered. You are to be hanged. You cannot feel harder about it than I do, but I could not help it if I would." "Don't say that," pleaded Plummer. "Cut out my tongue and strip me naked this freezing night, and let me go. Spare my life. I cannot go blood-stained," he sobbed, "into the presence of the Eternal." He exhausted every argument and plea, but the Vigilantes were inexorable. Death was their only punishment. They were pledged to it. Finally, with tears and sobs, Plummer confessed his numerous crimes. He was frantic at the prospect of death. Witnessing the death-throes of so many of his victims had not hardened him to meet his own fate bravely.

"Buck" Stinson and "Ned" Ray, who were captured at the same time with Plummer, were sent to death first. The order "Bring up Plummer" was then given and repeated, but no one stirred. Sympathy for this heartless outlaw was working in the breasts of his executioners. Plummer himself was trying to gain a few moments respite by saying some rusty prayers which stuck pitifully in his throat, but he finally rose as stoically as he could to the fate before him. Standing under the gallows, Plummer slipped off his necktie and tossed it over his shoulder to a young friend who had thrown himself weeping on the ground, saying: "Here is something to remember me by." He died without a struggle.

The work of implacable justice continued. Ives, Yager, Brown, Plummer, Stinson, Ray and others were dead; but Boone Helm, Jack Gallagher, Frank Parrish, Hayes Lyons and "Club-foot" George Lane, together with scores of other leaders, were at large. Every man who had taken part in the pursuit of the road-agents thus far was marked for death. No security was possible until the last of the outlaws was placed beyond the power of ever again giving the command "Hands up."

The executive committee on January 13, 1864, determined on hanging six of the ringleaders without delay. One of the doomed men — Bill Hunter — suspecting the purpose of the committee, or being secretly warned by some friend, managed to crawl along a drain ditch through the line of pickets that surrounded the town, and make his escape. In his flight he suffered greatly from exposure to the cold, and he was afterwards captured and executed in the Gallatin Valley. It is said that after the drop fell, his arms being free, he unconsciously went through the motion of reaching for his pistol, cocking and discharging it six different times.

While the executive committee were deliberating on these sentences, some of the men whose death-warrants were being signed were playing faro in a room two doors away. Express messengers were sent to warn the Vigilantes of the neighboring towns in the Gulch. They flew up and down the Gulch with the fateful message that night.

The following morning, the first gleams of light showed the pickets of the Vigilantes stationed on every eminence and point of vantage about Virginia City. The news flew like wild-fire. Hearts quaked and lips turned pale. Detachments of Vigilantes, stern, erect, determined-looking, marched from Nevada City, Junction, Summit, Pine

Grove, Highland, Fairweather. As soon as all was in readiness, the search for the road-agents began.

Frank Parrish was the first marauder captured by the Vigilantes. He was apprehended in one of the town stores and took the officer aside and asked why he was arrested. "For being accessory to the murders and the robberies of the road," was the brief rjeoinder. He pleaded innocence at first, but at last admitted his guilt. He gave some hasty directions about articles of clothing belonging to him and the settlement of some debts.

"Club-foot" George Lane was supposed to be a respectable shoemaker whose kit occupied a corner in Dane & Stuart's combination store and express office in Virginia City, but his occupation was a blind. His business as the spy of the road-agents was to overhear conversations which might give information of intended shipments of gold. Lane was arrested at a gambling-house. He was perfectly cool when he was taken. He was told that his sentence was immediate death and he sat for some time, his face covered with his hands. He then asked for a minister, and one was found who consoled him on the march to the gallows.

Next came Boone Helm, the most hardened of the gang. They tell, in the mountains, this story of Boone Helm. Back at his home in Missouri a neighbor named Littelbury Shoot had promised to accompany Helm to Texas. At the last moment Shoot decided not to go. Helm called at his house one night after Shoot had retired. He roused him up.

"I hear you've backed down on the Texas question," said Helm as Shoot opened the door.

"Well,"— said Shoot, starting to explain.

"Yes or no," said Helm. "Are you going?"

"No."

And Helm, with his left hand on Shoot's right shoulder, buried his bowie-knife hilt-deep in the heart of his friend.

Helm's arrest by the Vigilantes took place in front of the Virginia Hotel. When made acquainted with his doom, he sat down for a moment on a bench. He declared his innocence and fought desperately for delay, but finally said: "I have dared death in every form, and am not afraid to die." He called for whisky and was boisterously irreverent and profane to the last.

Jack Gallagher was found in a gambling-room, rolled up in bedding, shot-gun and revolver beside him. He had determined to kill his captors, but his heart failed him at the last. He knew that the reign of the road-agents was over. He was sent forward.

THE MINER'S DREAM.

The frontispiece of Mark Twain's "Roughing It," gives a contemporary idea of the gold-seeker's confident expectations

Hayes Lyons was at breakfast in his cabin. "Throw up your hands" was the command that greeted him as the Vigilantes opened the door. He was told to step out. He came out in his shirt-sleeves and when his coat was handed to him he was so agitated that he could hardly get into it.

The prisoners were ordered to stand in row, facing the guards, and were informed that they were about to proceed to execution. They were marched in the center of a hollow square, flanked by four lines of Vigilantes, armed with shot-guns and rifles. Pistol-men were dispersed throughout the crowd.

The line moved forward. Eight thousand people lined the streets and gazed from roofs and open windows. As the procession advanced slowly up the street, Gallagher alternately cursing and crying, called to an acquaintance on one of the roofs:

"Say, old fellow, I'm going to Heaven. I'll be there in time to open the gate for you."

"Hello, Bill," said Boone Helm to another in the crowd. "They've got me this time, and no mistake."

The last halt was made, and five boxes were placed under a beam in an unfinished, open building. They were the drops. "Clubfoot" George Lane asked leave to pray and knelt down. Jack Gallagher knelt with him, but called for whisky a moment later, and cursed the guard for not slacking the rope enough to let him drink. "I hope God Almighty will curse every one of you, and that I'll meet you all in the lowest pit of Hell," he shouted. Hayes Lyons was penitent and talked of his mother to those around him. Boone Helm cracked ribald jokes. "Kick away, old fellow," he said, as the oscillating figure of Gallagher cleaved the air. "I'll be in Hell with you in a minute" — and then shouting "Every man for his principles. Hurrah for Jeff Davis. Let her rip"— was swung into eternity. Frank Parrish stood silent and pensive. He dropped his black necktie over his face before his name was called.

The work of the Vigilantes was drawing to a close. Other executions followed. Between thirty and forty desperate men were hanged. Under the gibbet Bob Zachary had prayed that "God would forgive the Vigilantes for what they were doing, as it was the only way to clear the country of road-agents."

"Johnny" Cooper was drawn to the scaffold in a sleigh, his wounded leg forbidding him to walk. "I want," he said, "a good smoke before I die. I always enjoyed a smoke." A heaping pipe was given him.

"Alex" Carter and Cyrus Skinner were executed at midnight by torchlight at the place where the thriving city of Missoula now stands, and within a few miles of where Daniel E. Bandmann, the old-time tragedian, now lives on his ranch.

George Shears said to those who captured him in the Bitter Root valley:

"I knew I would have to come to this, but I thought I might run another season."

To save the trouble of procuring a drop, he was asked to ascend a ladder, and politely complied.

"I am not used to this business, gentlemen," he said, when he had mounted the ladder. "Am I to jump off or slide off?"

One of the last official acts of the Vigilantes was the hanging February 10, 1864, of Capt. J. A. Slade, of whom it was said that "West of Fort Kearney he was feared a great deal more than the Almighty."

He had not been one of the road-agents; on the contrary, he was a member of the Vigilantes; but in his revels he was a menace to society in Alder Gulch. He was warm-hearted toward a friend, but a perfect demon to those who had incurred his displeasure. His favorite pastime when intoxicated was, like Ives's, to ride his horse into saloons and other public places, buying wine for himself and horse, and demolishing everything in sight. He would go into a saloon where perhaps fifty men were playing cards, and insist that they should all stop and drink with him at the same moment. He would raise his glass with the rest of them, but, instead of drinking, would wait until the others had finished, when he would bring his glass on a level with his eyes, and stare at it with intentness for a minute. Then suddenly he would raise the glass, dash it from him with terrific force at the mirror, the floor or the barkeeper, then draw his revolver and begin shooting indiscriminately. Slade was the leader of the only lawless element that remained in Virginia City after the extermination of the road-agents. A favorite diversion of this crowd of toughs was to dash down the mountain side from their cabin homes, "load up" at the first convenient saloon, and proceed to the town stews. In the morning when the peaceful citizens got up, they would see a pile of logs and a group of shivering, crying women. One morning, after the Vigilante court had organized, news came that Slade and some of his friends had spent the night at one of these houses and in the morning had destroyed it as usual. The marshal was ordered to arrest Slade. He was brought before the court, tried and found guilty. Having been guilty of the same offense frequently before, he was now fined $400. He did not have the money with him, but promised to bring it the next time he was in town. He was again arrested for the same offense and brought into court. As the marshal started to read the warrant, Slade sprang at him and tore it from his hands, at the same time leveling a revolver at the heart of the Judge. "Now," said he, "I am about tired of this business, and

WILBUR F. SANDERS

Late United States Senator from Montana. In the early days he was the head of the Vigilante organization which hung between forty and fifty of the road-agents

I am not going to recognize your authority, or pay that $400 I shall hold you personally responsible for my safety, and if any of your committee attempts to touch me, I'll blow your heart out.''

Within a half hour the house to which Slade had gone was surrounded by armed men. The next minute they were in the room. One of them said, "We want you, Mr. Slade.'' Slade turned pale, but gave himself up. In order to preserve the forms of the crude law of the time, he was sentenced to death for high treason, for exciting others to rebellion, and for seeking to overthrow the Vigilante form of government.

Slade's execution has been criticized, and no doubt with reason ; but one must assuredly conclude that while Slade may not have deserved death, the demands of the hour called imperiously for stern measures.

Slade's execution was rendered the more dramatic by his wife's heroic ride in an endeavor to save him. She arrived only in time to see his body cut down.*

With the death of Slade, the reign of law began. A peace that had been unknown since the coming of the first gold-seekers settled over the communities of Alder Gulch. Justice had at last asserted itself, and the rewards of the miner were his own. The curtain had fallen on the first act of the making of a commonwealth.

* Mark Twain tells in "Roughing It" another anecdote illustrating the heroism of Slade's wife. The incident occurred perhaps ten years before his execution.

Slade was captured, once, by a party of men who intended to lynch him They disarmed him, and shut him up in a strong log-house, and placed a guard over him. He prevailed on his captors to send for his wife, so that he might have a last interview with her. She was a brave, loving, spirited woman. She jumped on a horse and rode for life and death. When she arrived they let her in without searching her, and before the door could be closed she whipped out a couple of revolvers, and she and her lord marched forth defying the party. And then, under a brisk fire, they mounted double and galloped away unharmed!

3

The Heroes
of the
Gunnison Tunnel

A.W. Rolker

BIRD'S EYE VIEW OF THE GUNNISON RIVER.

The Heroes of the Gunnison Tunnel

By A. W. Rolker in Collaboration With Day Allen Willey

ON September 27th the eyes of the people of the United States will be centered on a desert town in the southwest corner of Colorado—Lujane.

From the roofs of rough board shacks, in the heart of the arid waste, flags will float. Clouds of red, white and blue bunting will flutter. Senators, governors, perhaps even the President himself will be there to celebrate. For there will be a ceremony worthy of an epoch-marking event—that of the completion of the first of those enormous irrigation systems on which the Government has been working for the past ten years.

At the hour of high noon President Taft, either at Lujane or wherever he may be, will touch an electric button releasing a spark; and miles away, out of a tunnel through a spur in the wilds of the Rockies, the Gun-

nison River will be diverted from the world-famous Black Cañon and will rush into the Uncompahgre Valley with the rumble and thunder of a cataract. Into a huge canal it will seethe and roar, a deluge of molten silver ten feet deep and eighty feet across, traveling at the rate of a mile a minute with a force of 6,000 horse power. At the rate of 8,000 gallons a minute it will flow, filling 400 miles of lateral canals that gridiron 200,000 acres of brown, lifeless desert, uninhabitable, bald as the palm of your hand, cracked open in seams and fissures with the bombardment of ages of suns.

As the flood gushes forth, dynamite mines will crash salute amid dust and rocks and pebbles, clouds of yellow fumes wafting lazily toward azure skies. Then the news that the first of our gigantic irrigation sys-

31

tems has been put into operation will be telegraphed throughout the land. A desert, where no creature could have lived, will have been reclaimed. Five thousand forty-acre farms, the home sites of 25,000 men, women and children will have been thrown open. Crops, herds, villages and towns with refineries, hay presses, and other factories will spring up amid that fertile soil—from the beginning of all time the range of the viper—through the wizard touch of the engineer, turned into a garden spot, a source of inestimable wealth to the nation.

But, wonderful though the economic feature of the Gunnison River Irrigation System may be, there is not space to go into it here. A story infinitely more interesting there is to tell. A story not of water but of rich, red blood; not of crops and herds and dollars and cents, but of stout hearts and suffering and despair and triumph, such a story as rarely comes even into the life of that professional adventurer and pioneer of civilization, the Civil Engineer. So listen, for, on Lujane's great day, three special guests of honor have been invited: a little Frenchman named Lauzon and two engineers of the Reclamation Bureau, W. W. Torrence and A. L. Fellows. Lauzon's importance ends with having conceived the idea of turning the Gunnison out of its course. But Torrence and Fellows are the conquerors of the Black Cañon, a subterranean inferno that none thought it possible to explore. The suffering and horrors which they underwent in following the torrent down its bed, 3,000 feet beneath daylight, are almost beyond the powers of human conception.

Nearly twenty years ago, in Montrose County, in the southwest of Colorado, half a dozen settlers lived in the upper part of the Uncompahgre Valley, and among these the little Frenchman. Not on our 470,000,000 acres of the Land that God Forgot was there

W. W. TORRENCE.

a more hopeless strip than this where Lauzon and his neighbors lived. Soil, rich beyond belief in the chemical elements that go to make up plant food, extended as far as eye could reach; but water, the one remaining element necessary to enable plants to take up this food and to turn the waste into a paradise of plenty —water there was none.

Six miles from this valley coursed the Uncompahgre River, a mountain stream; in summer it was a sickly brooklet, in spring a roaring torrent swollen with deluges from cloudbursts and melting snows. At cost of infinite labor, Lauzon and his friends led the Uncompahgre into their valley to flood their little farms of something like forty acres each. There were seasons when the water needed to irrigate this small tract was sufficient, and crops abundant past belief were raised. But other seasons there were when Lauzon and his friends grew anxious; for not only was water low, but other settlers, attracted by the success of the six pioneers, had come in to share in the supply.

Of an evening Lauzon would sit dreaming in the door of his farmhouse, before him his forty, sappy-green acres studded with cattle, lambs and sheep; beyond, far as eye could reach, a gray-brown waste alive with heat devils and reflecting the shimmer of crimson and gold shed by the setting sun. Water, and within a week that desolation would be unrecognizable; that area of powdered alkali dust, whereon bones of men and beasts bleached under a temperature like that of an oven, would be transformed into a garden spot with an inexhaustible deposit of wealth, richer than any gold mine on earth.

Twenty miles away, in the Black Cañon, running through an unnamed spur of the Rocky Mountains, the Gunnison River coursed through a cleft that seemed to yawn into the very center of the earth. No eye had ever seen this river in all of its cañon bed. Gunnison, the explorer who gave his name

HOW IRRIGATION CAN CONVERT A DESERT INTO A LAND OF HOMES.

to the stream, had followed its surging waters down mountain sides, through peaceful valleys, past forests of stately spruce and pine and broad meadows of waving grass, until he found it swallowed in a recess so dark and so forbidding that it was named the Black Cañon. He looked into its ink-black depths and went no farther. And twenty years later, Professor Hayden, who made a general geological survey for the

THE GUNNISON CAÑON WHERE THE ENGINEERS BEGAN THEIR PERILOUS JOURNEY.

FELLOWS SWIMMING DOWN STREAM WITH THE
RUBBER MATTRESS.

which no human eye had dared to ferret out, and to lead it into the Uncompahgre, it would be necessary to bring it underground through a tunnel measuring at least six miles and through a mountain base. For months the Frenchman pondered, weighing the vastness of the idea against the might of the Government if it were thrown into the project.

Then one morning at the headquarters of the Reclamation Bureau, thousands of miles away in Washington, D. C., a telegram from Lauzon was received.

"Can the Gunnison River be made to water the Uncompahgre Valley?"

A. L. Fellows, engineer in the Reclamation Bureau who received this telegram, read and re-read it. Then, silently, he handed it to W. W. Torrence, one of his brother engineers. There was not another pair of men in the bureau more expert in the perilous specialty of cañon work than these two young men. Never in the history of the Bureau was a more dangerous undertaking proposed. To enter the cañon at a point where it was

Government, pronounced the cañon impenetrable. Geologists who had been lowered down the rocky walls returned after descending a thousand feet and declared that no man could go farther and live. Indians who had dared the cañon had never again been seen alive.

But Lauzon, a dreamer, saw what a marvelous thing it would be to capture the turbulent stream running waste, and to deflect it out of its fastness into the Uncompahgre and so through canals across the 200,000 acres of the valley — 203 square miles. But even to the dreamer this seemed absurd. To subject that stream, flowing in its cañon bed

surmised the tunnel might be driven, was out of all question. Should a reckless one venture to have himself lowered down those 3,000 feet, the stoutest silk rope would be chafed in two against projecting rocks, and the man would whirl headlong into eternity. The one way to reach the point in question was to enter the cañon fourteen miles upstream where a wall 1,500 feet high presented a single vulnerable spot, and from this point to follow the river, a veritable under-

SHOOTING ONE OF THE GUNNISON RAPIDS IN A CANVAS BOAT.

ground torrent hurling itself with the impact of a maelstrom through the bowels of the earth into a vast Unknown.

Whether the river on its course broke into cataracts that would smash boats like egg shells, whether it would lead over falls down which a boat would shoot to destruction, or whether it would suddenly dip underground, sucking men into the earth like so many flies down a sink hole, none could foretell. The only thing certain was that once a man entered on this trip he would have to finish it to the bitter end; he would no more be able to fight his way back *against* that current than he would be able to climb the perpendicular walls that led to the ribbon of daylight, a half-mile above him.

To those with an inkling of the terrors of the Black Cañon it seemed almost like suicide when, after shaking hands with the party of explorers left above, Torrence and four volunteer assistants of the Reclamation Service let themselves down by ropes into the cañon. The boats the men took down with them were made of stout oak frames covered with canvas, so that when they struck against rocks, instead of shattering and splintering into uselessness, they could

FELLOWS SWIMMING WHERE THE WALLS COULD NOT BE SCALED.

readily be repaired. Tinned meats and vegetables and hard tack enough for a month the men loaded into the boats, along with cameras, surveying instruments and note books in watertight tins. Then they signaled with revolver shots that the expedition was under way, for it had been arranged that men should be stationed at intervals along the edge of the cañon to observe the movements of those below and to report each day to their families and friends.

Down in the cañon, where

ONE OF THE EASIER FALLS THEY HAD TO PASS.

daylight was turned into dusk, where all was barren rock, where the terrorizing note of the torrent roared so that men had to shout into one another's ears, hardship had begun. The river, still swollen with melted snows, was cold as ice. In spots it hurled itself against rocks and bowlders and against the walls of the cañon, sending up spray twenty feet high and filling the air with an ice cold mist that drenched their clothes and dripped again from rocks worn smooth as glass. Over these, varying in size from the height of a table to that of a tall horse, the men boosted and pulled one another, while they held fast to long ropes attached to the boats that would have shot down stream like bullets out of a rifle had they not been hard held. In spots where the river had worn deep, there were basins, stretches of one or two hundred feet of placid water, and here the men would embark and venture forward as far as they dared. In other spots, the river was a mass of shallow rapids, churned into white foam from wall to wall, and so swift that men immersed to the knees could

THE POINT WHERE THE FIRST EXPEDITION
GAVE UP.

scarcely retain a footing. To slip and fall into the swirl would have meant being whisked like a feather over a mill dam only to be dashed to atoms; wherefore the men tied themselves to a common rope like alpine climbers, lifting boats and provisions on their shoulders and staggering with them through rapids to stretches of safety beyond.

At four o'clock in the afternoon the dusk faded quickly into blackness. Broad daylight reflected half way down the eastern wall of the cañon; but down at the bottom of the cleft which the water had gouged through the earth's crust, all was pitch black, filled with the incessant drone that reverberated from wall to wall and throbbed in the ears, stupefying the senses.

Despite the heartbreaking work of the day the men had not covered three quarters of a mile. After a meal of cold things, they stretched themselves, damp and chilled, on bare rocks for a long biting cold night in which they could not have even the comforts of talk. And this would endure until eight o'clock in the morning, when the sun would have risen sufficiently to make safe progress possible.

Stiff, miserable and tired, they scrambled from their hard beds. One of the boats parted its line that day, and neither rib nor shred of it ever was seen again. But late that afternoon, in a wall of the cañon, they found a cave so long that they were unable to explore to the end of it; and here they found shelter for the night and driftwood with which to light a fire and cook a meal and warm themselves.

For five days they traveled, working their hearts out, slipping and floundering up and down wet, glassy bowlders, treacherous as glare ice, and by night twisting miserably through long hours. Worst of all, owing to the loss of a boat with its load of provisions, it was necessary to cut rations. They were growing weak for want of rest and proper food, for lack of the sunshine and the blue sky, a patch of which they could see by looking straight up, and more than a narrow strip of which they might never see again. By night they lay, face upturned, amid spume and spray and din, in an atmosphere like that of a tomb, while overhead hung a strip of placid stars. With energy and vitality running low, courage dwindled, and to the suffering of the body were added the torments of the soul. Retreat against that volume of hurling water was out of question. Somewhere ahead, where the cañon grew deeper and deeper, there was one chance in a thousand of finding an unknown watercourse, or a fissure up which they might climb. Failing this, starvation stared them in the face, and the fate that comes to the human as it comes to the wolf, when food is gone, and the Ten Commandments are swallowed by the first of all laws of nature.

Meanwhile up above, on the brink of the

ONE OF THE WATER ARTERIES THAT WILL BRING NOURISHMENT TO THE UNCOMPAHGRE VALLEY.

cañon where watchers peered for a glimpse of the struggling men, the hope of seeing them alive was abandoned. During the five days not a sign of life had come out of the abyss. Wire nets were being lowered at the mouth of the cañon in the hope of recovering the bodies—when way, way down among the rocks a watcher spied them. At first he did not trust his eyes, for they appeared not much larger than good-sized jack rabbits. Field glasses showed rents and tatters of their clothing as the five were seen limping forward, helping each other. In vain the watchers shouted and fired volleys to attract attention. Into ears deafened by the never ceasing roar of the cataracts no other sound could penetrate.

The sight of those given up for dead set

A DETAIL FROM THE OLD PART OF THE VALLEY SHOWING HOW THE WATER WILL BE USED.

men's hearts thumping wildly in the hope of sending down a message of cheer. And at the prospect that those below might pass without looking up, one of the watchers could not resist the temptation to throw down a small stone. This stone loosened a larger one, and this in turn a still larger one, and so on, the rocks gaining in weight until, with a splash that sent water a hundred feet into the air, a ton of stone went crashing down into the stream a hundred yards in front of the climbing men. Only then did they look up, waving hats and bandannas. For half an

It became apparent that, with their present equipment and in their present condition, they could not hope to proceed much farther, but must bend all their remaining energies toward escape if they hoped to save their lives.

Pale, emaciated, weak and hollow-eyed they proceeded, searching for a chance whereby, even at risk of their necks, they could hope to escape. Directly ahead of them the river suddenly disappeared, shooting beneath millions of tons of house-high rocks and bowlders that had crashed from

AN IRRIGATION CANAL IN OPERATION.

hour they sat, gazing upward, without chance to communicate more than by wave of hand, yet unable to tear themselves from the bare sight of the men in the land of the living. Then they arose, crawling and limping on their way.

The men had traveled for three weeks when they realized that they had come to their rope's end. The farther they penetrated, the harder grew their trail. The gorge narrowed and deepened. The river, which until now had consisted of cataracts and rapids, grew into a swirling torrent often without banks, so that they had to swim, clutching the gunwale of the boat as a drowning person clutches a life preserver. The cañon had deepened to 2,300 feet, the walls being almost straight up and down.

the walls. Over the rocks they climbed and scrambled and pushed and hoisted each other, dragging the boats and provisions after them, taking an entire day to cover a scant hundred yards; then to discover that the cañon had risen to 2,500 feet and narrowed to twenty-eight, with walls literally perpendicular and worn smooth as glass. The volume of water hurled into this narrow passage found egress with the rapidity of a mill race.

To venture into this water by boat would have meant suicide. Thunderstruck, like so many men lined up at the brink of a grave, Torrence's assistants stood in silence, unable to turn eyes from the spot which they felt must mark their end. Hopelessly they gazed at the towering walls. A single giant pine, overhanging the brink directly over-head, was no taller than a toothpick. Tor-rence gave his men one glance and under-stood. No longer were they the intrepid engineers. Weakness, exhaustion and pri-vation had taken the heart out of them. Common, ordinary humans they were, foot-sore, battered, half-starved, stripped to the bare souls, fighting only for love of the lives within them. "The Falls of Sorrows" they named the gorge in front of them; and then they did what all humans do when at the end of their own strength and resource—they took off their hats and stood with bowed heads and prayed for help from Above.

"With our present equipment we can go no farther. The Black Cañon is *not* im-penetrable. If I get out of this scrape alive I shall come back." This was the last entry Torrence made in his note book; for even if he should lose his life, he expected that his notes, as well as a roll of negatives that he had been able to click off on his camera, might be found on his body so that his work would not have been in vain.

It was this same Torrence who discovered for these hopeless ones what appeared to be the bed of a water course leading precipi-tously into the cañon, 2500 feet deep; the course was narrow, and in spots stood at an angle of eighty degrees; but crags and rifts of rocks protruded, permitting foothold, and whatever might be its possibilities high up where the fissure went out of sight, here at the foot it looked promising, considering that there was no alternative of escape.

In their weakened condition it was im-possible to begin the perilous ascent; more-over, to begin the climb except in early morning would have meant to be overtaken by night on the face of the precipice. There-fore the men sat and rested, and for the first time in two weeks gorged themselves, leav-ing enough only for the next morning's meal. To stop during the climb to par-take of sustenance would be impossible.

When morning came they started upward. Tied to a common rope and armed with the spike shod tripod legs of the transits, to be used like so many *alpenstocks*, the men ascended, one after another; Torrence led, each man making a firm foothold and haul-ing in slack or cautiously paying out rope in case of a sudden slip. At snail's pace they gingerly picked their way, the greatest dan-ger being that those above might loosen

stones that would crash down upon those coming after.

By noon the men clung to the precipice like flies, beneath them a thousand dizzy feet up which came the note of the white-churned stream, above them a towering 1500 feet, arched with blue skies and fra-grant with the perfume of sunshine. The violent exercise had stirred appetites until hunger gnawed at empty vitals. On top of this was a raging thirst that filled their throats as if with dry cotton. In their veins was the fever of exertion and excitement, in their hearts the sickening dread that the leader might suddenly announce that the course terminated impassably in a vertical wall of smooth rock. But still the men pressed on, buoyed with the nervous energy of those that fight for life.

Toward late afternoon, despair came to one of the men who realized that night would overtake him in this plight, and that for twelve, interminable hours he would have to stand clinging to a rock, waiting for day-light; and it was with difficulty that he was restrained from leaping into the abyss at once.

Two thousand feet up, within 500 feet of salvation, night closed in. It found the climbers in a dreadful plight. Their lips were purple and swollen to triple size for want of water. Their hands were cut, the palms worn raw from contact with jagged rocks and from the chafing of the rope. Eyes were swollen and bloodshot, and faces were covered with a quarter-inch thick mask where a layer of rock dust had settled and had been baked in with the perspiration.

To spend a night clinging to the side of a precipice, within 500 feet of their goal, was more than could be expected of human for-titude, even if those ready to drop in their tracks from sheer exhaustion should by some miracle have managed to survive the night. It was therefore decided to take chances on groping their way in the dark, and for five hours they proceeded until, with a shout, Torrence grasped the stem of an overhang-ing sage brush, and pulled himself clear beneath God's own starry sky.

Panting, dripping perspiration, one after another the men climbed on to the brink and on hands and knees crawled clear of the edge and collapsed.

Fourteen miles in twenty-one days was all that they had covered. "This time the Black Cañon won," declared Torrence when, still showing signs of the grueling experience he had undergone, he entered the office of Fellows, district engineer of the Reclamation Bureau.

Off and on, for nearly a year, Torrence and Fellows planned how to conquer the Gunnison and its cañon. Whatever horrors might await them beyond the Falls of Sorrows, Torrence's report showed that up to this point at least the cañon might be explored. What was far more important, the data Torrence had obtained proved that, at least up to the Falls of Sorrows the project of turning the Gunnison out of its course would not only be feasible, but that it promised to become one of the most important in the undertakings of the Government.

Had the men dreamed of the unspeakable ordeal awaiting them down in that monster ditch, not all the fortunes of earth could have tempted them again into the undertaking. As it was, however, they planned a campaign of attack based on Torrence's first experience, and within a year after the failure of the first expedition the two men stood side by side in the upper cañon, ready to begin the fight all over again.

Just as much as possible by water, and just as little as possible over the rock-strewn banks, the two engineers had decided to move forward. Boats, experience had shown, were little more than useless in a torrent of this sort. Instead of a boat, therefore, the men had invented a contrivance of their own whereon to transport instruments and provisions. This was simply a rubber air-mattress measuring four by six feet, subdivided into independent air-tight compartments, provided with lashing to secure a load, and with hand ropes which the men could grasp to support themselves and keep their heads above water. Wading-boots, sealed water-tight about their legs, permitting them to swim without danger that the boots would fill and drag them down, and oil skin-covered note books and film bags fitting into sealable rubber pockets, completed the outfit.

For two weeks they climbed and waded and swam, fighting exhaustion, fatigue, the icy river and the obstacles in the dankness of the pitiless ditch. Then they reached the Falls of Sorrows, and from there the journey began once more into the heart of the Great Unknown.

Through the gorge they went, swimming,

holding fast to their unsinkable raft. In places wherever the channel widened and deepened they proceeded in this manner, either pulling the mattress behind them or pushing it ahead. For days on end they had not a dry stitch on them, and worked with blue lips and chattering teeth. A number of times they had become so exhausted in the water that, had they not taken the precaution to lash themselves to the raft, they would have gone down, never to come up again. And still, the further they went, the deeper and wilder and more difficult became the cañon. In spots the channel became so narrow that water roared over the bowlder-strewn bed with such force that the men could hardly retain their feet when immersed only to the depth of their ankles. In one place, where they had to work the raft over rock fragments in the midst of the stream, they struggled so hard to keep the mat from being torn to shreds that they spent three hours covering a distance of sixty feet. For hours at a stretch they were immersed, now swimming, now wading hip deep, in what was practically ice water. And added to these hardships of the day were those of the night; for so narrow became the cañon that often for several hundred yards water flowed in eddies from shore to shore, side ledges becoming so narrow that the men had to take turns to stretch in sleep, one sitting guard to prevent the other from rolling off into the water.

No matter how strong and brave a man may be, pit him against a torrent at the bottom of a cañon, deprive him of proper sustenance, of sunlight and of even a reasonable fighting chance for his life, and he becomes a mite. That is what was happening to these two men whose provisions were running low, and whose only hope of escape lay somewhere in the black, winding distance. Foot by foot, the cañon grew higher and higher and narrower and wilder, as if before long the two walls must come together, leaving the river to dash downward through a subterranean water course into which they would be sucked and buried alive, like rats drawn into the swirl of a sewer hole. What was more disturbing still, instruments showed that the descent of the river was increasing at an alarming rate, as if it might be heading toward an underground waterfall.

Cautiously, bearing the danger of a fall in mind, the men proceeded and had rounded a corner when, of a sudden, a hundred feet ahead, the river fell sheer out of sight. The depth of the water shallowed here so that the men could stand on bottom, despite the swift current. They ventured as near as possible to the brink; but whether the falls hurled themselves a hundred feet deep onto the rocks below, whether they boiled into a deep basin that would give them a chance for life, or whether the river disappeared and continued underground—these things they could not see.

For the first time during these hardships the heart went out of the men, and they sat side by side, head in hands. To have been caught unexpectedly and whirled over the falls would have been a quick mercy; but to be pent up hopelessly, with no alternative save deliberately to take a desperate leap— this was inhuman strain. But there was no other way out; and it was decided that Fellows should plunge first, that Torrence should then launch the raft with the instruments and what provisions were left, and come after.

Fellows leaped; and like a pine chip over the top of a mill dam his body flashed for an instant into view and was gone. For five minutes Torrence stood, awed by the stupendous force, picturing to himself the smashed and mangled remains of his friend. Then, quickly, he released the raft, and unable to bear the suspense, leaped in after him. He must have been whirled into temporary unconsciousness because, barring the sensation of plunging into the water, he had recollection of nothing until he found himself beyond the foot of the falls, clutching at an overhanging rock. Fellows lay collapsed on a stone shelf upon which he had drawn himself, gazing as if in a dream at the silver veil which roared and thundered, falling house-high, churning itself white against jagged black rocks that studded the basin into which they had landed.

For hours the men lay, panting, weakly turning their heads from side to side, slowly coming back to life after the frightful impact to which they had been subjected. But a new danger threatened them. Rations had run so low that for sixteen hours they had not had a mouthful to eat, and they divided a last spoonful of baked beans between them. They hobbled along, now limping, arms about each other's shoulder, now crawling on hands and knees, dragging their raft after them, sighting, recording notes and taking photographs while they swayed on their tottering feet.

They had made very little progress because of the hunger within them, and had sunk down at the mouth of a cleft in the wall to rest, when suddenly a mountain sheep bounded up beside them. Torrence clutched it and hung on like grim death as it tried to escape him. How the sheep got into the cañon and how it had managed to subsist there is a mystery. It was the only living thing the men encountered on their trip, and they ate it in a manner that may not be told, but just as any of us would have eaten it were we dying by inches for want of food.

According to survey the men knew they must now be within a few miles of the foot of the Black Cañon and they hastened on, the fire of new strength and courage in their veins. Between them and the end, however, was such an ordeal as comes into the lives of few who live to tell a tale.

Centuries, perhaps ages ago, the river had gnawed, undermining banks until, with a rumble like an earthquake, a landslide of thousands of tons of rock had crashed into the stream, making a mass hundreds of feet in height. For centuries, then, the torrents had bombarded against the base of this heap, wearing a tortuous channel and disappearing a short distance on into a grim tunnel. It was this obstacle by which the men were now confronted.

Of all the harrowing adventures that they had encountered, none could begin to compare with this. Behind them, in front of them, to either side of them, escape was cut off clean as if they were at the bottom of a 3,000-foot well. Like a pair of beetles running round and round the rim of a saucer, hunting the jumping-off place, the men coursed round and round. But the more they sought, the more they realized that their one hope of escape was to throw themselves into the maelstrom, taking blind chances of being hurled against rocks or being sucked under water and so perishing.

At the entrance of the pitch-dark tunnel they sat gazing at the vortex of a funnel-shaped eddy of the black, swirling water. Long, in silence, the men gazed into each other's eyes. Like two condemned men standing on the brink of eternity they clasped each other's hands in vise-like grasp.

Fellows leaped first. Twice his body whirled around like lightning. The single glimpse of a foot, and Torrence stood alone, petrified with horror; in his mind was the picture of the death struggle going on in the yawning hole before him.

He threw the raft into the eddy and watched it sucked and whirled out of sight. With his face buried in his hands he sat quaking, lacking the nerve to take the horrifying leap, yet remembering his promise to follow within ten minutes of his partner.

Finally he took a long, deep breath and dived head first into the funnel. For an instant he felt himself spinning round and round. A tearing, wrenching sensation as if he were being torn apart in a thousand directions, a pressure as if a mountain were closing in upon him, then a shooting forward like the speed of an arrow; and just as his senses were leaving him he was spat out of the water into clear air, and Fellows clutched his collar as he was whirling past a rock, drawing him upward to safety. Like frightened children suddenly snatched out of jaws of death, these two men of iron locked arms about each other and laughed and wept—laughed and wept hysterically like women.

"Who says the Black Cañon is impassable?" cried Fellows, and over and over they repeated the grim joke until they collapsed into the nervous sleep of exhaustion.

Two days later, they climbed 2,000 feet up the Devil's Slide at the lower end of the cañon, having traveled thirty miles along its bed, having swum the river seventy-two times from bank to bank, and having done what man born of woman never dared before and what none in his right senses will ever undertake again.

For a year, the Reclamation Bureau pondered over the survey of Fellows and Torrence, and mapped and planned. Then it sent an army of rockmen, laborers, mechanics and engineers to assault the Gunnison in its stronghold and turn it into the Uncompahgre.

Barring the world-famed Hoosac tunnel, and a railway tunnel through the Rockies, this one through which the Gunnison must be deflected through the base of the mountain range would be the longest in the country—in round numbers 30,600 feet. Out of the desert at Lujane rose a power plant, machine shops and bunk and mess houses, and from the Uncompahgre end a battery of fifteen power drills were set to work munching into the rock. At the same time the Black Cañon itself was assaulted. Against a precipitous wall hung men and steam drills in mid-air. The tremor and rumble of dynamite charges, followed by the clatter of tons of rock crashing into the abyss, drowned out the drone of the treacherous stream. Foot by foot, a wagon road, winding steeply upon itself, was hewn out of the solid rock. Where not even a goat could have found foothold, power houses, machine shops, and quarters for men were stuck like hornets' nests against the side of the cliff.

West from the River Portal, and east from the Uncompahgre end, the gnawing of the tunnel measuring eight feet high and ten and one half feet wide was begun. Through solid rock they bored, through quicksands that had to be timbered foot by foot. In the west end of the tunnel, the men tapped an underground stream charged with carbonic acid gas, which doused them with a 100-gallon-a-minute soda fountain and drove all hands helter-skelter toward daylight.

For ten years, working in three shifts, day and night, the engineers drove the gigantic bore, averaging a progress of 250 feet a month and removing more than 5,000,000 two-horse wagon-loads of material. Then came a day when the men in the eastern heading could make out the pounding of the drills of the men in the western heading, and two weeks later came the final charge that ripped through the separating wall of rock, while men leaped joyously from one heading into the other; for the long, dangerous, tedious work at last was done.

From the Uncompahgre end of the tunnel a canal, wide and deep enough to float a good sized ship, leads to the Uncompahgre River into which the unruly Gunnison, now harnessed, must flow—first grinding out electricity for power and light to be supplied to farms below, then subdividing itself throughout 400 miles of lateral canals, ready to spread itself meekly over corn and potato fields and to do men's bidding in every fertile form.

When that official opening day comes for the canal, as the President touches the button, Lauzon may be jubilant; but Fellows and Torrence, heroes of the gigantic undertaking in the Land that God Forgot, may stand where they see their old arch enemy as he emerges out of the sluice gate, and as it was twelve years ago at the whirlpool they will clasp each other by the hand and look down upon their work in a satisfaction none may measure, but this time to look down on the greatness of accomplished work.

4

Taming
The Frontier

"Bucky" O'Neill

TAMING THE FRONTIER

"BUCKY" O'NEILL

By WILLIAM MACLEOD RAINE

IN Arizona, men's eyes light up when they talk of "Bucky" O'Neill. He was a splendid type of the chivalrous frontiersman dear to the Western heart. His father was Captain John O'Neill, an officer of Co. K, 116th Pennsylvania Volunteers, which was a part of the celebrated Meagher's Irish Brigade so prominently mentioned in the annals of the Civil War. Captain O'Neill was five times wounded at Fredericksburg, and during the war received fourteen wounds, being obliged to walk on crutches for the rest of his life. Captain William O'Neill, familiarly known as "Bucky," received an excellent classical and legal education. He graduated in 1879 from the law course of the National University, and went straight to Phœnix, Arizona, where he became editor and manager of the *City Herald*.

From that time until his death, O'Neill was prominent as a miner, journalist, politician, business man, judge, soldier, and sheriff. He was a born soldier, and by grace of natural fitness, a leader of men.

"Bucky" was a reckless, soft-spoken, dark-eyed man of unflinching nerve. Personally he was very bashful among strangers. His soft brown eyes grew frightened at thought of making a speech. His daring was Irish in its extravagance, but it covered a very tender heart. At one time the Prescott Grays, of which body he was an officer, were called upon to guard the scaffold during a public hanging. As the trap was sprung one of the officers keeled over in a faint. It was "Bucky" O'Neill, a man whose nerve was famous all over a country full of plucky men. He explained afterwards that he could not bear to see a man killed without giving him a chance to fight for his life.

When the Santa Fé railroad was being built through the territory a gang of its workmen "jumped" a spring belonging to the Navajo Indians. The Navajos were a company of peaceable shepherds, and they were not ready to fight for their rights although their sheep were about to perish with thirst. Along rode "Bucky" O'Neill,

looking out for some of his many diverse interests, and discovered the pitiable condition of the Indian flocks.

His quick Celtic blood boiled. He did not wait for any help but rode straight to the gang of toughs.

"By God! you'll either treat these people decent and give them their water or I'll drive you out," said this Don Quixote of the desert, roundly.

O'Neill armed the Indians and told them to get ready to rush the spring. But the bullies had no mind to fight a body of men led by "Bucky" O'Neill. They retired voluntarily. The head chief of the Navajos was so grateful that he gave to "Bucky" a great silver ring as a mark of his esteem. This ring always commanded for O'Neill the respect due to a chief. He afterward presented it to Thurlow Weed in his generous way.

"Bucky" came into conflict with railroad interests later when he ran for sheriff. He had had inserted in the platform of his party a plank to the effect that the Republican candidates if elected would assess the railroad the full value of its land holdings. The sheriff was at that time the ex-officio assessor of Yavapai County. "Bucky" was the sole issue of the campaign, and though bitterly opposed by corporate interests, ran far ahead of his ticket and was elected.

The sheriff fulfilled his pledge and incurred the enmity of the railroads to such an extent that they were not willing to ask his services to capture the train robbers who had held up an express in Cañon Diablo. They told "Bucky" that very little money had been secured and the affair was of very little importance.

"Bucky" disagreed with them. A robbery had been committed in his county and he proposed to catch the bandits. He was refused inside information by the railroad authorities, but he took up the trail nevertheless. Cañon Diablo is a rough gorge lying in a mountainous country where the trail could easily be lost. Through barren mountain ranges, across

"Bucky" O'Neill.

a country where honest white men had seldom ridden, he and his posse followed the outlaws.

More than once the robbers were engaged at close range. Several times they tried to ambush their pursuers. All the horses ahead of the sheriff's posse were impressed or stampeded. It became imperative to change the jaded horses of the posse. The nearest ranch was thirty miles away, near the border line between Utah and Colorado. To this refuge O'Neill's party was making its way when a volley poured in on the men from a buttress of rock. "Bucky" led the charge which followed. None of the posse were injured, but two of the robbers were wounded in the running fight which followed. With fresh horses the whole party could have been captured, but the delay necessary to secure fresh mounts allowed the outlaws to escape.

"Bucky" was after them hotfoot a day later. The robbers were met again, and two more of them killed. The pursuers were again delayed on account of the jaded condition of their bronchos. O'Neill himself was at no needs to secure a fresh mount. He was riding a horse called Sandy, which had twice swam the Colorado river with his master on his back. "Bucky" had a standing offer to bet that Sandy could cover more and rougher country than any horse in the territory. Since leaving Yavapai County "Bucky" had not once changed horses. Sandy was still hitting the trail with the reliable gait that made him the wonder of everybody.

"Bucky's" impatience got the better of his prudence. He was hot on the trail and he did not want to wait for his men. He hurried forward alone, keeping an eye open for the robbers. He came upon them camped in Wah Weep Cañon in a sort of cave. With his usual quickness O'Neill had them covered before they could reach for a gun.

"Hello, boys, what's new?" was his easy greeting.

For a full hour he held the desperadoes under his gun before the rest of his party came up. By taking them in camp he secured all their baggage, concealed in which was $350,000—the loss that the railroad had said was of no consequence.

"Bucky" had covered the expenses of his posse both ways, expecting to be reimbursed. But the supervisors were friends of the railroads and refused to pay the expenses because the sheriff had technically violated the law by leaving the county without asking their permission. He carried his case from court to court, but lost in the end.

The sheriff who went out of his county after a desperado in those early days always faced the probability of having to fight for his prisoner. His friends were likely to line up in defence of their pet outlaw. On one occasion "Bucky" followed a criminal into New Mexico. He rode into a town where the man had just passed through. The people eyed the sheriff suspiciously and declared no such man had been there. O'Neill knew they were lying

and followed his man. He came up with him a short distance beyond the settlement.

The robber opened fire on the sheriff, and had his leg broken by "Bucky's" return shot. When the sheriff reached the settlement with his prisoner he found himself confronted by a mob. Smith, the captured outlaw, was himself of a chivalrous turn. He had that morning met a school teacher lost on the desert and had brought her back to the settlement. This struck a responsive chord in the Western heart, and the New Mexicans were convinced that Smith was "a gentleman."

Smith was quick to perceive his advantage and declared that O'Neill had shot him over a difference about a woman. The crowd closed in to rescue him. Things looked squally for the Yavapai sheriff. O'Neill backed his prisoner and his horse into an adobe hut.

"When a man crosses that doorway, I'll shoot him and then the prisoner," he said, his soft eyes grown hard as steel.

New Mexico understands that kind of talk. O'Neill got away with his prisoner in safety.

While "Bucky" was a resident of Phœnix the Hardy "outfit" rode in from the cow-camps to "shoot up" the town. They camped outside and sent word that they would presently be in. Henry Garfio, a Mexican, was sheriff. He was a good man and a nervy one. O'Neill was a deputy, and the two men rode out to meet the cow-punchers who were racing down Washington Street in a cloud of dust, their smoking Winchesters swinging from side to side.

O'Neill and Garfio stepped out of a doorway. The vaqueros drew rein for a moment and O'Neill advised them to be gone. Their leader, Hardy, laughed, and fired at him. O'Neill's answering shot threw him from his saddle.

"I told you to stop," said "Bucky" in gentle apology as he stepped across to the wounded man.

While he was sheriff of Yavapai some notorious cut-throats rode into Prescott and alighted at Cavanaugh's saloon. Word came to the court-house that they were in town. Presently a quiet young man sauntered up to the bar and joined the "bad men." It was "Bucky" O'Neill. A tense silence filled the room. Some believed that "Bucky" would not tackle this job. But he did.

His rather effeminate voice announced to the leader that he had come to arrest them. The man reached for his gun, but "Bucky's" fearless eyes met his fair and full. For a moment the man hesitated, looking into the sheriff's pistol. Then he threw down his gun with a curse. His men followed his example.

So gentle was "Bucky's" manner that those who did not know him were likely to be deceived. At Tucson he was once walking down the street with a rough-spoken citizen who prided himself on being blunt in talk and bold in action. O'Neill made a remark that caused his companion to spit out that he lied.

"Beg pardon?" said "Bucky," astonished.

"I say you lie," was the brusque retort.

"Bucky" took the would-be bold man by the ears and churned him up and down in the hope of teaching him better manners.

Despite his early fears of speechmaking O'Neill became one of the greatest politicians in the state. He was billed once to speak at Mammoth to deliver an election speech. Neal, the stage driver, was taking him in one of his "rigs." They came to the wash of the Cañon Del Oro, and found it a raging torrent.

Neal, himself a man of acknowledged courage, drew rein and asked "Bucky" what he should do.

"I've got to get to Mammoth to-night," said the other.

"I'll take you through if you say so," returned Neal nonchalantly.

"Fire ahead then."

They were nearly drowned, but "Bucky" spoke at Mammoth that night.

Only once was "Bucky" O'Neill known to turn his back to a foe. This was when he was acting as probate judge of Yavapai County. He had offended a woman and she opened fire at him with her tongue and an umbrella. "Bucky" hurriedly announced that court was adjourned and fled incontinently through the back door.

There was nothing O'Neill would not tackle. He took always the side of the underdog and did not care how many were against him. It was the vivid abandon with which he plunged into the frontier life that gave him his universal nickname of "Bucky." He gambled "with the lid off" at any game and for any stakes his opponent chose to name.

The first volunteer mustered into the army for the war with Spain was "Bucky" O'Neill. He entered as a private, but was afterwards made Captain of Troop A of Roosevelt's Rough Riders. His laconic expression, "Who wouldn't gamble for a star?" in response to somebody who remonstrated with him for enlisting as a private, made the rounds of the country. Whether the star he meant was Cuba, statehood for Arizona through the gallantry of her sons, or a brigadier's rank for himself, has never been definitely settled. A fellow captain of the Rough Riders, who was present when the remark was made, told me that a brigadier's star was meant.

"Bucky" O'Neill was killed at the battle of San Juan, July, 1898, as he walked up and down before his line of waiting men, talking to Captain Howse of the Artillery. Bullets were zipping all about him. Somebody remonstrated with him for exposing himself so recklessly. "You'll be killed sure, Captain."

"The Spanish bullet that will kill me is not yet moulded," he said with a laugh.

"As he turned on his heel a bullet struck him in the mouth and came out at the back of his head; so that even before he fell his gallant soul had gone out into the darkness."

In this sentence, Colonel Roosevelt tells of the passing of "Bucky" O'Neill, that strange character who smoked cigarettes and quoted Whitman on the battlefield, who fought all his gusty lifetime against injustice to the weak, but loved a row as a schoolboy does a holiday. His life work is written deep in a territory redeemed from lawlessness. To understand "Bucky" O'Neill you must know Arizona—its turbulent youthful energy, its bigness and its breadth, above all, its unflinching loyalty to manhood.

5

Billy the Kid
— A Man
All "Bad"

Arthur Chapman

BILLY THE KID—A MAN ALL "BAD"

By ARTHUR CHAPMAN

IT is one of the anomalies of Western life that a pale, slender, high voiced, light-haired, and altogether effeminate individual named William Antrim, sometimes called Billy Bonny, and generally known as Billy the Kid, should be the worst desperado in the history of the frontier. Yet, in considering the so-called "bad men" of the West, his name must stand forth as the superlative of badness. Some of the gun-fighters of frontier days killed in self-defense, and others killed when they were in liquor or inflamed with anger—but Billy the Kid was the only white man who slew out of pure wantonness. Three of his victims—Mexicans they were—he bowled over "just to see them kick," as he laughingly explained afterward. If he had a grudge against a man he never harbored it long, but simply confronted his victim and slew without making explanation. Only sturdy John Chisholm bade defiance to Billy to the end of the desperado's red career, and only one man ever proved himself a quicker shot—Patrick A. Garrett, one of the nerviest sheriffs that ever served in the days when the Southwest needed nervy men in that office.

Billy the Kid was only twenty-one years of age when he gasped out his life at the feet of his most implacable foe, and it was known that he had killed one man for every year of his existence. In early boyhood he was a New York street waif, from where he was sent to Silver City, New Mexico, where a stepfather volunteered to make him a worthy member of society. But at the mature age of fifteen, Billy quarreled with his step-father—one of the few quarrels in which the Kid's pistol did not speak the final word—and the youth left home, becoming a waiter in a hotel at Silver City. Soon Billy was convicted of stealing supplies from the hotel larder, and clothes from a Chinese laundryman. He was put in jail, but the jailer little reckoned with the budding desperado in his charge. Billy worked his slender form up through the chimney and made his escape. It was not to be his last successful jail-break, for no desperado since the days of Jack Sheppard

showed the Kid's wonderful faculty of turning the devices of locksmith and the watchfulness of guards to naught. After his escape from the Silver City jail he began life anew as a blacksmith's apprentice at Camp Apache. But one day he quarreled with the blacksmith. The apprentice shot the forge-master dead and made his escape. Thereafter Billy's ways were the ways of the desperado, for at last he had reached the proud distinction of having a price put on his head.

At the time of Billy's first essay in supreme crime the Lincoln County Cattle War was making Southwestern New Mexico a delectable place for gentlemen who cared not so much for clear consciences as for well-notched gun-handles. This war was waged between the horse thieves and cattle rustlers on one side and cattle owners on the other. A few bold cattlemen had entered the Pecos country with their herds, despite the fact that in so doing they were invading the haunts of men who had been driven out of the more settled portions of the territory by sheriff's posses and vigilance committees. One class determined to despoil the other class of its herds and to drive it out of Lincoln county, and the other class determined to fight for its range. A guerrilla warfare went on for two years and upwards, and Emerson Hough, in his "The Story of the Cowboy," estimates that two or three hundred men on both sides lost their lives in the long series of assassinations.

Chief among the stock owners was John Chisholm, whose brand was on thousands of range cattle. Billy worked for Chisholm a short time, but soon he had his inevitable quarrel with his employer. It was over a question of wages, Billy claiming that Chisholm had not squared their account. Only the fact that Chisholm was surrounded by a guard of hard-fighting cowboys, with reputations as "killers," kept him from assassination when he and the young desperado parted. As it was, Billy managed finally to exact a terrible penalty from Chisholm. It is more than likely that the Kid swore his vendetta against Chisholm and other cattle owners simply as a matter of course instead of a punctilious affair of principle. Billy would naturally take sides with the rustlers who were making life miserable for honest men in Lincoln county. He soon became a leader of the desperate crew and was in the thick of many of the deadly encounters that took place during the course of the "war." It is estimated that he put a round dozen of notches on his gun-handle during this fiercest of range feuds, every notch representing a human life. Two of his victims were a sheriff and his deputy, who had driven him and part of his gang into an adobe house.

The name of Billy the Kid became such a terror in the Southwest that the people of Lincoln county cast about for the right sort of a man to literally camp on the trail of this outlaw and rid the world of his presence. For this sole purpose Pat Garrett was elected. Garrett, who is now Collector of Customs at El Paso, and who looks mildly bored when anyone mentions Billy the Kid, had earned a reputation as a man who never wasted speeches or lead. Cool headed at all times, skilled in handling firearms, and thoroughly acquainted with the habits and haunts of the ruffians of the Southwest, the tall, easy-going Garrett was elected to try conclusions with the desperado. It was not an enviable task this, to essay to overmatch a man who knew the desert as the average matinee idol knows his Broadway, and whose "gameness" matched his ferocity, but Garrett undertook the responsibility with open eyes. He invaded the territory of Billy the Kid and carried out his plans so cleverly that he succeeded in trapping the desperado.

Organizing a posse of twenty-five determined men, many of whom had lost friends at the hands of the Kid, Garrett set out after his man. Bob Ollinger, who was as brave, faithful and skilled a man as ever hunted a desperado in frontier days, and a deputy named Stewart, were Garrett's lieutenants. On the Kid's side there was a resolute band, including Billy Wilson, Dave Rudebaugh and Tom Pickett, these three being almost as desperate criminals as their beardless leader. Garrett's posse divided in two bands, the larger, consisting of fifteen men, being headed by the sheriff and his two lieutenants. Garrett's party succeeded in bringing the Kid, Billy Wilson,

Tom Pickett, and one other at bay in an old cabin at Stinking Springs. The outlaws fastened their horses near the cabin and fortified the place. Garrett stationed his men about fifty yards from the cabin behind some natural rock fortifications, and at 3.30 o'clock in the afternoon the battle opened. A continuous fire was kept up on both sides. The posse kept well under cover and none of Garrett's men was hurt, but one of the outlaws was killed by a bullet that penetrated the cabin door. About twilight, when their ammunition ran low, the outlaws made a break for liberty. The Kid stole out to where the horses stood, intending to lead them to the cabin where all could mount and ride away. He succeeded in getting the bunch as far as the door, when one of the animals was killed, falling against the entrance in such a way that it was partially blocked. Billy once more took his stand with the besieged, but, when the posse began to surround the house with the intention of firing it when it became dark, the outlaws concluded to surrender. Dave Rudebaugh stepped out in the dusk and held up his hands, shouting as he did so that he surrendered. Billy Wilson and Pickett followed, and all were securely shackled hand and foot and taken to Las Vegas.

When it became noised about Las Vegas that Billy the Kid was made captive, a mob soon formed. Garrett had anticipated a lynching, and had put his prisoners in a box car, over which he, Ollinger, Stewart and their little band stood guard. Three hundred Mexicans and whites swept down upon Garrett and his men, demanding the prisoners. The sight of the Kid, who shook his manacled hands at the crowd and begged Garrett to "turn him loose with a brace of pistols," inflamed the mob to fury. The train could not move for an hour, but during that long sixty minutes Garrett and his bold deputies, with weapons drawn, held the mob at bay. Could the crowd have laid hands on the outlaws, short work would have been made of them, but every man in the mob knew the temper of Pat Garrett and the men at his back, and the train finally pulled out with the desperados unscathed.

The outlaws were duly tried, and Billy the Kid and Rudebaugh were sentenced to be hanged, the latter for having murdered a jailer at Las Vegas the year before, in an attempt to rescue some imprisoned partners in crime. The judge, in pronouncing sentence on Billy the Kid, made it impressive by declaring severely:

"And you are sentenced to be hanged by the neck until you are dead, dead, dead!"

was constantly on the watch for a chance to make his escape. When the day of his hanging was but two weeks distant, Billy saw his chance. The redoubtable Ollinger, who was one of the Kid's guards, was eating supper at a coffee house across the street. Another deputy, J. W. Bell, guarded the

Pat Garrett, who as Sheriff of Lincoln County closed the career of Billy the Kid.

Whereupon the boyish prisoner laughed in the judge's face and chanted in mockery:

"And you can go to h—l, h—l, h—l!"

Not for an instant did the Kid's confidence desert him. Though shackled hand and foot and guarded day and night, he

Kid while the desperado ate. In order to permit Billy to carry the food to his mouth, both handcuffs had been fastened to one wrist. Bell relaxed his vigilance an instant, when within striking distance of his prisoner. Quick as thought Billy's manacled hand came down on the deputy's head, stretching him out, half stunned. Snatching Bell's pistol, Billy shot the deputy through the body, the man staggering to his feet, and lurching down the back stairs, when he fell dead in the yard. Ollinger heard the shot and ran across the street. As he entered the jail yard someone called his name. Just as the deputy looked up and saw the Kid at a window, Billy fired Ollinger's own shotgun, which was heavily charged with buckshot. Ollinger fell dead, and Billy broke the weapon across the window sill, crying:

"There; you won't corral me with that any more."

Kicking open the door to an adjoining room where the weapons were kept, Billy gathered up six rifles and a number of revolvers. Then he forced the first person he met to break the shackles from his legs and bring up a horse. Taking a Winchester and four revolvers, Billy rendered the rest of the weapons useless and rode away.

At the time of the Kid's escape, Sheriff Garrett was at White Oaks. On his return to Lincoln he at once took the trail in search of the man who had killed his faithful assistants. But in the meantime Billy's everready revolver was playing havoc on the borders of Lincoln county. Soon after his escape from the Lincoln jail the Kid killed one William Matthews and a companion, whom he encountered in the desert. Such was the tribute of fear levied by the outlaw, that he was practically sure of securing food and shelter, no matter where he turned. Nor were people likely to give out information concerning his whereabouts, for the reason that, if it ever came to the outlaw's ears, it was equivalent to a death-warrant. Now camping with sheep-herders in the desert, now appearing at some round-up camp, and again walking boldly into some settlement, the Kid remained in Lincoln county for weeks, laughing at Garrett's efforts to trace him.

One day the Kid turned up at one of the Chisholm cow-camps. He had not forgotten his old feud with the cattle king of the Pecos. Three of the cowboys were at a fire, cooking supper, and twenty yards away Barrett Howell was hobbling a cow pony. Billy rode up to Howell and asked him if he worked for John Chisholm. On being answered in the affirmative, the Kid shot the

cowboy through the head, at the same time crying, in his high-pitched voice: "Well, there's your pay."

The cowboys at the fire sprang to their feet, as they saw their comrade fall, but Billy's revolver spoke twice more and two of them fell dead. Then, covering the remaining cowboy with his revolver, Billy shrilled this message:

"You tell John Chisholm he owes me money. I'll credit him with five dollars on the bill every time I kill one of his men. If I kill him the account is wiped out."

In July, 1881, after Billy had been at large some two months, Sheriff Garrett heard that the Kid had been seen in the vicinity of Fort Sumner. Accompanied by two deputies, Garrett remained in the vicinity of Fort Sumner a week, but information about the Kid was hard to get, in view of the bonds of terror in which the desperado held the entire community. One night, after vainly watching a suspected house until midnight, Garrett suggested that a call be made on Peter Maxwell, who lived in one of the old buildings at the fort, and who was brave enough to tell what he knew about the Kid's whereabouts. Garrett stepped into Maxwell's room to talk to him, while his deputies sat on the porch in the bright New Mexican moonlight. Soon a man, clad in shirt and trousers, and carrying a knife in one hand and a revolver in the other, hurried toward the building, and as he stepped on the porch, cried:

"*Quien es? Quien es?*" ("Who is it?")

One of the deputies, having no idea that this could be Billy the Kid, told him to put up his gun and not be alarmed. At the same time he rose and walked toward Billy, but, lithe as a cat, the desperado leaped through the open doorway into Maxwell's room.

Something—probably the sixth sense said to be given to all hunted things—told Billy that all was not right in the room. Coming into the dark from the bright moon-light he could not make out objects distinctly, consequently he could not see Garrett sitting at the foot of the bed. Coming to the edge of the bed, and putting his hand on the coverlet within a few inches of Garrett, Billy asked Maxwell:

"Say, Pete, who are those fellows out there?"

Garrett recognized the voice as that of

Billy the Kid, and slipped his holster around so he could get at his revolver. At the same time Billy caught sight of the figure on the bed. Covering Garrett with his revolver, he sprang backward, crying:

"*Quien es?*"

The instant's pause was fatal to Billy the Kid, for, almost before the Spanish words had dropped from the desperado's lips, Garrett's revolver had spoken. The Kid fell to the floor, shot through the heart, his revolver being discharged by his convulsive movement as he fell.

The qualities that caused Pat Garrett to be known as the coolest head in the Southwest were shown in this encounter. As he fired, Garrett leaned to the left, thinking that he could get Billy's bullet in the right side. "That would give me a chance to get another shot at him," explained the sheriff grimly.

As soon as the shots were heard, the deputies outside called Garrett's name, but again the presence of mind of the born gun fighter was manifested. Garrett did not answer, thinking that perhaps his gasping foe on the floor, was not fatally wounded, and that the sound of the sheriff's voice would give Billy the Kid a chance to get in an effective shot.

Could a Lombroso have studied this mere boy, who seemed to have been born with a tiger's blood thirst, no doubt science would have received an interesting contribution. Without a spark of pity for his numerous victims, and with no fear of his enemies in his heart, Billy the Kid presented a peculiar phenomenon. His desire was to kill, and it seemed to make little difference to him whether he killed in the most cowardly manner or whether he boldly faced the weapons of his enemies. Few men have been the Kid's equal with the revolver, and none ever made a more terrifying record with that universal weapon of the frontier.

Dying, as he had lived, like a wild beast, this beardless, soulless youth who had about him none of the attributes that usually gain the Western desperado a certain sort of admiration, must remain wholly the most unaccountable figure in frontier history.

6

The Plains Across

Noah Brooks

THE CENTURY MAGAZINE

APRIL, 1902.

"THE PLAINS ACROSS."[1]

BY NOAH BROOKS,

WITH ILLUSTRATIONS BY FREDERIC REMINGTON.

DURING the ten years immediately following the discovery of gold in California, the main-traveled road across the continent was what was known as the Platte River route. Starting from Council Bluffs, Iowa, a town then famous as the "jumping-off place" for California emigrants, the adventurers crossed the Missouri by a rope ferry and clambered up a steep, slippery bank to the site of the modern city of Omaha. The only building of any considerable dimensions in the early fifties was a large, unpainted, barn-like structure, which, we were proudly told, was to be the capitol of the Territory of Nebraska, the Territorial organization of which was authorized by Congress in 1854.

Crossing the Elkhorn during our first day's journey, we soon after struck the Platte, and our long, long tramp across the Great Plains had fairly begun. "Plains" very fairly describes the country lying along the Platte valley; for where the land was not a dead level, it was an undulating meadow skirting the river and belted along the stream with cottonwoods and willows. Thence the trail followed the river for about two hundred miles, and then, at the junction of the North Fork of the Platte, deflected northward, and, striking the Sweetwater, after crossing the upper waters of the North Fork, followed that beautiful stream through a hilly and picturesque country to the South Pass of the Rocky Mountains and over the Great Divide.

The trail from the Rocky Mountains to Salt Lake valley grew more and more difficult as we approached the rocky fastnesses of the Wahsatch range of mountains, that defends the land of the Latter-Day Saints on its eastern border. Leaving the valley and skirting the northern end of Great Salt Lake, the route followed the general course of the Humboldt, crossed the dreadful desert which takes its name from the river, and we finally caught sight once more of civilization

---

[1] In the rude ballads and songs of the time, the phrase for crossing the plains was "the plains across"; never by any chance did the verse-maker write "across the plains." This form of locution was at once adopted by the plainsmen, who unconsciously drifted into the use of the more poetic phrase, "the plains across"; and to this day you will find old pioneers scattered among the solitudes of the far Northwest who never admit that they came across the plains; they came the plains across.

in Honey Lake valley, at the eastern base of the Sierra Nevada. Here the trail began a toilsome ascent of the gigantic mountain wall, and scaling the roof of the world, as it seemed to us, slid down into the valley of the Sacramento through the wooded ridges of the Plumas mining region.

The distances from Council Bluffs, roughly

HALF-TONE PLATE ENGRAVED BY F. H. WELLINGTON.

A BULL-WHACKER.

The loaded whip was used with two hands and was twenty feet long, or more, in the lash. In some cases it had a horseshoe-nail in the end of the snapper.

estimated at the time, were as follows: 487 miles to Fort Laramie; 802 to South Pass; 900 to Fort Bridger; 984 to Salt Lake; 1340 to the head of the Humboldt; 1767 to Big Meadows, in the heart of the Sierras; and 1878 to the floor of the Sacramento valley. We left Omaha on the 27th of May, and made our first camp in the valley of the Sacramento on the 4th of October.

The average cost of a journey to California in those days did not greatly vary whether one took the water route by the way of Cape Horn or the land route by the trail just described. In either case the emigrants usually clubbed together, and the cost per man was therefore considerably reduced. A party of overland emigrants, supplied with a team of horses or oxen,— preferably the latter,—and numbering four or five men, were expected to invest about five hundred dollars for their outfit. This included the cost of provisions, clothing, tent, wagon, and animals, and a small sum of ready money for emergencies by the way. The necessaries of life were few and simple. The commissariat was slender, and included flour, dried beans, coffee, bacon or "side-meat," and a few small stores—sugar, salt, baking-powder, and the like. In those days the art of canning goods had not been invented, and the only article in that category was the indispensable yeast-powder, without which bread was impossible. The earliest emigrants experimented with hard bread, but soft bread, baked fresh every day, was found more economical and portable, as well as more palatable.

But, after all, beans and coffee were the mainstay of each well-seasoned and well-equipped party. In our own experience, good luck (more than good management) furnished us with enough of these two necessaries of life to last us from the Missouri to the Pacific. The coffee, it should be explained, was bought in its green state, and was browned and ground as occasion required. That variety of pork product known as side-meat was a boneless slab from the side of a mast-fed porker, salted and smoked. In western Iowa and Missouri we usually found this meat corded up in piles after it had been cured. Corn-meal, that beloved staff of life on the Western frontier, was an unprofitable addition to the stores of the emigrant. It was not "filling," and its nutriment was out of all proportion to its bulk. Hot flour bread, made into the form of biscuits, and dipped in the "dope," or gravy, made by mixing flour and water with the grease extracted from the fried bacon, was our mainstay.

Does the imagination of the epicure revolt at the suggestion of so rude a dish? To hundreds of thousands of weary emigrants, trudging their way across the continent, spending their days and nights in the open air and breathing an atmosphere bright with ozone, even ruder viands than this were as nectar and ambrosia.

The evolution of cooks, teamsters, woodsmen, and herders from the raw materials of a party of emigrants was one of the interesting features of life on the Great Plains. Here was a little company made up of a variety of experiences and aptitudes. Each man's best faculty in a novel service must be discovered. At the outset, none knew who should drive the oxen, who should do the cooking, or whose ingenuity would be taxed to mend broken wagon or tattered clothing. Gradually, and not altogether without grumbling and objection, each man filled his own proper place. No matter if the members of the party were college-bred, society men, farmers' sons, or ex-salesmen; each man found his legitimate vocation after a while. The severest critic of another's work was eventually charged with the labor which he had all along declared was not rightly performed by others. By the time the journey was fairly undertaken, the company was manned in every section as completely as if each worker had been assigned to his place in a council of the Fates. It was just and fit that he who had steadily derided the cooking of every other should show the others how cooking should be done; and common consent gave to the best manager of cattle the arduous post of driver. There was no place for drones, of course, for this was a strenuous life. Before the continent had been crossed the master spirits had asserted themselves. It was an evolution of the fittest.

I have said that these assignments to duty were not accomplished without grumbling and objection. Indeed, the division of labor in a party of emigrants was a prolific cause of quarrel. In our own little company of five there were occasional angry debates while the various burdens were being adjusted, but no outbreak ever occurred. We saw not a little fighting in the camps of others who sometimes jogged along the trail in our company, and these bloody fisticuffs were invariably the outcome of disputes over divisions of labor.

I recall one company from southern Illinois made up of an elderly man, his three sons, and a son-in-law. Their fights were many and violent, and, oddly enough, it was the son-in-law who usually sided with the gray-haired sire against his undutiful boys. In a sophisticated condition of society, I dare say, we should have regarded these bouts with something like horror; but I am bound to say that, in the simple savagery of our nearness to nature, we looked on with equanimity, if not amusement, while this happy family fought and mauled one another like wild beasts. They appeared to enjoy the fight, and we never could see that any bad blood was engendered by their frequent battles.

It should not be understood that the length of time required to traverse the distance between the Missouri and the Sacramento was wholly consumed in traveling. Nobody appeared to be in a feverish haste to finish the journey; and it was necessary to make occasional stops on the trail, where conditions were favorable, for the purpose of resting and refitting. A pleasant camping-place, with wood, water, and grass in plenty, was an invitation to halt and take a rest. This was called a "lay-by," and the halt sometimes lasted several days, during

miles; an uncommonly good day with favorable conditions would give us twenty-five miles. The distances from camping-place to camping-place were usually well known to all wayfarers. By some subtle agency, information (and sometimes misinformation) was dis-

HALF-TONE PLATE ENGRAVED BY R. C. COLLINS.

FRESH BUFFALO MEAT.

which wagon-tires were reset, ox-yokes repaired, clothes mended, and a general clean-up of the entire outfit completed preparatory to another long and uninterrupted drive toward the setting sun. If the stage of the journey immediately before us was an unusually difficult one, the stop was longer and the overhauling more thorough.

A day's march averaged about twenty

seminated along the trail before us and behind us, and we generally knew what sort of camping-place we should find each night, and how far it was from the place of the morning start. So, when we halted for the night, we knew pretty accurately how many miles we had covered in that day's tramp.

Of course riding was out of the question. We had one horse, but he was reserved for emergencies, and nobody but a shirk would think of crawling into the wagon, loaded down as it was with the necessaries of life, unless sickness made it impossible for him to walk. In this way we may be said to have walked all the way from the Missouri to the Sacramento. Much walking makes the human leg a mere affair of skin, bone, and sinew. We used to say that our legs were like chair-posts. But then the exercise was "good for the health." Nobody was ever ill.

Some of the difficulties of the way would appal a teamster used only to the smooth tracks of civilized life. Wagons were hauled through obstructions that seemed to a tyro simply insurmountable. The trail, for a great part of the way after leaving the valley of the Platte and before entering the desert plains of the far interior, was rough and rocky, now climbing steep hills and now dropping abruptly down steeper declivities. Crossing rivers and creeks was often perilous and attended with loss and hardship by the upsetting of wagons and the damage done to stores. At the worst of these crossings we always found companies detained by the stress of circumstances who were engaged in helping one another over the stream. All hands resorted to the process of "doubling up," as many yoke of cattle as were required being drafted from the assembled caravans to "snake across" the various wagons one after another. The cheerfulness with which these emigrants, total strangers to one another, buckled to the work, never leaving it until all were safely over, was beautiful to behold.

We had privately ridiculed an enormous prairie-schooner in one of the larger caravans that we passed at long intervals. It was as big as a small house, and required four yoke of oxen to draw it. When we came to the Malade, a small but very difficult stream beyond the South Pass, we found our big friend, with many other lesser craft, stalled on the banks of the river, puzzled to discover means of crossing. The stream was deep, swift, and narrow, and the banks were steep almost to perpendicularity. Lower down, the creek was a good fording-place for light wagons, but loaded teams like ours would be stalled in the oozy bottom. Finally, the uncouth owner of the great prairie-schooner, with the aid of many yoke of cattle and a large company of men, managed to get his wagon across the stream in such a way that the forward end rested on the farther bank and the hinder end on the hither brink, thus making a safe and commodious bridge. The wagons were now unloaded, and their contents were carried across on this novel bridge. The lightened wagons were driven across lower down, and, the entire day being spent in this adventure, all hands went into camp on the farther side of the never-to-be-forgotten Malade.

Grass, wood, and water were three necessities of life on the trail. But these were sometimes very difficult to find. Usually one or two of the party went on ahead of the rest and looked out a suitable camping-place where those essentials could be found. Fuel was sometimes absolutely unobtainable, possibly a few dry weeds and stalks being the only combustible thing to be found. In the buffalo region we depended wholly on the buffalo-chips with which the ground was plentifully bestrewn. The dung of the buffalo, some of which had lain there for countless ages, exposed to the action of sun, wind, and rain, became in time a desiccated mass of chewed and digested grass, as light as cork and as dry as tinder. This made a fire like that from charcoal.

There was something impressive to an imaginative mind in striking one of these lonely haunts of the buffalo on a short cut-off from the main-traveled trail. Here was no trace of human activity, and the innumerable signs of herds of buffalo were as undisturbed as they were before a white man trod the plains. A sentimental person might say that the existence of the buffalo, now becoming prehistoric, was a providential dispensation for the coming emigrant across these treeless spaces. The much-despised sage-brush, sure sign of a barren soil, and the far more despised and sticky greasewood, an ill-flavored herb, supplemented the buffalo-chips as we pressed farther to the westward and into the region of alkaline deserts.

Emigrants who were dependent upon open fires for cooking were often in very hard case. We were fortunate in the possession of a small sheet-iron camp-stove, for the heating of which a small amount of fuel was sufficient. This handy little apparatus was lashed to the rear end of the wagon when on the trail, and when it was in use, every sort of our simple cookery could be carried on by it with the most satisfactory results. When we were obliged to camp for the night on wet ground after a rain, the flat-bottomed camp-stove, well heated and light, was moved from place to place inside the tent until the surface on which we must make our bed was fairly dry. Sometimes, however, we camped

HALF-TONE PLATE ENGRAVED BY H. C. MERRILL.

SEARCHING FOR AN EASY FORD.

down on the damp ground; and sometimes, before we learned the trick of digging a ditch around the tent when signs of rain appeared, we woke to find ourselves lying in puddles of water. In such a case it was better to lie in the water that had been slightly warmed by the heat of one's body than to turn over into a colder stream on the other side. These experiences were novel and interesting; nobody ever suffered seriously from them.

But no wetness, no wind and rain, ever discomposed us as did the mosquitos in the valley of the Platte. I used to think that Lewis and Clark, in the journal of their expedition across the continent in 1804–06, laid too much stress upon the nuisance of the "moschetoes," as they called these pests. I had not then made the acquaintance of the Platte River insect. The mosquitos did not trouble us by day, but at dusk they seemed to rise out of the ground in clouds, filling the air and being taken into the breathing apparatus of sufferers. The cattle were tormented almost to madness, and sleep for us was impossible except by surrounding the camp with "smudges," or low fires built to make smoke without heat. The tent was smoked out before we turned in for the night, and the fly-entrance was carefully secured; but no precaution would exclude all of the winged inquisitors. Two mosquitos in a tent, among five men, were as efficient for mischief as two hundred. After a night of fighting these enemies to sleep, one rose in the morning unrefreshed, jaded, and weary beyond words of description. More than once, after a night of sleepless torment, I went to sleep while walking by the side of the patiently plodding ox-team, stumbling into wakefulness just as I lost consciousness. In such a plight it was good to get on ahead of the teams, when one was at liberty to go, and dropping by the side of the trail, sleep the sleep of the just until the teams came along to wake the weary one. Nobody wore garments that could be soiled or disfigured by dust or mud, and it was a great comfort to those of us who were city-bred to feel that abandon which rough clothing and a community of roughness give to a wayfarer in the wilderness.

In the matter of the necessaries of life, we had times of plenty and times of scarcity. There were places where our cattle were knee-deep in wild, succulent grasses, and there were times when they had nothing but the coarse and wilted sheaves of grass

carried along the trail from the last camp. Flour, coffee, and bacon never failed us; and there were times when we had more fresh meat than we could eat. In the buffalo country, of course, we had the wholesome beef of that then multitudinous animal in every possible variety. In the Rocky Mountain region, antelope, prairie-dogs,[1] black-tail deer, jack-rabbits, and occasionally sage-hens gave us an enjoyable change from our staple diet of bacon and bread. The antelope were very wild and timid, and no one thought of chasing them; they were brought down by stratagem. A bright-colored handkerchief fastened to a ramrod stuck into the ground was a lure which no antelope could resist. A small drove of these inquisitive creatures would circle distantly round and round the strange flag: but ever drawing nearer, sometimes pausing as if to discuss among themselves what that thing could possibly be, they would certainly come at last within gunshot of the patient hunter lying flat on the ground; a rifle-ball would bring down one of the herd, and the rest would disappear as if the earth had swallowed them.

In the heart of the buffalo country the buffaloes were an insufferable nuisance. Vast herds were moving across our trail from south to north, trampling the moist and grassy soil into a black paste, and so polluting the streams and springs that drinking-water was often difficult to obtain. The vastness of some of these droves was most impressive, in spite of the calamitous ruin they left behind them. As far as the eye could reach, the surface of the earth was a heaving mass of animal life; the ground seemed to be covered with a brown mantle of fur. As we advanced along the trail, the droves would quietly separate to our right and left, leaving a lane along which we traveled with herds on each side of us. From an eminence, looking backward and forward, one could see that we were completely hemmed in before and behind; and the space left for us by the buffalo moved along with us. They never in the least incommoded us by any hostile action; all they asked, apparently, was to be let alone.

A great herd of buffalo, moving rapidly, made a sound like a muffled roar of thunder; and when such an army struck a stream of water, the silvery flood was instantaneously transformed into a turbid tide. If a few scattered buffalo were cantering away from dreaded man, not one of them could resist

[1] A species of marmot, delicate of flesh and feeding on vegetable products.

HALF-TONE PLATE ENGRAVED BY H. C. MERRILL.

A LANE THROUGH THE BUFFALO HERD.

the temptation to fall and roll in a buffalo "wallow," if one chanced in his way. A bare spot of ground on which the buffalo have rolled is a wallow, and, once bare, it is kept so for ages. The buffalo is not the clumsy animal he looks in captivity or in pictures. It is a fleet horse that can overtake him; and to see him drop into a wallow while on a keen run, roll over and over two or three times, and skip to his feet and away with his comrades with the nimbleness of a kitten, is a sight to be remembered.

In the early fifties the buffalo country embraced nearly the whole of what is now the State of Nebraska. We killed our first buffalo at the mouth of Wood River, ten days from the Missouri, and I do not remember that we saw any after passing Fort Laramie. In those days it did not seem possible that the buffalo could ever be exterminated. But white men and Indians were alike moved by a spirit of destruction; they killed for the mere sake of killing. At several places along the rivers we saw heaps of skeletons of buffalo at the foot of bluffs over which they had been driven by the Indians to indiscriminate and needless slaughter. We passed countless numbers of carcasses left by reckless white butchers, untouched save by the coyote and the wolf of the night. One morning, just after moving out of camp, we came to the camping-place of a party of emigrants who had abandoned one of their wagons, and from it had made a big bonfire in which were slowly roasting the carcasses of four mighty buffalo from which the choice parts only had been removed. It is needless now to waste sentiment over the extermination of the buffalo. He can never be replaced, and we may solace ourselves with the reflection that the extinction of the big game greatly helped to solve the Indian problem. No game, no wild Indian.

Our last glimpse of civilization was "Grand Island City," a village of six or eight houses, on the Platte, in what is now Hall County, Nebraska. This was on the 6th of June, and a few days before we had passed through Columbus, another paper city. Columbus boasted an inn, a blacksmith-shop, and a trading-post. The passage of the Loup at that place was accomplished by means of a rope ferry, for which service the ferryman, before landing us on a sand-bar near the farther bank of the stream, exacted a fee of a dollar and a half for each team; the cattle were swum across. The tide of travel was so great that we were obliged to wait all day for our turn to cross. I asked the proprietor

of the ferry if he had had any touch of the California fever. With a twinkle of his eye he surveyed his ferry and his smithy, and said: "Wal, I allow this yere is Californy enough for me."

Our trail, after leaving the last settlements, was strewn with lame and abandoned cattle and the discarded material of those who had preceded us. As large companies passed on, they found their burdens lightened by the needful consumption of food-supplies; wagons were left along the trail, and the next comers helped themselves to such parts as they needed, or fancied they needed. I knew of more than one such thrifty party who picked up and mended a broken wagon, only to find, later on, that they had encumbered themselves with something that they did not want. Queer-looking contrivances for mining, worn-out clothing, and even valuable tools, were plentifully scattered along the trail. Everybody seemed to be stripping for the conflict with the rude forces of nature that was to come when we reached the heart of the continent. It was our habit to gather fuel from the flotsam and jetsam of the plains; but it often happened, in spite of this forethought, that the only fuel to be found in an otherwise excellent camping-place would be a few handfuls of dry grass, a cluster of dead weeds, or a clump of the ill-smelling greasewood.

Although we traveled a part of the time through what was known as a hostile Indian country, we were never molested by the red men. Friendly Indians came into our camps to beg, to pilfer, or to sell buckskins and moccasins. Before us and behind us were several attacks upon caravans, the victims usually being few in number and unprepared for a skirmish. But while we were in the region deemed dangerous from Indians we massed in with other companies of emigrants, so that we were seldom less than one hundred and fifty strong; a regular watch was kept by night, and the wagons were parked in a circle which could be used as a defense in case of an attack. The Sioux and the Cheyennes were on the warpath, but their field of action was far to the north of our trail. The "Goshoots," as they were called, committed the depredations of which we heard many terrifying tales. The proper title for that tribe, as we afterward learned, was Gosiutes; they were a branch of the Utah Indians. As soon as the amalgamated caravans were fairly clear of the hostile territory they resumed their individuality,

HALF-TONE PLATE ENGRAVED BY H. DAVIDSON.

MOONLIGHT IN THE WESTERN DESERT.

each company moving on at such a distance from those behind and before as would preclude the possibility of rivalry at the places for drinking and feeding cattle.

In the regions where alkali was abundant it was difficult to find streams that were not more or less impregnated with the dreadful stuff. In some places the shallow ponds formed by springs were dark brown in color and fairly burning to the taste with alkali. In others the limpid liquid, which looked harmless enough, tasted so strongly of the alkali that it was dangerous for the cattle to drink of it. Around some of the alkaline ponds we saw multitudes of small animals that had been poisoned by drinking at the margin. Usually our cattle shunned the more noxious of these deadly reservoirs; but sometimes their frantic thirst urged them to drink of the waters less impregnated with alkali, and the result was that, in the course of weeks, the whole interior economy of a poor creature would become so corrupted with the poison that it would stagger along for a brief space and then lie down to rise no more. It was also impossible to prevent the cattle from nibbling at the bunch-grass into which alkaline dust had been blown; and in this way they got the poison into their stomachs.

We had a camp pet, a mongrel dog, a large yellow creature, affectionate of disposition, and a most vigilant sentinel at night. He came to us on the Platte River trail, having apparently lost his master; and a faithful and lovable friend he proved to be. As he selected me for his special guardian, I found it necessary to shoe him when we were in the alkali region, the stuff having so penetrated the soft parts of his feet that he could not walk without pain. With thick, soft buckskin I made Pete (for that was his name) a set of moccasins, and having greased his feet with bacon fat, a sovereign remedy for alkali poison, I sewed on his novel coverings. Instead of wagging his tail with gratitude, Pete deliberately lay down on the ground, and with his teeth tore off his moccasins, licked his well-greased feet, and limped along the trail barefoot.

Another pet was a little steer with a crumpled horn, Tiger by name, but dog-like by nature. He, too, was a personal friend of mine, and, when unyoked, he would follow me about the camp with all the affectionateness that Pete could show. Poor Tige managed to absorb enough alkali to lay him low very soon after we reached the wholesome heights of the Sierra Nevada, but while he was with us he was our most devoted servant. He never shirked his share of the load, and in the most trying crises of our wearisome journey he was always patient, gentle, and hard-working. He was extravagantly fond of sugar, and if I held out my hand with a few grains of it in the palm, he would canter up to the yoke from afar with great cheerfulness. On the desert, where food and water were not to be had except as we carried them in the wagon, Tige refused to eat the wilted grass brought from the last green spot; but, one day, resting his nose on my shoulder, as I sat on the wagon-tongue taking my spare noonday luncheon, he fancied the dish, and with his big red tongue he calmly licked up my portion of stewed beans.

In the course of weeks, the camp, wherever it might be pitched, took on the semblance of a home. The tent was our house; the rude cooking- and eating-apparatus and the comfortable bedding were our household furniture, and the live stock about us was our movable property. Except in the most trying and difficult straits, evening found us busy with household cares and amusements. Our neighbors were changeable, it is true, but we often found new and pleasant acquaintances, and sometimes old friends from whom we had been separated for weeks would trundle up and camp near us. In a party that joined forces with us and accompanied us from the Upper Platte to the Sacramento there was a fiddle,—it would be a misnomer to call it a violin, as played by the owner,—and in our camp was a flute. Occasionally we were joined by other fiddles and by big, manly voices. The favorite songbook on the trail was "Old Put's Songster," a copy of which has been preserved with pious care in the library of the Society of California Pioneers. It was in this classic that was to be found the celebrated ballad of "Joe Bowers," a name subsequently immortalized by Bret Harte in one of his poems. The opening stanza of the ballad ran thus:

My name it is Joe Bowers, I 've got a brother Ike;
I came from old Missouri, yes, all the way from Pike.
I 'll tell you why I left thar, and how I came to roam,
And leave my poor old mammy, so far away from home.

Pike County, Missouri, was so numerously represented on the trail that year that every Missourian was known as a Pike. Ar-

OLD FORT BRIDGER, EAST OF SALT LAKE CITY.

kansas, too, had a large share in the migration, and it was safe to say that at least one half of those we met on the way across the continent were either Pikes or Pukes: by this last epithet were the Arkansians cheerfully known. Pike County emigrants were blessed with children, and their big prairie-schooners were overflowing with white-headed tots in assorted sizes. On one Missouri wagon we saw this tender plaint:

O Missouri, O Missouri, I much regret to see
You so much altered for the worse from what
  you used to be.
Time was when all the people were all happy and
  content,
But now they are so very poor, scarce one can
  get a cent.

Death, as well as life and song, was on the trail. In the summer of 1850 there was an outbreak of cholera which spread all along the territory now known as Wyoming. The graves of the fallen were to be seen dotting the plains, usually defended from prowling beasts by sections of wagon-tires driven into the earth over the mounds that covered the forsaken dead. In our own time we assisted at more than one funeral, generally that of a feeble woman, or an infant child, borne down by the hardships of the journey. In one or two instances, where affection had conquered many obstacles, we saw large cairns made to mark the graves of loved ones, built of stones that had been brought from a considerable distance. The north side of Independence Rock plunges perpendicularly into the ground, and along its foot appeared to have been a choice burial-ground. On the smooth face of the rock were painted, or rudely chiseled, the epitaphs of many who slept with the great precipice for their colossal headstone.

Independence Rock, on the Sweetwater (one of the affluents of the North Platte), was a landmark to which we had looked forward with exceeding longing, inasmuch as it marked one of the long stages of the journey. The rock is a huge ledge, several acres in extent, nearly level on top and inaccessible on all sides but one. Chimney Rock was another landmark on the Upper Platte. It is a tall, chimney-shaped mass, over two hundred feet in height, and visible for a long distance before it is reached. Laramie Peak, about forty miles west of Fort Laramie, was seen, sharp and well defined against the sky, seventy miles away; it is one of the salient peaks of the Rockies. Naturally, however, we regarded with the greatest interest the South Pass of the Rocky Mountains. In one respect the pass was a disappointment. The trail ran westward over a broad and gradually ascending route, with the mountains retiring discreetly to a considerable distance on each side.

The peaks of the loftiest and most distant ranges discernible from the pass were those of the Wind River Mountains, far to the north and west. They were sharp and needle-like against the tender azure of the sky, and their thin blue sides were laced with snow. On each side of the route, which in the pass had all the appearance of a wide boulevard (if I may use an urban illustration here), the scenery was rich and varied. Openings amid the undulating forests were lordly parks, and winding cañons gleaming with creeks and rivers lent a pleasing brightness to the scene. One could almost fancy he saw orchards and meadows scattered through the hills and valleys in the middle distance. It was hard to realize that this was a primitive wilderness as yet untrodden by the white man's foot.

It was here, in July, that we did realize how far "up above the world so high" we were. The rarefied air was invigorating, and accelerated heart-beats, as we climbed, gave token of a thinness of the atmosphere we had never known before. The nights were very cold, and a bucket of water left outside the tent would be found well skimmed with ice in the morning. What kept the mosquitos alive was to us incomprehensible. They did not trouble us at night, but they were seen drifting about during the day. At a short distance up one of the hillsides of the pass, we climbed to a snow-bank and had some boyish fun at snowballing; and fluttering over the coarse, granulated snow was an immense cloud of yellow butterflies. Butterflies, mosquitos, and snow—a curious combination for the delectation of the emigrant tenderfoot.

One of the famous landmarks to which we had looked forward with great interest was the Devil's Gate of the Rockies, through which we passed before beginning the climb of the backbone of the continent. It was a far more impressive spectacle than the pass. The gate is double, and through one of its tall, black portals murmurs the Sweetwater on its way to join the North Platte. The trail lies through the other fissure, trail and stream being only a few hundred rods apart.

In the South Pass we gazed with a certain awe upon Pacific Spring, a memorable bit of water that marked the dividing of the ways. It was a few yards to the south of the trail, a mossy spring welling out of a rocky chasm and flowing southward. Fifteen or twenty feet from the fountain, a spur of rock separated the rivulet, so that a part flowed to the eastward and eventually found its way into the Sweetwater and thence into the Platte, the Missouri, the Mississippi, the Gulf of Mexico, and the rude Atlantic. The other half of the stream flowed westward and slipped down into a woody cañon, where it found one of the affluents of the Big Sandy, and thence into Green River, the Colorado, and the Gulf of California, and was finally absorbed in the Pacific Ocean.

Another memorable object of natural scenery in this region was the fantastic formation known as Ancient Ruins Bluffs. A lofty structure, apparently of stone and marble, lifts itself from the plain through which Green River winds its way. The material is sandstone and indurated clay, which the winds and the whirling sands have wrought into an impressive monument of castles, turrets, donjon-keeps, parapets, towers, and frowning walls. These airy structures are several hundred feet high, and at a distance it is difficult to believe that they are not the work of men's hands. The natural disposition of young folks is to climb any impressive cliff or mountain; but these enchanted castles offer no coign of vantage by which even the most expert can find a way to the soaring battlements above. Point of Rocks, on Sulphur Creek, in what is now the western part of Wyoming, was another mighty agglomeration of spires and turrets, reminding one of a castellated city rather than a single group of rocks, wind-worn and ragged. Near Fort Bridger, farther along the trail to the westward, we saw a very curious formation of basaltic rock. The crystals were hexagonal in form, dark-

colored, and varying in size from a sixteenth of an inch, and even smaller, to eighteen inches in diameter. It was wonderful to see how in the minute interstices between the larger columns the fragile crystals had insinuated themselves.

At Fort Bridger we had a slight taste of civilized life, though we were yet on the savage frontier. Here were four companies of dragoons with all the paraphernalia of war, to say nothing of women, dogs, and sheep. Here was a large and well-stocked store kept by an army sutler, where one could buy pretty much anything that civilized people really need. One man's want manifested itself in a hand of tobacco; for another nothing short of a handful of raisins would suffice, and a third hankered for a stick of red-and-white candy. Here, too, we got our first newspaper since leaving the Missouri. It was "The Valley Tan," published in Salt Lake City, and then more than two weeks old. No matter, it was a newspaper. The first domestic manufacture introduced into the Mormon settlement was that of leather; and to that was given the distinctive title of "valley tan," it being tanned in the valley. As other articles were made by the isolated people, each was called "valley tan" to distinguish it from the imported sample; and, very naturally, the first newspaper was given the same name.

Two days from Fort Bridger we entered Echo Cañon, one of the most delightful spots which I remember on the long, long trail. The cañon is about twenty miles long, and could be readily traversed in a single day; but we loitered through it, so that we were more than two days in its charmed fastnesses. On each side of the route the cliffs tower to a great height, marked with columnar formations and clouded with red, white, yellow, and drab, like some ancient wall of brick and stone. The crests of these towers are crowned with verdure, and here and there are trees and vines that line the cañon and climb upward to the flying buttresses of the rocky walls. A delicious stream of water crosses and recrosses the trail; and while we were in the cañon, grass and fuel were abundant. To make our comfort complete, great quantities of wild berries hung invitingly from the bushes by the sides of the way. Silvery rivulets fell from the walls of the cañon, and wild vines and flowers in great variety bloomed against the buttresses and donjon-keeps of the formations through which we threaded our way.

Crossing the Weber, we entered one more

FROM 'AN OLD SKETCH.   HALF-TONE PLATE ENGRAVED BY H. DAVIDSON.

FIRST VIEW OF SALT LAKE FROM A MOUNTAIN PASS.

cañon, and suddenly, one afternoon, emerging from the mouth of Emigrant Cañon, we looked down upon one of the fairest scenes on which the eye of man has ever gazed— the Great Salt Lake valley. It was like a jewel set in the heart of the continent. Deep below us, stretching north and south, was the level floor of the valley. Far to the westward rose a wall of mountains, purple, pink, and blue in the distance. Nearer sparkled the azure waters of the Great Salt Lake, and in the lush greenness of the valley was the sylvan city of the Latter-Day Saints. The city was embowered in trees, as if it were a congeries of farms spread over a large space, a few tall buildings rising here and there to denote that this was indeed a city in the midst of the wilderness. The descent to the floor of the valley was steep and dangerous. Looking fearfully over the parapet of rock that guarded one side of the narrow trail, we saw more than once the mangled wrecks of unfortunate emigrants—wagons, cattle, and impedimenta heaped in wild confusion and ruin far down in the rocky ravines.

There were no welcoming embassies to meet us; no brass-band and municipal delegation came out to escort us into the city of the Latter-Day Saints. Two low-browed men, surly and unwelcoming, told us where we could camp in the ragged suburbs of the city, that particular open space being named Emigrant Square, for the benefit of such as we; but Emigrant Square was not sufficient to hold us all. Camps rose in the fields and vacant lots all about us, and it was evident that our company was not longed for by the Saints. Before us there had been a few invasions of the long-enjoyed privacy of the Mormon settlement. The scattered drops of the overland migration had been resolved into a shower. The tide had risen. It was an inundation.

Two or three days sufficed us for a stay at Salt Lake City. The Saints took every opportunity to let us see that we were not welcome, and frequent thefts of cattle and horses at night, among our neighbors, warned us that it would be well to "light out" as soon as possible. For the Mormons it should be said that the irruption of emigrants was certainly undesirable. There was no downright lawlessness, but the campers were not careful to avoid giving offense to the citizens. At that time the city was supplied by water from the mountains, the clear, cool streams flowing through the streets in open channels lined with gravel and kept scrupulously clean, so that one could drink from any place without fear of taking in base matter; and these watercourses were let in or shut off at the boundary of each man's lot at his own pleasure. The newcomers, with their innumerable herds of cattle, were untidy in a settlement where animals were not allowed at large, and where the watercourses were kept pure by strict regulations with heavy penalties attached.

While we stayed, the Mormon women flocked around the camps peddling fresh vegetables and milk, in exchange for which they always asked for tea, never for cash unless the coveted herb was not to be had. A goodly supply of excellent fresh vegetables could be bought for a single "drawin' of tea," a measure too vague for the masculine understanding. The fresh provisions which we found so plentiful were a luxury to men long used to the spare diet of the plains, and the poor women who brought them to camp were generously treated. For the most part, these women had a washed-out and faded look; they never ventured upon any light talk with us; their sad appearance was in their mild dickering as well as in their forlorn garb.

The route from the city of the Saints lay around the northern end of the lake, but, in order to reach the road to Bear River, we were obliged to cross a few fenced fields, and this involved long parleys with surly owners. We passed through a string of small towns on our way up to the main-traveled trail, the last of these being Box Elder, now known as Brigham City. Box Elder was a settlement of about three hundred people, and boasted a post-office, a blacksmith's shop, a trading-post, and a brewery. At this last-named establishment we bought some fresh yeast, which served us a good turn in bread-making for many a day thereafter. We bought new flour in Salt Lake City at a fair price, having skimped ourselves on that article for some time on account of the exorbitant cost of it at the trading-posts on the trail. At Fort Bridger, flour was thirty-five dollars a barrel, and bacon was one dollar a pound. But the Mormons could sometimes ask big prices for what they had to sell. At the crossing of Bear River the ferryman demanded three dollars for each team carried across the stream, the cattle being swum over even at that price. We went on ten miles up the river, where we found a good crossing and saved our money.

Two days after leaving Box Elder we left the valley and struck Deep Creek, one of the numerous streams in that forbidding land, which "run well for a season," and then sink into the sandy, barren ground. Here we passed into what is now Idaho, Pilot Springs and Stony Creek being the first water we found beyond the present boundary-line. The trail over the Goose Creek Mountains was very difficult and stony, but the beauty of the view somewhat compensated for the labors of the climb. The surface of the earth seemed tossed up into a tumult of waves that had stiffened as it rose and fell. Winding among the peaks were belts of forest and undergrowth, lush and rich in color, but far away from our trail, which led through broken plains and steep valleys.

No dweller on the sea-coast can realize the exceeding clearness of the atmosphere in these great altitudes. Mountains that we knew to be at least one hundred miles away seemed to be within easy walking distance. Two of our number, while we were lying by one day, set out to explore a snow-field apparently two miles off. They were gone nearly all day, and reported the field to be about twenty miles from camp.

At the City of Rocks, in what is now Cassia County, Idaho, we learned the particulars of a so-called "Indian massacre" that had taken place on the trail ahead of us, and had caused great alarm among the emigrants. As was apt to be the case, white men were the aggressors, and the red men were goaded to attack. Five white men were killed, and when we reached their camping-place, a day or two later, we came upon the wrecks of their wagons, punctured with bullet-holes and stained with blood.

We were now approaching the edge of the Great Desert, which, stretching from the Bitter Root Mountains, in northern Idaho, to the southern boundary of Arizona, interposed for many years a barrier that was supposed to be impassable to the hardy emigrant. Now came long night marches and dreary days spent in traversing a region intolerable with dust, heat, rocky trails, and sideling hills. After leaving the Sink of the Humboldt the trail ran westward over a vast chaos of split boulders, broken stones, and powdery soil. Crossing occasional bluffs and wearily traversing winding cañons, the emigrants toiled on their way, hoping for rest and refreshment at some of the springs whose names had been given us, but whose actual condition belied their reputation. At Antelope Springs, for example, we found only a confused mass of mud and mire

packed with splintered rock and befouled by droves of cattle that had preceded us.

Sage-brush offered us fuel, and, dipping up water by the spoonful, we secured enough to make a pot of coffee; but our poor animals could only sniff thirstily of the wet ground and swallow their disappointment. Twenty miles away were Rabbit-hole Springs, where water was always to be had, and a night drive took us there. Mounting a rocky ridge, we plunged down on the farther side about midnight, and, to our great surprise, found that we had driven into an encampment of weary emigrants who had pitched their tents directly on the trail and on both sides thereof. In the twinkling of an eye, confusion dire and inextricable reigned. The angry campers swarmed out of their tents like wasps, repelling the invaders with hard words. But, advising them never to camp on a trail again, we gathered up our herds and wagons and swept on down the defile that led to the long, sandy plain on whose farther edge were the much-desired springs.

It was a clear, starlight night, and the trail was over a plateau, the sandy surface of which was undulating and springy. It was an ideal road for an ideal night. Passing ahead of the train, one could fancy, in the deadly stillness of the mysterious desert, shut in by darkness and the billowy sand, that he was a lost man, a mere waif on the great ocean of those "unexplored regions" which we have seen marked on ancient maps. The stillness was so utter that my faithful Pete, who followed at my heels, frightened by its deadliness, would occasionally trot up to my side, whining in his loneliness, and, reassured by a kindly word, drop back to his place in the rear-guard. Darkness, silence, and unfathomable mystery covered the Great Desert.

Rabbit-hole Springs did not disappoint us with a scant supply of water. A dry, rounded hilltop, covered with a baked crust of earth, rose by the side of the trail, and on its summit was a group of wells, sunk in square holes, with rude steps leading down thereto. The precious fluid was plentiful and good; we and all our cattle drank and were abundantly refreshed.

Camping at four o'clock in the morning, we had a short rest, and then pressed on over a rocky ridge, below which stretched another long and undulating plain, torrid in the blinding heat, and at noon giving us the spectacle of an extraordinary mirage. The long caravans ahead of us seemed to carry on their wagon-tops shadowy duplicates of each vehicle; and on the top of these, which had their wheels in the air, were other ghostly teams driven through the hazy atmosphere, their wheels on the wheels of those below. It was an astonishing and most unusual sight. Far to the westward and northward, the ranges of hills were punctuated with needle-like summits that pierced the sky. The peaks, flaming in red and blue, looked like masses of heated metal turned out to cool on the arid waste.

The last day's drive in the desert was the hardest of all. Twenty miles lay between us and the Honey Lake valley. It was to be traveled in the night; and as the numerous trains and caravans swept down into the plain from the point of rocks on which I was sitting, waiting for our wagons to come up, it was pathetic to note the intentness with which this multitude of home-seekers and gold-seekers set their faces westward. There was no haste, no fussy anxiety, but the vast multitude of men, women, and children who had left all behind them to look for a new life in an unknown land trooped silently down into the desert waste. The setting sun bathed the plain in golden radiance, and eastward the rocky pinnacles of the ranges through which we had toiled were glorified with purple, gold, and crimson. It was a sight to be remembered—as beautiful as a dream, hiding a wilderness as cruel as death.

Honey Lake belied the sweetness of its name. It was a small sheet of muddy water, but emptying into it was a sparkling river, or creek, known as Susan's River, which, meandering through an emerald valley and watering many a meadow, gave unwonted beauty to a scene the like of which had not been gazed upon by the toil-worn plainsmen for many a day. Here, too, we got our first glimpse of the Sierra Nevada. It was a majestic sight. The pale green of the lower hills broke against the dark olive that defined the base of the pine-clad foot-hills. Above, and broken by many a densely shadowed gulch and ravine, rose the high Sierra, bald with rocks and slides in places, and bristling with sharp, snowy peaks that were lifted to the skies.

After the privation and poverty of the desert, the wild abundance of the forests of the Sierra was luxury indescribable. We camped by crystal waterfalls with rank and succulent grasses all about us; overhead were the spreading branches of noble pines, and our camp-fires were heaped with an extravagance of fuel. But we soon found how hard it was to climb the mountain-range;

and when, after a day's solid rest and comfort, we reached the crest of the ridge, we saw that the trail pitched almost perpendicularly over the sharp backbone of the Sierra. Two or three trees that grew by the place where the track led to the brink were

THE SKULL OF A GRIZZLY BEAR.

scarred and worn nearly through by ropes that had been wound around them to let down the heavy wagons into the abyss below. The cattle were taken out of the teams and driven down through the undergrowth of thickets; and then, making a rope fast to the rear axle of each wagon, one wagon at a time was carefully lowered down the steep declivity.

That arduous labor over, we passed through the "Devil's Corral" and camped in Mountain Meadows, a very paradise of a spot, in which it seemed as if we were surrounded by every luxury imaginable, albeit we had nothing but what uncultivated nature gave us. Here we left our faithful Tige; the poor little steer died in the midst of plenty. Pressing on, we passed through mining settlements of queer names and no names, and, late in September, making the summit of Chaparral Hill, the Sacramento valley burst upon our view.

The vale of the new Eldorado was tawny and gold with sear grass and wild oats. In the distance rose the misty mountain wall of the Coast Range; nearer a heroic outline of noble peaks broke the yellow abundance of the valley's floor. This was the group known as Sutter's Buttes, near the base of which was Nye's Ranch (now Marysville), the goal of our long tramp. Dogtown, Inskip, and a little host of other mining hamlets, claimed our attention briefly as we swept down into the noble valley, on whose farther edge, by the historic Yuba, we found our last camp.

Here we met the wave of migration that earlier broke on the shores of the Pacific. In the winter of 1849–50 two hundred and fifty vessels sailed for San Francisco from the ports of the Atlantic States; and their multitudes of men were reinforced by other multitudes from other lands. In a single year the population of the nascent State was augmented by an influx of more than one hundred thousand persons, arriving by sea and by land. We were late, but behind us toiled other thousands, some of whom, blockaded in the snow-bound mountains, paid dearly for their tardiness in starting on their way to the Golden Land. They were never missed in the final make-up of the State. For without Territorial tutelage, full-orbed and panoplied in Freedom, California sprang into Statehood.

7

A Colorado Glacier

Junius Henderson

ARAPAHOE GLACIER, SEPTEMBER 2, 1902

A Colorado Glacier

BY JUNIUS HENDERSON

Curator of the Museum, University of Colorado

AGES ago, when the climate of the Rocky Mountain region was very different from that of the present day, when the annual snowfall greatly exceeded the annual loss by melting and evaporation, snow accumulated to an enormous depth along all the higher portions of the range. As the snow continued to pile up and pressure increased, it formed ice, which began to flow slowly to lower levels. The glaciers thus formed extended their icy tongues down preexisting mountain gorges, sometimes for many miles, until they reached levels where the mean annual temperature was sufficient to melt the ice as rapidly as it moved downward. The ice reached a thickness of hundreds, sometimes even thousands,

of feet, as shown by perched boulders, glacial scratches and *roches moutonnées*. These ice-streams greatly modified the valleys in which they flowed, changing their V shape, characteristic of stream-formed gorges, to the U shape of glacial valley topography. They rounded off angular rocks and produced on a grand scale the *roches moutonnées* typical of glaciated mountain regions. They built great moraines, well defined and having steep sides, as would be expected in a region where valleys were bordered by precipitous cliffs and material was so abundant and accessible. Then the climate again changed and the glaciers slowly retreated, until now they are represented chiefly by remnants of *névé* rest-

A VIEW OF GOOSE LAKE
Roches moutonnées, with Arapahoe Cirque in the background

ing in the arms of glacial cirques at altitudes of from 12,000 to 14,000 feet above sea-level.

It had long been supposed that no true glaciers remain in the Rockies south of Wyoming, a supposition now known to be incorrect. North of Long's Peak two ice-fields have been described and referred to as glaciers by men whose determinations are entitled to considerable weight, though on the whole they partake more of the nature of *névé* and are so considered by some geologists. This difference of opinion is entirely excusable on the ground that the dividing line between *névé* and glacier is indistinct, "the one passing into the other by insensible gradation." However, explorations carried on in the last five years have brought to light an ice-stream which is so distinctly a glacier as to leave no chance for a dispute as to its character. It has been visited by experienced geologists, mapped, photographed and thoroughly studied.

Arapahoe Glacier is about a mile long, and is situated amid scenery as inspiring as any in the southern Rockies. It occupies an amphitheatre or glacial cirque upon the east side of the Arapahoe Peaks, the peaks and their thin, sharp, serrated connecting ridge forming the semicircular rim of the cirque, the ridges running eastward from the north and south peaks forming the walls of the ancient glacial valley. The highest point on the rim of the cirque is 13,700 feet above sea-level.

The glacier once extended down North Boulder Valley about eight miles, and has left in its retreat a great network of moraines to delight the student of glacial geology, and a magnificent chain of glacial lakes to please the eye of the landscape artist. Upon the banks of one or another of these lakes our annual exploring expeditions have camped in early September for a number of years, living close to Nature, surrounded by scenery which in a large measure compensated for the hardship of climbing rugged peaks and picking our way through an untrodden wilderness of stunted conifers, huge boulders, high precipices, and deep canyons. At night the music of a dozen waterfalls lulled us to sleep as we stretched our weary limbs upon beds of fragrant fir and spruce boughs. Among these peaks the fauna and flora are quite different from those of lower levels, and the trees tell in unmistakable language of deep snows and continual west winds, in some cases growing flat upon the rocks, in others holding their heads erect but throwing their branches out horizontally to the eastward, in order to oppose the least possible resistance to the wind.

On the ice we find all the phenomena of well-defined alpine glaciers the world over, but the first evidence of present glacial work we noticed in the stream and lakes fed by the melting ice. The lakes most remote from the glacier were clear as crystal; but as we approached the ice, the water took on at first a greenish tinge, gradually deepening and whitening as we progressed, until at the end of the ice-tongue we found it milky white, made so by the contained sediment or "rock-flour" ground from its granitic bed by the moving ice-stream.

The next thing to attract attention was the perfect freshness of the terminal moraine. All along the valley we had passed and crossed ancient moraines

from which the fine mud had been removed by the storms of centuries, but here at the present terminus is a heterogeneous mixture of wet materials varying from the finest silt to boulders weighing many tons, looking as if the mass had just been deposited there by a gigantic steam-shovel. The lake for which it operates as a retaining dam is evidence of a recent recession of the ice front. The moraine is the omnivorous recipient of everything that falls upon or into the ice, in addition to the rock-flour and other material carried along beneath it.

Another striking feature of the glacier is the stratification and banding of the ice, characteristic of all glaciers. These were once supposed to be distinct features due to two very different causes, but in the light of recent investigations this

THE "BERGSCHLUND," ARAPAHOE GLACIER

may be doubted without danger of being considered a heretic. It seems quite possible that the banding and stratification, considered as a whole, simply represent successive seasons or falls of snow, first

A Crevasse on Arapahoe Glacier

appearing in a poorly defined way in the *névé* and acquiring better definition with the downward progress of the ice. Another feature which serves to distinguish glacier-ice from *névé* is the distinct granular crystalline structure.

Arapahoe Glacier is remarkable in the definite symmetry of its *Bergschlund*, the great semicircular crevasse extending across the face of the ice-stream and marking the point where the glacier proper, by accelerated movement, breaks

away from the *névé*. Its crevassing systems, too, are very definitely outlined. Where the ice flows over a sudden change in the slope of the valley floor, yawning crevasses are opened to unknown depths by the stretching of the ice. They vary from a few inches to many feet in width, and are often several hundred feet in length. In making his way amid the maze of crevasses a sudden slip may plunge the explorer to an instant death; and, be it remembered, ice does not afford the most secure foothold in the world, so that a slip is altogether too easy. Furthermore, caverns sometimes form with but a thin covering of ice, and a heavy fall of moist snow, drifting with the wind, often covers crevasses of sufficient width to engulf a human being. Such covered crevasses are particularly apt to occur early in the season, before the preceding winter's snows have been melted back. Men have unconsciously and unconcernedly crossed Arapahoe Glacier on what they supposed was solid ice, where a few weeks later the melting of the slight crust of frozen snow exposed the *Bergschlund* twenty feet in width. In the Swiss Alps at least one instance is known where a man has fallen into a crevasse, and his body has been carried downward and years later deposited on the terminal moraine. On

LAKE DAMMED BY PRESENT TERMINAL MORAINE OF ARAPAHOE GLACIER
Ice-tongue extends into lake. Photographed August 30, 1902

the terminal moraine of Arapahoe Glacier we recently found the carcass of a mountain-sheep melting out of the ice, where it had been in cold storage for many years, perhaps even centuries. The most reasonable supposition, in view of all the circumstances, is that it broke through or slipped into a crevasse and was carried downward to the terminus by the movement of the ice. Crevasses may open slowly and quietly, or with astonishing suddenness. The writer was once treated to a perfect cannonading upon Arapahoe Glacier, the ice cracking almost beneath his feet several times in succession, with thunderous roars, forcibly reminding him that he had business imperatively requiring his instant presence elsewhere.

Another source of danger from which there have been some narrow escapes at the terminus of Arapahoe Glacier is the instability of boulders upon the fresh moraine. On ancient mountain moraines one may generally feel safe in trusting his weight upon the edges of large boulders, because they have been for ages settling into more and more secure positions. On fresh moraines, however, they are often deposited in nicely balanced positions, or reduced to such condition by the washing away of the finer materials around them, so that the slightest pressure may overturn boulders weighing several tons. For this reason experienced glacialists avoid the fresh deposits whenever practicable, and when forced upon them, proceed with the utmost caution.

No measurements were necessary to convince our first exploring party that the ice was moving. To the student of glacial phenomena the evidence on every hand was as easily read as a printed page and as convincing as a mathematical demonstration, but it remained to determine the rate of movement. Consequently, on a later visit, we set up the instruments on the granitic north wall and placed a line of zinc tablets across the face of the ice. Returning exactly one year later, we found that the tablets had moved in amounts varying from 11.15 feet at a point 300 feet from the edge, to 27.7 feet at a point near the centre.

The existence of this glacier within a few miles of civilization for so long a time before recognition of its true char-

SILVER LAKE, WITH ARAPAHOE IN THE DISTANCE

acter seems rather astounding. Hundreds of tourists had gazed upon it from the rim of the amphitheatre, late enough in the season for the melting of the surface snow to disclose the crevassed and stratified ice, which should have attracted attention. It may be that other glaciers in the less accessible fastnesses of the Colorado Rockies await discovery by observant explorers able to recognize them when found, and the pleasure of making new discoveries and adding to the sum total of human knowledge should be sufficient incentive for the lover of Nature whose eyes are keen, whose lungs are elastic enough for high altitudes, whose muscles are strong, and whose nerves are steady enough for hard climbing in a rugged land. Even though no new discoveries be made, what pleasure can be greater than getting away from the well-beaten paths, where everything is new

and strange, and where Nature's building has been on a grand scale A school-teacher, after following the writer along the difficult ridge from the south spur to the north spur of Arapahoe Peaks, and reaching a point attained by but few of the tourists, gazed out over the awe-inspiring expanse of mountains and valleys, visible for at least 150 miles to the north, south, and west, and many miles to the east, and at last broke the silence of the mountain solitude with the exclamation, "I tell you, it makes a man a better American to see this!"

Why should Americans go abroad to see the sights of foreign lands, who have not the faintest conception of the wonders of our own land to be found by getting away from the regular lines of travel, which naturally and almost necessarily follow the lines of least resistance, which lead them away from the grander views?

8

Flying Down a Fifty-Mile Flume

Bailey Millard

Everybody's Magazine

JULY, 1903.

SHOOTING DOWN KING'S RIVER CAÑON.

Flying Down a Fifty-Mile Flume

By BAILEY MILLARD

With Photographs by W. J. Street

CRISP and terse were the orders that attended the launching of the Mary Ann from the Millwood skids, up in the Sierran heights. The Mary Ann was a rough boat, made to fit into a V-shaped chute, and she was knocked together in half an hour for the floating of a pair of more or less intrepid voyagers who had undertaken the unusual journey from Millwood, Cal., down the longest and steepest lumber flume in the world, to Sanger, in the San Joaquin Valley. It is a distance of fifty-four miles, and, in the first

thirteen miles, the descent is over 4,300 feet.

"Slide her in, boys!" yelled the solemn-looking flume boss. "Look out there, kids! Stern first. In she goes."

Splash!

The Mary Ann was afloat in the swift-running flume.

"Hold her fast now," called the boss. "All ready, gentlemen. Stow their stuff aboard, Jim."

Springing nimbly upon the rough little

87

deck, the flume voyagers, with a bravado which concealed the blank misgivings of creatures moving about in worlds unrealized and

Going to meet their fate
In a highly nervous state,

took their seats, one on a cracker-box aft, the other on a redwood block forward.

"You want to hold on," cautioned Jim, who moored the boat with a stout grip on his "picaroon." "She'll run like the mill-tails of hell."

We did not know what the infernal mill-tails were or how they ran, but the idea of holding on appealed to us as a practical one.

"Let her go, boys! Good-by, gentlemen!" The flume boss waved his hand.

"Good-by!"

The "picaroon" was raised and the thrill of life ran along the Mary Ann's keel. She lurched a little to the right, settled down astern where the water was swelling high, and darted like a hounded deer down the long, gleaming, tragic, watery way.

The sharp sunlight of noon in the Sierras, edged and whitened by the snows that lay all about, glared with unmitigable intensity upon the scene. But to the voyagers of the Mary Ann, in the first stage of that mad whirl down the mountains, the sugar pines, the snow-laden cedars, the great blocks of freckled granite and the snow-drifts, with the alternating patches of low-growing bear clover, were bits of the haziest impressionist picture that ever obscured a dream-daubed canvas—a mere swinging chaos of trees and rocks and snows—a swaying streak of tumbled beauty, to be imbibed in quick breaths with the heady air of the high Sierras.

Swish!

A light balsam bough whipped my shoulders, and somehow its familiar odor inspired me with confidence.

It gave me something more than Dutch courage. I could go down to Gehenna with that smell in my nostrils. And it looked like Gehenna ahead. For the angle of descent on which we had been gliding along seemed like a dead level to what lay before. We had come to the brink of the Devil's Slide—a neat little half-mile plunge which, the flume men had declared, would give us "a pompadour hair-cut."

There were two deep in-takes of breath, a shrinking down off the seats to the safer and solider deck of the boat, a humming of mountain-air in the ears, and then the whizzing landscape fused into a long, filmy, biographic blur that raced before the uncertain eyes of the voyagers.

Out of this nightmare flung the words of Manager Boole of the Sanger Lumber Company, uttered while he sat in his comfortable swivel-chair two days before we made the long stage journey to Millwood, near the head of the flume:

"I wouldn't ride down that flume for the whole plant."

Then again, all too late, came the warning words of Secretary Young:

"I consider the trip a very hazardous one. Lumber is constantly jumping out of the flume, why not a boat or raft?"

But we were in

TAKING LUMBER FROM THE FLUME.

for it, whatever the hazard. We ran down the slide faster than the water, having greater bulk, in one particular place, and greater weight, and thus being capable of greater momentum.

Z-z-z-z-eee-up!

It was the terror-inspired protest of the Mary Ann, as she scraped her flat nose against the side of the flume.

EVERYDAY WORK OF THE FLUME.

She retarded swiftly, pitching us forward. The water rose quickly over her stern, wetting my legs and the edge of my coat, and splashing over the sides of the flume, down the trestle and into the deep gulch below.

"Here we are at the foot of the slide. That must be Mount Patterson up there," said the photographer, pointing to a white peak off to the north.

But I had no eye for the calm beauty of Patterson. From the stiller waters I looked back up the flume and marvelled at the awful descent. I could not time the swiftness of the Devil's Slide any more than a man riding a cyclone can manage a stop-watch, but it seemed to me that no express train ever equalled it. You can work a camera from the window of a whirling Pullman, but the flight of the Mary Ann down that slide defied the swiftest shutter in the hands of an expert.

How does it feel to shoot the Devil's Slide? The ride is such a bit of brisk living as sets the blood all a-tingle and gives one a taste of the recklessness of Phaëton trying to drive the chariot of the sun. One feels that to make such a voyage every day would in time fill even the commonest of men with the abandon of the gods.

We passed the Lower Mill, about two miles below Millwood, still sailing at a pretty pace, then on by a little flat called the Strawberry Patch, and then by high, tragic cliffs on the edge of which the flume clung by a

sort of miracle in which even the gnarled pines had come to have faith. The speed increased a little and we swam dizzily out upon a terrible trestle, the spindling timbers of which, as seen from an oncoming curve, seemed the flimsiest of supports. But no matter how little we might fancy the outlook at any of these ticklish points, we had to stand by the ship. Once in the flume, on those upper grades, there is no stopping and but little slackening until you reach a station.

No end of trestles. We crossed one creek thirteen times, darting out upon the bridges unexpectedly from curves that nearly swayed one to perdition. But in those wild aërial flights the Mary Ann proved herself a skyworthy craft, and I can recommend her as the safest airship I have ever seen. There is nothing hyperbolical about this, for remember that the flume is away up in the air, higher, for the most part, than New York's elevated railroad, and that the stations are all on tall stilts.

After passing the awe-inspiring Dingwald's Trestle and the Shotgun Trestle, our swaying perspective took in a long vista of the cañon of Mill Creek, down which we were racing at a speed far exceeding that of its turbulent waters. We soared over Davidson's Flat leaning out from heaven to see where a grub-boat had dashed through the flume on a certain fateful flight. There lay the splintered fragments far below, and the wreck of a cook-stove which had gone down with it—a scrappy pile of junk which not even the covetous Indians had seen fit to carry away.

Across Dry Creek, fringed by fragrant pines, the Mary Ann sailed more slowly. Near here, James A. Grant, a flume herder, fell off the narrow, rickety sidewalk the other day into two feet of snow and was carried down to Station Three and One-Half with an injured spine.

Samson Creek runs into the cañon a little way below, and joins its white tumult with that of Mill Creek. Now we feel the strange elation of gathering speed, and away down the longest slide of the flume we plunge profanely amid masses of virgin mountain green, flecked by snow-drifts and pencilled with the straight Titanic trunks of sugar pines. Misgivings are melting away, and our nerves are becoming those of seasoned voyagers. Despite the swiftness of the downward whirl and the cutting of our faces by the keen-edged atmosphere through which we race, we can descry the objects along the way with something of satisfaction.

We had dropped over one thousand feet from the Millwood altitude in four and one-half miles, and in the flight to Three, the next station, we made a corresponding change in height. We were running out of the district of the yellow and sugar pines and were reaching the Digger pine levels. The last trace of snow had disappeared. Before us lay tall buttes, and nearer ridges all in purplish-browns, umbers, ochres and the softer hues that lay between; and down on the sloping cañon sides the white oaks, touched by the mystic wand of April, were sending forth delicate firstlings from their branch-tips, which now and again rustled against our faces, sometimes as gently as the caresses of a lover and then sharply, so that we threw up our arms to shield our eyes.

Two awe-inspiring trestles were crossed,

A GRUB BOAT HAD DASHED THROUGH.

one over Bear and the other over Granite Creek, and we looked down with terror and rapture commingled into the little streams that ran nearly one hundred and fifty feet below.

The air grew warmer and I took off my coat. It was not so bracing down here and we missed the pervasive pine scents. We gave a shout as a great mass of poppies on a steep scarp flung into view. There were acres of the Californian beauties, and they grew so closely together that they painted the hillside a dazzling orange on which the sun played warmly. Farther on, the cañon side was blued by lupins and yellowed by buttercups, while the cornflowers and the baby blue-eyes made saucy little faces at us. Then a long stretch of open country and soon we were sailing high over the tree-tops in a dreamy mood into which words fitted not at all; for the eye was tranced by the delicate beauty that lay all about.

Flitting silently, swiftly on, we passed the Twin Trestles, each 106 feet high, and came to a great jutting point where there lay below us a big spill of lumber. Some of it was splintered and bent as it lay in the bottom of the gulch, but there was much that would have been serviceable for building purposes. From the head of the flume down the fifty-mile run to Sanger there is enough waste lumber to build a good-sized town. The planks and stringers, floated down in long trains from the mill to the valley below, wedge together in great jams, and the lumber that follows is diverted by the rising water thus banked up in the flume and is thrown down into the cañon.

A short stop at Three and we glided swiftly down to Four and One-Half, where we caught sight of the first flutter of a woman's skirt we had seen in the cañon. The young woman at Four and One-Half was the wife of one of the flume herders. It was a rough household there at the flume-side in the cabin on stilts, among the beetling crags and the Digger pines, but she had imported a bit of art in the shape of Indian baskets, of which she had a pretty collection. She seemed cheerful, and laughed and joked with the men of the flume, with an air of gay comradeship.

Wild poppies made fine dashes of deep color below the station, and we rejoiced in them and in the soft air of springtime as we floated down the cañon. Red-bud bushes bloomed with the profusion of an apple orchard. Along the edge of the flume ahead, a whimsical gray squirrel ran and chattered and whisked away, with flashing tail, as our boat neared him.

We ran around a great curve in "sweet aërial freedom, wild and high," and lo! before us sprawled the racing waters of the famed Kings River, a wide-spread "crystal rapture," gleaming in the bright sunlight and challenging us to a contest of speed down the great cañon in which we now found ourselves.

On our left rose giant cliffs, and on our right, across the river, lay the sharply rising buttes, while behind impended the snow-white Sierras, thrilled by their own silence— a picture of the eternal immensities framed in the nearer crags. It was a scene to stir the blood of a tethered city man and to make the brick perspective of the town seem wofully mean in comparison.

The Kings foamed over the granite blocks, rippled over gravel bars in glinting whiteness and purity, showing here a passionate burst and there, in the blue stretches of stiller water, a thoughtful passivity and a grand content.

THE AWE-INSPIRING TWIN TRESTLE.

"Low bridge!" yelled the man with the camera.

A lantern arm hung down over the flume and had to be neatly dodged. A shanty loomed up ahead, and we ran into the slack water at Station Four.

"The boss has telephoned down that you can't run your boat any farther than this," said the flume-herder, a clean-looking young fellow in a rough shirt and overalls, "but we'll build you a couple of rafts and you can go the rest of the way on them. It will be faster, anyway."

"Why not the boat?" I asked.

"Because a boat strikes through the riffles and its keel scratches the bottom of the flume, disturbing the stuff that is collected there and making a leak. We can't stand for leaks. A lot of our time is used repairing the flume anyway."

The rafts were built in about twenty minutes by the flume-herder and his assistants, two bright, active young men, who handled the heavy sticks of lumber as though they were walking-canes. First came two 4 × 6 stringers, sixteen feet long. On top of these was nailed a sixteen-inch board, and on that were spiked two ten-inch planks, two inches thick. The top planks were laid side by side and held together by small cleats. This made a raft twelve inches wide at the bottom and twenty inches wide at the top. Rather a narrow craft, flume-worthy enough, but inclined to turn turtle if the raftsman were not good at balancing.

At Four the altitude is only 1,038 feet, so we had descended in the thirteen miles from Millwood over 4,300 feet. This considerable descent in so short a distance accounts for the swiftness of our flight.

Here we met Blake, a husky young fellow

with a world of good cheer in his make-up, who gave us excellent bread, some well-cooked red beans, and an apple-pie. We were drawn to Blake as much because of his sunny optimism, as the fact that we had suffered for nearly a week in the mountains from the sad and bedraggled cookery which prevails in the outlying regions of California.

The two rafts were hinged together tandem fashion, by a short piece of narrow

began to enjoy the new mode of travel, and made the cañon echo with our whoops. The north fork of the Kings River joins its brawling mate here, and materially augments the rapid flood. An oak limb drooped low over the flume, and in leaning to one side to dodge the seemingly inevitable blow, I lost my balance. At the same time the nails that held my seat to the raft parted under the strain and I was pitched backward and

THROUGH GROVES GORGEOUS WITH ORANGES.

board and tied, for further security, with stout rope. Seats were nailed amidships of each raft. They were not upholstered reclining chairs, but merely short pieces of 4×4 lumber, with a little board nailed on top. A five-gallon petroleum can, fastened behind each seat, made a receptacle for stowing luggage, but the big camera had to be handled very gingerly, being lifted aboard and placed between the knees of the photographer, who sat on the after raft, balancing for dear life.

This added responsibility of balancing proved irksome, but in a half-hour we accustomed ourselves to the usages of rafting,

sidewise off the crazy little craft and found myself floundering in the flume. I had pictured the circumstance over and over at night before the journey was begun, so, although the water was a little colder than I had thought—my tub being prepared by the handmaiden of the genius of the cold Sierras and not much warmed in its swift run down the mountains—I took less account of my ducking than I did of the wild and unconfined glee of my raftmate, to whom the incident was irresistibly piquant. He was, in fact, so overcome by his hilarity, that he was wholly unable to assist me in the work of rescue, which was simple enough and consisted in merely grasping the side of the raft and pulling myself aboard. The sun soon dried my clothing. At the next station we

LAUNCH OF THE
MARY ANN.

rigged up good seats with comfortable backs, and went sailing down the cañon with larger content. But soon we bumped into an ugly looking plank, suspended from a frame-work over the flume. The plank swung low in the water, and we had to grasp it and swing it over our heads—a clumsy operation that came near smashing the big camera, to say nothing

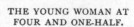

HIGH IN THE
SIERRAS.

of two sacred heads. The plank was attached to a wire that rang a bell in the station shanty, to let the flume-herder know that lumber was coming.

At Station Five, Mrs. Parker, who was at home alone, her husband being down the flume on his work of inspection, greeted us in the kindly mountain fashion, though evidently frightened at first by the appearance of two strangers, and kept her children close about her. She gave us some idea of the lonely life of a flume-herder's wife—a life which did not seem to

depress the cheery little spirit, living there in the wild cañon, with no reminder of the great outside world save the strings of lumber that ran all day down the flume —the one duct that connected her with the civilization of which she read in the papers; nor did I gather that she envied the women about whom she read—the women whose diamonds gleamed in electric-lighted drawing-rooms, who came and went in parlor-car and steam-yacht, and were wedded and divorced in the remote region beyond the flume's end.

Toward dusk, we glided silently over the steel bridge hanging high above Kings River, and were soon at Maxon's Flat, thirty miles from the head of the flume. An old man came out with a lantern and conducted us to his cottage, where we ate canned salmon and hot biscuits. Afterward we found quarters in a rough shed known by the lumbermen who

THE YOUNG WOMAN AT
FOUR AND ONE-HALF.

sleep there as "Cold Storage." Our rafts had been moored by a couple of hempen ropes, and, as the lumber strings would not come down until late next morning, were safe enough. We slept soundly in sheetless beds in "Cold Storage," though the crickets essayed, with strident notes, to deprive us of slumber.

In the cool hush of one of the most inspiring mornings I have ever known, we walked abroad on the flat. Near by was an orange orchard, and we gathered a store of yellow globes, which we treasured up in the boxes on the rafts.

WHERE THE WATER ENTERS THE FLUME.

AT THE JOURNEY'S END.

The sun blazed down with fierce intensity. In a great meadow where many cattle herded and looked up at us inquisitively, as who should say, "Those be strange vacqueros riding up there," a big brown bull took a lively interest in us, for the reason, as the photographer would have it, that I had taken off my shoes and was displaying a pair of luridly red stockings, stuck high upon my foot-rest. Nor did Taurus relish the bits of orange-peel I threw at him as we lazed along, but pawed the ground, as if he felt it to be a beautiful morning and that he must manifest his strength and courage by goring someone. Near Centreville, a small town among the lemon groves, we looked down upon a little graveyard strung about with barbed wire. So slowly we sailed along that I counted the headstones. There were twenty-three of them, and a lonely one outside the fence—a more ambitious and towering stone than any of the others. Whose was this grave, set apart beyond the pale? Was its occupant less worthy than the rest? In what had he sinned that he might not lie where the rude forefathers of the hamlet slept?

It was near Centreville that other fiendish obstructions were encountered—planks, stringers, and boards lying across the flume— and our lives for that afternoon were full of a vexed sense of being held back when we should have been going forward. In the

Slowly, out over the tops of the orange trees, we floated, past Trimmer Springs, where an old lady in a big sunbonnet called out a pleasant "Good-morning!" and remarked, "Yer having a lovely sail!" A fat turkey gobbler gave us a spasmodic greeting, and a big black dog barked surlily at us. We passed some quartz mines, one of which dumped its débris from a chute that ran over the flume, and displayed a curious sign, "Outsiders Don't Burn Your Fingers." As to the meaning of which we speculated long and fruitlessly.

As Mount Morrow loomed to the left of us, we saw the last of the pines, and in an hour or two we were floating out over the valley of San Joaquin. Far behind we had left the demesne of tragic peaks and crags and cañons, the wintry skylands and their robes of snow, and we had come to a green, laughing land of lemon orchards, alfalfa meadows and waving palms, where the canals flowed slowly along willow-fringed banks, where linnets twittered, heat-bugs droned, and humming-birds fanned the still, warm air of summer.

cool of the afternoon the Sanger house-tops came in view, and in an hour or two we were at the end of our flume journey and had seen our rafts torn asunder by brawny lumbermen and flung down the skids.

It is a great structure, this flume. There are over 10,000,000 feet of lumber in the fifty-four miles, and it has cost about half a million. In the busy season it brings down from the mountains 200,000 feet of lumber a day, chiefly redwood (sawed from the *Sequoia gigantea*, the largest tree in the world), sugar pine, yellow pine, and fir. It was Homeric labor erecting the great chute, and it required an army of men for half a year. The work of building the iron suspension bridge on which the flume crossed Kings River was a tremendous task and has all gone for naught, for the water, running in uneven volume, caused the bridge to sway and made it unsafe. A new steel bridge had

to be built. Some of the high wooden trestles and miles of common fluming have had to be abandoned and new structures built, because of age and consequent dilapidation and insecurity.

So rarely is the flume journey made from end to end that, when it became known in Sanger that we had boated and rafted down from Millwood, we were pointed out as objects of curiosity, and were asked so many questions that we were not unhappy when we boarded the train and were hurried out of the town. But looking up at the high peaks among which Millwood snuggled so restfully, breathing that glorious breath of life, which, if it be anywhere, is in the mountains, I felt that I had left my heart behind. White old Patterson beckoned me back, with an injured look because of my truantry, and I thought I could see the pines vainly waving their homing signals.

WINDING THROUGH THE VALLEY OF KING'S RIVER.

9

The Round Table of Dodge City

E.G. Little

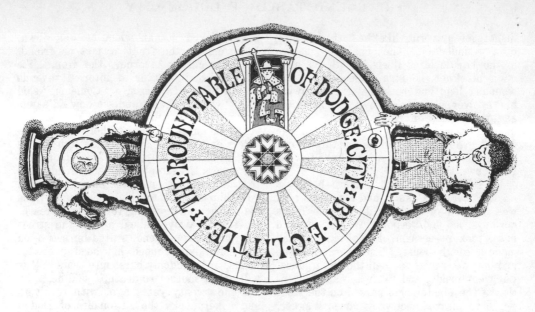

THE·ROUND·TABLE·OF·DODGE·CITY·BY·E·G·LITTLE·

BORDER MEN KNIGHTS-ERRANT WHO SURPASSED THE ACHIEVEMENTS OF HEROES OF ROMANCE.

FOR a dozen years Dodge City was the rallying-point of the Knights of the Border. Through the streets of that buffalo-grass village rode a greater cavalcade of men at arms than ever followed King Arthur through the alleys of Camelot. Wyatt Earp at Tombstone slew the men who killed his brothers Virgil and Morgan, and made good the reputation he held at Dodge as the coolest head of all that reckless company. William Tilghlman, quiet and deadly as an Oklahoma marshal, captured Bill Doolin single-handed. Ben Daniels fought with the First United States Volunteer Cavalry in its two Cuban battles, and won Colonel Roosevelt's commendation as a good soldier. Ben Thompson returned to Texas and became celebrated as the chief fighting man of the Lone-Star State. Clay Allison's trail to Dodge City, lined with graves almost as frequent as those Napoleon left to mark his retreat from Moscow, had already stamped him as a bad man. Doc Holliday, Luke Short, Bill Thompson, Fred Singer, Dave Black, Charley Coulter, and Charley Bassett at Dodge and elsewhere established a name for courage and daring but little less than that of their better known comrades. But William Barclay Masterson, Patrick

Shugrue, and David Mather were the distinctive personalities of the Round Table of Dodge City.

Twenty-seven years ago a handsome young fellow known as Bat Masterson was employed as a scout in the vicinity of Fort Elliott or Cantonment in the Texas Pan-Handle. At Sweetwater, close by, a good-looking young woman conducted a music and dance hall, which was a rendezvous for the soldiers, scouts, traders, and buffalo hunters who pervaded that region. Her failings and her virtues were those of her sisters, the Nell Gwynns and Peg Woffingtons of other generations. Among them she numbered courage, unselfishness, faithfulness to her friends, and the capacity for self-sacrifice. Jealous of her preference for his brown-eyed young rival, a big sergeant from the Fort beat upon the doors of the dance hall, and, gaining admission, at once opened fire upon the scout. The girl was the first to observe his move, and, springing between the men, received the bullet and fell dead. But the slender figure of the Thespian was a poor bulwark, and the same bullet entered the hip of the youthful plainsman, till then a mere lad of the farm and the border. Flat on his back, his left leg quivering like the fluttering wing of a wounded bird, the cool, fierce nature of the boy declared itself. With one hand upon his knee, he straightened down the wounded leg; and with the other, drawing his revolver, slew his enemy where he stood, and passed into a man's estate. A few months later he was one of twenty men who fought five hundred Indians for three days, and made the battle of Adobe Walls famous forever on the border.

In 1877 Bat, though a mere boy, was Sheriff of Ford County, and his brother Ed was marshal of Dodge City. Some Texas cowboys, led by Corporal Walker, a herd boss, took possession of a dance hall and made a rough house. The sheriff and the marshal went over to quell the disturbance. Bat went inside, and Ed, who was the gentler of the Mastersons, paused on the front porch to disarm a cowboy named Wagner. "I will have to take your gun," said Ed Masterson. Wagner, short, stout, dark, and surly, placed his gun against Masterson's breast and fired, even setting fire to his victim's clothing by the shot. Bat ran out, and Ed staggered toward him saying, "I've got my dose, Bat; I'm done for." Some men would have caught their brothers in their arms, others would have begun firing without a word; but Bat Masterson did one of the things which prove him, his old comrades say, a great general. His mentality covered every feature of the situation. First he sprang from the lighter sidewalk into the darker street. Then he said to his dying brother, "Ed, put the fire out of your clothes, go across the street and get help. I'll stay here and tend to this." Wagner fell at his first fire, shot through the abdomen, and died that evening in terrible agony. Next he shot the leader Walker through the lungs and through the side, and, still firing rapidly, chased the other cowboys out of sight from where he stood. In the twinkling of an eye he had whipped a drunken mob of mad killers, slain two men, avenged his brother's death, and restored order in Dodge City. The tall figure of the fair-faced Walker, with death hanging over his head, walked slowly up the sidewalk to the next saloon-door, and quietly through that saloon to the rear, where he fell in a heap. Masterson, showing his continuity of purpose, ran swiftly after him, found him, as he supposed, dead at the back door, and came away, for he never kicked a man when he was down. Returning to the front he met his friend, the prosecuting attorney, the Hon. Mike Sutton, now collector of internal revenue for the State of Kansas. "Come on," said Bat, "we'll go quick and see how Ed's getting along," and walked swiftly across the street in quest of his brother. The spectators on the other side, by the light of his burning raiment, watched Ed Masterson stagger across the street and the railroad track to the north, then gathered him up and gave him every attention. Bat came in as his brother was gasping for his last breath. He turned away, walked across the street with his lawyer friend, seated himself upon the sidewalk, dropped his head upon his hands, and suddenly burst into tears. "It will grieve mother to death," said he.

Some twenty years ago, with revolvers and poker decks the Argonauts of Dodge City went to Tombstone, Arizona, in quest of the Golden Fleece, Bat Masterson among them. His brother James, the least forceful of the family, remained in Dodge and got the worst of a quarrel with Peacock of the Lady Gay, and Updegraff, his barkeeper. Though it was generally understood that Jim and Bat were not on speaking terms, Charley Ronan wired the brother at Tombstone, and he took the first train to Dodge to fight for the reputation of his brother. At eleven A.M. the train reached Dodge. Masterson alighted, walked across the street to Mike Sutton's law office, stepped into the adjoining bedroom, laid off coat, collar, and cuffs, and removed the travel stains, as is customary with gentlemen when they have travelled fifteen hundred miles to shoot up a town. Casually remarking that Jim seemed to have been having some trouble, he walked down-stairs and out on the north side of Front Street. The railroad runs through the heart of Dodge, and on each side is a highway, giving Front Street the effect of a double avenue. On the north and south it was lined with saloons, dance halls, and business houses. The Lady Gay Dance Hall was over on the south side, and Mr. Masterson on the north. Shaking hands with Shugrue, he glanced across the railroad track and saw Peacock and Updegraff walking diagonally across the open space south of the track from the Lady Gay to the railroad station. Hastily remarking that he had some business, he ran out on the track and accosted them.

"Oh, Updegraff!" said he, throwing up his left hand. As they looked he called, "I'm after you, come a-shootin'," and the modern tournament of Ashby-de-la-Zouch had begun. If Ivanhoe was ready and fearless with his challenge, Bois-Guilbert and Front de Bœuf were sufficiently spirited in reply. They promptly returned the fire, the opposing forces slowly advancing. But suddenly Peacock's friends from the south and Masterson's from the north opened fire, and Shotgun Collins put in an appearance on the railroad track, back of Masterson, with his simple weapon. He had, it appears, come all the way from Tombstone with Masterson simply to demonstrate his friendship. Damon did no more for Pythias. The allied forces skipped behind the little calaboose which stood in the centre of the open space, and, Peacock taking one corner and Updegraff the other, continued the vendetta. Charley Ronan, backing up his telegram, and Neil Brown, sportively known by his friends as "Skinny" Brown, began firing in open order from Beason and Harris's on the north. The Hon. Robert Wright, a prominent and wealthy business man, known in the Southwest for forty years as Bob Wright, and the Grand Duke Alexis's famous friend, Mr. Chalk Beason, who were well known peace-makers, finding their efforts as unnoticed and unavailing as Mrs. Partington's equally celebrated endeavor at the Atlantic with her broom, strategically secured situations which best united dignity and safety with a view of the conflict.

Dodge City divided itself into three classes of people. One class arrayed itself in support of the respective gladiators; another, following the examples of Wright and Beason, secured the best view possible and filled the parquet; the rest of the town lay on its faces and listened to the rattle of the guns. The windows of the buildings were shot to pieces; a hundred hair-breadth escapes have been enumerated; but, recovering enough, the only man hurt, and he recovered, was Updegraff, who had precipitated the conflict by his treatment of Jim Masterson. He was shot through the lungs, and, jumping a seven-wire fence, made his way to his quarters in the dance hall, in the midst of the fusillade. The conflict ended almost as suddenly as it began, principally, I think, because everybody was out of ammunition. Collins was making so much noise with his shotgun that he failed to realize hostilities were discontinued, so Bob Wright went down and pulled his sleeve and called his attention to the fact. Mr. Collins apologized very nicely for his remissness, put on his blanket, and came back on the reservation.

Masterson walked up from the railroad track endeavoring to reload a very badly heated revolver. Mayor A. B. Webster, who as representative of a vigilance committee had killed his man at Hays City, and was quite a stickler for law and order, was very much disgusted with this promiscuous violation of the city ordinances and the apparent inefficiency of his police force, due probably to their sympathy with the various contending factions. By this time Webster had secured his own shotgun, and, coming out, he promptly covered Masterson, saying, "Put down that gun." The Ivanhoe of this affair could hardly decide what the mayor's attitude was, and suggested, "I will bring it to you"; to which the mayor responded, "Put down that gun or I'll kill you." Bat hesitated, but in response to the call of his friends dropped his pistol and surrendered, and the tournament was completed. Masterson was immediately taken to the police judge's office, and at twelve o'clock very properly fined five dollars and costs, which he paid. Even his best friends admitted that the police judge only did right. He had arrived at eleven, paid his fine at twelve, and at three P.M. Mr. Masterson, accompanied by his fidus Achates, took the train for Tombstone. He had vindicated the family reputation, restored the prestige of the Masterson name, and demonstrated to the world that there are still knights-errant who will travel three thousand miles and risk their lives in fair and open conflict to uphold a brother's cause.

Nor did these strange individuals fail to appreciate the fact that they were modern additions of ancient knighthood. Some sneaking imitation of a man under the cover of the law had wronged and insulted Masterson as such hypocrites do. He came to Masterson and held out his hand, pretending a friendship he did not feel. The frontiersman caught the hand in his, looked the fellow in the eye a moment, slapped his face twice with his open left hand, and pushed the other away. "Now, you —— —— ——, go and shake hands with somebody who wants to shake with you. 'The hand of Douglass is his own,'" he said.

The Modred of the Dodge City Round Table was David Mather, a Connecticut Yankee, and a descendant of the Cotton Mather family. Furtive, suspicious, secretive, he was known from Los Vegas to Dodge City as "Mysterious Dave." He and Cyrus were the sons of a Yankee sea-captain who was lost at sea. They undertook to farm in the Solomon Valley, but the Indian troubles drove them out. They came to Dodge City and engaged in breaking prairie for the settlers, soon turning their attention to buffalo hunting. The Indians stole their horses, and they proceeded to retaliate by establishing a large trade in Indian ponies. Dave sold a herd of forty in Dodge City at fourteen dollars a head at one time. The soldiers interfered with their business in a measure by attempting to protect the Indians, and it has been charged that Dave took out letters of marque and levied on the Government stock of horses. This was done, however, in a purely playful spirit, if at all. The Mathers soon desired a more settled life, and turned their attention to playing poker at Dodge City. Dave served as deputy sheriff, and, I believe, as marshal. He seems to have been a faithful officer. At one time he was playing poker in his brother's saloon with a man named Barnes. Just as Sheriff Shugrue came in, Dave Mather swept the stakes off the table and slapped Barnes. The sheriff warned him to desist, when Cy Mather suddenly called out, "Look out, Pat, the other Barnes is pulling his gun." Shugrue immediately caught the other Barnes, but the original Barnes went after his gun and fired at Dave Mather, just grazing his forehead. Cy Mather opened fire in defence of his brother, and everybody took a hand, in fact, with results eventually fatal to one of the Barnes boys; but Shugrue finally secured peace and told the Barnes family that they might "consider themselves under arrest." He then escorted his special captive Barnes to the jail, and said to Dave Mather, "I put you in charge of the other Barnes. Keep him here till I return." This, however, was merely a bit of strategy, as he promptly returned, and arrested all three of them, the two Mathers and the remaining Barnes. The Irishman shrewdly calculated that Dave Mather, put in charge of the prisoner, would consider it his duty to stay. Evidently the Yankee had a code of honor up to which he lived.

There was and still is a considerable prejudice against Dave Mather. Many declare him to have been a cur who would not fight on the square, that he was a horse-thief and a highwayman. Mather complained frequently of this prejudice. He once said to a friend, "If I sit down in a crowd of twenty-five, and some son-of-a-gun of a stranger comes along looking for a fight, he passes twenty-four men by and jumps on me." It is doubtful if a Connecticut Yankee of the Cotton Mather blood would particularly commend himself to the genial spirits of the Southwest. His appearance furthered the prejudice. Five feet and ten inches high, slender, stoop-shouldered, walking always with his face toward the ground, never looking a man straight in the eye, quiet, reserved, coming and going unheralded and unadvertised, it is not at all surprising that he was known as "Mysterious Dave." He had a steel-blue eye, over which he always pulled down his hat closely. He had a simple and gentle face, as little like a fighter as you could imagine. My observation has been that most of the bad men of the border were blue-eyed. A man with a soft blue eye will always be selected by a bully as a victim in preference to these snapping black, brown, or cold gray eyes. On the average, men possess about the same amount of courage, and when the blue-eyed man has been imposed on sufficiently he resents it; one combat precipitates another, till he gets a reputation up to which he feels he must live. There is your fighting man. Mather was a good example.

However, there was not an entire lack of justification for the criticisms. He once remarked, "These killers are all murderers. All of 'em look for the best of it. If I made up my mind I had to kill a man, I'd rather find him asleep than any other way." When he was deputy marshal at Los Vegas, a man stepped up to him, put a pistol in his face, and said, "You're the fellow who goes around here killin' people. I'll just fix you out right now." Mather threw his hands before his face and backed off. "No, no!" said he, "you are mistaken. I'm your friend. I'm no killer. I'm peaceable. I'm your friend. I'm your friend." The puzzled avenger hesitated and dropped his gun-hand by his side. As Mather shoved his pistol back in the holster, he glanced at the corpse and remarked, "Now don't make any more mistakes." Somebody told him one day to look out, that Bat Master-

"THE ONLY DESCENDANT OF COTTON MATHER WHO HAS DISTINGUISHED HIMSELF"

son would kill him. Sometimes he stuttered slightly. He said, "No, I may kill him. He will shove his gun in my stomach and orate. I'll turn 'round, put my hand in the middle of my back, and say, 'You shoot me right there; you can do it.' He will drop his hand by his side, and then he'll c-c-climb the golden stairs." Mr. Owen Wister, in a recent number of this magazine, had a very logical discussion of the bad man. Dave Mather was about as correct a type of the bad man as could be found. Take notice that he was simply a modern buffalo-grass edition of that Cotton Mather who burned witches and abused everybody who did not happen to believe just as he did.

The story they tell of Mather's Los Vegas experience was probably correct. The Henry gang took possession of a dance hall and began to make life a burden for the peaceful denizens of Los Vegas. Marshal Tom Carson, followed by the stoop-shouldered figure of policeman Dave Mather, stalked into the room and called for order. At the first shot all the lights went out except one. A terrific fusillade in the darkness followed, and the marshal, with both arms broken, walked unsteadily to the door and died. For several minutes the affray continued so fiercely that no policemen cared to enter. Gradually the cowboys appeared, running for their horses. When the smoke cleared away and other officers ventured in, the silent and stoop-shouldered figure of Dave Mather was found holding two prisoners, one badly wounded, while four dead cowboys scattered over the floor certified to the craftiness, the gameness, and the good pistol practice of the only descendant of Cotton Mather who has distinguished himself.

In 1879 he was employed by the Santa Fé as a gladiator to protect their right of way near Pueblo against the Denver and Rio Grande. In 1885 he was hired by the Northern cattlemen to prevent the passage of Texas cattle across the Cherokee strip. In both instances he was merely a member of a company. When put in danger, Mather was exceedingly dangerous, and it is likely that more bad men were afraid of him than of any other walking arsenal who patrolled the border line. Returning to Dodge he found himself so out of favor with the administration, that after he and Dave Black had barricaded their rooms for several days

they were glad to escape between two suns. Three days after, as Bill Tilghman, who had been the chief instrument of his expatriation, was purchasing a ticket at the Kansas City Union Depot, somebody touched him on the shoulder. He turned to confront the simple face of "Mysterious Dave Mather," to suppose that Mather, as usual, had the drop on him and that he was a dead man. But the austere and sombre Puritan merely put out his hand, said, "Hello, Bill!" and drifted out of the life of Dodge City forever. From the British Northwest territories came the report that he had enlisted as one of the mounted police, looted the stage he was sent to guard, and escaped with twenty thousand pounds. His brother Cy reports that he was killed by the moonshiners in the mountains of Tennessee. Did this last of the Puritans terminate his career as a hero or a highwayman? Quien Sabe? Like Tennessee's Pardner, he played a lone hand.

I am afraid that the Round Table of Dodge City, with the little hole in the centre, can exhibit no green baize-covered Sir Galahad. Probably, if the truth were known there was no Sir Galahad at the other Round Table; but one of the Dodge City members was neither a gambler, a killer, nor a bad man. Patrick Shugrue disclaims even ever having had any difficulties in arresting bad men. He seemed to think that, "You may consider yourself under arrest," had a hypnotic effect, for he always used that form. According to his own diffident version he must have been a sort of a Pied Piper around whom his captives sportively played. Pat is five feet seven inches high, and weighs about one hundred and sixty pounds. His sturdy and rather awkward figure; his strong, shrewd face, as homely as Abraham Lincoln's; his unique and original, though simple and unaffected utterance; mark him as a peculiar man. He and his twin brother Mike were the sons of an Irish schoolmaster, born in County Kerry, Ireland. Pat was raised by his grandmother in the mountains of Kerry, and came to America at ten years of age unable to speak a word of English. While Masterson was hunting buffalo and Mather was stealing horses from the Indians in the territory, this little sawed-off Irish blacksmith was shoeing horses for the United States of America at Fort Dodge. He moved into Dodge City and opened a blacksmith shop. At that time hunting buffalo and stealing horses were the principal avocations in the Southwest. Stealing horses from the Indians was, of course, a legitimate industry. Stealing horses and mules from the Government was sometimes regarded with indifference, with the same tolerance that we extend to a tramp stealing a ride on a train. Patrick Shugrue, of course, enjoyed an extensive business among the horsemen. While he was too honest to be involved in anything wrong, he was too good a business man to become inquisitive.

In 1878, however, he was accidentally elected constable. His brother Michael, who was wagon-master at Fort Dodge, requested his aid in running down a horse-thief who had taken a fine Government horse, which was presumably in a big stable south of the river at Dodge City. While Pat deprecated the loss of custom that would ensue, he determined to do his duty. "What did you come here fer?" said the suspicious landlord of the horse hostelry. "Nawthin'," said Pat. "I'll play you a game of seven-up fer the drinks." The game ended, Pat expressed a desire to inspect and purchase a couple of ponies, and soon located the Government property in the stable. "Whose horse is that?" said the constable. "I dunno," said the landlord. "You don't?" said Pat. "You may consider yourself under arrest." "What fer?" said the landlord. "Fer receivin' stolen Government property," said Pat. "Heavens," said the landlord, "if I tell you, they'll kill me!" but he gave the man's name. Pat knew the fellow was sleeping in a dug-out, with a bunch of horse-thieves near town, and went home and secured a shotgun and a warrant. They wanted him to take a posse. "No," said the blacksmith, "that would simply stir up a row with them," and he walked out to the dug-out, pushed the door open, and stepped in, shoving the shotgun ahead. Six lay in the bunks about dozing. "Mr. Jones, git up," said the Irishman. "I've got a warrant fer you. Consider yourself under arrest." One young man stirred in his bunk and reached for his gun. The new peace officer threw the shotgun on him. "Young feller, you make another break like that an' I'll kill you. I didn't come down here to make no gun trouble, but I kin tell you right now I didn't come down here to git the worst of it. You come along with me," said he to his prisoner. "Read the warrant," said that gentleman, who stood on ceremony. Accordingly Patrick, holding his gun on the fellow, held the warrant above it like a sheet of music and read it to him. "I'll go peaceable," said the prisoner, "but I'm lame and can't walk." "Well, you'll walk out o' here fast enough," said Shugrue. "Git out o' that bunk before I shoot a hole in it." The gentleman responded with alacrity, and the constable marched his prisoner to town. The horse-thief is now a rich banker, and the captor is a poor man. "I thought the thing over," said Pat, "an' right there I declared myself agin horse-stealin'."

In 1883 Patrick Shugrue was put forward for sheriff with the city administration against him. The mayor appointed forty deputies. Pat went to him and demurred, saying they did not need so many, that it would cause friction. The official vigorously and somewhat rudely declared his determination to maintain the number. Pat regarded it as an attempt to bulldoze his friends. "You may not have so many tomorrow," said he. When the polls opened next morning, Wyatt Earp and Bat Masterson, summoned from the Far West, stood on either side. "What are you fellows here for? Do you think you're going to vote?" said one of the deputies. "No," said Wyatt Earp, "we are here to see that Pat Shugrue gits a square deal." A consultation followed, the deputies went out of business, and all the sporting and fighting gentlemen gave their attention to betting on the election. Pat carried the town by eighty-six, every precinct in the county, and was triumphantly elected. A stranger might wonder how he could command such loyal support from such men, but it was because the little Irishman was made of the right kind of stuff, and he remembers his friends.

Shugrue served two terms as sheriff of Ford and the fourteen counties attached to it for judicial purposes. He never lost a prisoner, and he got the men he went after, but he never found it necessary to kill any one. When we remember that some of the worst men in the world were included within his jurisdiction, it must be conceded that Pat and his brother Mike, who was for ten years sheriff of Clarke County, with a similar record, though Mike killed two men, were two of the most efficient peace officers the West ever knew. Pat, modest in regard to his own merits, is almost loquacious in relating those of his brother, who is indeed regarded by some as perhaps the better of the two.

In response to Ed Julian's request, the sheriff went to his place of business only to find a big pistol shoved in his face. As the assassin fired, Patrick caught the pistol in his hand and held it up. The bullet grazed his face, and the powder left its terrific marks all around one eye, where they will remain till Pat Shugrue follows his twin brother to where all good Irish Catholics go. Julian was a strong man, but the wrathful and powerful little Irish blacksmith wrested the weapon from him, and, quivering with indignation, faced the trembling figure of the assassin. "I ought to kill you," said he; and then, pausing a moment, added, "You may consider yourself under arrest."

Of course there are those who think the Shugrues should have killed more people. The criticism is similar to the one Seth Mabry passed on Ben Thompson. Twenty-five hundred delegates held a cattlemen's convention at Austin. A banquet was given to a select fifty-two. The local Congressman, for some reason, was not invited, an affront which his friend Ben Thompson determined to resent. Accordingly when the banquet hall was opened, Mr. Thompson stepped in with his six-shooter, and in a pleasant and quiet way broke every plate, and knocked every wine bottle off the table. Seth Mabry said to Bob Wright, "They say this Ben Thompson is such a brave man. I don't think he's such a brave man. He cut off a little party of fifty-two of us and jumped on us, but if he's such a brave man, why didn't he tackle that convention of twenty-five hundred men?" Patrick Shugrue was not a bad man and never claimed to be a killer, but he was a fine type of the border peace officer, who did his duty without fear or favor, and that is as high an encomium as can be passed upon the most dashing knight that ever rode out of Camelot with his lance across his shoulder.

Mather's chief characteristic was the instinct of self-preservation. That dormant, he was an ordinary, commonplace fellow; that instinct aroused, he became a cruel, ruthless, and scientific slayer of men, a veritable stick of dynamite. If he had added to his treasures the instinct of ac-

quisition, he might have grown wealthy at some business which permitted him to levy tribute on his fellow-men. Shugrue, shrewd, sturdy, sensible, was simply the average man, exceptionally endowed with the idea of doing his duty under the only code he knew—the statutory law. W. B. Masterson had talents which in other walks of life would have commanded success. He might have been an excellent newspaper man very easily, as he showed capacity in that direction; but a restless youth on the Western border, he loved excitement, and it carried him into his mode of life. He really had little confidence in the accepted standards of society. His observation was that they most frequently sheltered cowardly rascals. He was a man of chivalric tendencies, and held as the sovereign principle of his career absolute loyalty to his friends.

The swish of the lariat, the shout of the cowboy, the crack of the pistol, and the Knights of the Border have passed away from Dodge City forever. Ancient Fort Dodge, that shook to the tread of the cavalry, that was the refuge for so many thousands against the raid of the Indian, is now the home of old veterans whose declining years are made easy by a grateful commonwealth. The Round Table of Dodge City has done its work and gone its way, as did Ulysses and his town burners, Romulus and his wife stealers, Roland and his henchmen, the good King Arthur and his friends and foes. In the path of them all follows a quieter civilization, better homes, and a higher life. But the bank wrecker succeeds the bank robber, the railroad wrecker follows the train robber, the bad man takes advantage of the unsophisticated, the bully coerces the helpless, and every vice of the border reappears in all the great channels of business but little better masked, while the sleek Pharisee boasts that he is not like the rude frontiersman. So will the story run forever, unless the precepts of the gentle Galilean shall obtain some actual hold on the instincts of the race—half-brother to the chimpanzee, that already endeavors to hold his head among the gods. Meanwhile, over against the storied shield of Sir Lancelot of the Lake, the Knights of the Border hang a stack of little ivory discs and four aces couchant, a six-shooter rampant on a baize-covered circle—the bullet-dented escutcheon of the House of Masterson.

10

Round-Up Days

Stewart Edward White

ROUND-UP DAYS

BY STEWART EDWARD WHITE

DRAWINGS BY J. N. MARCHAND

I

THE DRIVE

A CRY awakened me. It was still deep night. The moon sailed overhead, the stars shone unwavering like candles, and a chill breeze wandered in from the open spaces of the desert. I raised myself on my elbow, throwing aside the blankets and the canvas tarpaulin. Forty other indistinct formless bundles on the ground all about me were sluggishly astir. Four figures passed and repassed between me and a red fire. I knew them for the two cooks and the horse wranglers. One of the latter was grumbling.

"Didn't git in till moon-up last night," he growled, "might as well trade my bed for a lantern and be done with it."

Even as I stretched my arms and shivered a little, the two wranglers threw down their tin plates with a clatter, mounted horses and rode away in the direction of the thousand acres or so known as the pasture.

I pulled on my clothes hastily, buckled in my buckskin shirt and dove for the fire. A dozen others were before me. It was bitterly cold. In the east the sky had paled the least bit in the world, but the moon and stars shone on bravely and undiminished. A band of coyotes were shrieking desperate blasphemies against the new day; and the stray herd, awakening, were beginning to bawl and bellow.

Two crater-like dutch ovens, filled with pieces of fried beef, stood near the fire; two galvanized water buckets, brimming with soda biscuits, flanked them; two tremendous coffee pots stood guard at either end. We picked us each a tin cup and a tin plate from the box at the rear of the chuck wagon; helped ourselves from a dutch oven, a pail, and a coffee pot, and squatted on our heels as close to the fire as possible. Men who came too late borrowed the shovel, scooped up some coals, and so started little fires of their own about which new groups formed.

While we ate the eastern sky lightened. The mountains under the dawn looked like silhouettes cut from slate-colored paper; those in the west showed faintly luminous. Objects about us became dimly visible. We could make out the windmill, and the adobe of the ranch houses, and the corrals. The cowboys arose one by one, dropped their plates into the dish-pan, and began to hunt out their ropes. Everything was obscure and mysterious in the faint gray light. I watched Windy Bill near his tarpaulin. He stooped to throw over the canvas. When he bent, it was before daylight; when he straightened his back, daylight had come. It was just like that, as though some one had reached out his hand to turn on the illumination of the world.

The eastern mountains were fragile; the plain was ethereal, like a sea of liquid gases. From the pasture we heard the shoutings of the wranglers, and made out a cloud of dust. In a moment the first of the remuda came into view, trotting forward with the free grace of the unburdened horse. Others followed in procession; those near, sharp and well defined, those in the background, more or less obscured by the dust, now appearing plainly, now fading like ghosts. The leaders turned unhesitatingly into the corral. After them poured the stream of the remuda—two hundred and fifty horses —with an unceasing thunder of hoofs.

Immediately the cook-camp was deserted. The cowboys entered the corral. The horses began to circulate around the edge of the inclosure as around the circumference of a circus ring. The men, grouped at the center, watched keenly, looking for the mounts they had already decided on. In no time each had recognized his choice and, his loop trailing, was walking toward that part of the revolving circumference where his pony dodged. Some few whirled the loop, but most cast it with a quick flip. It was really marvelous to observe the accuracy with which the noose would fly, past a dozen tossing heads and over a dozen backs, to settle firmly about the neck of an animal perhaps in the very center of the group. But again, if the first throw failed, it was interesting to see how the selected pony would dodge, double back, twist, turn and hide to escape a second cast. And it was equally interesting to observe how his companions would help him. They seemed to realize that they were not wanted, and would push themselves between the cowboy and his intended mount with the utmost boldness. In the thick dust that instantly arose, and with the bewildering thunder of galloping, the flashing change of grouping, the rush of the charging animals, recognition alone would seem almost impossible, yet in an incredibly short time each had his mount, and the others, under convoy of the wranglers, were meekly wending their way out over the plain. There, until time for a change of horses, they would graze in a loose and scattered band, requiring scarcely any supervision. Escape? Bless you, no, that thought was the last in their minds.

In the meantime the saddles and bridles were adjusted. Always in a cowboy's "string" of from six to ten animals the boss assigns him two or three broncos to break in to the cow business. Therefore, each morning we could observe a half dozen or so men gingerly leading wicked looking little animals out to the sand "to take the pitch out of them." One small black belonging to a cowboy called "The Judge," used to more than fulfill expectations of a good time.

"Go to him, Judge!" some one would always remark.

"If he ain't goin' to pitch, I ain't goin'

to make him," the Judge would grin as he swung aboard.

The black would trot off quite calmly and in a most matter of fact way, as though to shame all slanderers of his lamb-like character. Then, as the bystanders would turn away, he would utter a squeal, throw down his head and go to it. He was a very hard bucker, and made some really spectacular jumps, but the trick on which he based his claims to originality consisted in standing on his hind legs at so perilous an approach to the perpendicular that his rider would conclude him about to fall backward, and then suddenly to spring forward in a series of stiff-legged bucks. The first maneuver induced the rider to loosen his seat in order to be ready to jump from under, and the second threw him before he could regain his grip.

"And they say a horse don't think!" exclaimed an admirer.

But as these were broken horses—save the mark—the show was all over after each had had his little fling. We mounted and rode away, just as the mountain peaks to the west caught the rays of a sun we should not enjoy for a good half hour yet.

I had five horses in my string, and this morning rode "that C S horse, Brown Jug." Brown Jug was a powerful and well-built animal, about fourteen-two in height, and possessed of a vast enthusiasm for cow-work. As the morning was frosty, he felt good.

At the gate of the water corral we separated into two groups. The smaller, under the direction of Jed Parker, was to drive the mesquite in the wide flats; the rest of us, under command of Homer, the round-up captain, were to sweep the country even as far as the base of the foothills near Mount Graham. Accordingly we put our horses to the full gallop.

Mile after mile we thundered along at a brisk rate of speed. Sometimes we dodged in and out among the mesquite bushes, alternately separating and coming together again; sometimes we swept over grassy plains apparently of illimitable extent; sometimes we skipped and hopped and buck-jumped through and over little gullies, barrancas and other sorts of malpais, but always without drawing rein. The men rode easily with no thought to the way nor care for the footing. The air came

A mad mother cow is a very demon at times.

Drawing by J. N. Marchand.

back sharp against our faces. The warm blood stirred by the rush flowed more rapidly. We experienced a delightful glow. Of the morning cold only the very tips of our fingers and the ends of our noses retained a remnant. Already the sun was shining low and level across the plains. The shadows of the cañons modeled the hitherto flat surfaces of the mountains.

After a time we came to some low hills helmeted with the outcrop of a rock escarpment. Hitherto they had seemed a termination of Mount Graham, but now when we rode around them we discovered them to be separated from the range by a good five miles of sloping plain. Later we looked back and would have sworn them part of the Dos Cabesas system did we not know them to be at least eight miles distant from that rocky rampart. It is always that way in Arizona. Spaces develop of whose existence you had not the slightest intimation. Hidden in apparently plane surfaces are valleys and prairies. At one sweep of the eye you embrace the entire area of an eastern state, but nevertheless the reality as you explore it foot by foot proves to be infinitely more than the vision has promised.

Beyond the hill we stopped. Here our party divided again, half to the right and half to the left. We had ridden directly away from camp; now we rode a circumference of which headquarters was the center. The country was pleasantly rolling and covered with grass. Here and there were clumps of soapweed. Far in a remote distance lay a slender dark line across the plain. This we knew to be mesquite, and once entered, we knew it too would seem to spread out vastly. And then this grassy slope on which we now rode would show merely as an insignificant streak of yellow. It is also like that in Arizona. I have ridden in succession through grassland, brush-land, flower-land, desert. Each in turn seemed entirely to fill the space of the plains between the mountains.

From time to time Homer halted us and detached a man. The business of the latter was then to ride directly back to camp, driving all cattle before him. Each was in sight of his right and left hand neighbor. Thus was constructed a dragnet, which contracted as home was neared.

I was detached when of our party only the cattleman and Homer remained. They would take the outside. This was the post of honor, and required the hardest riding, for as soon as the cattle should realize the fact of their pursuit, they would attempt to "break" past the end and up the valley. Brown Jug and I congratulated ourselves on an exciting morning in prospect.

Now wild cattle know perfectly well what a drive means, and they do not intend to get into a round-up if they can help it. Were it not for the two facts, that they are afraid of a mounted man, and cannot run quite so fast as a horse, I do not know how the cattle business would be conducted. As soon as a band of them caught sight of any one of us, they curled their tails and away they went at a long easy lope that a domestic cow would stare at in wonder. This was all very well, in fact we yelled and shrieked and otherwise uttered cow-calls to keep them going, to "get the cattle started," as they say. But pretty soon a little band of the many scurrying away before our thin line, began to bear farther and farther to the east. When in their judgment they should have gained an opening, they would turn directly back and make a dash for liberty. Accordingly, the nearest cowboy clapped spurs to his horse and pursued them.

It was a pretty race. The cattle ran easily enough, with long, springy jumps that carried them over the ground faster than appearances would lead one to believe. The cow-pony, his nose stretched out, his ears slanted, his eyes snapping with joy of the chase, flew fairly "belly to earth." The rider sat slightly forward, with the cowboy's loose seat. A whirl of dust, strangely insignificant against the immensity of a desert morning, rose from the flying group. Now they disappeared in a ravine, only to scramble out again the next instant, pace undiminished. The rider merely rose slightly and threw up his elbows to relieve the jar of the rough gulley. At first the cattle seemed to hold their own, but soon the horse began to gain. In a short time he had come abreast of the leading animal. The latter stopped short with a snort, dodged back, and set out at right angles to his former course. From a dead run the pony came to a stand in two fierce plunges, doubled back like a shot, and was off on the other tack. An un-

Hold hard along the river banks.

Drawing by J. N. Marchand.

accustomed rider would here have lost his seat. The second dash was short. With a final shake of the head, the steers turned to the proper course in the direction of the ranch. The pony dropped unconcernedly to the shuffling jog of habitual progression.

Far away stretched the arc of our cordon. The most distant rider was a speck, and the cattle ahead of him were like maggots endowed with a smooth, swift, onward motion. As yet the herd had not taken form; it was still too widely scattered. Its units, in the shape of small bunches momently grew in numbers. The distant plains were crawling and alive with minute creatures making toward a common, tiny center.

Immediately in our front the cattle at first behaved very well. Then far down the long gentle slope I saw a break for the upper valley. The mannikin that represented Homer at once became even smaller as it departed in pursuit. The cattleman moved down to cover Homer's territory until he should return, and I in turn edged farther to the right. Then another break from another bunch. The cattleman rode at top speed to head it. Before long he disappeared in the distant mesquite. I found myself in sole charge of a front three miles long.

The nearest cattle were some distance ahead, and trotting along at a good gait. As yet they had not discovered the chance left open by unforeseen circumstance. I descended and took in on my cinch while yet there was time. Even as I mounted, an impatient movement on the part of experienced Brown Jug told me that the cattle had seen their opportunity.

I gathered the reins and spoke to the horse. He needed no further direction, but set off at a wide angle nicely calculated to intercept the truants. Brown Jug was a powerful beast. The spring of his leap was as whalebone. The yellow earth began to stream past as water. Always the pace increased with a growing thunder of hoofs. It seemed that nothing could turn us from the straight line, nothing check the headlong momentum of our rush. My eyes filled with tears from the wind of our going. Saddle strings streamed behind. Brown Jug's mane whipped my bridle hand. Dimly I was conscious of soapweed, sacatone, mesquite, as we passed them. They were abreast and gone before I could think of them or how they were to be dodged. Two antelope bounded away to the left; birds rose hastily from the grasses. A sudden *chirk, chirk, chirk,* rose all about me. We were in the very center of a prairie dog town, but before I could formulate in my mind the probabilities of holes and broken legs, the *chirk, chirk, chirking* had fallen astern. Brown Jug had skipped and dodged successfully.

We were approaching the cattle. They ran stubbornly and well, evidently unwilling to be turned until the latest possible moment. A great rage at their obstinacy took possession of us both. A broad, shallow wash crossed our way, but we plunged through its rocks and bowlders recklessly, angered at even the slight delay they necessitated. The hard land on the other side we greeted with joy. Brown Jug extended himself with a snort.

Suddenly a jar seemed to shake my very head loose. I found myself staring over the horse's head directly down into a deep and precipitous gulley, the edge of which was so cunningly concealed by the grasses as to have remained invisible to my blurred vision. Brown Jug, however, had caught sight of it at the last instant, and had executed one of the wonderful stops possible only to a cow-pony.

But already the cattle had discovered a passage above, and were scrambling down and across. Brown Jug and I, at more sober pace, slid off the almost perpendicular bank, and out the other side.

A moment later we had headed them. They whirled, and without the necessity of any suggestion on my part Brown Jug turned after them, and so quickly that my stirrup actually brushed the ground. After that we were masters. We chased the cattle far enough to start them well in the proper direction, and then pulled down to a walk in order to get a breath of wind.

But now we noticed another band, back on the ground over which we had just come, doubling through in the direction of Mount Graham. A hard run set them to rights. We turned. More had poured out from the hills. Bands were crossing everywhere, ahead and behind. Brown Jug and I set to work.

Being an indivisible unit, we could chase only one bunch at a time; and while we

One mired steer gives more trouble than a hundred on the loose.

Drawing by J. N. Marchand.

were after one, a half dozen others would be taking advantage of our preoccupation. We could not hold our own. Each run after an escaping bunch had to be on a longer diagonal. Gradually we were forced back, and back, and back, but still we managed to hold the line unbroken. Never shall I forget the dash and clatter of that morning. Neither Brown Jug nor I thought for a moment of sparing horse-flesh, nor of picking a route. We made the shortest line, and paid little attention to anything that stood in the way. A very fever of resistance possessed us. It was like beating against a head wind, or fighting fire, or combating in any other way any of the great forces of nature. We were quite alone. The cattleman and Homer had vanished. To our left the men were fully occupied in marshaling the compact brown herds that had gradually massed, for these antagonists of mine were merely the outlying remnants.

I suppose Brown Jug must have run nearly twenty miles with only one check. Then we chased a cow some distance and into the dry bed of a stream, where before we could stop she whirled on us savagely. By luck her horn hit only the leather of my saddle skirts, so we left her, for when a cow has sense enough to "get on the peck," as I shall tell you later, there is no driving her farther. We gained nothing, and had to give ground; but we succeeded in holding a semblance of order, so that the cattle did not break and scatter far and wide.

The sun had by now well risen and was beginning to shine hot. Brown Jug still ran gamely and displayed as much interest as ever, but he was evidently tiring. We were both glad to see Homer's gray showing in the fringe of mesquite. Together we soon succeeded in throwing the cows into the main herd; and, strangely enough, as soon as they had joined their fellows, their wildness left them.

As my horse was somewhat winded, I joined the "drag" at the rear. Here, by course of natural sifting soon accumulated all the lazy, gentle, and sickly cows, and the small calves. The difficulty now was to prevent them from lagging and dropping out. To that end we indulged in a great variety of the picturesque cow-calls peculiar to the cowboy. One found an old tin can which by the aid of a few pebbles he converted into a very effective rattle.

The dust rose in clouds and eddied in the sun. We slouched easily in our saddles. The cowboys compared notes as to the brands they had seen. Our ponies shuffled along, resting, but always ready.

Thus we passed over the country, down the long, gentle slope to the "sink" of the valley, whence another long, gentle slope ran to the base of the other ranges. At greater or lesser distances we caught the dust, and made out dimly the masses of the other herds collected by our companions and by the party under Jed Parker. They went forward toward the common center with a slow ruminative movement, and the dust they raised went with them.

Little by little they grew plainer to us, and the home ranch, hitherto merely a brown shimmer in the distance, began to take on definition as the group of buildings, windmills, and corrals we knew. Miniature horsemen could be seen galloping forward to the open white plain where the herd would be held. Then the mesquite enveloped us, and we knew little more, save the anxiety lest we overlook laggards in the brush, until we came out on the edge of that same white plain.

Here were more cattle, thousands of them, and billows of dust, and a great bellowing, and dim mounted figures riding and shouting ahead of the herd. Soon they succeeded in turning the leaders back. These threw into confusion those that followed. In a few moments the cattle had stopped. A cordon of horsemen sat at equal distances to ring them in.

"Pretty good haul," said the man next to me—"a good five thousand head."

Homer galloped down the line, designating rapidly the men who were first to change their horses while the others held the herd. He named me, so I rode away with the group to where the remuda, thrown together by the horse wranglers was waiting.

Their former kingdom has been pre-empted.

Drawing by J. N. Marchand.

THE OUTING MAGAZINE

NOVEMBER, 1907

ROUND-UP DAYS

CUTTING OUT

BY STEWART EDWARD WHITE

PHOTOGRAPHS BY THE AUTHOR

Y somewhere near noon we had bunched and held in a smooth, wide flat, free from bushes and dog holes, the herd of four or five thousand head. Each sat at ease on his horse facing the cattle, watching lazily the clouds of dust and the shifting beasts, but ready at any instant to turn back the restless or independent individuals that might break for liberty.

Out of the haze came Homer, the round-up captain, on an easy lope. As he passed successively the sentries he delivered to each a low command, but without slacking pace. Some of those spoken to wheeled their horses and rode away. The others settled themselves in their saddles and began to roll cigarettes.

"Change horses; get something to eat," said he to me; so I swung after the file trailing away at a canter over the low swells beyond the plain.

The remuda had been driven by its herders to a corner of the pasture's wire fence, and there held. As each man arrived, he dismounted, threw off his saddle, and turned his animal loose. Then he flipped a loop in his rope and disappeared in the eddying herd. The discarded horse, with many grunts, indulged in a satisfying roll; shook himself vigorously, and walked slowly away. His labor was over for the day; and he knew it, and took not the slightest trouble to get out of the way of the men with the swinging ropes.

Not so the fresh horses, however. They had no intention of being caught, if they could help it, but dodged and twisted, hid and doubled behind the moving screen of their friends. The latter seemed to know they were not wanted, made no effort to avoid the men, and probably accounted in great measure for the fact that the herd as a body remained compact, in spite of the cowboys threading it and in spite of the lack of an inclosure.

Our horses caught, we saddled as hastily as possible, and then at the top speed of our fresh and eager ponies we swept down on the chuck wagon. There we fell off our saddles and descended on the meat and bread like ravenous locusts in a cornfield.

The herd of cow-ponies—some have done their day's work and stand quietly; the others dodge about to avoid the rope of a rider.

The ponies stood where we left them, "tied to the ground" in the cattle-country fashion.

As soon as a man had stoked up for the afternoon, he rode away. Some finished before others, so across the plain formed an endless procession of men returning to the herd, and of those whom they replaced coming for their turn at the grub.

We found the herd quiet. Some were even lying down chewing their cuds as peacefully as any barnyard cows. Most, however, stood ruminative or walked slowly to and fro in the confines allotted by the horsemen; so that the herd looked from a distance like a brown carpet whose pattern was constantly changing—a dusty brown carpet in the process of being beaten. I relieved one of the watchers, and settled myself for a wait.

At this close inspection the different sorts of cattle showed more distinctly their characteristics. The cows and calves generally rested peacefully enough, the calf often lying down while the mother stood guard over it. Steers, however, were more restless. They walked ceaselessly, threading their way in and out among the standing cattle, pausing in brutish amazement at the edge of the herd, and turning back immediately to endless journeyings. The bulls, excited by so much company forced on their accustomed solitary habit, roared defiance at each other until the air fairly trembled. Occasionally two would clash foreheads. Then the powerful animals would push and wrestle, trying for a chance to gore. The decision of supremacy was a question of but a few minutes, and a bloody top-knot the worst damage. The defeated one side-stepped hastily and clumsily out of reach, and then walked away.

Most of the time all we had to do was to sit our horses and watch these things; to enjoy the warm bath of the Arizona sun, and to converse with our next neighbors. Once in a while some enterprising cow, observing the opening between the men, would start to walk out. Others would fall in behind her until the movement would become general. Then one of us would swing his leg off the pommel and jog his pony over to head them off. They would return peacefully enough.

But one black muley cow with a calf as black and muley as herself was more persistent. Time after time, with infinite patience, she tried it again the moment my back was turned. I tried driving her far into the herd. No use; she always returned. Quirtings and stones had no effect on her mild and steady persistence.

"She's a San Simon cow," drawled my neighbor. "Everybody knows her. She's at every round-up, just naturally raisin' hell."

When the last man had returned from chuck, Homer made the dispositions for the cut. There were present probably thirty men from the home ranches round about, and twenty representing owners at a distance, here to pick up the strays inevitable to the season's drift. The round-up captain appointed two men to hold the cow-and-calf cut, and two more to hold the steer cut. Several of us rode into the herd, while the remainder retained their positions as sentinels to hold the main body of cattle into shape.

Little G and I rode slowly among the cattle looking everywhere. The animals moved sluggishly aside to give us passage, and closed in as sluggishly behind us so that we were always closely hemmed in wherever we went. Over the shifting sleek backs, through the eddying clouds of dust, I could make out the figures of my companions moving slowly, apparently aimlessly, here and there.

Our task for the moment was to search out the unbranded J H calves. Since in ranks so closely crowded it would be physically impossible actually to see an animal's branded flank, we depended entirely on the ear marks.

Did you ever notice how any animal, tame or wild, always points his ears inquiringly in the direction of whatever interests or alarms him? Those ears are for the moment his most prominent feature. So when a brand is quite indistinguishable because, as at present, of press of numbers, or, as in winter, from extreme length of hair, the cropped ears tell plainly the tale of ownership. As every animal is so marked when branded, it follows that an uncut pair of ears means that its owner has never felt the iron.

So now we had to look first of all for calves with uncut ears. After discovering one, we had to ascertain his ownership by examining the ear-marks of his mother, by

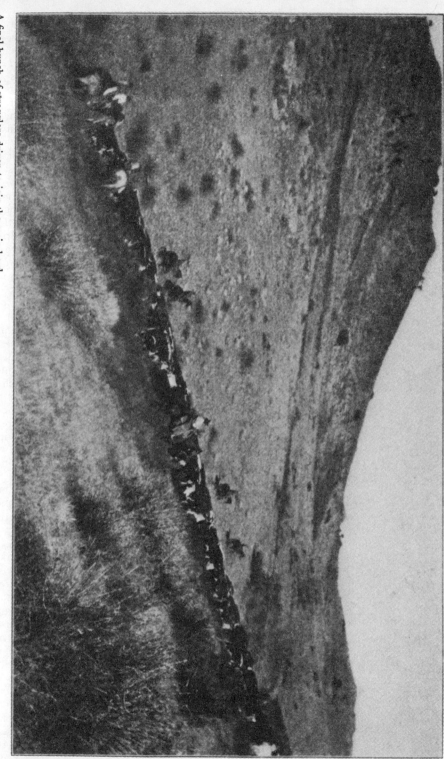

A final bunch of stragglers driven to join the main herd.

It takes untiring vigilance and a good pony to head off every independent-minded steer in the herd.

You can chase a cow just so far, and then it is as well to give up and turn back.

The cows with calves are cut out from the main herd and stand about lazily.

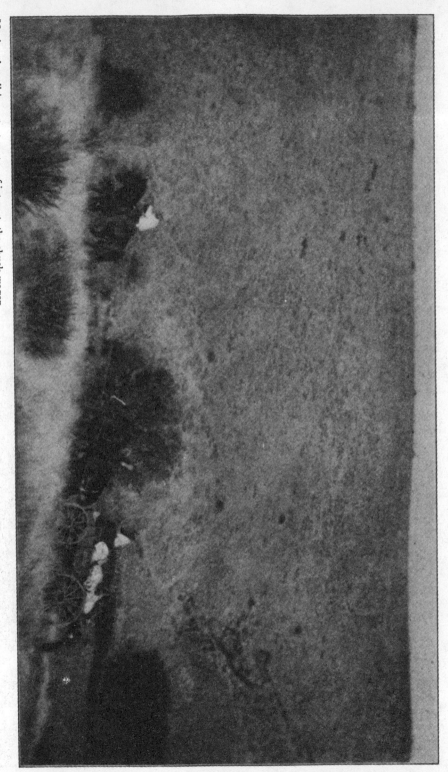

Moving that all-important center of interest, the chuck wagon.

whose side he was sure in this alarming multitude to be clinging faithfully.

Calves were numerous, and J H cows everywhere to be seen, so in somewhat less than ten seconds I had my eye on a mother and son. Immediately I turned Little G in their direction. At the slap of my quirt against the stirrup, all the cows immediately about me shrank suspiciously aside. Little G stepped forward daintily, his nostrils expanding, his ears working back and forth, trying to the best of his ability to understand which animals I had selected. The cow and her calf turned in toward the center of the herd. A touch of the reins guided the pony. At once he comprehended. From that time on he needed no further directions. Cautiously, patiently, with great skill, he forced the cow through the press toward the edge of the herd. It had to be done very quietly, at a foot pace, so as to alarm neither the objects of pursuit, nor those surrounding them. When the cow turned back, Little G somehow happened always in her way. Before she knew it she was at the outer edge of the herd. There she found herself, with a group of three or four companions, facing the open plain. Instinctively she sought shelter. I felt Little G's muscles tighten beneath me. The moment for action had come. Before the cow had a chance to dodge among her companions, the pony was upon her like a thunderbolt. She broke in alarm, trying desperately to avoid the rush. There ensued an exciting contest of dodgings, turnings, and doublings. Wherever she turned Little G was before her. Some of his evolutions were marvelous. All I had to do was to sit my saddle, and apply just that final touch of judgment denied even the wisest of the lower animals. Time and again the turn was so quick that my stirrup swept the ground. At last the cow, convinced of the uselessness of further effort to return, broke away on a long lumbering run to the open plain. She was stopped and held by the men detailed, and so formed the nucleus of the new cut-herd. Immediately Little G, his ears working in conscious virtue, jogtrotted back into the herd, ready for another.

After a dozen cows had been sent across to the cut-herd, the work simplified. Once a cow caught sight of this new band, she generally made directly for it, head and tail up. After the first short struggle to force her from the herd, all I had to do was to start her in the proper direction and keep her at it until her decision was fixed. If she was too soon left to her own devices, however, she was likely to return. An old cowman knows to a second just the proper moment to abandon her.

Sometimes in spite of our best efforts a cow succeeded in circling us and plunging into the main herd. The temptation was then strong to plunge in also, and to drive her out by main force; but the temptation had to be resisted. A dash into the thick of it might break the whole band. At once, of his own accord, Little G dropped to his fast shuffling walk, and again we addressed ourselves to the task of pushing her gently to the edge.

This was all comparatively simple—almost any pony is fast enough for the calf cut—but now Homer gave orders for the steer cut to begin, and steers are rapid and resourceful and full of natural cussedness. Little G and I were relieved by Windy Bill, and betook ourselves to the outside of the herd.

Here we had leisure to observe the effects that up to this moment we had ourselves been producing. The herd, restless by reason of the horsemen threading it, shifted, gave ground, expanded and contracted, so that its shape and size were always changing in the constant area guarded by the sentinel cowboys. Dust arose from these movements, clouds of it, to eddy and swirl, thicken and dissipate in the currents of air. Now it concealed all but the nearest dimly outlined animals; again it parted in rifts through which mistily we discerned the riders moving in and out of the fog; again it lifted high and thin so that we saw in clarity the whole herd and the outriders and the mesas far away. As the afternoon waned, long shafts of sun slanted through this dust. It played on men and beasts magically, expanding them to the dimensions of strange genii appearing and effacing themselves in the billows of vapor from some enchanted bottle.

We on the outside found our sinecure of hot noontide filched from us by the cooler hours. The cattle, wearied of standing and perhaps somewhat hungry

At top speed the hungry band sweeps down upon the grinning cook and his steaming pots.

and thirsty, grew more and more impatient. We rode continually back and forth, turning the slow movement in on itself. Occasionally some particularly enterprising cow would conclude that one or another of the cut-herds would suit her better than this mill of turmoil. She would start confidently out, head and tail up, find herself chased back, get stubborn on the question, and lead her pursuer a long, hard run before she would return to her companions. Once in a while one would even have to be roped and dragged back. For know, before something happens to you, that you can chase a cow safely only until she gets hot and winded. Then she stands her ground and gets emphatically "on the peck."

I remember very well when, in South Dakota, I first discovered this. It was after I had had considerable cow work too. I thought of cows as I had always seen them—afraid of a horseman, easy to turn with the pony, and willing to be chased as far as necessary to the work. Nobody told me anything different. One day we were making a drive in an exceedingly broken country. I was bringing in a small bunch I had discovered in a pocket of the hills, but was excessively annoyed by one old cow that insisted on breaking back. In the wisdom of further experience, I now conclude that she probably had a calf in the brush. Finally she got away entirely. After starting the bunch well ahead, I went after her.

Well, the cow and I ran nearly side by side for as much as half a mile at top speed. She declined to be headed. Finally she fell down and was so entirely winded that she could not get up.

"Now, old girl, I've got you," said I, and set myself to urging her to her feet.

The pony acted somewhat astonished, and suspicious of the job. Therein he knew a lot more than I did. But I insisted, and like a good pony he obeyed. I yelled at the cow, and slapped my hat, and used my quirt. When she had quite recovered her wind, she got slowly to her feet, and charged me in a most determined manner.

Now a bull, or a steer, is not difficult to dodge. He lowers his head, shuts his eyes, and comes in on one straight rush. But a cow looks to see what she is doing; her eyes are open every minute, and it overjoys her to take a side hook at you even when you succeed in eluding her direct charge.

The pony I was riding did his best, but even then could not avoid a sharp prod that would have ripped him up had not my leather *bastos* intervened. Then we retired to a distance in order to plan further; but we did not succeed in inducing that cow to revise her ideas, so at last we left her. When, in some chagrin, I mentioned to the round-up captain the fact that I had skipped one animal, he merely laughed.

"Why, kid," said he "you can't do nothin' with a cow that gets on the prod that away 'thout you ropes her; and what could you do with her out there if you *did* rope her?"

So I learned one thing more about cows.

After the steer cut had been finished, the men representing the neighboring ranges looked through the herd for strays of their brands. These were thrown into the stray-herd, which had been brought up from the bottom lands to receive the new accessions. Work was pushed rapidly, as the afternoon was nearly gone.

In fact so absorbed were we that until it was almost upon us we did not notice a heavy thunder shower that arose in the region of the Dragoon Mountains, and swept rapidly across the zenith. Before we knew it the rain had begun. In ten seconds it had increased to a deluge; and in twenty we were all to leeward of the herd striving desperately to stop the drift of the cattle down wind.

We did everything in our power to stop them, but in vain. Slickers waved, quirts slapped against leather, six-shooters flashed but still the cattle, heads lowered, advanced with a slow and sullen persistence that would not be stemmed. If we held our ground, they divided around us. Step by step we were forced to give way—the thin line of nervously plunging horses sprayed before the dense mass of the cattle.

"No they won't stampede," shouted Charley to my question. "There's cows and calves in them. If they was just steers or grown critters, they might."

The sensations of those few moments were very vivid—the blinding beat of the storm in my face, the unbroken front of horned heads bearing down on me resistless as fate, the long slant of rain with the sun shining in the distance beyond it.

Abruptly the down-pour ceased. We shook our hats free of water, and drove the herd back to the cutting grounds again.

But now the surface of the ground was slippery, and the rapid maneuvering of horses had become a matter precarious in the extreme. Time and again the ponies fairly sat on their haunches and slid when negotiating a sudden stop; while quick turns meant the rapid scramblings that only a cow horse could accomplish. Nevertheless the work went forward unchecked. The men of the other outfits cut their cattle into the stray-herd. The latter was by now of considerable size, for this was the third week of the round-up.

Finally every one expressed himself as satisfied. The largely diminished main herd was now started forward by means of shrill cowboy cries and beating of quirts. The cattle were only too eager to go. From my position on a little rise above the stray herd, I could see the leaders breaking into a run, their heads thrown forward as they snuffed their freedom. On the mesa side the sentinel riders quietly withdrew. From the rear and flank the horsemen closed in. The cattle poured out in a steady stream through the opening thus left toward the mesa. The fringe of cowboys followed, urging them on. Abruptly the cavalcade turned and came loping back. The cattle continued ahead on a trot, gradually spreading abroad over the landscape, losing their integrity as a herd. Some of the slower or hungrier dropped out and began to graze. Certain of the more wary disappeared to right or left.

Now, after the day's work was practically over, we had our first accident. The horse ridden by a young fellow from Dos Cabesas slipped, fell, and rolled quite over his rider. At once the animal lunged to his feet, only to be immediately seized by the nearest rider. But the Dos Cabesas man lay still, his arms and legs spread abroad, his head doubled sideways in a horribly suggestive manner. We hopped off. Two men straightened him out, while two more looked carefully over the indications on the ground.

"All right," sang out one of these, "the horn didn't catch him."

He pointed to the indentation left by the pommel. Indeed five minutes brought the man to his senses. He complained of a very twisted back. Homer sent one of the men in after the bed-wagon, by means of which the sufferer was shortly transported to camp. By the end of the week he was again in the saddle. How men escape from this common accident with injuries so slight has always puzzled me. The horse rolls completely over his rider, and yet it seems to be the rarest thing in the world for the latter to be either killed or permanently injured.

Now each man had the privilege of looking through the J H cuts to see if by chance strays of his own had been included in them. When all had expressed themselves as satisfied, the various bands were started to the corrals.

From a slight eminence where I had paused to enjoy the evening, I looked down on the scene. The three herds, separated by generous distances one from the other, crawled leisurely along; the riders, their hats thrust back, lolled in their saddles, shouting conversation to each other, relaxing after the day's work; through the clouds strong shafts of light belittled the living creatures, threw into proportion the vastness of the desert.

ROUND-UP DAYS

III—CORRAL BRANDING

BY STEWART EDWARD WHITE

PHOTOGRAPHS BY THE AUTHOR

T night we slept like sticks of wood. No dreams visited us, but in accordance with the immemorial habit of those who live out—whether in the woods, on the plains, among the mountains, or at sea— once during the night each of us arose on his elbow, looked about him, and dropped back to sleep. If there had been a fire to replenish, that would have been the moment to do so; if the wind had been changing and the seas rising, that would have been the time to cast an eye aloft for indications, to feel whether the anchor cable was holding; if the pack horses had straggled from the alpine meadows under the snow, this would have been the occasion for intent listening after the faintly tinkling bell so that next day one would know in which direction to look. But since there existed for us no responsibility, we each reported dutifully at the roll-call of habit, and dropped back into our blankets with a grateful sigh.

I remember the moon sailing a good gait among apparently stationary cloudlets; I recall a deep black shadow lying before distant silvery mountains; I glanced over the stark motionless canvasses, each of which concealed a man; the air trembled with the bellowing of cattle in the corrals.

Seemingly but a moment later the cook's howl brought me to consciousness again. A clear licking little fire danced in the blackness. Before it moved silhouettes of men already eating.

I piled out and joined the group. Homer was busy distributing his men for the day. Three were to care for the remuda; five were to move the stray-herd from the corrals to good feed; three branding crews were told to brand the calves we had collected in the cut of the afternoon before. That took up about half the men. The rest were to take a short drive in the salt grass. I joined the Cattleman, and together we made our way afoot to the branding pen.

We were the only ones who did go afoot, however, although the corrals were not more than two hundred yards distant. When we arrived, we found the string of ponies standing around outside. Between the upright bars of greasewood, we could see the cattle, and near the opposite side the men building a fire next the fence. We pushed open the wide gate and entered. The three ropers sat their horses, idly swinging the loops of their ropes back and forth. Three others brought wood and arranged it carefully in such a manner as to get the best draught for heating—a good branding fire is most decidedly a work of art. One stood waiting for them to finish, a sheaf of long J H stamping irons in his hand. All the rest squatted on their heels along the fence, smoking cigarettes, and chatting together. The first rays of the sun slanted across in one great sweep from the remote mountains.

In ten minutes Charley pronounced the irons ready. Homer, Wooden, and old California John rode in among the cattle. The rest of the men arose and stretched their legs and advanced. The Cattleman and I climbed to the top bar of the gate, where we roosted, he with his tally-book on his knee.

Each rider swung his rope above his head with one hand, keeping the broad loop open by a skillful turn of the wrist at the end of

"He was sliding majestically along on his belly."

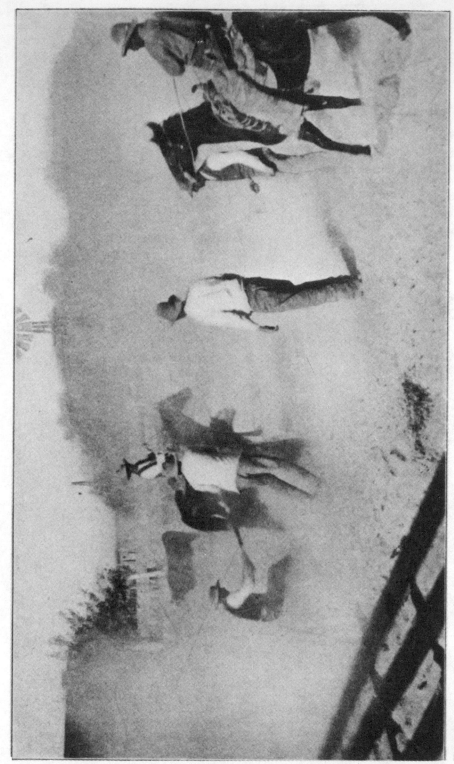

The tail-hold. "This is the production of some fun if it fails."

A branding in the mountains.

each revolution. In a moment Homer leaned forward and threw. As the loop settled, he jerked sharply upward, exactly as one would strike to hook a big fish. This tightened the loop and prevented it from slipping off. Immediately, and without waiting to ascertain the result of the maneuver, the horse turned and began methodically, without undue haste, to walk toward the branding fire. Homer wrapped the rope twice or thrice about the horn, and sat over in one stirrup to avoid the tightened line and to preserve the balance. Nobody paid any attention to the calf.

The latter had been caught by the two hind legs. As the rope tightened, he was suddenly upset, and before he could realize that something disagreeable was happening, he was sliding majestically along on his belly. Behind him followed his anxious mother, her head swinging from side to side.

Near the fire the horse stopped. The two "bull-doggers" immediately pounced upon the victim. It was promptly flopped over on its right side. One knelt on its head and twisted back its foreleg in a sort of hammer-lock; the other seized one hind foot, pressed his boot heel against the other hind leg close to the body, and sat down behind the animal. Thus the calf was unable to struggle. When once you have had the wind knocked out of you, or a rib or two broken, you cease to think this unnecessarily rough. Then one of the others threw off the rope. Homer rode away, coiling the rope as he went.

"Hot iron!" yelled a bull-dogger.

"Marker!" yelled the other.

Immediately two men ran forward. The brander pressed the iron smoothly against the flank. A smoke and the smell of scorching hair arose. Perhaps the calf blatted a little as the heat scorched. In a brief moment it was over. The brand showed cherry, which is the proper color to indicate due peeling and a successful mark.

In the meantime the marker was engaged in his work. First with a sharp knife he cut off slanting the upper quarter of one ear. Then he nicked out a swallow-tail in the other. The pieces he thrust into his pocket in order that at the completion of the work he could thus check the Cattleman's tally-board as to the number of calves branded. The bull-dogger let go.

The calf sprang up, was appropriated and smelled by his worried mother, and the two departed into the herd to talk it over.

It seems to me that a great deal of unnecessary twaddle is abroad as to the extreme cruelty of branding. Undoubtedly it is to some extent painful, and could some other method of ready identification be devised, it might be as well to adopt it in preference. But in the circumstance of a free range, thousands of cattle and hundreds of owners, any other method is out of the question. I remember a New England movement looking toward small brass tags to be hung from the ear. Inextinguishable laughter followed the spread of this doctrine through Arizona. Imagine a puncher examining politely the ear-tags of wild cattle on the open range or in a round-up!

But, as I have intimated, even the inevitable branding and ear-marking are not so painful as one might suppose. The scorching hardly penetrates below the outer tough skin—only enough to kill the roots of the hair—besides which it must be remembered that cattle are not as sensitive as the higher nervous organisms. A calf usually bellows when the iron bites, but as soon as released, he almost invariably goes to feeding or to looking idly about. Indeed, I have never seen one even take the trouble to lick his wounds, which is certainly not true in the case of the injuries they inflict on each other in fighting. Besides which it happens but once in a lifetime, and is over in ten seconds; a comfort denied of us who have our teeth filled.

In the meantime two other calves had been roped by the two other men. One of the little animals was but a few months old, so the rider did not bother with its hind legs, but tossed his loop over its neck. Naturally, when things tightened up, Mr. Calf entered his objections, which took the form of most vigorous bawlings, and the most comical bucking, pitching, cavorting and bounding in the air. Mr. Frost's bull calf alone in pictorial history shows the attitudes. And then, of course, there was the gorgeous contrast between all this frantic and uncomprehending excitement and the absolute matter-of-fact imperturbability of horse and rider. Once at the fire one of the men seized the tightened rope in one hand, reached well over the animal's back to get a slack of the loose hide next the belly,

Sometimes three or four calves were on the ground at once.

"Bull-dogging by the tail hold."

Corral branding—method of holding down a calf.

lifted strongly, and tripped. This is called "bull-dogging." As he knew his business, and as the calf was a small one, the little beast went over promptly, hit the ground with a whack, and was seized and held.

Such good luck did not always follow, however. An occasional and exceedingly husky bull yearling declined to be upset in any such manner. He would catch himself on one foot, scramble vigorously, and end by struggling back to the upright. Then ten to one he made a dash to get away. In such case he was generally snubbed up short enough at the end of the rope, but once or twice he succeeded in running around a group absorbed in branding. You can imagine what happened next. The rope, attached at one end to a conscientious and immovable horse and at the other to a reckless and vigorous little bull, swept its taut and destroying way about mid-knee high across that group. The brander and marker, who were standing, promptly sat down hard; the bull-doggers, who were sitting, immediately turned several most capable somersaults; the other calf arose and inextricably entangled his rope with that of his accomplice. Hot irons, hot language and dust filled the air.

Another method, and one requiring slightly more knack, is to grasp the animal's tail and throw it by a quick jerk across the pressure of the rope. This is productive of some fun if it fails.

By now the branding was in full swing. The three horses came and went phlegmatically. When the nooses fell, they turned and walked toward the fire as a matter of course. Rarely did the cast fail. Men ran to and fro busy and intent. Sometimes three or four calves were on the ground at once. Cries arose in a confusion. "Marker!" "Hot iron!" "Tally one!" Dust eddied and dissipated. Behind all were clear sunlight, and the organ roll of the cattle bellowing.

Toward the middle of the morning the bull-doggers began to get a little tired.

"No more necked calves," they announced, "catch 'em by the hind legs, or bull-dog 'em yourself."

And that went. Once in a while the rider, lazy, or careless, or bothered by the press of numbers, dragged up a victim caught by the neck. The bull-doggers flatly refused to have anything to do with it. An obvious way out would have been to flip off the loop and try again, but of course that would have amounted to a confession of wrong.

"You fellows drive me plumb weary," remarked the rider, slowly dismounting. "A little calf like that! What you all need is a nigger to cut up your food for you!"

Then he would spit on his hands and go at it alone. If luck attended his first effort, his sarcasm was profound.

"There's yore little calf," said he, "would you like to have me tote it to you, or do you reckon you could toddle this far with yore little old iron?"

But if the calf gave much trouble, then all work ceased while the unfortunate puncher wrestled it down.

Toward noon the work slacked. Unbranded calves were scarce. Sometimes the men rode here and there for a minute or so before their eyes fell on a pair of uncropped ears. Finally Homer rode over to the Cattleman and reported the branding finished. The latter counted the marks in his tally-book.

"One hundred and seventy-six," he announced.

The markers, squatted on their heels, told over the bits of ears they had saved. The total amounted to but an hundred and seventy-five. Everybody went to searching for the missing bit. It was not forthcoming. Finally Wooden discovered it in his hip pocket.

"Felt her thar all the time," said he, "thought it must be a chaw of tobacco."

This matter satisfactorily adjusted, the men all ran for their ponies. They had been doing a wrestler's heavy work all the morning, but did not seem to be tired.

Through the wide gates the cattle were urged out to the open plain. There they were held for over an hour while the cows wandered about looking for their lost progeny. A cow knows her calf by scent and sound, not by sight—the noise was deafening and the motion incessant.

Finally the last and most foolish cow found the last and most foolish calf. We turned the herd loose to hunt water and grass at its own pleasure, and went slowly back to chuck.

11

In the
Days
of the
Deadwood
Treasure Coach

W.H. Taylor

In the Days of the Deadwood Treasure Coach

A Chapter from the Personal Recollections of W. H. Taylor

Drawings by C. S. Price

NOTABLE event in the annals of the frontier was the robbery at Cold Springs of the Deadwood Treasure Coach, carrying bullion, gold dust, expressage and United States mail from the Black Hills mines in South Dakota to Cheyenne, Wyoming. The few statements appearing in print at different times have seemed, to a person knowing somewhat of the circumstances at first hand, to be either sensational or inaccurate, and generally both. Hence, it is essayed herein to put down such statements only as will properly line up with the facts.

The robbery took place on the twenty-sixth of September, 1878, the second season of the noted gold excitement, by which time there had been drawn to the region from both near and abroad a horde of outlaws that rivalled in numeri-

cal strength anything of the particular kind ever collected together in this country. Well organized and mounted, they seemed to have a roving commission to operate as a piratical land force, as it were, under letters of marque. Taken by and large, they met all requirements and represented the standard article of highway robber; human life counted with them no more than did the weight of a feather. There were particular gangs under leaders answering to the cognomens: Charley Price, Frank Toll, Doug Goodale, Big-Nosed George, Bill Bivens, McLaughlin, and McDonald—the latter was probably Frank James. Additional to these were the Wall and Blackburn gangs. This list implies no disparagement to others who were operating in such a manner as to be less well known.

Along the three hundred miles of stage line there were numerous scenes of violence, and it is said that over a hundred lives were lost on this trail in one season. The Sioux Indians were also in the field, more or less, and played their part with their usual skill; albeit there were placed to their credit numerous dastardly acts of which they were not guilty.

On the Cut-Off Trail that led to the mines through Custer City was what was known as Red Cañon. This was a fatal place to many an unfortunate gold-seeker. Any small party stood about an equal chance of being attacked in passing through there, and in many places along this cañon were raised mounds, with head-boards or without, that indicated the last resting places of ambitious mortals who there had met an untimely end. One fellow of a classical turn of mind had placed up at the entrance a sign on which he had written:

ABANDON HOPE
ALL YE WHO ENTER
HERE

On my way to the Hills in the early part of the season of '78 I met W. M.

W. H. TAYLOR, THE AUTHOR, ABOUT 1879.

Ward, of the company's employes, who invited me to take passage with him in a light rig in which he was about to embark for Deadwood. Between Fort Laramie and Jenny's Stockade he pointed out to me eleven places where stages had been robbed that season. In September, when reaching Fort Laramie again on my return trip, I met General Adams, a special agent of the Postal Department, and joined him and a posse of five or six men that he had collected with a view to preventing interference with the United States mails. Equipped with Government horses from the Fort we

started back in the direction of the Hills intending to make a camp near the Stockade on Beaver Creek, and reconnoitre the country around there. We traveled mostly at night to avoid observation, and when riding along Lance Creek, a little before sundown, we came to the scene of a hold-up that had taken place two nights before, when Boone May, who was in our outfit, had fired a heavy charge of buckshot into one of the robbers at close range. He stoutly asserted that he must have killed him, and there were signs there that bore out his statement, although some searching done the day before had not revealed much but an abandoned saddle with some leathers missing, but after passing on a little distance we looked back and could make out two or three vultures on dusky wings fanning their way in a direct line towards something with which we thought they might have already made themselves familiar. They were not going at random, as was evident in the following spring, when the skeleton of Frank Toll was found in a deep gulch, and partly covered with sagebrush, about a fourth of a mile from the trail.

After reaching Jenny's Stockade we scouted around there for several days, and at one camp in the mountains, vacated temporarily, we found several hams hanging in storage, and a pile of discarded horseshoes, showing they were putting themselves on an Indian footing, for obvious reasons. Things were very quiet for several days following our arrival, yet occasional vague rumors in the air indicated trouble. In about a week

General Adams took a trip over to Deadwood, and on the twenty-sixth, the coach not appearing about the usual time—six P. M.—we all got into saddle and on general principles started up the line. It was thought they might be in some slight difficulty only; a hold-up had not, with one or two exceptions, occurred in that direction at any time theretofore, the general policy being to operate in a more open country, away from the mountains, where fewer obstacles were in the way of escape. Five or six miles up we met a horseman coming at break-neck speed.

We here picked up an old hunter named Phillips, and reinforced by Davis also, pushed ahead again. From the Stockade to the Springs was about twenty miles up grade, so when we pulled up in proximity to the place, the unfortunate horses were punished to about their limit.

We stopped quite a distance short of the stable, *cached* our horses and guided by Phillips made a little circuit so as to approach the place from the rear. As we reached there, we were, in the darkness, at a loss to understand the situa-

A LIGHT LOAD.

He was from what was called the Milk Ranch, and urged us to hurry, as the coach had been held up just as it reached the stable at Cold Springs. We crowded on all steam at once and at the ranch met Scott Davis, who had been in charge of the guards and had made his escape after resistance had become a hopeless affair. He swore they were just as hard a lot as he ever met up with.

"They killed Campbell," said he, "at the first fire, and then I think all the rest as well, but we can probably get there before they open the safe."

tion properly. We could hear more or less banging and noise of some kind, and as any of our people could hardly be alive after all the shooting Davis had seen and heard, it only remained to suppose that the enemy were yet in possession of the place; hence we had to proceed with some caution. Then followed a night of uncertainty and cross purposes seldom equalled.

We took positions on all sides and then hailed the place repeatedly, calling our people by name, but got no response. Then Davis, Pache and myself came around to the stage road on the west side and were lying in a short cover about forty feet from the trail when we heard two horsemen coming up. Knowing that no friendly or sane person would ride boldly along from that direction, we thought it was some of their scouts sent out a little way to watch the approaches.

By that time the moon had arisen, and a break in the tree-tops that loomed up over in front of us, gave a clear view for thirty feet or more. As they approached this space we drew down on them, intending to put an end to their careers right then and there, but suddenly an impulse came over me to make *sure* who they were, and I said to Scott, "Let's halt them," but by that time he was getting impatient and at the same instant cut loose. Pache did likewise and *ahoom! ahoom!* went booming and rolling over across the cañon, giving things in the stillness of the night, a rattling shake-up. One horse, riderless, bolted and went straight ahead, and the other whirled on the back trail, got

GALE E. HILL, WHO WAS "ALL SHOT UP."

tangled in the bridle reins and was thrashing around in the cover all night.

Shortly we turned our attention again to the stable, but the possession of the veriest modicum of horse sense forbade our rushing the place, unless willing to be like Falstaff's soldiery, "mere food for powder." So we decided to shoot up the place, and did so, pouring in round after round. Even this produced nothing definite, and it was not until broad daylight that we could get anybody smoked out, or even obtain a tail hold of the situation proper. "Big Gene," the stage

driver, then showed himself, and very frankly allowed that standing off road agents was no part of his vocation; he was all broke up.

"Boys, we were too much rattled to say anything. We thought it was the gang come back to murder us and take the horses," said he. One of these latter, crazy with hunger, had got into some predicament and helped in the noises we had heard during the night, and the luck that attends all fools and crazy men had stood the two mounted *hombres* in good stead, for the boys had missed them only by the margin of a hair, and they were not the right parties at all.

Just here it is well to hark back a little and explain the movements of the road agents up to this point. As a matter of fact, learned from captured parties later on, the whole outfit had for some time previously included at least ten men, and the arrangements were made to rob the coach at a point a mile or two further down the line to the west, where some big rocks were located right close to the road.

Several of the gang were in ambush there as already agreed upon, and wondering what had become of their leader and something like half their band. They told that when we passed there on the way up they could have nearly touched us with their guns, and regretted not having taken us in, as it was evident that in some way their plans had miscarried; the reason being that on the evening previous, these several worthies, to include at least Spear, Bill Mansfield, McBride, Charley Carey and

THE SHERIFF'S POSSE.

Goodale, happened together a little off by themselves, and in giving directions the leader said: "We will blaze away and do them all up the first thing, then we will have no bother and can open the safe and get away lively." One then suggested that if that was to be the method they could easily operate alone and thus take all the plunder, and this was the plan they carried out. Coming to the stable a little before the coach was due, they captured Miner, the stock tender, and also Zimmers, one of the guards, who happened there in some way. These they bucked and gagged and placed in the granary, out of the way; then they punched out the adobe from the spaces between the logs, to give loopholes for their guns.

General Adams, who was already booked at the Deadwood office to come back on the coach that morning, appeared at the last moment and stated that something had turned up to delay him another day or so. Right there his guiding star was in the ascendant, for every outlaw in the district had been aware of his activity in trying to carry out plans for their capture, and it was particularly intended to make sure of him when they loosed off the first volley fired in the attack; but another was killed in. his stead. Campbell, an operator in the stage company's employ, had been waiting a chance to get down the line to one of the stations and was then told to get aboard. He was a tall, fine-looking man, and of course a non-combatant in the company's affairs; but his days were already numbered.

The treasure coach left with Scott

SCOTT W. DAVIS.
Captain of the Treasure Coach, Deadwood to Cheyenne, Wyoming.

Davis, Gale Hill and Capt. (?) Smith as guards, and Campbell, as aforesaid. They reached the stable at Cold Springs at about three P. M., and as there was a slight declivity in front, the driver remained on the box, while Hill, who was also on the outside, got down to block the wheel. He was bent over in the act of doing so, with his Winchester retained in one hand, when there was the roar of a volley from all the robbers' guns, and at a frightfully close range. Probably the coach was no more than twenty feet from the stable door. Campbell was mortally struck and Hill got one ball through the wrist and another entirely through his body, entering rather close to the backbone, piercing his left lung and tearing a big hole out through his breast.

This supposedly would have killed any man, afloat or ashore, yet it did nothing of the kind to Hill, for he instantly whirled and brought up his rifle. The first thing that he could realize was that Carey, who had stepped out of the stable door to see clear of the smoke, had a gun almost in his face, so close in fact, as he told me later, he could feel the hot air on the side of his neck as it came from the gun barrel. Simultaneously they blazed away, and both missed. Carey then fell back into the stable, and Hill made a dash for the corner of the building, then on along the side to the rear, crossed the end and then looked back up the side opposite to that he had just traversed. A rattling fusillade was still going on and he saw a man up in front who was down on one knee and pumping a Winchester for all he was worth. I am stating this just as he told it to me. He was beginning to feel a little weak then, and so thought he would take no chances, but laid his gun over the cross logs of the stable for a rest, and deliberately cut loose. The man seemed paralyzed to feel and hear any shot from the rear and he incontinently dropped his weapon and took a header through the square hole out of which refuse was cast. Hill said he noticed his resemblance to a frog and had to smile, badly as he felt. This was McBride, at whom he had taken a pot shot, striking him in the groin and putting him among the sick and disabled to the effect that he was a big burden to them in their flight. Hill was then hardly able to stand, so he

time that he took shelter behind a tree on the bank of the cañon about forty yards away. He fired for a while at any loose fish he could distinguish through the smoke, but as he was the only one then making any resistance and they were all having a go at him, he dropped over the bank and made his way down the mountain to the ranch, as stated. This left the enemy a clear swing, and they started in to see what booty they had taken. Campbell had fallen with nine ball holes in his body, and in his death struggles kept calling for water; the driver was anxious to get this for him, but Carey said, "Stay where you are. He dont need anything." The bold

Dooley, Photographer.

THE OLD DEADWOOD TREASURE COACH WHICH, AFTER MANY ADVENTURES WITH "BAD MEN," CROSSED THE ATLANTIC AND WAS "RIDDEN IN BY FOUR KINGS."

sat down with his back against the building, but it occurred to him that they might easily slip up and take a shot at him there, and so he started for a large tree some fifty yards away, and this was the last he remembered.

In reality Hill became insane and deliberately walked back among the robbers. They saw that he was unarmed and talking at random and so paid no further attention to him. They said he was actually "babbling of green fields" and things he had seen when a boy.

When the row opened, Scott Davis jumped out of the coach on the opposite side, to get a chance to swing his gun, but the firing became so hot in a short

Captain (?) they found dormant in the bottom of the coach, and although he had a sawed-off shotgun in his grasp, it did not appear that he had cut any figure in the scrimmage. They tied him up and placed him back in the coach, told Gene to drive on, and taking the outfit back into the cover, a little off the trail, went at the safe hammer and tongs. It was a chilled steel affair, sent out from Cincinnati to the company, under guarantee to resist all burglars operating *al fresco*. They, however, had stolen a big striking hammer out of some mine, and with this implement knocked the thing into smithereens in less than twenty minutes. They were also otherwise prepared with a coil of fuse and about ten pounds of giant powder. They made a haul of twenty-six thousand dollars in gold bullion, and from Adams' Express and Registered United States mail, some three thousand dollars more. The Adams Company offered a reward of $5,000 for the capture of the robbers.

Fixing up McBride as well as they could, they struck out south and east, in the general direction of the Missouri River. Bill Mansfield, who was wounded in the fight, died that night and they buried him about five miles down the creek from the station. Once they were well out of the way, the survivors took stock of themselves and found they were in a sorry plight. Miner and Zimmers, on being released, started to Deadwood to raise an alarm. The others dragged the body of Campbell inside, made a rough kind of resting place for Hill, piled up sacks around the room for a sort of breastworks, and exhausted and terrified, crouched down to spend the night.

When, as stated, we approached in the morning, the place resembled shambles more than otherwise. In the dust in front, not far from where the coach stopped, there was a space three or four feet across, completely saturated with blood where Campbell had been struggling and calling, though vainly, for a mouthful of water. There were actually crimson trails leading about the place in all directions. Hill appeared so near death that nothing much could be done for him, yet we broke open Miner's cabin, took him in there, and piling up all the robes and blankets available for a bed, did what we could for his comfort.

At every expiration the air could be heard coming out of his back as well as the wound in his breast. That a man shot in such a frightful manner could be kept alive was, at that time, a revelation to me, yet it was a matter of ten years thereafter before the Grim Ferryman actually got him as a passenger aboard his craft, and I believe it was conceded that no braver man had preceded him. Doubtless great credit was due to Doctor L. V. Babcock, who came from Deadwood to his aid; and I know it was even said that but two or three cases were then known of recovery under just the same conditions. The notorious Frank Howard, however, who was a member of the posse of which I had charge in the January following, was shot in a very similar manner as we were returning from the Big Horn country, yet he lived to put in more than fifteen years to the good (or bad) before being eventually and properly hanged, at a point somewhere in Idaho. That is another story, though, but the arrival of the old time Sheriff of Deadwood, Seth Bullock,

COLONEL LUKE VOORHEES, OF CHEYENNE, WYOMING.

Manager of the Cheyenne-Deadwood Stage Line.

and his taking up the trail of the successful robbers while our own outfit hit off that of the less important half-dozen or so who were fleeing the country on general principles, might be referred to here.

By nightfall a number of horsemen, including the doctor, Sheriff's posse, and others had come up over the trail from Deadwood, and as they went about with lanterns examining the dead man and looking over the situation, the scene appeared rather weird. One suspicious character had been taken in custody off-hand, and a grim discussion was going on as to the propriety of making every-- thing tight and sure by hanging him. We had spent a good part of the day in difficult efforts to trace the robbers, for they had separated like a band of quail. Two days in saddle and one strenuous night without sleep brought us to a point where nature rebelled, and we rolled into our blankets vaguely wondering whose arguments would prevail, but too much exhausted to take active interest in the proceedings.

In the morning we started to return for a pack animal and a week's rations from the stockade. A mile or so short of there was the cabin of the notorious "Mother Ogden," who was well under- stood to be keeping a rendezvous for road agents and such of that ilk as had scruples against appearing anywhere in person for their supplies. In appearance she was simply tall, masculine and fierce, yet in the face of these disqualifications her blandishments had cast a spell over one Boris, whom from the first we had wanted to arrest. There was a thick cover along the stream conveniently near, and from prudential motives, Boris had been "lying out" since our advent in the neighborhood.

As we came along about noon, we no- ticed a dense smoke going out the chimney of Mother Ogden's abode, and rightly conjecturing that our man might chance to be there, awaiting luncheon, came up on the blind side of the cabin and around to the door in time to see him make a frantic grab for a rifle he had standing against the wall; in an in- stant, though, he saw that two guns were drawn on him, and assumed the most unconcerned air in the world. That this gaunt female just aforesaid kept a fence for thieves and industrious chevaliers, was about as certain as any- thing need be, yet at first glance the place seemed bare and destitute of any- thing like plunder. She, however, had an immense bed, standing well up on its legs, and draped around with a suitable curtain. Our official zeal prompted in- spection of this concern, in spite of a verbal protest that was forcible, but not worded in fine phrases. It proved a combined magazine and arsenal that car-

ried a surprising stock; between the mat- tresses, and in the hold, it was just bulg- ing with hams, flour, saddles, ammuni- tion, whole bolts of cloth, silk and what not. Of course it was no particular busi- ness of ours to declare the stuff contra- band, so we went on into camp. General Adams also reached there directly, and that evening we all collected in the stage stable to hold a kind of drum-head court martial on Boris.

I remember the old General getting out his note book and pencil with quite an air of authority, but he had reckoned without the defendant; that worthy was the most reticent man possible; he simply knew nothing detrimental to the accused. After a while Boone May reached down from the bunk he was sitting on and picked up a lariat, which he threw across to the General, saying:

"What's the use of fooling with him? He's the biggest liar in the world."

At the time I thought this was simply a ruse, but really there were plans for serious harm to him, offered in deadly earnest. The effect of the move was that he speedily changed his mind, and stated that he had been in three hold-ups that season, but was then in bad repute with the gang through having squan- dered the money for a band of stolen horses entrusted to him for sale. Their plans were, he said, to go from the Hills to Medicine Bow, Wyoming, to rob the store of Trabing Brothers, a branch of which concern, located on the Crazy Woman's fork of Powder River, had already been looted earlier in the season.

The next morning it was in order to resume search for the trail. Also it dawned on us that in the person of Boris we had a doggone questionable asset—a white elephant, not to be let go, nor held on to, very easily. We finally made shift to requisition an extra horse on which we placed him, and underneath the belly of which we lashed him firmly by the heels, and then set out; at night we slept with him handcuffed to one of us.

Finding marks of the fugitives was hard work, but at last we saw where they had come out into the open, nearly as far north as the Inyan Kara, and thence had taken a line westward. Of course we were not aware of being in pursuit of the inferior wing of the combination until later. We made rather slow progress, but managed to hold the trail until one night when there came up a terrific rain storm that obliterated every hoof-mark, or possible trace of them. We then set a compass course for Fort Fetterman, this country being at the time an unbroken wilderness; roads or any kind of traveled trails there were none. At the Fort we disbanded for the time, to resume operations later on.

The posse brought over by the Sheriff from Deadwood was naturally composed of the best material available, and included Stocking, a noted trailer and gunman, afterward captain of the Stipendary Fighters employed at the Iron Mine in Leadville. They, however, found their work cut out for them, although by a lucky fluke they got wind of the right parties almost from the first. The latter, for one thing, had quite a start, and were familiar with every twist and turn in the mountains, besides they were going for their lives.

The morning after the robbery I found, under the tree where McBride had been lying when they tried to care for him, a black leather cartridge belt saturated with blood. We were wondering how they could make headway with such a handicap as a badly wounded man must be, but Pache, who used to know Carey, declared that he in particular would never bother very much with him, but would kill him to get him safely out of the way. Now, quite to the contrary of this, we learned later, it was Goodale, the son of respectable parents and all that, that proposed this very thing, while Carey declared that as long as the trip lasted, if alive himself, he would stick by McBride, and he did. When they were passing near some fellow's ranch he, by some hook or crook, laid hold of a light wagon, and by gearing up a broncho to it, hauled the wounded man over fifty miles.

Sheriff Bullock at last crowded them so close that one night their camp-fire was seen off to one side of the trail and they were heard talking. In the night time it is mighty hard to break through a cover in such a case in a way to surprise anybody, so when they closed in on the place everyone had fled—"to the devil with the hindmost." They were flushed so suddenly that they lost quite a lot of stuff. One sack that they had partly buried contained about a fourth of the plunder. Pursuit was given up after a while and for a time they went clear.

Spear, of this gang, next attracted attention over at Plum Creek, Nebraska, by spending money too freely to square with his general make-up, and when arrested much of his holding was recovered also. I believe that his confession gave the clew to Goodale, and detectives were sent to Atlantic City, Iowa, where he was found posing as a rich prospector returned from the mines. His people were living over a bank and he had placed a hatful of so of the loot, gold watches, jewelry, nuggets, etc., in the safe. It was late in the day when he was arrested. McBride was seen on the street and in sight at the same time, and pursued, but he reached cover in one of those immense cornfields they have there, and as night came on directly, he was lost.

Much satisfaction was expressed at the capture of Goodale, and the stage company sent on an employe deputized expressly to bring him and his plunder back to their headquarters in Wyoming, but when the train arrived in Cheyenne he was not aboard. Very naturally different views of the matter were held at the time. It was claimed that as they were coming up somewhere a little west of Grand Island, in the night, he had bolted headlong through a lavatory window, with the train running at full speed, and although handcuffed and shackled, made his escape. The remarks and comments made on the subject by Voorhees, Hill and some of those most interested were edifying, but difficult to sort out for printing. They were not poetry by any means, and were too lurid even for blank verse. But there was no Goodale, and as far as I know, none of the lot, outside of Spear, was ever again heard of.

Colonel Luke Voorhees, of Cheyenne, is the only one living of the old frontier stage company of Gilmer, Saulsbury and Patrick. The iron horse is now steaming over much of their former territory, and their occupation gone, but they were an important feature in their day.

The old Treasure Coach itself was built in Concord, New Hampshire, and was eventually presented by Colonel Voorhees, superintendent of the line, to Buffalo Bill, and for the last twenty years or more has been shown at his "Wild West" exhibitions. According to Cody's assertion it is the only vehicle that, as it were, ever deliberately crossed the Atlantic Ocean to be ridden in by four kings.

12

Timber Titans

George Dollar

Timber Titans.

By George Dollar.

A GERMAN ship named *Maria Hackfeld* was lately dispatched from San Francisco to London with a cross-section of a California redwood tree, consigned, it is said, to Mr. William Waldorf Astor. The shipment is reported to be the result of a bet recently made by Mr. Astor, who, at a dinner party, told his English friends some astonishing stories about the size of the redwoods. Mr. Astor wagered that he could procure a cross-section of a redwood large enough to form a table for forty guests. This wager will undoubtedly be won with ease. The cross-section is 2ft. in thickness, showing the greater diameter of the tree to be 16ft. 6in., and the smaller diameter 14ft. 11in. The circumference is, therefore, about 52ft., which ought to accommodate forty average men without difficulty.

Odd to say, also, this section, notwithstanding its great size, is but a tiny thing, after all. Many redwoods in California measure 60ft. in circumference, and some have measured 75ft. These, again, are outstripped in size by the so-called "big trees" of the Calaveras and Mariposa groves, the like of which are seen in no other part of the world. Many English people know them only through whisky and wine advertisements. The irrepressible advertising agent has, in fact, seized upon the very tree shown on this page, in order that public attention may be strongly drawn to the merits of the juicy Californian grape. Others know of them through frequent visits to the Crystal Palace, where the bark of the grand old "Mother of the Forest," which measured 90ft. in girth and 321ft. in height, has been exhibited for years.

Botanically speaking, both the redwoods and the "big trees" are species of the genus Sequoia—a pretty name given to them in honour of Sequoyah, the Cherokee Indian who invented letters for his people. They are both natives of California, the redwoods being confined to the coast ranges and the "big trees" to the western slopes of the Sierra Nevada Mountains. They are distinguished by their peculiar fibrous bark and their rich colour of cinnamon brown. The redwood grows in such large quantities that it is a fit material for commerce, and the redwood industry of Humboldt County, California, where the trees abound, is enormous. The "big trees," on the other hand, are carefully guarded by the Government. The Mariposa Grove, which contains over seven hundred majestic trees, has been set apart by Congress as a national park, and the Government commissioners are able to resist the encroachments of everything except forest fires, which, at times, have sadly decimated and destroyed the trees.

Many of the trees are known throughout the world by characteristic names given to them in honour of popular heroes and favourites of the hour. A section of one of the fallen kings of the Mariposa

A BIG TREE OF CALIFORNIA.
Photo. from the Pacific Illustrating Bureau, San Fran., Cal.

The "big trees" were discovered in 1852 by a white hunter named Dowd, who in that year found himself in the neighbourhood of Calaveras Grove. The date 1850 is carved on one of the trees, and this has led many people to think that the big trees had been visited previously to 1852. Since that time, the trees have been one of the remarkable natural "sights" of the United States. Botanists have quarrelled over the proper name to give them, and have estimated their age from the rings in the fallen logs. Cross-sections have been cut and forwarded to different parts of the country, in order that people might see for themselves that the stories of the "big trees" were true. In Boston, several years ago, one of these cross-sections was erected in a public square, and dances were held on its polished surface. The idea of using a tree for such a purpose

"CHIP OF THE OLD BLOCK," IN MARIPOSA GROVE, CALIFORNIA.
From a Photo. by Underwood & Underwood, London.

group is called "Chip of the Old Block," and our illustration gives but a faint idea of what the "old block" must have been in the day of its towering grandeur. Another tree, shown on the following page, has been called "Uncle Tom's Cabin," on account of the tent-like opening at its base—an opening in which the stalwart figure of a man is dwarfed. The most famous tree is called "Grizzly Giant," which is over 93ft. in circumference at the ground, and over 64ft. at a distance of 11ft. from the base. It reaches a height of 200ft. before throwing out a branch, and its first branch is 8ft. in diameter. "Grizzly Giant" is the largest living tree in the world, and stands over 275ft. high. These figures can, however, but barely suggest the mammoth girth of this celebrated sequoia, which people travel from all parts of the world to see. Nor can the visitor realize that it and its neighbours have been standing for 2,500 years. Yet such is the estimated age of these forest giants. They were but bushes when Nero fiddled before burning Rome.

originated in California, where a stump of one of the trees has had a house built upon it, to serve as a ball-room.

A glance at our illustration of the primeval redwood forest in Humboldt County, California, the first of several redwood photographs lent to us by the Humboldt Chamber of Commerce, will give an idea of the massive trunks of these valuable trees, which stretch out for 100 miles along the coast, "not in sentinel groves," according to a poetical writer, "but in

"UNCLE TOM'S CABIN."
From a Photo. by Underwood & Underwood, London.

one continuous belt — dense, stately, dark, and forbidding." The forests are apparently imperishable, except through the axe of the woodsman, and this is wielded with care. The trees are never injured by fire. The wood resists combustion, and is hard to burn even when dry. The redwood is the only lumber that can take the place of the white pine, answer as a satisfactory substitute for mahogany and black walnut, displace oak for redwood ties, cypress and cedar for shingles, and surpass

From a]   PRIMEVAL REDWOOD FOREST IN HUMBOLDT COUNTY, CALIFORNIA.   *[Photograph.*

From a Photo. by]   CUTTING DOWN THE REDWOOD.   *[A. W. Ericson, Arcata, Cal.*

to perish or even to die, but send forth shoots and sprouts which, if left undisturbed, would renew the forests in course of centuries.

With such superb natural resources at hand, it is not strange that the redwood forests should resound with the cry of the lumberman and the crash of the falling tree. With these may be heard the grating of the saw as it cuts its swath through the heart of the tree, the

all other woods for durability when in contact with earth, or when exposed to moisture. These qualities make the redwood industry important to the builders of cities and homes, of railroads, flumes, and conduits, to those engaged in mining, manufacture, and agriculture all over the country. It is important to the consumers, and they should feel as gratified as do the people of Humboldt, that there is still a reserve forest containing 50,000,000,000ft. of timber, which can be utilized for so many purposes. Redwood will make an enduring foundation, solid walls, and an imperishable roof. Thus it provides the substantial equipment for any structure. But it may be made to embellish and adorn the home, as well as shelter the inmates. As a finishing wood it is unequalled, and for cabinet material some qualities of it are superior. Even the stumps, it is said, refuse

LOGGING WITH OXEN IN THE MOUNTAINS.
Photo. from the Pacific Illustrating Bureau, San Fran., Cal.

LOADING REDWOOD LOGS ON A CAR.
From a Photo. by A. W. Ericson, Arcata, Cal.

try, mostly rugged, also introduces a distinct element into logging operations. Ingenuity combined with capital has intervened, and almost every extensive redwood mill-plant in Humboldt includes several miles of railroad, with locomotives, cars, and other equipments for transporting logs and lumber, numerous donkey-engines for hauling logs out into the road, several miles of electric wire with instruments to supply telephone service to the remotest camps and connect them with the mill and yard, and, in many cases, a system of wire cable on the endless chain principle, with stationary engine to "snake" the logs to the railway landing. Oxen are still used in some camps, and it is an interesting sight to watch a long string of tugging oxen toiling down through the hills amid a cloud of dust, the logs after them like a gigantic snake.

steady click of the axe, the buzzing of fifty saw-mills in the neighbourhood, and the puff of powerful locomotives engaged in pulling the heavy logs out of the woods. It is a scene of eternal hurry in the very heart of Nature.

In order to cut down the trees, the choppers stand on platforms raised around the tree at some little distance from the base. The steady movement of the axe makes a quick impression on the massive timber, but it sometimes takes two weeks for two men to start the tree on its crashing fall to the ground. Most of the unskilled labourers of the county are employed in felling, although even this class of work requires a special amount of skill.

The great bulk and weight of redwood logs, and the fact that operations in the logging regions are in progress only during summer months and the absence of snow, make lumbering in Humboldt differ from the methods used elsewhere. The character of the coun-

A redwood is ready for the donkey-engine as soon as it has been sawed into sections. Chains and ropes are then attached to the log, and it is drawn through the forest towards the platform-cars or trolleys, upon which it is deposited. In the illustration at the top of this page we may see one of these mammoth sections in position on the car. When all the cars are loaded in this manner, they are made up into a train and attached to a powerful locomotive.

A not uncommon sight in the redwood region, but one which, to strangers, would appear remarkable, is illustrated at the bottom of this page, where we get a full view of a

From a Photo. by]   TRAIN-LOAD OF TWENTY-FOUR REDWOOD LOGS.   *[A. W. Ericson, Arcata, Cal.*

Photo. from]   A LOGGING CHUTE.   [*The Pacific Illustrating Bureau, San Fran., Cal.*

train-load of twenty-four redwood logs winding slowly from among the hills.

By many lumbermen in California the rivers are used with great effect in the transport of logs. In the summer the logs are dumped into the bed of the stream to await a winter freshet, which carries the mass along with great speed to the mills, where they lie until they are ready to be sawed.

The greater part of the logs, however, are transported by the railways direct to the side of the river or pond, and there shot into the water by means of inclined ways made of other logs. The logs dash down with great swiftness, and enter the water with a huge splash, casting the spray high into the air with the force almost of a torpedo explosion. The illustrations on this page show a log-chute and the magnificent column of water sent up by the diving log.

From the log-

pond to the saw-mill is usually but a step. In some mills the logs are pulled up on small cars; in others, they are drawn up on greased ways by means of long cables. In the forest of the Bridal Veil Lumbering Company, at Bridal Veil, in Oregon, the logs are transferred to the mill by means of a curious railway, illustrated on the following page. The train, so-called, is made up of an ordinary locomotive and a string of logs, each one as large in diameter

DIVING LOG
Photo. from The Pacific Illustrating Bureau, San Fran., Cal.

A RAILROAD WITHOUT CARS.
By courtesy of " Cassier's Magazine."   From a Photo. by Browning, Portland, Oregon.

and some even larger than the boiler of the engine. Boards are nailed to the sleepers between the rails, and on these the logs slide. Except on descending grades, the boards are greased, and the train moves at good speed. Where the road is level or slightly ascending the engine pulls the logs, and where it is descending it holds them back. At the mills of the company the manufactured lumber, regardless of size, is run into a flume, and this is carried about two miles to the planing-mill and shipping yard, the flume descending about 1,200ft. in that distance.

One of the great items of expense in the lumber business is the cost of transportation from the forests to the consumer. Huge sums which might otherwise have been left in the pockets of householders have been placed in the coffers of railway and steamship companies. It was in order to lessen the cost of transport that the cigar-shaped log-raft was designed. These extraordinary rafts, of which we give five excellent illustrations, are the invention of Mr. Hugh R. Robertson, of St. John, New Brunswick. The first raft was built at Joggins, in Nova Scotia, and on account of its novelty quickly gained the nickname of the "Joggins raft." It was built in 1887, and its dimensions, of which a fair idea is given in the illustration below, were : length, 560ft. ; depth, 35ft. It took several months

CIGAR-SHAPED LOG-RAFT BUILT AT JOGGINS, NOVA SCOTIA, 1887.
From a Photo. by Mr. J. Fraser-Gregory, St. John, New Brunswick.

THE JOGGINS RAFT FROM BENEATH, SHOWING SUPPORTS.
From a Photo. by Mr. J. Fraser Gregory, St. John, New Brunswick.

to build, and was composed of several hundred thousand logs, closely bound together in a cradle of logs, which rested upon timber foundations. The raft was pointed at one end, and lay on the shore slant-wise in order that it might be quickly and easily launched. During the process of construction the inventor was much laughed at, but, nothing daunted in his scheme, he launched the raft and dispatched it to New York in tow. The first Joggins raft, however, quickly bore out the prophecies of Mr. Robertson's opponents, and came to grief in the wild and wintry Atlantic. The hawser which attached it to the tug was snapped by the force of the waves, the raft burst in pieces, and the huge logs, which represented many thousand pounds in gold, were rapidly distributed over the surface of the Atlantic, to the deep chagrin of the inventor, and the danger of mariners.

Notwithstanding this accident, the Joggins raft had really come to stay. A second raft

LAUNCHING THE JOGGINS RAFT.
From a Photo. by Mr. J. Fraser Gregory, St. John, New Brunswick.

CIGAR-SHAPED RAFT BUILT ON THE PACIFIC COAST.   LENGTH 528FT., CONTAINING 560,000 LINEAL FEET OF TIMBER.
Photo. from the Pacific Illustrating Bureau, San Fran., Cal.

was quickly built in co-operation with Mr. J. D. Leary, and sent to New York, a distance of 700 miles, in ten days, where the lumber of which it was made was sold at a profit enormous in itself, and yet at a price remarkable for cheapness. The much-derided inventor made a fortune, and, selling his idea to Mr. Leary, left for the Pacific Coast, where he is engaged to this day in transporting lumber by means of cigar-shaped rafts with wonderful success. Our last two illustrations show the side and top view of one of these rafts lately built on the Columbia River. Its value was £9,000, and its length 528ft., with the width of 52ft. and a draught of 24ft. The heavy chains, which are so plainly seen in the illustration, inclose 560,000 lineal feet of timber.

THE TOP OF A CIGAR-SHAPED RAFT.
Photo. from the Pacific Illustrating Bureau, San Fran., Cal.

13

The Old Régime
in the
Southwest

Albert E. Hyde

HALF-TONE PLATE ENGRAVED BY J. TINKEY.

PROSPECTING IN NEW MEXICO, IN THE EARLY EIGHTIES.

THE OLD RÉGIME IN THE SOUTHWEST.

THE REIGN OF THE REVOLVER IN NEW MEXICO.

BY ALBERT E. HYDE.

WITH PICTURES BY J. N. MARCHAND.

EARLY in my youth, in November, 1880, armed with letters of introduction to General Lew Wallace, then governor of the Territory of New Mexico, I left my home in Tennessee for Santa Fé.

From the governor I heard the story of the lawless condition of the Territory and the doings of that dreaded desperado "Billy the Kid." His recital of some of the incidents of this "bad" young man's career inspired the writer with a keen desire to see the beardless boy who killed inoffensive people "just to see 'em kick," and incidentally to secure their "valuables."

In a few weeks I moved to Las Vegas, making the Grand View Hotel in "Oldtown" my headquarters. "Newtown," near the railroad, was growing rapidly. Its streets were already marked with scattering adobe buildings, frame houses, and rough board shacks. Oldtown was an interesting study in sun-

baked mud, the dingy color of which was relieved here and there by a dab of white-wash. The streets were narrow and, like a very large percentage of the population, crooked. The Grand View Hotel, also adobe, was distinguished mainly by reason of its euphonious and suggestive name; at least, we had the view with regularity and precision three times a day. The amusements of the town were Mexican monte and cock-fighting among the Mexicans, and all kinds of gambling, enlivened by numerous "killings," among the whites.

In this day and time, when the faithful execution of the law is upheld by a majority of the people in every community, it would seem impossible that a moral code so lax as that which cursed New Mexico twenty-one years ago could exist in any section of the United States, however remote. The Territory was a rendezvous for reckless, wild, and lawless men, a refuge for fleeing criminals. Of course there were men, adventurous spirits, who were not fleeing from outraged justice, but they were, for the most part, rough specimens who were willing enough to leave the settlement of a dispute to the arbitrament of the six-shooter. In 1880 the percentage of peaceably inclined white population was deplorably small.

FRONTIER CONDITIONS IN 1880.

THE Santa Fé Railroad had just strung its line of shining steel across that desert of uncertain sands. Deming, a town of tents near the Texas line, was its terminal. Its single branch line was the eighteen miles of road-bed from Lamy Junction to Santa Fé. On each side of the main line, which divided the Territory from north to south, stretched miles and miles of uninhabited country. The fertile river valleys held a majority of the Mexican population, but the arid desert, the pine-covered slopes and mountains, were marked here and there by Mexican hamlets or Indian pueblos. A vast sea of shifting, treacherous sand constantly menaced the new road-bed of the Santa Fé. Time and again rods of track were displaced and covered up during the period of a sand-storm. Such incidents made railway travel on

schedule time, south of Santa Fé, as uncertain as the disposition of a Mescalero Apache Indian. The ranges in the Southwest grazed countless thousands of cattle, owned by him whose brand burned the hide and who had the nerve to hold. Wild horses roamed the foot-hills and plains; wild game inhabited the mountains and valleys; and the shifty coyote, unmolested by man, sat upon his haunches under the stars and sent his blood-curdling howl echoing among the hills.

Silver City, in the mountains near the Arizona line, and the San Juan district in southern Colorado, had been opened up, and the overflow of prospectors and miners began to penetrate the middle ground. Already Whiteoaks, a small mining town in Lincoln County, had sprung into existence. This little place was about the center of the largest operations of Billy the Kid. Men crossed this great inland country by bronco or stage. In those days he was a fearless man who would accept the ribbons on a New Mexico stage-coach.

The cattle-men in Lincoln County employed an army of cow-boys—"cow-punchers," they called themselves. They were as wild and reckless a set as ever tamed a bucking bronco or pulled the trigger of a Colt's 45. Witness the long, terrible conflict

HALF-TONE PLATE ENGRAVED BY PETER AITKEN.

AN INCIDENT OF THE "LINCOLN COUNTY WAR."

between the cattle-men and the thieves, known as the Lincoln County War, a struggle in which hundreds of lives were sacrificed.

A Colt's 45-caliber single-action revolver was circulating medium. It was good for its exact cost, about sixteen dollars, in any "game," or over the bar. It was a common thing to see a man who was "down on his luck" stake his last cent and then "cash in" his "gun." Cow-punchers, mule-drivers, tie-cutters, miners, ranchmen, gamblers, and all "bad men" generally, wore their revolvers openly on the hip. Those who rode added the deadly Winchester to their armament, carrying it in a leather holster fastened to the saddle under the rider's left leg.

Men knew one another by given name or "nickname," for the most part. It was dan-

HALF-TONE PLATE ENGRAVED BY C. W. CHADWICK.

A HOLD-UP.

gerous to be too curious about a man's antecedents. It was a rare thing to hear a man boast of his ancestry.

A BIT OF NECESSARY CAUTION.

I WAS charged to look up a man at one time prominent in an Eastern community, who had suddenly disappeared, and when last heard of was somewhere in New Mexico. Standing in a popular resort in Las Vegas, one night, conversing with the man behind the counter, it occurred to me to inquire about Hillyar, the man whom I sought. As the name was pronounced, a big fellow, standing a few feet away, turned square upon me and proceeded to bore me with a pair of remarkably keen brown eyes. Growing somewhat restless

under the steady gaze of so formidable a stranger, I felt much relief when, after a moment's hesitation, he motioned me aside. With his eyes still searching mine, he said, in a low voice: "I heerd ye inquirin' fur a man name' Hillyar. What 's yer business with him?"

The situation began to dawn upon me.

"Merely social," I replied, with a smile.

His look did not indicate that he was entirely convinced.

"I knowed a feller by that name wunst," he continued. "He wus a big feller an' wore a heavy brown beard. Is he wanted fur anything?"

"No," I replied; "that is, the law is not looking for him, if that 's what you mean, but some friends are anxious to know where he is. If you can give me the information, I will appreciate the favor."

With another penetrating look, he said: "I ain't right shore, but I think he 's gone up in the San Juan country; heerd him talkin' about goin'."

I was satisfied by this time that he knew where my man was and could easily reach him.

"What can I do to convince you that I am his friend and one whom he would be glad to see?"

He reflected a moment, and then said: "I 'm goin' back to Tie-camp No. 2 ter-mor-rer,—that 's thirty-odd miles from here,—and I 'll inquire. Ef you 'll put yer name down on a piece of paper, so 's ef I git on his trail he 'll know who wants him, I 'll do the best I kin fur ye. I 'll be back in Vegas this day week arter next. Meet me here."

At the time appointed I met him, and he accosted me thus: "Young feller, I 've found yer man, an' here 's a letter from him. I knowed whar he wus all the time, but thar 's so many fellers huntin' cover hyar I wanted

Tie-camp No. 2. I had last seen Hillyar about the year 1877. He was then thirty-six years of age and a splendid specimen of

HALF-TONE PLATE ENGRAVED BY F. H. WELLINGTON.

"'I CAIN'T SHOOT A BRAVE MAN DOWN LIKE A DOG.'"

to make dead shore it wus all right with Hillyar 'fore I said too much."

Later I learned that my messenger was himself one of those "fellers huntin' cover," having killed his man in the East.

AN ASTONISHING TRANSFORMATION.

HILLYAR urged me to visit him, and I left Las Vegas one bright winter morning for

vigorous manhood. He was a professional man and an elegant, polished, faultlessly dressed gentleman.

Inquiring at the saloon at the switch, a crude one-room building constructed of rough pine boards, I was told that Hillyar had come down from the tie-camp that morning, and that I would find him in the tie-yard.

Walking in the direction indicated, I saw my man, and knew him by his beard, sun-

HALF-TONE PLATE ENGRAVED BY M. HAIDER.

"THE MEN WERE ORDERED OFF THE CAR."

burnt and unkempt as it was, but, shade of Beau Brummell, what a change! The man, rapidly approaching with outstretched hand and a string of picturesque oaths of cordial welcome, wore a wide sombrero, a blue flannel shirt, a red bandana handkerchief tied loosely about the throat, brown overall trousers, tucked into heavy high top-boots and held in place at the waist by a cartridge-belt, from which dangled a Colt's 45 six-shooter. I could hardly credit my senses.

He introduced me formally to "Dad," the proprietor and bartender of the lone saloon. He kept up his rough talk and ready invective until we were safely in his tent. Then,

unbuckling his six-shooter, he grabbed both my hands and became at once the gentlemanly, grammatical Hillyar of old.

AN EXHIBITION OF NERVE.

AT the switch I met "Territory Bill," a white man, tall, angular, with small grayish-blue eyes, a pronounced hooked nose, and scattering sandy whiskers. Territory's business, when he was not engaged in a "killing" or playing cards, was stealing cross-ties. He had the habit of "snaking off" two tie-sticks from the cut and inspected timber of the W. & W. million-tie contract. While the occupation proved lucrative and pleasant enough to Territory, his attempt to earn an honest living in this way was looked upon with disfavor by the contractors. They therefore promptly "sicked the dog" on him.

One morning, after a particularly satisfactory haul, Territory was drinking at Dad's saloon, where I had been listening to accounts of "hair-breadth 'scapes." There was not a soul in the saloon but Dad, Territory, and myself.

Suddenly the sound of rapidly approaching hoofs was heard, a horseman drew up with a sharp clatter at the platform in front, and swinging from the saddle, came dashing through the door. He had a deadly Colt's 45 pushed well to the front, and I could catch the gleam of a pair of cold, determined eyes behind the barrel. This was the "dog," no doubt of it.

The moment he found himself inside and master of the situation, he advanced to within a few paces of Territory Bill, who was leaning carelessly with one elbow on the bar, one hand to his cheek, while the other toyed with his whisky-glass. Bill made no move, the hand upon the whisky-glass growing quiet. He knew he was "up against it." Death stared him in the face; there was no escape. Not a muscle moved. His eyes, glancing along the threatening revolver, gazed calmly, fearless and unconcerned, into the eyes behind. In quiet, even tones, which scarcely moved a facial muscle, he said: "You 've got the drop, Charley. It 's all right if you don't pull the trigger."

There were probably ten seconds of agonizing suspense. Dad and myself were speechless. To me, unused to such scenes, those terrible seconds seemed like minutes. Every moment I expected to see the brains of Territory scattered over the rough bar.

Yielding to the spell of Bill's wonderful nerve, Charley muttered, "By ——, I cain't shoot a brave man down like a dog"; then quickly retreating to the door, he threw the weapon into its holster, was on his horse instantly, and, with a vicious dig of his spurs, galloped away.

We three stood looking at one another in eloquent silence, first broken by Territory's remark, "Close call, Dad; give us a drink."

It was a victory for nerve.

A TYPICAL ENCOUNTER BETWEEN "TIE MEN" AND MEXICANS.

I ACCOMPANIED Hillyar to Tie-camp No. 2, situated in the mountains about twelve miles from the switch.

Here I not only heard a graphic description of the then recent fight at Cow Creek Hill, but saw the horribly mutilated bodies of the two white men who were killed.

An ancient little Mexican hamlet marks the crest of Cow Creek Hill. It lies on the tie wagon-road, about half-way between the switch and the camp. One evening, returning from the switch, the teamsters learned that a Mexican dance was soon to take place. A number of the drivers determined to go, and when the time arrived they procured an extra supply of whisky in honor of the event. The camp boss readily gave his consent, and about eight o'clock in the evening twelve white men rode over in one of the big "Studebakers." On the way they drank freely, and passed the time singing, shouting, and firing their big 45's.

Arriving on the scene, they hobbled the mules and sought admission to the dance. This was graciously granted, accompanied, however, with the polite request that they deposit their arms with the master of ceremonies until they were ready to return.

This they foolishly refused to do, and trouble followed. The Mexicans, while assuming to excuse this breach of etiquette, began quietly to arm themselves.

The house was the usual one-story adobe, originally planned in the form of a square, with the *patio*, or court, in the center. For some reason, three sides only had been completed, leaving the building U-shaped, with the opening facing the road. It was near this opening that the teamsters left their wagon.

Shortly before midnight the white men had monopolized all the available floor-space, crowding the Mexican men entirely out of the dance. The master of ceremonies mildly expostulated, but the teamsters were then too drunk to listen to reason or care for consequences, and one of them knocked the Mexican down. The lights instantly disappeared, the women were quickly and safely removed, no one knows how, and the Americans found themselves barred in a dark room, while a score or more of infuriated, well-armed Mexicans were on the outside, thirsting for their blood.

The seriousness of the situation soon began to dawn upon the whisky-addled brain of Doc Hodgson, the powerful and dangerous wagon boss, and it almost sobered him.

"Boys," he roared, "we must git outen here quick and fight it out in the open."

A long bench was converted into a bat-

HALF-TONE PLATE ENGRAVED BY C. W. CHADWICK.

THE DASH ACROSS THE PLAZA TO THE JAIL.

tering-ram, and a vigorous attack was made upon the door, which failed to yield, though it was much weakened. Hodgson, growing uncontrollably desperate, ordered the men to stand back. Rushing through the dark, he hurled his great bulk against the obstacle, and the shattered door flew from its hinges. Crowding out, the men faced a heavy fire directed upon them from the top, openings, and corners of the building.

"Come on, boys; we must git to cover!" yelled Hodgson, as he ran for the wagon, followed by his men. A terrible fusillade was kept up as fast as both sides could load and reload.

The last words his companions heard Hodgson utter were: "Boys, hain't got another cartridge left. We must run fer it. Scatter. Don't git in a bunch."

Abandoning the friendly shelter of the wagon, they separated and ran down the hill, every man for himself, the Mexicans in hot pursuit.

That morning, between two and four o'clock, the weary, smoke-begrimed stragglers began to arrive at the camp. By 5 A.M. nine men had reported; three were missing. No cross-tie teams left the camp that day. A council was held, and it was decided to put the men on the mules, ride down to the scene of battle, and search for the missing men. There were about thirty armed men in the party. When they arrived at the foot of the hill they saw almost a hundred well-armed Mexicans occupying the crest.

A pitched battle seemed imminent. During parleys and threatenings, however, continued till long past noon, small parties were searching the patches of mesquit on the sides of the hill for the missing men. They found the bodies of Hodgson and a teamster known as "Red," both shot, beaten with stones and sticks, and partly burned.

In the meantime it was learned that the third missing man was a prisoner held for trial before a Mexican alcalde in a neighboring town. This man owed his life to the fact that he could not run, having been lamed by a bullet early in the fight. He had crawled into the bed of the wagon, and when found, several hours later, he expected to be torn to pieces, so furiously did the young hot-bloods demand his instant execution; but the wild passions of the night had, in a measure, abated, and cooler counsel prevented his immediate slaughter.

The tie-camp party peremptorily demanded the instant release of the prisoner, but were met with shouts of derision. At this critical moment two contractors, who spoke Mexican patois like natives, arrived upon the scene. They arranged a compromise, and prevented another deadly conflict. The trial, which was a great farce, was set for that afternoon, and picked men from the camp were selected to attend and see that "justice" was done. The frightened alcalde released the man, who returned to the camp in triumph. It was impossible to ascertain how many Mexicans were killed in the fight. They never give out information of this kind. The Americans attributed their "good luck" to the notorious bad marksmanship of the "Greasers."

Each of the ten white survivors of the fight soon received a note, written in good Spanish, ordering him to leave the country without delay. Some of them heeded the warning, but the majority continued at their work. It was necessary for the latter to pass through the hamlet on Cow Creek Hill twice a day. They did not know at what moment they might be shot, but judging from their demeanor, they cared little if they could only get a chance at the enemy during the shooting.

Such was the condition of society in New Mexico during the reign of the Colt's 45 and in the days of Faro Charley, Stuttering Joe, and Billy the Kid.

There was no municipal or State system worthy the name for the apprehension and conviction of criminals. It would have taken a most powerful Law and Order League backed by incorruptible courts, or the more speedy punishment of "Judge Lynch," to have stemmed that current of reckless, riotous lawlessness and daredeviltry which overflowed the vast Southwestern "no-man's-land" twenty-one years ago.

In the cities of Las Vegas and Santa Fé the constabulary was only a weak pretense, and the machinery of the courts was rusty and unoiled. Under the eye of the police every form of gambling and every shade of vice went on day and night. Murders were committed in dance-halls and gambling-resorts without fear of arrest. The "song of the six-shooter" was heard in the land, but it seldom attracted official investigation.

When a crowd of cow-boys came to town to "blow in their money," pandemonium broke loose. The dance-halls blazed all night unless temporarily darkened by some hilarious marksman's unerring aim.

A SANTA FÉ DANCE-HALL

THE usual dance-hall was a low adobe building, possibly one hundred feet long, with the entire street front wide open. On the right of the entrance was located the bar. Along the left wall stood a row of gambling-tables with gaming devices from "rolling faro" and "high-ball poker" (two extremely popular games) to Mexican monte, a game in evidence in every resort in the Territory. The tables extended back from the entrance to the edge of the floor-space set apart for the dancers, and at the extreme end of the room was a crude vaudeville stage. What a travesty upon histrionic art was the miserable performance to be seen here! I heard a poor, painted, lost thing sing the "Holy City" in one of these dens, and while not a Christian young man, my soul sickened at the sacrilege and the pity of it.

These places were lighted brilliantly enough at night by rows of oil-lamps along the walls. At dark the music began, and a little later the dancing. Gambling never stopped. Mexican women, some of them very young, sat quietly waiting for an invitation to dance. There were a few American women, but the Mexicans predominated. One paid fifty cents for the privilege of dancing with a girl. The fee also entitled the couple to a drink at the bar at the conclusion of each dance, the woman being permitted to take a check, its equivalent, if she preferred. At midnight the crowd was largest and the revel reached flood-tide.

If no killing marred the evening, one might have looked upon a wonderful picture, which in all probability will be seen no more. The gambling-tables were crowded with "cappers" and whisky-heated players, whose operations were feverishly watched by a nondescript crowd of game-hungry humanity. Cow-boys, ranchmen, miners, teamsters, and soldiers lined the tables and staked their last dollar with a nonchalance worthy of a better cause. When a seat at the tables was vacated, it was instantly filled. Whisky was served free at the tables.

Beyond this intense scene was an animated picture. To the cracked music of a half-drunken Mexican band, gaily dressed girls were whirling in the figures of the Spanish quadrille. Their partners were men of all types representing untamed Western life. The prevailing style of dress was the wide hat, red silk neckerchief, blue flannel shirt, fringed leggings and moccasins, or plain overalls and high-heeled boots, with the inevitable cartridge-belt, revolver, and big spurs. A few of the men were dressed in corduroy or the regulation army blue. There were only two styles of hat worn

by the men, however otherwise dressed. They were the wide-brimmed, heavy, cone-shaped Mexican sombrero, and the large, soft, fine wool hat, either white (the favorite color) or black.

In the winter of 1880–81 there were many such resorts in Las Vegas and Santa Fé.

Once I saw one of these brilliant scenes vanish as quickly as if some one had cut off an electric wire. A dispute arose over a Mexican girl. The two contestants were trying to decide which merited the honor of the next dance. When the battle began, the roar of the revolvers was deafening, and in an incredibly short time all was darkness, except for the lightning flashes of the big 45's.

SHERIFF VERSUS DESPERADO.

THESE incidents of country and city life are particularly noted in order that the reader may get an intelligent grasp of the social conditions which made it possible for Billy the Kid to mark out for five years his career of crime, unmolested by law and order. It was these conditions which made it necessary, at last, to vest in one man the civil and military authority of the Territory in an effort to kill Billy the Kid and thus break up his gang. The man selected for this hazardous undertaking was Pat Garrett, who was chosen solely upon the understanding that he would kill or capture this desperado.

Garrett's election was the legal challenge from law to lawlessness. Without other preliminaries, personal quarrel, or malice, the contest was between the most dangerous law-breaker of the century and a cool-headed, clear-eyed, courageous, and resourceful man. It was to be a man-hunt to the death, and both men so accepted the coming struggle.

I met Pat Garrett at Las Vegas shortly after he became sheriff. He was a tall, spare man, with noticeably long legs and arms. He was a silent man, but nevertheless pleasant enough socially. Coolness, courage, and determination were written on his face.

Billy the Kid, on the other hand, was utterly reckless, relentless, and cruel. He was as quick as lightning with the revolver, and a dead shot. He was twenty-one years of age at the time of his death and had killed twenty-one men. He was supported by as desperate a gang of "killers" and thieves as were ever recorded in the annals of crime. This was the man Pat Garrett had pledged himself to deliver to the authorities dead or alive.

One day Garrett was missing from his usual

haunts. He had silently disappeared. The people knew that he was about to make his first move in this game of life and death, and the whole population of New Mexico awaited the issue in nervous suspense.

THE CAPTURE OF BILLY THE KID.

I WAS lounging on the veranda of the Grand View Hotel one afternoon when a man on a horse covered with foam galloped past. He shouted to Dr. Sutfin, the proprietor, as he rode by: "Garrett's got the Kid and three of the gang. He's bringing 'em in to Vegas."

In half an hour, Oldtown, usually peaceful and quiet in the afternoon, was seething with excitement.

The news of the capture of the Kid spread like a prairie fire. People began at once to line up on each side of the road by which Garrett would enter the town. As it terminated in the street in front of the Grand View, I merely moved my position from the veranda to the adobe fence which inclosed the yard.

The news was not generally believed. The capture of Billy the Kid alive was simply beyond belief. A rumor, however, was sufficient to turn the entire populace to curious expectancy.

It was a beautiful afternoon, and the elevation of the Grand View afforded a wide range of vision across the plains, stretching to the blue line of distant hills.

As the hours passed, the crowds began to grow more impatient and distrustful. All had become skeptical, when from our point of vantage we discerned a cloud of dust in the southwest. When the cause of it advanced close enough for the people to descry a wagon outfit accompanied by mounted men, a mighty shout went up. The good news was indeed true. Billy the Kid was a prisoner, and Pat Garrett was a hero.

As the wagon, pulled by four mules, approached, we saw four men sitting in the bed, two on a side, facing each other. The Kid, whom Dr. Sutfin had known in his cow-boy days and instantly recognized, was on the hotel side of the wagon, chained to a fierce-looking, dark-bearded man, who kept his slouch-hat pulled well down over his eyes, and who looked neither to the right nor to the left. This was the daring and dangerous Dave Rudabaugh, who, among many other crimes, had killed the Mexican jailer at Las Vegas a short time before, making good his escape along with the companions he released. He feared recognition, as well he might, for the Mexican population thirsted for his blood. The other two prisoners were Pickett and Wilson, prominent members of the Kid's gang.

Billy the Kid was in a joyous mood. He was a short, slender, beardless young man. The marked peculiarity of his face was a pointed chin and a short upper lip which exposed the large front teeth and gave a chronic grin to his expression. He wore his hat pushed far back, and jocularly greeted the crowd. Recognizing Dr. Sutfin, he called: "Hello, doc! Thought I jes drop in an' see how you fellers in Vegas air behavin' yerselves."

Heavily armed deputies rode on each side of the wagon, with two bringing up the rear. Garrett rode in front. The large crowd evidently surprised and annoyed him. Fearing for the safety of Rudabaugh, he turned and gave a low order to the mule-driver, who instantly whipped up his team, and a run was made across the plaza to the jail.

Garrett heard enough during the next few hours to convince him that an attempt would be made to lynch Rudabaugh. He promptly increased his force to thirty men, who guarded the jail that night. In the meantime he planned to take the prisoners next day to Santa Fé for safe-keeping. Not a suspicion of this move was allowed to get out.

Just before train-time Garrett dressed the men in plain clothes. He waited until the train was due, and then placed the prisoners in a closed carriage and drove rapidly to the depot. He placed his men in the smoking-car, and but for the accident of a delayed north-bound train his ruse would have been entirely successful. Las Vegas was the meeting-point, and the south-bound train had received orders to side-track. The Kid was still chained to Rudabaugh, and as they brushed past me on the platform I had a good look at the wild animal, and met the gaze of a pair of round, cold gray eyes.

THE CAREER OF BILLY THE KID.

THERE were many conflicting stories about the origin of Billy the Kid. Dr. Sutfin maintained that Billy was a Chicago boot-black whose mind had become inflamed by reading dime novels. He arrived in New Mexico when sixteen years of age, and went to work on a cattle-ranch in Lincoln County. When the long and deadly cattle-men's war broke out he fought for his employer. His record of killings began then. He was to receive five dollars per day for his services, but when the day of payment came a dispute arose between "the man behind the gun" and the man behind the cash. Billy quit ugly and dissatisfied. He swore he would get even. He became an outlaw. He ran off his former employer's cattle and killed his employees at sight. Soon he began to enlarge his operations. He gathered about him a band of reckless rough-riders and deadly pistol-shots, among whom Dave Rudabaugh was the chief and the Kid's right-hand man.

The deeds of murder, robbery, and fiendish deviltry accredited to Billy and his gang would fill a volume. His remarkable career developed only one chivalrous or generous impulse. For some inscrutable reason he gave liberally to the poor out of his murderous levies, and consequently many grateful blessings followed the little fiend as he rode from the doors of squalor, poverty, and distress. He had no other redeeming quality, unless his attachment to a Mexican girl could be so considered. His pastime, his greatest amusement and delight, was the taking of human life. The name of this youthful "killer" carried such terror into the homes of the Southwest that not a man could be induced to discuss his crimes. When a stranger introduced the subject, the host would look furtively around, and say: "Oh, Billy's all right. There are worse men than Billy. He's kind-hearted enough." Then the subject was hurriedly dropped.

The story of Billy's capture is that Garrett and his posse of carefully selected deputies, aided by a light fall of snow, tracked the Kid and his party to a lonely ranch and surrounded them. The order was to shoot the Kid dead on sight, and a young man who resembled him, coming to the door, was mistaken for Billy and instantly killed. This deplorable mistake gave the besieged knowledge of the situation. They were fairly caught. Garrett's men were all under cover commanding the only exit from the house. The Kid wanted to fight it out. He swore that he would rather be killed than taken. He raved, stormed, and cursed his men. Rudabaugh held out the hope of escape to him, and thus persuaded him to give up. Making known their desire to surrender, Garrett ordered them to leave their arms in the house and to step out one at a time with hands up. This was done, the men were shackled, and the homeward march began. Garrett had achieved the impossible.

FIGHTING A MOB.

Now this cruel, slender, boyish-looking man sat in the smoker of the south-bound train, handcuffed to Rudabaugh and chained to the seat. When the train backed in on the siding, I and a companion started back to the hotel. We had gone only a few yards when we heard men shouting, and soon met crowds of Mexicans armed with Winchesters running in our direction. It flashed upon me at once that Garrett's move was known, and that a mob was coming to take Rudabaugh.

Opposite the side-track on which the passenger-train stood, and only fifty feet away, was another siding holding several empty freight-cars. I suggested to my friend that we occupy the top of one of the cars. We could not have selected a better place. Our position commanded an excellent view of the interior of the smoker, and we could observe every movement of its occupants.

The moment Garrett was informed of the approaching danger, he requested the passengers to leave the train and seek a place of safety, which advice they were not slow to follow. Fearing that Rudabaugh might be shot from the outside, he unchained him from the Kid and moved him across the aisle, pulling down the lattice-shade. Walking up and down the car from door to door, his Winchester across his arm, Garrett calmly awaited developments.

We could see Rudabaugh through the window at which the Kid still sat, but he was not visible to those standing on the ground. He leaned back against the window-shade, quietly puffing a cigar. He did not appear to be disturbed by the thought that his life hung in the balance, and that a horrible death awaited him should the mob succeed in its purpose. His expression was that of a man absolutely indifferent to his fate.

The mob arrived and assembled between the freight-cars and the passenger-train. Two men with Winchesters were stationed at the engine. The leaders, three in number, mounted the steps of the smoker and demanded admittance. This was promptly refused, and the men were ordered off the car. They came back to the main body and demanded the prisoner Rudabaugh.

"I have reason to believe that these prisoners are not safe here," replied Garrett, "and I am taking them to Santa Fé, where they can be more securely guarded."

This explanation failed to satisfy the crowd.

"Take the other prisoner to Santa Fé," replied their spokesman, "but give Rudabaugh to us. His crime was committed here against one of our own people, and you have no right to remove him."

Slowly Garrett replied: "I have risked my life to bring these men to justice alive, and I will risk it again to protect them, for this is my sworn duty. I solemnly warn you that an attempt to take them from me will fail, unless you kill me first."

During this exciting colloquy, Billy the Kid, with his head thrust out of the window, was an amused listener. Unable to restrain himself, he began in rapid Greaser Spanish to tell the crowd what he thought of them, and judging from the interpretation of my friend, his regard for them and their forebears was not of a complimentary kind. He turned rapidly to Garrett, and said: "Pat, take these things off [holding up his manacled hands], give me a couple of guns, and turn me loose in that crowd of Greasers. If you will do that I 'll walk right back in here and hold out my hands for the bracelets."

Wise old Garrett said nothing, but shook his head.

The spokesmen of the Mexicans, after considerable discussion among themselves, changed the form of their demand. They wanted Rudabaugh returned to the Las Vegas jail.

Garrett refused to yield the point.

Then there was a cry of rage. Some one yelled "Look out!" and there was instantly a hurried scattering of the mob.

The Mexicans hastily sought cover. They dropped behind piles of cross-ties, the trucks of the freight-cars, and other shelter, and then the ugly muzzles of guns covered the smoking-car from all directions.

We thought the battle was squarely on, and quickly flattened ourselves on the top of the car, expecting every minute to hear the roar of guns; but seconds passed, and not a shot disturbed the stillness. Venturing a look into the car, we saw Garrett, his face pale but sternly set, his hand upon the lever of his rifle, waiting grimly the first shot. Rudabaugh had not moved his position, but was chewing viciously at the stump of his cigar. The Kid, still begging Garrett to turn him loose temporarily, seemed perfectly wild to get actively into the excitement. He

was in his element, but for the first time in his life his hands were tied, and the novelty of the situation galled him.

Gradually the Mexicans came out and assembled for another parley. Twice more was this stirring scene repeated.

Garrett began to weary, and at last declared that at the first shot he would arm the prisoners. This settled it. A compromise was quickly arranged. Garrett proposed that two citizens, representing the Mexicans of Las Vegas, accompany him to see that he turned the prisoners over to the proper authorities at Santa Fé.

Amid the cheers of belated passengers and white spectators, the train, held up for an hour, pulled out from the station. The coolness, nerve, and resource of Pat Garrett had saved the day.

Governor Wallace's threat to use the military power to end the Lincoln County War and to break up the Kid's gang did not in the least disturb the murderous robbers. They were too well aware of the military situation at the time. The truth was that the soldiers had their hands full during the winter of 1880–81 keeping Victorio and his marauding bands of Mescalero Apaches under some sort of surveillance. The Kid, knowing this, laughed derisively at the governor's threats, and rejected contemptuously his offers of personal pardon.

I saw Billy the Kid twice after the Las Vegas incident. The first time was during his incarceration at Santa Fé. He was hobbling about the open court of the jail, his ankles heavily ironed. The second time he was on the train being conveyed back to Lincoln County, the scene of his gravest crimes.

The treacherous murder of his two white jailers at Lincoln, his dramatic escape, and finally his death at the hands of Pat Garrett, which occurred at Maxwell's ranch, near Las Cruces, has been graphically told by a writer in a recent magazine.

His death was the signal for rejoicing throughout the Territory. To only one living soul in all the world did Garrett's fatal bullet carry sorrow that moonlit night on the Bonito: the poor Mexican girl, his faithful sweetheart, to see whom for the last time he risked and forfeited his life, alone mourned him. He died as he had lived, a wild, untamable, remorseless human fiend. With him passed the old order of things. The reign of the revolver in New Mexico was over forever.

14

Pioneer Days in San Francisco

John Williamson Palmer

PIONEER DAYS IN SAN FRANCISCO.

BUILDING OF THE "ALTA CALIFORNIA."

WHEN Captain Montgomery first gave the American flag to the breeze on the Plaza of Yerba Buena on the 8th of July, 1846, let us hope that a certain person was there to see—that native woman who, in Los Angeles in 1842, sang in the hearing of Duflot de Mofras her song of prophecy: "When the Frenchmen come, the women will surrender; when the Americans come, good-by to California!"

On the day of that flag-raising Yerba Buena was an amiable as well as a picturesque village, and its tenscore of inhabitants,—native Californians, English, Scotch, and Irish, with a sprinkling of Swiss, Swedes, Danes, Kanakas, and Indians,—unvexed by prophetic dreams of the feverish days of gold, were content to hail that gaudy bunting, and the promise of all that it stood for; were content to wait till the commerce of all the seas should find its way to the noblest anchorage the world could offer it.

The ever-expectant citizen of Yerba Buena who, spy-glass in hand, on the last day of that same July, mounted the hill above the cove ("Telegraph Hill" it was to be called) was greeted with a prospect that justified his highest hopes, and inspired him with the raptures to which Benjamin Morell had given expression fifteen years before—"a bay that might float the whole British navy without crowding; a circling grassy shore indented with convenient coves; a verdant, blooming country round about." Here were waving woodlands, and pastures flecked with grazing herds; hill and dale, mountain and valley, rolling rivers and gurgling brooks. And, looking seaward to where the Pacific pounded at the rocky headlands of the Golden Gate, he descried a ship under all sail, heading for the straits and the bay; a ship carrying the American ensign at her peak, but not a man-of-war, for her decks, and even her lower rigging, were black with passengers—men, women, and children! Again and again, with leveled glass, he peered, confirming the witness of his eyes; then he turned and ran down the hill and around the curving beach of the cove that rested sleepily between the arms of Clark's Point and the Rincon; and presently all the motley multitude of his fellow citizens were swarming from their adobes and their shanties, stirred with the news as the leafy ridges of the Contra Costa were stirred with the sea-breeze.

The ship that let go her anchor that day, off the little island of the "good herb," was the *Brooklyn* from New York, bringing "Bishop" Brannan (the redoubtable "Sam" of a later day) and his colony of Latter-day Saints; and these brought stout hearts, strong arms, and cunning hands; money, tools, pluck, keen wits, and a printing-press. And so, although they quarreled with their very mundane bishop, and went to law with him, and abandoned their scheme of Mormon colonization, and presently made game of Brigham Young in their tents among the sand-hills, nevertheless they gave to San Francisco her first prayer-meeting, her first jury trial, her first local advertising, her first newspaper; for with the same types and press that had once done duty for "The Prophet" in New York, they printed blank deeds, alcaldes' grants, and pronunciamientos, and early in the following January issued the first number of the "California Star," pledged "to eschew with the greatest caution everything that tends to the propagation of sectarian dogmas." A progressive folk, those Mormons of Yerba Buena!

Toward the close of January, 1847, Yerba Buena underwent a change of name, and by summary process and proclamation of the alcalde became San Francisco; for the chief magistrates of those days were a very summary folk, doing a mildly autocratic business each in his little bailiwick, and having small reverence for precedents or principles, but just setting up or casting down according to certain loose notions of their own regarding Mexican judicature or Californian traditions. And so the first alcalde of Yerba Buena under the American flag, being a naval lieutenant (Mr. Washington A. Bartlett) appointed by Captain Montgomery, and invested with ample powers, military as well as civil, to administer the affairs of the embryo metropolis according to Mexican practice conformed to American ideas, proceeded to the making of history in a small way, building better than he knew. He first changed the name of the place to San Francisco, and then vouchsafed to explain that Yerba Buena was but a paltry cognomen taken from a lot of vulgar mint overrunning an insignificant island; that it was a merely local name, "unknown beyond the district," while San Francisco had long had the freedom of the maps; and finally that it was an outlandish name, which Americans would mangle in pronouncing. "Therefore, to prevent confusion and mistakes in public documents, and that the town may have the advantage of the name given on the public map, it is hereby ordained," etc.

And the alcalde was right: for in 1836 Alexander Forbes had written "the port of San Francisco is hardly surpassed by any in the world"; and ten years later (eighteen months in advance of the Bartlett coup) George Bancroft, then Secretary of the Navy, had instructed Commodore Sloat in relation to the blockade or occupation of "the port of San Francisco," in the event of his (Sloat's) ascertaining with certainty that Mexico had declared war against the United States.

The 5th of March, 1847, brought the ship *Thomas H. Perkins*, with a detachment of the New York regiment commanded by Colonel Stevenson. These men were pledged by the terms of their enlistment to make permanent settlement in California at the close of the war, and they had been chosen·for the most part with an eye to their prospective usefulness as skilled artisans or shrewd traders. Thus they constituted an important accession to the population, and, joined with their Mormon predecessors, showed a bold front of energy and confident resources. The air began to be stirred with the bustle of business, and all the talk was of town lots. General Kearney had ceded to the town all the beach- and water-lots on the east front, between Fort Montgomery and Rincon Point; and on the 20th of July two hundred of these lots, lying between the limits of high- and low-water marks, were sold at public auction for from $50 to $100 each. These lots measured 45 × 137 feet, and were for the most part uncovered at low tide. In December, 1853, the water-lots between Clay and Sacra-

mento streets fetched from $8000 to $16,000 each, although they were but 25 × 60 feet, and at all times under water. In 1847 a fifty-vara lot north of Market street could be bought for $16. A vara, the Spanish yard, is about 33⅓ inches, and six of these lots made a building block bounded by four streets. Hittell [1] records that, in the seventeen months ending on the 1st of August, "157 houses had been built in a place which had only 30 houses before"; and already it was a city of two newspapers, for in May the "Californian" had come from Monterey and cast in its fortunes with the "smart little settlement on the cove," which, having secured two notable importations of unterrified hustlers, had begun to set competition at defiance, with a total population of nearly five hundred, composed of all nationalities under the sun. Of this number fully one half were citizens of the United States; and these, being stirred by municipal aspirations, bethought them that it was time to give the place a town council and call it a city. So a public meeting was held under a call from the governor, and six gentlemen were elected to constitute an *ayuntamiento*, or council. These were Messrs. Glover, Jones, Howard, Parker, Leidesdorff, and Clark, and their functions were the laying out of streets, the award of building privileges, the regulation of business, the granting of licenses, the appointment of town officers and constables, etc. The enforcement of ordinances and general execution of the laws devolved upon the first alcalde, who was Mr. George Hyde. He was assisted by Dr. T. M. Leavenworth as second alcalde, and by Mr. Leidesdorff as treasurer. Messrs. Glover, Leidesdorff, and Clark were appointed a committee to take measures for the establishment of a public school for the youth of both sexes; but it was not until April 3, 1848, that the school was formally opened. By that time the population had increased to about 850, all told, and the buildings of all kinds numbered two hundred, including two considerable hotels, besides public houses and saloons, stores, warehouses, and two wharves in course of construction. Already the characteristic enterprise of San Francisco had begun to express itself in a brisk development of its peculiar industry : gambling-houses were springing up on every corner, and an ordinance of the ayuntamiento provided for the seizure, for the benefit of the town, of all moneys found on any table used for gambling with cards. "Such an ordinance, if enforced a year later, would have enriched the city in a single night; but the act was repealed at the next meeting." [2]

Early in the spring of 1848 there began to be rumors of gold to be found in the foothills

[1] J. S. Hittell, "A History of the City of San Francisco."

[2] Soulé, Gihon, and Nisbet, "The Annals of San Francisco": New York, 1855.

of the Sierra Nevada; and presently actual miners appeared in town, showing small parcels of dust and telling tales of wonder that turned the heads of gaping groups met at the landing on the cove and in every place convenient for assembling from Telegraph Hill to Happy Valley. Then the cry went up, and bedlam was let loose. Sailors deserted from the shipping and soldiers from the barracks; the laborer dropped his shovel and his pick, only to return and take them up again — shovels and picks would be useful in the diggings; the mechanic turned his back upon his job; the builder left his house unroofed; the blacksmith and the baker let their fires go out; and the merchant stripped his shelves, huddled his goods into boxes and bales, and shouted at the cove for a launch bound for the Sacramento Valley. The cry of "Gold!" was caught up and reëchoed on the docks and in the market-places of Atlantic seaports, until the world was turned upside down. Every day added to the number of those who were hurrying to the "placers," and the bay was alive with freighted launches crawling up the Sacramento. In May and June the "Californian" and the "California Star" stopped their presses with a farewell fly-sheet. In the middle of July the "Californian" revived with news of affairs in the mines. For two months the ayuntamiento had not met; the city fathers and officials had all gone to the diggings. The public school, which had been closed for two months, was reopened in December, and on Sundays public worship was held there by a Protestant chaplain imported from Honolulu, on a salary of $2500, raised by subscription.

The first brick house in San Francisco was built by Mellus and Howard on the corner of Clay and Montgomery streets, in September, 1848. In December flour was $20 a barrel, butter ninety cents a pound, brandy $8 a gallon, and gold-dust dull at $10.50 an ounce. Common laborers were getting $10 a day, and ordinary mechanics $20. Gold-dust at $16 the ounce soon became the circulating medium for all purposes of trade. The bay was bustling with small craft, and the sand-hills were thickly flecked with canvas tents and such makeshifts as could be rigged with a pole and two blankets, while the Plaza, and Clay and Montgomery streets, rioted in music and drink and gambling. "Men," says Hittell, "who had lived on five dollars a month now spent hundreds; men who had been idlers formerly were now among the most industrious, and men who had never before wasted a day became loungers and gamblers." And, let us add, men who at home had been blithe, cheery, vital, became despondent, moody, inert, stunned by the mad scramble about them; and men refined, sensitive, keenly susceptible to impressions of coarseness and depravity, became home-sick, heart-sick, desperate, ready to plunge into the unknown out of the ghastly brutality of such a training as this.

On the last day of February came the steamship *California*, bringing General Persifer Smith to the command of the Military Department, comprising California and Oregon; and on the last day of March the Pacific mail-steamer *Oregon* brought about three hundred and fifty passengers, including Colonel John W. Geary, who bore government despatches to the commanders of the military and naval forces on the Pacific, and brought the first regular mail that was opened in San Francisco. Colonel Geary had been appointed postmaster of the new city, with powers to create post-offices, appoint postmasters, and establish mail routes throughout the territory. Within the next three months more than three hundred square-rigged vessels were lying in the harbor stranded and disabled for want of sailors, the crews having deserted in a body almost as soon as the anchors were let go. Some of these vessels eventually rotted where they were moored; some were hauled up on the beach and in the mud to serve as store-houses, lodging-houses, and saloons; and, at a later period, more than one of them, flanked by buildings and wharves, and forming part of a street, appeared as an original and startling feature of that most surprising town. Thus, the brig *Euphemia* was purchased by the ayuntamiento and converted into the first jail, and the store-ship *Apollo* was used as a lodging-house and drinking-saloon; and as lots were piled or filled in on the flat covered by the bay, the Apollo saloon in course of time presented the extraordinary spectacle of the hull of a large ship looming up among the houses. The *Niantic*, stripped of her masts and rigging, and propped with piles on each side, lay at the corner of Sansome and Clay streets and served for the storing of merchandise, and when the May fire of 1851 consumed all but the deeper parts of her hull and some of her ribs, a hotel was built on the wreck and called the Niantic.

In the first six months of 1849 fifteen thousand souls were added to the population of San Francisco; in the latter half of that year about four thousand arrived every month by sea alone. At first the immigrants were from Mexico, Chile, Peru, and the South American ports generally; but soon our own Americans began to swarm in, coming by way of Cape Horn and Panama, or across the plains; and the number of these was swelled by the addition of thousands of deserters from the shipping, and by a straggling contingent from China, Australia, and the Hawaiian Islands. Probably two thirds of these newcomers proceeded at once to the mines, but those that remained to try their fortunes in the city were enough to give to San Francisco at the end of the year a population of twenty-five thousand—mostly men, young or of middle age, very few women, fewer children, with here and there a bewildered matron or maiden of good repute. Here were British subjects, Frenchmen, Germans, and Dutch, Italians, Spaniards, Norwegians, Swedes, and Swiss, Jews, Turks, Chinese, Kanakas, New Zealanders, Malays, and Negroes, Parthians, Medes, and Elamites, Cretes and Arabians, and the dwellers in Mesopotamia and Cappadocia, in Boston and New Orleans, Chicago and Peoria, Hoboken and Hackensack.

And how did they all live? In frame-houses of one story, more commonly in board shanties and canvas tents, pitched in the midst of sand or mud and various rubbish and strange filth and fleas; and they slept on rude cots, or on "soft planks" under horse-blankets, on tables, counters, floors, on trucks in the open air, in bunks braced against the weather-boarding, forty of them in one loft; and so they tossed and scratched, and swore and laughed, and sang and skylarked—those who were not tired or drunk enough to sleep. And in the working-hours they bustled, and jostled, and tugged, and sweated, and made money—always made money. They labored and they lugged: they worked on lighters, drove trucks, packed mules, rang bells, carried messages, "waited" in restaurants, "marked" for billiard-tables, served drinks in bar-rooms, "faked" on the Plaza, "cried" at auctions, toted lumber for houses, ran a game of faro or roulette in the El Dorado or the Bella Union, or manipulated three-card monte on the head of a barrel in front of the Parker House; they speculated in beach- and water-lots, in lumber, pork, flour, potatoes; in picks, shovels, pans, long boots, slouch-hats, knives, blankets, and Mexican saddles. There were doctors, lawyers, politicians, preachers, even gentlemen and scholars among them; but they all speculated, and as a rule they gambled. Clerks in stores and offices had munificent salaries; $5 a day was about the smallest stipend even in the custom-house, and one Baptist preacher was paid $10,000 a year. Laborers received a dollar an hour; a pick or a shovel was worth $10; a tin pan or a wooden bowl, $5; and a butchers' knife, $30. At one time the carpenters who were getting $12 a day struck for $16. Lumber rose to $500 per thousand feet, "and every brick in a house cost a dollar, one way or another."[1] Wheat flour and salt pork sold at $40 a barrel; a small loaf of bread was fifty cents, and a hard-boiled egg a dollar. You paid $3 to get into the circus, and $55 for a private box. Men talked dollars, and a copper

[1] "Annals of San Francisco."

coin was an object of antiquarian interest. Forty dollars was the price for ordinary coarse boots; and a pair that came above the knees and would carry you gallantly through the quagmires brought a round hundred. When a shirt became very dirty, the wearer threw it away and bought a new one. Washing cost $15 a dozen in 1849. Rents were simply monstrous: $3000 a month in advance for a "store" hurriedly built of rough boards. Wright and Co. paid $75,000 for the wretched little place on the corner of the Plaza that they called the Miners' Bank, and $36,000 was asked for the use of the Old Adobe as a custom-house. The Parker House paid $120,000 a year in rents, nearly one half of that amount being collected from the gamblers who held the second floor; and the canvas tent next door, used as a gambling-saloon, and called the El Dorado, was good for $40,000 a year. From 10 to 15 per cent. a month was paid in advance for the use of money borrowed on substantial security. The prices of real estate went up among the stars: $8000 for a fifty-vara lot that had been bought in 1848 for $20. Yet, for all that, everybody made money, although a man might stare aghast at the squalor of his lodging, and wish that he might part with his appetite at any price to some other man. It was some such man as this who preserved the bill of fare of the Ward House for the dinner there on the 27th of October, 1849.

Oxtail soup	$1.00
Baked trout, anchovy sauce	1.50
Roast beef	1.00
Roast lamb, stuffed	1.00
Roast mutton, stuffed	1.00
Roast pork, with apple sauce	1.25
Baked mutton, caper sauce	1.25
Corned beef and cabbage	1.25
Ham	1.00
Curried sausages	1.00
Lamb and green peas	1.25
Venison, wine sauce	1.50
Stewed kidney, champagne sauce	1.25
Fresh eggs	1.00 each
Sweet potatoes	.50
Irish potatoes	.50
Cabbage	.50
Squash	.50
Bread pudding	.75
Mince pie	.75
Brandy peaches	2.00
Rum omelette	2.00
Jelly omelette	2.00
Cheese	.50
Prunes	.75

At the El Dorado Hotel at Hangtown (a mining-camp) the dainty menu offered "beef with one potato, fair size," $1.25; "beef, up along," $1; "baked beans, greased," $1; "new potatoes, peeled," 75 cents; "hash, low grade," 75 cents; "hash, 18 karats," $1; "roast grizzly," $1; "jackass rabbit,

IN FRONT OF THE EMPIRE SALOON.

DRAWN BY GILBERT GAUL.

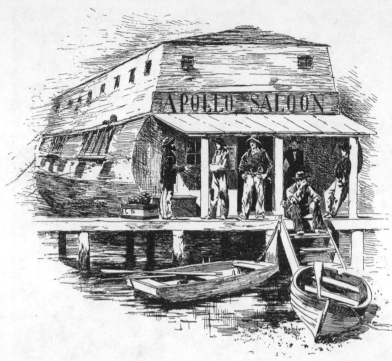

OLD STORE-SHIP "APOLLO," USED AS A SALOON.

and barrels. Men waded through the slough, and thought themselves lucky when they sank no deeper than their waists. Lanterns were in request at night, and poles in the daytime. In view of the scarcity and great cost of proper materials and labor, such make-shifts were the only means at hand. A traveler who came by sea in 1849 describes with graphic interest "the peculiar construction of the sidewalk between the store of Simmons, Hutchinson & Co. and the Adams Express office." This place was bridged with cooking-stoves, sacks of

whole," $1.50; "rice with brandy peaches," $2; and "a square meal" for $3. "All payable in advance. Gold-scales on the end of bar." But the small, cheap gold-scales cost $30, and the coarse knives and forks not less than $25 the pair.

The aspect of the streets of San Francisco at this time was such as one may imagine of an unsightly waste of sand and mud churned by the continual grinding of heavy wagons and trucks, and the tugging and floundering of horses, mules, and oxen; thoroughfares irregular and uneven, ungraded, unpaved, unplanked, obstructed by lumber and goods; alternate humps and holes, the actual dumping-places of the town, handy receptacles for the general sweepings and rubbish and indescribable offal and filth, the refuse of an indiscriminate population "pigging" together in shanties and tents. And these conditions extended beyond the actual settlement into the chaparral and underbrush that covered the sand-hills on the north and west.

The flooding rains of winter transformed what should have been thoroughfares into treacherous quagmires set with holes and traps fit to smother horse and man. Loads of brushwood and branches of trees, cut from the hills, were thrown into these swamps; but they served no more than a temporary purpose, and the inmates of tents and houses made such bridges and crossings as they could with boards, boxes,

Chile flour, bags of coffee, and boxes of tobacco; and one yawning pit was stopped with a piano. Nevertheless, there were clumsy or drunken pedestrians who would have sunk out of sight but for timely rescue. Hittell tells of two horses that were left in the mud of Montgomery street to die of starvation, and of three drunken men who were suffocated between Washington and Jackson streets. And yet the rains that were productive of conditions so desperate and deadly in the city brought showers of gold to the miners in the diggings, and the monthly yield of dust and nuggets was three times greater after November than it had been in the summer.

Standing on the piazza of the Old Adobe custom-house, on the upper side of the Plaza, or Portsmouth Square, and looking eastward across the open space, you had before you the Parker House and Dennison's Exchange, center and focus of all interest and all news to the San Franciscan of '49; and adjoining the Parker House, on the corner of the Plaza formed by the intersection of Kearney and Washington streets, was the El Dorado, most reckless of gambling-resorts and phenix of many fires. Amidships, on the north side of the square, was the original office of the "Alta California" newspaper, a journal which terminated its existence only a few months ago; and adjoining that, the Bella Union and Washington Hall—alike infamous, the former as a den of gambling desperados and cutthroats, and the latter as a stew of polyglot debauchery.

Southward, on the Clay street side of the Plaza, and on the corner of Kearney street, was that historic adobe, the old City Hotel, the first important hostelry of Yerba Buena; and when the placers began to give out their treasures it was the headquarters of gambling miners, and overflowed with gold. "Scenes such as never before were and never again will be witnessed," said the "Alta California," "were common in the old City Hotel in 1848 and '49." In the spring of '49 the building was leased for $16,000 per annum, cut up into small stores and offices, and subleased at an enormous advance; but the City Hotel was "gobbled up" in the great fire of June, 1851. Higher up, on the south side, was Sam Brannan's office, where that redoubtable Mormon arraigned the "Hounds" before a concourse

Leavenworth or a Geary; and midway between the Old Adobe and the Parker House stood the original flag-staff, boldly flaunting Uncle Sam's title-deed to the land of gold.

The Old Adobe was a conspicuous landmark in the San Francisco of those wild times, and most dear to the memory of every Forty-niner. In the early days of the American occupation it had been used as a military barrack and guard-house, and later it became the first custom-house of San Francisco. A sedate, drowsy-looking structure, with sturdy brown walls, a low-pitched roof, tiled in the true rancho fashion, a long, rickety porch with planking all adrift, and posts and railings elaborately whittled, the Old Adobe from its coign of vantage on the higher ground overlooked the Plaza and took note of the various devilment that marked its reckless doings; while, with that handy cross-beam at the south end of the porch, it seemed

A MUDDY STREET IN SAN FRANCISCO.

of exasperated citizens, and demanded their summary stamping out. Across the way, on the southwest corner of the Plaza, was the little frame school-house—the first school-house, which became, afterward, a concert-hall for Steve Massett's musical eccentricities, and then a police-station for a most inefficient constabulary. Between the school-house and the south end of the Old Adobe was the alcalde's office, where justice was informally dispensed by a

to wait with cynical patience until the coming vigilance committee should bring their first victim their short shrift and their long rope. The ever-open portal admitted you to a wide vestibule which divided the house into unequal wings, and showed you on one side the desks of the inspectors and deputies, and on the other the sanctum of the collector—an imperturbable and dapper little man whose supernatural equanimity was the admiration of the time and place,

DRAWN BY A. CASTAIGNE.

ENGRAVED BY J. H. E. WHITNEY.

THE POST-OFFICE IN SAN FRANCISCO, 1849–50.

imparting an air of repose and hospitality to all his surroundings, and making even his iron safe, which should have been the grim receptacle of the public treasure, seem but a pleasing and confiding joke, seeing that he usually kept it as open as his own countenance, and free to display its golden lining to the day.

On the 22d of June, 1851, the Old Adobe disappeared from the map of San Francisco, swallowed up in that last great fire which devoured the City Hotel and the City Hospital, the Jenny Lind Theater and the office of the "Alta California." Other adobe houses characteristic of the old California life were the Mowry dwelling and the residence of Señora Briones, both on the northwestern skirt of the town. These were all of one story, and roofed with tiles. The entrance was set fairly in the middle of the front, and there was usually a hall extending from the front to the back door and equally dividing the house, so as to give a large sitting-room, which was also used for a guest-room, on one side of the hall, and on the other a bed-chamber in front and a kitchen at the back. In several of these houses the guest-room and the bed-chamber were floored with tiles of marble in alternate black and white, and the cornices showed some fair attempts at carving; these apartments were always hospitably furnished, and on occasions of entertainment made pretensions to luxury.

The post-office of that time was a frame building of one story and an attic on the corner of Clay and Pike streets. There was but small accommodation here for clerks and "handlers," and still less for the impatient and peremptory crowd of home-hungry men who came daily, but most of all on mail-day, which was once a month, and took the small windows and loopholes by storm. To avoid confusion and dangerous conflict, long queues were formed, extending from the windows along Clay street to the Plaza, and along Pike street sometimes as far as Sacramento, and even to the chaparral beyond. Here traders, miners, merchants, gamblers, and adventurers of every complexion waited in their places, often from the afternoon of one day, all night long, to the morning of the next, in the mud and the soaking rain, with weary limbs and anxious hearts. Men whose strength was unequal to the strain were glad to employ others to hold their places for them through the long hours; and there were those who, while not seeking or expecting letters for themselves, secured good standings in the line before the coming of the crowd, only to sell their right of place to richer men whose time was money. From ten to twenty dollars was a common price for such service.

The gamblers of '49 constituted a controlling class with whom all the physical, moral, and financial force. Abounding in ready resources of a mixed and mysterious kind, and unscrupulous in the application of them; themselves well stocked with the adventurer's courage, and their courage imposingly backed up with six-shooters; numbering in their society, whether as professionals or amateurs, many of the "first men" of the city; having the largest show of "smartness," if not of a finer intellectuality and higher wisdom; of sophisticated observation, reckless speculation, and, most important of all, cash; paying the highest rents, monopolizing the most desirable business sites; prompt in applying every new and admirable improvement, commanding every comfort that invention or expensive labor could supply, every luxury that fine raiment, and pictures, and shows, and music, and wine, and a motley "world of ladies" could stand for — no wonder that they swayed the city, and carried the day with a high hand. For they paid twelve per cent. a month for money, and were ready to take all they could get at that price, offering securities in the good-will and fixtures of one "saloon" or another, a house, a lease, a water-lot, a bank.

Moreover, the gambler of '49 was no vulgar villain of the sordid stripe; he had his aspirations; it was proud game he hunted, and he put his own life into the chase. The law being to play fair or die, and the finest distinctions of the *meum* and *tuum* being defined by the pistol, it is easy to understand that there were honest gamblers in San Francisco in '49; in fact, I will go so far as to assert that, as a class, no others were so strict and punctual in all their dealings. No investment was safer or more profitable than a loan to a gambler; no rightful claim was more easy of collection. Nor were these men, though most dangerous on certain points of professional prerogative, by any means habitually quarrelsome. On the contrary, they were often the peacemakers of a fierce crowd whose explosive passions were stirred, constituting themselves an extemporaneous vigilance committee, in the name of the law and order they had themselves set up for the occasion; and then woe to the refractory!

As I have elsewhere said,

not uncommonly the professional faro-banker of '49 was a farmer-like and homespun man, with a kindly composition of features and expression, patriarchal in his manners, a man to go to for advice, abounding in instructive experiences of life, and full of benevolent leanings toward the world; a man to lounge about the porticos of hotels, reading his "Alta," or the latest home papers, projecting city improvements and public charities, discussing important enterprises, overhauling the business of the ayuntamiento, considering at large the state of the country, defining the duties of

OLD ADOBE, USED AS CUSTOM-HOUSE.

Congress toward California, portraying the future of the State ; and then — starting out to make the round of the tables, and deliberately to set about "breaking the bank." I have known such a man to take, in one day and night, five out of seven monte banks, besides a faro bank or two, seat his own dealers at them to keep the game going, and then subside into his pipe and newspaper, his political economy and projects of benevolence.

Of such was the fraternity that swayed the city in those days, and the secret of their paramount influence lay, partly, in their harmonious combination of the preëminently American traits—a faculty of taking accurately and at once the bearings of new and strange situations, fixity of purpose, persistence of endeavor, audacity of enterprise, ready hazard of life, ever fresh elasticity of sanguine temperament, but principally in the imposing figures of an omnipotent cash capital, wherewith they knew how to feed the enormous cravings of the people, and mitigate their privations and their pains.[1]

The people eagerly accepted the treacherous comforts and solacements so seductively displayed on the green cloth; and gambling became the recreation of the honest toiler or trader, as well as the revel of the reckless bucaneer. While occupations were as various as the needs and makeshifts of those who had recourse to them, it may be said that in all that din and bustle and hurly-burly there was but one pursuit. Miners and boatmen, laborers, mechanics, and builders, merchants and clerks and peddlers, thimbleriggers and fakirs from the streets, lawyers, physicians, judges, clergymen—all alike found a rapture in faro or bluff, a distraction in roulette or rondo, an edifying experience in monte or rouge-et-noir. The bar and the green table went into partnership, and, with a joint stock of cards and chips, decanters, fiddles, and pictures, and reckless women, did a madly merry business. There were hundreds of such places where, in the evening and all night long, keen fellows, horribly quiet, shuffled the fateful cards with deadly deliberation, or where bedeviled women, horribly beautiful, greedy, and cruel, twirled roulette-wheels to the mockery of music.

The great "saloons" were on the Plaza : all of the east side and the greater part of the north and south sides were given up to them. In each of these from ten to a dozen tables waited for players—for the man whose "blood was up," or the man who was bored, or the pleasant fellow who "might as well amuse himself." The man whose blood was up usually began with a stake of a thousand dollars and ended with fifty cents, and lost it; and the pleasant fellow who would amuse himself usually began with fifty cents and ended with a thousand dollars, and lost it; while the bored man won and won, and "took no interest." Piles of coin in gold and silver, bags of dust, and gold in nuggets, lay in the middle of the table; and the game went on in sweet repose and pensiveness, not even broken when the stakes were at their highest, and the spectators, standing three lines deep, waited for the luck of "that long-haired stranger who came to break the bank."

"Everybody gambled"—that was the excuse for everybody else. The phenomenal exception was the man who, having lost his all at three-card monte on the head of a barrel in the Plaza, was thereupon seized with acute compunctions on moral grounds, and a luminous theory of the ratio of chances. "While profits and wages were so high, while there were no homes, no comfort or decency to be found in lofts and bunks, men thought to take refuge in riotous excess, seeking for rest and recreation

[1] J. W. Palmer, "The New and the Old."

in gambling-hells, and bar-rooms, and dance-houses."[1] To find the few virtuous and worthy women of that time, you must have sought for them in tents and makeshift harbors, safely withdrawn from the public gaze, or else in the struggling beginnings of churches that feebly held their little forts against the banded forces of a multifarious godlessness.

From the upper corner on Washington street to the lower corner on Clay street, the people filed across the Plaza, between the Old Adobe and the Parker House, in an unending procession, or broke into motley groups of many colors and many tongues, and loitered by the flag-staff, among the trucks, and the oxen, and

that they had sown the wind to reap the whirl-wind. The Chinese quarter in San Francisco became, it was charged, a hotbed of depravity and crime. The opium-habit spread among the white youth of both sexes, and fetid dens were open day and night."[2] The oath of a Chinaman became a joke in the courts, and it was proved that in the Chinese quarter rewards were covertly offered for the slaying of innocent witnesses. Thus anti-Chinese legislation, for the suppression of the Chinese high-binder, became a foregone conclusion.

But there are Chinese and Chinese; they are not all coolies and highbinders. In " Little China," as the district which includes Dupont

CORNER OF THE PLAZA, FEBRUARY, 1850.

the mules, the stalls of the small venders, and the handy boxes and barrels of the fakirs and thimbleriggers, and the dealers of three-card monte; while from time to time some jingling ranchero, picturesque in serape, sombrero, and silver bell-buttons, and heeled with formidable spurs, would come caracoling across the square, making a circus of himself for the delectation of señora and madame. Always conspicuous among these was the ubiquitous Chinaman, " child-like and bland," but slyly twinkling with the conscious smartness of ways that are as hard to find out as the thimble-rigger's pea, which he so cunningly resembles.

There is record of two Chinese men and one woman who came to California on the bark *Eagle* from Hong-Kong in 1848. By February, 1850, these had been followed by 787 men and two women, and still they came. Beginning in the mines, they spread into the farms and gardens, and thence into workshops and factories, out-bidding the Caucasian with longer hours of work and smaller pay. " Then the men who had given them employment, displacing the American and European workmen, soon found

street and the upper part of Sacramento street is called, were many respectable and wealthy Chinese merchants, men who trafficked in the goods and wares of their country, and were regarded by their Caucasian neighbors as shrewd, polite, and well informed, having consideration for their social caste, holding themselves aloof from the washermen and the porters, and, so far as the exigencies of their business permitted, living retired. In common fairness they were not to be reckoned with the keepers of gambling-dens, opium-joints, and brothels, but rather to be accepted as an honorable protest and appeal in the interest of that class of their people who are industrious, decent in their lives and manners, and of good report, who are contented, peaceable, and thrifty, and who hold it a point of honor that the Chinaman who cannot pay his debts must kill himself for the credit of the survivors.

Even in those days a sentiment of Sunday-ness might be found in the suburbs of San Francisco; and in an equestrian scamper to the Lagoon, the Presidio (the old Spanish cantonment), or the Mission San Dolores, one might

1 " Annals of San Francisco."

2 San Francisco " Chronicle," September 7, 1890.

MISSION SAN DOLORES — SUNDAY AFTERNOON.

give his heart an airing. The Mission, so intimately associated with the early history of Yerba Buena and the later San Francisco, though it had been projected ever since the discovery of the bay in 1769, was not founded till 1776. The site was a small, fertile plain, embosomed among green hills, about two miles from the center of the present city. Several rivulets of clear, sweet water mixed their streams to form the larger Mission Creek. Further north were the bleak and sterile sand-hills on which the site of the present city was pitched; but the Presidio was more happily placed, and the small cove on the east, within the narrow entrance to the bay, afforded shelter and good anchorage.

The old Mission Church of 1850 was a spacious building of adobe, very plain without and partly whitewashed, except the front, which was relieved by certain crude architectural decorations, and showed several handsome bells. The interior was somber, grim, and cold. On the walls were rude paintings of saints and sacred subjects, and tinsel ornaments decorated the altar. But mass was still celebrated in the gloomy pile for the spiritual comfort of a small company of worshipers, mostly women of the Spanish races.

But the Mission was the favorite resort of holiday-makers from the city, especially of the Sunday revelers. Here bull-fights were held, and bear-baitings, and prize-fights of pugilists, and horse-races, and duels, and all the other mild diversions of the Forty-niner; and bars and gambling-tables supplied abundantly the indispensable refreshment and risk. Over the plank road, constructed in 1850, came an endless cavalcade of dashing equestrians of both sexes, and the highways extending southward to San José invited to pleasant excursions among green fields and hills.

But, after all, it was but a ghastly jollity, for under and all around it were destitution and disease, crime and despair and death. For the sick, the friendless, and the utterly broken there were, for many months, no infirmary, no hospital fund, no city physician.

"Your honor, and gentlemen," said the eccentric Mr. Krafft, addressing an imaginary ayuntamiento, "we are very sick, and hungry, and helpless, and wretched. If somebody does not do something for us we shall die; and that will be bad, considering how far we have come, and how hard it was to get here, and how short a time we have been here, and that we have not had a fair chance. All we ask is a fair chance; and we say again, upon our honor, gentlemen, if somebody does not do something for us, we shall die, or we shall be setting fire to the town first, and cutting all our throats."[1]

For these were the times when scurvied men were landing from the ships, and men crippled with rheumatism, and wasted with dysentery, and delirious with pneumonia and typhoid fever, were taking refuge in the city, to find only the bare, wet earth for a bed, under a leaky tent, or a foul bunk in the loft of a shanty, where a man had never a chance to die like a man, because of the cruel, carousing crew in the den below; no doctor, no nurse, no balm, no wine or oil, no cup of cold water, no decent deathbed. And so we found their poor, cold, silent corpses in lonely tents apart, or in the bush, or under the lee of a pile of lumber in Sacramento or Montgomery street; and we dug a hole and buried them right there, and the city of San Francisco is their gravestone, and this story is their epitaph.

Here is a passage from the address of the alcalde, Colonel John W. Geary, to the ayuntamiento in August, 1849:

At this time we are without a dollar in the public treasury, and it is to be feared the city is greatly in debt. You have neither an office for your magistrate, nor any other public edifice. You are without a single police officer or watchman, and you have not the means of confining a prisoner for one hour; neither have you a place to shelter sick and unfortunate strangers who

1 J. W. Palmer, "The New and the Old."

may be cast upon our shores, or to bury them when dead. Public improvements are unknown in San Francisco. In short, you are without a single requisite for the promotion of prosperity, for the protection of property, or for the maintenance of order.

Organized bands of ruffians, including thieves, burglars, and roughs, ever ready with knife and pistol, roamed unchallenged. Depredation and assault became familiar incidents them fast bound with his " Thus saith the Lord your God!"

Most dangerous, and for a time most numerous, of the immigrant criminals who came to recruit the gangs of " Sydney-town " were the old convicts and ticket-of-leave men from Van Diemen's Land and New South Wales, who feared nothing but the gallows anywhere, and even that not at all in this land of devil-may-care, where prosecutors and witnesses were too

" HOUNDS " ATTACKING CHILIANS.

in the life of the town. The conflagrations which subsequently laid waste the most valuable districts were traced or ascribed to the handiwork of " Sydney coves " and " Hounds," who plundered under cover of the general confusion and dismay incident to a great fire. And everywhere was the reckless apathy of " every man for his own hand," every man a law to himself, and the six-shooter his only constable. Only on a Sunday afternoon, on the piazza of the Old Adobe, was the voice of the prophet heard in righteous rebuke and warning—the voice of brave old Father Taylor, lifted up in stentorian psalm and prayer, arresting the passing miner and gambler, the " Sydney cove " and the courtezan, and holding busy to concern themselves with courts ; where judges were ignorant, careless, or corrupt; where trials were too costly for a bankrupt city ; and where a man might hide easily and utterly under an alias or an alibi, a pea-jacket or a serape, a smooth face or a ragged beard.

The quarter known as " Sydney-town," the " Five Points" and the " Seven Dials " of San Francisco, lay around Clark's Point, in Broadway and Pacific street. Here a policeman hardly dared to enter, night was made hideous with debauchery and assaults, and for a few ounces a fellow could be hired to kill a man or fire a house, and no questions asked. "Although hundreds of murders had been committed " by the desperate denizens of these and other

THE FIRST HOTEL AT SAN FRANCISCO.

quarters, "and many murderers had been arrested, not one had been hanged, either legally or at the hands of self-appointed executioners; and the very courts themselves had become a by-word." [1]

But the very excesses and intolerable outrages of this state of things presently compelled their own stamping out by methods that were short and summary. On the 15th of July, 1849, a gang of young men who called themselves "Regulators," but were commonly known as "Hounds," and who were the "Mohawks" and "thugs" and "plug-uglies" of that time, proceeded to "take the town" after a fashion which they had made their own. This gang, which had been first heard of toward the close of 1848, began to make itself felt and feared in the spring of the following year. Under the pretense of mutual defense against the encroachments of foreigners, especially Chileans, Peruvians, and Mexicans, they had adopted a sort of military organization with a regular headquarters, which they called Tammany Hall, in a tent near the City Hotel. They paraded the town in broad daylight, with flag and fife and drum, armed with revolvers and bludgeons; and at night, when the streets were dark and unguarded, they often raided saloons and taverns, eating and drinking at the charge of the proprietors, and afterward making a wreck of stock and furniture in the very devilment of wantonness and fun.

Returning from a marauding excursion to the Contra Costa on the afternoon of Sunday, the 15th of July, they made the rounds of the town, equipped in fantastic toggery of ponchos

and Canton crape shawls, pillaged from Spanish-American and Chinese shops; and in the evening they marched upon the tents of the Chileños, cuffing and kicking the women and children, and clubbing and shooting the men, tearing down the tents, destroying their scanty furniture, and plundering them of clothing and valuables.

The limit of that criminal apathy which had so long passed for patience was reached at last. On the 16th the community of "all good citizens" met on the Plaza in response to a proclamation of Alcalde Leavenworth, who had been urged to vigorous action by a committee of merchants and others. The meeting was organized with Mr. W. D. M. Howard as chairman and Dr. Fourgeaud as secretary. Sam Brannan addressed the multitude, and denounced the "Hounds," and the whole foul herd of criminals and miscreants, in unmeasured terms. A subscription was opened for the relief of those who had suffered by the outrages of the 15th; a volunteer police force was organized, consisting of 230 special constables, armed with muskets and revolvers, and commanded by Captain W. E. Spofford; and that same afternoon twenty of the "Hounds," including Sam Roberts, their leader, were captured and lodged on board the United States ship *Warren*. On Tuesday a grand jury of twenty-four citizens found a true bill against the prisoners, who were brought to trial on Wednesday before a jury specially impaneled. Sam Roberts and his mate, Saunders, were sentenced to ten years' imprisonment with hard labor, and the others to shorter terms with fines. But these penalties were never enforced. Several of the leaders were sent out of the country, the rest were set at liberty; and although the "Hounds" were muz-

[1] San Francisco "Chronicle," September 7, 1890.

zled, other criminals and desperados, more daring and dangerous than they, were encouraged to show a bold front and strike deadlier blows. The famous Vigilance Committee of 1851, with its swift and tragic executions, was the inevitable response to the general cry for retribution and protection.[1]

The hotels of San Francisco may be regarded as the consummate product of that primitive system of coarse feeding-places which began in 1848 in the makeshifts of a mining-camp, and was developed in the growth of "saloons" and restaurants of every imaginable description: dining-rooms, chop-houses, cabarets, and fondas. There were cooks for every people and tribe under the sun — American, English, German, French, Italian, Chilean, Mexican, Chinese, Kanaka, Negro. There were beef and mutton from the ranches, fish from the bay and rivers, bear, elk, antelope, hare, squirrel, quail, duck, snipe, and plover from the inland hills and valleys, vegetables from the Pacific islands, and fruits from more distant ports. A hungry man might make a tolerable meal on beef at fifty cents, pork or mutton at seventy-five cents, a dozen canned oysters for a dollar, and a baked potato for half a dollar; or if his appetite was dainty and his pouch full, he might indulge in roast duck at five dollars, broiled quail at two dollars, and "top off" with sardines and *pâté de foie gras* regardless of expense.

Mr. Winn, the proprietor of the Fountain Head and Branch, arrived in San Francisco in 1849 without a dollar. He started business by making candy with his own hands, and peddling it about the streets on a tray slung from his shoulders by a pair of old suspenders. The San Francisco "Commercial Advertiser" of the 6th of April, 1854, notes that Mr. Winn "paid for ice and eggs last season (five months), $28,000; for one month's advertising, $1600; receipts at his two houses average $57,000 a month; has paid $200 a month for water; to one man in his employ, $1000 a month and his board; has paid $3000 for potatoes, and $5000 for eggs, for the same time; and fed poor and hungry people at a daily cost to him of $20."

The first of the San Francisco hostelries, in point of time, was the old City Hotel, which was built of adobes in 1846 at the corner of Clay and Kearney streets, and, until after the discovery of gold, was the only notable public house. Then followed, in 1849 and the succeeding years, the Parker House, the Graham

House (afterward the City Hall), the St. Francis, the Union (destroyed in the fire of May 4, 1851), the Oriental, the Tehama, Wilson's Exchange, the Rasette House, and others.

The public amusements of San Francisco may be said to have begun at the old school-house on the Plaza on the evening of June 22, 1849, when Mr. Stephen C. Massett appeared in a sort of musical monologue, with recitations and imitations. The small room was filled, "front seats" being "reserved" for the four ladies who were present. The piano used on this occasion was loaned by Mr. Harrison, the collector of the port, and was said to be the only one in California; the charge for admission was $3, and $16 was the price paid for removing the piano from the custom-house to the school-house, half-way across the

THE FIRST SCHOOL-HOUSE, SAN FRANCISCO.

Plaza. In 1849 and 1850 there were equestrian and acrobatic performances in tents,— Rowe's and Foley's circuses,— and in January, 1850, the first dramatic performance was given in Washington Hall, "The Wife" and "Charles II." being indifferently played by a small company to a large audience. In April, 1850, a French vaudeville company appeared in a neat little house on Washington street near Montgomery, and, in September following, the original Jenny Lind Theater offered its attractions over the Parker House saloon on Kearney street. This house was destroyed in the fire of May, 1851. The large brick and stone building known as the New Jenny Lind, afterward the City Hall, was opened on the 4th of October, 1851, and the American Theater on Sansome street on the 20th.[2]

The school-house on the Plaza was appropriated as a place of public worship in October,

1 See this magazine for November and December, 1891.
2 "Annals of San Francisco."

1848, the services being conducted by the Rev. Dwight Hunt, a missionary from the Sandwich Islands, who is remembered as the first Protestant clergyman in California. The little house was filled at every meeting, and on the first Sunday in January, 1849, the first Sacrament of the Lord's Supper was administered to twelve communicants of different denominations. That congregation was composed of people who were not hampered by sectarian prejudices, or concerned to cavil about creeds and forms. The steamship *California*, which arrived in February, brought four missionaries from New York — Messrs. Wheeler, Baptist, and Woodbridge, Douglass, and Willey, Presbyterians. On the 1st of April the steamer *Oregon* brought the Rev. Albert Williams, who, after preaching for a while in the school-house, on the 20th of May organized the first Protestant society in the new city, — the "First Presbyterian Church," — which was started with six members. In this small but notable group were Sarah B. Gillespie of the Presbyterian Missionary Church at Macao, China, and Mr. Frederick J. Billings, of the First Congregational Church at Woodstock, Vermont. This gentleman, by the early and earnest part he took in the moral sanitation of the city, won for himself an honorable name in her annals as a conspicuous pioneer in all good works; he was associated with General Halleck in the practice of law. The place of worship of this brave little congregation was on Dupont street in a tent that had been the marquee of a military company in Boston. This temporary accommodation was superseded in the fall of 1850 by a church edifice, complete with pulpit, pews, lamps, and bells, which was brought out from New York and set up in Stockton street near Broadway; but five months later it was burned, in the great fire of June 2, 1851. Although this represented the first religious society organized in San Francisco, it was preceded as a church edifice by the "First Baptist Church," on Washington street between Dupont and Stockton streets, erected to accommodate the congregation gathered by the Rev. O. C. Wheeler, who had arrived in the *California* in February, 1849. Then followed the "First Congregational Church," organized in July, 1849; "Trinity Church" (Episcopalian), and Grace Chapel, under the rectorship of that devoted missionary, Dr. Vermehr, who, in February, 1854, resigned the principal charge to Bishop Kip.

The early Roman Catholic "Church of St. Patrick," in Happy Valley, with its school and orphan-asylum, and those at the Mission San Dolores and in Vallejo street, were largely attended, and services were held in English, French, and Spanish. Jewish synagogues and Buddhist temples have their place in the religious history of the city, which, beginning with the Mormon elder, Sam Brannan, became in time worthy of the ministrations of Bishops Alemany and Kip; and no man did more to pilot her skittish flock to nobler heights than that brave, pertinacious, and magnetic Methodist, William Taylor, whose church was the open Plaza, and his pulpit the porch of the Old Adobe.

On the 4th of January, 1849, the "Californian," which in November, 1848, had been consolidated with the "Star," changed its name to the "Alta California." At first it appeared as a weekly, then three times a week, and finally it became the first daily paper in California. Then came in quick succession the "Journal of Commerce," the "Pacific News," and the "Daily Herald." On the 1st of August appeared the "Picayune," the fifth daily, but the first evening paper. These were followed by the "Courier," the "Chronicle," the "Bulletin," and others, including German, French, Italian, Spanish, and even Chinese newspapers, all of them marked in a greater or less degree by the ability, enterprise, pluck, and vim which are the characteristics of the country.

In describing the familiar features which should appear in a picture of the San Francisco of those golden years, the auction is not to be forgotten — that last resort of the consignee or supercargo who could find no storage for his shipment, no ready purchaser at any price. There were neither wharves nor warehouses to accommodate the overflowing freights brought by incoming fleets of merchantmen. Lighterage from ship to shore cost four dollars a ton, and the monthly rate for storage was ten dollars a ton. Perishable goods were often a total loss; cargoes were, in some cases, reshipped to the Atlantic States without breaking bulk. Excessive and indiscriminate shipments could but result in wholesale waste and recklessness, and the only relief was to be found in auctions of a slap-dash kind, conducted by any man who might see fit to put up a sign near the water-front.

At first the principal landing-place was at Clark's Point, where the water was deep at the rocky shore; but by October, 1850, there were wharves of considerable length at Market, California, Sacramento, Clay, Washington, Jackson, and Pacific streets. The aggregate length of all the wharves exceeded six thousand feet, and the cost to that date amounted to a round million.

The famous clippers which had excited the admiration of the world of men who "go down to the sea in ships" by the beauty of their lines, their buoyant grace, and their capacity to carry great spreads of canvas, were racing against time around Cape Horn to land on the wharves of San Francisco cargoes for which there might be no market, but at rates of freight that nearly paid the cost of the ship in a single run. Those were the days of the *Gray Eagle* and the *Grayhound*, the *White Squall* and the *Flying Cloud*, the *Typhoon* and the *Trade Wind*, and the *Sovereign of the Seas* — true couriers and wild riders of the main, that made the very storms their servants.

On Telegraph Hill — on the very spot where in 1847 our citizen of Yerba Buena had stood

was made in not less than seven or eight days, "fares, $30 cabin, $20 deck, and $5 extra for berths; meals on board, $2." In 1855 a good boat could make the distance in half a day.

It is usual to speak of the conflagrations which from time to time laid waste the most populous and bustling parts of San Francisco as the "great fires," because any one of them sufficed to fill the measure of a citizen's conception of ruthless devastation and dismay. There were six of them, beginning with that of Christmas Eve, 1849. Then thin boards

A LODGING-HOUSE INTERIOR.

watching the incoming of the *Brooklyn* with her dispensation of Mormons — Messrs. Sweeny and Baugh erected early in 1849 a lookout, or observatory, which commanded the approach and entrance to the Golden Gate, and by means of a code of signals kept their patrons of the city informed of the approach of vessels of every class, from coasting craft to man-of-war. At a later day a station was established nearer the ocean, which transmitted earlier intelligence by signaling the inner telegraph-house.

Until the fall of 1849 small schooners and launches had afforded the only means of navigation across the bay and up the Sacramento and San Joaquin rivers; but in September a little iron steamer called the *Pioneer* began to ply the waters of the Sacramento, and was shortly followed by the *Mint*, the steam-propeller *McKim*, and the *Senator*. At first the run

and lath, and flimsy cotton cloth, and painted canvas, were licked up like tinder by the lapping tongues of flame. The fire began in Dennison's Exchange, on the Plaza, in the early morning. That notable landmark of the Forty-niner, the Parker House, and all the buildings on Kearney street between Clay and Washington streets, were obliterated from the map of the city. It was the work of minutes, and the loss was a million. On May 4, 1850, the second great fire broke out on the site of the first, and swept away in its amazing rush and roar three entire blocks in the heart of the city. This time the loss was four millions. In the first conflagration it was the gamblers who had chiefly suffered; now it was the merchants. Six weeks later, on the 14th of June, when the wind was high, the entire district bounded by Clay and California streets, Kearney street and

FREDERICK J. BILLINGS.

the water's edge, was swept away, buildings and goods being almost totally consumed.

On the 4th of May, 1851, the anniversary of the second great fire, the city was desolated by a conflagration which is remembered as *the* great fire. It made a jest and mock of "fire-proof" buildings, and iron frames and doors and shutters curled up in the flames like card-board. It began late on the night of the 3d, in a store on the south side of the Plaza. The wind rose with the flames, and whirled them south and north; the streets beneath the planking became great flues; the whole business part of the city was a roaring furnace; and the reflection is said to have been visible in the sky at Monterey, a hundred miles away. Ten hours sufficed for the destruction of nearly two thousand houses; eighteen whole squares, with portions of five others, in the most important part of the city, were almost totally obliterated, and the loss was estimated at $12,-000,000. On what had been the streets, men said, "Well, the bay is here, and the people are here, and the placers are left!" And they went straightway to work and built a new city, richer, stronger, handsomer than before. Hittell says of these fires that they exercised an important influence upon the politics and trade of the city. "The fire of May, 1851, was attributed to incendiarism. The amount of property exposed in the streets was so great that the citizens banded themselves into a committee of vigilance, which soon extended its jurisdiction and hanged murderers as well as protected property. Merchants put their goods into store-ships, and the harbor was filled with old hulks until 1854, when brick stores, really fire-proof, began to furnish room and safety on shore. Unable to make bricks or cut stone except at terrific cost, orders were sent abroad for incombustible building materials. Granite was brought from China or from Quincy, lava from Honolulu, and bricks from Sydney, London, and New York." Out of the ruin and waste sprang new life, new forces, higher hopes, and nobler endeavors.

By 1852 the characteristics of a Spanish town had well-nigh disappeared from San Francisco. From Clark's Point to the Rincon, all had become American. The jingling ranchero, ostentatiously sombrero'd and bespurred, had been superseded by equipages familiar in the Eastern cities; omnibuses plied between the Plaza and the Mission; the "steam paddy" was busy in Happy Valley; and the sand-hills at the back of the town were being dumped into the water-lots in front. The city was moving bayward, and new streets were growing upon piles. "Where once floated ships of a thousand tons, now were great tenements of brick securely founded in the solid earth."

The sleepy little Yerba Buena of 1847 had become a metropolis of factories and great stores, of schools and churches, of newspapers and theaters, of benevolent institutions and public works, of stage-coaches and mails, expresses and steamers; a city of brilliant bustle and magnificent dissipations. But a dollar was no longer paid for a pill, nor ten dollars for an ounce of carpet-tacks; for everybody was trying to sell, and everywhere was glut in spite of the ravenous extravagance and waste. Auctioneers tossed off ship-loads of merchandise for a song, and the enormous loss fell upon the foreign shippers; so "happy-go-lucky" was the temper of the hour, and a canter to the Presidio or the Mission, or a picnic excursion to the Contra Costa, was the usual diversion in the intervals of business.

In August, 1850, the Society of California Pioneers was called into being, mainly through the influence and efforts of Messrs. Howard, Brannan, Bryant, Wadsworth, Folsom, and others; and its first appearance as a civic organization, preceding all others in California, was in the public obsequies appointed to honor the memory of President Zachary Taylor, on the 29th of that month. The officers first

invested all his means in the sterile sand-lots of Yerba Buena, and waited for the coming of the great city he foresaw.

The records of that parent society were destroyed in the great fire of May, 1851, with the exception of one book containing the constitution and the signatures of a few members. The officers, who had been chosen to serve a twelve-month, were compelled by the exigencies of that memorable period of disaster, danger, and turmoil to hold their respective places for three years; but in the imposing demonstration by which the admission of California into the Union of States was celebrated on the 29th of October, 1850, the Society of Pioneers appeared in force, and made a conspicuous impression by their moral and intellectual prestige. On the 6th of July, 1853, the association, which owing to the local troubles had so long been unable to meet, was reorganized at the Oriental Hotel, when Mr. Brannan was elected president; Messrs. Larkin, Snyder, and Lippincott, vice-presidents; and William Tecumseh Sherman, treasurer. The society as at present constituted is a social and benevolent, as well as a historical, scientific, and

DENNISON'S EXCHANGE AND PARKER HOUSE, BEFORE THE FIRE OF DECEMBER, 1849.

elected were Messrs. Howard, president; Brannan and Snyder, vice-presidents; Bryant, Parker, Folsom, and Wadsworth, secretaries; and Talbot H. Green, treasurer. Among these associated pioneers Captain Folsom was a conspicuous figure. He came to California as a staff-officer in the quartermaster's department of Stevenson's regiment, and was eventually made chief of that department on the North Pacific coast. With notable foresight, long before the apparition of the golden wizard, he

literary association; and its objects are to collect and preserve information relating to the early settlement and subsequent history of the country, and "in all appropriate matters to advance the interests and perpetuate the memory of those whose sagacity and enterprise induced them to settle in the wilderness and become the founders of a new State."

In the impressive list of honorary members and distinguished guests who in the past have imparted distinction to the meetings of this

PHOTOGRAPHED BY TABER.

CAPTAIN J. L. FOLSOM.

most interesting association are to be found the names of Generals Sherman, Rosecrans, Wool, Frémont, Halleck, Schofield, Sutter, and Vallejo, and the Revs. Henry W. Bellows and Thomas Starr King.

Originally it was a condition of membership that the applicant should have arrived in California prior to the 1st of January, 1850; but the constitution has since been amended so as to admit the sons of pioneers.

John Williamson Palmer.

15

Ranch Life in the Far West

Theodore Roosevelt

THE CENTURY MAGAZINE.

FEBRUARY, 1888.

RANCH LIFE IN THE FAR WEST.

IN THE CATTLE COUNTRY.

ILLUSTRATIONS BY FREDERIC REMINGTON.

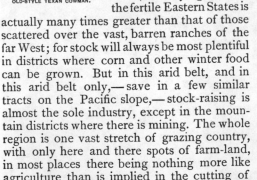

OLD-STYLE TEXAN COWMAN.

THE great grazing lands of the West lie in what is known as the arid belt, which stretches from British America on the north to Mexico on the south, through the middle of the United States. It includes New Mexico, part of Arizona, Colorado, Wyoming, Montana, and the western portion of Texas, Kansas, Nebraska, and Dakota. It must not be understood by this that more cattle are to be found here than elsewhere, for the contrary is true, it being a fact often lost sight of that the number of cattle raised on the small, thick-lying farms of the fertile Eastern States is actually many times greater than that of those scattered over the vast, barren ranches of the far West; for stock will always be most plentiful in districts where corn and other winter food can be grown. But in this arid belt, and in this arid belt only,—save in a few similar tracts on the Pacific slope,—stock-raising is almost the sole industry, except in the mountain districts where there is mining. The whole region is one vast stretch of grazing country, with only here and there spots of farm-land, in most places there being nothing more like agriculture than is implied in the cutting of some tons of wild hay or the planting of a gar-

den patch for home use. This is especially true of the northern portion of the region, which comprises the basin of the Upper Missouri, and with which alone I am familiar. Here there are no fences to speak of, and all the land north of the Black Hills and the Big Horn Mountains and between the Rockies and the Dakota wheat-fields might be spoken of as one gigantic, unbroken pasture, where cowboys and branding-irons take the place of fences.

The country throughout this great Upper Missouri basin has a wonderful sameness of character; and the rest of the arid belt, lying to the southward, is closely akin to it in its main features. A traveler seeing it for the first time is especially struck by its look of parched, barren desolation; he can with difficulty believe that it will support cattle at all. It is a region of light rainfall; the grass is short and comparatively scanty; there is no timber except along the beds of the streams, and in many places there are alkali deserts where nothing grows but sage-brush and cactus. Now the land stretches out into level, seemingly endless plains or into rolling prairies; again it is broken by abrupt hills and deep, winding valleys; or else it is crossed by chains of buttes, usually bare, but often clad with a dense growth of dwarfed pines or gnarled, stunted cedars. The muddy rivers run in broad, shallow beds, which after heavy rainfalls are filled to the brim by the swollen torrents, while in droughts the larger streams dwindle into sluggish trickles of clearer water, and the smaller ones dry up entirely, but in occasional deep pools.

All through the region, except on the great

Indian reservation, there has been a scanty and sparse settlement, quite peculiar in its character. In the forest the woodchopper comes first; on the fertile prairies the granger is the pioneer; but on the long stretching uplands of the far West it is the men who guard and follow the horned herds that prepare the way for the settlers who come after. The high plains of the Upper Missouri and its tributary rivers were first opened, and are still held, by the stockmen, and the whole civilization of the region has received the stamp of their marked and individual characteristics. They were from the South, not from the East, although many men from the latter region came out along the great transcontinental railway lines and joined them in their northern migration.

They were not dwellers in towns, and from the nature of their industry lived as far apart from each other as possible. In choosing new ranges, old cow-hands, who are also seasoned plainsmen, are invariably sent ahead, perhaps a year in advance, to spy out the land and pick the best places. One of these may go by himself, or more often, especially if they have to penetrate little known or entirely unknown tracts, two or three will go together, the owner or manager of the herd himself being one of them. Perhaps their herds may already be on the border of the wild and uninhabited country: in that case they may have to take but a few days' journey before finding the stretches of sheltered, long-grass land that they seek. For instance, when I wished to move my own elkhorn steer brand on to a new ranch I had to spend barely a week in traveling north among the Little Missouri Bad Lands before finding what was then untrodden ground far outside the range of any of my neighbors' cattle. But if a large outfit is going to shift its quarters it must go much farther; and both the necessity and the

AN EXPLORING OUTFIT.

AN EPISODE IN THE OPENING UP OF A CATTLE COUNTRY.

THE MIDDAY MEAL.

chance for long wanderings were especially great when the final overthrow of the northern Horse Indians opened the whole Upper Missouri basin at one sweep to the stockmen. Then the advance-guards or explorers, each on one horse and leading another with food and bedding, were often absent months at a time, threading their way through the trackless wastes of plain, plateau, and river-bottom. If possible they would choose a country that would be good for winter and summer alike; but often this could not be done, and then they would try to find a well-watered tract on which the cattle could be summered, and from which they could be driven in fall to their sheltered winter range—for the cattle in winter eat snow, and an entirely waterless region, if broken, and with good pasturage, is often the best possible winter ground, as it is sure not to have been eaten off at all during the summer, while in the bottom the grass is always cropped down soonest. Many outfits regularly shift their herds every spring and fall; but with us in the Bad Lands all we do, when cold weather sets in, is to drive our beasts off the scantily grassed river-bottom

back ten miles or more among the broken buttes and plateaux of the uplands to where the brown hay, cured on the stalk, stands thick in the winding *coulées*.

These lookouts or forerunners having returned, the herds are set in motion as early in the spring as may be, so as to get on the ground in time to let the travel-worn beasts rest and gain flesh before winter sets in. Each herd is accompanied by a dozen, or a score, or a couple of score, of cowboys, according to its size, and beside it rumble and jolt the heavy four-horse wagons that hold the food and bedding of the men and the few implements they will need at the end of their journey. As long as possible they follow the trails made by the herds that have already traveled in the same direction, and when these end they strike out for themselves. In the Upper Missouri basin, the pioneer herds soon had to scatter out and each find its own way among the great dreary solitudes, creeping carefully along so that the cattle might not be overdriven and might have water at the halting-places. An outfit might thus be months on its lonely journey, slowly making its way over melancholy, pathless plains, or down the valleys of the lonely rivers. It was tedious, harassing work, as the weary cattle had to be driven carefully and quietly during the day and strictly guarded at night, with a perpetual watch kept for Indians or white horse-thieves. Often they would skirt the edges of the streams for days at a time, seeking for a ford or a good swimming crossing, and if the water was up and the quicksand deep the danger to the riders was serious and the risk of loss among the cattle very great.

At last, after days of excitement and danger and after months of weary, monotonous toil, the chosen ground is reached and the

by several yoke of oxen, or perhaps by six or eight mules. To guard against the numerous mishaps of prairie travel, two or three of these prairie schooners usually go together, the brawny teamsters, known either as "bull-whackers" or as "mule-skinners," stalking beside their slow-moving teams.

The small outlying camps are often tents, or mere dug-outs in the ground. But at the main ranch there will be a cluster of log buildings, including a separate cabin for the foreman or ranchman; often another in which to cook and eat; a long house for the men to sleep in; stables, sheds, a blacksmith's shop, etc.,— the whole group forming quite a little settle-

THE OUTLYING CAMP.

final camp pitched. The footsore animals are turned loose to shift for themselves, outlying camps of two or three men each being established to hem them in. Meanwhile the primitive ranch-house, out-buildings, and corrals are built, the unhewn cottonwood logs being chinked with moss and mud, while the roofs are of branches covered with dirt, spades and axes being the only tools needed for the work. Bunks, chairs, and tables are all home-made, and as rough as the houses they are in. The supplies of coarse, rude food are carried perhaps two or three hundred miles from the nearest town, either in the ranch-wagons or else by some regular freighting outfit, whose huge canvas-topped prairie schooners are each drawn

ment, with the corrals, the stacks of natural hay, and the patches of fenced land for gardens or horse pastures. This little settlement may be situated right out in the treeless, nearly level open, but much more often is placed in the partly wooded bottom of a creek or river, sheltered by the usual background of somber brown hills.

When the northern plains began to be settled, such a ranch would at first be absolutely alone in the wilderness, but others of the same sort were sure soon to be established within twenty or thirty miles on one side or the other. The lives of the men in such places were strangely cut off from the outside world, and, indeed, the same is true to a hardly less extent at the present day. Sometimes the wagons are sent for provisions, and the beef-steers are at stated times driven off for shipment. Parties of hunters and trappers call now and then. More rarely small bands of emigrants go by in search of new homes, impelled by the restless, aimless craving for change so deeply grafted in the breast of the American borderer: the white-topped wagons are loaded with domestic goods, with sallow, dispirited-looking women, and with tow-headed children; while the gaunt, moody frontiermen slouch alongside, rifle on shoulder, lank, homely, uncouth, and yet with a curious suggestion of grim strength underlying it all. Or cowboys from neighboring ranches will ride over, looking for lost horses, or seeing if their cattle have strayed off the range. But this is all. Civilization seems as remote as if we were living in an age long past. The whole existence is patriarchal in character: it is the life of men who live in the open, who tend their herds on horseback, who go armed and ready to guard their lives by their own prowess, whose wants are very simple, and who call no man master. Ranching is an occupation like those of vigorous, primitive pastoral peoples, having little in common with the humdrum, workaday business world of the nineteenth century; and the free ranchman in his manner of life shows more kinship to an Arab sheik than to a sleek city merchant or tradesman.

By degrees the country becomes what in a stock-raising region passes for well settled. In addition to the great ranches smaller ones are established, with a few hundred, or even a few score, head of cattle apiece; and now and then miserable farmers straggle in to fight a losing and desperate battle with drought, cold, and grasshoppers. The wheels of the heavy wagons, driven always over the same course from one ranch to another, or to the remote frontier towns from which they get their goods, wear ruts in the soil, and roads are soon formed, perhaps originally following the deep trails made by the vanished buffalo. These roads lead down the river-bottoms or along the crests of the divides or else strike out fairly across the prairie, and a man may sometimes travel a hundred miles along one without coming to a house or camp of any sort. If they lead to a shipping point whence the beeves are sent to market, the cattle, traveling in single file, will have worn many and deep paths on each side of the wheel-marks; and the roads between important places which are regularly used either by the United States Government, by stage-coach lines, or by freight teams become deeply worn

landmarks — as, for instance, near us, the Deadwood and the old Fort Keogh trails.

Cattle-ranching can only be carried on in its present form while the population is scanty; and so in stock-raising regions, pure and simple, there are usually few towns, and these are almost always at the shipping points for cattle. But, on the other hand, wealthy cattlemen, like miners who have done well, always spend their money freely; and accordingly towns like Denver, Cheyenne, and Helena, where these two classes are the most influential in the community, are far pleasanter places of residence than cities of five times their population in the exclusively agricultural States to the eastward.

A true "cow town" is worth seeing, — such a one as Miles City, for instance, especially at the time of the annual meeting of the great Montana Stock-raisers' Association. Then the whole place is full to overflowing, the importance of the meeting and the fun of the attendant frolics, especially the horse-races, drawing from the surrounding ranch country many hundreds of men of every degree, from the rich stock-owner worth his millions to the ordinary cowboy who works for forty dollars a month. It would be impossible to imagine a more typically American assemblage, for although there are always a certain number of foreigners, usually English, Irish, or German, yet they have become completely Americanized; and on the whole it would be difficult to gather a finer body of men, in spite of their numerous shortcomings. The ranch-owners differ more from each other than do the cowboys; and the former certainly compare very favorably with similar classes of capitalists in the East. Anything more foolish than the demagogic outcry against "cattle kings" it would be difficult to imagine. Indeed, there are very few businesses so absolutely legitimate as stock-raising and so beneficial to the nation at large; and a successful stock-grower must not only be shrewd, thrifty, patient, and enterprising, but he must also possess qualities of personal bravery, hardihood, and self-reliance to a degree not demanded in the least by any mercantile occupation in a community long settled. Stockmen are in the West the pioneers of civilization, and their daring and adventurousness make the after settlement of the region possible. The whole country owes them a great debt.

The most successful ranchmen are those, usually South-westerners, who have been bred to the business and have grown up with it; but many Eastern men, including not a few college graduates, have also done excellently by devoting their whole time and energy to their work, — although Easterners who invest their money in cattle without knowing anything of the business, or who trust all to their subordinates, are naturally enough likely to incur heavy losses. Stockmen are learning more and more to act together; and certainly the meetings of their associations are conducted with a dignity and good sense that would do credit to any parliamentary body.

during their long drives with every kind of team, through every kind of country, and in every kind of weather, who, proud of their really wonderful skill as reinsmen and conscious of their high standing in any frontier community, look down on and sneer at the plodding teamsters; trappers and wolfers, whose business is to poison wolves, with shaggy, knock-kneed

A ROW IN A CATTLE TOWN.

But the cowboys resemble one another much more and outsiders much less than is the case even with their employers, the ranchmen. A town in the cattle country, when for some cause it is thronged with men from the neighborhood round about, always presents a picturesque sight on the wooden sidewalks of the broad, dusty streets. The men who ply the various industries known only to frontier existence jostle one another as they saunter to and fro or lounge lazily in front of the straggling, cheap-looking board houses: hunters, in their buckskin shirts and fur caps, greasy and unkempt, but with resolute faces and sullen, watchful eyes, that are ever on the alert; teamsters, surly and self-contained, with slouch hats and great cowhide boots; stage-drivers, their faces seamed by hardship and exposure

ponies to carry their small bales and bundles of furs—beaver, wolf, fox, and occasionally otter; silent sheep-herders, with cast-down faces, never able to forget the absolute solitude and monotony of their dreary lives, nor to rid their minds of the thought of the woolly idiots they pass all their days in tending,— these are the men who have come to town, either on business or else to frequent the flaunting saloons and gaudy hells of all kinds in search of the coarse, vicious excitement that in the minds of many of them does duty as pleasure, the only form of pleasure they have ever had a chance to know. Indians too, wrapped in blankets and with stolid, emotionless faces, stalk silently round among the whites, or join in the gambling and horse-racing. If the town is on the borders of the mountain country, there will also be sinewy lumbermen, rough-looking miners and packers, whose business it is to guide the long mule trains that go where wagons can not and whose work in packing needs special and peculiar skill; and mingled with and drawn from all these classes are desperadoes of every grade, from the gambler up through the horse-thief to the murderous professional bully, or, as he is locally called, "bad man"—now, however, a much less conspicuous object than formerly.

But everywhere among these plainsmen and mountain-men, and more important than any, are the cowboys,—the men who follow the calling that has brought such towns into being. Singly, or in twos or threes, they gallop their wiry little horses down the street, their lithe, supple figures erect or swaying slightly as they sit loosely in the saddle; while their stirrups are so long that their knees are hardly bent, the bridles not taut enough to keep the chains from clanking. They are smaller and less muscular than the wielders of ax and pick; but they are as hardy and self-reliant as any men who ever breathed—with bronzed, set faces, and keen eyes that look all the world straight in the face without flinching as they flash out from under the broad-brimmed hats. Peril and hardship, and years of long toil broken by weeks of brutal dissipation, draw haggard lines across their eager faces, but never dim their reckless eyes nor break their bearing of defiant self-confidence. They do not walk well, partly because they so rarely do any work out of the saddle, partly because their *chaperajos* or leather overalls hamper them when on the ground; but their appearance is striking for all that, and picturesque too, with their jingling spurs, the big revolvers stuck in their belts, and bright silk handkerchiefs knotted loosely round their necks over the open collars of the flannel shirts. When drunk on the villainous whisky of the frontier towns, they cut mad antics, riding their horses into the saloons, firing their pistols right and left, from boisterous lightheartedness rather than from any viciousness, and indulging too often in deadly shooting affrays, brought on either by the accidental contact of the moment or on account of some long-standing grudge, or perhaps because of bad blood between two ranches or localities; but except while on such sprees they are quiet, rather self-contained men, perfectly frank and simple, and on their own ground treat a stranger with the most whole-souled hospitality, doing all in their power for him and scorning to take any reward in return. Although prompt to resent an injury, they are not at all apt to be rude to outsiders, treating them with what can almost be called a grave courtesy. They are

much better fellows and pleasanter companions than small farmers or agricultural laborers; nor are the mechanics and workmen of a great city to be mentioned in the same breath.

The bulk of the cowboys themselves are South-westerners; but there are also many from the Eastern and the Northern States, who if they begin young do quite as well as the Southerner. The best hands are fairly bred to the work and follow it from their youth up. Nothing can be more foolish than for an Easterner to think he can become a cowboy in a few months' time. Many a young fellow comes out hot with enthusiasm for life on the plains, only to learn that his clumsiness is greater than he could have believed possible; that the cowboy business is like any other and has to be learned by serving a painful apprenticeship; and that this apprenticeship implies the endurance of rough fare, hard living, dirt, exposure of every kind, no little toil, and month after month of the dullest monotony. For cowboy work there is need of special traits and special training, and young Easterners should be sure of themselves before trying it: the struggle for existence is very keen in the far West, and it is no place for men who lack the ruder, coarser virtues and physical qualities, no matter how intellectual or how refined and delicate their sensibilities. Such are more likely to fail there than in older communities. Probably during the past few years more than half of the young Easterners who have come West with a little money to learn the cattle business have failed signally and lost what they had in the beginning. The West, especially the far West, needs men who have been bred on the farm or in the workshop far more than it does clerks or college graduates.

Some of the cowboys are Mexicans, who generally do the actual work well enough, but are not trustworthy; moreover, they are always regarded with extreme disfavor by the Texans in an outfit, among whom the intolerant caste spirit is very strong. Southern-born whites will never work under them, and look down upon all colored or half-caste races. One spring I had with my wagon a Pueblo Indian, an excellent rider and roper, but a drunken, worthless, lazy devil; and in the summer of 1886 there were with us a Sioux half-breed, a quiet, hard-working, faithful fellow, and a mulatto, who was one of the best cow-hands in the whole round-up.

Cowboys, like most Westerners, occasionally show remarkable versatility in their tastes and pursuits. One whom I know has abandoned his regular occupation for the past nine months, during which time he has been in succession a bartender, a school-teacher,

COWBOY FUN.

and a probate judge! Another, whom I once employed for a short while, had passed through even more varied experiences, including those of a barber, a sailor, an apothecary, and a buffalo-hunter.

As a rule the cowboys are known to each other only by their first names, with, perhaps, as a prefix, the title of the brand for which they are working. Thus I remember once over-hearing a casual remark to the effect that "Bar Y Harry" had married "the seven Open A girl," the latter being the daughter of a neighboring ranchman. Often they receive nicknames, as, for instance, Dutch Wannigan, Windy Jack, and Kid Williams, all of whom are on the list of my personal acquaintances.

No man traveling through or living in the country need fear molestation from the cowboys unless he himself accompanies them on their drinking-bouts, or in other ways plays the fool, for they are, with us at any rate, very good fellows, and the most determined and effective foes of real law-breakers, such as horse and cattle thieves, murderers, etc. Few of the outrages quoted in Eastern papers as their handiwork are such in reality, the average Easterner apparently considering every individual who wears a broad hat and carries a six-shooter a cowboy. These outrages are, as

IN A BOG-HOLE.

a rule, the work of the roughs and criminals who always gather on the outskirts of civilization and who infest every frontier town until the decent citizens become sufficiently numerous and determined to take the law into their own hands and drive them out. The old buffalo-hunters, who formed a distinct class, became powerful forces for evil once they had destroyed the vast herds of mighty beasts whose pursuit had been their means of livelihood. They were absolutely shiftless and improvident; they had no settled habits; they were inured to peril and hardship, but entirely unaccustomed to steady work; and so they afforded just the materials from which to make the bolder and more desperate kinds of criminals. When the game was gone they hung round the settlements for some little time, and then many of them naturally took to horse-stealing, cattle-killing, and highway robbery, although others, of course, went into honest pursuits. They were men who died off rapidly, however; for it is curious to see how many of these plainsmen, in spite of their iron nerves and thews, have their constitutions completely undermined, as much by the terrible hardships they have endured as by the fits of prolonged and bestial revelry with which they have varied them.

The "bad men," or professional fighters and man-killers, are of a different stamp, quite a number of them being, according to their light, perfectly honest. These are the men who do most of the killing in frontier communities; yet it is a noteworthy fact that the men who are killed generally deserve their fate. These men are, of course, used to brawling, and are not only sure shots, but, what is equally important, able to "draw" their weapons with marvelous quickness. They think nothing whatever of murder, and are the dread and terror of their associates; yet they are very chary of taking the life of a man of good standing, and will often weaken and back down at once if confronted fearlessly. With many of them their courage arises from confidence in their own powers and knowledge of the fear in which they are held; and men of this type often show the white feather when they get in a tight place. Others, however, will face any odds without flinching. On the other hand, I have known of these men fighting, when mortally wounded, with a cool, ferocious despair that was terrible. As elsewhere, so here, very quiet men are often those who in an emergency show themselves best able to hold their own. These desperadoes always try to "get the drop" on a foe — that is, to take him at a disadvantage before he can use his own weapon. I have known more men killed in this way, when the affair was wholly one-sided, than I have known to be shot in fair fight; and I have known fully as many who were shot by accident. It is wonderful, in the event of a street-fight, how few bullets seem to hit the men they are aimed at.

During the last two or three years the stockmen have united to put down all these dangerous characters, often by the most summary exercise of lynch law. Notorious bullies and murderers have been taken out and hung, while the bands of horse and cattle thieves have been regularly hunted down and destroyed in pitched fights by parties of armed

ern Montana shot or hung nearly sixty — not, however, with the best judgment in all cases.

A stranger in the North-western cattle country is especially struck by the resemblance the settlers show in their pursuits and habits to the Southern people. Nebraska and Dakota, east of the Missouri, resemble Minnesota and Iowa and the States farther east, but Montana and the Dakota cow country show more kinship with Texas; for while elsewhere in America settlement has advanced along the parallels of latitude, on the great plains it has followed the meridians of longitude and has gone northerly rather than westerly. The business is carried on as it is in the South. The rough-rider of the plains, the hero of rope and revolver, is first cousin to the backwoodsman of the southern Alleghanies, the man of the ax and

Frederic Remington '87

PULLING A COW OUT OF THE MUD.

the rifle; he is only a unique offshoot of the frontier stock of the South-west. The very term "round-up" is used by the cowboys in the exact sense in which it is employed by the hill people and mountaineers of Kentucky, Tennessee, and North Carolina, with whom also labor is dear and poor land cheap, and whose few cattle are consequently branded and turned loose in the woods exactly as is done with the great herds on the plains.

But the ranching industry itself was copied from the Mexicans, of whose land and herds the South-western frontiermen of Texas took forcible possession; and the traveler in the North-west will see at a glance that the terms and practices of our business are largely of Spanish origin. The cruel curb-bit and heavy stock-saddle, with its high horn and cantle, prove that we have adopted Spanish-American horse-gear; and the broad hat, huge blunt spurs, and leather *chaperajos* of the rider, as well as the corral in which the stock are penned, all alike show the same ancestry. Throughout the cattle country east of the Rocky Mountains, from the Rio Grande to the Saskatch-

cowboys; and as a consequence most of our territory is now perfectly law-abiding. One such fight occurred north of me early last spring. The horse-thieves were overtaken on the banks of the Missouri; two of their number were slain, and the others were driven on the ice, which broke, and two more were drowned. A few months previously another gang, whose headquarters were near the Canadian line, were surprised in their hut; two or three were shot down by the cowboys as they tried to come out, while the rest barricaded themselves in and fought until the great log-hut was set on fire, when they broke forth in a body, and nearly all were killed at once, only one or two making their escape. A little over a year ago one committee of vigilantes in east-

ewan, the same terms are in use and the same system is followed; but on the Pacific slope, in California, there are certain small differences, even in nomenclature. Thus, we of the great plains all use the double *cincha* saddle, with one girth behind the horse's fore legs and another farther back, while Californians prefer one with a single *cincha*, which seems to us much inferior for stock-work. Again, Californians use the Spanish word "lasso," which with us has been entirely dropped, no plainsman with pre-

or quite as highly as good horsemanship, and is much rarer. Once a cowboy is a good roper and rider, the only other accomplishment he values is skill with his great army revolver, it being taken for granted that he is already a thorough plainsman and has long mastered the details of cattle-work; for the best roper and rider alive is of little use unless he is hard-working, honest, keenly alive to his employer's interest, and very careful in the management of the cattle.

A DISPUTE OVER A BRAND.

tensions to the title thinking of any word but "rope," either as noun or verb.

The rope, whether leather lariat or made of grass, is the one essential feature of every cowboy's equipment. Loosely coiled, it hangs from the horn or is tied to one side of the saddle in front of the thigh, and is used for every conceivable emergency, a twist being taken round the stout saddle-horn the second the noose settles over the neck or around the legs of a chased animal. In helping pull a wagon up a steep pitch, in dragging an animal by the horns out of a bog-hole, in hauling up logs for the fire, and in a hundred other ways aside from its legitimate purpose, the rope is of invaluable service, and dexterity with it is prized almost

All cowboys can handle the rope with more or less ease and precision, but great skill in its use is only attained after long practice, and for its highest development needs that the man should have begun in earliest infancy. A really first-class roper can command his own price, and is usually fit for little but his own special work.

It is much the same with riding. The cowboy is an excellent rider in his own way, but his way differs from that of a trained school horseman or cross-country fox-hunter as much as it does from the horsemanship of an Arab or of a Sioux Indian, and, as with all these, it has its special merits and special defects — schoolman, fox-hunter, cowboy, Arab, and

Indian being all alike admirable riders in their respective styles, and each cherishing the same profound and ignorant contempt for every method but his own. The flash riders, or horse-breakers, always called " bronco busters," can perform really marvelous feats, riding with ease the most vicious and unbroken beasts, that no ordinary cowboy would dare to tackle. Although sitting seemingly so loose in the saddle, such a rider cannot be jarred out of it by the wildest plunger, it being a favorite feat to sit out the antics of a bucking horse with silver half-dollars under each knee or in the stirrups under each foot. But their method of breaking is very rough, consisting only in sad-dling and bridling a beast by main force and then riding him, also by main force, until he is exhausted, when he is turned over as " broken." Later on the cowboy himself may train his horse to stop or wheel instantly at a touch of the reins or bit, to start at top speed at a signal, and to stand motionless when left. An intelligent pony soon picks up a good deal of knowledge about the cow busi-ness on his own account.

All cattle are branded, usually on the hip, shoulder, and side, or on any one of them, with letters, numbers, or figures, in every com-bination, the outfit being known by its brand. Near me, for instance, are the Three Sevens, the Thistle, the Bellows, the OX, the VI., the Sev-enty-six Bar (⁷⁶), and the Quarter Circle Dia-mond (◇) outfits. The dew-lap and the ears may also be cut, notched, or slit. All brands are registered, and are thus protected against imi-tators, any man tampering with them being punished as severely as possible. Unbranded animals are called *mavericks*, and when found on the round-up are either branded by the owner of the range on which they are, or else are sold for the benefit of the association. At every shipping point, as well as where the beef cattle are received, there are stock in-spectors who jealously examine all the brands on the live animals or on the hides of the slaughtered ones, so as to detect any foul play, which is immediately reported to the associa-tion. It becomes second nature with a cow-boy to inspect and note the brands of every bunch of animals he comes across.

Perhaps the thing that seems strangest to the traveler who for the first time crosses the bleak plains of this Upper Missouri grazing country is the small number of cattle seen. He can hardly believe he is in the great stock region, where for miles upon miles he will not see a single head, and will then come only upon a straggling herd of a few score. As a matter of fact, where there is no artificial food put up for winter use cattle always need a good deal of ground per head; and this is peculiarly the case with us in the North-west, where much of the ground is bare of vegetation and where what pasture there is is both short and sparse. It is a matter of absolute necessity, where beasts are left to shift for themselves in the open during the bitter winter weather, that they then should have grass that they have not cropped too far down; and to insure this it is necessary with us to allow on the average about twenty-five acres of ground to each animal. This means that a range of coun-try ten miles square will keep between two and three thousand head of stock only, and if more are put on, it is at the risk of seeing a severe winter kill off half or three-quarters of the whole number. So a range may be in re-ality overstocked when to an Eastern and un-practiced eye it seems hardly to have on it a number worth taking into account.

Overstocking is the great danger threaten-ing the stock-raising industry on the plains. This industry has only risen to be of more than local consequence during the past score of years, as before that time it was confined to Texas and California; but during these two decades of its existence the stockmen in dif-ferent localities have again and again suffered the most ruinous losses, usually with over-stocking as the ultimate cause. In the south the drought, and in the north the deep snows, and everywhere unusually bad winters, do im-mense damage; still, if the land is fitted for stock at all, they will, averaging one year with another, do very well so long as the feed is not cropped down too close.

But, of course, no amount of feed will make some countries worth anything for cattle that are not housed during the winter; and stock-men in choosing new ranges for their herds pay almost as much attention to the capacity of the land for yielding shelter as they do to the abundant and good quality of the grass. High up among the foot-hills of the mountains cattle will not live through the winter; and an open, rolling prairie land of heavy rainfall, and where in consequence the snow lies deep and there is no protection from the furious cold winds, is useless for winter grazing, no matter how thick and high the feed. The three es-sentials for a range are grass, water, and shel-ter: the water is only needed in summer and the shelter in winter, while it may be doubted if drought during the hot months has ever killed off more cattle than have died in con-sequence of exposure on shelterless ground to the icy weather, lasting from November to April.

The finest summer range may be valueless either on account of its lack of shelter or be-cause it is in a region of heavy snowfall — por-tions of territory lying in the same latitude

BRONCO BUSTERS SADDLING.

and not very far apart often differing widely in this respect. This loss, of course, had nothing to do with overstocking; and the same was true of the loss that visited the few herds which spent the very hard winter of 1880 on the northern cattle plains. These were the pioneers of their kind, and the grass was all that could be desired; yet the extraordinary severity of the weather proved too much for the cattle. This was especially the case with those herds consisting of "pilgrims," as they are called—that is, of animals driven up on to the range from the south, and therefore in poor condition. One such herd of pilgrims on the Powder River suffered a loss of thirty-six hundred out of a total of four thousand, and the survivors kept alive only by browsing on the tops of cottonwoods felled for them. Even seasoned animals fared very badly. One great herd in the Yellowstone Valley lost about a fourth of its number, the loss falling mainly on the breeding cows, calves, and bulls,— always the chief sufferers, as the steers, and also the dry cows, will get through almost anything. The loss here would have been far heavier than it was had it not been for a curious trait shown by the cattle. They kept in bands of several hundred each, and during the time of the deep snows a band would make a start and travel several miles in a straight line, plowing their way through the drifts and beating out a broad track; then, when stopped by a frozen watercourse or chain of buttes, they would turn back and graze over the trail thus made, the only place where they could get at the grass.

A drenching rain, followed by a severe snap of cold, is even more destructive than deep snow, for the saturated coats of the poor beasts are turned into sheets of icy mail, and the grass-blades, frozen at the roots as well as above, change into sheaves of brittle spears as uneatable as so many icicles. Entire herds have perished in consequence of such a storm. Mere cold, however, will kill only very weak animals, which is fortunate for us, as the spirit in the thermometer during winter often sinks to fifty degrees below zero, the cold being literally arctic; yet though the cattle become thin during such a snap of weather, and sometimes have their ears, tails, and even horns frozen off, they nevertheless rarely die from the cold alone. But if there is a blizzard blowing in at such a time, the cattle need shelter, and if caught in the open, will travel for scores of miles before the storm, until they reach a break in the ground, or some stretch of dense woodland, which will shield them from the blasts. If cattle traveling in this manner come to some obstacle that they can not pass, as, for instance, a wire fence or a steep railway embankment,

they will not try to make their way back against the storm, but will simply stand with their tails to it until they drop dead in their tracks; and, accordingly, in some parts of the country— but luckily far to the south of us— the railways are fringed with countless skeletons of beasts that have thus perished, while many of the long wire fences make an almost equally bad showing. In some of the very open country of Kansas and Indian Territory, many of the herds during the past two years have suffered a loss of from sixty to eighty per cent., although this was from a variety of causes, including drought as well as severe winter weather. Too much rain is quite as bad as too little, especially if it falls after the 1st of August, for then, though the growth of grass is very rank and luxuriant, it yet has little strength and does not cure well on the stalk; and it is only possible to winter cattle at large at all because of the way in which the grass turns into natural hay by this curing on the stalk.

But scantiness of food, due to overstocking, is the one really great danger to us in the north, who do not have to fear the droughts that occasionally devastate portions of the southern ranges. In a fairly good country, if the feed is plenty, the natural increase of a herd is sure shortly to repair any damage that may be done by an unusually severe winter— unless, indeed, the latter should be one such as occurs but two or three times in a century. When, however, the grass becomes cropped down, then the loss in even an ordinary year is heavy among the weaker animals, and if the winter is at all severe it becomes simply appalling. The snow covers the shorter grass much quicker, and even when there is enough, the cattle, weak and unfit to travel around, have to work hard to get it by exertion tending to enfeeble them and render them less able to cope with the exposure and cold. Again, the grass is, of course, soonest eaten off where there is shelter; and, accordingly, the broken ground to which the animals cling during winter may be grazed bare of vegetation though the open plains, to which only the hardiest will at this season stray, may have plenty; and insufficiency of food, although not such as to actually to starve them, weakens them so that they succumb readily to the cold or to one of the numerous accidents to which they are liable— as slipping off an icy butte or getting cast in a frozen washout. The cows in calf are those that suffer most, and so heavy is the loss among these and so light the calf crop that it is yet an open question whether our northern ranges are as a whole fitted for breeding. When the animals get weak they will huddle into some nook or corner or empty hut and simply stay there till they die.

Overstocking may cause little or no harm for two or three years, but sooner or later there comes a winter which means ruin to the ranches that have too many cattle on them; and in our country, which is even now getting crowded, it is merely a question of time as to when a winter will come that will understock the ranges by the summary process of killing off about half of all the cattle throughout the North-west

In our northern country we have "free grass"; that is, the stockmen rarely own more than small portions of the land over which their cattle range, the bulk of it being unsurveyed and still the property of the National Government—for the latter refuses to sell the soil except in small lots, acting on the wise principle of distributing it among as many owners as possible. Here and there some ranchman has acquired title to narrow strips of territory peculiarly valuable as giving water-right; but the amount of land thus occupied is small with us,—although the reverse is the case farther south,—and there is practically no fencing to speak of. As a consequence, the land is one vast pasture, and the man who overstocks his own range damages his neighbors as much as himself. These huge northern pastures are too dry and the soil too poor to be used for agriculture until the rich, wet lands to the east and west are occupied; and at present we have little fear from grangers. Of course, in the end much of the ground will be taken up for small farms, but the farmers that so far have come in have absolutely failed to make even a living, except now and then by raising a few vegetables for the use of the stockmen; and we are inclined to welcome the incoming of an occasional settler, if he is a decent man, especially as, by the laws of the Territories in which the great grazing plains lie, he is obliged to fence in his own patch of cleared ground, and we do not have to keep our cattle out of it.

At present we are far more afraid of each other. There are always plenty of men who for the sake of the chance of gain they themselves run are willing to jeopardize the interests of their neighbors by putting on more cattle than the land will support—for the loss, of course, falls as heavily on the man who has put on the right number as on him who has put on too many; and it is against these individuals that we have to guard so far as we are able. To protect ourselves completely is impossible, but the very identity of interest that renders all of us liable to suffer for the fault of a few also renders us as a whole able to take some rough measures to guard against the wrong-doing of a portion of our number; for the fact that the cattle wander intermixed over the ranges forces all the ranchmen of a locality to combine if they wish to do their work effectively. Accordingly, the stockmen of a neighborhood, when it holds as many cattle as it safely can, usually unitedly refuse to work with any one who puts in another herd. In the cow country a man is peculiarly dependent upon his neighbors, and a small outfit is wholly unable to work without their assistance when once the cattle have mingled completely with those of other brands. A large outfit is much more master of its destiny, and can do its own work quite by itself; but even such a one can be injured in countless ways if the hostility of the neighboring ranchmen is incurred. So a certain check is put to undue crowding of the ranges; but it is only partial.

The best days of ranching are over; and though there are many ranchmen who still make money, yet during the past two or three years the majority have certainly lost. This is especially true of the numerous Easterners who went into the business without any experience and trusted themselves entirely to their Western representatives; although, on the other hand, many of those who have made most money at it are Easterners, who, however, have happened to be naturally fitted for the work and who have deliberately settled down to learning the business as they would have learned any other, devoting their whole time and energy to it. As the country grows older, stock-raising will in some places die out, and in others entirely change its character; the ranches will be broken up, will be gradually modified into stock-farms, or, if on good soil, may even fall under the sway of the husbandman.

In its present form stock-raising on the plains is doomed, and can hardly outlast the century. The great free ranches, with their barbarous, picturesque, and curiously fascinating surroundings, mark a primitive stage of existence as surely as do the great tracts of primeval forests, and like the latter must pass away before the onward march of our people; and we who have felt the charm of the life, and have exulted in its abounding vigor and its bold, restless freedom, will not only regret its passing for our own sakes only, but must also feel real sorrow that those who come after us are not to see, as we have seen, what is perhaps the pleasantest, healthiest, and most exciting phase of American existence.

Theodore Roosevelt.

16

The Home Ranch

Theodore Roosevelt

MARCH, 1888.

THE HOME RANCH.

BY THEODORE ROOSEVELT.

ILLUSTRATIONS BY FREDERIC REMINGTON.

A MONTANA TYPE.

MY home ranch lies on both sides of the Little Missouri, the nearest ranchman above me being about twelve, and the nearest below me about ten, miles distant. The general course of the stream here is northerly, but, while flowing through my ranch, it takes a great westerly reach of some three miles, walled in, as always, between chains of steep, high bluffs half a mile or more apart. The stream twists down through the valley in long sweeps, leaving oval wooded bottoms, first on one side and then on the other; and in an open glade among the thick-growing timber stands the long, low house of hewn logs.

Just in front of the ranch veranda is a line of old cottonwoods that shade it during the fierce heats of summer, rendering it always cool and pleasant. But a few feet beyond these trees comes the cut-off bank of the river, through whose broad, sandy bed the shallow stream winds as if lost, except when a freshet fills it from brim to brim with foaming yellow water. The bluffs that wall in the river-valley curve back in semicircles, rising from its alluvial bottom generally as abrupt cliffs, but often as steep, grassy slopes that lead up to great level plateaus; and the line is broken every mile or two by the entrance of a coulée,

or dry creek, whose head branches may be twenty miles back. Above us, where the river comes round the bend, the valley is very narrow, and the high buttes bounding it rise, sheer and barren, into scalped hill-peaks and naked knife-blade ridges.

The other buildings stand in the same open glade with the ranch house, the dense growth of cottonwoods and matted, thorny underbrush making a wall all about, through which we have chopped our wagon roads and trodden out our own bridle-paths. The cattle have now trampled down this brush a little, but deer still lie in it, only a couple of hundred yards from the house; and from the door sometimes in the evening one can see them peer out into the open, or make their way down, timidly and cautiously, to drink at the river. The stable, sheds, and other outbuildings, with the hayricks and the pens for such cattle as we bring in during winter, are near the house; the patch of fenced garden land is on the edge of the woods; and near the middle of the glade stands the high, circular horse-corral, with a snubbing-post in the center, and a wing built out from one side of the gate entrance, so that the saddle band can be driven in without trouble. As it is very hard to work cattle where there is much brush, the larger cow-corral is some four miles off on an open bottom.

A ranchman's life is certainly a very pleasant one, albeit generally varied with plenty of hardship and anxiety. Although occasionally he passes days of severe toil,—for example, if he goes on the round-up he works as hard as any of his men,—yet he no longer has to undergo the monotonous drudgery attendant upon the tasks of the cowboy or of the apprentice in the business. His fare is simple; but, if he chooses, it is good enough. Many ranches are provided with nothing at all but salt pork, canned goods, and bread; indeed, it is a curious fact that in traveling through this cow country it is often impossible to get any milk or butter; but this is only because the owners or managers are too lazy to take enough trouble to insure their own comfort. We ourselves always keep up two or three cows, choosing such as are naturally tame, and so we invariably have plenty of milk and, when there is time for churning, a good deal of butter. We also keep hens, which, in spite of the damaging inroads of hawks, bob-cats, and foxes, supply us with eggs, and in time of need, when our rifles have failed to keep us in game, with stewed, roast, or fried chicken also. From our garden we get potatoes, and unless drought, frost, or grasshoppers interfere (which they do about every second year), other vegetables as well. For fresh meat we depend chiefly upon our prowess as hunters.

During much of the time we are away on the different round-ups, that "wheeled house," the great four-horse wagon, being then our home; but when at the ranch our routine of life is always much the same, save during

ELK HORN RANCH BUILDINGS.

the scattered groups of the saddle band, our six or eight mares, with their colts, keep by themselves, and are rarely bothered by us, as no cowboy ever rides anything but horses, because mares give great trouble where all the animals have to be herded together. Once every two or three days somebody rides round and finds out where each of these smaller bands is, but the man who goes out in the morning merely gathers one bunch. He drives these into the corral, the other men (who have been lolling idly about the house or stable, fixing their saddles or doing any odd job) coming out with their ropes as soon as they hear the patter of the unshod hoofs and the shouts of the cowboy driver. Going into the corral, and standing near the center, each of us picks out some one of his own string from among the animals that are trotting and running in a compact mass round the circle; and after one or more trials, according to his skill, ropes it and leads it out. When all have caught their horses the rest are again turned loose, together with those that have been kept up overnight. Some horses soon get tame and do not need to be roped; my pet cutting pony, little Muley, and good old Manitou, my companion in so many

hunting trips, will neither of them stay with the rest of their fellows that are jamming and jostling each other as they rush round in the dust of the corral, but they very sensibly walk up and stand quietly with the men in the middle, by the snubbing-post. Both are great pets, Manitou in particular; the wise old fellow being very fond of bread and sometimes coming up of his own accord to the ranch house and even putting his head into the door to beg for it.

Once saddled, the men ride off on their different tasks; for almost everything is done in the saddle, except that in winter we cut our firewood and quarry our coal,—both on the

the excessively bitter weather of midwinter, when there is little to do except to hunt, if the days are fine enough. We breakfast early—before dawn when the nights have grown long, and rarely later than sunrise, even in midsummer. Perhaps before this meal, certainly the instant it is over, the man whose duty it is rides off to hunt up and drive in the saddle band. Each of us has his own string of horses, eight or ten in number, and the whole band usually split up into two or three companies. In addition to

ranch,—and in summer attend to the garden and put up what wild hay we need.

If any horses have strayed, one or two of the men will be sent off to look for them; for hunting lost horses is one of the commonest and most irksome of our duties. Every outfit always has certain of its horses at large; and if they remain out long enough they become

If the men do not go horse-hunting they may ride off over the range; for there is generally some work to be done among the cattle, such as driving in and branding calves that have been overlooked by the round-up, or getting some animal out of a bog-hole. During the early spring months, before the round-up begins, the chief work is in haul-

ROPING IN A HORSE-CORRAL.

as wild and wary as deer and have to be regularly surrounded and run down. On one occasion, when three of mine had been running loose for a couple of months, we had to follow at full speed for at least fifteen miles before exhausting them enough to enable us to get some control over them and head them towards a corral. Twice I have had horses absent nearly a year before they were recovered. One of them, after being on the ranch nine months, went off one night and traveled about two hundred miles in a straight line back to its old haunts, swimming the Yellowstone on the way. Two others were at one time away nearly eighteen months, during which time we saw them twice, and on one occasion a couple of the men fairly ran their horses down in following them. We began to think they were lost for good, as they were all the time going farther down towards the Sioux country, but we finally recovered them.

ing out mired cows and steers; and if we did not keep a sharp lookout, the losses at this season would be very serious. As long as everything is frozen solid there is, of course, no danger from miring; but when the thaw comes, along towards the beginning of March, a period of new danger to the cattle sets in. When the ice breaks up, the streams are left with an edging of deep bog, while the quicksand is at its worst. As the frost goes out of the soil, the ground round every little alkali-spring changes into a trembling quagmire, and deep holes of slimy, tenacious mud form in the bottom of all the gullies. The cattle, which have had to live on snow for three or four months, are very eager for water, and are weak and in poor condition. They rush heedlessly into any pool and stand there, drinking gallons of the icy water and sinking steadily into the mud. When they try to get out they are already too deep down, and are too weak to make a prolonged struggle. After one or two fits of desperate floundering, they resign themselves to their fate with dumb apathy and are lost, unless some one of us riding about discovers and hauls them out. They may be thus lost in wonderfully small mud-holes; often they will be found dead in a gulch but two or three feet across, or in the quicksand of a creek so narrow that it could almost be jumped. An alkalihole, where the water oozes out through the thick clay, is the worst of all, owing to the ropy tenacity with which the horrible substance sticks and clings to any unfortunate beast that gets into it.

In the spring these mud-holes cause very serious losses among the cattle, and are at all times fruitful sources of danger; indeed, during an ordinary year more cattle die from getting mired than from any other cause. In addition to this they also often prove very annoying to the rider himself, as getting his steed mired or caught in a quicksand is one of the commonest of the accidents that beset a horseman in the far West. This usually happens in fording a river, if the latter is at all high, or else in crossing one of the numerous creeks; although I once saw a horse and rider suddenly engulfed while leisurely walking over what appeared to be dry land. They had come to an alkali mud-hole, an old buffalo-wallow, which had filled up and was covered with a sun-baked crust, that let them through as if they had stepped on a trap-door. There being several of us along, we got down our ropes and dragged both unfortunates out in short order.

When the river is up it is a very common thing for a horseman to have great difficulty in crossing, for the swift, brown water runs

A DEEP FORD.

over a bed of deep quicksand that is ever shifting. An inexperienced horse, or a mule, —for a mule is useless in mud or quicksand,— becomes mad with fright in such a crossing, and, after speedily exhausting its strength in wild struggles, will throw itself on its side and drown unless the rider gets it out. An old horse used to such work will, on the contrary, take matters quietly and often push along through really dangerous quicksand. Old Manitou never loses his head for an instant; but, now resting a few seconds, now feeling his way cautiously forward, and now making two or three desperate plunges, will go on wherever a horse possibly can. It is really dangerous crossing some of the creeks, as the bottom may give way where it seems hardest; and if one is alone he may work hours in vain before getting his horse out, even after taking off both saddle and bridle, the only hope being to head it so that every plunge takes it an inch or two in the right direction.

Nor are mud-holes the only danger the

horseman has to fear; for in much of the Bad Lands the buttes are so steep and broken that it needs genuine mountaineering skill to get through them, and no horse but a Western one, bred to the business, could accomplish the feat. In many parts of our country it is impossible for a horseman who does not know the land to cross it, and it is difficult enough even for an experienced hand. For a stretch of nearly ten miles along the Little Missouri above my range, and where it passes through it, there are but three or four places where it is possible for a horseman to get out to the eastern prairie through the exceedingly broken country lying back from the river. In places this very rough ground comes down to the water; elsewhere it lies back near the heads of the creeks. In such very bad ground the whole country seems to be one tangled chaos of cañon-like valleys, winding gullies, and washouts, with abrupt, unbroken sides, isolated peaks of sandstone, marl, or "gumbo" clay, which rain turns into slippery glue, and hill chains whose ridges always end in sheer cliffs. After a man has made his way with infinite toil for half a mile, a point will be reached around which it is an absolute impossibility to go, and the adventurer has nothing to do but painfully retrace his steps and try again in a new direction, as likely as not with the same result. In such a place the rider dismounts and leads his horse, the latter climbing with cat-like agility up seemingly inaccessible heights, scrambling across the steep, sloping shoulders of the bluffs, sliding down the faces of the clay cliffs with all four legs rigid, or dropping from ledge to ledge like a goat, and accepting with unruffled composure an occasional roll from top to bottom. But, in spite of the climbing abilities of the ponies, it is difficult, and at times — for our steeds, at any rate — dangerous work to go through such places, and we only do it when it cannot be avoided. Once I was overtaken by darkness while trying to get through a great tract of very rough land, and, after once or twice nearly breaking my neck, in despair had to give up all attempts to get out, and until daybreak simply staid where I was, in a kind of ledge or pocket on the side of the cliff, luckily sheltered from the wind. It was midsummer and the nights were short, but this particular one seemed quite long enough; and though I was on the move by dawn, it was three hours later before I led the horse, as hungry, numb, and stiff as myself, out on the prairie again.

Occasionally, it is imperatively necessary to cross some of the worst parts of the Bad Lands with a wagon, and such a trip is exhausting and laborious beyond belief. Often the wagon will have to be taken to pieces every few hundred yards in order to get it over a ravine, lower it into a valley, or drag it up a cliff. One outfit, that a year ago tried to take a short cut through some of the Bad Lands of the Powder River, made just four miles in three days, and then had to come back to their starting-point after all. But with only saddle-horses we feel that it must be a very extraordinary country indeed if, in case of necessity, we cannot go through it.

The long forenoon's work, with its attendant mishaps to man and beast, being over, the men who have been out among the horses and cattle come riding in, to be joined by their fellows — if any there be — who have been hunting, or haying, or chopping wood. The midday dinner is variable as to time, for it comes when the men have returned from their work; but, whatever be the hour, it is the most substantial meal of the day, and we feel that we have little fault to find with a table on whose clean cloth are spread platters of smoked elk meat, loaves of good bread, jugs and bowls of milk, saddles of venison or broiled antelope steaks, perhaps roast and fried prairie chickens, with eggs, butter, wild plums, and tea or coffee.

The afternoon's tasks are usually much the same as the morning's, but this time is often spent in doing the odds and ends; as, for instance, it may be devoted to breaking-in a new horse. Large outfits generally hire a bronco-buster to do this; but we ourselves almost always break our own horses, two or three of my men being very good riders, although none of them can claim to be anything out of the common. A first-class flash rider or bronco-buster receives high wages and deserves them, for he follows a most dangerous trade, at which no man can hope to grow old; his work being infinitely harder than that of an Eastern horse-breaker or rough-rider, because he has to do it in such a limited time. A good rider is a good rider all the world over; but an Eastern or English horse-breaker and Western bronco-buster have so little in common with each other as regards style or surroundings, and are so totally out of place in doing each other's work, that it is almost impossible to get either to admit that the other has any merits at all as a horseman, for neither could sit in the saddle of the other or could without great difficulty perform his task. The ordinary Eastern seat, which approaches more or less the seat of a cross-country rider or fox-hunter, is nearly as different from the cowboy's seat as from that of a man who rides bareback. The stirrups on a stock saddle are much farther back than they are on an ordinary English one (a difference far more important than the high horn and cantle of the former), and the man stands nearly erect in them, instead of having his legs bent; and he grips with the thighs and not with the knees, throwing his feet well out. Some of the things he teaches his horse would be wholly useless to an Eastern equestrian: for example, one of the first lessons the newly caught animal has to learn is not to "run on a rope"; and he is taught this by being violently snubbed up, probably turning a somersault, the first two or three times that he feels the noose settle round his neck, and makes a mad rush for liberty. The snubbing-post is the usual adjunct in teaching such a lesson; but a skillful man can do without any help and throw a horse clean over by holding the rope tight against the left haunch, at the same time leaning so far back, with the legs straight in front, that the heels dig deep into the ground when the

A HARD TRAIL.

strain comes, and the horse, running out with the slack of the rope, is brought up standing, or even turned head over heels by the shock. Cowboys are probably the only men in the world who invariably wear gloves, buckskin gauntlets being preferred, as otherwise the ropes would soon take every particle of skin off their hands.

A bronco-buster has to work by such violent methods in consequence of the short amount of time at his command. Horses are cheap, each outfit has a great many, and the wages for breaking an animal are but five or ten dollars. Three rides, of an hour or two each, on as many consecutive days, are the outside number a bronco-buster deems necessary before turning an animal over as "broken." The average bronco-buster, however, handles horses so very rudely that we prefer, aside from motives of economy, to break our own; and this is always possible, if we take enough time. The best and most quiet horses on the ranch are far from being those broken by the best riders; on the contrary, they are those that have been handled most gently, although firmly, and that have

sires and dams, yet are quite as wild as the antelope on whose domain they have intruded. Ranchmen run in these wild horses whenever possible, and they are but little more difficult to break than the so-called "tame" animals. But the wild stallions are, whenever possible, shot; both because of their propensity for driving off the ranch mares, and because their incurable viciousness makes them always unsafe companions for other horses still more than

IN WITH THE HORSE HERD.

had the greatest number of days devoted to their education.

Some horses, of course, are almost incurably vicious, and must be conquered by main force. One pleasing brute on my ranch will at times rush at a man open-mouthed like a wolf, and this is a regular trick of the range-stallions. In a great many—indeed, in most—localities there are wild horses to be found, which, although invariably of domestic descent, being either themselves runaways from some ranch or Indian outfit, or else claiming such for their

for men. A wild stallion fears no beast except the grizzly, and will not always flinch from an encounter with it; yet it is a curious fact that a jack will almost always kill one in a fair fight. The particulars of a fight of this sort were related to me by a cattle man who was engaged in bringing out blooded stock from the East. Among the animals under his charge were two great stallions, one gray and one black, and a fine jackass, not much over half the size of either of the former. The animals were kept in separate pens, but one day both horses got into the same inclosure, next to the jack-pen, and began to fight as only enraged stallions can, striking like boxers with their fore feet, and biting with their teeth. The gray was getting the best of it; but while clinched with his antagonist in one tussle they rolled against the jack-pen, breaking it in. No sooner was the jack at liberty than, with ears laid back and mouth wide open, he made straight for the two horses, who had for the moment separated. The gray turned to meet him, rearing on his hind legs and striking at him with his fore feet; but the jack slipped in, and in a minute grasped his antagonist by the throat with his wide-open jaws, and then held on like a bull-dog, all four feet planted stiffly in the soil. The stallion made tremendous efforts to shake him off: he would try to whirl round and kick him, but for that the jack was too short; then he would rise up, lifting the jack off the ground, and strike at him with his fore feet; but all that he gained by this was to skin his foe's front legs without making him loose his hold. Twice they fell, and twice the stallion rose, by main strength dragging the jack with him; but all in vain. Meanwhile the black horse attacked both the combatants with perfect impartiality, striking and kicking them with his hoofs, while his teeth, as they slipped off the tough hides, met with a snap like that of a bear-trap. Undoubtedly the jack would have killed at least one of the horses had not the men come up, and with no small difficulty separated the maddened brutes.

If not breaking horses, mending saddles, or doing something else of the sort, the cowboys will often while away their leisure moments by practicing with the rope. A man cannot practice too much with this if he wishes to attain even moderate proficiency; and as a matter of fact he soon gets to wish to practice the whole time. A cowboy is always roping something, and it especially delights him to try his skill at game. A friend of mine, a young ranchman in the Judith basin, about three years ago roped a buffalo, and by the exercise of the greatest skill, both on his own part and on his steed's, actually succeeded, by alternate bullying and coaxing, in getting the huge brute almost into camp. I have occasionally known men on fast horses to rope deer, and even antelope, when circumstances all joined to favor them; and last summer one of the cowboys on a ranch about thirty miles off ran into and roped a wounded elk. A forty-foot lariat is the one commonly used, for the ordinary range at which a man can use it is only about twenty-five feet. Few men can throw forty feet; and to do this, taking into account the coil, needs a sixty-foot rope.

When the day's work is over we take supper, and bed-time comes soon afterward, for the men who live on ranches sleep well and soundly. As a rule, the nights are cool and bracing, even in midsummer; except when we occasionally have a spell of burning weather, with a steady, hot wind that blows in our faces like a furnace blast, sending the thermometer far up above a hundred and making us gasp for breath, even at night, in the dry-baked heat of the air. But it is only rarely that we get a few days of this sort; generally, no matter how unbearable the heat of the day has been, we can at least sleep pleasantly at night.

A ranchman's work is, of course, free from much of the sameness attendant upon that of a mere cowboy. One day he will ride out with his men among the cattle, or after strayed horses; the next he may hunt, so as to keep the ranch in meat; then he can make the tour of his outlying camps; or, again, may join one of the round-ups for a week or two, perhaps keeping with it the entire time it is working. On occasions he will have a good deal of spare time on his hands, which, if he chooses, he can spend in reading or writing. If he cares for books, there will be many a worn volume in the primitive little sitting-room, with its log walls and huge fireplace; but after a hard day's work a man will not read much, but will rock to and fro in the flickering firelight, talking sleepily over his success in the day's chase and the difficulty he has had with the cattle; or else may simply lie stretched at full length on the elk-hides and wolf-skins in front of the hearthstone, listening in drowsy silence to the roar and crackle of the blazing logs and to the moaning of the wind outside.

In the sharp fall weather the riding is delicious all day long; but even in the late spring, and all through the summer, we try, if we can, to do our work before the heat of the day, and if going on a long ride, whether to hunt or for other purposes, leave the ranch house by dawn.

The early rides in the spring mornings have a charm all their own, for they are taken when, for the one and only time during the year, the same brown landscape of these high plains turns to a vivid green, as the new grass sprouts and the trees and bushes thrust forth the young leaves; and at dawn, with the dew glittering everywhere, all things show at their best and freshest. The flowers are out and a man may gallop for miles at a stretch with his horse's hoofs sinking at every stride into the carpet of prairie roses, whose short stalks lift the beautiful blossoms but a few inches from the ground. Even in the waste places the cactuses are blooming; and one kind in particular, a dwarfish, globular plant, with its mass of splendid crimson flowers, glows against the sides of the gray buttes like a splash of flame.

The ravines, winding about and splitting out farther to the flat prairie land on the divide. Here, in places, the level, grassy plains are strewn with mounds and hillocks of red or gray scoria, that stand singly or clustered into little groups, their tops crested, or their

A BUCKING BRONCO.

into a labyrinth of coulées, with chains of rounded hills to separate them, have groves of trees in their bottoms, over the sides of the water-courses. In these are found the black-tail deer, and his cousin, the whitetail, too, with his flaunting flag; but in the spring-time, when we are after antelope only, we must go sides covered, by queer, detached masses of volcanic rock, wrought into strange shapes by the dead forces whose blind, hidden strength long ago called them into being. The road our wagons take, when the water is too high for us to come down the river bottom, stretches far ahead — two dark, straight, parallel furrows which merge into one in the distance. Quaint little horned frogs crawl sluggishly along in the wheel tracks, and the sickle-billed curlews run over the ground or soar above and around the horsemen, uttering their mournful, never-ceasing clamor. The grass-land stretches out in the sunlight like a sea, every wind bending the blades into a ripple, and flecking the prairie with shifting patches of a different green from that around, exactly as the touch of a light squall or wind-gust will fleck the smooth surface of the ocean. Our Western plains differ widely in detail from those of Asia; yet they always recall to my mind Arnold's description of the Scythian steppes in "The Strayed Reveller."

In the spring mornings the rider on the plains will hear bird songs unknown in the East. The Missouri sky-lark sings while soaring above the great plateaus so high in the air that it is impossible to see the bird; and this habit of singing while soaring it shares with some sparrow-like birds that are often found in company with it. The white-shouldered lark-bunting, in its livery of black, has rich, full notes, and as it sings on the wing it reminds one of the bobolink; and the sweet-voiced lark-finch also utters its song in the air. These birds, and most of the sparrows of the plains, are characteristic of this region.

But many of our birds, especially those found in the wooded river bottoms, answer to those of the East; only almost each one has some marked point of difference from its Eastern representative. The bluebird out West is very much of a blue bird indeed, for it has no "earth tinge" on its breast at all; while the indigo-bird, on the contrary, has gained the ruddy markings that the other has lost. The flicker has the shafts of its wing and tail quills colored orange instead of yellow. The towhee has lost all title to its name, for its only cry is a mew like that of a cat-bird; while, most wonderful of all, the meadow-lark has found a rich, strong voice, and is one of the sweetest and most incessant singers we have.

Throughout June the thickets and groves about the ranch house are loud with bird music from before dawn till long after sunrise. The thrashers have sung all the night through from among the thorn-bushes if there has been a moon, or even if there has been bright starlight; and before the first glimmer of gray the bell-like, silvery songs of the shy woodland thrushes chime in; while meadow-lark, robin, bluebird, and song sparrow, together with many rarer singers, like the grosbeak, join in swelling the chorus. There are some would-be singers whose intention is better than their execution. Blackbirds of several

kinds are plenty round the house and stables, walking about with a knowing air, like so many dwarf crows; and now and then a flock of yellow-heads will mix for a few days with their purple or rusty-colored brethren. The males of these yellow-headed grakles are really handsome, their orange and yellow heads contrasting finely with the black of the rest of their plumage; but their voices are discordant to a degree. When a flock has done feeding it will often light in straggling order among the trees in front of the veranda, and then the males will begin to sing, or rather to utter the most extraordinary collection of broken sounds — creakings, gurglings, hisses, twitters, and every now and then a liquid note or two. It is like an accentuated representation of the noise made by a flock of common blackbirds. At night-fall the poor-wills begin to utter their boding call from the wooded ravines back in the hills; not "whip-poor-will," as in the East, but with two syllables only. They often come round the ranch house. Late one evening I had been sitting motionless on the veranda, looking out across the water and watching the green and brown of the hill-tops change to purple and umber and then fade off into shadowy gray as the somber darkness deepened. Suddenly a poor-will lit on the floor beside me and staid some little time; now and then uttering its mournful cries, then ceasing for a few moments as it flitted round after insects, and again returning to the same place to begin anew. The little owls, too, call to each other with tremulous, quavering voices throughout the livelong night, as they sit in the creaking trees that overhang the roof. Now and then we hear the wilder voices of the wilderness, from animals that in the hours of darkness do not fear the neighborhood of man: the coyotes wail like dismal ventriloquists, or the silence may be broken by the strident challenge of a lynx, or by the snorting and stamping of a deer that has come to the edge of the open.

In the hot noontide hours of midsummer the broad ranch veranda, always in the shade, is almost the only spot where a man can be comfortable; but here he can sit for hours at a time, leaning back in his rocking-chair as he reads or smokes, or with half-closed, dreamy eyes gazes across the shallow, nearly dry river-bed to the wooded bottoms opposite, and to the plateaus lying back of them. Against the sheer white faces of the cliffs, that come down without a break, the dark green tree-tops stand out in bold relief. In the hot lifeless air all objects that are not near by seem to sway and waver. There are few sounds to break the stillness. From the upper branches of the cottonwood-trees overhead, whose shimmering, tremulous leaves are hardly ever quiet, but if the wind stirs at all, rustle and quaver and sigh all day long, comes every now and then the soft, melancholy cooing of the mourning dove, whose voice always seems far away and expresses more than any other sound in

toss it up with their horns. At times the horses, too, will come down to drink, and to splash and roll in the water.

The prairie-dogs alone are not daunted by the heat, but sit at the mouths of their burrows with their usual pert curiosity. They are both-

CRUISING FOR STOCK.

nature the sadness of gentle, hopeless, never-ending grief. The other birds are still; and very few animals move about. Now and then the black shadow of a wheeling vulture falls on the sun-scorched ground. The cattle, that have strung down in long files from the hills, lie quietly on the sand-bars, except that some of the bulls keep traveling up and down, bellowing and routing or giving vent to long, surly grumblings as they paw the sand and

ersome little fellows, and most prolific, increasing in spite of the perpetual war made on them by every carnivorous bird and beast. One of their worst foes is the black-footed ferret, a handsome, rather rare animal, somewhat like a mink, with a yellow-brown body and dark feet and mask. It is a most bloodthirsty little brute, feeding on all small animals and ground birds. It will readily master a jack-rabbit, will kill very young fawns if it finds them in the mother's absence, and work extraordinary havoc in a dog town, as it can follow the wretched little beasts down into the burrows. In one instance, I knew of a black-footed ferret making a succession of inroads on a ranchman's poultry, killing and carrying off most of them before it was trapped. Coyotes, foxes, swifts, badgers, and skunks also like to lurk about the dog towns. Of the skunks, by the way, we had last year altogether too much; there was a perfect plague of them all along the river, and they took to trying to get into the huts, with the stupid pertinacity of the species. At every ranch house dozens were killed, we ourselves bagging thirty-three, all slain near the house, and one, to our unspeakable sorrow, in it.

In making a journey over ground we know, during the hot weather we often prefer to ride by moonlight. The moon shines very brightly through the dry, clear night air, turning the gray buttes into glimmering silver; and the horses travel far more readily and easily than under the glaring noonday sun. The road between my upper and lower ranch houses is about forty miles long, sometimes following the river-bed, and then again branching off inland, crossing the great plateaus and winding through the ravines of the broken country. It is a five-hours' fair ride; and so, in a hot spell, we like to take it during the cool of the night, starting at sunset. After nightfall the face of the country seems to alter marvelously, and the cool moonlight only intensifies the change. The river gleams like running quicksilver, and the moonbeams play over the grassy stretches of the plateaus and glance off the wind-rippled blades as they would from water. The Bad Lands seem to be stranger and wilder than ever, the silvery rays turning the country into a kind of grim fairy-land. The grotesque, fantastic outlines of the higher cliffs stand out with startling clearness, while the lower buttes have become formless, misshapen masses, and the deep gorges are in black shadow; in the darkness there will be no sound but the rhythmic echo of the hoof-beats of the horses, and the steady, metallic clank of the steel bridle-chains.

But the fall is the time for riding; for in the keen, frosty air neither man nor beast will tire, though out from the dawn until the shadows have again waxed long and the daylight has begun to wane, warning all to push straight for home without drawing rein. Then deer-saddles and elk-haunches hang from the trees near the house; and one can have good sport right on the sand of the river-bed, for we always keep shot-gun or rifle at hand, to be ready for any prairie chickens, or for such of the passing water-fowl as light in the river near

us. Occasionally we take a shot at a flock of waders, among which the pretty avocets are the most striking in looks and manners. Prairie fowl are quite plenty all round us, and occasionally small flocks come fairly down into the yard, or perch among the trees near by. At evening they fly down to the river to drink, and as they sit on the sand-bars offer fine marks for the rifles. So do the geese and ducks when they occasionally light on the same places or paddle leisurely down stream in the middle of the river; but to make much of a bag of these we have to use the heavy No. 10, choke-bore shot-gun, while the little 16-bore fowling-piece is much the handiest for prairie fowl. A good many different kinds of water-fowl pass, ranging in size from a teal duck to a Canada goose, and all of them at times help to eke out our bill of fare. Last fall a white-fronted goose lit on the river in front of the ranch house, and three of us, armed with miscellaneous weapons, went out after him; we disabled him, and then after much bad shooting, and more violent running through thick sand and thick underbrush, finally overtook and most foully butchered him. The snow geese and common wild geese are what we usually kill, however.

Sometimes strings of sandbill cranes fly along the river, their guttural clangor being heard very far off. They usually light on a plateau, where sometimes they form rings and go through a series of queer antics, dancing and posturing to each other. They are exceedingly wide-awake birds, and more shy and wary than antelope, so that they are rarely shot; yet once I succeeded in stalking up to a group in the early morning, and firing into them rather at random, my bullet killed a full-grown female. Its breast, when roasted, proved to be very good eating.

Sometimes we vary our diet with fish — wall-eyed pike, ugly, slimy catfish, and other uncouth finny things, looking very fit denizens of the mud-choked water; but they are good eating withal, in spite of their uncanny appearance. We usually catch them with set lines, left out overnight in the deeper pools.

The cattle are fattest and in best condition during the fall, and it is then that the bulk of the beef steers are gathered and shipped — four-year-olds as a rule, though some threes and some fives go along with them. Cattle are a nuisance while hunting on foot, as they either take fright and run off when they see the hunter, scaring all game within sight, or else, what is worse, follow him, blustering and bullying and pretending that they are on the point of charging, but rarely actually doing so. Still, they are occasionally really dangerous,

LINE RIDING IN WINTER.

and it is never entirely safe for a man to be on foot when there is a chance of meeting the droves of long-horned steers. But they will always bluster rather than fight, whether with men or beasts, or with one another. The bulls and some of the steers are forever traveling and challenging each other, never ceasing their hoarse rumbling and moaning and their long-drawn, savage bellowing, tearing up the banks with their horns and sending little spurts of dust above their shoulders with their fore hoofs; yet they do not seem especially fond of real fighting, although, of course, they do occasionally have most desperate and obstinate set-tos with one another. A large bear will make short work of a bull: a few months ago one of the former killed a very big bull near a ranch house a score of miles or so distant, and during one night tore up and devoured a large part of his victim. The ranchman poisoned the carcass and killed the bear.

In the winter there is much less work than at any other season, but what there is involves great hardship and exposure. Many of the men are discharged after the summer is over, and during much of the cold weather there is little to do except hunt now and then, and in very bitter days lounge about the house. But some of the men are out in the line camps, and the ranchman has occasionally to make the round of these; and besides that, one or more of the cowboys who are at home ought to be out every day when the cattle have become weak, so as to pick up and drive in any beast that will otherwise evidently fail to get through the season — a cow that has had an unusually early calf being particularly apt to need attention. The horses shift for themselves and need no help. Often, in winter, the Indians cut down the cottonwood trees and feed the tops to their ponies; but this is not done to keep them from starving, but only to keep them from wandering off in search of grass. Besides, the ponies are very fond of the bark of the young cottonwood shoots, and it is healthy for them.

The men in the line camps lead a hard life, for they have to be out in every kind of

CATTLE DRIFTING BEFORE THE STORM.

weather, and should be especially active and watchful during the storms. The camps are established along some line which it is proposed to make the boundary of the cattle's drift in a given direction. For example, we care very little whether our cattle wander to the Yellowstone; but we strongly object to their drifting east and south-east towards the granger country and the Sioux reservation, especially as when they drift that way they come out on flat, bare plains where there is danger of perishing. Accordingly, the cowmen along the Little Missouri have united in establishing a row of camps to the east of the river, along the line where the broken ground meets the prairie. The camps are usually for two men each, and some fifteen or twenty miles apart; then, in the morning, its two men start out in opposite ways, each riding till he meets his neighbor of the next camp nearest on that side, when he returns. The camp itself is sometimes merely a tent pitched in a sheltered coulée, but ought to be either made of logs or else a dug-out in the ground. A small corral and horse-shed is near by, with enough hay for the ponies, of which each rider has two or three. In riding over the beat each man drives any cattle that have come near it back into the Bad Lands, and if he sees by the hoof-marks that a few have strayed out over the line very recently, he will follow and fetch them home. They must be shoved well back into the Bad Lands before a great storm strikes them; for if they once begin to drift in masses before an icy gale it is impossible for a small number of men to hold them, and the only thing is to let them go, and then to organize an expedition to follow them as soon as possible. Line riding is very cold work, and dangerous too, when the men have to be out in a blinding snow-storm, or in a savage blizzard that takes the spirit in the thermometer far down below zero. In the worst storms it is impossible for any man to be out.

But other kinds of work besides line riding necessitate exposure to bitter weather. Once, while spending a few days over on Beaver Creek hunting up a lost horse, I happened to meet a cowboy who was out on the same errand, and made friends with him. We started home together across the open prairies, but were caught in a very heavy snow-storm almost immediately after leaving the ranch where we had spent the night. We were soon completely turned round, the great soft flakes—for, luckily, it was not cold—almost blinding us, and we had to travel entirely by compass. After feeling our way along for eight or nine hours, we finally got down into the broken country near Sentinel Butte and came across an empty hut, a welcome sight to men as cold, hungry, and tired as we were.   In this hut we passed the night very comfortably, picketing our horses in a sheltered nook near by, with plenty of hay from an old stack. To while away the long evening, I read Hamlet aloud, from a little pocket Shakspere. The cowboy, a Texan,— one of the best riders I have seen, and also a very intelligent as well as a thoroughly good fellow in every way,— was greatly interested in it and commented most shrewdly on the parts he liked, especially Polonius's advice to Laertes, which he translated into more homely language with great relish, and ended with the just criticism that "old Shakspere saveyed human natur' some"—savey being a verb presumably adapted into the limited plains' vocabulary from the French.

Even for those who do not have to look up stray horses, and who are not forced to ride the line day in and day out, there is apt to be some hardship and danger in being abroad during the bitter weather; yet a ride in mid-winter is certainly fascinating.   The great white country wrapped in the powdery snow-drift seems like another land; and the familiar landmarks are so changed that a man must be careful lest he lose his way, for the discomfort of a night in the open during such weather is very great indeed. When the sun is out the glare from the endless white stretches dazzles the eyes; and if the gray snow-clouds hang low and only let a pale, wan light struggle through, the lonely wastes become fairly appalling in their desolation.   For hour after hour a man may go on and see no sign of life except, perhaps, a big white owl sweeping noiselessly by, so that in the dark it looks like a snow-wreath; the cold gradually chilling the rider to the bones, as he draws his fur cap tight over his ears and muffles his face in the huge collar of his wolf-skin coat, and making the shaggy little steed drop head and tail as it picks its way over the frozen soil. There are few moments more pleasant than the home-coming, when, in the gathering darkness, after crossing the last chain of ice-covered buttes, or after coming round the last turn in the wind-swept valley, we see, through the leafless trees, or across the frozen river, the red gleam of the firelight as it shines through the ranch windows and flickers over the trunks of the cottonwoods outside, warming a man's blood by the mere hint of the warmth awaiting him within.

Theodore Roosevelt.

17

Custer's Last Battle

E.S. Godfrey

INDIAN SCOUTS WATCHING CUSTER'S ADVANCE.

CUSTER'S LAST BATTLE.

BY ONE OF HIS TROOP COMMANDERS.

ON the 16th of April, 1876, at McComb City, Missouri, I received orders to report my troop ("K," 7th Cavalry) to the Commanding General of the Department of Dakota, at St. Paul, Minnesota. At the latter place about twenty-five recruits fresh from civil life joined the troop, and we were ordered to proceed to Fort Abraham Lincoln, Dakota, where the Yellowstone Expedition was being organized. This expedition consisted of the 7th United States Cavalry, commanded by General George A. Custer, 28 officers and about 700 men; two companies of the 17th United States Infantry, and one company of the 6th United States Infantry, 8 officers and 135 men; one platoon of Gatling guns, 2 officers and 32 men (of the 20th United States Infantry); and 40 "Ree" Indian scouts. The expeditionary forces were commanded by Brigadier-General Alfred H. Terry, the Department Commander, who with his staff arrived several days prior to our departure.

On the 17th day of May, at 5 A.M., the "general"[1] was sounded, the wagons were packed and sent to the Quartermaster, and by

[1] The signal to take down tents and break camp.

six o'clock the wagon-train was on the road escorted by the infantry. By seven o'clock the 7th Cavalry was marching in column of platoon around the parade-ground of Fort Lincoln, headed by the band playing "Garry Owen," the Seventh's battle tune, first used when the regiment charged at the battle of Washita. The column was halted and dismounted just outside the garrison. The officers and married men were permitted to leave the ranks to say "good-by" to their families. General Terry, knowing the anxiety of the ladies, had assented to, or ordered, this demonstration, in order to allay their fears and satisfy them, by the formidable appearance we made, that we were able to cope with any enemy that we might expect to meet. Not many came out to witness the pageant, but many tear-filled eyes looked from the windows.

During this halt the wagon-train was assembled on the plateau west of the post and formed in column of fours. When it started off the "assembly" was sounded and absentees joined their commands. The signals "Mount" and "Forward" were sounded, and the regiment marched away, the band playing "The girl I left behind me."

The 7th Cavalry was divided into two columns, designated right and left wings, commanded by Major Marcus A. Reno and Captain F. W. Benteen. Each wing was subdivided into two battalions of three troops each. After the first day the following was the habitual order of march: one battalion was advance-guard, one was rear-guard, and one marched on each flank of the train. General Custer, with one troop of the advance-guard, went ahead and selected the route for the train and the camping-places at the end of the day's march. The other two troops of the advance-guard reported at headquarters for pioneer or fatigue duty, to build bridges and creek crossings. The rear-guard kept behind everything; when it came up to a wagon stalled in the mire, it helped to put the wagon forward. The battalions on the flanks were to keep within five hundred yards of the trail and not to get more than half a mile in advance or rear of the train. To avoid dismounting any oftener than necessary, the march was conducted as follows: one troop marched until about half a mile in advance of the train, when it was dismounted, the horses unbitted and allowed to graze until the train had passed and was about half a mile in advance of it, when it took up the march again; each of the other two troops would conduct their march in the same manner, so that two troops would be alongside the train all the time. If the country was much broken, a half dozen flankers were thrown out to guard against surprise. The flankers regulated their march so as to keep abreast of their troop. The pack-animals and beef herd were driven alongside the train by the packers and herders.

One wagon was assigned to each troop, and transported five days' rations and forage and the mess kit of the troop; also the mess kit, tents, and baggage of the troop officers and ten days' supplies for the officers' mess. The men were armed with the carbine and revolver; no one, not even the officer of the day, carried the saber. Each troop horse carried, in addition to the rider, between eighty and ninety pounds. This additional weight included all equipments and about one hundred rounds of ammunition. The wagon-train consisted in all of about one hundred and fifty wheeled vehicles. In it were carried thirty days' supplies of forage and rations (excepting beef), and two hundred rounds of ammunition per man. The two-horse wagons, hired by contract, carried from fifteen hundred to two thousand pounds. The six-mule government wagons carried from three to five thousand pounds, depending on the size and condition of the mules. The Gatling guns were each hauled by four condemned cavalry horses and marched in advance of the train. Two light wagons, loaded with axes, shovels, pickaxes and some pine boards and scantling, sufficient for a short bridge, accompanied the

"pioneer" troops. The "crossings," as they are termed, were often very tedious and would frequently delay the train several hours. During this time the cavalry horses were unbitted and grazed, the men holding the reins. Those men not on duty at the crossing slept, or collected in groups to spin yarns and take a whiff at their "dingy dudeens." The officers usually collected near the crossing to watch progress, and passed the time in conversation and playing practical jokes. About noon the "strikers," who carried the haversacks, were called, and the different messes had their luncheon, sometimes separately, sometimes clubbing together. When the haversacks were opened, the horses usually stopped grazing and put their noses near their riders' faces and asked very plainly to share the hardtack; if their polite request did not receive attention they would paw the ground, or even strike their riders. The old soldier was generally willing to share with his beast.

The length of the day's march, varying from ten to forty miles, was determined in a great measure by the difficulties or obstacles encountered, by wood, water, and grass, and by the distance in advance where such advantages were likely to be found. If, about two or three o'clock in the afternoon, a column of smoke was seen in the direction of the trail and a mile or two in advance, it was a pretty sure indication that a camp had been selected. The cavalry, excepting the rear-guard, would then cut loose from the train and go directly to camp. The rear-guard would send details to collect fuel and unpack their wagons. The adjutant showed the wing commanders the general direction their lines of tents were to run, and the latter then directed the battalion or troop commanders to their camping-places. Generally one flank of each line would rest near the creek. The general form of the camp was that of a parallelogram. The wings camped on the long sides facing each other, and the headquarters and guard were located at one end nearest to the creek; the wagon-train was parked to close the other end and was guarded by the infantry battalion. The troops, as they arrived at their places, were formed in line, facing inward, dismounted, unsaddled, and, if the weather was hot and the sun shining, the men rubbed the horses' backs until dry. After this the horses were sent to water and put out to graze, with side-lines and lariats, under charge of the stable guard, consisting of one non-commissioned officer and three or six privates. The men of the troop then collected fuel, sometimes wood, often a mile or more distant from the camp; sometimes "buffalo chips." The main guard, consisting, usually, of four or five non-commissioned officers and twelve or fifteen privates, reported mounted at headquarters, and were

MAJOR-GENERAL GEORGE A. CUSTER.
(FROM A PHOTOGRAPH BY BRADY.)

was performed by an officer designated as " Officer of the Herd." To preserve the grazing in the immediate vicinity of the camp for evening and night grazing, all horses were required to be outside of the camp limits until retreat. When the train arrived, the headquarters and troop wagons went directly to the camping-place of their respective commands. The officers' baggage and tents were unloaded first; then the wagons went near the place where the troop kitchen was to be located, always on that flank of the troop farthest from headquarters. The teamsters unharnessed their mules and put them out to graze. The old stable guard reported to the troop commander for fatigue duty to put up the officers' tents and collect fuel for their mess. The troop officers' tents were usually placed twenty-five yards in rear of the line of men's tents and facing toward them. Their cook or mess tent was placed about ten or fifteen yards further to the rear. The " striker " made down the beds and arranged the " furniture," so to speak, which generally consisted of a camp-stool, tin washbasin, and a looking-glass. The men put up their tents soon after caring for their horses. The fronts of their tents were placed on a line established by stretching a picket-rope. The first sergeant's was on that flank of the line nearest to the headquarters. The horse equipments were placed on a line three yards in front of the tents. The men were not prohibited from using their saddles as pillows. A trench was dug for the mess fire, and the grass was burned around it for several yards to prevent prairie fires. After this the cooks busied themselves preparing supper. Beef was issued soon after the wagon-train came in, and the necessary number of beeves were butchered for the

directed to take posts on prominent points overlooking the camp and surrounding country, to guard against surprise. Each post consisted of one non-commissioned officer and three privates. The officer of the day, in addition to his ordinary duties in camp, had charge of the safety of the cavalry herds. Sometimes this latter duty

next day's issue; this was hauled in the wagons. Stable call was sounded about an hour before sunset. The men of each troop were formed on the parade and marched to the horse herds by the first sergeant. Each man went to his own horse, took off the side-lines and fastened them around the horse's neck, then pulled the picket-pin, coiled the lariat, noosed the end fastened to the head halter around the horse's muzzle, mounted, and assembled in line at a place indicated by the first sergeant. The troop was then marched to the watering-place, which was usually selected with great care because of the boggy banks and miry beds of the prairie streams. After watering, the horses were lariated outside but in the immediate vicinity of the camp. The ground directly in rear of the troop belonged to it, and was jealously guarded by those concerned against encroachment by others. After lariating their horses, the men got their curry-combs, brushes, and nose-bags, and went to the troop wagon, where the quartermaster-sergeant and farrier measured, with tin cups, the forage to each man, each watching jealously that he got as much for his horse as those before him. He then went at once to feed and groom his horse. The officer whose duty it was to attend stables and the first sergeant superintended the grooming, examining each horse's back and feet carefully to see if they were all right. When a horse's back got sore through the carelessness of the rider, the man would generally be compelled to lead his horse until the sore was well. Immediately after stables, the cooks announced in a loud tone "supper." The men with haversack and tin cup went to the mess fire and got their hardtack, meat, and coffee. If game had been killed the men did a little extra cooking themselves.

The troop officers' mess kits consisted of a sheet-iron cooking-stove, an iron kettle, stewing, frying, baking, and dish pans; a small Dutch oven, a camp-kettle, a mess-chest holding tableware for four persons, and a small folding-table. The table in fair weather was spread in the open air. The early part of the meal was a matter of business, but after the substantials were stowed away, the delicacies were eaten more leisurely and time found for conversation. After supper the pipes were lighted, and the officers, if the weather was cold, went to the windward side of the camp-fire. Each man as he took his place was sure to poke or kick the fire, turn his back, hitch up his coat-tail, and fold his hands behind him.

Retreat was sounded a little after sunset and the roll was called, as much to insure the men having their equipments in place as to secure their presence, for it was not often we were near enough to any attraction to call the men away. (In 1876 there was not a ranch west of Bismarck, Dakota, nor east of Bozeman, Montana.) The stable guards began their tours of duty at this time. The non-commissioned officer reported to the troop commander for instructions for the night; these usually designated whether the horses were to be tied to the picket-line or kept out to graze, and included special instructions for the care of sick or weak horses. At dusk all horses were brought within the limits of the camp. The picket-line was stretched over three wagons in front of the men's tents, or three posts were used when remaining in camp over a day.

During the evening the men grouped about the fires and sang songs and spun yarns until "taps." The cooks prepared the breakfast, which usually consisted of hard bread, bacon, and coffee. If beans or fresh meat were to be cooked, the food was put into the Dutch ovens or camp-kettles, which were placed in the fire trench, covered over with hot ashes and coals, and a fire built over them. If the wind blew hard all fires were extinguished, to prevent prairie fires. The cooks were called an hour or an hour and a half before reveille. At the first call for reveille, usually 4.20 A. M., the stable guard awakened the occupants of each tent and the officer whose duty it was to attend roll-call. Stable call followed reveille and was superintended by an officer. This occupied about three-quarters of an hour. Two hours after reveille, the command would be on the march. Of course there were incidents that occasionally relieved the monotony.

Antelope were very plentiful, and the men were encouraged by troop commanders to hunt. General Custer had a number of stag-hounds, which amused themselves and the command in their futile attempts to catch them. One morning they started up a large buck near where the column was marching; Lieutenant Hare immediately followed the hounds, passed them, drew his revolver, and shot the buck. Nothing of special interest occurred until the 27th of May, when we came to the Bad Lands of the Little Missouri River. On the 30th General Custer was sent with four troops to make a scout up the Little Missouri, for about twenty miles. He returned the same day, without having discovered any recent "Indian signs." On the 31st we crossed the Little Missouri without difficulty. On the 1st and 2d of June we were obliged to remain in camp on account of a snow-storm.

We remained in camp on the Powder River for three days. General Terry went to the Yellowstone to communicate with the supply steamer *Far West*, which was at the mouth of the Powder River. He also went up the Yellowstone to communicate with General Gibbon's command, known as the "Montana Column," composed of four troops of the 2d Cavalry and several companies of the 7th Infantry. Before General Terry left it was given out that the 7th Cavalry would be sent to scout up the Powder River, while the wagon-train, escorted by the infantry, would be sent to establish a supply camp at the mouth of the Powder.

Eleven pack-mules, saddles, and aparejos were issued to each troop for this scout. This was a new departure; neither officers, men, nor mules had had any experience with this method of transportation. There were a few "packers" (civilian employés) to give instructions. Short, compactly built mules, the best for the purpose, were selected from the teams. A non-commissioned officer and four men of each troop were detailed for packers. After some instruction had been given by the professionals, especially how to tie the "diamond hitch," we concluded to make our maiden attempt by packing two empty water-casks. The mule was blinded and he submitted, with some uneasiness, to the packing. We supposed the packs were securely fastened and did not anticipate any trouble; but it is always the unexpected that happens with a mule. The blind was lifted; the mule gave a startled look first to one side, then to the other, at the two casks bandaged to his sides. He jumped to one side, causing to rattle a bung-plug that had fallen inside one of the casks. This startled him still more, and with head and tail high in the air he jumped again. He snorted and brayed, bucked and kicked, until the casks fell off. One was fastened to the saddle by the sling-rope. He now began to run, braying and making such a "rumpus" that the camp turned out as spectators. The affair excited serious concern lest all the animals in camp would be stampeded. When the cask was loose we got him back and made a second attempt with two sacks of grain. These he soon bucked off and then regaled himself with the spilt grain. As a final effort we concluded to try the aparejo, and pack two boxes of ammunition. This done, the mule walked off with as little concern as if he had been a pack-mule all his life.

General Terry having returned, orders were issued on the 10th for the right wing, six troops, under Major Reno, to make a scout up the Powder, provided with twelve days' rations. The left wing was ordered to turn over all forage and rations; also the pack-mules, except four to each troop. Major Reno left at 3 P. M., and the next day the rest of the command marched to the mouth of the Powder. My troop was rear-guard, and at times we were over three miles in rear of the wagon-train waiting on the packers, for we had taken this opportunity to give them practical instruction.

Up to this time we had not seen an Indian, nor any recent signs of them, except one small trail of perhaps a half dozen tepees, evidently of a party of agency Indians on their way to join the hostile camps. The buffalo had all gone west; other game was scarce and wild. The indications were that the Indians were west of the Powder, and information from General Gibbon placed them south of the Yellowstone. Some of the officers of the right wing before they left expressed their belief that we would not find any Indians, and were sanguine that we would all get home by the middle of August.

Major Reno was ordered to scout to the forks of the Powder, then across to Mizpah Creek, follow it down to near its confluence with the Powder; then cross over to Pumpkin Creek, follow it down to the Tongue River, scout up that stream, and then rejoin the regiment at the mouth of the Tongue by the time his supplies were exhausted; unless, in the mean time, he should make some discovery that made it necessary to return sooner to make preparations for pursuit. A supply depot was established at the mouth of the Powder, guarded by the infantry, at which the wagon-train was left.

General Terry, with his staff and some supplies, took passage on the supply steamer *Far West*, and went up to the mouth of the Tongue. General Custer, with the left wing, marched to the mouth of the Tongue, where we remained until the 19th waiting tidings from Reno's scout. The grounds where we camped had been occupied by the Indians the previous winter. (Miles City, Montana, was first built on the site of this camp.) The rude shelters for their ponies, built of driftwood, were still standing and furnished fuel for our camp-fires. A number of their dead, placed upon scaffolds, or tied to the branches of trees, were disturbed and robbed of their trinkets. Several persons rode about exhibiting trinkets with as much gusto as if they were trophies of their valor, and showed no more concern for their desecration than if they had won them at a raffle. Ten days later I saw the bodies of these same persons dead, naked, and mutilated.

On the 19th of June tidings came from Reno that he had found a large trail that led up the Rosebud River. The particulars were not generally known. The camp was full of rumors; credulity was raised to the highest pitch, and we were filled with anxiety and curiosity until we reached Reno's command, and learned the details of their discoveries. They had found a large trail on the Tongue River, and had followed it up the Rosebud about forty miles. The number of lodges in the deserted villages was estimated by the number of camp-fires remaining to be about three hundred and fifty. The indications were that the trail was about three weeks old. No Indians had been seen, nor any recent signs. It is not probable that Reno's movements were known to the Indians, for on the very day Reno reached his farthest point up the Rosebud, the battle of the Rosebud, between General Crook's forces and the Indians, was fought. The two commands were then not more than forty miles apart, but neither knew nor even suspected the proximity of the other.

We reached the mouth of the Rosebud about noon on the 21st, and began preparations for the march and the battle of the Little Big Horn.

There were a number of Sioux Indians who never went to an agency except to visit friends and relatives. They camped in and roamed about the Buffalo Country. Their camp was the rendezvous for the agency Indians when they went out for their annual hunts for meat and robes. They were known as the "Hostiles," and comprised representatives from all the different tribes of the Sioux nation. Many of them were renegade outlaws from the agencies. In their visits to the agencies they were usually arrogant and fomenters of discord. Depredations had been made upon the commerce to the Black Hills, and a number of lives taken by them or by others, for which they were blamed. The authorities at Washington had determined to compel these Indians to reside at the agencies — hence the Sioux War. Sitting Bull, an Uncpapa Sioux Indian, was the chief of the hostile camp; he had about sixty lodges of followers on whom he could at all times depend. He was the host of the Hostiles, and as such received and entertained their visitors. These visitors gave him many presents, and he was thus enabled to make many presents in return. All visitors paid tribute to him, so he gave liberally to the most influential, the chiefs, i. e., he "put it where it would do the most good." In this way he became known as the chief of the hostile Indian camp, and the camp was generally known as "Sitting Bull's camp." Sitting Bull was a heavy-set, muscular man, about five feet eight inches in stature, and at the time of the battle of the Little Big Horn was forty-two years of age. He was the autocrat of the camp — chiefly because he was the host. In council his views had great weight, because he was known as a great medicine man. He was a chief, but not a warrior chief. In the war councils he had a voice and vote the same as any other chief. A short time previous to the battle he had "made medicine," had predicted that the soldiers would attack them and that the soldiers would all be killed. He took no active part in the battle, but, as was his custom in time of danger, remained in the village "making medicine." Personally he was regarded as a great coward and a very great liar, " a man with a big head and a little heart." The command passed the remains of a "Sun-dance" lodge which took place about June 5, and to which I shall again refer. This was always a ceremony of great importance to the Indians. It ranks in interest and importance to the Indians with the graduation or commencement exercises of our civilized communities. In anticipation of this event, the Indians from the agencies had assembled at this camp.

Major James McLaughlin, United States Indian Agent, stationed at the Devil's Lake Agency, Dakota, from 1870 to 1881, and at Standing Rock Agency, Dakota, from 1881 to the present time, has made it a point to get estimates of the number of Indians at the hostile camp at the time of the battle. In his opinion, and all who know him will accept it with confidence, about one-third of the whole Sioux nation, including the northern Cheyennes and Arapahoes, were present at the battle; he estimates the number present as between twelve and fifteen thousand; that one out of four is a low estimate in determining the number of warriors present; every male over fourteen years of age may be considered a warrior in a general fight such as was the battle of the Little Big Horn; also, considering the extra hazards of the hunt and expected battle, fewer squaws would accompany the recruits from the agencies. The minimum strength of their fighting men may then be put down as between twenty-five hundred and three thousand. Information was despatched from General Sheridan that from one agency alone about eighteen hundred lodges had set out to join the hostile camp; but that information did not reach General Terry until several days after the battle. The principal warrior chiefs of the hostile Indians were: "Gall," "Crow King," and "Black Moon," Uncpapa Sioux; "Low Dog," "Crazy Horse," and "Big Road," Ogallala Sioux; "Spotted Eagle," Sans-Arc Sioux; "Hump" of the Minneconjous; and "White Bull" and "Little Horse," of the Cheyennes. To these belong the chief honors of conducting the battle, of whom, however, "Gall," "Crow King," and "Crazy Horse" were the ruling spirits.

Generals Terry, Gibbon, and Custer had a conference on board the steamer Far West. It was decided that the 7th Cavalry, under General Custer, should follow the trail discovered by Reno. "Officers' call" was sounded as soon as the conference had concluded. Upon assembling, General Custer gave us our orders. We were to transport on our pack-mules fifteen days' rations of hard bread, coffee, and sugar; twelve days' rations of bacon, and fifty rounds of carbine ammunition per man. Each man was to be supplied with 100 rounds of carbine and 24 rounds of pistol ammunition, to be carried on his person and in his saddle-bags. Each man was to carry on his horse twelve pounds of oats. The pack-mules sent out with Reno's command were badly used up, and promised seriously to embarrass the expedition. General Custer recommended that some extra forage be carried on the pack-mules. In endeavoring to carry out this recommendation some troop commanders foresaw the difficulties, and told the General that some of the mules would certainly break down, especially if the extra forage was packed. He replied in an excited manner, quite unusual with him: "Well, gentlemen, you may carry what supplies you please; you will be held responsible for your companies. The extra forage was only a suggestion, but this fact bear in mind, we will follow the trail for fifteen days unless we catch them before that time expires, no matter how far it may take us from our base of supplies; we may not see the supply steamer again;" and, turning as he was about to enter his tent, he added, "You had better carry along an extra supply of salt; we may have to live on horse meat before we get through." He was taken at his word, and an extra supply of salt was carried. "Battalion" and "wing" organizations were broken up, and troop commanders were responsible only to General Custer. His written instructions were as follows:

CAMP AT MOUTH OF ROSEBUD RIVER, MONTANA TERRITORY, June 22d, 1876. LIEUTENANT-COLONEL CUSTER, 7TH CAVALRY. COLONEL: The Brigadier-General Commanding directs that, as soon as your regiment can be made ready for the march, you will proceed up the Rosebud in pursuit of the Indians whose trail was discovered by Major Reno a few days since. It is, of course, impossible to give you any definite instructions in regard to this movement, and were it not impossible to do so the Department Commander places too much confidence in your zeal, energy, and ability to wish to impose upon you precise orders which might hamper your action when nearly in contact with the enemy. He will, however, indicate to you his own views of what your action should be, and he desires that you should conform to them unless you shall see sufficient reason for departing from them. He thinks that you should proceed up the Rosebud until you ascertain definitely the direction in which the trail above spoken of leads. Should it be found (as it appears almost certain that it will be found) to turn towards the Little Horn, he thinks that you should still proceed southward, perhaps as far as the headwaters of the Tongue, and then turn towards the Little Horn, feeling constantly, however, to your left, so as to preclude the possibility of the escape of the Indians to the south or southeast by passing around your left flank. The column of Colonel Gibbon is now in motion for the mouth of the Big Horn. As soon as it reaches

that point it will cross the Yellowstone and move up at least as far as the forks of the Big and Little Horns. Of course its future movements must be controlled by circumstances as they arise, but it is hoped that the Indians, if upon the Little Horn, may be so nearly inclosed by the two columns that their escape will be impossible.

The Department Commander desires that on your way up the Rosebud you should thoroughly examine the upper part of Tulloch's Creek, and that you should endeavor to send a scout through to Colonel Gibbon's column, with information of the result of your examination. The lower part of this creek will be examined by a detachment from Colonel Gibbon's command. The supply steamer will be pushed up the Big Horn as far as the forks if the river is found to be navigable for that distance, and the Department Commander, who will accompany the column of Colonel Gibbon, desires you to report to him there not later than the expiration of the time for which your troops are rationed, unless in the mean time you receive further orders. Very respectfully, your obedient servant, E. W. SMITH, Captain 18th Infantry, Acting Assistant Adjutant-General.

These instructions are explicit, and fixed the location of the Indians very accurately. Of course as soon as it was determined that we were to go out, nearly every one took time to write letters home, but I doubt very much if there were many of a cheerful nature. Some officers made their wills; others gave verbal instructions as to the disposition of personal property and distribution of mementos; they seemed to have a presentiment of their fate.

At twelve o'clock, noon, on the 22d of June, the "Forward" was sounded, and the regiment marched out of camp in column of fours, each troop followed by its pack-mules. Generals Terry, Gibbon, and Custer stationed themselves near our line of march and reviewed the regiment. General Terry had a pleasant word for each officer as he returned the salute. Our pack-trains proved troublesome at the start, as the cargoes began falling off before we got out of camp, and during all that day the mules straggled badly. After that day, however, they were placed under the charge of an officer, who was directed to report at the end of each day's march the order of merit of the efficiency of the troop packers. Doubtless General Custer had some ulterior design in this. It is quite probable that if he had had occasion to detach troops requiring rapid marching, he would have selected those troops whose packers had the best records. At all events the efficiency was much increased, and after we struck the Indian trail the pack-trains kept well closed.

We went into camp about 4 P. M., having marched twelve miles. About sunset "officers' call" was sounded, and we assembled at General Custer's bivouac and squatted in groups about the General's bed. It was not a cheerful assemblage; everybody seemed to be in a serious mood, and the little conversation carried on, before all had arrived, was in undertones. When all had assembled the General said that until further orders trumpet-calls would not be sounded except in an emergency; the marches would begin at 5 A. M. sharp; the troop commanders were all experienced officers, and knew well enough what to do, and when to do what was necessary for their troops; there were two things that would be regulated from his headquarters, i. e., when to move out of and when to go into camp. All other details, such as reveille, stables, watering, halting, grazing, etc., on the march would be left to the judgment and discretion of the troop commanders; they were to keep within supporting distance of each other, not to get ahead of the scouts, or very far to the rear of the column. He took particular pains to impress upon the officers his reliance upon their judgment, discretion, and loyalty. He thought, judging from the number of lodge-fires reported by Reno, that we might meet at least a thousand warriors; there might be enough young men from the agencies, visiting their hostile friends, to make a total of fifteen hundred. He had consulted the reports of the Commissioner of Indian Affairs as to the probable number of "Hostiles" (those who had persistently refused to live or enroll themselves at the Indian agencies), and he was confident, if any reliance was to be placed upon those reports, that there would not be an opposing force of more than fifteen hundred. General Terry had offered him the additional force of the battalion of the 2d Cavalry, but he had declined it because he felt sure that the 7th Cavalry could whip any force that would be able to combine against him; that if the regiment could not, no other regiment in the service could; if they could whip the regiment, they would be able to defeat a much larger force, or, in other words, the reinforcement of this battalion could not save us from defeat. With the regiment acting alone there would be harmony, but another organization would be sure to cause jealousy. He had declined the offer of the Gatling guns for the reason that they might hamper our movements or march at a critical moment, because of the difficult nature of the country through which we would march. The marches would be from twenty-five to thirty miles a day. Troop officers were cautioned to husband their rations and the strength of their mules and horses, as we might be out for a great deal longer time than that for which we were rationed, as he intended to follow the trail until we could get the Indians, even if it took us to the Indian agencies on the Missouri River or in Nebraska. All

officers were requested to make to him, then or at any time, any suggestions they thought fit.

This "talk" of his, as we called it, was considered at the time as something extraordinary for General Custer, for it was not his habit to unbosom himself to his officers. In it he showed a lack of self-confidence, a reliance on somebody else; there was an indefinable something that was not Custer. His manner and tone, usually brusque and aggressive, or somewhat rasping, was on this occasion conciliating and subdued. There was something akin to an appeal, as if depressed, that made a deep impression on all present. We compared watches to get the official time, and separated to attend to our various duties. Lieutenants McIntosh, Wallace,[1] and myself walked to our bivouac, for some distance in silence, when Wallace remarked: "Godfrey, I believe General Custer is going to be killed." "Why, Wallace," I replied, "what makes you think so?" "Because," said he, "I have never heard Custer talk in that way before."

I went to my troop and gave orders what time the "silent" reveille should be and as to other details for the morning preparations; also the following directions in case of a night attack: the stable guard, packers, and cooks were to go out at once to the horses and mules to quiet and guard them; the other men were to go at once to a designated rendezvous and await orders; no man should fire a shot until he received orders from an officer to do so. When they retired for the night they should put their arms and equipments where they could get them without leaving their beds. I then went through the herd to satisfy myself as to the security of the animals. During the performance of this duty I came to the bivouac of the Indian scouts. "Mitch" Bouyer, the half-breed interpreter, "Bloody Knife," the chief of the Ree scouts, "Half-Yellow-Face," the chief of the Crow scouts, and others were having a "talk." I observed them for a few minutes, when Bouyer turned toward me, apparently at the suggestion of "Half-Yellow-Face," and said, "Have you ever fought against these Sioux?" "Yes," I replied. Then he asked, "Well, how many do you expect to find?" I answered, "It is said we may find between one thousand and fifteen hundred." "Well, do you think we can whip that many?" "Oh, yes, I guess so." After he had interpreted our conversation, he said to me with a good deal of emphasis, "Well, I can tell you we are going to have a —— big fight."

At five o'clock, sharp, on the morning of the 23d, General Custer mounted and started up the Rosebud, followed by two sergeants, one

[1] Killed at the battle of Wounded Knee, December 29, 1890.

carrying the regimental standard and the other his personal or headquarters flag, the same kind of flag as used while commanding his cavalry division during the Rebellion. This was the signal for the command to mount and take up the march. Eight miles out we came to the first of the Indian camping-places. It certainly indicated a large village and numerous population. There were a great many " wicki-ups " (bushes stuck in the ground with the tops drawn together, over which they placed canvas or blankets). These we supposed at the time were for the dogs, but subsequent events developed the fact that they were the temporary shelters of the transients from the agencies. During the day we passed through three of these camping-places and made halts at each one. Everybody was busy studying the age of pony droppings and tracks and lodge trails, and endeavoring to determine the number of lodges. These points were the all-absorbing topics of conversation. We went into camp about five o'clock, having marched about thirty-three miles.

June 24th we passed a great many camping-places, all appearing to be of nearly the same strength. One would naturally suppose these were the successive camping-places of the same village, when in fact they were the continuous camps of the several bands. The fact that they appeared to be of nearly the same age, that is, having been made at the same time, did not impress us then. We passed through one much larger than any of the others. The grass for a considerable distance around it had been cropped close, indicating that large herds had been grazed there. The frame of a large " Sun-dance " lodge was standing, and in it we found the scalp of a white man, probably one of General Gibbon's command who had been killed some weeks previously. It was whilst here that the Indians from the agencies had joined the Hostiles' camp. The command halted here and " officers' call " was sounded. Upon assembling we were informed that our Crow scouts, who had been very active and efficient, had discovered fresh signs, the tracks of three or four ponies and of one Indian on foot. At this time a stiff southerly breeze was blowing; as we were about to separate, the General's headquarters flag was blown down, falling toward our rear. Being near the flag, I picked it up and stuck the staff in the ground, but it fell again to the rear. I then bored the staff into the ground where it would have the support of a sage-bush. This circumstance made no impression on me at the time, but after the battle an officer asked me if I remembered the incident; he had observed it, and regarded the fact of its falling to the rear as a bad omen, and felt sure we would suffer a defeat.

The march during the day was tedious. We made many long halts so as not to get ahead of the scouts, who seemed to be doing their work thoroughly, giving special attention to the right, toward Tulloch's Creek, the valley of which was in general view from the divide. Once or twice signal smokes were reported in that direction. The weather was dry and had been for some time, consequently the trail was very dusty. The troops were required to march on separate trails so that the dust clouds would not rise so high. The valley was heavily marked with lodge-pole trails and pony tracks, showing that immense herds of ponies had been driven over it. About sundown we went into camp under the cover of a bluff, so as to hide the command as much as possible. We had marched about twenty-eight miles. The fires were ordered to be put out as soon as supper was over, and we were to be in readiness to march again at 11.30 P. M. Lieutenant Hare and myself lay down about 9.30 to take a nap; when comfortably fixed we heard some one say, " He 's over there by that tree." As that described our locality pretty well, I called out to know what was wanted, and the reply came : " The General's compliments and wants to see all the officers at headquarters immediately." So we gave up our much-needed rest and groped our way through horse herds, over sleeping men, and through thickets of bushes trying to find headquarters. No one could tell us, and as all fires and lights were out we could not keep our bearings. We finally espied a solitary candle-light, toward which we traveled, and found most of the officers assembled at the General's bivouac. The General said that the trail led over the divide to the Little Big Horn ; the march would be taken up at once, as he was anxious to get as near the divide as possible before daylight, where the command would be concealed during the day, and give ample time for the country to be studied, to locate the village and to make plans for the attack on the 26th. We then returned to our troops, except Lieutenant Hare, who was put on duty with the scouts. Because of the dust it was impossible to see any distance, and the rattle of equipments and clattering of the horses' feet made it difficult to hear distinctly beyond our immediate surroundings. We could not see the trail, and we could only follow it by keeping in the dust cloud. The night was very calm, but occasionally a slight breeze would waft the cloud and disconcert our bearings ; then we were obliged to halt to catch a sound from those in advance, sometimes whistling or hallooing, and getting a response we would start forward again. Finally troopers were put ahead, away from the noise of our column, and where they could hear the noise of those in front. A little after 2 A. M., June 25, the command was halted to await further tidings from the scouts; we had marched about ten miles. Part of the command unsaddled to rest the horses. After daylight some coffee was made, but it was almost impossible to drink it; the water was so alkaline that the horses refused to drink it. Some time before eight o'clock, General Custer rode bareback to the several troops and gave orders to be ready to march at eight o'clock, and gave information that scouts had discovered the locality of the Indian villages or camps in the valley of the Little Big Horn, about twelve or fifteen miles beyond the divide. Just before setting out on the march I went to where General Custer's bivouac was. The General, "Bloody Knife," and several Ree scouts and a half-breed interpreter were squatted in a circle having a "talk," after the Indian fashion. The General wore a serious expression and was apparently abstracted. The scouts were doing the talking, and seemed nervous and disturbed. Finally "Bloody Knife" made a remark that recalled the General from his reverie, and he asked in his usual quick, brusque manner, "What's that he says?" The interpreter replied, "He says we'll find enough Sioux to keep us fighting two or three days." The General smiled and remarked, "I guess we'll get through with them in one day."

We started promptly at eight o'clock and marched uninterruptedly until 10.30 A. M., when we halted in a ravine and were ordered to preserve quiet, keep concealed, and not do anything that would be likely to reveal our presence to the enemy; we had marched about ten miles.

It is a rare occurrence in Indian warfare that gives a commander the opportunity to reconnoiter the enemy's position in daylight. This is particularly true if the Indians have a knowledge of the presence of troops in the country. When following an Indian trail the "signs" indicate the length of time elapsed since the presence of the Indians. When the "signs" indicate a "hot trail," *i. e.*, near approach, the commander judges his distance and by a forced march, usually in the night-time, tries to reach the Indian village at night and make his disposition for a surprise attack at daylight. At all events his attack must be made with celerity, and generally without other knowledge of the numbers of the opposing force than that discovered or conjectured while following the trail. The dispositions for the attack may be said to be "made in the dark," and successful surprise to depend upon luck. If the advance to the attack be made in daylight it is next to impossible that a near approach can be made without discovery. In all our previous experiences, when the immediate presence of the troops was once known to them, the warriors swarmed to the attack, and resorted to all kinds of ruses to mislead the troops, to delay the advance toward their camp or village, while the squaws and children secured what personal effects they could, drove off the pony herd, and by flight put themselves beyond danger, and then scattering made successful pursuit next to impossible. In civilized warfare the hostile forces may confront each other for hours, days, or weeks, and the battle may be conducted with a tolerable knowledge of the numbers, position, etc., of each other. A full knowledge of the immediate presence of the enemy does not imply immediate attack. In Indian warfare the rule is "touch and go." These remarks are made because the firebrand nature of Indian warfare is not generally understood. In meditating upon the preliminaries of an Indian battle, old soldiers who have participated only in the battles of the Rebellion are apt to draw upon their own experiences for comparison, when there is no comparison.

The Little Big Horn River, or the "Greasy Grass" as it is known to the Indians, is a rapid mountain stream, from twenty to forty yards wide, with pebbled bottom, but abrupt, soft banks. The water at the ordinary stage is from two to five feet in depth, depending upon the width of the channel. The general direction of its course is northeasterly down to the Little Big Horn battle-field, where it trends northwesterly to its confluence with the Big Horn River. The other topographical features of the country which concern us in this narrative may be briefly described as follows: Between the Little Big Horn and Big Horn Rivers is a plateau of undulating prairie; between the Little Big Horn and the Rosebud are the Little Chetish or Wolf Mountains. By this it must not be misunderstood as a rocky upheaval chain or spur of mountains, but it is a rough, broken country of considerable elevation, of high precipitous hills and deep, narrow gulches. The command had followed the trail up a branch of the Rosebud to within, say, a mile of the summit of these mountains, which form the "divide." Not many miles to our right was the divide between the Little Big Horn and Tulloch's Fork. The creek that drained the watershed to our right and front is now called "Sundance," or Benteen's, Creek. The trail, very tortuous, and sometimes dangerous, followed down the bed and valley of this creek, which at that time was dry for the greater part of its length. It was from the divide between the Little Big Horn and the Rosebud that the scouts had discovered the smoke rising above the village, and the pony herds grazing in the valley of the Little Big Horn, somewhere about twelve or fifteen miles away. It was to their point of view that General Custer had gone while the column was halted in the ravine. It was impossible for him to discover more of the enemy than had already been reported by the scouts. In consequence of the high bluffs which screened the village, it was not possible in following the trail to discover more. Nor was there a point of observation near the trail from which further discoveries could be made until the battle was at hand.

It was well known to the Indians that the troops were in the field, and a battle was fully expected by them; but the close proximity of our column was not known to them until the morning of the day of the battle. Several young men had left the hostile camp on that morning to go to one of the agencies in Nebraska. They saw the dust made by the column of troops; some of their number returned to the village and gave warning that the troops were coming, so the attack was not a surprise. For two or three days their camp had been pitched on the site where they were attacked. The place was not selected with the view to making that the battle-field of the campaign, but whoever was in the van on their march thought it a good place to camp, put up his tepee, and the others as they arrived followed his example. It is customary among the Indians to camp by bands. The bands usually camp some distance apart, and Indians of the number then together would occupy a territory of several miles along the river valley, and not necessarily within supporting distance of each other. But in view of the possible fulfilment of Sitting Bull's prophecy the village had massed.

Our officers had generally collected in groups and discussed the situation. Some sought solitude and sleep, or meditation. The Ree scouts, who had not been very active for the past day or two, were together and their "medicine man" was anointing them and invoking the Great Spirit to protect them from the Sioux. They seemed to have become satisfied that we were going to find more Sioux than we could well take care of. Captain Yates's troop had lost one of its packs of hard bread during the night march from our last halting-place on the 24th. He had sent a detail back on the trail to recover it. Captain Keogh came to where a group of officers were, and said this detail had returned and reported that when near the pack they discovered an Indian opening one of the boxes of hard bread with his tomahawk, and that as soon as the Indian saw the soldiers he galloped away to the hills out of range and then moved along leisurely. This information was taken to the General at once by his brother, Colonel Tom Custer. The General came back and had "officers' call" sounded. He recounted Captain

Keogh's report, and also said that the scouts had seen several Indians moving along the ridge overlooking the valley through which we had marched, as if observing our movements; he thought the Indians must have seen the dust made by the command. At all events our presence had been discovered and further concealment was unnecessary; that we would march at once to attack the village; that he had not intended to make the attack until the next morning, the 26th, but our discovery made it imperative to act at once, as delay would allow the village to scatter and escape. Troop commanders were ordered to make a detail of one non-commissioned officer and six men to accompany the pack; to inspect their troops and report as soon as they were ready to march; that the troops would take their places in the column of march in the order in which reports of readiness were received, and that the last one to report would escort the pack-train.

The inspections were quickly made and the column was soon en route. We crossed the dividing ridge between the Rosebud and Little Big Horn valleys a little before noon. Shortly afterward the regiment was divided into battalions. The advance battalion, under Major Reno, consisted of troop "M," Captain French; troop "A," Captain Moylan and Lieutenant De Rudio; troop "G," Lieutenants McIntosh and Wallace; the Indian scouts under Lieutenants Varnum and Hare and the interpreter Girard; Lieutenant Hodgson was Acting Adjutant and Doctors De Wolf and Porter were the medical officers. The battalion under General Custer was composed of troop "I," Captain Keogh and Lieutenant Porter; troop "F," Captain Yates and Lieutenant Reily; troop "C," Captain Custer and Lieutenant Harrington; troop "E," Lieutenants Smith and Sturgis; troop "L," Lieutenants Calhoun and Crittenden; Lieutenant Cook was the Adjutant, and Dr. G. E. Lord was medical officer. The battalion under Captain Benteen consisted of troop "H," Captain Benteen and Lieutenant Gibson; troop "D," Captain Weir and Lieutenant Edgerly, and troop "K," Lieutenant Godfrey. The pack-train, Lieutenant Mathey in charge, was under the escort of troop "B," Captain McDougall.

Major Reno's battalion marched down a valley that developed into the small tributary to the Little Big Horn, now called "Sun-dance," or Benteen's, Creek. The Indian trail followed the meanderings of this valley. Custer's column followed Reno's closely, and the pack-train followed their trail. Benteen's battalion was ordered to the left and front, to a line of high bluffs about three or four miles distant. Benteen was ordered if he saw anything to send word to Custer, but to pitch into anything he

"BOOTS AND SADDLES."

came across; if, when he arrived at the high bluffs, he could not see any enemy, he should continue his march to the next line of bluffs and so on, until he could see the Little Big Horn Valley. He marched over a succession of rough, steep hills and deep valleys. The view from the point where the regiment was organized into battalions did not discover the difficult nature of the country, but as we advanced farther it became more and more difficult and more forbidding. Lieutenant Gibson was sent some distance in advance but saw no enemy, and so signaled the result of his reconnaissance to Benteen. The obstacles threw the battalion by degrees to the right until we came in sight of and not more than a mile from the trail. Many of our horses were greatly jaded by the climbing and descending, some getting far to the rear of the column. Benteen very wisely determined to follow the trail of the rest of the command, and we got into it just in advance of the pack-train. During this march on the left we could see occasionally the battalion under Custer, distinguished by the troop mounted on gray horses, marching at a rapid gait. Two or three times we heard loud cheering and also some few shots, but the occasion of these demonstrations is not known.

Some time after getting on the trail we came to a water-hole, or morass, at which a stream of running water had its source. Benteen halted the battalion. While watering we heard some firing in advance, and Weir became a little impatient at the delay of watering and started off with his troop, taking the advance, whereas his place in column was second. The rest of the battalion moved out very soon afterward and soon caught up with him. Just as we were leaving the water-hole the pack-train was arriving, and the poor thirsty mules plunged into the morass in spite of the efforts of the packers to prevent them, for they had not had water since the previous evening. We passed a burning tepee, fired presumably by our scouts, in which was the body of a warrior who had been killed in the battle with Crook's troops on the Rosebud on the 17th of June.

The battalions under Reno and Custer did not meet any Indians until Reno arrived at the burning tepee; here a few were seen. These Indians did not act as if surprised by the appearance of troops; they made no effort to delay the column, but simply kept far enough in advance to invite pursuit. Reno's command and the scouts followed them closely, until he received orders "to move forward at as rapid a gait as he thought prudent, and charge the village afterward, and the whole outfit would support him." The order was received when Reno was not very far from the Little Big Horn

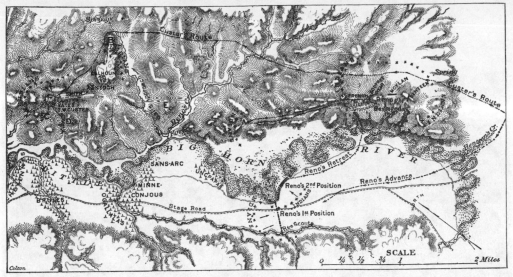

MAP OF CUSTER'S LAST BATTLE.

A — Hill where Custer was seen by some of Reno's men during the fight in the valley ; also the point reached by Reno's advance after the retreat from the valley, from which he fell back to the position in which he was besieged. B — Here Keogh's and Calhoun's troops dismounted and advanced along the ridge to where the bodies of their commands were found. C — A few bodies mostly from the commands of Yates and T. W. Custer, who for the greater part died with General Custer on the hill above, now known as Custer's Hill, and on which stands the monument shown on page 383. D — Ravine where were found bodies of many of Smith's troop who had formed in line on the ridge between Custer's and Keogh's position ; Lieutenant Smith's body was found on Custer's Hill. E — Hill where Sergeant Butler's body was found ; empty cartridge-shells lay about him. He belonged to Captain Custer's troop, and may have been carrying a message to Reno.

River. His battalion moved at a trot to the river, where Reno delayed about ten or fifteen minutes watering the horses and reforming the column on the left bank of the stream. Reno now sent word to Custer that he had everything in front of him and that the enemy was strong. Custer had moved off to the right, being separated from Reno by a line of high bluffs and the river. Reno moved forward in column of fours about half a mile, then formed the battalion in line of battle across the valley with the scouts on the left ; after advancing about a mile further he deployed the battalion as skirmishers. In the mean time the Hostiles, continually reinforced, fell back, firing occasionally, but made no decided effort to check Reno's advance. The horses of two men became unmanageable and carried them into the Indian camp. The Indians now developed great force, opened a brisk fire, mounted, and made a dash

RENO'S CROSSING, IN RETREAT, SHOWING VALLEY TO THE WEST. (FROM A PHOTOGRAPH BY D. F. BARRY.)

RENO'S CROSSING, IN RETREAT, THE BLUFF WHERE HE WAS BESIEGED APPEARING ON THE RIGHT.
(FROM A PHOTOGRAPH BY D. F. BARRY.)

toward the foot-hills on the left flank where the Ree scouts were. The scouts ignominiously fled, most of them abandoning the field altogether.

Reno, not seeing the " whole outfit " within supporting distance, did not obey his orders to charge the village, but dismounted his command to fight on foot. The movements of the Indians around the left flank and the flight of the scouts caused the left to fall back until the command was on the defensive in the timber and covered by the bank of the old river-bed. Reno's loss thus far was one wounded. The position was a strong one, well protected in front by the bank and fringe of timber, somewhat open in the rear, but sheltered by timber in the bottom. Those present differ in their estimates of the length of time the command remained in the bottom after they were attacked in force. Some say " a few minutes "; others, " about an hour." While Reno remained there his casualties were few. The Hostiles had him nearly surrounded, and there was some firing from the rear of the position by Indians on the opposite bank of the river. One man was killed close to where Reno was, and directly afterward Reno gave orders to those near him to " mount and get to the bluffs." This order was not generally heard or communicated; while those who did hear it were preparing to execute it, he countermanded the order, but soon afterward he repeated the same order, " to mount and get to the bluffs," and again it was not generally understood. Individuals, observing

the preparations of those on the left, near Reno, informed their troop commanders, who then gave orders to mount. Owing to the noise of the firing and to the absorbed attention they were giving to the enemy, many did not know of the order until too late to accompany the command. Some remained concealed until the Indians left and then came out. Four others remained until night and then escaped. Reno's command left the bottom by troop organizations in column. Reno was with the foremost in this retreat or " charge," as he termed it in his report, and after he had exhausted the shots of his revolvers he threw them away. The hostile strength pushed Reno's retreat to the left, so he could not get to the ford where he had entered the valley, but they were fortunate in striking the river at a fordable place; a pony-trail led up a funnel-shaped ravine into the bluffs. Here the command got jammed and lost all semblance of organization. The Indians fired into them, but not very effectively. There does not appear to have been any resistance, certainly no organized resistance, during this retreat. On the right and left of the ravine into which the pony-path led were rough precipitous clay bluffs. It was surprising to see what steep inclines men and horses clambered up under the excitement of danger.

Lieutenant Donald McIntosh was killed soon after leaving the timber. Dr. De Wolf was killed while climbing one of the bluffs a short distance from the command. Lieutenant B. H. Hodgson's horse leaped from the bank into the river and fell dead; the lieutenant was wounded in the leg, probably by the same bullet that killed the horse. Hodgson called out, " For God's sake, don't abandon me "; he was assured that he would not be left behind. Hodgson then took hold of a comrade's stirrup-strap and was taken across the stream, but soon after was shot and killed. Hodgson, some days before the battle, had said that if he was dismounted in battle or wounded, he intended to take hold of somebody's stirrup to assist himself from the field. During the retreat Private Dalvern, troop " F," had a hand-to-hand conflict with an Indian; his horse was killed; he then shot the Indian, caught the Indian's pony, and rode to the command.

Reno's casualties thus far were three officers, including Dr. J. M. De Wolf, and twenty-nine enlisted men and scouts killed; seven enlisted men wounded; and one officer, one interpreter, and fourteen soldiers and scouts missing. Nearly all the casualties occurred during the retreat and after leaving the timber. The Ree scouts continued their flight until they reached the supply camp at the mouth of the Powder, on the 27th. The Crow scouts remained with the command.

CAVALRY OFFICER IN CAMPAIGN DRESS.

We will now go back to Benteen's battalion. Not long after leaving the water-hole a sergeant met him with an order from Custer to the commanding officer of the pack-train to hurry it up. The sergeant was sent back to the train with the message; as he passed the column he said to the men, " We 've got 'em, boys." From this and other remarks we inferred that Custer had attacked and captured the village.

Shortly afterward we were met by a trumpeter bearing this message signed by Colonel Cook, Adjutant: "Benteen, come on. Big village. Be quick. Bring packs," with the postscript, " Bring packs." The column had been marching at a trot and walk, according as the ground was smooth or broken. We now heard firing, first straggling shots, and as we advanced the engagement became more and more pronounced and appeared to be coming toward us. The column took the gallop with pistols drawn, expecting to meet the enemy which we thought Custer was driving before him in his effort to communicate with the pack-train, never suspecting that our force had been defeated. We were forming in line to meet our supposed enemy, when we came in full view of the valley of the Little Big Horn. The valley was full of horsemen riding to and fro in clouds of dust and smoke, for the grass had been fired by the Indians to drive the troops out and cover their own movements. On the bluffs to our right we saw a body of troops and that they were engaged. But an engagement appeared to be going on in the valley too. Owing to the distance, smoke, and dust, it was impossible to distinguish if those in the valley were friends or foes. There was a short time of uncertainty as to the direction in which we should go, but some Crow scouts came by, driving a small herd of ponies, one of whom said " Soldiers," and motioned for the command to go to the right. Following his directions, we soon joined Reno's battalion, which was still firing. Reno had lost his hat and had a handkerchief tied about his head, and appeared to be very much excited.

Benteen's battalion was ordered to dismount and deploy as skirmishers on the edge of the bluffs overlooking the valley. Very soon after this the Indians withdrew from the attack. Lieutenant Hare came to where I was standing and, grasping my hand heartily, said with a good deal of emphasis : " We 've had a big fight in the bottom, got whipped, and I am —— glad to see you." I was satisfied that he meant what he said, for I had already suspected that something was wrong, but was not quite prepared for such startling information. Benteen's battalion was ordered to divide its ammunition with Reno's men, who had apparently expended nearly all in their personal possession. It has often been a matter of doubt whether this was a fact, or the effect of imagination. It seems most improbable, in view of their active movements and the short time the command was firing, that the " most of the men " should have expended one hundred and fifty rounds of ammunition per man.

While waiting for the ammunition pack-mules, Major Reno concluded to make an effort to recover and bury the body of Lieutenant Hodgson. At the same time we loaded up a few men with canteens to get water for the command; they were to accompany the rescuing party. The effort was futile; the party was ordered back after being fired upon by some Indians who doubtless were scalping the dead near the foot of the bluffs.

A number of officers collected on the edge of the bluff overlooking the valley and were discussing the situation; among our number was Captain Moylan, a veteran soldier, and a good one too, watching intently the scene below. Moylan remarked, quite emphatically: " Gentlemen, in my opinion General Custer has made the biggest mistake of his life, by not taking the whole regiment in at once in the first attack." At this time there were a large number of horsemen, Indians, in the valley. Suddenly they all started down the valley, and in a few minutes scarcely a horseman was to be seen. Heavy firing was heard down the river. During this time the questions were being asked : " What 's the matter with Custer, that he don't send word what we shall do? " " Wonder what we are staying here for? " etc., thus showing some uneasiness; but still no one seemed to show great anxiety, nor do I know that any one felt any serious apprehension but that Custer could and would take care of himself. Some of Reno's men had seen a party of Custer's command, including Custer himself, on the bluffs about the time the Indians began to develop in Reno's front. This party was heard to cheer, and seen to wave their hats as if to give encouragement, and then they disappeared behind the hills or escaped further attention from those below. It was about the time of this incident that Trumpeter Martini left Cook with Custer's last orders to Benteen, viz.: " Benteen, come on. Big village. Be quick. Bring packs. Cook, Adjutant. P. S. Bring packs." The repetition in the order would seem to indicate that Cook was excited, flurried, or that he wanted to emphasize the necessity for escorting the packs. It is possible, yes probable, that from the high point Custer could then see nearly the whole camp and force of the Indians and realized that the chances were desperate; but it was too late

to reunite his forces for the attack. Reno was already in the fight and his (Custer's) own battalion was separated from the attack by a distance of two and a half to three miles. He had no reason to think that Reno would not push his attack vigorously. A commander seldom goes into battle counting upon the failure of

LIEUTENANT B. H. HODGSON,   LIEUTENANT DONALD McINTOSH.
ACTING ADJUTANT.   COMMANDING TROOP " G."

OFFICERS WITH RENO, WHO WERE KILLED.

his lieutenant; if he did, he certainly would provide that such failure should not turn into disaster.

During a long time after the junction of Reno and Benteen we heard firing down the river in the direction of Custer's command. We were satisfied that Custer was fighting the Indians somewhere, and the conviction was expressed that " our command ought to be doing something or Custer would be after Reno with a sharp stick." We heard two distinct volleys which excited some surprise, and, if I mistake not, brought out the remark from some one that " Custer was giving it to them for all he was worth." I have but little doubt now that these volleys were fired by Custer's orders as signals of distress and to indicate where he was.

Captain Weir and Lieutenant Edgerly, after driving the Indians away from Reno's command, on their side, heard the firing, became impatient at the delay, and thought they would move down that way, if they should be permitted. Weir started to get this permission, but changed his mind and concluded to take a survey from the high bluffs first. Edgerly, seeing Weir going in the direction of the firing, supposed it was all right and started down the ravine with the troop. Weir, from the high point, saw the Indians in large numbers start for Edgerly, and signaled for him to change his direction, and Edgerly went over to the high point, where they remained, not seriously molested, until the remainder of the troops marched down there; the Indians were seen by them to ride about what afterward proved to be Custer's battle-field, shooting into the bodies of the dead men.

McDougall came up with the pack-train and reported the firing when he reported his arrival

GENERAL CUSTER IN HIS BUCKSKIN SUIT.
This was his dress on his last campaign, with cavalry boots and sombrero added. The portrait is from a photograph of General Custer and the Grand Duke Alexis, taken at the time of their hunting expedition, not long before General Custer's death.

Indians, but they drove them away and were not again molested.

My recollection is that it was about half-past two when we joined Reno. About five o'clock the command moved down toward Custer's supposed whereabouts, intending to join him. The advance went as far as the high bluffs where the command was halted. Persons who have been on the plains and have seen stationary objects dancing before them, now in view and now obscured, or a weed on the top of a hill, projected against the sky, magnified to appear as a tree, will readily understand why our views would be unsatisfactory. We could see stationary groups of horsemen, and individual horsemen moving about; from their grouping and the manner in which they sat their horses we knew they were Indians. On the left of the valley a strange sight attracted our attention. Some one remarked that there had been a fire that scorched the leaves of the bushes, which caused the reddish-brown appearance, but this appearance was changeable; watching this intently for a short time with field-glasses, it was discovered that this strange sight was the immense pony-herds of the Indians.

Looking toward Custer's field, on a hill two miles away we saw a large assemblage. At first our command did not appear to attract their attention, although there was some commotion observable among those nearer to our position. We heard occasional shots, most of which seemed to be a great distance off, beyond the large groups on the hill. While watching this group the conclusion was arrived at that Custer had been repulsed, and the firing was the parting shots of the rear-guard. The firing ceased, the groups dispersed, clouds of dust arose from all parts of the field, and the horsemen converged toward our position. The command was now dismounted to fight on foot. Weir's and French's troops were posted on the high bluffs and to the front of them; my own troop along the crest of the bluffs next to the river; the rest of the command moved to the rear, as I supposed to occupy other points in the vicinity, to make this our defensive position. Busying myself with posting my men, giving direction about the use of ammunition, etc., I was a little startled by the remark that the command was out of sight. At this time Weir's and French's troops were being attacked. Orders were soon brought to me by Lieutenant Hare,

to Reno. I remember distinctly looking at my watch at twenty minutes past four, and made a note of it in my memorandum-book, and although I have never satisfactorily been able to recall what particular incident happened at that time, it was some important event before we started down the river. It is my impression, however, that it was the arrival of the pack-train. It was about this time that thirteen men and a scout named Herendeen rejoined the command; they had been missing since Reno's flight from the bottom; several of them were wounded. These men had lost their horses in the stampede from the bottom and had remained in the timber; when leaving the timber to rejoin, they were fired upon by five

Acting-Adjutant, to join the main command. I had gone some distance in the execution of this order when, looking back, I saw French's troop come tearing over the bluffs, and soon after Weir's troop followed in hot haste. Edgerly was near the top of the bluff trying to mount his frantic horse, and it did seem that he would not succeed, but he vaulted into his saddle and then joined the troop. The Indians almost immediately followed to the top of the bluff, and commenced firing into the retreating troops, killing one man, wounding others and several horses. They then started down the hillside in pursuit. I at once made up my mind that such a retreat and close pursuit would throw the whole command into confusion, and, perhaps, prove disastrous. I dismounted my men to fight on foot, deploying as rapidly as possible without waiting for the formation laid down in tactics. Lieutenant Hare expressed his intention of staying with me, "Adjutant or no Adjutant." The led horses were sent to the main command. Our fire in a short time compelled the Indians to halt and take cover, but before this was accomplished, a second order came for me to fall back as quickly as possible to the main command. Having checked the pursuit we began our retreat, slowly at first, but kept up our firing. After proceeding some distance the men began to group together, and to move a little faster and faster, and our fire slackened. This was pretty good evidence that they were getting demoralized. The Indians were being heavily reinforced, and began to come from their cover, but kept up a heavy fire. I halted the line, made the men take their intervals, and again drove the Indians to cover; then once more began the retreat. The firing of the Indians was very heavy; the bullets struck the ground all about us; but the "ping-ping" of the bullets overhead seemed to have a more terrifying influence than the "swish-thud" of the bullets that struck the ground immediately about us. When we got to the ridge in front of Reno's position I observed some Indians making all haste to get possession of a hill to the right. I could now see the rest of the command, and I knew that that hill would command Reno's position. Supposing that my troop was to occupy the line we were then on, I ordered Hare to take ten men and hold the hill, but, just as he was moving off, an order came from Reno to get back as quickly as possible; so I recalled Hare and ordered the men to run to the lines. This movement was executed, strange to say, without a single casualty.

The Indians now took possession of all the surrounding high points, and opened a heavy fire. They had in the mean time sent a large force up the valley, and soon our position was entirely surrounded. It was now about seven o'clock.

Our position next the river was protected by the rough, rugged steep bluffs which were cut up by irregular deep ravines. From the crest of these bluffs the ground gently declined away from the river. On the north there was a short ridge, the ground sloping gently to the front and rear. This ridge, during the first day, was occupied by five troops. Directly in rear of the ridge was a small hill; in the ravine on the south of this hill our hospital was established, and the horses and pack-mules were secured. Across this ravine one troop, Moylan's, was posted, the packs and dead animals being utilized for breastworks. The high hill on the south was occupied by Benteen's troop. Everybody now lay down and spread himself out as thin as possible. After lying there a few minutes I was horrified to find myself wondering if a small sage-bush, about as thick as my finger, would turn a bullet, so I got up and walked along the line, cautioned the men not to waste their ammunition; ordered certain men who were good shots to do the firing, and others to keep them supplied with loaded guns.

The firing continued till nearly dark (between nine and ten o'clock), although after dusk but little attention was paid to the firing, as everybody moved about freely.

Of course everybody was wondering about Custer—why he did not communicate by courier or signal. But the general opinion seemed to prevail that he had been defeated and driven down the river, where he would probably join General Terry, and with whom he would return to our relief. Quite frequently, too, the question, "What's the matter with Custer?" would evoke an impatient reply.

Indians are proverbial economists of fuel, but they did not stint themselves that night. The long twilight was prolonged by numerous bonfires, located throughout their village. The long shadows of the hills and the refracted light gave a supernatural aspect to the surrounding country, which may account for the illusions of those who imagined they could see columns of troops, etc. Although our dusky foes did not molest us with obtrusive attentions during the night, yet it must not be inferred that we were allowed to pass the night in perfect rest; or that they were endeavoring to soothe us into forgetfulness of their proximity, or trying to conceal their situation. They were a good deal happier than we were; nor did they strive to conceal their joy. Their camp was a veritable pandemonium. All night long they continued their frantic revels; beating tom-toms, dancing,

DISMOUNTED — THE FOURTH TROOPERS MOVING THE LED HORSES.

whooping, yelling with demoniacal screams, and discharging firearms. We knew they were having a scalp-dance. In this connection the question has often been asked "if they did not have prisoners at the torture?" The Indians deny that they took any prisoners. We did not discover any evidence of torture in their camps. It is true that we did find human heads severed from their bodies, but these probably had been paraded in their orgies during that terrible night.

Our casualties had been comparatively few since taking position on the hill. The question of moving was discussed, but the conditions coupled to the proposition caused it to be indignantly rejected. Some of the scouts were sent out soon after dark to look for signs of Custer's command, but they returned after a short absence saying that the country was full of Sioux. Lieutenant Varnum volunteered to go out, but was either discouraged from the venture or forbidden to go out.

After dark the troops were arranged a little differently. The horses were unsaddled, and the mules were relieved of their packs; all animals were secured to lariats stretched and picketed to the ground.

Soon after all firing had ceased the wildest confusion prevailed. Men imagined they could see a column of troops over on the hills or ridges, that they could hear the tramp of the horses, the command of officers, or even the trumpet-calls. Stable-call was sounded by one of our trumpeters; shots were fired by some of our men, and familiar trumpet-calls were sounded by our trumpeter immediately after, to let the supposed marching column know that we were friends. Every favorable expression or opinion was received with credulity, and then ratified with a cheer. Somebody suggested that General Crook might be coming, so some one, a civilian packer, I think, mounted a horse, and galloping along the line yelled: "Don't be discouraged, boys, Crook is coming." But they gradually realized that the much-wished-for reinforcements were but the phantasma of their imaginations, and settled down to their work of digging rifle-pits. They worked in pairs, in threes and fours. The ground was hard and dry. There were only three or four spades and shovels in the whole command; axes, hatchets, knives, table-forks, tin cups, and halves of canteens were brought into use. However, everybody worked hard, and some were still digging when the enemy opened fire at early dawn, between half-past two and three o'clock, so that all had some sort of shelter, except Benteen's men. The enemy's first salutations were rather feeble, and our side made scarcely any response; but as dawn advanced to daylight their lines

were heavily reinforced, and both sides kept up a continuous fusillade. Of course it was their policy to draw our fire as much as possible to exhaust our ammunition. As they exposed their persons very little we forbade our men, except well-known good shots, to fire without orders. The Indians amused themselves by standing erect, in full view for an instant, and then dropping down again before a bullet could reach them, but of that they soon seemed to grow tired or found it too dangerous; then they resorted to the old ruse of raising a hat and blouse, or a blanket, on a stick to draw our fire; we soon understood their tactics. Occasionally they fired volleys at command. Their fire, however, was not very effective. Benteen's troop suffered greater losses than any other, because their rear was exposed to the long-range firing from the hills on the north. The horses and mules suffered greatly, as they were fully exposed to long-range fire from the east.

Benteen came over to where Reno was lying, and asked for reinforcements to be sent to his line. Before he left his line, however, he ordered Gibson not to fall back under any circumstances, as this was the key of the position. Gibson's men had expended nearly all their ammunition, some men being reduced to as few as four or five cartridges. He was embarrassed, too, with quite a number of wounded men. Indeed, the situation here was most critical, for if the Indians had made a rush, a retreat was inevitable. Private McDermott volunteered to carry a message from Gibson to Benteen urging him to hasten the reinforcements. After considerable urging by Benteen, Reno finally ordered French to take "M" troop over to the south side. On his way over Benteen picked up some men then with the horses. Just previous to his arrival an Indian had shot one of Gibson's men, then rushed up and touched the body with his "coup-stick," and started back to cover, but he was killed. He was in such close proximity to the lines and so exposed to the fire that the other Indians could not carry his body away. This, I believe, was the only dead Indian left in our possession. This boldness determined Benteen to make a charge, and the Indians were driven nearly to the river. On their retreat they dragged several dead and wounded warriors away with them.

The firing almost ceased for a while, and then it recommenced with greater fury. From this fact, and their more active movements, it became evident that they contemplated something more serious than a mere fusillade. Benteen came back to where Reno was, and said if something was not done pretty soon the Indians would run into our lines. Waiting a short

UNHORSED.

time, and no action being taken on his suggestion, he said rather impatiently: "You 've got to do something here pretty quick; this won't do, you must drive them back." Reno then directed us to get ready for a charge, and told Benteen to give the word. Benteen called out "All ready now, men. Now 's your time. Give them hell. Hip, hip, here we go!" and away we went with a hurrah, every man, but one who lay in his pit crying like a child. The Indians fired more rapidly than before from their whole line. Our men left the pits with their carbines loaded, and they began firing without orders soon after we started. A large body of Indians had assembled at the foot of one of the hills, intending probably to make a charge, as Benteen had divined, but they broke as soon as our line started. When we had advanced 75 or 100 yards, Reno called out "Get back, men, get back," and back the whole line came. A most singular fact of this sortie was that not a man who advanced with the lines was hit; but directly after every one had gotten into the pits again, the one man who did not go out was shot in the head and killed instantly. The poor fellow had a premonition that he would be killed, and had so told one of his comrades.

Up to this time the command had been without water. The excitement and heat made our thirst almost maddening. The men were forbidden to use tobacco. They put pebbles in their mouths to excite the glands; some ate grass roots, but did not find relief; some tried to eat hard bread, but after chewing it awhile would blow it out of their mouths like so much flour. A few potatoes were given out and afforded some relief. About 11 A. M. the firing was slack, and parties of volunteers were formed to get water under the protection of Benteen's lines. The parties worked their way down the ravines to within a few yards of the river. The men would get ready, make a rush to the river, fill the camp-kettles, and return to fill the canteens. Some Indians stationed in a copse of woods, a short distance away, opened fire whenever a man exposed himself, which made this a particularly hazardous service. Several men were wounded, and the additional danger was then incurred of rescuing their wounded comrades. I think all these men were rewarded with medals of honor. By about one o'clock the Indians had nearly all left us, but they still guarded the river; by that time, however, we had about all the water we needed for immediate use. About two o'clock the Indians came back, opened fire, and drove us to the trenches again, but by three o'clock the firing had ceased altogether.

Late in the afternoon we saw a few horsemen in the bottom apparently to observe us, and then fire was set to the grass in the valley. About 7 P. M. we saw emerge from behind this screen of smoke an immense moving mass crossing the plateau, going toward the Big

Horn Mountains. A fervent "Thank God" that they had at last given up the contest was soon followed by grave doubts as to their motive for moving. Perhaps Custer had met Terry, and was coming to our relief. Perhaps they were short of ammunition, and were moving their village to a safe distance before making a final desperate effort to overwhelm us. Perhaps it was only a ruse to get us on the move, and then clean us out.

The stench from the dead men and horses was now exceedingly offensive, and it was decided to take up a new position nearer the river. The companies were assigned positions, and the men were put to work digging pits with the expectation of a renewal of the attack. Our loss on the hill had been eighteen killed and fifty-two wounded.

During the night Lieutenant De Rudio, Private O'Neal, Mr. Girard, the interpreter, and Jackson, a half-breed scout, came to our line. They had been left in the bottom when Reno made his retreat.

In this narrative of the movements immediately preceding, and resulting in, the annihilation of the men with Custer, I have related facts substantially as observed by myself or as given to me by Chief Gall of the Sioux. His statements have been corroborated by other Indians, notably the wife of "Spotted Horn Bull," an intelligent Sioux squaw, one of the first who had the courage to talk freely to any one who participated in the battle.

In 1886, on the tenth anniversary, an effort was made to have a reunion of the survivors at the battle-field. Colonel Benteen, Captains McDougall and Edgerly, Dr. Porter, Sergeant Hall, Trumpeter Penwell, and myself met there on the 25th of June. Through the kind efforts of the officers and of the ladies at Fort Custer our visit was made as pleasant as possible. Through the personal influence of Major McLaughlin, Indian agent at Standing Rock Agency, Chief Gall was prevailed upon to accompany the party and describe Custer's part in the battle. We were unfortunate in not having an efficient and truthful interpreter on the field at the reunion. The statements I have used were, after our return to the agency, interpreted by Mrs. McLaughlin and Mr. Farribault, of the agency, both of whom are perfectly trustworthy and are familiar with the Sioux language.

It has been previously noted that General Custer separated from Reno before the latter crossed the Little Big Horn under orders to charge the village. Custer's column bore to the right of the river (a sudden change of plan, probably); a ridge of high bluffs and the river separated the two commands, and they could not see each other. On this ridge, however, Custer and staff were seen to wave their hats, and heard to cheer just as Reno was beginning the attack; but Custer's troops were at that time a mile or more to his right. It was about this time that the trumpeter was sent back with Custer's last order to Benteen. From this place [see A on map] Custer could survey the valley for several miles above and for a short distance below Reno; yet he could only see a part of the village; he must, then, have felt confident that all the Indians were below him; hence, I presume, his message to Benteen. The view of the main body of the village was cut off by the highest points of the ridge, a short distance from him. Had he gone to this high point he would have understood the magnitude of his undertaking, and it is probable that his plan of battle would have been changed. We have no evidence that he did not go there. He could see, however, that the village was not breaking away toward the Big Horn Mountains. He must, then, have expected to find the squaws and children fleeing to the bluffs on the north, for in no other way do I account for his wide detour to the right. He must have counted upon Reno's success, and fully expected the "scatteration" of the non-combatants with the pony herds. The probable attack upon the families and the capture of the herds were in that event counted upon to strike consternation in the hearts of the warriors, and were elements for success upon which General Custer fully counted in the event of a daylight attack.

When Reno's advance was checked, and his left began to fall back, Chief Gall started with some of his warriors to cut off Reno's retreat to the bluffs. On his way he was excitedly hailed by "Iron Cedar," one of his warriors, who was on the high point, to hurry to him, that more soldiers were coming. This was the first intimation the Indians had of Custer's column; up to the time of this incident they had supposed that all the troops were in at Reno's attack. Custer had then crossed the valley of the dry creek, and was marching along and well up the slope of the bluff forming the second ridge back from the river, and nearly parallel to it. The command was marching rapidly in column of fours, and there was some confusion in the ranks, due probably to the unmanageableness of some excited horses.

The accepted theory for many years after the battle, and still persisted in by some writers, was that Custer's column had turned the high bluffs near the river, moved down the dry (Reno's) creek, and attempted to ford the river near the lowest point of these bluffs; that he was there met by an overpowering force and driven back; that he then divided his battalion, moved down the river with the view of attacking the village, but met with such resistance

CAPTAIN M. W. KEOGH, COMMANDING TROOP "I."

from the enemy posted along the river bank and ravines that he was compelled to fall back, fighting, to the position on the ridge. The numerous bodies found scattered between the river and ridge were supposed to be the first victims of the fight. I am now satisfied that these were men who either survived those on the ridge or attempted to escape the massacre.

Custer's route was as indicated on the map, and his column was never nearer the river or village than his final position on the ridge. The wife of Spotted Horn Bull, when giving me her account of the battle, persisted in saying that Custer's column did not attempt to cross at the ford, and appealed to her husband, who supported her statement. On the battle-field, in 1886, Chief Gall indicated Custer's route to me, and it then flashed upon me that I myself had seen Custer's trail. On June 28, while we were burying the dead, I asked Major Reno's permission to go on the high ridge east or back of the field to look for tracks of shod horses to ascertain if some of the command might not have escaped. When I reached the ridge I saw this trail, and wondered who could have made it, but dismissed the thought that it had been made by Custer's column, because it did not accord with the theory with which we were then filled, that Custer had attempted to cross at the ford, and this trail was too far back, and showed no indication of leading

toward the ford. Trumpeter Penwell was my orderly and accompanied me. It was a singular coincidence that in 1886 Penwell was stationed at Fort Custer, and was my orderly when visiting the battle-field. Penwell corroborated my recollection of the trail.

The ford theory arose from the fact that we found there numerous tracks of shod horses, but they evidently had been made after the Indians had possessed themselves of the cavalry horses, for they rode them after capturing them. No bodies of men or horses were found anywhere near the ford, and these facts are conclusive to my mind that Custer did not go to the ford with any body of men.

As soon as Gall had personally confirmed Iron Cedar's report he sent word to the warriors battling against Reno, and to the people in the village. The greatest consternation prevailed among the families, and orders were given for them to leave at once. Before they could do so the great body of warriors had left Reno, and hastened to attack Custer. This explains why Reno was not pushed when so much confusion at the river crossing gave the Indians every opportunity of annihilating his command. Not long after the Indians began to show a strong force in Custer's front, Custer turned his column to the left, and advanced in the direction of the village to near a place now marked as a spring, halted at the junction of the ravines just below it, and dismounted two troops, Keogh's and Calhoun's, to fight on foot. These two troops advanced at double-time to a knoll, now marked by Crittenden's monument. The other three troops, mounted, followed them a short distance in their rear. The led horses remained where the troops dismounted. When Keogh and Calhoun got to the knoll the other troops marched rapidly to

CAPTAIN G. W. YATES, COMMANDING TROOP "F."

the right; Smith's troop deployed as skirmishers, mounted, and took position on a ridge, which, on Smith's left, ended in Keogh's position (now marked by Crittenden's monument), and, on Smith's right, ended at the hill on which Custer took position with Yates and Tom Custer's troops, now known as Custer's Hill, and marked by the monument erected to the command. Smith's skirmishers, holding their gray horses, remained in groups of fours.

The line occupied by Custer's battalion was the first considerable ridge back from the river, the nearest point being about half a mile from it. His front was extended about three fourths of a mile. The whole village was in full view. A few hundred yards from his line was another but lower ridge, the further slope of which was not commanded by his line. It was here that the Indians under Crazy Horse from the lower part of the village, among whom were the Cheyennes, formed for the charge on Custer's Hill. All Indians had now left Reno. Gall collected his warriors, and moved up a ravine south of Keogh and Calhoun. As they were turning this flank they discovered the led horses without any other guard than the horse-holders. They opened fire upon the horse-holders, and used the usual devices to stampede the horses—that is, yelling, waving blankets, etc.; in this they succeeded very soon, and the horses were caught up by the squaws. In this disaster Keogh and Calhoun probably lost their reserve ammunition, which was carried in the saddle-bags. Gall's warriors now moved to the foot of the knoll held by Calhoun. A large force dismounted and advanced up the slope far enough to be able to see the soldiers when standing erect, but were protected when squatting or lying down. By jumping up and firing quickly, they exposed themselves only for an instant, but drew the fire of the soldiers, causing a waste of ammunition. In the mean time Gall was massing his mounted warriors under the protection of the slope. When everything was in readiness, at a signal from Gall the dismounted warriors rose, fired, and every Indian gave voice to the war-whoop; the mounted Indians put whip to their ponies, and the whole mass rushed upon and crushed Calhoun. The maddened mass of Indians was carried forward by its own momentum over Calhoun and Crittenden down into the depression where Keogh was, with over thirty men, and all was over on that part of the field.

In the mean time the same tactics were being pursued and executed around Custer's Hill. The warriors, under the leadership of Crow-King, Crazy Horse, White Bull, "Hump," and others, moved up the ravine west of Custer's Hill, and concentrated under the shelter of the ridges on his right flank and back of his position. Gall's bloody work was finished before the annihilation of Custer was accomplished, and his victorious warriors hurried forward to the hot encounter then going on, and the frightful massacre was completed.

Smith's men had disappeared from the ridge, but not without leaving enough dead bodies to mark their line. About twenty-eight bodies of men belonging to this troop and other organizations were found in one ravine nearer the river. Many corpses were found scattered

CAPTAIN T. W. CUSTER, COMMANDING TROOP "C."

over the field between Custer's line of defense, the river, and in the direction of Reno's Hill. These, doubtless, were of men who had attempted to escape; some of them may have been sent as couriers by Custer. One of the first bodies I recognized and one of the nearest to the ford was that of Sergeant Butler of Tom Custer's troop. Sergeant Butler was a soldier of many years' experience and of known courage. The indications were that he had sold his life dearly, for near and under him were found many empty cartridge-shells.

All the Indian accounts that I know of agree that there was no organized close-quarters fighting, except on the two flanks; that with the annihilation at Custer's Hill the battle was virtually over. It does not appear that the Indians made any advance to the attack from the direction of the river; they did have a defensive force along the river and in the ravines which destroyed those who left Custer's line.

There was a great deal of firing going on over the field after the battle by the young men and boys riding about and shooting into the dead bodies.

LIEUTENANT W. W. COOK, ADJUTANT.

LIEUTENANT W. VAN W. REILY.

LIEUTENANT J. J. CRITTENDEN.

LIEUTENANT JAMES CALHOUN,
COMMANDING TROOP "L."

LIEUTENANT A. E. SMITH,
COMMANDING TROOP "E."

LIEUTENANT H. M. HARRINGTON.

LIEUTENANT J. E. PORTER.

LIEUTENANT J. G. STURGIS.

PORTRAITS (ON THIS AND THE TWO PREVIOUS PAGES) OF OFFICERS WHO DIED WITH CUSTER.
These portraits are from photographs, or copies, for the most part by D. F. Barry of West Superior, Wis., who has taken many pictures of the Custer battle-field. Those of Lieutenants Reily and Sturgis are by Scholten, St. Louis, and Pach, New York.

Tuesday morning, June 27, we had reveille without the "morning guns," enjoyed the pleasure of a square meal, and had our stock properly cared for. Our commanding officer seemed to think the Indians had some "trap" set for us, and required our men to hold themselves in readiness to occupy the pits at a moment's notice. Nothing seemed determined except to stay where we were. Not an Indian was in sight, but a few ponies were seen grazing down in the valley.

About 9.30 A. M. a cloud of dust was observed several miles down the river. The assembly was sounded, the horses were placed in a protected situation, and camp-kettles and canteens were filled with water. An hour of suspense followed; but from the slow advance we concluded that they were our own troops. "But whose command is it?" We looked in vain for a gray-horse troop. It could not be Custer; it must then be Crook, for if it was Terry, Custer would be with him. Cheer after cheer was given for Crook. A white man, Harris, I think, soon came up with a note from General Terry, addressed to General Custer, dated June 26, stating that two of our Crow scouts had given information that our column had been whipped and nearly all had been killed; that he did not believe their story, but was coming with medical assistance. The scout said that he could not get to our lines the night before, as the Indians were on the alert. Very soon after this Lieutenant Bradley, 7th Infantry, came into our lines, and asked where I was. Greeting most cordially my old friend, I immediately asked, "Where is Custer?" He replied, "I don't know, but I suppose he was killed, as we counted 197 dead bodies. I don't suppose any escaped." We were simply dumfounded. This was the first intimation we had of his fate. It was hard to realize; it did seem impossible.

General Terry and staff, and officers of General Gibbon's column soon after approached, and their coming was greeted with prolonged, hearty cheers. The grave countenance of the General awed the men to silence. The officers assembled to meet their guests. There was scarcely a dry eye; hardly a word was spoken, but quivering lips and hearty grasping of hands gave token of thankfulness for the relief and grief for the misfortune.

During the rest of that day we were busy collecting our effects and destroying surplus property. The wounded were cared for and taken to the camp of our new friends of the Montana column. Among the wounded was saddler "Mike" Madden of my troop, whom I promoted to be sergeant, on the field, for gallantry. Madden was very fond of his grog. His long abstinence had given him a famous thirst. It was necessary to amputate his leg, which was done without administering any anesthetic; but after the amputation the surgeon gave him a good, stiff drink of brandy. Madden eagerly gulped it down, and his eyes fairly danced as he smacked his lips and said, "M-eh, doctor, cut off my other leg."

On the morning of the 28th we left our intrenchments to bury the dead of Custer's command. The morning was bright, and from the high bluffs we had a clear view of Custer's battle-field. We saw a large number of objects that looked like white boulders scattered over the field. Glasses were brought into requisition, and it was announced that these objects were the dead bodies. Captain Weir exclaimed, "Oh, how white they look!"

All the bodies, except a few, were stripped of their clothing. According to my recollection nearly all were scalped or mutilated, but there was one notable exception, that of General Custer, whose face and expression were

natural; he had been shot in the temple and in the left side. Many faces had a pained, almost terrified expression. It is said that "Rain-in-the-face," a Sioux warrior, has gloried that he had cut out and had eaten the heart and liver of one of the officers. Other bodies were muti-

VIEW, FROM THE SIDE TOWARD THE RIVER, OF CUSTER'S HILL AND THE BATTLE MONUMENT. (FROM A PHOTOGRAPH BY D. F. BARRY.)

lated in a disgusting manner. The bodies of Dr. Lord and Lieutenants Porter, Harrington, and Sturgis were not found, at least not recognized. The clothing of Porter and Sturgis was found in the village, and showed that they had been killed. We buried, according to my memoranda, 212 bodies. The killed of the entire command was 265, and of wounded we had 52.

The question has been often asked, "What were the causes of Custer's defeat?" I should say:

First. The overpowering numbers of the enemy and their unexpected cohesion.

Second. Reno's panic rout from the valley.

Third. The defective extraction of the empty cartridge-shells from the carbines.

Of the first, I will say that we had nothing conclusive on which to base calculations of the numbers—and to this day it seems almost incredible that such great numbers of Indians should have left the agencies, to combine against the troops, without information relating thereto having been communicated to the commanders of troops in the field, further than that heretofore mentioned. The second has been mentioned incidentally. The Indians say if Reno's position in the valley had been held, they would have been compelled to divide their strength for the different attacks, which would have caused confusion and apprehension, and prevented the concentration of every able-bodied warrior upon the battalion under Custer; that, at the time of the discovery of Custer's advance to attack, the chiefs gave orders for the village to move, to break up; that, at the time of Reno's retreat, this order was being carried out, but as soon as Reno's retreat was assured the order was countermanded, and the squaws were compelled to return with the pony herds; that the order would not have been countermanded had Reno's forces remained fighting in the bottom. Custer's attack did not begin until after Reno had reached the bluffs.

Of the third we can only judge by our own experience. When cartridges were dirty and corroded the ejectors did not always extract the empty shells from the chambers, and the men were compelled to use knives to get them out. When the shells were clean no great difficulty was experienced. To what extent this was a factor in causing the disaster we have no means of knowing.

A battle was unavoidable. Every man in Terry's and Custer's commands expected a battle; it was for that purpose, to punish the Indians, that the command was sent out, and with that determination Custer made his preparations. Had Custer continued his march southward — that is, left the Indian trail — the Indians would have known of our movement on the 25th, and a battle would have been fought very near the same field on which Crook had been attacked and forced back only a week before; the Indians never would have remained in camp and allowed a concentration of the several columns to attack them. If they had escaped without punishment or battle Custer would undoubtedly have been blamed.

E. S. Godfrey,
Captain 7th Cavalry.

"TAPS." (CAVALRY BUGLER IN FULL UNIFORM.)

18

The Great Northwest

Ray Stannard Baker

THE CENTURY MAGAZINE

MARCH, 1903

THE GREAT NORTHWEST

BY RAY STANNARD BAKER

WITH PICTURES BY ERNEST BLUMENSCHEIN

WHEN the new settler crosses the Rockies, the altitude, or the rarefied atmosphere, or some vapor of the West yet unnamed by science, seems to endow him with the roseate vision, so that ever afterward all that he beholds is good and beautiful—and bigger than anywhere else. There is something refreshing and edifying in the way the Northwesterner shows off his town to the stranger: his boundless admiration for the new Episcopal church; his pride in the paving of Main street; his brotherly interest in the development of the First National Bank; the imagination with which he prophesies the glorious future of the place, and exhibits the acres and acres of desert and hillside which the town is presently to populate. It is an adamantine visitor indeed who goes away without taking a deed or two for hopeful corner lots in the residential district.

I recall a little town in western Washington where the train stopped for a twenty-minute breakfast—a dusty road, and a distant spire rising above a row of dry cottonwoods. Fate had set the town back from the railroad, where its charms were invisible from passing trains; but the people, proud of their place, were not to be outdone. Close to the platform, where it could not escape attention, they had set up an enormous frame hung with photographic views of the town: the Cascade Hotel with a row of arm-chairs in front, the residence of the Hon. John Smith, the interior of Roe's hardware-store, prize apples raised by Joseph Jones, Esq., and so on. In the corner they had placed a little pocketful of circulars labeled, "Take one."

I took one. It gave a beguiling picture of the hopes of this new, struggling, ambitious, engaging town. I wish now that I had stopped and walked up the dusty road and found out what was under the spire and the dry cottonwoods. I might have been disappointed in the Hon. John Smith's residence, and even in the interior of Roe's store, but I should have felt, at least, the irresistible spirit of these towns—youth, enthusiasm, health, hospitality. You never go amiss for a friend in a Western town.

Seattle, Tacoma, Spokane, Portland, throb with enterprise and rivalry. Nor can they be called boom towns—not now. Ten years ago they were in the very heyday of municipal intoxication, expanding in a most extraordinary manner; and they were shortly sorry for their excesses. The crisis of 1893 left them all prostrate, their rich men poor, pretentious buildings half completed, and boom additions to towns behind for taxes. Unlike the mushroom towns of early Kansas, however, they had genuine reasons for being, and a superb natural strength that brought speedy convalescence, so that to-day the visitor finds them reveling in the full joy of life. There is something immensely attractive in the pugnacity with which Seattle advances her fine new shipyard, while Tacoma counters with a low death-rate and enormous wheat shipments, and Portland opens her batteries with an unequaled fresh-water harbor. One soon enters into the spirit of the animated population combats and climate battles and prevalence-of-crime skirmishes. With what enthusiasm Spokane, acquiring a new flour-mill, hurls it, figuratively, in the teeth of her rivals! Fairhaven offers battle with its salmon industry, and no one who visits Washington can escape the belligerent banner of Everett—the smoke from her manufacturing chimneys. Every city on the coast has made up its mind firmly, if not quietly, to become the metropolis of the West.

Oftentimes the rivalry has its humorous side. While in Seattle I heard much of Mount Rainier, the splendid volcanic peak which rises cloud-white southeast by south of the city. It is one of the most magnificent of American mountains, now set apart, with wise forethought, as a national reserve. The people of Seattle are proud of Mount Rainier; they regard it as a special Seattle attraction, and have even named a certain brew of beer after the

Drawn by Ernest Blumenschein

A FRONTIER TOWN HOTEL-KEEPER

mountain. When I reached Tacoma one of the first things to which my attention was called was Mount Tacoma, rising gloriously in the southeast. It struck me that it bore a singular resemblance to Mount Rainier, and I said as much.

" It *is* sometimes called Mount Rainier," said my informant; " but if you call it anything but Mount Tacoma over here you can't get anything to eat."

And so the mountain is the dear scenic possession, under separate names, of two cities.

Here in the Northwest one encounters the living representation of the strenuous life. Here men work together in a way unknown anywhere else. The East is insular, every man for himself. The Northwest —indeed, the whole West —has learned the value of coöperation and community interest. Migrating to a new country with difficulties and dangers on every hand, the people have been forced to combine and stand with solid front to the world. As a result, innumerable organizations have sprung up having for their purpose the advancement of some community interest. Here the chamber of commerce is seen in its true glory—an organization of the leading business men of the town, supported by voluntary but liberal contributions, the object being to " boom " the city. A Western town that begrudges an appropriation of a hundred dollars for repairing the pavement of the main street will cheerfully empty its pockets of a thousand dollars for heralding the glories of the place. Let 's grow, they say; never mind the patches—a youthfulness that we can't help liking. So the chamber circulates broadcast advertising matter showing the superiority of its town over all rivals, the purity of its waters, the sweetness of its air, its unequaled business opportunities, until the fluttering visitor, dazzled by this display of charms, casts here his fortunes. And it is the curious and wonderful property of this expansiveness

Drawn by Ernest Blumenschein.   Half-tone plate engraved by F. H. Wellington

BUILDING THE NEW HOME, MOUNT RAINIER (MOUNT TACOMA) IN THE BACKGROUND

that, once within its spell, the unwary one remains bedazzled for ever and ever, so that he sees no longer wood and stone, but marble and gold and precious stones.

The chamber of commerce engages itself in gathering plums. A plum, in the Western sense, is a new railroad, a new coaling-station, a new manufacturing plant; it falls to the most energetic shaking. Behold, then, these associations bringing down

such expenditures are looked upon as reasonable and even necessary. The legislature is asked for an appropriation to construct a building, all of native woods, to be located near the depot in a certain town and to contain a permanent display of prize fruits and grains; and, what is more, the appropriation is granted. While I was in Portland the chamber of commerce was preparing to send a man East with a fine

Drawn by Ernest Blumenschein

AN OLD SEATTLE INDIAN

plums to the right joyous cheering of their respective constituencies, and you will appreciate one factor, at least, in the Western joy of life.

And then there are numberless lesser organizations—to advance Oriental trade, to secure wheat shipments, to boom the mines of a certain county, to prevent the shipment of poor fruit, to kill jack-rabbits. It would be difficult indeed to imagine the State of New York—much less private individuals—appropriating money to advertise the resources of Oneida County for watermelon-growing; but here in the West

mineral exhibit to boom the mines of Oregon. The fruit-growers, the cattlemen, the irrigation farmers, all have organizations which direct in a really amazing degree the methods of the industry, the shipment of products, and so on.

A whole farming community may turn out, at a day's notice, to help kill jack-rabbits or catch grasshoppers, and with a zest and hilarity that would astonish an Eastern farmer. While I was in Utah the ranchers were giving what they called "grasshopper balls." The price of admission to these was a bushel of fresh-gathered grasshoppers, a part of the jollification being a huge bonfire in which the grasshoppers were cremated.

As a result of this spirit, it requires only a breath to raise a crowd in a Western town, whether for a wedding, a barn-raising, or a lynching. An Eastern village may continue a century without being stirred with a moment of crowd enthusiasm, but the people of the Northwestern town are constantly rising and doing things, sometimes amusing, sometimes serious, always interesting. People work together naturally. An expression of this social helpfulness is manifested by the prevalence of the secret society. In the hotel at Tacoma I met a jovial man with a double chin, who had a singularly hearty way of shaking hands. He asked me at once, in a big, husky voice, if I was an Eagle. I was not.

"Then perhaps you are a Concatenated Hoo-Hoo?"

I was not a Hoo-Hoo, and there was real anxiety in his voice when he inquired further as to whether I was an Elk, a Mason, a Forester, or a Knight of Pythias.

"If you stay long in the West," he said, "you 'll have to join something or other."

Indeed, nearly every man in the Northwest wears the badge of some order, often several of them. In one extreme case I counted six badges on one person, four on the coat lapels, one pendent from the watch-charm, and one worn as the seal-setting for a ring. Imagine this man going about with his grips and passwords; he could not long escape brothers in any direction in which fate led him. In some comparatively small towns the lodges are numbered by scores, some of them housed in resplendent club-rooms. At Butte City, for instance, I counted the announcements, in the daily papers, of no fewer than twelve lodges of Masons, fifteen of Odd Fellows, nine of Knights of Pythias,

Drawn by Ernest Blumenschein

A PROSPECTOR

Drawn by Ernest Blumenschein

A FRONTIER LAWYER

ten of the Ancient Order of United Workmen, and thirty-eight lodges of other orders, to say nothing of the Elks and Eagles, nor forty lodges and branches of labor organizations. The importance of the place which these societies occupy in the life of the country is indicated by frequent and often gorgeous parades, street fairs, carnivals, balls, the record of which in the newspapers is given an importance quite unfamiliar to the Easterner. Several new orders have had an extraordinary recent growth in the West, notably the Elks. No Western city of importance is now without its Elks' home, often one of the finest buildings in town, where the Elks resort for their

Drawn by Ernest Blumenschein

A TRAVELING PHOTOGRAPHER

Drawn by Ernest Blumenschein. Half-tone plate engraved by J. W. Evans

A FOREST RANGER. ONE OF HIS DUTIES IS TO PREVENT FOREST
FIRES FROM SPREADING

mystic and hilarious rites. Combined with their social features, these organizations usually possess a distinct benevolent purpose—the relief of unfortunate members and their families. In short, they express one of the most engaging characteristics of the country—in Western parlance, its "good-heartedness," its "good-fellowship," its willingness to help and be friendly.

A traveler in the West soon becomes aware of this infectious spirit of good humor. Your neighbor in the car or in the hotel lobby is much more likely to speak to you than he would be in the East. Ride anywhere in the country, and every man you meet will salute you with a "Howdy" or a "Fine day." If you give him half a chance, he will stop, throw one leg over the pommel of his saddle, and "swap lies." The distances are so great that he has probably come a long way without seeing any one, and he wants to talk a bit. Meet a Connecticut farmer, and he begins at once to ask personal questions; but the Westerner, traditionally shy of confidences, much prefers to talk horse or the lore of the road. And the very necessity of crowding a good deal of stored-up cogitation into brief talk-

ing opportunities has developed a singular sententiousness and picturesqueness of speech. Meeting a genuine Westerner, I always felt that he was just ready to burst with an epigram. I recall the reply of an irrigation farmer when I commented on the evident prosperity of the ranches of the neighborhood.

"They 're doin' well, all right," he said, "but you 'll still find a good many of 'em jumpin' sideways for a hot biscuit."

A country virtually without millionaires, and with none of the rooted aristocracy that comes from the long continuance of a wealthy family in one neighborhood, it is free from many of the formalities of the East. Your waiter at the hotel tells you enthusiastically about the last base-ball game or prize-fight; your bell-boy asks what might be an impertinent question in an older community, but without impertinence here. I inquired of the conductor of a car in Seattle if I was on the right way to the university. "You bet your life," he said heartily. Even when a man intends to hold you up, the next moment he will be good-humored about it. And if you are truly Western, you will be equally good-humored in return, even though you experience an uncomfortable sensation at the pit of the stomach. An Idaho rancher, Lon Daw by name, told me of an experience of his. It seems that, when driving through the country, he always kept a Colt's army revolver—one of the old ugly, long-barreled guns—on the seat beside him, within easy reach of his hand. One day a masked man stepped out of the bushes at the roadside and laid his hand on the bridle of one of Daw's horses, stopping the team.

"I was always waiting for just such a chance," said Daw, "so I threw my gun over my arm and drew a bead on his stomach."

It must have been a moment of some embarrassment to the outlaw, for he had been careless in getting his revolver up. But he was not at all disconcerted.

"Excuse me, pardner," he said. "I reckon I've got the wrong outfit."

To which Daw replied:

"Sure, neighbor; we're all liable to make mistakes."

And then they both laughed, and the outlaw stepped back into the bushes.

In the Northwest everything seems to have happened within the last ten years; events which would be of epoch-making importance in any country at any time have here crowded one upon another with wanton prodigality, so that the Northwesterner, plumped down in the whirl of great things, can himself hardly grasp their full significance, contenting himself with confused superlatives.

Think of this march of events! It was barely eight years ago that the gold-fields of the Klondike were brought to the knowledge of the world, causing a rush of Americans to the Northwest, and building up suddenly a new and important business for the Puget Sound ports, where the miners outfitted and took ship. Following the Klondike excitement, came the various Alaska discoveries, and Seattle and Tacoma were and are the natural headquarters for most of the supplies shipped northward, as well as the entry point for the returning miners with their treasure, not a little of which is left to enrich the people of the ports.

Hardly had the gold excitement calmed to the paces of a steady business enterprise when the Spanish War broke out, and these Pacific cities were thrown into the turmoil of visiting battle-ships and of provisioning and transporting the army of the Philippines. Then came the opening trade with our new insular possessions in the Pacific, the Chinese War and its call for equipment and its stir of soldiery and transports, followed by the recent commercial expansion of Japan, with its trade demands. And now an element has just entered into the calculations of the coast—the construction of the Panama Canal—which will revolutionize whole departments of the world's trade and exercise a profound influence for good or evil on the cities of the Northwestern coast.

Many of the events, it is true, notably the opening of the door to the far East, are mostly promissory assets; and yet their prophecy of a golden future has not been without its profound effect on the growth of the Pacific cities and the attraction of energetic men with money. To the Pacific ports will ultimately come most of the trade of the Philippines, worth sixty million dollars annually, and a growing share of the billion dollars or more of the annual business of China, Japan, Siberia, and the Dutch East Indies, to say nothing of the large foreign trade of Australia and New Zealand. Alaska, once regarded as a hopelessly distant and irreclaimable waste of mountains and snow, is also progressing with wonderful rapidity, not only in its mines, but in the development of its fisheries and in the utilization of its forests and its agricultural resources, so that to-day the Alaskan trade is of much importance.

While these world-events were crowding upon one another, the development of the country tributary to the coast, upon which the solid progress of the cities must ultimately rest, was going forward with unprecedented rapidity. Western Canada was opening to settlement, is opening now, in a marvelous manner; railroads were building; schemes for irrigating the arid lands were in course of development; crop production was increasing; timber was being cut from an almost inexhaustible supply, to supplement the waning forests of Maine and Michigan; coal-mines were being opened, and salmon caught—all the forces of industry working together with a rapidity which must always remain a world's wonder.

Except in the general phenomena of its

development, it is difficult to treat the Northwest as an entirety, owing to the great diversity in the character of its climate, soil, altitude, and natural resources, as well as in the great dissimilarity of its industries.

and Wyoming, the coastal strip contains a good deal more than a third of the population (roughly, 604,000), with Portland, Seattle, and Tacoma as its chief cities. The only towns exceeding 25,000 inhabitants in the arid or semi-arid Northwest, to the east of the Cascades, are Spokane and Butte, the entire population of the immense territory of Montana, Wyoming, Idaho, and the eastern three quarters of Washington and Oregon being less than 900,000.

At present the range of the Rocky Mountains is the real boundary between

It would not be easy to imagine two regions in the same zone more different in character than the low, rainy, heavily forested, richly productive coastal regions of Oregon and Washington and the high, barren, arid or semi-arid plains lying only a few miles to the eastward on the other side of the Cascade Mountains. Western Washington and Oregon, though of the latitude of northern New England and New Brunswick, the city of Seattle being of higher latitude than the northernmost point of Maine, are warmed by the Japan Current, so that the climate is wonderfully like that of southern England, while the country beyond the mountains possesses many of the characteristics of the Great American Desert, of which it is, in reality, a part. Comprising less than a twentieth of the area of the five Northwestern States of Oregon, Washington, Idaho, Montana,

Drawn by Ernest Blumenschein

SKETCHES OF TYPES IN SEATTLE

the East and the West; it is the continental divide of commerce. The business of Montana and Wyoming, generally speaking, flows to the eastward, while that of

Idaho, Washington, and Oregon takes its course to the Pacific coast. But with the development of Oriental markets, the opening of Alaska, and the increase of manufacturing industries, the coast cities will draw from regions more remote, crowding the commercial divide to the eastward until it approaches more nearly the geographical center line of the country. This, at least, is the great ambition of the coast cities—a unified Northwest.

Indeed, the conditions which account for Seattle and Portland are exactly those which built up New York, Boston, and Chicago. Most Western towns trace their origin to a gold-mine or a cattle chance. If great gold discoveries had been made in the Northwest at the time Marshall found gold in California, Portland and Seattle would to-day be cities as large and important as San Francisco. But the storekeeper, the ship-builder, the manufacturer, is never so venturesome as the miner, and the cities of the Pacific Northwest had to await the growth influences exerted by their natural advantages as ports, distributing-points, and manufacturing centers. The miner, always lured by the vision of gold, crossed the mountains in the face of every obstacle; the trader, the lumberman, and the fisher awaited the railroad.

In the Southwest, where the settlement is much older and the conditions those of the arid land, one is able to distinguish a type, not yet fully outlined perhaps, but readily recognizable—a type that may some day be as distinct as the Kentucky colonel or the Connecticut Yankee. A somewhat similar type may also be traced in the arid Northwest—the descendant of the cow-boy and the miner, a product of desert, mountain, and irrigated valley, with the free life which is even to-day a distinctive feature of all this great country. But it would be difficult indeed to discern any special type-differentiation in the Pacific Northwest, and there is no indication that the American of Portland, Oregon, will ever be specially different from the American of Portland, Maine. The people of western Washington and Oregon present a wonderful mixture of Americans, largely from the Middle States, but with no small sprinkling of the far East and South. Recently a good many Scandinavians have been coming to the farms, and a few other foreigners to the cities, and there is a large substratum of Japanese, Chinese, negroes, and Indians; but the population thus far, as in the Southwest, is to a singular degree pure American. Chicago seems, somehow, to possess a German cast of countenance,—an impression that has deepened in the writer's mind with recent visits,—and St. Paul is distinctively Scandinavian; but these far-Western cities give one the impression of being intensely American: I mean Anglo-Saxon. The reason for this is clearly to be found in the fact that the Anglo-Saxon American is the real pioneer, with a training in the opening of new countries that reaches back to the days of the *Mayflower* and of the Virginia cavalier.

One finds it difficult to tell of the wonders of the coastal Northwest without in some degree sharing the enthusiasm of the American of Puget Sound and the Willamette valley. In the words of an old writer describing California, it is "a country of diverse and manifold blessings, designed by Almighty God for a perfect and complete State." Compared with the enormous stretches of the Northwest as a whole, or even of the States of Washington and Oregon, it seems a mere strip of land crowded between the mountains and the sea. Though five hundred miles in length, the extent north and south of the two States of Washington and Oregon, it is only from fifty to one hundred and twenty-five miles in width, and much even of this comparatively small territory is made up of rugged mountains. Nature has blessed it with a singularly equable climate—few really hot days in summer and a winter which better deserves the name rainy season. Most of the moisture of the entire Northwest falls on this favored coastal strip, for heavy rain-clouds, floating in from the sea, meet the barrier of the Cascade Mountains, and the country to the eastward is left arid, a part of the Great Desert. Portland has five times as much rain as Umatilla, one hundred and sixty miles to the east on the other side of the mountains, and at Astoria, near the mouth of the Columbia River, it is said to rain most of the time, so that the people of the coast are sometimes called "web-footers." Despite the universality of the umbrella, however, statistics show that the annual rainfall in Portland and Seattle is not greater than that of Boston and New York, but there is this difference: Portland drizzles; New York pours, and is done with it. The prevailing condition of moisture and the mild climate have combined to produce an unmatched vegetation throughout the whole region. No visitor can fail to be impressed with the luxuriance of the trees, shrubs, crops. Here the dandelion grows in thick clumps as high as one's waist; the dogwood is here a large and beautiful tree; clover grows rank beyond belief. Here are the greatest and most valuable forests on the continent, if not in the world, an apparently inexhaustible supply of timber. While the trees do not grow as large as the big trees, the sequoias of California, they are very much larger than any in the forests of Maine or Michigan, splendid firs and cedars, four hundred years old, often two hundred and fifty feet tall, twenty-five feet or more in circumference at the base, without a branch for one hundred and fifty feet from the ground. Though lumbering has become so important an industry in Oregon and Washington that the product of the mills is shipped to New York and even to Maine, to say nothing of the cargoes sent to foreign lands, yet one may travel for days through the primeval forests and see not the slightest evidence of men. So dense is the timber that an entire logging crew will work for months on a few acres of land.

In the great lumbering districts of Maine and Michigan the land is often of poor quality, so that when it is denuded of timber it possesses small value for agricultural purposes. But in Washington the decay of centuries of rich vegetation has left in some of the heavily forested districts a singularly deep and productive soil, so that farmers have come in and planted apple-trees and clover among the stumps. These little

Drawn by Ernest Blumenschein
A COW-PUNCHER

farms are a constant marvel to the visitor: a little log house, hardly larger than many of the great stumps, sometimes even built against a stump, a rude barn, a fence, and a rich green field. In many places where the great trees stand close above-ground, coal deposits have been discovered underneath, the remains of the forests of an earlier day. At one favored spot I saw land which had yielded a large return in lumber, was then being farmed on the surface, while a coal-mine was in process of development underneath—a sort of threefold increment, which must remain a marvel of the far Northwest. The mills of Oregon and Washington to-day produce one fourteenth of all the lumber manufactured in the United States, a percentage which will increase largely within the next few years.

It is a region, also, of almost unbounded agricultural advantages, the meadow-like valleys of the streams having already reached a high state of cultivation. Indeed, the Willamette valley, in Oregon, is not only the oldest cultivated region of the far West, but it is one of the most beautiful agricultural valleys in all America. It was first settled as far back as 1843 by emigrants from Missouri, and for years was the chief source of food-supply for the early mining-camps of the California gold-fields. Portland, at the mouth of the Willamette, was its business city. To-day railroads run down each side of the Willamette River, and the valley supports a score of beautiful towns.

So rapid, indeed, has been the development of Oregon and Washington in recent years that few people realize the important part they now play in the agricultural production of the country. Washington, including the production of the semi-arid eastern part of the State,—the Spokane country,—has become one of the great wheat States. Twenty years ago Washington produced no wheat worth mentioning; in 1900 the crop of the State was over twenty-five million bushels—nearly equal to that of California. Only three States—Minnesota, Kansas, and California—exceed it in production. In the same year Oregon produced sixteen million bushels. And none of the great wheat States averaged so many bushels to the acre as Washington, which shows the remarkable fertility of its soil. The average for the crop of 1900 was twenty-three and a half bushels to the acre, while Minnesota, which has long been the very name for wheat, produced only ten and a half bushels, and Kansas seventeen and seven tenths bushels. Of all the wheat exported from the United States, Washington and Oregon to-day furnish about a quarter, mostly shipped around Cape Horn to Cork, Ireland, and to England and Scotland. Corn, the great crop of the Middle West, is not raised to any extent in Washington and Oregon, owing to the absence of continued hot weather; but both States produce large quantities of alfalfa, which in the far West, especially in the irrigated districts, has assumed first importance as a cattle-food.

Compared with the arid regions, the coastal strip is not a great cattle country, though it is building up considerable dairy interests. Hop-culture on a large scale is also assuming great importance, Oregon being the greatest producer of all the States, and Oregon and Washington together shipping more than half the American crop. In the hop season there are sections of the Willamette valley which remind one strongly of the fields of Kent, England. Both States are also taking an important part in the development of the new American beet-sugar industry. And Oregon and Washington fruit has a reputation only second to that of California.

It is a somewhat singular fact that most of the great fisheries of the world are located off coasts which are rocky and inhospitable and often scantily and meanly populated, but the favored American Northwest furnishes an example of a rich and fertile land washed by a hardly less fertile sea; for the salmon-fisheries of Puget Sound and the Columbia River must now be numbered among the great fishing industries of the world. Every year millions of salmon, swarming from the ocean into the rivers to spawn, are taken in nets and traps, canned, and shipped the world over. In the Columbia River salmon-fishing has long been an important industry, with numerous canneries at Astoria and at other points up the river. More recently the fisheries of Puget Sound have been developed until they are of first importance. In 1901, a phenomenal year, Washington packed over seven million dollars' worth of fish and Oregon over two million dollars' worth.

But the sea, and not its fisheries,—nor even the wonderful resources of the soil, nor mines, nor lumber,—is the great hope and opportunity of the Pacific Northwest. For here is the gateway of empire; here on the sea-edge, in magnificent harbors, cities have sprung up which will take toll on the products of a million farms and ranges. Without its harbors the coastal strip would still become a densely populated and prosperous land, but with them it will become great in cities and great in commercial power. It is the characteristic of the Pacific shore of the continent that it turns a rude shoulder to the sea. Here are mountains, and here at their base is the sea, abrupt, final, inhospitable, unlike the Atlantic shore, which runs out tentatively in bars and sheltering headlands, with scattering islands and wide-opening deltas where ships may easily run to shelter. Only in three or four places in fifteen hundred miles of coast are there indentations in the rude mountain wall where vessels can find safe haven, but these harbors make up in excellence what they lack in numbers. The three chief openings are at the bay of San Francisco, at the mouth of the Columbia River, and in Puget Sound; and here the greater cities of the coast have naturally sprung into existence, and are struggling with fine spirit for supremacy in the growing trade of the far East. Each harbor-opening has been made a terminal point for one or more transcontinental railway lines, and already most of the ports have their own fleets of ships ready to carry the products of the empire behind the mountains and return with the goods of far countries. As an example of the world-wide extent of their commerce, nothing could be more striking than the record of the foreign grain-fleet which went out loaded from Portland in the year 1901.

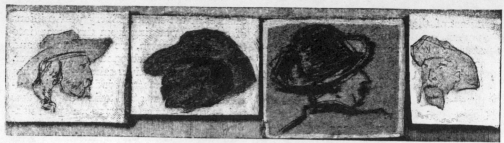

Drawn by Ernest Blumenschein

COW-BOYS

There were seventy-seven British vessels, two Danish, one Dutch, eleven French, thirty-four German, two Italian, and one Norwegian, and their cargoes went to nearly every part of the world.

The Eastern visitor finds the cities of the Northwestern coast brimful of life, color, significance, picturesque interest; and though the forces which have combined in their making are somewhat similar, each has a distinct character and individuality. "Lively," a word of the West, may well be applied to them—a sort of brisk activity, youthfulness, ozone. They have the rather unusual capacity of doing big things and talking about them lustily at the same time. It is the cry of the street corners: "Just watch us grow. See us getting to the front."

Portland (90,426 people in 1900) and Seattle (80,671 people in 1900), the largest of the Northwestern cities, are about the size of Scranton, Pennsylvania, or Lowell, Massachusetts, but they give the impression of being much larger, more important, more metropolitan. A Western town of twenty thousand makes more noise than an Eastern city of several times the size. One invariably overestimates Western populations. Seattle and Tacoma, spread out on hillsides, with chimneys smoking, buildings looming above the sky-line of the hills, and harbors full of busy ships, seem at first glance to be Chicagos, at the very least, and when one is actually inside of them there seems a sort of conspiracy to keep him so busy that he will have no opportunity of correcting his early impressions. Last spring, when I arrived in Seattle, the ships were loading for Nome and the Klondike, and it seemed evident that every one was going and had only ten minutes to reach the dock. But when the ships weighed anchor and sailed away into the sunset, the people were still hurrying, and I began to see why they had accomplished so much in twenty years.

Every citizen possesses an extraordinary knowledge of his city; in five minutes he will give you fifty reasons why it is to be, shortly, the very greatest in the world. He has such a hearty way of rubbing his hands and telling you he likes it out West that you are almost convinced that you ought to come out and live beside him. He is perfectly invincible, indisputable, the Northwesterner. In Seattle he convinces you beyond argument that Seattle is the only port of any consequence on the coast; at Tacoma he causes your memory to blot out Seattle as completely as if you had never heard of it; and at Portland you are certain that the Columbia River is the only true inlet from the Pacific Ocean. Even the smaller towns, Everett, Fairhaven, New Whatcom, and ancient Astoria, will give you convincing proofs of future greatness. And there is quite enough truth to assure each of these towns its share of bigness.

The Easterner who visits Portland usually has his mind made up to see a new, crude Western town; what he really sees is a fine old city, a bit, as it might be, of central New York—a square with the post-office in the center, tree-shaded streets, comfortable homes, and plenty of churches and clubs, the signs of conservatism and solid respectability. And yet no decay, for if there are signs of the order which comes of long settlement, there is an equal show of brisk energy. Few cities of the size of Portland can exhibit finer store and office buildings, a better street-car service, or more comfortable residences. Unlike almost any other Western town, save San Francisco perhaps, it has got beyond its first generation; it has acquired the momentum of stored riches and passed the stage of pioneer crudities. The sons of the pioneers are now coming into power. They have been educated in the East, have traveled in Europe, and they have come back to make homes in their beautiful city. Wealth and education have blossomed, as always, in conservatism and comfort and a greater attention to society, art, music. Portland is noted for the solidity of its financial institutions, its fine clubs and hotels, its good schools and libraries. It is beginning to take a solicitous interest in its history, a true sign of the self-consciousness which comes of assured success. Pioneer societies spring up only when the pioneer has become a curiosity. They will tell you that there are two classes of society in Portland, each as proud as the sons of the *Mayflower* themselves: one the descendants of those who came around Cape Horn in pre-railroad days, the other the descendants of those who crossed the plains.

Portland is in no sense a boom city; it is probably less known in the East than any other important Western town: it has had little advertising compared, for instance, with Seattle and Tacoma, and for many years its growth was slow, though substantial. Yet during the ten years ended in 1900 only three important cities in the United States had a greater percentage of gain in population. In 1890 it had only 46,385 inhabitants; in 1900 it had 90,426, nearly double. In the same time San Francisco increased only 14.6 per cent. But the exposition of 1905, by which Portland will celebrate the centennial of Lewis and Clark's discovery of Oregon, will probably make the city thoroughly known in every quarter of the land.

Portland is a singular combination of the seaport and the inland town. Probably seven out of ten Eastern people, with the question suddenly put, would place Portland on the Pacific Ocean, and a considerable proportion of the remainder would have it on the Columbia River. But it is one hundred miles from the ocean, and several miles from the Columbia, in the Willamette valley, the region of fine farms and orchards. The Willamette River at Portland is a majestic stream, so deep that great ocean vessels come from all the world to load at its docks. Portland is the fifth city in the United States as a wheat-exporter, the total shipment for 1901 being over thirteen million bushels—nearly equal

to that of San Francisco, and largely exceeding those of Seattle and Tacoma put together. It also has a large lumber, flour, fruit, and fish business.

Two views in Portland stand out in the writer's memory above all others: the first, the wide, busy river as seen from one of the bridges, the city rising on both sides, and tall-masted ships moored at the docks; the second, the view at sunset of the rose-colored, snow-capped peak of Mount Hood from the beautiful drives in the outskirts of the town.

The cities of Puget Sound give a very different impression from Portland. Puget Sound is one of the finest harbors in the world, if not the finest—a deep bay, over a hundred miles long, cut off from the ocean by the mountainous western peninsula of Washington. The waters nearly everywhere are deep, the shores abrupt, and the tide is moderate. Ships may go from Tacoma half-way to Alaska without passing out of this great sound and its extensions northward.

From Olympia, at the south, to Blaine, on the Canadian boundary, a dozen ports have sprung into existence along this great landlocked harbor, and two of them have become important cities—Tacoma, at the head of Commencement Bay, with 37,714 people (in 1900), and Seattle, thirty miles northward, with a population of 80,671 (1900); then, farther north, Everett (7838 people), Fairhaven (4228), New Whatcom (6834), and several other small but ambitious seaport towns. Still farther to the north, just over the Canadian line in British Columbia, on the northern extension of Puget Sound, is the growing and important town of Vancouver (13,685 people), destined to play the part of rival to the American cities below. Across the sound, on Vancouver Island, is the quaint old British capital of Victoria (16,841 people), full of soldiers, Indians, and Chinamen, but wonderfully well built and well kept, with a solid British conservatism and respectability.

Seattle clings to a steep hillside; a little shake, it seems, would send it sliding down into the sea. A shelf of piling has been built out into the water at the bottom for docks, and here, also, run the railroads. The main streets are notches cut in the hillside, and it is a wonder indeed, and a source of alarm to the visitor, to see the little flat-topped cable-cars running up and down the perilous grades of the cross-streets. Loaded teams go tacking zigzag up these hills like a sailing-ship in the wind, and pedestrians are given cleats and railings on some of the sidewalks to help them make the climb. But, in the face of these difficulties, Seattle has built a fine city, a great harbor and docks, a ship-building plant, a coaling-depot, a navy-yard, and many manufacturing industries. No other American city that I know of gives such an impression of boundless activity, such a stir of enterprise and noise, as Seattle, such a determination to grow and be big. They will tell you of the "Seattle spirit," the willingness of the citizens to pay their money to help the town. Desiring a railroad terminal, they promptly collect a hundred and fifty thousand dollars by popular subscription, and build a branch from the rival town of Tacoma; they give their ship-builder a hundred thousand dollars outright to enable him to secure the contract for a United States warship. A city of many beautiful homes and schools, it has also a large floating population always in evidence on the streets, young men mostly, for it is the gateway to the Alaska mines. Here the miners outfit, and here they return either poverty-stricken or with gold to spend, giving the town some of the freedom and spirit of the mining-camp. Living expenses, a few years ago so high that they were a national marvel, are now not more exorbitant than in the East, a reduction due to the development of the surrounding agricultural country.

Tacoma, like Seattle, is located on a hillside, a bright, clean, attractive city, a great lumbering and shipping center, with a growing flour-milling business and a prospective smelting industry. Its docks are a marvel to the visitor: one of the warehouses is nearly half a mile long, so arranged that the railroads come in at one side and the ships at the other—a system which renders the handling of goods remarkably cheap. Being the chief outlet for the wheat-fields of eastern Washington and the vast forests and coal-mines to the south and southeast of Puget Sound, it has built up a great commerce both domestic and foreign, its total foreign business exceeding that of any other Pacific port except San Francisco. In the far West wheat is shipped in sacks instead of in bulk, as in the East, and the method of handling by electrically operated conveyors is a revelation to the visitor, great ships loading for far-away ports with a rapidity simply astonishing. Here, also, come the vessels of the Orient. I walked through long warehouses packed with tea and matting and hemp and other products of the far East, brought in exchange for American breadstuffs. Here lumber-schooners back up to the very doors of the sawmills and receive their cargoes. Here, also, are great coaldocks where steamers can fill their bunkers within a few rods of the place where they take their cargo. All this business is growing at a rate hardly conceivable, the entire commerce of Puget Sound having increased four hundred and seventy-four per cent. in ten years' time.

We now come to the consideration of the greater arid and semi-arid Northwest beyond the Cascade Mountains, differentiated as it is from the rich coastal strip by the lack of sufficient rain, but already possessing great importance in agriculture,—chiefly irrigation farming, stock-raising, and mining,—with the promise of a greater future. A large part of this territory is made up of high plateaus, rising in Montana, Idaho, and Wyoming to the stupendous, rugged heights of the Rocky Mountains. The mountains were at once a help and a hindrance in the settlement of the country—a help because they are full of rich mineral deposits, with plenty of game in the wilder uplands, streams full of fish, and scenery of unmatched grandeur, attractive to adventurers from every part of the world. But by delaying road- and railroad-building the mountains held back for long the settled occupation of the country. A few years ago both the Rockies and the Cascades might well have been classed as "only scenery and rocks"; but it is typical of modern development that even the snow-clad peaks should now be made to serve the practical purposes of man. For they furnish the water for the irrigated fields of the valleys below, and render possible the habitation of plateaus once regarded as irreclaimable deserts. The Federal government has wisely taken possession of a large portion of the summits of both the ranges, creating vast national forest reserves and parks in extent comparable only to small States, so that the sources of the life-giving waters of the western half of the

Drawn by Ernest Blumenschein.   Half-tone plate engraved by H. Davidson

HELENA WOMEN ON HORSEBACK

continent may be forever protected and conserved. In no part of the entire United States has the Federal government such large interests as in the Northwest, for it controls not only the area of the forest reserves, but vast tracts of land yet unclaimed by settlers, and immense Indian and military reservations. It is probable that the people of the United States still own or control over three fourths of the entire territory of the five Northwestern States, and much of it will be forever a wilderness and a national playground. But the habitable parts of the country are large enough to support an immense population, the development thus far having barely begun.

More than a century ago hardy, wilderness-loving trappers and hunters had entered this country, laying the foundation for the free life which followed. Then came the inevitable prospector tramping the hills, the real though unintentional founder of empire; for every pan of gold he washed from the mountain gulches brought in a settler from the East. The trappers were pure nomads, passing on, and leaving only the burnt embers of their camp-fires; but with the pioneers came ugly shack towns, ragged and boisterous, but the virile germs of advancing civilization. In Idaho and Montana many of these mining towns still exist, Butte City itself being only an overgrown mining-camp. Indeed, new ones are constantly appearing, exact prototypes of the old, and hardly less reckless and free. Only yesterday the Thunder Mountain country of Idaho was opened; a dozen little camps sprang into existence, the

Drawn by Ernest Blumenschein

FULL-BLOODED BANNOCK INDIAN JUST RETURNED FROM SCHOOL

stories of the doings of which brought back memories of the fifties in California and the sixties in Montana. Even to-day the prospector is one of the familiar figures of the Rocky Mountain Northwest, for while settlement has been rapid, the country is immense and rugged, with vast areas of free land, even unsurveyed land, to be had for the taking, and the prospector has as good a chance now as he ever had—perhaps better, for low-grade ores that were worthless ten years ago can now be worked with profit. Parts of the interior of Idaho to-day are as much a wilderness and almost as difficult of access as the goldfields of Alaska.

Following the miners, came the cattle and sheepmen, swarming up from Texas, spreading widely over the free range, building up the unique cow-town of the plains, and molding that most distinct of Western types, the cow-boy, with a civilization as quick on the trigger, as wild and free, as that of the mining-camps themselves. This life still exists, to a large extent, in the arid Northwest, but much toned down, it is true, much more businesslike, with an eye always open to the Chicago market reports, and cattle too valuable to "punch." Even to-day the chief industries of Wyoming, Idaho, and much of western Washington and Oregon are cattle- and sheep-raising. In Montana, though the cattle and sheep business is of high importance, it is overshadowed as an industry by the copper, silver, and gold of the mines. The cow-town still exists; not quite the cow-town of the older West, but spirited enough to satisfy the most exacting Easterner. Wyo-

Drawn by Ernest Blumenschein.   Half-tone plate engraved by H. Davidson

A COPPER-MINE AT BUTTE

ming has changed the least of any of the Western States: it is still distinctly a cattle State—rolling plains, mountains, desert, with a few rich and fertile valleys, and a population so scattered that one may sometimes travel for days without seeing a sign of human habitation. Twice the size of Pennsylvania, it has a bare one seventh as many people, or only a fraction more than one inhabitant to each square mile of territory.

Yet in Wyoming, as in all other parts of the arid Northwest, ranchers are crowding into the irrigable valleys, many of which have become thickly populated and wonderfully well cultivated and beautiful to look upon. The Big Horn basin of Wyoming, for instance, only a few years ago an Indian wilderness and a resort for hunters, is now rapidly settling up; so is the valley of the Snake River in Idaho and in Washington, the Yellowstone and the Missouri and their branches in Montana, the Yakima in the west, and also many lesser streams. These new ranchers are helping to revolutionize the cattle and sheep industries, which will probably be long the most important of any in the arid West. The old wild, long-horned cattle have all but disappeared, and their places have been taken by well-bred Hereford, Galloway, and Shorthorn stock, which is carefully fed and well protected. The herds are not as large as they were, nor are they dependent entirely upon the free range, to survive or starve as the snow is shallow or deep, or the grass rich or poor;

Drawn by Ernest Blumenschein.   Half-tone plate engraved by J. Tinkey

BUFFALO JONES, FAMOUS IN WYOMING

for the irrigation farmer's chief crop in all this region is hay—alfalfa mostly. He cuts several crops a year; his yield is as certain as the water in his ditches, and his profits sure. He feeds his own small herds, and sells the remainder of his crop to the big ranchmen; and the cattle go to market in good condition. Sheep are increasing in numbers, though the cattlemen wage unremitting war upon them for the possession of the free range, even to exterminating large flocks, and sometimes killing the herders. A third of all the sheep in the United States are owned in the Northwest, and Billings in Montana and The Dalles in Oregon are the greatest initial wool-markets in the country.

But agriculture in the dry Northwest is by no means confined to cattle and sheep, with the dependent industry of hay-raising. One of the important discoveries of recent years, relative to this region, is the fact that there are varying degrees of aridity. There are vast stretches of land where little or no rain ever falls, where no crops will ever grow except under irrigation; but in certain localities a little heavier rainfall enables the settlers to practise what has come to be known as "dry farming," a development of the first importance. Between the Cascade Mountains and the Rockies a large territory in eastern Washington, northeastern Oregon, and northwestern Idaho is thus farmed. Here there is double the rainfall of most of the arid Northwest, though the total precipitation is

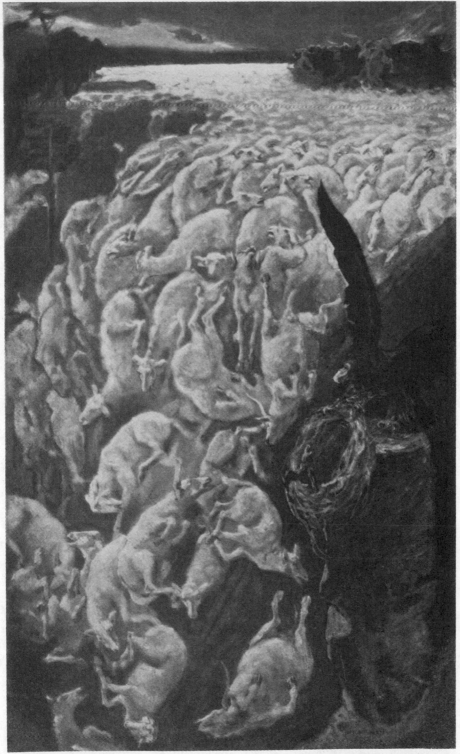

Drawn by Ernest Blumenschein.   Half-tone plate engraved by H. C. Merrill

AN EPISODE OF THE SHEEP AND CATTLE WAR—FIVE THOUSAND SHEEP
DRIVEN TO DEATH OVER A PRECIPICE

only a small fraction of that in humid western Washington. This is the famous Palouse, Walla Walla, and Lewiston country, which has become, within a few years, one of the most important wheat centers in the United States. The soil is exceedingly rich, raising without fertilization often as high of 36,848 (1900), an increase of eighty-five per cent. over that of 1890, and it is yearly growing in importance as a railroad and business center. Other towns of this notable district are Umatilla and Pendleton in Oregon, Walla Walla and Colfax in Washington, and Lewiston in Idaho.

Drawn by Ernest Blumenschein

A MAIDEN OF THE TETON MOUNTAINS

as thirty-five bushels to the acre, though the country is often so dry that it seems as if the fields must blow away in dust. In some regions water must be hauled for miles, often by railroad, for culinary purposes. Yet here grow these wonderful wheat crops, and here has sprung up a fine new civilization, with many prosperous towns. Spokane, in Washington, is the great center of this agricultural district —a beautiful, clean, well-ordered town, with fine water-power, flour-mills, electric lights, and car lines. It has a population

One may safely prophesy that here will grow up ultimately one of the important agricultural districts of the Union.

Fruit-raising is also becoming yearly a more valuable resource of the arid land. Nothing can exceed the beauty of the orchards and fields of such irrigated valleys as the Yakima in Washington, Hood River in Oregon, the Boisé and the Snake in Idaho, the Yellowstone in Montana, and others. In half a dozen years the strawberry-raisers of Hood River have made themselves famous, shipping their product for hundreds

Drawn by Ernest Blumenschein

MAIN STREET IN A PLAINS TOWN

of miles in every direction. Indeed, it is to irrigation that all this region must look for its greatest future development. Alfalfa hay, as I have said, is now the chief crop, and a very profitable one, but the farmers are gradually working out into other lines. Most of the smaller streams are now utilized pretty fully, but almost nothing has so far been done to take out the almost limitless supply of water from the Columbia, Snake, Yellowstone, and Missouri. With the storage reservoirs assured by the now promised assistance of the Federal government, and the more careful distribution of water already in use, the irrigated area of all the arid Northwest can be greatly increased.

In mining the arid Northwest occupies a place of first importance. Montana is to-day the third State in the Union in mineral wealth, and the greatest copper-producing center of the world. The value of its output of copper, gold, silver, and coal is nearly seventy million dollars a year, Butte City being the center of the industry, a city so full of picturesque interest that I shall write about it more fully in another article of this series. Idaho is the eleventh State in the Union in mineral wealth, with an annual product of nearly ten million dollars. Wyoming has important coal deposits worth nearly six million dollars a year.

This, in barest outline, is the new Northwest. An instantaneous photograph has been almost a necessity, so rapidly is the country changing. Two things the visitor is sure of: immense basic resources and a superb activity of growth. What he sees to-day will be different and better to-morrow, and he can only faintly foreshadow the ultimate greatness of the country. As an enthusiastic Westerner has asserted, "the development of the United States began at the back door" (meaning the Atlantic coast); "you shall see one day what the front door is like."

And so the Northwesterner, looking never behind, has anchored his confidence firmly in the unmatched resources of his country and in the surety of reaching in trade the millions of Asia and the new population of Alaska.

19

The Round-Up

Theodore Roosevelt

AN ARIZONA TYPE.

THE ROUND-UP.

BY THEODORE ROOSEVELT.

ILLUSTRATIONS BY FREDERIC REMINGTON.

DURING the winter-time there is ordinarily but little work done among the cattle. There is some line riding, and a continual lookout is kept for the very weak animals; but most of the stock are left to shift for themselves, undisturbed. Almost every stock-grower's association forbids branding any calves before the spring round-up. If great bands of cattle wander off the range, parties may be fitted out to go after them and bring them back; but this is only done when absolutely necessary, as when the drift of the cattle has been towards an Indian reservation or a settled granger country, for the weather is very severe, and the horses are so poor that their food must be carried along.

The bulk of the work is done during the summer, including the late spring and early fall, and consists mainly in a succession of round-ups, beginning, with us, in May and ending towards the last of October. But a good deal may be done by riding over one's range. Frequently, too, herding will be practiced on a large scale.

More important than herding is "trail" work; cattle, while driven from one range to another, or to a shipping point for beef, being said to be "on the trail." For years, the over-supply from the vast breeding ranches to the south, especially in Texas, has been driven northward in large herds, either to the shipping towns along the great railroads, or else to the fattening ranges of the North-west; it having been found, so far, that while the calf crop is larger in the South, beeves become much heavier in the North. Such cattle, for the most part, went along tolerably well-marked routes or trails, which became for the time

293

being of great importance, flourishing — and extremely lawless — towns growing up along them; but with the growth of the railroad system, and above all with the filling-up of the northern ranges, these trails have steadily become of less and less consequence, though many herds still travel them on their way to the already crowded ranges of western Dakota and Montana, or to the Canadian regions beyond. The trail work is something by itself. The herds may be on the trail several months, averaging fifteen miles or less a a day. The cowboys accompanying each have to undergo much hard toil, of a peculiarly same and wearisome kind, on account of the extreme slowness with which everything must be done, as trail cattle should never be hurried. The foreman of a trail outfit must be not only a veteran cowhand, but also a miracle of patience and resolution.

Round-up work is far less irksome, there being an immense amount of dash and excitement connected with it; and when once the cattle are on the range, the important work is done during the round-up. On cow ranches, or wherever there is breeding stock, the spring round-up is the great event of the season, as it is then that the bulk of the calves are branded. It usually lasts six weeks, or thereabouts; but its end by no means implies rest for the stockman. On the contrary, as soon as it is over, wagons are sent to work out-of-the-way parts of the country that have been passed over, but where cattle are supposed to have drifted; and by the time these have come back the first beef round-up has begun, and thereafter beeves are steadily gathered and shipped, at least from among the larger herds, until cold weather sets in; and in the fall there is another round-up, to brand the late calves and see that the stock is got back on the range. As all of these round-ups are of one character, a description of the most important, taking place in the spring, will be enough.

In April we begin to get up the horses. Throughout the winter very few have been kept for use, as they are then poor and weak, and must be given grain and hay if they are to be worked. The men in the line camps need two or three apiece, and each man at the home ranch has a couple more; but the rest are left out to shift for themselves, which the tough, hardy little fellows are well able to do. Ponies can pick up a living where cattle die; though the scanty feed, which they may have to uncover by pawing off the snow, and the bitter weather often make them look very gaunt by spring-time. But the first warm rains bring up the green grass, and then all the live-stock gain flesh with wonderful rapidity. When the spring round-up begins the horses should be as fat and sleek as possible. After running all winter free, even the most sober pony is apt to betray an inclination to buck; and, if possible, we like to ride every animal once or twice before we begin to do real work with him. Animals that have escaped for any length of time are almost as bad to handle as if they had never been broken. One of the two horses mentioned in a preceding article as having been gone eighteen months has, since his return, been suggestively dubbed "Dynamite Jimmy," on account of the incessant and eruptive energy with which he bucks. Many of our horses, by the way, are thus named from some feat or peculiarity. Wire Fence, when being broken, ran into one of the abominations after which he is now called; Hackamore once got away and remained out for three weeks with a hackamore, or breaking-halter, on him; Macaulay contracted the habit of regularly getting rid of the huge Scotchman to whom he was intrusted; Bulberry Johnny spent the hour or two after he was first mounted in a large patch of thorny bulberry bushes, his distracted rider unable to get him to do anything but move round sidewise in a circle; Fall Back would never get to the front; Water Skip always jumps mud-puddles; and there are a dozen others with names as purely descriptive.

The stock-growers of Montana, of the western part of Dakota, and even of portions of extreme northern Wyoming, — that is, of all the grazing lands lying in the basin of the Upper Missouri, — have united, and formed themselves into the great Montana Stock-growers' Association. Among the countless benefits they have derived from this course, not the least has been the way in which the various round-ups work in with and supplement one another. At the spring meeting of the association, the entire territory mentioned above, including perhaps a hundred thousand square miles, is mapped out into round-up districts, which generally are changed but slightly from year to year, and the times and places for the round-ups to begin refixed so that those of adjacent districts may be run with a view to the best interests of all. Thus the stockmen along the Yellowstone have one round-up; we along the Little Missouri have another; and the country lying between, through which the Big Beaver flows, is almost equally important to both. Accordingly, one spring, the Little Missouri round-up, beginning May 25 and working down-stream, was timed so as to reach the mouth of the Big Beaver about June 1, the Yellowstone round-up beginning at that date and place. Both then worked up the Beaver together to its head, when the Yellowstone men turned to the west and we bent back to our own river; thus the bulk of the strayed cattle of each were brought back to their respective ranges. Our own round-up district covers the Big and Little Beaver creeks, which rise near each other, but empty into the Little Missouri nearly a hundred and fifty miles apart, and so much of the latter river as lies between their mouths.

The captain or foreman of the round-up, upon whom very much of its efficiency and success depends, is chosen beforehand. He is, of course, an expert cowman, thoroughly acquainted with the country; and he must also be able to command and to keep control of the wild rough-riders he has under him — a feat needing both tact and firmness.

At the appointed day all meet at the place from which the round-up is to start. Each ranch, of course, has most work to be done in its own round-up district, but it is also necessary to have representatives in all those surrounding it. A large outfit may employ a dozen cowboys, or over, in the home district, and yet have nearly as many more representing its interest in the various ones adjoining. Smaller outfits generally club together to run a wagon and send outside representatives, or else go along with their stronger neighbors, they paying part of the expenses. A large outfit, with a herd of twenty thousand cattle or more, can, if necessary, run a round-up entirely by itself, and is able to act independently of outside help; it is therefore at a great advantage compared with those that can take no step effectively without their neighbors' consent and assistance.

If the starting-point is some distance off, it may be necessary to leave home three or four days in advance. Before this we have got everything in readiness; have overhauled the wagons, shod any horse whose fore feet are tender, — as a rule, all our ponies go barefooted, — and left things in order at the ranch. Our outfit may be taken as a sample of every one else's. We have a stout four-horse wagon to carry the bedding and the food; in its rear a mess-chest is rigged to hold the knives, forks, cans, etc. All our four team-horses are strong, willing animals, though of no great size, being originally just "broncos," or unbroken native horses, like the others. The teamster is also cook: a man who is a really first-rate hand at both driving and cooking — and our present teamster is both — can always command his price. Besides our own men, some cowboys from neighboring ranches and two or three representatives from other round-up districts are always along, and we generally have at least a dozen "riders," as they are termed, — that is, cowboys, or "cow-punchers," who do the actual cattle-work, — with the wagon. Each of these has a string of eight or ten ponies; and to take charge of the saddle-band, thus consisting of a hundred odd head, there are two herders, always known as "horse-wranglers" — one for the day and one for the night. Occasionally there will be two wagons, one to carry the bedding and one the food, known, respectively, as the bed and the mess wagon; but this is not usual.

While traveling to the meeting-point the pace is always slow, as it is an object to bring the horses on the ground as fresh as possible. Accordingly, we keep at a walk almost all day, and the riders, having nothing else to do, assist the wranglers in driving the saddle-band, three or four going in front, and others on the side, so that the horses shall keep on a walk. There is always some trouble with the animals at the starting out, as they are very fresh and are restive under the saddle. The herd is likely to stampede, and any beast that is frisky or vicious is sure to show its worst side. To do really effective cow-work a pony should be well broken; but many even of the old ones have vicious traits, and almost every man will have in his string one or two young horses, or broncos, hardly broken at all. In consequence, very many of my horses have to this day traits not calculated to set a timid or a clumsy rider at his ease. One or two run away and cannot be held by even the strongest bit; others can hardly be bridled or saddled until they have been thrown; two or three have a tendency to fall over backward; and half of them buck more or less, some so hard that only an expert can sit them.

In riding these wild, vicious horses, and in careering over such very bad ground, especially at night, accidents are always occurring. A man who is merely an ordinary rider is certain to have a pretty hard time. On my first round-up I had a string of nine horses, four of them broncos, only broken to the extent of having each been saddled once or twice. One of them it was an impossibility to bridle or to saddle single-handed; it was very difficult to get on or off him, and he was exceedingly nervous if a man moved his hands or feet; but he had no bad tricks. The second soon became perfectly quiet. The third turned out to be one of the worst buckers on the ranch: once, when he bucked me off, I managed to fall on a stone and broke a rib. The fourth had a still worse habit, for he would balk and then throw himself over backward: once, when I was not quick enough, he caught me and broke something in the point of my shoulder, so that it was some weeks before I could raise the arm freely. My hurts were far from serious, and did not interfere with my riding and working as usual through the round-up; but I was heartily glad when it ended, and ever since have religiously done my best to get none but gentle horses in my own string. However, every one gets falls from or with his horse now and then in the cow country; and even my men, good riders though they are, are sometimes injured. One of them once broke his ankle; another a rib; another was on one occasion stunned, remaining unconscious for some hours; and yet another had certain of his horses buck under him so hard and long as finally to hurt his lungs and make him cough blood. Fatal accidents occur annually in almost every district, especially if there is much work to be done among stampeded cattle at night; but on my own ranch none of my men have ever been seriously hurt, though on one occasion a cowboy from another ranch, who was with my wagon, was killed, his horse falling and pitching him heavily on his head.

For bedding, each man has two or three pairs of blankets, and a tarpaulin or small wagon-sheet. Usually, two or three sleep together. Even in June the nights are generally cool and pleasant, and it is chilly in the early mornings; although this is not always so, and when the weather stays hot and mosquitoes are plenty, the hours of darkness, even in midsummer, seem painfully long. In the Bad Lands proper we are not often bothered very seriously by these winged pests; but in the low bottoms of the Big Missouri, and beside many of the reedy ponds and great sloughs out on the prairie, they are a perfect scourge. During the very hot nights, when they are especially active, the bed-clothes make a man feel absolutely smothered, and yet his only chance for sleep is to wrap himself tightly up, head and all; and even then some of the pests will usually force their way in. At sunset I have seen the mosquitoes rise up from the land like a dense cloud, to make the hot, stifling night one long torture; the horses would neither lie down nor graze, traveling restlessly to and fro till daybreak, their bodies streaked and bloody, and the insects settling on them so as to make them all one color, a uniform gray; while the men, after a few hours' tossing about in the vain attempt to sleep, rose, built a little fire of damp sage brush, and thus endured the misery as best they could until it was light enough to work.

But if the weather is fine, a man will never sleep better nor more pleasantly than in the open air after a hard day's work on the round-up; nor will an ordinary shower or gust of wind disturb him in the least, for he simply draws the tarpaulin over his head and goes on sleeping. But now and then we have a wind-

storm that might better be called a whirlwind and has to be met very differently; and two or three days or nights of rain insure the wetting of the blankets, and therefore shivering discomfort on the part of the would-be sleeper. For two or three hours all goes well; and it is rather soothing to listen to the steady patter of the great raindrops on the canvas. But then it will be found that a corner has been left open through which the water can get in, or else the tarpaulin will begin to leak somewhere; or perhaps the water will have collected in a hollow underneath and have begun to soak through. Soon a little stream trickles in, and every effort to remedy matters merely results in a change for the worse. To move out of the way insures getting wet in a fresh spot; and the best course is to lie still and accept the evils that have come with what fortitude one can. Even thus, the first night a man can sleep pretty well; but if the rain continues, the second night, when the blankets are already damp, and when the water comes through more easily, is apt to be most unpleasant.

Of course, a man can take little spare clothing on a round-up; at the very outside two or three clean handkerchiefs, a pair of socks, a change of underclothes, and the most primitive kind of washing apparatus, all wrapped up in a stout jacket which is to be worn when night-herding. The inevitable "slicker," or oil-skin coat, which gives complete protection from the wet, is always carried behind the saddle.

At the meeting-place there is usually a delay of a day or two to let every one come in; and the plain on which the encampment is made becomes a scene of great bustle and turmoil. The heavy four-horse wagons jolt in from different quarters, the horse-wranglers rushing madly to and fro in the endeavor to keep the different saddle-bands from mingling, while the "riders," or cowboys, with each wagon jog along in a body. The representatives from outside districts ride in singly or by twos and threes, every man driving before him his own horses, one of them loaded with his bedding. Each wagon wheels out of the way into some camping-place not too near the others, the bedding is tossed out on the ground, and then every one is left to do what he wishes, while the different wagon bosses, or foremen, seek out the captain of the round-up to learn what his plans are.

There is a good deal of rough but effective discipline and method in the way in which a round-up is carried on. The captain of the whole has as lieutenants the various wagon foremen, and in making demands for men to do some special service he will usually merely

THE ROUND-UP.

designate some foreman to take charge of the work and let him parcel it out among his men to suit himself. The captain of the round-up or the foreman of a wagon may himself be a ranchman; if such is not the case, and the ranchman nevertheless comes along, he works and fares precisely as do the other cowboys.

While the head men are gathered in a little knot, planning out the work, the others are dispersed over the plain in every direction, racing, breaking rough horses, or simply larking with one another. If a man has an especially bad horse, he usually takes such an opportunity, when he has plenty of time, to ride him; and while saddling he is surrounded by a crowd of most unsympathetic associates who greet with uproarious mirth any misadventure. A

may reserve all his energies for the rider. In the last case, the man, keeping tight hold with his left hand of the cheek-strap, so as to prevent the horse from getting his head down until he is fairly seated, swings himself quickly into the saddle. Up rises the bronco's back into an arch; his head, the ears laid straight back, goes down between his fore feet, and, squealing savagely, he makes a succession of rapid, stiff-legged, jarring bounds. Sometimes he is a "plunging" bucker, who runs forward all the time while bucking; or he may buck steadily in one place, or "sunfish,"— that is, bring first one shoulder down almost to the ground and then the other,— or else he may change ends while in the air. A first-class rider will sit throughout it all without moving from the sad-

THE ROPE CORRAL.

man on a bucking horse is always considered fair game, every squeal and jump of the bronco being hailed with cheers of delighted irony for the rider and shouts to "stay with him." The antics of a vicious bronco show infinite variety of detail, but are all modeled on one general plan. When the rope settles round his neck the fight begins, and it is only after much plunging and snorting that a twist is taken over his nose, or else a hackamore — a species of severe halter, usually made of plaited hair — slipped on his head. While being bridled he strikes viciously with his fore feet, and perhaps has to be blindfolded or thrown down; and to get the saddle on him is quite as difficult. When saddled, he may get rid of his exuberant spirits by bucking under the saddle, or

dle, quirting * his horse all the time, though his hat may be jarred off his head and his revolver out of its sheath. After a few jumps, however, the average man grasps hold of the horn of the saddle — the delighted onlookers meanwhile earnestly advising him not to "go to leather "— and is contented to get through the affair in any shape provided he can escape without being thrown off. An accident is of necessity borne with a broad grin, as any attempt to resent the raillery of the bystanders — which is perfectly good-humored — would be apt to result disastrously. Cowboys are certainly extremely good riders. As a class they

* Quirt is the name of the short flexible riding-whip used throughout cowboy land. The term is a Spanish one.

have no superiors. Of course, they would at first be at a disadvantage in steeple-chasing or fox-hunting, but their average of horsemanship is without doubt higher than that of the men who take part in these latter amusements. A cowboy would learn to ride across country in a quarter of the time it would take a cross-country rider to learn to handle a vicious bronco or to do good cow-work round and in a herd.

On such a day, when there is no regular work, there will often also be horse-races, as each outfit is pretty sure to have some running pony which it believes can outpace any other. These contests are always short-distance dashes, for but a few hundred yards. Horse-racing is a mania with most plainsmen, white or red. A man with a good racing pony will travel all about with it, often winning large sums, visiting alike cow ranches, frontier towns, and Indian encampments. Sometimes the race is "pony against pony," the victor taking both steeds. In racing the men ride bareback, as there are hardly any light saddles in the cow country. There will be intense excitement and very heavy betting over a race between two well-known horses, together with a good chance of blood being shed in the attendant quarrels. Indians and whites often race against each other as well as among themselves. I have seen several such contests, and in every case but one the white man happened to win. A race is usually run between two thick rows of spectators, on foot and on horseback, and as the racers pass, these rows close in behind them, every man yelling and shouting with all the strength of his lungs, and all waving their hats and cloaks to encourage the contestants, or firing off their revolvers and saddle guns. The little horses are fairly maddened, as is natural enough, and run as if they were crazy: were the distances longer, some would be sure to drop in their tracks.

Besides the horse-races, which are, of course, the main attraction, the men at a round-up will often get up wrestling matches or foot-races. In fact, every one feels that he is off for a holiday; for after the monotony of a long winter, the cowboys look forward eagerly to the round-up, where the work is hard, it is true, but exciting and varied, and treated a good deal as a frolic. There is no eight-hour law in cowboy land: during round-up time we often count ourselves lucky if we get off with much less than sixteen hours; but the work is done in the saddle, and the men are spurred on all the time by the desire to outdo one another in feats of daring and skillful horsemanship. There is very little quarreling or fighting; and though the fun often takes the form of rather rough horse-play, yet the practice

of carrying dangerous weapons makes cowboys show far more rough courtesy to each other and far less rudeness to strangers than is the case among, for instance, Eastern miners, or even lumbermen. When a quarrel may very probably result fatally, a man thinks twice before going into it: warlike people or classes always treat one another with a certain amount of consideration and politeness. The moral tone of a cow-camp, indeed, is rather high than otherwise. Meanness, cowardice, and dishonesty are not tolerated. There is a high regard for truthfulness and keeping one's word, intense contempt for any kind of hypocrisy, and a hearty dislike for a man who shirks his work. Many of the men gamble and drink, but many do neither; and the conversation is not worse than in most bodies composed wholly of male human beings. A cowboy will not submit tamely to an insult, and is very ready to avenge his own wrongs; nor has he an overwrought fear of shedding blood. He possesses, in fact, few of the emasculated, milk-and-water moralities admired by the pseudo-philanthropists; but he does possess, to a very high degree, the stern, manly qualities that are so valuable to a nation.

The method of work is simple. The mess-wagons and loose horses, after breaking camp in the morning, move on in a straight line for some few miles, going into camp again before midday; and the day herd, consisting of all the cattle that have been found far off their range, and which are to be brought back there, and of any others that it is necessary to gather, follows on afterwards. Meanwhile the cowboys scatter out and drive in all the cattle from the country round about, going perhaps ten or fifteen miles back from the line of march, and meeting at the place where camp has already been pitched. The wagons always keep some little distance from one another, and the saddle-bands do the same, so that the horses may not get mixed. It is rather picturesque to see the four-horse teams filing down at a trot through a pass among the buttes—the saddle-bands being driven along at a smart pace to one side or behind, the teamsters cracking their whips, and the horse-wranglers calling and shouting as they ride rapidly from side to side behind the horses, urging on the stragglers by dexterous touches with the knotted ends of their long lariats that are left trailing from the saddle. The country driven over is very rough, and it is often necessary to double up teams and put on eight horses to each wagon in going up an unusually steep pitch, or hauling through a deep mud-hole, or over a river crossing where there is quicksand.

The speed and thoroughness with which a

DRIVING TO THE ROUND-UP.

country can be worked depends, of course, very largely upon the number of riders. Ours is probably about an average round-up as regards size. The last spring I was out, there were half a dozen wagons along; the saddle-bands numbered about a hundred each; and the morning we started, sixty men in the saddle splashed across the shallow ford of the river that divided the plain where we had camped from the valley of the long winding creek up which we were first to work.

In the morning, the cook is preparing breakfast long before the first glimmer of dawn. As soon as it is ready, probably about 3 o'clock, he utters a long-drawn shout, and all the sleepers feel it is time to be up on the instant, for they know there can be no such thing as delay on the round-up, under penalty of being set afoot. Accordingly, they bundle out, rubbing their eyes and yawning, draw on their boots and trousers,—if they have taken the latter off,—roll up and cord their bedding, and usually without any attempt at washing crowd over to the little smoldering fire, which is placed in a hole dug in the ground, so that there may be no risk of its spreading. The

men are rarely very hungry at breakfast, and it is a meal that has to be eaten in shortest order, so it is perhaps the least important. Each man, as he comes up, grasps a tin cup and plate from the mess-box, pours out his tea or coffee, with sugar, but of course no milk, helps himself to one or two of the biscuits that have been baked in a Dutch oven, and perhaps also to a slice of the fat pork swimming in the grease of the frying-pan, ladles himself out some beans, if there are any, and squats down on the ground to eat his breakfast. The meal is not an elaborate one; nevertheless a man will have to hurry if he wishes to eat it before hearing the foreman sing out, "Come, boys, catch your horses"; when he must drop everything and run out to the wagon with his lariat. The night wrangler is now bringing in the saddle-band, which he has been up all night guarding. A rope corral is rigged up by stretching a rope from each wheel of one side of the wagon, making a V-shaped space, into which the saddle-horses are driven. Certain men stand around to keep them inside, while the others catch the horses: many outfits have one man to do all the roping. As soon as each has caught his horse — usually a strong, tough animal, the small, quick ponies being reserved for the work round the herd in the afternoon — the band, now in charge of the day wrangler, is turned loose, and every one saddles up as fast as possible. It still lacks some time of being sunrise, and the air has in it the peculiar chill of the early morning. When all are saddled, many of the horses bucking and dancing about, the riders from the different wagons all assemble at the one where the captain is sitting, already mounted. He waits a very short time — for laggards receive but scant mercy — before announcing the proposed camping-place and parceling out the work among those present. If, as is usually the case, the line of march is along a river or creek, he appoints some man to take a dozen others and drive down (or up) it ahead of the day herd, so that the latter will not have to travel through other cattle; the day herd

Meanwhile the two bands, a score of riders in each, separate and make their way in opposite directions. The leader of each tries to get such a "scatter" on his men that they will cover completely all the land gone over. This morning work is called circle riding, and is peculiarly hard in the Bad Lands on account of the remarkably broken, rugged nature of the country. The men come in on lines that tend to a common center — as if the sticks of a fan were curved. As the band goes out, the leader from time to time detaches one or two men to ride down through certain sections of the country, making the shorter, or what are called inside, circles, while he keeps on; and finally, retaining as companions the two or three whose horses are toughest, makes the longest or outside circle himself, going clear back to the divide, or whatever the point may be that marks the limit of the round-up work, and then turning and working straight to the meet-

SADDLING FRESH HORSES.

itself being driven and guarded by a dozen men detached for that purpose. The rest of the riders are divided into two bands, placed under men who know the country, and start out, one on each side, to bring in every head for fifteen miles back. The captain then himself rides down to the new camping-place, so as to be there as soon as any cattle are brought in.

ing-place. Each man, of course, brings in every head of cattle he can see.

These long, swift rides in the glorious spring mornings are not soon to be forgotten. The sweet, fresh air, with a touch of sharpness thus early in the day, and the rapid motion of the fiery little horse combine to make a man's blood thrill and leap with sheer buoyant light-heartedness and eager, exultant pleasure in the boldness and freedom of the life he is leading. As we climb the steep sides of the first range of buttes, wisps of wavering mist still cling in the hollows of the valley; when we come out on the top of the first great plateau, the sun flames up over its edge, and in the level, red beams the galloping horsemen throw long fantastic shadows. Black care rarely sits behind a rider whose pace is fast enough; at any rate, not when he first feels the horse move under him.

Sometimes we trot or pace, and again we lope or gallop; the few who are to take the outside circle must needs ride both hard and fast. Although only grass-fed, the horses are tough and wiry; and, moreover, are each used but once in four days, or thereabouts, so they

wet weather the Bad Lands are absolutely impassable; but if the ground is not slippery, it is a remarkable place that can shake the matter-of-course confidence felt by the rider in the capacity of his steed to go anywhere.

When the men on the outside circle have reached the bound set them,—whether it is a low divide, a group of jagged hills, the edge of the rolling, limitless prairie, or the long, waste reaches of alkali and sage brush,—they turn their horses' heads and begin to work down the branches of the creeks, one or two riding down the bottom, while the others keep off to the right and the left, a little ahead and fairly high up on the side hills, so as to command as much of a view as possible. On the level or rolling prairies the cattle can be seen a long way off, and it is an easy matter to gather and to drive them; but in the Bad Lands

ROPED!

stand the work well. The course out lies across great grassy plateaus, along knife-like ridge crests, among winding valleys and ravines, and over acres of barren, sun-scorched buttes, that look grimly grotesque and forbidding, while in the Bad Lands the riders unhesitatingly go down and over places where it seems impossible that a horse should even stand. The line of horsemen will quarter down the side of a butte, where every pony has to drop from ledge to ledge like a goat, and will go over the shoulder of a soapstone cliff, when wet and slippery, with a series of plunges and scrambles which if unsuccessful would land horses and riders in the bottom of the cañon-like washout below. In descending a clay butte after a rain, the pony will put all four feet together and slide down to the bottom almost or quite on his haunches. In very

every little pocket, basin, and coulée has to be searched, every gorge or ravine entered, and the dense patches of brushwood and spindling, wind-beaten trees closely examined. All the cattle are carried on ahead down the creek; and it is curious to watch the different behavior of the different breeds. A cowboy riding off to one side of the creek, and seeing a number of long-horned Texans grazing in the branches of a set of coulées, has merely to ride across the upper ends of these, uttering the drawn-out "ei-koh-h-h," so familiar to the cattle-men, and the long-horns will stop grazing, stare fixedly at him, and then, wheeling, strike off down the coulées at a trot, tails in air, to be carried along by the center riders when they reach the main creek into which the coulées lead. Our own range cattle are not so wild, but nevertheless are easy to drive; while Eastern-raised beasts have little fear of a horseman, and merely stare stupidly

CUTTING OUT A STEER.

at him until he rides directly towards them. Every little bunch of stock is thus collected, and all are driven along together. At the place where some large fork joins the main creek another band may be met, driven by some of the men who have left earlier in the day to take one of the shorter circles; and thus, before coming down to the bottom where the wagons are camped and where the actual "round-up" itself is to take place, this one herd may include a couple of thousand head; or, on the other hand, the longest ride may not result in the finding of a dozen animals. As soon as the riders are in, they disperse to their respective wagons to get dinner and change horses, leaving the cattle to be held by one or two of their number. If only a small number of cattle have been gathered, they will all be run into one herd; if there are

many of them, however, the different herds will be held separate.

A plain where a round-up is taking place offers a picturesque sight. I well remember one such. It was on a level bottom in the bend of the river, which here made an almost semi-circular sweep. The bottom was in shape a long oval, hemmed in by an unbroken line of steep bluffs so that it looked like an amphitheater. Across the faces of the dazzling white cliffs there were sharp bands of black and red, drawn by the coal seams and the layers of burned clay: the leaves of the trees and the grass had the vivid green of spring-time. The wagons were camped among the cottonwood trees fringing the river, a thin column of smoke rising up from beside each. The horses were grazing round the outskirts, those of each wagon by themselves and kept from going

BRANDING A HORSE.

too near the others by their watchful guard. In the great circular corral, towards one end, the men were already branding calves, while the whole middle of the bottom was covered with lowing herds of cattle and shouting, galloping cowboys. Apparently there was nothing but dust, noise, and confusion; but in reality the work was proceeding all the while with the utmost rapidity and certainty.

As soon as, or even before, the last circle riders have come in and have snatched a few hasty mouthfuls to serve as their midday meal, we begin to work the herd — or herds, if the one herd would be of too unwieldy size. The animals are held in a compact bunch, most of the riders forming a ring outside, while a couple from each ranch successively look the herds through and cut out those marked with their own brand. It is difficult, in such a mass of moving beasts,— for they do not stay still, but keep weaving in and out among each other,— to find all of one's own animals: a man must have natural gifts, as well as great experience, before he becomes a good brand-reader and is able to really "clean up a herd"— that is, be sure he has left nothing of his own in it.

To do good work in cutting out from a herd, not only should the rider be a good horseman, but he should also have a skillful, thoroughly trained horse. A good cutting pony is not common, and is generally too valuable to be used anywhere but in the herd. Such an one enters thoroughly into the spirit of the thing,

and finds out immediately the animal his master is after; he will then follow it closely of his own accord through every wheel and double, at top speed. When looking through the herd, it is necessary to move slowly; and when any animal is found it is taken to the outskirts at a walk, so as not to alarm the others. Once at the outside, however, the cowboy has to ride like lightning; for as soon as the beast he is after finds itself separated from its companions it endeavors to break back among them, and a young, range-raised steer or heifer runs like a deer. In cutting out a cow and a calf two men have to work together. As the animals of a brand are cut out they are received and held apart by some rider detailed for the purpose, who is said to be "holding the cut."

All this time the men holding the herd have their hands full, for some animal is continually trying to break out, when the nearest man flies at it at once and after a smart chase brings it back to its fellows. As soon as all the cows, calves, and whatever else is being gathered have been cut out, the rest are driven clear off the ground and turned loose, being headed in the direction contrary to that in which we travel the following day. Then the riders surround the next herd, the men holding cuts move them up near it, and the work is begun anew.

If it is necessary to throw an animal, either to examine a brand or for any other reason, half a dozen men will have their ropes down at once; and then it is spur and quirt in the rivalry to see which can outdo the other until the beast is roped and thrown. A first-class hand will, unaided, rope, throw, and tie down a cow or steer in wonderfully short time: one of the favorite tests of competitive skill among the cowboys is the speed with which this feat can be accomplished. Usually, however, one man ropes the animal by the head and another at the same time gets the loop of his lariat over one or both its hind legs, when it is twisted over and stretched out in a second. In following an animal on horseback the man keeps steadily swinging the rope round his head, by a dexterous motion of the wrist only, until he gets a chance to throw it; when on foot, especially if catching horses in a corral, the loop is allowed to drag loosely on the ground. A good roper will hurl out the coil with marvelous accuracy and force; it fairly whistles through the air, and settles round the object with almost infallible certainty. Mexicans make the best ropers; but some Texans are very little behind them. A good horse takes as much interest in the work as does his rider, and the instant the noose settles over the victim wheels and braces himself to meet the shock, standing with his legs firmly planted, the steer or cow being thrown with a jerk. An unskillful rider and an untrained horse will often themselves be thrown when the strain comes.

Sometimes an animal — usually a cow or steer, but, strangely enough, very rarely a bull — will get fighting mad, and turn on the men. If on the drive, such a beast usually is simply dropped out; but if they have time, nothing delights the cowboys more than an encounter of this sort, and the charging brute is roped and tied down in short order. Often such a one will make a very vicious fight, and is most dangerous. Once a fighting cow kept several of us busy for nearly an hour; she gored two ponies, one of them, which was, luckily, hurt but slightly, being my own pet cutting horse. If a steer is hauled out of a mud-hole, its first act is usually to charge the rescuer.

As soon as all the brands of cattle are worked, and

the animals that are to be driven along have been put in the day herd, attention is turned to the cows and calves, which are already gathered in different bands, consisting each of all the cows of a certain brand and all the calves that are following them. If there is a corral, each band is in turn driven into it; if there is none, a ring of riders does duty in its place. A fire is built, the irons heated, and a dozen men dismount to, as it is called, "wrestle" the calves. The best two ropers go in on their horses to catch the latter; one man keeps tally, a couple put on the brands, and the others seize, throw, and hold the little unfortunates. A first-class roper invariably catches the calf by both hind feet, and then, having taken a twist with his lariat round the horn of the saddle, drags the bawling little creature, extended at full length, up to the fire, where it is held before it can make a struggle. A less skillful roper catches round the neck, and then, if the calf is a large one, the man who seizes it has his hands full, as the bleating, bucking animal develops astonishing strength, cuts the wildest capers, and resists frantically and with all its power. If there are seventy or eighty calves in a corral, the scene is one of the greatest confusion. The ropers, spurring and checking the fierce little horses, drag the calves up so quickly that a dozen men can hardly hold them; the men with the irons, blackened with soot, run to and fro; the calf-wrestlers, grimy with blood, dust, and sweat, work like beavers; while with

BRANDING A CALF.

the voice of a stentor the tally-man shouts out the number and sex of each calf. The dust rises in clouds, and the shouts, cheers, curses, and laughter of the men unite with the lowing of the cows and the frantic bleating of the roped calves to make a perfect babel. Now and then an old cow turns vicious and puts every one out of the corral. Or a *maverick* bull,— that is, an unbranded bull,— a yearling or a two-years-old, is caught, thrown, and branded; when he is let up, there is sure to be a fine scatter. Down goes his head, and he bolts at the nearest man, who makes out of the way at top speed, amidst roars of laughter from all of his companions; while the men holding down calves swear savagely as they dodge charging mavericks, trampling horses, and taut lariats with frantic, plunging little beasts at the farther ends.

Every morning certain riders are detached to drive and to guard the day herd, which is most monotonous work, the men being on from 4 in the morning till 8 in the evening, the only rest coming at dinner-time, when they change horses. When the herd has reached the camping-ground there is nothing to do but to loll listlessly over the saddle-bow in the blazing sun, watching the cattle feed and sleep, and seeing that they do not spread out too much. Plodding slowly along on the trail through the columns of dust stirred up by the hoofs is not much better. Cattle travel best and fastest strung out in long lines; the swiftest taking the lead in single file, while the weak and the lazy, the young calves and the poor cows, crowd together in the rear. Two men travel along with the leaders, one on each side, to point them in the right direction; one or two others keep by the flanks, and the rest are in the rear to act as "drag-drivers" and hurry up the phalanx of reluctant weaklings. If the foremost of the string travels too fast, one rider will go along on the trail a few rods ahead, and thus keep them back so that those in the rear will not be left behind.

Generally all this is very tame and irksome; but by fits and starts there will be little flurries of excitement. Two or three of the circle riders may unexpectedly come over a butte near by with a bunch of cattle, which at once start for the day herd, and then there will be a few minutes' furious riding hither and thither to keep them out. Or the cattle may begin to run, and then get "milling"—that is, all crowd together into a mass like a ball, wherein they move round and round, trying to keep their heads towards the center, and refusing to leave it. The only way to start them is to force one's horse in among them and cut out some of their number, which then begin to travel off by themselves, when the

others will probably follow. But in spite of occasional incidents of this kind, day-herding has a dreary sameness about it that makes the men dislike and seek to avoid it.

. From 8 in the evening till 4 in the morning the day herd becomes a night herd. Each wagon in succession undertakes to guard it for a night, dividing the time into watches of two hours apiece, a couple of riders taking each watch. This is generally chilly and tedious; but at times it is accompanied by intense excitement and danger, when the cattle become stampeded, whether by storm or otherwise. The first and the last watches are those chosen by preference; the others are disagreeable, the men having to turn out cold and sleepy, in the pitchy darkness, the two hours of chilly wakefulness completely breaking the night's rest. The first guards have to bed the cattle down, though the day-herders often do this themselves: it simply consists in hemming them into as small a space as possible, and then riding round them until they lie down and fall asleep. Often, especially at first, this takes some time—the beasts will keep rising and lying down again. When at last most become quiet, some perverse brute of a steer will deliberately hook them all up; they keep moving in and out among one another, and long strings of animals suddenly start out from the herd at a stretching walk, and are turned back by the nearest cowboy only to break forth at a new spot. When finally they have lain down and are chewing their cud or slumbering, the two night guards begin riding round them in opposite ways, often, on very dark nights, calling or singing to them, as the sound of the human voice on such occasions seems to have a tendency to quiet them. In inky black weather, especially when rainy, it is both difficult and unpleasant work; the main trust must be placed in the horse, which, if old at the business, will of its own accord keep pacing steadily round the herd, and head off any animals that, unseen by the rider's eyes in the darkness, are trying to break out. Usually the watch passes off without incident, but on rare occasions the cattle become restless and prone to stampede. Anything may then start them — the plunge of a horse, the sudden approach of a coyote, or the arrival of some outside steers or cows that have smelt them and come up. Every animal in the herd will be on its feet in an instant, as if by an electric shock, and off with a rush, horns and tail up. Then, no matter how rough the ground nor how pitchy black the night, the cowboys must ride for all there is in them and spare neither their own nor their horses' necks. Perhaps their charges break away and are lost altogether; perhaps, by

THE HERD AT NIGHT.

desperate galloping, they may head them off, get them running in a circle, and finally stop them. Once stopped, they may break again, and possibly divide up, one cowboy, perhaps, following each band. I have known six such stops and renewed stampedes to take place in one night, the cowboy staying with his ever-diminishing herd of steers until daybreak, when he managed to get them under control again, and, by careful humoring of his jaded, staggering horse, finally brought those that were left back to the camp several miles distant. The riding in these night stampedes is wild and dangerous to a degree, especially if the man gets caught in the rush of the beasts. It also frequently necessitates an immense amount of work in collecting the scattered animals. On one such occasion a small party of us were thirty-six hours in the saddle, dismounting only to change horses or to eat. We were almost worn out at the end of the time; but it must be kept in mind that for a long spell of such work a stock-saddle is far less tiring than the ordinary Eastern or English one, and in every way superior to it.

By very hard riding, such a stampede may

sometimes be prevented. Once we were bringing a thousand head of young cattle down to my lower ranch, and as the river was high were obliged to take the inland trail. The third night we were forced to make a dry camp, the cattle having had no water since the morning. Nevertheless, we got them bedded down without difficulty, and one of the cowboys and myself stood first guard. But very soon after nightfall, when the darkness had become complete, the thirsty brutes of one accord got on their feet and tried to break out. The only salvation was to keep them close together, as, if they once got scattered, we knew they could never be gathered; so I kept on one side, and the cowboy on the other, and never in my life did I ride so hard. In the darkness I could but dimly see the shadowy outlines of the herd, as with whip and spurs I ran the pony along its edge, turning back the beasts at one point barely in time to wheel and keep them in at another. The ground was cut up by numerous little gullies, and each of us got several falls, horses and riders turning complete somersaults. We were dripping with sweat, and our ponies quivering and trembling like quaking aspens, when, after more than an hour of the most violent exertion, we finally got the herd quieted again.

On another occasion while with the round-up we were spared an excessively unpleasant night only because there happened to be two or three great corrals not more than a mile or so away. All day long it had been raining heavily, and we were well drenched; but towards evening it lulled a little, and the day herd, a very large one, of some two thousand head, was gathered on an open bottom. We had turned the horses loose, and in our oil-skin slickers cowered, soaked and comfortless, under the lee of the wagon, to take a meal of damp bread and lukewarm tea, the sizzling embers of the fire having about given up the ghost after a fruitless struggle with the steady downpour. Suddenly the wind began to come in quick, sharp gusts, and soon a regular blizzard was blowing, driving the rain in stinging level sheets before it. Just as we were preparing to turn into bed, with the certainty of a night of more or less chilly misery ahead of us, one of my men, an iron-faced personage, whom no one would ever have dreamed had a weakness for poetry, looked towards the plain where the cattle were, and remarked, "I guess there's 'racing and chasing on Cannobie Lea' now, sure." Following his gaze, I saw that the cattle had begun to drift before the storm, the night guards being evidently unable to cope with them, while at the other wagons riders were saddling in hot haste and spurring off to their help through the blinding rain. Some of us at once ran out to our own saddle-band. All of the ponies were standing huddled together, with their heads down and their tails to the wind. They were wild and restive enough usually; but the storm had cowed them, and we were able to catch them without either rope or halter. We made quick work of saddling; and the second each man was ready, away he loped through the dusk, splashing and slipping in the pools of water that studded the muddy plain. Most of the riders were already out when we arrived. The cattle were gathered in a compact, wedge-shaped, or rather fan-shaped mass, with their tails to the wind—that is, towards the thin end of the wedge or fan. In front of this fan-shaped mass of frightened, maddened beasts was a long line of cowboys, each muffled in his slicker and with his broad hat pulled down over his eyes, to shield him from the pelting rain. When the cattle were quiet for a moment every horseman at once turned round with his back to the wind, and the whole line stood as motionless as so many sentries. Then, if the cattle began to spread out and overlap at the ends, or made a rush and broke through at one part of the lines, there would be a change into wild activity. The men, shouting and swaying in their saddles, darted to and fro with reckless speed, utterly heedless of danger—now racing to the threatened point, now checking and wheeling their horses so sharply as to bring them square on their haunches, or even throw them flat down, while the hoofs plowed long furrows in the slippery soil, until, after some minutes of this mad galloping hither and thither, the herd, having drifted a hundred yards or so, would be once more brought up standing. We always had to let them drift a little to prevent their spreading out too much. The din of the thunder was terrific, peal following peal until they mingled in one continuous, rumbling roar; and at every thunder-clap louder than its fellows the cattle would try to break away. Darkness had set in, but each flash of lightning showed us a dense array of tossing horns and staring eyes. It grew always harder to hold in the herd; but the drift took us along to the corrals already spoken of, whose entrances were luckily to windward. As soon as we reached the first we cut off part of the herd, and turned it within; and after again doing this with the second, we were able to put all the remaining animals into the third. The instant the cattle were housed five-sixths of the horsemen started back at full speed for the wagons; the rest of us barely waited to put up the bars and make the corrals secure before galloping after them. We had to ride right in the teeth of the driv-

IN A STAMPEDE.

ing storm; and once at the wagons we made small delay in crawling in under our blankets, damp though the latter were, for we were ourselves far too wet, stiff, and cold not to hail with grateful welcome any kind of shelter from the wind and the rain.

All animals were benumbed by the violence of this gale of cold rain: a prairie-chicken rose from under my horse's feet so heavily that, thoughtlessly striking at it, I cut it down with my whip; while when a jack rabbit got up ahead of us, it was barely able to limp clumsily out of our way.

But though there is much work and hardship, rough fare, monotony, and exposure connected with the round-up, yet there are few

TRAILING CATTLE.

men who do not look forward to it and back to it with pleasure. The only fault to be found is that the hours of work are so long that one does not usually have enough time to sleep. The food, if rough, is good. The men are good-humored, bold, and thoroughly interested in their business, continually vying with one another in the effort to see which can do the work best. It is superbly health-giving, and is full of excitement and adventure, calling for the exhibition of pluck, self-reliance, hardihood, and dashing horsemanship; and of all forms of physical labor the easiest and pleasantest is to sit in the saddle.

The scenery is often exceedingly striking in character, especially in the Bad Lands, with their queer fantastic formations. Among the most interesting features are the burning mines. These are formed by the coal seams that get on fire. They vary greatly in size. Some send up smoke-columns that are visible miles away, while others are not noticeable a few rods off. The old ones gradually burn away, while new ones unexpectedly break out. Thus, last fall, one suddenly appeared but half a mile from the ranch house. We never knew it was there until one cold moonlight night, when we were riding home, we rounded the corner of a ravine and saw in our path a tall white column of smoke rising from a rift in the snowy crags ahead of us. As the trail was over perfectly familiar ground, we were for a moment almost as startled as if we had seen a ghost.

The burning mines are uncanny places, anyhow. A strong smell of sulphur hangs round them, the heated earth crumbles and cracks, and through the long clefts that form in it we can see the lurid glow of the subterranean fires, with here and there tongues of blue or cherry colored flame dancing up to the surface.

The winters vary greatly in severity with us. During some seasons men can go lightly clad even in January and February, and the cattle hardly suffer at all; during others there will be spells of bitter weather, accompanied by furious blizzards, which render it impossible for days and weeks at a time for men to stir out-of-doors at all, save at the risk of their lives. Then line rider, ranchman, hunter, and teamster alike all have to keep within doors. I have known of several cases of men freezing to death when caught in shelterless places by such a blizzard, a strange fact being that in about half of them the doomed man had evidently gone mad before dying, and had stripped himself of most of his clothes, the body when found being nearly naked. On our ranch we have never had any bad accidents, although every winter some of us get more or less frost-bitten. My last experience in this line was while returning by moonlight from a successful hunt after mountain sheep. The thermometer was 26° below zero, and we had had no food for twelve hours. I got numbed, and before I was aware of it had frozen my face, one foot, both knees, and one hand. Luckily, I reached the ranch before serious damage was done. About once every six or seven years we have a season when these storms follow one another almost without interval throughout the winter months, and then the loss among the stock is frightful. One such winter occurred in 1880-81. The grass was then so good that the few cattle raised on the range escaped fairly well, but even then the trail herds were almost destroyed. This was when there were very few ranchmen in the country. The next severe winter was that of 1886-87, when the rush of incoming herds had overstocked the ranges, and the loss was in consequence fairly appalling, especially to the outfits who had just put on cattle.

The snow-fall was unprecedented, both for its depth and for the way it lasted; and it was this, and not the cold, that caused the loss. About the middle of November the storms began. Day after day the snow came down, thawing and then freezing and piling itself higher and higher. By January the drifts had filled the ravines and coulées almost level. The snow lay in great masses on the plateaus and river bottoms; and this lasted until the end of February. The preceding summer we had been visited by a prolonged drought, so that the short, scanty grass was already well cropped down; the snow covered what pasturage there was to the depth of several feet, and the cattle could not get at it at all, and could hardly move round. It was all but impossible to travel on horseback, except on a few well-beaten trails. Even on the level it was very tiresome to try to break through the snow, and it was dangerous to attempt to penetrate the Bad Lands, whose shape had been completely altered by the great white mounds and drifts. The starving cattle died by scores of thousands before their helpless owners' eyes. The bulls, the cows who were suckling calves, or who were heavy with calf, the weak cattle that had just been driven upon the trail, and the late calves suffered most; the old range animals did better, and the steers best of all; but the best was bad enough. Even many of the horses died. An outfit near me lost half its saddle-band, the animals having been worked so hard that they were very thin when fall came.

In the thick brush the stock got some shelter and sustenance. They gnawed every twig and bough they could get at. They browsed the bitter sage brush down to where the branches were the thickness of a man's finger. When near a ranch they crowded into the out-houses and sheds to die, and fences had to be built around the windows to keep the wild-eyed, desperate beasts from thrusting their heads through the glass panes. In most cases it was impossible either to drive them to the haystacks or to haul the hay out to them. The deer even were so weak as to be easily run down; and on one or two of the plateaus where there were bands of antelope, these wary creatures grew so numbed and feeble that they could have been slaughtered like rabbits. But the hunters could hardly get out, and could bring home neither hide nor meat, so the game went unharmed.

It would be impossible to imagine any sight more dreary and melancholy than that offered by the ranges when the snow went off in March. The land was a mere barren waste; not a green thing to be seen; the dead grass eaten off till the country looked as if it had been shaved with a razor. Occasionally among the desolate hills a rider would come across a band of gaunt, hollow-flanked cattle feebly cropping the sparse, dry pasturage, too listless to move out of the way; and the blackened carcasses lay in the sheltered spots, some stretched out, others in as natural a position as if the animals had merely lain down to rest. It was small wonder that cheerful stockmen were rare objects that spring. Our only comfort was that we did not, as usual, suffer a heavy loss from weak cattle getting mired down in the springs and mud-holes when the ice broke up — for all the weak animals were dead already. The truth is, ours is a primitive industry, and we suffer the reverses as well as enjoy the successes only known to primitive peoples. A hard winter is to us in the north what a dry summer is to Texas or Australia — what seasons of famine once were to all peoples. We still live in an iron age that the old civilized world has long passed by. The men of the border reckon upon stern and unending struggles with their iron-bound surroundings; against the grim harshness of their existence they set the strength and the abounding vitality that come with it. They run risks to life and limb that are unknown to the dwellers in cities; and what the men freely brave, the beasts that they own must also sometimes suffer.

Theodore Roosevelt.

20

Artist Wanderings Among the Cheyennes

Frederick Remington

ARTIST WANDERINGS AMONG THE CHEYENNES.

WRITTEN AND ILLUSTRATED BY FREDERIC REMINGTON.

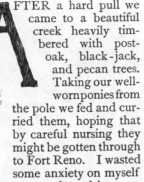

A CHEYENNE.

AFTER a hard pull we came to a beautiful creek heavily timbered with post-oak, black-jack, and pecan trees. Taking our well-worn ponies from the pole we fed and curried them, hoping that by careful nursing they might be gotten through to Fort Reno. I wasted some anxiety on myself as I discovered that my cowboy driver unrolled from a greasy newspaper the provisions which he had assured me before starting was a matter which had been attended to. It was "poor picking" enough, and I did not enjoy and coax him along. The road was heavy with sand and we lost a parallel trail made by the passage of the Eighth Cavalry some weeks before. We hoped to discover the "breaks"[1] of the South Canadian River before darkness set in; but the land rose steadily away in front, and we realized that something must be done. At last coming suddenly upon a group of miserable pole cabins, we saw two Caddoes reclining on a framework of poles. I conceived the idea of hiring one of these to guide us through in the darkness. The wretches refused to understand us, talk English, sign language, or what we would. But after a hard bargain one saddled his pony and consented to lead the way through the darkness. On we traveled, our valuable guide riding so far ahead that we could not see him, and at last we came suddenly in sight of the bright surface of the

THE SIGN LANGUAGE.

my after-dinner smoke when I realized that the situation was complicated by the fact that we had eaten everything for dinner and were then miles from Reno, with a pair of played-out ponies.

Hooking up again, we started on. On a little hill one jaded beast "set back in the breeching" and we dismounted to push the wagon

South Canadian. The sun was fast sinking, and by the time we had crossed the wide sand-bars and the shallow water of the river bottom a great red gleam was all that remained on the western horizon. About a mile to the left flickered the camp-fires about a group of lodges

[1] The lowering of the land, cut by streams tending towards the basin of a large river.

315

AN ARAPAHO SCOUT.

of Arapahoes. We fed our team and then ourselves crunched kernels of "horse-trough corn" which were extracted from the feed box. Our Caddo sat on his horse while we lay stretched on the grassy bank above the sand flats. A dark-skinned old Arapaho rode up, and our Caddo saluted him. They began to converse in the sign language as they sat on their ponies, and we watched them with great interest. With graceful gestures they made the signs and seemed immediately and fully to comprehend each other. As the old Arapaho's face cut dark against the sunset I thought it the finest Indian profile I had ever seen. He was arrayed in the full wild Indian costume of these latter days, with leggings, beaded moccasins, and a sheet wrapped about his waist and thighs. The Caddo, on the contrary, was a progressive man. His hair was cropped in Cossack style; he wore a hat, boots, and a great "slicker," or cowboy's oil-skin coat. For the space of half an hour they thus interested each other. We speculated on the meaning of the signs, and could often follow them; but they abbreviated so much and did it all so fast that we missed the full meaning of their conversation. Among other things the Caddo told the Arapaho who we were, and also made arrangements to meet him at the same place at about 10 o'clock on the following day.

Darkness now set in, and as we plunged into the timber after the disappearing form of our guide I could not see my companions on the seat beside me. I think horses can make out things better than men can under circumstances like these; and as the land lay flat before us, I had none of the fears which one who journeys in the mountains often feels.

The patter of horses' hoofs in the darkness behind us was followed by a hailing cry in the guttural tone of an Indian. I could just make out a mounted man with a led horse beside the wagon, and we exchanged inquiries in English and found him to be an acquaintance of the morning, in the person of a young Cheyenne scout from Fort Reno who had been down to buy a horse of a Caddo. He had lived at the Carlisle school, and although he had been back in the tribe long enough to let his hair grow, he had not yet forgotten all his English. As he was going through to the post, we dismissed our Caddo and followed him.

Far ahead in the gloom could be seen two of the post lights, and we were encouraged. The little ponies traveled faster and with more spirit in the night, as indeed do all horses. The lights did not come nearer, but kept at the indefinite distance peculiar to lights on a dark night. We plunged into holes, and the old wagon pitched and tipped in a style which insured keeping its sleepy occupants awake. But there is an end to all things, and our tedious trail brought us into Fort Reno at last. A sleepy boy with a lamp came to the door of the post-trader's and wanted to know if I was trying to break the house down, which was a natural conclusion on his part, as sundry dents in a certain door of the place will bear witness to this day.

On the following morning I appeared at the headquarters office, credentials in hand. A smart, well-gotten up "non-com." gave me a chair and discreetly kept an eye on the articles of value in the room, for the hard usage of my recent travels had so worn and soiled my clothing that I was more picturesque than assuring in appearance. The colonel came soon, and he too eyed me with suspicious glances until he made out that I was not a Texas horse thief nor an Oklahoma boomer. After finding that I desired to see his protégés of the prairie, he sent for the interpreter, Mr. Ben. Clark, and said, "Seek no farther; here is the best Cheyenne in the country."

Mr. Clark I found to be all that the colonel had recommended, except that he did not look like a Cheyenne, being a perfect type of the frontier scout, only lacking the long hair, which to his

BEN. CLARK, INTERPRETER.

practical mind a white man did not seem to require. A pair of mules and a buckboard were provided at the quartermaster's corral, and Mr. Clark and I started on a tour of observation.

We met many Cheyennes riding to some place or another. They were almost invariably tall men with fine Indian features. They wore the hair caught by braids very low on the shoulders, making a black mass about the ears, which at a distance is not unlike the aspect of an Apache. All the Indians now use light "cow-saddles," and ride with the long stirrups peculiar to Western Americans, instead

back, although I have never heard any one with enough temerity to question his ability. I always like to dwell on this subject of riding, and I have an admiration for a really good rider which is altogether beyond his deserts in the light of philosophy. In the Eastern States the European riding-master has proselyted to such an extent that it is rather a fashionable fad to question the utility of the Western method. When we consider that for generations these races of men who ride on the plains and in the Rocky Mountains have been literally bred on a horse's back, it seems reasonable to suppose they ought to be riders; and when

A CHEYENNE CAMP.

of "trees" of their own construction with the short stirrup of the old days. In summer, instead of a blanket, a white sheet is generally worn, which becomes dirty and assumes a very mellow tone of color. Under the saddle the bright blue or red Government cloth blanket is worn, and the sheet is caught around the waist, giving the appearance of Zouave trousers. The variety of shapes which an Indian can produce with a blanket, the great difference in wearing it, and the grace and naturalism of its adjustment, are subjects one never tires of watching. The only criticism of the riding of modern Indians one can make is the incessant thumping of the horse's ribs, as though using a spur. Outside of the far South-west, I have never seen Indians use spurs. With the awkward old "trees" formerly made by the Indians, and with the abnormally short stirrup, an Indian was anything but graceful on horse-

one sees an Indian or a cowboy riding up precipices where no horses ought to be made to go, or assuming on horseback some of the grotesque positions they at times affect, one needs no assurance that they do ride splendidly.

As we rattled along in the buckboard, Mr. Clark proved very interesting. For thirty odd years he has been in contact with the Cheyennes. He speaks the language fluently, and has discovered in a trip to the far North that the Crees use almost identically the same tongue. Originally the Cheyennes came from the far North, and they are Algonquin in origin. Though their legend of the famous "medicine arrow" is not a recent discovery, I cannot forbear to give it here.

A long time ago, perhaps about the year 1640, the Cheyennes were fighting a race of men who had guns. The fighting was in the vicinity of the Devil's Lake country, and the Cheyennes had been repeatedly worsted in combat and were in dire distress. A young Horatius of the tribe determined to sacrifice himself for the common weal, and so wandered away. After a time he met an old man, a mythical personage, who took pity on him. Together they entered a great cave, and the old man gave him various articles of "medicine" to choose from, and the young man selected the "medicine arrows." After the old man had performed the proper incantations, the hero went forth with his potent fetish and rejoined the tribe. The people regained courage, and in the fight which soon followed they conquered and obtained guns for the first time. Ever since the tribe has kept the medicine arrows, and they are now in the Indian Territory in the possession of the southern Cheyennes. Years ago the Pawnees captured the arrows and in ransom got vast numbers of ponies, although they never gave back all of the arrows, and the Cheyennes attribute all their hard experiences of later days to this loss. Once a year, and oftener should a situation demand it, the ceremony of the arrows takes place. No one has ever witnessed it except the initiated priests.

The tribal traditions are not known thoroughly by all, and of late years only a very few old men can tell perfectly the tribal stories. Why this is so no one seems to know, unless the Indians have seen and heard so much through the white men that their faith is shaken.

Our buckboard drew gradually nearer the camp of the Cheyennes. A great level prairie of waving green was dotted with the brown toned white canvas lodges, and standing near them were brush "ramadas," or sheds, and also wagons. For about ten years they have owned wagons, and now seldom use the *travaux*. In little groups all over the plain were scattered pony herds, and about the camp could be seen forms wearing bright blankets or wrapped in ghostlike cotton sheets. Little columns of blue smoke rose here and there, and gathered in front of one lodge was squatted a group of men. A young squaw dressed in a bright calico gown stood near a ramada and bandied words with the interpreter while I sketched. Presently she was informed that I had made her picture, when she ran off, laughing at what she considered an unbecoming trick on the part of her entertainer. The women of this tribe are the only squaws I have ever met, except in some of the tribes of the northern plains, who have any claim to be considered good looking. Indeed, some of them are quite as I imagine Pocahontas, Minnehaha, and the rest of the heroines of the race appeared. The female names are conventional, and have been borne by the women ever since the oldest man can remember. Some of them have the pleasant sound which we occasionally find in the Indian tongues: "Mut-say-yo," "Wau-hi-yo," "Mo-ka-is," "Jok-ko-ko-me-yo," for instance, are examples; and with the soft guttural of their Indian pronunciation I found them charming. As we entered the camp all the elements which make that sort of scene interesting were about. A medicine-man was at work over a sick fellow. We watched him through the opening of a lodge and our sympathies were not aroused, as the patient was a young buck who seemed in no need of them. A group of young men were preparing for a clan dance. Two young fellows lay stretched on the grass in graceful attitudes. They were what we call "chums." Children were playing with dogs; women were beading moccasins; a group of men lay under a wagon playing monte; a very old man, who was quite naked, tottered up to our vehicle and talked with Mr. Clark. His name was Bull Bear, and he was a strange object with his many wrinkles, gray hair, and toothless jaws.

From a passing horseman I procured an old "buck saddle" made of elk horn. They are now very rare. Indian saddlery is interesting, as all the tribes had a different model, and the women used one differing from that of the men.

We dismounted at the lodge of Whirlwind, a fine old type who now enjoys the prestige of head chief. He was dignified and reserved, and greeted us cordially as he invited us to a seat under the ramada. He refused a cigar, as will nearly all Indians, and produced his own cigarettes.

Through the interpreter we were enabled to converse freely. I have a suspicion that the old man had an impression that I was in some way connected with the Government. All Indians somehow divide the white race into three parts. One is either a soldier, a Texas cowboy, or a "big chief from Washington," which latter distinction I enjoyed. I explained that I was not a "big chief," but an artist, the significance of which he did not grasp. He was requested to put on his plumage, and I then proceeded to make a drawing of him. He looked it over in a coldly critical way, grunted several times, and seemed more mystified than ever; but I do not think I diminished in his estimation. In his younger days Whirlwind had been a war chief; but he traveled to Washington and there saw the power and numbers of the white man. He advised for peace after that, and did not take the warpath in the last great outbreak. His people were defeated, as he said they would be, and confidence in his judgment was restored. I asked him all sorts of questions to draw on his reminiscences of the old Indian life before the conquest, all of which were answered gravely and without boasting. It was on his statesmanlike mind, however, to make clear to me the condition of his people, and I heard him through. Though not versed in the science of government, I was interested in the old man's talk. He had just returned from a conference of the tribes which had been held in the Cherokee country, and was full of the importance of the conclusions there evolved. The Indians all fear that they will lose their land, and the council advised all Indians to do nothing which would interfere with their tenure of the land now held by them. He told with pride of the speech he made while there and of the admiration with which he was regarded as he stood, dressed in the garb of the wild Indian, with his tomahawk in hand. However, he is a very progressive man, and explained that while he was too old to give up the methods of life which he had always observed, yet his son would be as the civilized Cherokees are. The son was squatted near,

FREDERIC REMINGTON-
AFTER PHOTOGRAPH.

CHEYENNE AGENCY.

and I believed his statement, as the boy was large of stature and bright of mind, having enjoyed some three years' schooling at a place which I have now forgotten. He wore white men's clothes and had just been discharged from the corps of scouts at Reno. When I asked the boy why he did not plow and sow and reap, he simply shrugged his shoulders at my ignorance, which, in justice to myself, I must explain was only a leading question, for I know that corn cannot be raised on this reservation with sufficient regularity to warrant the attempt. The rainfall is not enough; and where white men despair, I, for one, do not expect wild Indians to continue. They have tried it

and have failed, and are now very properly discouraged. Stock-raising is the natural industry of the country, and that is the proper pursuit of these people. They are only now recovering by natural increase from the reverses which they suffered in their last outbreak. It is hard for them to start cattle herds, as their ration is insufficient, and one scarcely can expect a hungry man to herd cattle when he needs the beef to appease his hunger. Nevertheless, some men have respectable herds and can afford to kill an animal occasionally without taking the stock cattle. In this particular they display wonderful forbearance, and were they properly rationed for a time and given stock cattle, there is not a doubt but in time they would become self-supporting. The present scheme of taking a few boys and girls away from the camps to put them in school where they are taught English, morals, and trades has nothing reprehensible about it, except that it is absolutely of no consequence so far as solving the Indian problem is concerned. The few boys return to the camps with their English, their school clothes, and their short hair. They know a trade also, but have no opportunity to be employed in it. They loaf about the forts for a time with nothing to do, and the white men talk pigeon English to them and the wild Indians sneer at them. Their virtues are unappreciated, and, as a natural consequence, the thousands of years of barbarism which is bred in their nature overcome the three little seasons of school training. They go to the camps, go back to the blanket, let their hair grow, and forget their English. In a year one cannot tell a school-boy from any other little savage, and in the whole proceeding I see nothing at all strange.

The camp will not rise to the school-boy, and so Mahomet goes to the mountain. If it comes to pass that the white race desires to aid these Indians to become a part of our social system instead of slowly crushing them out of it, there is only one way to do it. The so-called Indian problem is no problem at all in reality, only that it has been made one by a long succession of acts which were masterly in their imbecility and were fostered by political avarice. The sentiment of this nation is in favor of no longer regarding the aborigines of this country as a conquered race; and except

AN AGENCY POLICEMAN.

that the great body of our citizens are apathetic of things so remote as these wards of the Government, the people who have the administration of their destinies would be called to account. No one not directly interested ever questioned that the Indian Department should have been attached to the War Department; but that is too patent a fact to discuss. Now the Indian affairs are in so hopeless a state of dry-rot that practical men, in political or in military circles, hesitate to attempt the rôle of reformers. The views which I have on the subject are not original, but are very old and very well understood by all men who live in the Indian countries. They are current among army officers who have spent their whole lives on the Indian frontier of the far West, but are not often spoken, because all men realize the impotency of any attempt to overcome the active work of certain political circles backed by public apathy and a lot of theoretical Indian regenerators. If anything is done to relieve the condition of the Indian tribes it must be a scheme which begins at the bottom and takes the "whole outfit," as a Western man would

say, in its scope. If these measures of relief are at all tardy, before we realize it the wild Indian tribes will be, as some writer has said, "loafers and outcasts, contending with the dogs for kitchen scraps in Western villages." They have all raised stock successfully when not interfered with or not forced by insufficient rations to eat up their stock cattle to appease their hunger, and I have never heard that Indians were not made of soldier stuff. A great many Western garrisons have their corps of Indian scouts. In every case they prove efficient. They are naturally the finest irregular cavalry on the face of this globe, and with an organization similar to the Russian Cossacks they would do the United States great good and become themselves gradually civilized. An irregular cavalry is every year a more and more important branch of the service. Any good cavalry officer, I believe, could take a command of Indians and ride around the world without having a piece of bacon, or a cartridge, or a horse issued by his Government. So far as effective police work in the West is concerned, the corps of Indian scouts do nearly all of that

THE BRANDING CHUTE AT THE BEEF ISSUE.

service now. They all like to be enlisted in the service, universally obey orders, and are never disloyal. But nothing will be done; so why continue this?

For hours we sat in the ramada of the old chief and conversed, and when we started to go I was much impressed by the discovery that the old Indian knew more about Indians, Indian policy, and the tendencies and impulses of the white men concerning his race than any other person I had ever met.

The glories of the reign of an Indian chieftain are past. As his people become more and more dependent on the Government his prestige wanes. For instance, at the time of our visit to this camp the people were at loggerheads regarding the locality where the great annual Sun Dance, or, more literally, "The Big Medicine," should be held. The men of the camp that I visited wanted it at one place, and those of the "upper camp" wanted it at another. The chief could not arrange the matter, and so the solution of the difficulty was placed in the hands of the agent.

The Cheyenne agency buildings are situated about a mile and a half from Fort Sill. The great brick building is imposing. A group of stores and little white dwelling-houses sur-

round it, giving much the effect of a New England village. Wagons, saddled ponies, and Indians are generally disposed about the vicinity and give life to the scene. Fifteen native policemen in the employ of the agency do the work and take care of the place. They are uniformed in cadet gray, and with their beaded white moccasins and their revolvers are neat and soldierly looking. A son of old Bent, the famous frontiersman, and an educated Indian do the clerical work, so that the agent is about the only white man in the place. The goods which are issued to the Indians have changed greatly in character as their needs have become more civilized. The hatchets and similar articles of the old traders are not given out, on the ground that they are barbarous. Gay colored clothes still seem to suit the esthetic sense of the people, and the general effect of a body of modern Indians is exceeding brilliant. Arabs could not surpass them in this respect.

They receive flour, sugar, and coffee at the great agency building, but the beef is issued from a corral situated out on the plain at some distance away. The distribution is a very thrilling sight, and I made arrangements to see it by procuring a cavalry horse from Colonel Wade at the fort and by following the ambulance containing an army officer who was detailed as inspector. We left the post in the early morning, and the driver "poured his lash into the mules" until they scurried along at a speed which kept the old troop-horse at a neat pace.

The heavy dew was on the grass, and clouds lay in great rolls across the sky, obscuring the sun. From the direction of the target range the "stump" of the Springfields came to our ears, showing that the soldiers were hard at their devotions. In twos, and threes, and groups, and crowds, came Indians, converg-

be given out. With loud cries the cowboys in the corral forced the steers into the chute, and crowding and clashing they came through into the scales. The gate of the scales was opened and a half-dozen frightened steers crowded down the chute and packed themselves in an unyielding mass at the other end. A tall Arapaho policeman seized a branding-iron, and mounting the platform of the chute poised his iron and with a quick motion forced it on the back of the living beast. With a wild but useless plunge and a loud bellow of pain the steer shrunk from the hot contact; but

WAITING FOR THE BEEF ISSUE.

ing on the beef corral. The corral is a great ragged fence made of an assortment of boards, poles, scantling, planks, old wagons, and attached to this is a little house near which the weighing scales are placed. The crowd collected in a great mass near the gate and branding-chute. A fire was burning, and the cattle contractors (cowboys) were heating their branding-irons to mark the "I. D." on the cattle distributed, so that any Indian having subsequently a hide in his possession would be enabled to satisfy roving cattle inspectors that they were not to be suspected of killing stock.

The agent came to the corral and together with the army officer inspected the cattle to

it was all over, and a long black "I. D." disfigured the surface of the skin.

Opposite the branding-chute were drawn up thirty young bucks on their ponies, with their rifles and revolvers in hand. The agent shouted the Indian names from his book, and a very engaging lot of cognomens they were. A policeman on the platform designated a particular steer which was to be the property of each man as his name was called. The Indian came forward and marked his steer by reaching over the fence and cutting off an ear with a sharp knife, by severing the tail, or by tying some old rag to some part of the animal. The cold-blooded mutilation was perfectly shocking, and I turned away in sickened disgust. After all

STEER-HUNTING.

had been marked, the terrified brutes found the gate at the end of the chute suddenly opened by the police guard; but before this had been done a frantic steer had put his head half through the gate, and in order to force him back a red-hot branding-iron was pushed into his face, burning it horribly. The worst was over; the gates flew wide, and the maddened brutes poured forth, charging swiftly away in a wild impulse to escape the vicinity of the crowd of humanity. The young bucks in the group broke away, and each one, singling out his steer, followed at top speed, with rifle or six-shooter in hand. I desired to see the whole proceeding, and mounting my cavalry horse followed two young savages who seemed to have a steer possessed of unusual speed. The lieutenant had previously told me that the shooting at the steers was often wild and reckless, and advised me to look sharp or I might have to "pack a bullet." Puffs of smoke and the "pop! pop!" of the guns came from all over the plain. Now a steer would drop, stricken by some lucky shot. It was buffalo-hunting over again, and was evidently greatly enjoyed by the young men. My two fellows headed their steer up the hill on the right, and when they had gotten him far enough away they "turned loose," as we say. My old cavalry horse began to exhibit a lively interest in the smell of gunpowder, and plunged away until he had me up and in front of the steer and the Indians, who rode on each side. They blazed away at the steer's head, and I could hear a misdirected bullet "sing" by uncomfortably near. Seeing me in front, the steer

dodged off to one side, and the young fellow who was in his way, by a very clever piece of horsemanship, avoided being run over. The whole affair demonstrated to me that the Indian boys could not handle the revolver well, for they shot a dozen rounds before they killed the poor beast. Under their philosophic outward calm I thought I could see that they were not proud of the exhibition they had made. After the killing, the squaws followed the wagons and proceeded to cut up the meat. After it had been divided among themselves, by some arrangement which they seemed to understand, they cut it into very thin pieces and started back to their camps.

Peace and contentment reign while the beef holds out, which is not long, as the ration is insufficient. This is purposely so, as it is expected that the Indians will seek to increase a scant food supply by raising corn. It does not have that effect, however. By selling ponies, which they have in great numbers, they manage to get money; but the financial future of the Cheyennes is not flattering.

Enlistment in the scouting corps at Reno is a method of obtaining employment much sought after by the young men. The camp is on a hill opposite the post, where the white tepees are arranged in a long line. A wall tent at the end is occupied by two soldiers who do the clerical work. The scouts wear the uniform of the United States army, and some of them are strikingly handsome in the garb. They are lithe and naturally "well set up," as the soldiers phrase it. They perform all the duties of soldiers; but at some of the irksome tasks, like standing sentry, they do not come out strong. They are not often used for that purpose, however, it being found that Indians do not appreciate military forms and ceremonies.

Having seen all that I desired, I procured passage in the stage to a station on the Santa Fe Railroad. In the far distance the train came rushing up the track, and as it stopped I boarded it. As I settled back in the soft cushions of the sleeping-car I looked at my dirty clothes and did not blame the negro porter for regarding me with the haughty spirit of his class.

Frederic Remington.

21

The Treasures of the Yosemite

John Muir

THE CENTURY MAGAZINE.

AUGUST, 1890.

THE TREASURES OF THE YOSEMITE.

THE Yosemite Valley, in the heart of the Sierra Nevada, is a noble mark for the traveler, whether tourist, botanist, geologist, or lover of wilderness pure and simple. But those who are free may find the journey a long one; not because of the miles, for they are not so many,—only about two hundred and fifty from San Francisco, and passed over by rail and carriage roads in a day or two,—but the way is so beautiful that one is beguiled at every step, and the great golden days and weeks and months go by uncounted. How vividly my own first journey to Yosemite comes to mind, though made more than a score of years ago. I set out afoot from Oakland, on the bay of San Francisco, in April. It was the bloom-time of the year over all the lowlands and ranges of the coast; the landscape was fairly drenched with sunshine, the larks were singing, and the hills were so covered with flowers that they seemed to be painted. Slow indeed was my progress through these glorious gardens, the first of the California flora I had seen. Cattle and cultivation were making few scars as yet, and I wandered enchanted in long, wavering curves, aware now and then that Yosemite lay to the eastward, and that, some time, I should find it.

One shining morning, at the head of the Pacheco Pass, a landscape was displayed that after all my wanderings still appears as the most divinely beautiful and sublime I have ever beheld. There at my feet lay the great central plain of California, level as a lake, thirty or forty miles wide, four hundred long,

one rich furred bed of golden Compositæ. And along the eastern shore of this lake of gold rose the mighty Sierra, miles in height, in massive, tranquil grandeur, so gloriously colored and so radiant that it seemed not clothed with light, but wholly composed of it, like the wall of some celestial city. Along the top, and extending a good way down, was a rich pearl-gray belt of snow; then a belt of blue and dark purple, marking the extension of the forests; and stretching along the base of the range a broad belt of rose-purple, where lay the miners' gold and the open foothill gardens — all the colors smoothly blending, making a wall of light clear as crystal and ineffably fine, yet firm as adamant. Then it seemed to me the Sierra should be called, not the Nevada or Snowy Range, but the Range of Light. And after ten years in the midst of it, rejoicing and wondering, seeing the glorious floods of light that fill it,—the sunbursts of morning among the mountain-peaks, the broad noonday radiance on the crystal rocks, the flush of the alpenglow, and the thousand dashing waterfalls with their marvelous abundance of irised spray,—it still seems to me a range of light. But no terrestrial beauty may endure forever. The glory of wildness has already departed from the great central plain. Its bloom is shed, and so in part is the bloom of the mountains. In Yosemite, even under the protection of the Government, all that is perishable is vanishing apace.

The Sierra is about 500 miles long, 70 miles wide, and from 7000 to nearly 15,000 feet high. In general views no mark of man is visible upon it, nor anything to suggest the wonderful depth and grandeur of its sculpture. None of its magnificent forest-crowned ridges seems to rise much above the general level to publish

which find anchorage on a thousand narrow steps and benches, the whole enlivened and made glorious with rejoicing streams that come dancing and foaming over the sunny brows of

VIEW OF THE YOSEMITE VALLEY FROM POINT LOOKOUT—EL CAPITAN ON THE LEFT, THE BRIDAL VEIL FALL ON THE RIGHT, THE HALF DOME IN THE DISTANCE.

its wealth. No great valley or river is seen, or group of well-marked features of any kind standing out as distinct pictures. Even the summit peaks, marshaled in glorious array so high in the sky, seem comparatively smooth and featureless. Nevertheless the whole range is furrowed with cañons to a depth of from 2000 to 5000 feet, in which once flowed majestic glaciers, and in which now flow and sing the bright Sierra rivers.

Though of such stupendous depth, these cañons are not raw, gloomy, jagged-walled gorges, savage and inaccessible. With rough passages here and there, they are mostly smooth, open pathways conducting to the fountains of the summit; mountain streets full of life and light, graded and sculptured by the ancient glaciers, and presenting throughout all their courses a rich variety of novel and attractive scenery—the most attractive that has yet been discovered in the mountain ranges of the world. In many places, especially in the middle region of the western flank, the main cañons widen into spacious valleys or parks of charming beauty, level and flowery and diversified like landscape gardens with meadows and groves and thickets of blooming bushes, while the lofty walls, infinitely varied in form, are fringed with ferns, flowering plants, shrubs of many species, and tall evergreens and oaks

the cliffs, and through side cañons in falls of every conceivable form, to join the shining river that flows in tranquil beauty down the middle of each one of them.

The most famous and accessible of these cañon valleys, and also the one that presents their most striking and sublime features on the grandest scale, is the Yosemite, situated on the upper waters of the Merced at an elevation of 4000 feet above the level of the sea. It is about seven miles long, half a mile to a mile wide, and nearly a mile deep, and is carved in the solid granite flank of the range. The walls of the valley are made up of rocks, mountains in size, partly separated from each other by side cañons and gorges; and they are so sheer in front, and so compactly and harmoniously built together on a level floor, that the place, comprehensively seen, looks like some immense hall or temple lighted from above.

But no temple made with hands can compare with Yosemite. Every rock in its walls seems to glow with life. Some lean back in majestic repose; others, absolutely sheer or nearly so for thousands of feet, advance beyond their companions in thoughtful attitudes, giving welcome to storms and calms alike, seemingly conscious, yet heedless of everything going on about them. Awful in stern, immovable majesty, how softly these mountain rocks are adorned and how fine and reassuring the company they keep — their feet set in groves and gay emerald meadows, their brows in the thin blue sky, a thousand flowers leaning confidingly against their adamantine bosses, bathed in floods of booming water, floods of light, while snow, clouds, winds, avalanches, shine and sing and wreathe about them as the years go by! Birds, bees, butterflies, and myriads of nameless wings stir the air into music and give glad animation. Down through the midst flows the crystal Merced — river of mercy — peacefully gliding, reflecting lilies and trees and the onlooking rocks, things frail and fleeting and types of endurance meeting here and blending in countless forms, as if into this one mountain mansion Nature had gathered her choicest treasures, whether great or small, to draw her lovers into close and confiding communion with her.

Sauntering towards Yosemite up the foothills, richer and wilder become the forests and streams. At an elevation of 6000 feet above the level of the sea the silver firs are 200 feet high, with branches whorled around the colossal shafts in regular order, and every branch beautifully pinnate like a fern leaf. The Douglas spruce and the yellow and sugar pines here reach their highest developments of beauty and grandeur, and the rich, brown-barked libocedrus with warm, yellow-green plumes. The majestic sequoia, too, is here, the king of conifers, "the noblest of a noble race." All these colossal trees are as wonderful in the fineness of their beauty and proportions as in stature, growing together, an assemblage of conifers surpassing all that have yet been discovered in the forests of the world. Here, indeed, is the tree-lover's paradise, the woods, dry and wholesome, letting in the light in shimmering masses half sunshine, half shade, the air indescribably spicy and exhilarating, plushy fir boughs for beds, and cascades to sing us asleep as we gaze through the trees to the stars.

On the highest ridges passed over on our way to Yosemite the lovely silver fir (*Abies amabilis*) forms the bulk of the woods, pressing forward in glorious array to the very brink of the walls on both sides and far beyond to a

DOWN GRADE INTO THE VALLEY.

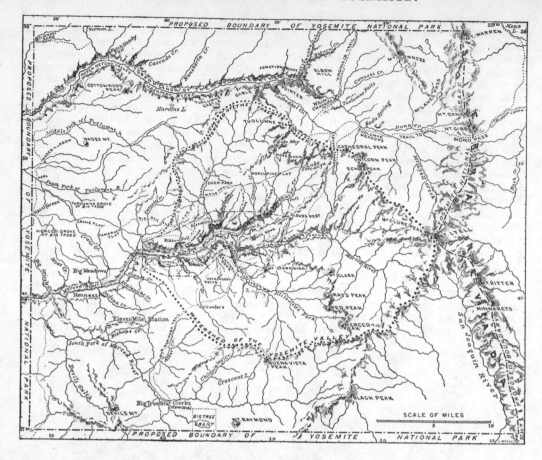

height of from 8000 to 9000 feet above the level of the sea. Thus it appears that Yosemite, presenting such stupendous faces of bare granite, is nevertheless embedded in magnificent forests. All the main species of pine, fir, spruce, and libocedrus are also found in the valley itself. But there are no "big trees" (*Sequoia gigantea*) in the valley or about the rim of it. The nearest are about ten miles beyond the boundary wall of the grant, on small tributaries of the Merced and Tuolumne. The sequoia belt extends along the western flank of the range, from the well-known Calaveras Grove on the north to the head of Deer Creek on the south, a distance of about two hundred miles, at an elevation of from about 5000 to 8000 feet above sea level. From the Calaveras to the south fork of King's River the species occurs only in small isolated groves or patches so sparsely distributed along the belt that two of the gaps that occur are nearly forty miles wide, one of them between the Stanislaus and Tuolumne groves, the other between those of the Fresno and King's River. Hence southward, instead of forming small sequestered groups among

the other conifers, the big trees sweep majestically across the broad, rugged basins of the Kaweah and Tule in noble forests a distance of nearly seventy miles, with a width of from three to ten miles, the continuity of this portion of the belt being interrupted only by deep cañons.

The Fresno, the largest of the northern groves, occupies an area of three or four square miles, and is situated a short distance to the southward of the famous Mariposa Grove. Along the beveled rim of the cañon of the south fork of King's River there is a stately forest of sequoia about six miles long and two miles wide. This is the northernmost assemblage of big trees that may fairly be called a forest. Descending the precipitous divide between King's River and the Kaweah one enters the grand forests that form the main continuous portion of the belt. Advancing southward the trees become more and more irrepressibly exuberant, heaving their massive crowns into the sky from every ridge, and waving onward in graceful compliance with the complicated topography. The finest of the Kaweah portion of the belt is on the broad ridge between Marble Creek and the middle fork, and extends from the granite headlands overlooking the hot plains back to within a few miles of the cool glacial fountains. The extreme upper limit of the belt is reached between the middle and south forks of the Kaweah, at an elevation of 8400 feet. But the finest block of sequoia in the entire belt is on the north fork of the Tule River. In the northern groups there are comparatively few young trees or saplings. But here for every old, storm-stricken giant there is one or more in all the glory of prime, and for each of these there are many young trees and crowds of eager, hopeful saplings growing heartily everywhere — on moraines, rocky ledges, along watercourses, and in the deep, moist alluvium of meadows, seemingly in hot pursuit of eternal life.

Though the area occupied by the species increases so much from north to south, there is no marked increase in the size of the trees. A height of two hundred and seventy-five feet and a diameter of twenty is perhaps about the average for full-grown trees: specimens twenty-five feet in diameter are not rare, and a good many are nearly three hundred feet high. The largest I have yet met in the course of my explorations is a majestic old monument in the new King's River forest. It is thirty-five feet and eight inches in diameter inside the bark four feet from the ground, and a plank of solid wood the whole width of the tree might be hewn from it without the slightest decay.

Under the most favorable conditions these giants live five or six thousand years, though few of even the larger specimens are more than half as old. The sequoia seems to be entirely exempt from the diseases that afflict and kill other conifers — mildew, dry rot, or any other kind of rot. I never saw a sick sequoia, or one that seemed to be dying of old age. Unless destroyed by man, they live on indefinitely until burned, smashed by lightning, or cast down by the giving way of the ground on which they stand.

These king trees, all that there are of their kind in the world, are surely worth saving, whether for beauty, science, or bald use. But as yet only the isolated Mariposa Grove has been reserved as a park for public use and pleasure. Were the importance of our forests at all understood by the people in general, even from an economic standpoint their preservation would call forth the most watchful attention of the Government. At present, however, every kind of destruction is moving on with accelerated speed. Fifteen years ago I found five mills located on or near the lower margin of the main sequoia belt, all of which were cutting big-tree lumber. How many more have been built since that time I am unable to say, but most of the Fresno group are doomed to feed the large mills established near them, and a company with ample means is about ready for work on the magnificent forests of King's River. In these mill operations waste far exceeds use. For after the young, manageable trees have been cut, blasted, and sawed, the woods are fired to clear the ground of limbs and refuse, and of course the seedlings and saplings, and many of the unmanageable giants, are destroyed, leaving but little more than black, charred monuments. These mill ravages, however, are small as yet compared with the comprehensive destruction caused by "sheepmen." Incredible numbers of sheep are driven to the mountain pastures every summer, and desolation follows them. Every garden within reach is trampled, the shrubs are stripped of leaves as if devoured by locusts, and the woods are burned to improve the pasturage. The entire belt of forests is thus swept by fire, from one end of the range to the

DESTRUCTIVE WORK IN YOSEMITE VALLEY: THE "LEIDIG MEADOWS" PLOWED UP IN OCTOBER, 1888, TO RAISE HAY. ("PROCESS" REPRODUCTION FROM A PHOTO-GRAPH.)

other; and, with the exception of the resinous *Pinus contorta*, the sequoia suffers most of all. Steps are now being taken towards the creation of a national park about the Yosemite, and great is the need, not only for the sake of the adjacent forests, but for the valley itself. For the branching cañons and valleys of the basins of the streams that pour into Yosemite are as closely related to it as are the fingers to the palm of the hand — as the branches, foliage, and flowers of a tree to the trunk. Therefore, very naturally, all the fountain region above Yosemite, with its peaks, cañons, snow fields, glaciers, forests, and streams, should be included in the park to make it an harmonious unit instead of a fragment, great though the fragment be; while to the westward, below the valley, the boundary might be extended with great advantage far enough to comprehend the Fresno, Mariposa, Merced, and Tuolumne groves of big trees, three of which are on roads leading to the valley, while all of them are in the midst of conifers scarcely less interesting than the colossal brown giants themselves.

From the heights on the margin of these glorious forests we at length gain our first general view of the valley — a view that breaks

MIRROR VIEW OF THE THREE BROTHERS.

suddenly upon us in all its glory far and wide and deep; a new revelation in landscape affairs that goes far to make the weakest and meanest spectator rich and significant evermore.

Along the curves and zigzags of the road, all the way down to the bottom, the valley is in sight with ever-changing views, and the eye ranges far up over the green grovy floor between the mighty walls, bits of the river gleaming here and there, while as we draw nearer we begin to hear the song of the waters. Gazing at random, perhaps the first object to gain concentrated attention will be the Bridal Veil, a beautiful waterfall on our right. Its brow, where it first leaps free from the rock, is about nine hundred feet above us; and as it sways and sings in the wind, with gauzy, sunsifted spray half falling, half floating, it seems infinitely gentle and fine; but the hymn it sings tells the solemn power that is hidden beneath the soft clothing it wears.

On the other side of the valley, opposite the Veil, there is another magnificent fall, called the Ribbon Fall, or Virgin's Tears. The "tears" fall from a height of about 3000 feet, and are most extravagantly copious when the snow is melting, coming hissing and roaring with force enough to drive a mile of mills, suggesting the "weeping skies" of cyclones and hurricanes.

Just beyond this glorious flood the El Capitan rock is seen through the pine groves pressing forward beyond the general line of the wall in most imposing grandeur. It is 3300 feet high, a plain, severely simple, glacier-sculptured face of granite, the end of one of the most compact and enduring of the mountain ridges, standing there in supreme height and breadth, a type of permanence.

Across the valley from here, above the Bridal Veil, are the picturesque Cathedral Rocks, nearly 2700 feet high, making a noble display of fine yet massive sculpture. They are closely related to El Capitan, having been hewn from the same mountain ridge by the Yosemite glacier when the valley was in process of formation.

Beyond El Capitan the next in succession of the most striking features of the north wall are the Three Brothers, an immense mountain mass with three gables fronting the valley one above the other, the topmost nearly 4000 feet high. They were named for three brothers captured here during the Indian war, sons of Tenaya, the old Yosemite chief.

On the south wall opposite the Brothers towers the Sentinel Rock to a height of more than 3000 feet, a telling monument of the icy past.

Sauntering up the valley through meadow and grove, in the company of these majestic rocks, which seem to follow as we advance gazing, admiring, looking for new wonders ahead where all about us is wonderful, the thunder of the Yosemite Fall is heard, and when we arrive in front of the Sentinel it is

EL CAPITAN.

revealed in all its glory from base to summit, half a mile in height, and seeming to gush direct from the sky. But even this fall, perhaps the most wonderful in the world, cannot at first control our attention, for now the wide upper portion of the valley is displayed to view, with the North Dome, Royal Arches, and Washington Column on our left; Glacier Point Rock, with its magnificent sculpture, on the right; and in the middle Tissiack or Half Dome, the most beautiful and most sublime of all the mountain rocks about the valley. It rises in serene majesty from the fertile level into the sky to a height of 4750 feet.

Here the valley divides into three branches, the Tenaya, Nevada, and Illilouette cañons and valleys, extending back into the fountains of the High Sierra, with scenery every way worthy the relation they bear to Yosemite.

In the south branch, a mile or two from the main valley, is the Illilouette Fall, 600 feet high, one of the most beautiful of all the Yosemite choir, but to most people inaccessible as yet on account of its rough, boulder-choked cañon. Its principal fountains of ice and snow lie in the beautiful and interesting mountains of the Merced group, while its broad, open basin in general is noted for the beauty of its lakes and extensive forests.

Going up the north branch of the valley, we pass between the North Dome and the Half Dome, and in less than an hour come to Mirror Lake, the Dome Cascades, and Tenaya Fall, each interesting in its own way. Beyond

MIRROR VIEW OF YOSEMITE FALLS.

gardens and meadows occur in filled up lake basins among the rock-waves in the bottom of the cañon, and everywhere the surface of the granite has a smooth-wiped appearance, and in many places, reflecting the sunbeams, shines like glass—phenomena due to glacial action, the cañon having been the channel of one of the main tributaries of the ancient Yosemite glacier.

Ten miles above the valley we come to the beautiful Tenaya Lake, and here the cañon terminates. A mile or two above the lake stands the grand Sierra Cathedral, a building of one stone, hewn from the living rock, with sides, roof, gable, spire, and ornamental pinnacles, fashioned and finished symmetrically like a work of art, and set on a well-graded plateau about 9000 feet high, as if Nature in making so fine a house had also been careful that it should be finely seen. From every direction its peculiar form and graceful beauty of expression never fail to charm. Its height from the floor to the ridge of the roof is about 2500 feet, and among the pinnacles that adorn the front glorious views may be gained of the upper basins of the Merced and Tuolumne.

Passing on each side of the Cathedral we descend into the delightful Tuolumne Valley, from which excursions may be made to Mount Dana, Mono Lake, Mount Lyell, to the many curious peaks that rise above the meadows on the south, and to the Big Tuolumne Cañon with its glorious abundance of rocks and falling, gliding, tossing water. For all these the spacious meadows near the Soda Springs form a delightful center.

Returning now to Yosemite, and ascending the middle or Nevada branch of the valley, which is occupied by the main Merced River, we come within a few miles to the Vernal and Nevada falls, 400 and 600 feet high, and set in the midst of most novel and sublime rock-work. Above these, tracing the river, we are led into the Little Yosemite, a valley like the great Yosemite in form, sculpture, and vegetation. It is about three miles long, with walls 1500 to 2000 feet high, cascades coming over them, and the river flowing through the meadows and groves of the level bottom in tranquil crystal reaches.

Beyond this there are four other little Yosemites in the main cañon, making a series of five in all, the highest situated a few miles below the base of Mount Lyell, at an elevation of about 7800 feet above the sea. To describe these, with all their wealth of Yosemite furniture, and the wilderness of lofty peaks above them, the home of the avalanche and treasury of the fountain snow, would take us far beyond the bounds of a magazine article. We cannot here consider the formation of these mountain landscapes—how the crystal rocks with

the fall, on the north side of the cañon, is the sublime El Capitan-like rock called Mount Watkins; on the south the vast granite wave of Cloud's Rest, a mile in height; and between them the fine Tenaya Cascade with silvery plumes outspread on smooth, glacier-polished folds of granite, making a vertical descent in all of about 700 feet.

Just beyond the Dome Cascades, on the shoulder of Mount Watkins, there is an old trail once used by the Indians on their way across the range to Mono, but in the cañon above this point there is no trail of any sort. Between Mount Watkins and Cloud's Rest the cañon is accessible only to mountaineers, and it is so dangerous in some places that I hesitate to advise even good climbers anxious to test their nerve and skill to pass through it. Beyond the Cascades no great difficulty will be encountered. A succession of charming lily

crystal snow were brought to the light, making beauty whose influence is so mysterious on everybody who sees it; the blooming of the clouds; the fall of the snow; the flight of the avalanches; the invisible march of the grinding glaciers; the innumerable forms of the falling streams.

Of the small glacier lakes so characteristic of these upper regions, there are no fewer than sixty-seven in the basin of the main middle branch, besides countless smaller pools, all their waters crisp and living and looking out on beautiful skies. In the basin of the Illilouette there are sixteen, in the Tenaya and its branches thirteen, in the Yosemite Creek basin fourteen, and in the Pohono or Bridal Veil one, making a grand total of a hundred and eleven lakes whose waters come to sing at Yosemite. So glorious is the background of the great valley, so harmonious its relations to its widespreading fountains. On each side also the same harmony prevails. Climbing out of the valley by the subordinate cañons, we find the ground rising from the brink of the walls—on the south side to the fountains of Pohono or Bridal Veil Creek, the basin of which is noted for the extent and beauty of its meadows and its superb forests of silver fir; on the north side through the basin of the Yosemite Creek to the dividing ridge along the Tuolumne Cañon and the fountains of the Hoffman spur.

In general views the Yosemite Creek basin seems to be paved with domes and smooth whaleback masses of granite in every stage of development — some showing only their crowns; others rising high and free above the girdling forests, singly or in groups. Others again are developed only on one side, forming bold outstanding bosses usually well fringed with shrubs and trees, and presenting the polished shining surfaces given them by the glacier that brought them into relief. On the upper portion of the basin broad moraine beds have been deposited, and on these fine, thrifty forests are growing. Lakes and meadows and small spongy bogs may be found hiding here and there among

the domes, in the woods, or back in the fountain recesses of Mount Hoffman, while a thousand gardens are planted along the banks of the streams. All the wide, fan-shaped upper portion of the basin is covered with a network of small rills that go cheerily on their way to their grand fall in the valley, now flowing on smooth pavements in sheets thin as glass, now diving under willows and laving their red roots, oozing through bogs, making tiny falls and cascades, whirling and dancing, calming again, gliding through bits of smooth glacier meadows with sod of Alpine agrostis mixed with blue and white violets and daisies, breaking, tossing among rough boulders and fallen trees, flow-

SENTINEL ROCK.

ing together until, all united, they go to their fate with stately, tranquil air like a full-grown river. At the crossing of the Mono trail, about two miles above the head of the Yosemite Fall, the stream is nearly forty feet wide, and when the snow is melting rapidly in the spring it is about four feet deep, with a current of two and a half miles an hour. This is about the volume of water that forms the fall in May and June when there has been much snow the preceding winter; but it varies greatly from month to month. The snow rapidly vanishes from the open portion of the basin, which faces southward, and only a few of the tributaries reach back to perennial snow and ice fountains in the shadowy amphitheaters on the northern slopes of Mount Hoffman. The total descent made by the stream from its highest sources to its confluence with the Merced in the valley is about 6000 feet, while the distance is only about ten miles, an average fall of 600 feet per mile. The last mile of its course lies between the sides of sunken domes and swelling folds of the granite that are clustered and

as if leaving a lake, it slips over the polished lip of the pool down another incline and out over the brow of the precipice in a magnificent curve thick sown with rainbow spray.

In tracing the stream for the first time, getting acquainted with the life it lived in the mountains, I was eager to reach the extreme verge to see how it behaves in flowing so far through the air; but after enjoying this view and getting safely away I have never advised any one to follow my steps. The last incline down which the stream journeys so gracefully is so steep and smooth one must slip cautiously forward on hands and feet alongside the rushing water, which so near one's head is very exciting. But to gain a perfect view one must go yet farther, over a curving brow to a slight shelf on the extreme brink. This shelf, formed by the flaking off of a fold of the granite, is

CATHEDRAL ROCKS. (2660 FEET HIGH.)

pressed together like a mass of bossy cumulus clouds. Through this shining way Yosemite Creek goes to its fate, swaying and swirling with easy, graceful gestures and singing the last of its mountain songs before it reaches the dizzy edge of Yosemite to fall 2600 feet into another world, where climate, vegetation, inhabitants, all are different. Emerging from this last cañon the stream glides, in flat, lace-like folds, down a smooth incline into a small pool where it seems to rest and compose itself before taking the grand plunge. Then calmly,

about three inches wide, just wide enough for a safe rest for one's heels. To me it seemed nerve-trying to slip to this narrow foothold and poise on the edge of such a precipice so close to the confusing whirl of the waters; and after casting longing glances over the shining brow of the fall and listening to its sublime psalm, I concluded not to attempt to go nearer, but did, nevertheless, against reasonable judgment. Noticing some tufts of artemisia in a cleft of rock, I filled my mouth with the leaves, hoping their bitter taste might help to keep caution keen and prevent giddiness; then I reached the little ledge, got my heels well set, and worked side-wise twenty or thirty feet to a point close to the out-plunging current. Here the view is perfectly free down into the heart of the bright irised throng of comet-like streams into which the whole ponderous volume of the fall separates a little below the brow. So glorious a display of pure wildness, acting at close range while one is cut off from all the world beside, is terribly impressive.

DESTRUCTIVE WORK IN YOSEMITE VALLEY: STUMP FOREST, MOSTLY OF YOUNG PINE, IN "STATE PASTURE," COVERING SOME EIGHT ACRES. CUT IN JUNE, 1887, AND STUMPS LEFT STANDING AND PERFECTLY SOUND. ABOUT 2000 TREES, OR MORE, FELLED IN THIS ONE SPOT. ("PROCESS" REPRODUCTION OF PHOTOGRAPH.)

About forty yards to the eastward of the Yosemite Fall on a fissured portion of the edge of the cliff a less nerve-trying view may be obtained, extending all the way down to the bottom from a point about two hundred feet below the brow of the fall, where the current, striking a narrow ledge, bounds out in the characteristic comet-shaped masses. Seen from here towards noon, in the spring, the rainbow on its brow seems to be broken up and mingled with the rushing comets until all the fall is stained with iris colors, leaving no white water visible. This is the best of the safe views from above, the huge steadfast rocks, the flying waters, and the rainbow light forming one of the most glorious pictures conceivable.

The Yosemite Fall is separated into an upper and a lower fall with a series of falls and cascades between them, but when viewed in front from the bottom of the valley they all appear as one.

The Nevada Fall usually is ranked next to the Yosemite in general interest among the five main falls of the valley. Coming through the Little Yosemite in tranquil reaches, charmingly embowered, the river is first broken into rapids on a moraine boulder bar that crosses the lower end of the valley. Thence it pursues its way to the head of the fall in a very rough channel, cut in the solid granite, dashing on side angles, heaving in heavy, surging masses against bossy knobs, and swirling and swashing in potholes without a moment's rest. Thus, already chafed and dashed to foam, over-folded and twisted, it

plunges over the brink of the precipice as if glad to escape into the open air. But before it reaches the bottom it is pulverized yet finer by impinging upon a sloping portion of the cliff about half way down, thus making it the whitest of all the falls of the valley, and altogether one of the most wonderful in the world.

On the north side, close to the head of the fall, a slab of granite projects over the brink, forming a fine point for a view over the throng of streamers and wild plunging thunderbolts; and through the broad drifts of spray we see the river far below gathering its spent waters and rushing on again down the cañon in glad exultation into Emerald Pool, where at length it grows calm and gets rest for what still lies before it. All the features of the view

DESTRUCTIVE WORK IN YOSEMITE VALLEY: SPECIMEN TREE TRIMMING DONE IN 1887–88. MUCH SIMILAR WORK HAS BEEN DONE IN OTHER PARTS OF THE VALLEY. ("PROCESS" REPRODUCTION OF PHOTOGRAPH.)

correspond with the waters. The glacier-sculptured walls of the cañon on either hand, with the sublime mass of the Glacier Point Ridge in front, form a huge triangular, pit-like basin,

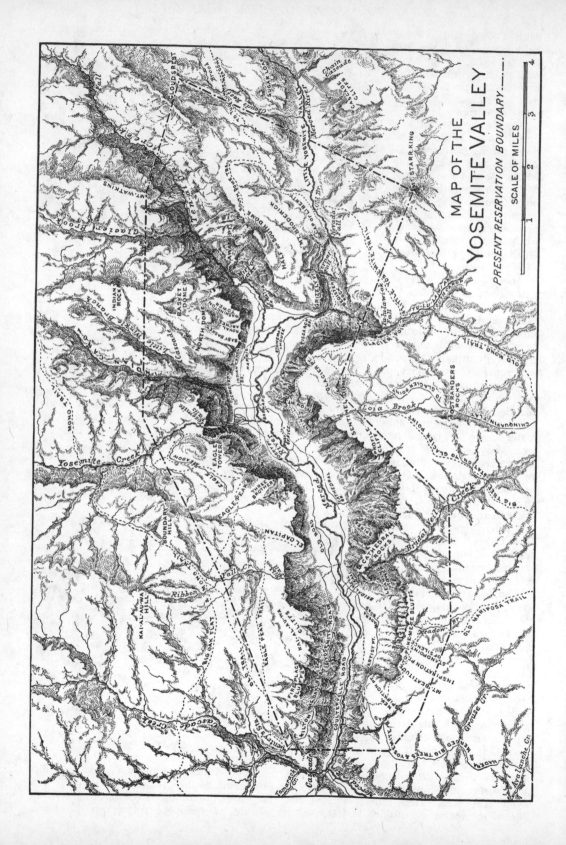

MAP OF THE
YOSEMITE VALLEY

PRESENT RESERVATION BOUNDARY------

SCALE OF MILES

which, filled with the roar of the falling river, seems as if it might be the hopper of one of the mills of the gods in which the mountains were being ground to dust.

The Vernal, famous for its rainbows, is a staid, orderly, easy-going fall, proper and exact in every movement, with scarce a hint of the passionate enthusiasm of the Yosemite or the Nevada. Nevertheless it is a favorite with most visitors, doubtless because it is better seen than any other. A good stairway ascends the cliff beside it, and the level plateau at the head enables one to saunter safely along the edge of the stream as it comes from Emerald Pool and to watch its waters, calmly bending over the brow of the precipice, in a sheet 80 feet wide and changing from green to purplish gray and white until dashed on the rough boulder talus below. Thence issuing from beneath the clouds of the out-wafting spray we can see the adventurous stream, still unspent, beating its way down the rugged cañon in gray continuous cascades, dear to the ousel, until it sweeps around the shoulder of the Half Dome on its approach to the head of the main valley.

The Illilouette in general appearance most resembles the Nevada. The volume of water is less than half as great, but it is about the same height (600 feet), and its waters receive the same kind of preliminary tossing in a rocky, irregular channel. Therefore it is a very white and fine-grained fall. When it is in full springtime bloom it is partly divided by rocks that roughen the lip of the precipice, but this division amounts only to a kind of fluting and grooving of the column, which has a beautiful effect. It is not nearly so grand a fall as the upper Yosemite, or so symmetrical as the Vernal, or so airily graceful and simple as the Bridal Veil, nor does it ever display so tremendous an outgush of snowy magnificence as the Nevada; but in the exquisite fineness and richness of texture of its flowing folds it surpasses them all.

One of the finest things I ever saw in Yosemite or elsewhere I found on the brow of this beautiful fall. It was in the Indian summer, when the leaf colors were ripe and the great cliffs and domes were transfigured in the hazy golden air. I had wandered up the rugged talus-dammed cañon of the Illilouette, admiring the wonderful views to be had there of the great Half Dome and the Liberty Cap, the foliage of the maples, dogwoods, rubus tangles, etc., the late goldenrods and asters, and the extreme purity of the water, which in motionless pools on this stream is almost perfectly invisible. The voice of the fall was now low, and the grand flood had waned to floating gauze and thin-broidered folds of linked and arrowy lace-work. When I reached the fall slant sunbeams were glinting across the head of it,

leaving all the rest in shadow; and on the illumined brow a group of yellow spangles were playing, of singular form and beauty, flashing up and dancing in large flame-shaped masses, wavering at times, then steadying, rising and falling in accord with the shifting forms of the water. But the color changed not at all. Nothing in clouds or flowers, on bird-wings or the lips of shells, could rival it in fineness. It was the most divinely beautiful mass of yellow light I ever beheld — one of nature's pre-

STAIRWAY ON CLOUD'S REST TRAIL.

cious sights that come to us but once in a lifetime.

For about a mile above Mirror Lake the cañon is level and well planted with fir, spruce, and libocedrus, forming a remarkably fine grove, at the head of which is the Tenaya Fall. Though seldom seen or described, this is, I think, the most picturesque fall in the valley. For a considerable distance above it Tenaya Creek comes rushing down, white and foamy, over a flat pavement inclined at an angle of about eighteen degrees. In time of high water this sheet of bright rapids is nearly seventy feet wide, and is varied in a very striking way by three parallel furrows that extend in the direction of the flow. These furrows, worn by the action of the stream upon cleavage joints, vary in width, are slightly sinuous, and have large boulders firmly wedged in them here and there in narrow places, giving rise, of course, to a complicated series of wild dashes, doublings, and arching bounds in the swift torrent. Just before it reaches the sheer precipice of the fall the current is divided, the left division making a vertical fall of about eighty feet in a romantic leafy nook, while the other forms a rugged cascade.

Lunar rainbows or spraybows also abound; their colors as distinct as those of the sun, and

the moon came round the domes and sent her beams into the wild uproar, I ventured out on the narrow bench that extends back of the fall from Fern Ledge and began to admire the dim-veiled grandeur of the view. I could see the fine gauzy threads of the outer tissue by having the light in front; and wishing to look at the moon through the meshes of some of the denser portions of the fall, I ventured to

LOOKING UP MERCED RIVER, ON THE WAY TO VERNAL FALLS.

as obviously banded, though less vivid. Fine specimens may be found any night at the foot of the upper Yosemite Fall, glowing gloriously amid the gloomy shadows of the cañon whenever there is plenty of moonlight and spray, silent interpreters of the heart-peace of Nature in the stormy darkness. Even the secondary bow is at times distinctly visible.

The best point from which to observe them is on Fern Ledge. For some time after moonrise the arc has a span of about five hundred feet, and is set upright; one end planted in the boiling spray at the bottom, the other in the edge of the fall, creeping lower, of course, and becoming less upright as the moon rises higher. This grand arc of color, glowing in mild, shapely beauty in so weird and huge a chamber of night shadows, and amid the rush and roar and tumultuous dashing of this thunder-voiced fall, is one of the most impressive and most cheering of all the blessed evangels of the mountains.

A wild scene, but not a safe one, is made by the moon as it appears through the edge of the Yosemite Fall when one is behind it. Once after enjoying the night-song of the waters, and watching the formation of the colored bow as

creep farther behind it while it was gently wind-swayed, without taking sufficient thought about the consequences of its swaying back to its natural position after the wind pressure should be removed. The effect was enchanting. Fine, savage music sounded above, beneath, around me; while the moon, apparently in the very midst of the rushing waters, seemed to be struggling to keep her place, on account of the ever-varying form and density of the water masses through which she was seen, now darkened by a rush of thick-headed comets, now flashing out through openings between them. I was in fairyland between the dark wall and the wild throng of illumined waters, but suffered sudden disenchantment; for, like the witch scene in Alloway Kirk, "in an instant all was dark." Down came a dash of spent comets, thin and harmless-looking in the distance, but desperately solid and stony in striking one's shoulders. It seemed like a mixture of choking spray and gravel. Instinctively dropping on my knees, I laid hold of an angle of the rock, rolled myself together with my face pressed against my breast, and in this attitude submitted as best I could to my thundering baptism. The heavier masses seemed to strike like cobblestones, and there was a confused noise of many waters about my ears — hissing, gurgling, clashing sounds that were not heard as music. The situation was easily realized. How fast one's thoughts burn at such times! I was weighing the chances of escape. Would the column be swayed a few inches away from the wall, or would it come yet closer? The fall was in flood, and not so lightly would its ponderous mass be swayed. My fate seemed to depend on a breath of the "idle wind." It was moved gently forward, the pounding ceased, and I once more revisited the glimpses of the moon. But fearing I might be caught at a disadvantage in making too hasty a retreat, I moved only a few feet along the bench to where a block of ice lay. Between the ice and the wall I wedged myself, and lay face downwards until the steadiness of the light gave encouragement to get away. Somewhat nerve-shaken, drenched, and benumbed, I made out to build a fire, warmed myself, ran home to avoid taking cold, reached my cabin before daylight, got an hour or two of sleep, and awoke sane and comfortable, better, not worse, for my wild bath in moonlit spray.

Owing to the westerly trend of the valley and its vast depth there is a great difference between the climates of the north and south sides — greater than between many countries far apart; for the south wall is in shadow during the winter months, while the north is bathed in sunshine every clear day. Thus there is mild spring weather on one side of the valley while winter rules the other. Far up the north-side cliffs many a nook may be found closely embraced by sun-beaten rock-bosses in which flowers bloom every month of the year. Even butterflies may be seen in these high winter gardens except when storms are falling and a few days after they have ceased. Near the head of the lower Yosemite Fall in January I found the ant lions lying in wait in their warm sand-cups, rock ferns being unrolled, club mosses covered with fresh growing points, the flowers of the laurel nearly open, and the honeysuckle rosetted with bright young leaves; every plant seemed to be thinking about summer and to be stirred with good vital sunshine. Even on the shadow side of the valley the frost is never very sharp. The lowest temperature I ever observed during four winters was +7°. The first twenty-four days of January had an average temperature at 9 A. M. of 32°, minimum 22°; at 3 P. M. the average was 40° 30', the minimum 32°.

Throughout the winter months the spray of the upper Yosemite Fall is frozen while falling thinly exposed and is deposited around the base of the fall in the form of a hollow truncated cone, which sometimes reaches a height of five hundred feet or more, into the heart of which the whole volume of the fall descends with a tremendous roar as if pouring down the throat of a crater. In the building of this ice-cone part of the frozen spray falls directly to its place, but a considerable portion is first frozen upon the face of the cliff on both sides of the fall, and attains a thickness of a foot or more during the night. When the sun strikes this ice-coating it is expanded and cracked off in masses weighing from a few pounds to several tons, and is built into the walls of the cone; while in windy, frosty weather, when the fall is swayed from side to side, the cone is well drenched, and the loose ice-masses and dust are all firmly frozen together. The thundering, reverberating reports of the falling ice-masses are like those of heavy cannon. They usually occur at intervals of a few minutes, and are the most strikingly characteristic of the winter sounds of the valley, and constant accompaniments of the best sunshine. While this stormy building is in progress the surface of the cone is smooth and pure white, the whole presenting the appearance of a beautiful crystal hill wreathed with folds of spray which are oftentimes irised. But when it is wasting and breaking up in the spring its surface is strewn with leaves, pine branches, stones, sand, etc., that have been brought over the fall, making it look like a heap of avalanche detritus.

After being engulfed and churned in the stormy interior of the crater the waters of the fall issue from arched openings at the base, seemingly scourged and weary and glad to escape, while belching spray spouted up out of the throat past the descending current is wafted away in irised drifts to the rocks and groves.

Anxious to learn what I could about the structure of this curious ice-hill, I tried to climb it, carrying an ax to cut footsteps. Before I had reached the base of it I was met by a current of spray and wind that made breathing difficult. I pushed on backward, however, and soon gained the slope of the hill, where by creeping close to the surface most of the blast was avoided. Thus I made my way nearly to the summit, halting at times to peer up through the wild whirls of spray, or to listen to the sublime thunder beneath me, the whole hill sounding as if it were a huge, bellowing, exploding drum. I hoped that by waiting until the fall was blown aslant I should be able to climb to the lip of the crater and get a view of the interior; but a suffocating blast, half air, half water, followed by the fall of an enormous mass of ice from the wall, quickly discouraged me. The whole cone was jarred by the blow, and I was afraid its side might fall in. Some fragments of the mass sped past me dangerously near; so I beat a hasty retreat, chilled and drenched, and laid myself on a sunny rock in a safe place to dry.

The Bridal Veil, upper Yosemite, and the Tu-ee-u-la-la of Hetch Hetchy (the next cañon to the north), on account of their height and exposure, are greatly influenced by winds. The common summer winds that come up the river cañon from the plains are never very strong, partly on account of the roughness of the way they have to travel. But the north winds of winter do some very wild work, worrying the falls and the forests, and hanging snow banners, a mile long, on the peaks of the summit of the range. One morning I was awakened by the pelting of pine cones on the roof of my cabin, and found, on going out, that the north wind had taken possession of the valley, filling it with a sea-like roar, and, arousing the pines to magnificent action, made them bow like supple willows. The valley had been visited a short time before by a succession of most beautiful snowstorms, and the floor, and the cliffs, and all the region round about were lavishly laden with winter jewelry. Rocks, trees, the sandy flats and the meadows, all were in bloom, and the air was filled with a dust of shining petals. The gale increased all day, and branches and tassels and empty burs of the silver pine covered the snow, while the falls were being twisted and torn and tossed about as if they were mere wisps of floating mist. In the morning the great ponderous column of the upper Yosemite Fall, increased in volume by the melting of the snow during a warm spell, was caught by a tremendous blast, bent upwards, torn to shreds, and driven back over the brow of the cliff whence it came, as if denied admission to the valley. This kind of work would be kept up for ten or fifteen minutes, then a partial lull in the storm would allow the vast torrent to arrange its tattered skirts, and come back again to sing on in its accustomed course. Amid all this rocking and bending and baffling of the waters they were lighted by a steady glare of sunlight, strangely white from spicules of snow crystals. The lower fall, though less exposed, was yet violently swirled and torn and thrashed about in its narrow cañon, and at times appeared as one resplendent mass of iris colors from top to bottom, as if a hundred rainbows had been doubled up into a mass four or five hundred feet in diameter. In the afternoon, while I watched the upper fall from the shelter of a pine tree, it was suddenly arrested in its descent at a point about half way down, and was neither blown upward nor driven aside, but was simply held stationary in mid air, as if gravitation below that point in the path of its descent had ceased

to act. The ponderous flood, weighing hundreds of tons, was sustained hovering, hesitating, like a bunch of thistledown, while I counted 190. All this time the ordinary amount of water was coming over the cliff and accumulating in the air, swedging and widening and forming an irregular cone 700 feet high tapering to the top of the wall, the whole standing still, resting on the invisible arm of the north wind. At length, as if commanded to go on again, scores of arrowy comets shot forth from the bottom of the suspended mass as if escaping from separate outlets.

The brow of El Capitan was decked with long streamers of snow-like hair, Cloud's Rest was enveloped in drifting gossamer films, and the Half Dome loomed up in the garish light like some majestic living creature clad in the same gauzy, wind-woven drapery, upward currents meeting overhead sometimes making it smoke like a volcano.

Glorious as are these rocks and waters when jumbled in storm winds, or chanting rejoicing in everyday dress, there is a glory that excelleth, when rare conditions of weather meet to make every valley, hollow, gorge, and cañon sing with flood waters. Only once have I seen Yosemite in full bloom of flood during all the years I have lived there. In 1871 the early winter weather was delightful; the days all sunshine, the nights clear and serene, calling forth fine crops of frost crystals for the withered ferns and grasses, the most luxuriant growths of hoar-frost imaginable. In the afternoon of December 16, when I was sauntering on the meadows, I noticed a massive crimson cloud growing in solitary grandeur above Cathedral Rocks, its form scarcely less striking than its color. It had a picturesque, bulging base like an old sequoia, a smooth, tapering stem, and a bossy, down-curling crown like a mushroom; all its parts colored alike, making one mass of translucent crimson. Wondering what the meaning of that lonely red cloud might be, I was up betimes next morning looking at the weather, but all seemed tranquil as yet. Towards noon gray clouds began to grow which had a close, curly grain like bird's-eye maple, and late at night rain fell, which soon changed to snow; next morning about ten inches lay on the meadows, and it was still falling in a fine, cordial storm.

During the night of the 18th a torrent of rain fell on the snow, but as the temperature was 34°, the snow line was only a few hundred feet above the bottom of the valley, and to get out of the rainstorm into the snowstorm one had only to climb a little above the tops of the pines. The streams, therefore, instead of being increased in volume, were diminished by the storm, because the snow sponged up part of their waters and choked the smaller tributaries. But about midnight the temperature suddenly rose to 42°, carrying the snow line far beyond the valley, over the upper basins perhaps to the summit of the range, and next morning Yosemite was rejoicing in a glorious flood. The warm, copious rain falling on the snow was at first absorbed and held back, and so also was that portion of the snow that the rain melted, and all that was melted by the warm wind, until the whole mass of snow was saturated and became sludgy, and at length slipped and rushed simultaneously from a thousand slopes into the channels in wild extravagance, heaping and swelling flood over flood, and plunging into the valley in one stupendous avalanche.

Awakened by the roar, I looked out and at once recognized the extraordinary character of the storm. The rain was still pouring in torrents, and the wind, blowing a gale, was working in passionate accord with the flood. The section of the north wall visible from my cabin was covered with a network of falls — new visitors that seemed strangely out of place. Eager to get into the midst of the show, I snatched a piece of bread for breakfast and ran out. The mountain waters, suddenly liberated, seemed to be holding a grand jubilee. The two Sentinel cascades rivaled the great falls at ordinary stages, and across the valley by the Three Brothers I caught glimpses of more falls than I could readily count; while the whole valley throbbed and trembled, and was filled with an awful, massive, solemn, sealike roar. After looking about me bewildered for a few moments I tried to reach the upper meadows, where the valley is widest, that I might be able to see the walls on both sides, and thus gain general views. But the meadows were flooded, forming an almost continuous lake dotted with blue sludgy islands, while innumerable streams roared like lions across my path and were sweeping forward rocks and logs with tremendous energy over ground where tiny gilias had been growing but a short time before. Climbing into the talus slopes, where these savage torrents were broken among earthquake boulders, I succeeded in crossing them, and forced my way up the valley to Hutchings' Bridge, where I crossed the river and waded to the middle of the upper meadow. Here most of the new falls were in sight, probably the most glorious assemblage of waterfalls ever displayed from any one standpoint in the world. On that portion of the south wall between Hutchings' and the Sentinel there were ten falls plunging and booming from a height of nearly 3000 feet, the smallest of which might have been heard miles away. In the neighborhood of Glacier Point there

were six; between the Three Brothers and Yosemite Fall, nine; between Yosemite and Royal Arch Falls, ten; from Washington Column to Mount Watkins, ten; on the slopes of Half Dome, facing Mirror Lake, eight; on the shoulder of Half Dome, facing the valley, three — fifty-six new falls occupying the upper end of the valley, besides a countless host of silvery threads gleaming everywhere. In all the valley there must have been upward of a hundred. As if celebrating some great event, falls and cascades came thronging in Yosemite costume from every groove and cañon far and near.

All summer visitors will remember the comet forms of the Yosemite Fall and the laces of the Bridal Veil and Nevada. In the falls of this winter jubilee the lace forms predominated, but there was no lack of thunder-toned comets. The lower portion of one of the Sentinel cascades was composed of two main white shafts, the space between them filled in with chained and beaded gauze of intricate pattern, through the singing threads of which the purplish-gray rock could be dimly seen. The series above Glacier Point was still more complicated in structure, displaying every form that one would imagine water might be dashed and combed and woven into. Those on the north wall between Washington Column and the Royal Arch Fall were so nearly related that they formed an almost continuous sheet, and these again were but slightly separated from those about Indian Cañon. The group about the Three Brothers and El Capitan, owing to the topography and cleavage of the cliffs back of them, were more broken and irregular. The Tissiack cascades were comparatively small, yet sufficient to give that noblest of mountain rocks a glorious voice. In the midst of all this rejoicing the Yosemite Fall was scarce heard until about three o'clock in the afternoon. Then I was startled by a sudden thundering crash as if a rock avalanche had come to join the chorus. This was the flood wave of Yosemite Creek, which had just arrived, delayed by the distance it had to travel, and by the choking snows of its widespread fountains. Now, with volume tenfold increased beyond its springtime fullness, it took its place as leader of the glorious choir. No idle, silent water was to be found anywhere; all sang loud or low in divine harmony.

And the winds sang too, playing on every pine, leaf, and rock, surging against the huge brows and domes and outstanding battlements, deflected hither and thither, broken into a thousand cascading currents that whirled in the hollow. And these again, reacting on the clouds, eroded immense cavernous spaces in their gray depths, sweeping forward the resulting detritus in ragged trains like the moraines of glaciers. These cloud movements in turn published the work of the winds, giving them a visible body, and enabling us to trace their wild career. As if endowed with independent motion, some detached cloud would rise hastily upon some errand to the very top of the wall in a single effort, examining the faces of the cliffs, and then perhaps as suddenly descend to sweep imposingly along the meadows, trailing draggled fringes through the pines, fondling their waving spires with infinite gentleness, or gliding behind a grove or a single tree bring it into striking relief, while all bowed and waved in solemn rhythm. Sometimes as they drooped and condensed, or thinned to misty gauze, half the valley would be veiled at once, leaving here and there some lofty headland cut off from all visible connection with the walls, looming alone, dim, spectral, as if belonging to the sky — visitors, like the new falls, come to take part in the festival. Thus for two days and nights in measureless extravagance the storm went on, and mostly without spectators, at least of a terrestrial kind. I saw nobody out — bird, bear, squirrel, or man.

Tourists had vanished months before, and the hotel people and laborers were out of sight, careful about getting cold and wet, and satisfied with views from doors and windows. The bears, I suppose, were in their boulder dens in the cañons, the squirrels in their knot-hole nests, the grouse in close fir groves, and the small singers in the chaparral. Strange to say, I did not see even the water-ousel, though he must have greatly enjoyed the storm.

This was the most sublime waterfall flood I ever saw — clouds, winds, rocks, waters, throbbing together as one. And then to contemplate what was going on simultaneously with all this in other mountain temples: the Big Tuolumne Cañon — how the white waters were singing there, and the winds, and how the clouds were marching. In Hetch Hetchy Valley also, and the great King's River Yosemite, and in all the other cañons and valleys of the Sierra from Shasta to the southernmost fountains of the Kern — five hundred miles of flooded waterfalls chanting together. What a psalm was that!

John Muir.

22

Pioneer Mining in California

E.G. Waite

PIONEER MINING IN CALIFORNIA.

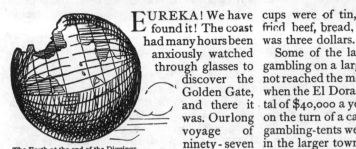

The Earth at the end of the Diggings.
(Reprinted from " Punch.")

EUREKA! We have found it! The coast had many hours been anxiously watched through glasses to discover the Golden Gate, and there it was. Our long voyage of ninety - seven days from Panama was about over. The old brigantine, leaking at every seam, was headed for the opening between the rocky headlands, and in the bright moonlight, August 4, 1849, she slowly made her way, all sails set, into the magnificent bay of San Francisco. She rounded Clark's Point, and before dawn swung with the tide up to the spot occupied by the rear end of Montgomery block, between Montgomery and Sansome streets, now a half-mile inland from the water-front of San Francisco.

It was an exciting hour. We had received no news from home since our departure from New York on the 1st of March, and everybody was eager to get ashore for letters and papers. Not far away was a little shell of a building, probably sixteen feet square, erected on four posts, each resting on a hogshead filled with stones and thus stayed in the mud. From this a plank ran to *terra firma*. The sun had not risen when we landed from our iron cockle-shell and wandered in squads through a straggling village, chiefly of tents ; only a few wooden houses had yet been built, while three or four adobe structures told of Mexican occupation. Sand-dunes were plenty, and when the winds came in from the Pacific the dust made lively work, and gave us our first lessons in Californian climatology.

With the morning light the tents gave forth their sleepers, and such a motley tenantry! And such a stir! Americans in great variety of dress, natives of the islands, with a picturesque mingling of Mexicans in wide trousers and short jackets with a profusion of small globular buttons, their shock heads thrust through slits in their serapes and topped off with brown, sugar-loaf-crowned, broad-brimmed, heavy felt sombreros.

Ship-fare had given us a longing for a fancy breakfast. A restaurant-sign attracted me, and I went in. The table was a bare plank against one of the walls of the tent ; the plates and cups were of tin, and the meal consisted of fried beef, bread, and black coffee. The bill was three dollars.

Some of the largest tents were devoted to gambling on a large scale, though the vice had not reached the magnitude of succeeding years, when the El Dorado gambling-tent paid a rental of $40,000 a year, and $20,000 were staked on the turn of a card. In those early days these gambling-tents were the most attractive places in the larger towns. They were commodious, and were about the only places warmed by fires ; they had well-furnished and somewhat tasteful bars, where liquors were dispensed at a dollar a glass. Tables were distributed along the sides, and in rows through the middle, at which monte, faro, vingt-et-un, roulette, lansquenet, and I do not know how many other games were played. When the whole was ablaze with lights of an evening, an occasional woman seen assisting at the games, and a band of music or singers giving forth a concourse of sweet sounds, crowds surged before the bar and around the tables, some attracted by the novelty, some to get warm, but more to try their luck.

Our stay in San Francisco was but for a day or two. We had come to mine for gold, and though the inducements for business in the incipient city were flattering, even wages commanding eight to ten dollars a day, or a dollar an hour, we determined to push on to the mines. Glowing accounts induced us to try the southern mines, and a passage to Stockton was secured on an old tub of a schooner at the rate of three ounces of gold, or thirty-six dollars, per head. The deck was crowded with men of every nationality. The rolling hills, tawny, and flecked with green trees, bounding the bays of San Francisco, Suisun, and San Pablo, were novel and interesting. The very color of the earth, covered with wild oats or dried grass, suggested a land of gold. The sight was inspiriting. But when we reached the mouth of the San Joaquin our miseries began. This river has an extraordinarily tortuous course almost entirely through tule, or marshlands, that in 1849 produced bushels of voracious mosquitoes to the acre. I had never known the like before. It seemed as if there was a stratum of swarming insect life ten feet thick over the surface of the earth. I corded my trousers tight to my boot-legs to keep them from pulling up, donned a thick coat, though the heat was intolerable, shielded my neck and face with handkerchiefs, and put on buckskin gloves, and in that condition parboiled and smothered. In spite of all precautions our faces were much swollen with the poison of numberless bites. To escape the hot sun we took refuge below deck, and to drive away the pests a smudge was made on some sand in the bottom of the boat, which filled the hold almost to suffocation. The mosquitoes were too ravenous to be wholly foiled by smoke. I think I never endured such vexation and suffering. Sleep was impossible. The boat had to be worked by hand around the numerous bends, and half the time the sails were useless for want of wind. It was a burning calm in the midst of a swamp. But even in our distress there was a humorous side, provoking grim smiles at least.

We finally arrived at Stockton, then also a village of tents. The newest style of architecture called for light frames on which canvas was tacked for sides and roof. There was no need of windows except for air currents, light enough coming through the cloth. We were impatient to go on to our destination, the Big Bar of the Mokelumne River, and soon were on the way with pack-mules and horses hired for the purpose. Camping on the bank of the Calaveras the first night, we were treated to our first serenade by coyotes. A peculiarity of this small wolf is that he can pipe in any key, fooling you with the belief that he has twenty companions, though one little wretch is making all the noise. We passed the plain of the San Joaquin Valley, with its dark, spreading live-oaks, like an old orchard miles in extent, and began the ascent of the foothills. Brown and red soil made its appearance hot and dusty; nut-pines were mingled with oaks and manzanitas, ceanothus, buckeye, and poison oak. Wild oats and burr clover still remained in patches unfound by the cattle of the plain. The air was dry, but grew more bracing. The trail wound among trees, around hills, through ravines, and sometimes up steep ascents, but at last, on the third day from Stockton, after a journey of more than seven thousand miles by land and sea, we reached the mines.

My first impressions were not pleasant. The first miner I saw at his work was a rough, dirty-looking man in a dry ravine. The banks were about as high as his shoulders. A double-barreled shot-gun lay on the edge of the bank within easy reach. He was picking up dry clay and gravel from the bottom of his claim, pulverizing it in his wooden pan with a stone, and then shaking it about till the lighter particles came to the top and were brushed over the rim. The pulverizing and shaking continued until a small quantity of dust and gold was left in the bottom. The dust was blown out with the breath. This process was called " dry washing."

The Big Bar of the Mokelumne lay in the gorge six or eight hundred feet below. The sight was not at all inspiring. What in mining parlance are called "bars" are deposits of sand, gravel, clay, and boulders made by rivers, usually opposite the angle of a bend. Sometimes these are small, and sometimes several acres in extent, and vary from a few inches to ten feet or more in depth to the bed-rock. Our bar, as its name denotes, was a large one, of perhaps five or six acres, covered with boulders from a few pounds' weight to several tons. A few tall pines were scattered over it, and here and there were a number of tents. Though perhaps a hundred miners were at work, the river went merrily on unstained to the sea. Down the steep banks of the gorge we went, stirring up the red dust and covering ourselves with it from head to foot. The animals did not like so steep a trail, and would have their own way among the timber, loosening the packs; but we made the descent with average success. On the bar we found friends that we had made in Panama, who had preceded us a few days, long enough to speak the vernacular of mining and to pride themselves on being "old miners," assuming as such to know just where the gold would be found in the largest quantities, and where to expect the least.

And now my mining life began. It was as free from restraint as the air that came through the soughing pines. Only Mexican law could be said to exist, and in all the mining region there were no officers to enforce its feeble demands. Every man was a law unto himself, and it is little to say in behalf of the pioneers of California that they carried the laws of justice and humanity in their hearts to such a degree that no more orderly society was ever known on the face of the earth than in those early days.

Pioneer mining life — what was it? The miner must have an outfit of a pick, pan, shovel, rocker, dipper and bucket of wood, or of rawhide. A tent was good to have, but he could make shift during the dry season with a substitute of boughs, for there was no fear of rain from May to October. A blanket of rubber spread on a stratum of leaves, on which his woolen blankets were laid, sufficed for a bed. His culinary utensils were confined to a frying-pan, a small iron pot, tin cups and plates, knife, fork, and spoon. His wardrobe consisted generally of a pair of serviceable shirts, a change of trousers, strong boots, and a slouch-hat. With these, and a supply of bacon, flour, salt, saleratus, beans, a few candles, and occasionally fresh beef, the miner was ready for work. His luxuries were tea and raw sugar, with occasionally the addition of dried peaches from Chili. His bread was made by mixing flour, water,

A TULE MARSH
ON THE
SAN JOAQUIN.

(DRAWN BY
HARRY FENN.)

and saleratus in the tin or iron pan which did double duty in the kitchen and in gathering gold, and baking it about two inches thick, like a shortcake. But slapjacks, the legitimate successors of the Mexican tortillas, were also a standard article of diet. Tin teapots were sometimes affected, but the small iron pot with a hollow handle did duty for both tea and beans or frijoles. The latter were of a brown variety grown in Chili, and were prepared after the Mexican style with a piece of bacon or fresh beef and plenty of chili colorado, or red pepper. They were allowed to cook a long time, often standing in the hot embers over night to be ready for breakfast in the morning. The bill-of-fare did not vary much for breakfast, dinner, and supper.

The most expensive instrument of the early miner was the rocker, which, though simple in construction, cost in the mines from fifty to a hundred dollars. In general appearance it was not unlike a baby's cradle as used by our grandmothers and as still seen on the frontier. It consisted of a flat bottom with two sides that flared outward, and an end board at the head, while the foot was open save a riffle about an inch and a half high at the bottom to catch the gold that might pass another riffle across the bottom near the middle. At the head of the cradle was a hopper about eighteen inches square, with a perforated sheet-iron bottom or wire screen. Under this was an apron, or board, sloping downward towards the head. Two substantial rockers under the whole completed the simple machine which gave to the world millions of dollars. The *modus operandi* may be described as follows: Two sticks of wood hewn on the upper side were imbedded at the river's brink, one four inches lower than the other, on which the rockers were to rest, thus securing a grade in the machine to facilitate the outward flow of the water and sand. Two miners usually worked together as partners. One shoveled the earth into the rocker, while the other, seated on a boulder or block of wood, dipped the water from the river, and poured it upon the earth in the hopper with one hand, all the time rocking with the other.

THE OLD SACRAMENTO TRAIL NORTH OF DONNER LAKE.

When the earth was thoroughly washed, he rose, lifted the hopper from its place, threw out the stones and gravel, replaced it, and thus the work went on. As the ground about the rocker became exhausted to the bed-rock, recourse was had to the bucket, and the earth was carried sometimes a few rods, making laborious work for the miner. To keep the rocker going another hand would be employed to carry earth, and each would carry two buckets at a time. Hard work of this kind suggested improvements in mining. At noon the gold and black sand collected above the riffles were taken up on a scraper and thrown into the pan, which was carried to the river and carefully washed to remove as far as possible all but the gold. The yield of the forenoon was carried to the camp, dried over a blaze, the dry sand blown out, and the gold weighed in scales or guessed at, and poured into the partnership purse and deposited under the bed or anywhere else out of sight. Few miners thought of weighing themselves down with gold, and few taxed their resources much to find places of concealment. I was in many camps down to 1854, and in none did I ever know of a theft of gold, and I heard of but one, and that was punished by a cat-o'-nine-tails, which was afterward nailed to the center-post of a trader's tent, as a warning to evil-doers.

The gold taken from the river bars was mostly in the form of scales resembling cucumber seeds, and of varying size. It was most plentiful on the bed-rock and in a few inches of soil above it, though sometimes three or four feet of earth would pay to wash. Where the bed-rock was hard the miner cleaned it, for a shovelful of dirt might contain a few dollars in small particles. Where the bed-rock was soft shale or slate on edge the miner picked away an inch or so and washed it, as frequently

the scales were found to be driven quite thickly into the crevices. When the ground was very rich the rocker was cleaned of gold every hour or two. When work was over, around the supper fire the events of the day were discussed, earnings compared, reports made of grizzly bears or deer being seen or killed, of better diggings of " coarse gold " discovered. This was the hour for speculations as to the origin of the gold in the rivers, and a strong opinion was entertained by many who were not well-read that immense masses of the precious metal would some day be brought to light in the snow-capped peaks towering to the east. " Coarse gold " was a charm to the ear of the ordinary miner. His claim might be paying him an ounce a day in fine gold, but he was always interested in some reported diggings far away where the product was in lumps, and not infrequently he left a good mine to seek some richer El Dorado. The characteristic and besetting fault of the early miner was unrest. He was forever seeking better fortune. Yet it was this passion for prospecting that resulted in the discovery of gold in an incredibly short time from the southern end of the San Joaquin Valley to the northern limit of the State. To " prospect " was to find a spot that looked favorable and make an examination of it. The miner would take a pan of earth, shake and gyrate it under water, raising and tipping it frequently to run the dirt and water off, then plunge it again, and so continue until a small residuum of black sand and gold remained. A speck of gold was the " color," several specks were " several colors," and the number and size determined the judgment of the miner whether he should go to work or move on. I have seen ounces taken in this way in a single pan, but in the earlier days

WORKING A CLAIM.

"NOT EVEN THE COLOR."
(COMPOSED FROM AN OLD PRINT.)

we counted a "bit" to the pan, twelve and a half cents, a fair prospect.

The average gain of the miner in those days can never be known. Though he was extraordinarily frank and confiding in the offhand conversations about the camp-fire, yet there is reason to believe that his largest receipts were sometimes not reported. My observation was that the industrious worker rarely brought to his supper less than ten dollars, often an ounce (reckoned at sixteen dollars), and sometimes six ounces, or even more. I myself took from the earth nearly one hundred and fifty ounces in seventeen successive working days. My largest clean-up was $224. One day, in less than half an hour, I took with my knife from a crevice in the rocks six and a half ounces of gold. When the river went down after it had been swollen by the first rains and had swept over the bed-rock of bars supposed to be worked out, hundreds of glittering scales were left exposed, affording pleasant picking for a day or two.

The nights in the mines were glorious for sleep. However hot the days,— and I have known a thermometer hung on the north side of a pine-tree to show 128° at two o'clock,—the nights were cool, requiring at least one good pair of blankets for comfort. Stretched on the ground under a tent or canopy of boughs, or with nothing but the purest air between him and the stars, the miner was lulled to rest by the murmur of the river or by a coyote, running his remarkable gamut. The great heat did not interfere with work, and there was not a case of sunstroke, nor was the atmosphere sultry or very oppressive. Eighty-eight degrees in the moist climate of Panama made life vastly more uncomfortable.

At first, and until the blue-shirted population became numerous, not much regard was had to the size of claims, the miner occupying about all the ground he desired. But a change soon came. The sense of justice of the first occu-

pants of a locality, inspired, it may be, by the fact that the swarms of new immigrants would soon compel a division, allowed a mining statute limiting claims to a certain size. This varied in the different camps, and depended somewhat on the richness of the earth. Generally each miner was restricted to about fifteen feet front on the river, the claim extending across the bar to the hill, but where the bar was a wide one the length was shortened. In some cases a claim was from fifteen to eighteen feet square. Back from the river and near the foot of the mountain the bed-rock was sometimes ten or twelve feet below the surface, and great labor was required to throw off the top earth to reach the auriferous stratum, and often such deep claims were very wet, calling for constant bailing. Of course such claims must be rich to pay, and some of them were, but it was not always so. I have known days and sometimes weeks of hard work to be spent in one of these pits, to find a smooth bed-rock at last with very little gold on it. Now and then, after long and tedious toil and discouragements, the miner "struck his pile," but as often he found nothing but barren rock or gravel.

Mining is one of the most fascinating and exciting of employments. But in the earlier days, when we knew less about genuine indications, mining was, more than now, a species of gambling. The effects are yet to be seen in hundreds of men still living near their old haunts, who, in common phrase, have "lost their grip"; others live in our memories who, after repeated disappointment, sleep on the mountain sides in nameless graves. Yet these same unfortunates did their part in giving to the world thousands of millions of dollars;

SURFACE SLUICING.

LONG TOM. (COMPOSED FROM A LITHOGRAPH, BY BRITTON & REY, PUBLISHED ABOUT 1849.)

thus stimulating progress probably more than was ever known in any other epoch of similar length in the history of mankind.

The early miner soon observed in working by the river's shore that the pay dirt sometimes extended down under the water, and he was not slow in going after the yellow metal wherever it was to be found. Large prospects suggested turning the stream from its bed to work the bottom, and this was usually done by digging a canal across the bar, or by carrying the water in a wooden flume over the channel or across the bends. I have seen companies of men, filled with enthusiasm and confidence, at work for weeks until the river-bed was laid bare, to find only a narrow strip of pay ground along the edge. But in some cases the reward was enormous.

One Sunday in September, 1849, putting on my "store clothes" and "biled shirt," brought along from the old home in utter ignorance of the real life I was to lead in the mines, I went on a pedestrian trip of observation down the river. The air of the morning was like champagne. The shaking of rockers or rattle of stones thrown from hoppers was little heard. Miners were washing their clothes by the side of the river. Camp-fires smoked everywhere, and many resting or sleeping men were stretched on buffalo-robes or blankets under trees and brush awnings. The trail was across rocky bars, stony points, and along the steep sides of the hills. I had sauntered for three or four miles when, on rounding a point, a busy and novel scene burst on my view. Files of Mexicans were coming and going, bearing earth in wooden bateas on their heads to make a dam in order to turn the stream. The work was being superintended by a stalwart American, the projector of the enterprise, in broad sombrero, and reclining on a serape spread on the bank, reminding one of a planter with his slaves. It proved to be Colonel James,

who was afterwards a distinguished criminal lawyer of San Francisco. I learned from him that the dam, after weeks of labor, was nearly completed; an hour more and the river would be flowing in an old channel. My curiosity was excited, and I remained to see the result of his venture. When the water was drawn off, the bed of the river presented the appearance of successive strata of hard slate, on edge, from three or four inches to a foot or more apart, the softer slate or shale between having been worn out and the depressions partly filled with sand and gravel. These strata on edge extended diagonally across the channel, forming an abundance of natural riffles to catch and retain the gold. My recollection is that the bed of the river had been laid bare to an extent of 200 yards in length by 60 feet in width. The great moment of expectation had come. By invitation I followed the colonel, who carried a pick, a pan, a shovel, and a small tin cup. It was plain there would be little gravel to wash, as the claim was on the slope of a "rapid," the grade being so great that most of the light material borne by the waters had been carried over. The shovel at once showed the wealth of one of the crevices, and I distinctly saw the colonel take his tin cup by the handle and scrape up from the bottom of the crevice a few handfuls that seemed to me to be half gold. I did not stay to see the gold washed, but I can safely say that I saw at least a thousand dollars go into the pan in half an hour.

I had seen enough to make a rosy report, and soon was a member of a company to turn the river near our camp on the bar. We dammed the river, the bed-rock of which was smooth and barren. It was no child's play, working in the water in the hot sun, sometimes up to our necks, laying boulders into a wall across the stream, and filling in above with the red clay of the mountain side. Miners would

MARYSVILLE BUTTES, A LANDMARK OF THE SACRAMENTO VALLEY.

A RUSH FOR NEW DIGGINGS.

pass and repass, envy us our claim, and chances were numerous to sell out interests at good figures; but we had come to California to make a fortune and return as soon as possible, and had no thought of selling a "sure thing" for a few thousand dollars. Alas, for great expectations! the river claim proved a failure. The earnings from washing the bar were nearly all gone, newcomers occupied all the ground not exhausted, and so we prepared to wander.

Pictures of camp-life crowd upon one. Who can forget the trains of loaded mules descending the mountain to the bar, with their attending Mexicans, raising a cloud of red dust and filling the air with their cries of "Hoopa!" "Mula!" and other expletives? Or the herds of wild cattle galloping down at breakneck speed, followed by swarthy and dust-begrimed *vaqueros*, "in sugar-loaf hats and legs of leather," and their headlong riding over the boulder-covered bar, swinging their riatas and lassoing the frightened bullocks for the butchers? Almost every store-tent had one or more rude tables where card-playing was indulged in "for the drinks," or where monte, the favorite gambling game, was played for dust, and at night these places were alive with miners purchasing supplies or trying their luck at the tables. As illustrative of the confidence of traders in the miners, I may here mention that in 1849 and for a year or two thereafter I never knew of a miner being refused credit for anything he wanted. A trader, a total stranger to me, who had heard a rumor of better diggings, once offered me his tent and contents at cost—about $2200, not a dollar to be paid until all the goods were sold. The miners on the bar were always ready to help others with purse or counsel, to share the last flapjack or frijole, or to espouse the cause of the injured. On Sunday or when the work of the day was over visits were exchanged without formality, and there was a general cordial mingling of men from all parts of the country and from every quarter of the globe. A considerable number of the first gold-seekers had brought books to the mines which passed from hand to hand, and there could be found a variety of volumes. Reading and argument were common sources of amusement, and in some of the tents one might hear the picking of improvised banjos.

The autumn of 1849 came on. The leaves had begun to fall; the winds in the towering pines and the murmur of the waters had more melancholy tones, the crickets sang more plaintively, the few birds were restless, and what with the want of claims to work and the coming of the rainy season it was needful that we

A ROUGH ROAD TO THE MINES.

seek another locality and prepare for the winter. I had already prospected the Rich Gulch of the Calaveras five or six miles away, had worked one day on a claim and had left a pick and shovel there as an evidence of ownership. The custom of the miners was to recognize mining tools in a claim as equivalent to possession, and in the absence of the claimant these tools were sufficient to hold the claim ten days. But my partner had fallen sick, and I was not able to leave him, and when we moved to the gulch eleven days after I had left it, we found the tools on the bank and two "jumpers" at work. We were too late, but we took the loss philosophically, as there was plenty of ground not taken. I understood afterward that the jumpers realized out of the claim about $7000 in six weeks, which was more than I pocketed from the gulch during the entire winter.

The Rich Gulch was a good type of what were called "dry diggings"—a long arroyo, dry in summer with a good stream running

A WOMAN IN THE MINES.

down it after a rain. Claims extended from bank to bank, and for sixteen feet in length. The brown and red soil from the hills had run down in the course of time and changed the channel of the stream in many places, and here the miners had to expend a good deal of labor on what they called "dead work," removing this hill soil, sometimes twenty feet in depth, to get to the old gold-bearing bed. As coöperation in the way of drainage had at this time been little thought of, each claim had to get rid of its own water in any way without much consideration for neighbors below. The amount of bottom dirt washed was slight compared with the whole removed, but in most claims it was exceedingly rich. Many a man had reason to remember with pleasure those winter diggings for the fortune they gave him. The gold was coarser and rougher than that of the rivers, not having been so much ground among the sand and gravel.

During the winter of 1849–50, the cost of living was extreme. As the season was a very wet one, the roads and trails were full of mudholes, in which supply wagons were stuck and mules and oxen mired. Wagons and animals were unloaded several times a day to extricate them from the mud, and in one instance at least fourteen days were spent on the road from Stockton, fifty miles away. Flour reached a dollar a pound, rice the same, pork and bacon a dollar and sixty cents a pound, saleratus sixteen dollars a pound, and spermaceti candles a dollar each. An ounce of gold was the price of a pick or shovel, and almost anything needed, except fresh beef, commanded a proportionate price. That all miners did not get rich is accounted for in the statement that it took a fair claim to pay expenses. The short duration of a placer claim, the loss of time in finding another, and the too general restlessness, tell the story of many failures to realize a fortune by even those who were the most lucky. Too often it was due to extravagance, gambling, or the guzzling of brandy or

the little community. Some of his decisions in cases of double ownership of claims did not square with our notions of justice. It was more than suspected that he had been " greased," *i. e.* bribed, to make them. A meeting of miners was called, and a committee was appointed to draft laws for the gulch. The alcalde, a stalwart and swarthy Creole, gathered his boon companions around him and tried to interrupt

PROSPECTING IN CALIFORNIA IN 1851.

whisky at eight dollars a bottle. But, drunk or sober, one was obliged to pay two ounces for a pair of pantaloons, a hundred dollars for a pair of long-legged boots, and four dollars expressage for a letter.

There were not more than four or five log-huts in the gulch, nine-tenths of all the miners living in common soldier tents, about eight feet square, the entire winter. Ours had a huge fireplace in front, that sent through our thin, cotton dwelling a warm glow from a fire of manzanita wood, which is nearly equal to hickory for fuel. The weather was at no time very cold, and we suffered no discomfort. February was like May in New York.

It was during this month that an alcalde, assuming to have derived his authority from an alcalde at Stockton, began to give law to

the reading of the proposed laws, loudly declaring that he was alcalde and was going to govern the camp at any hazard. But the odds against him soon cooled his courage, and though pistols were exhibited and violence was threatened, no blows were struck. The next morning the blustering alcalde retired from the gulch forever. The new laws constituted the first code (so far as I know) adopted in the mines, and sufficed for the settlement of disputes for a long time.

I neglected to state in the proper place that in the early part of October business took me to Sacramento, and I only go back to relate an incident which will help to illustrate mining life as it was in California. The trip was made in a large mule-wagon dignified with the name of stage, and consumed nearly three days. Late

A MINERS' BALL.

in the afternoon of the first day, the driver said it was about time to camp, but he remarked that at a house four miles farther on there was a woman. Now a woman in the mines was a rarity; we had had a glimpse of one on the bar during the summer, and that was all. It was at once put to vote to determine whether we should camp or go on. Of course there can be no doubt of the result. In the evening we halted in front of a log house with a very steep roof made of tules, and applied for supper. The hostess, a tall, raw-boned Missourian, on presenting our bill in the morning, to weigh the dust put a cube of lead in the scales that approximated the size of a hymn-book, but the generosity and chivalry of the early miner and the rarity of women combined to make us ignore it.

In the spring of 1850 I returned to San Francisco, and in May, with one companion and four animals, went around the bay to Sonoma and from thence began the exploration of that unknown region from Sonoma to Oregon. Wandering miners we knew had already gone over the mountains and found gold on the Trinity. Were there not other streams flowing into the Pacific north of San Francisco, and might not all be auriferous as well? It was a tedious, eventful, but fruitless journey of forty-seven days, almost wholly over mountains trodden by Digger Indians and, what was more perilous, by ferocious grizzlies, of which we saw five at one time. No gold was found in any stream till we reached the Trinity, thirty-six days from San Francisco, and there the diggings were not remarkably rich. The hardest toilers reported but from eight to ten dollars a day. The style of mining did not differ from that which I have described, except that the pay dirt was carried a considerable distance in buckets from high and dry bars down to the river to be washed. Something better must be found, and a prospecting party was sent on an exploring expedition farther north.

There were some queer distinctions in those days. One Sunday, going to the butcher's booth, I found a customer ahead of me, who inquired if he could not have a piece of a liver which was hanging on a tree in plain sight.

"Don't know if you can or not," said the butcher.

"I'd like to know why? I've been trading with you all along, and never asked for liver before; but I want some variety now."

"Stand around and let me look at you. No, you can't have any liver."

"Well, why?"

"There ain't enough to go round. I have to have some rule about givin' it out, and I have decided that no miner can have a scrap of liver from me unless he wears a canvas patch on the seat of his pants."

The canvas patch was a badge of precedence as well recognized in our camp on the Trinity as the star of the Order of the Garter is in Great Britain.

On the 3d of July two of our prospecting party returned and whispered the news that rich bars had been found on a stream full of salmon farther north, and the next morning we were off. The night of the fourth and fifth gave us the variety of a snow-storm, from which we took shelter under a roof of spruce boughs inclosed on three sides with the same material. After eleven days of exhausting climbing and descending steep and lofty mountains, tearing our clothes in the tangled chaparral, camping at night in the chilly air where the water from melting snows made green pastures for our mules, we reached the virgin diggings on Salmon River. There was no evidence that any white man had preceded us. The bars by the river were untouched; an interminable forest stretched all over the mountain sides and up and down the winding river, unmarked by the woodman's ax — not dense, but relieved by glades and openings, and but for the steepness of the mountains easily traveled.

Here was a newer scene and a more novel life. There were but eleven Americans of us all told, and a wide and rugged region lay between us and others of our race. Indians came in squads, shyly viewed us, made their comments, and passed on. They were superior to the Diggers of the California valleys, and were of the blood of the Modocs, who committed such atrocities in the lava-beds twenty years after.

My partner in the new diggings was a printer from the establishment of Harper & Brothers, who had come around the Horn as one of Stevenson's regiment in 1847. Displeased with our allotment of claims, which were too wet, we resolved to take chances alone with the Indians. So one fine morning we quietly packed the mules, forded the river at a shallow place, and proceeded to go we knew not whither. A tramp of eight or nine miles on elk and Indian paths, along a ridge that rose two hundred feet above the river, brought us to a point at the junction of streams. Crossing the north fork we made our camp on a high bar covered with young pines and oaks and already occupied by an Indian family, with whom we hastened to make friends by gifts of beads, bracelets, and other trinkets captivating to the savage. We had no tent, and made our camp by inclosing a small space with ropes tied to saplings for corner posts, to keep the mules, turned loose upon the bar, away from our bed and provisions.

Here, again, was a still fresher and wilder

CORRESPONDING AGENT

Cargo of Hams value $ 5000
Burnt at the last fire ___ 2000
Rats eaten ___ 1000
Customs & duties ___ 1000
Freigth ___ 1000
Summa All square !!

Cheap and easy way of going to the mines.

Gent. How much ?
Waiter. Dinner 10. Wine 20. Desert 30.
Gent. Shillings ?
Wait. Shillings? No !!! Dollars !!!

DEPARTURE FOR EL DORADO

Life preserver in the mines:

TO ADMIRERS OF MUSIC

Gentl. & Ladies take your seats The best chance to make your Fortune in five hours is opened for you !! Quick ! Quick ! if you dont do it this time you will never do it again !!!

Jenny Lind can be heard every evening for only two Rials a glass !!!

As I am in want of patients for my Sarsaparilla, and as it is the only thing I have to live upon, I shall swallow it myself.

Director of the X. Mining Company

A Company of prospecting miners.

Gamblers.

SAN FRANCISCO CARICATURES.
(FROM AN OLD LITHOGRAPH BY JUSTH AND QUIROT, IN THE COLLECTION OF COMMANDER JOHN R. BARTLETT.)

life. Cut loose from our kind we trusted to uncorrupted natives, and did not trust in vain. A little prospecting gave glowing promise. Fifty cents to the pan was not infrequent. The rocker was speedily screwed together and real work begun. The river was high from melting snows on the mountains, and the portions of the bars out of water were small, but our first day's work yielded about fourteen ounces. Thus we

passed two weeks, mining in patches and with varying success, when miners on the Klamath, hearing from the Indians that white men were working on one of the branches above, pushed up the country to see if somebody had not something better than they. Among the new-comers were a few Texans who laid claim to a very wet bar down the river, and were soon doing well. Somehow a rumor came to our isolated camp that big lump diggings had been found to the northeast on Scott River, and the Texans were on the wing. My partner took the big lump fever and went along. I associated myself with three others, entire strangers, and we took possession of Texas Bar, threw a slight breakwater of clay along the river's edge to stop the water from spreading over the bar, and then cutting a drain to the bed rock from the lower end, we had comparatively dry ground and went to washing. We worked early and late, sometimes not ceasing till starlight, for all our provisions except flour were exhausted, and our only reliance was on the Indians, who supplied us with salmon in exchange for trinkets. This kind of living could not last, and we strained every nerve to get as much gold from the claim as possible. The average spoil of a day was rather more than a hundred dollars to the man. About the middle of September a conference of the few miners left on the river was held at the Forks, and as the diggings were too good to abandon it was agreed to despatch six men and twenty mules to Trinidad on the coast for supplies to last the winter. The train was made up and took the trail at once. Haste was necessary, as even flour, the last link to civilization, was nearly gone.

Meanwhile the mining went on. Few in numbers, and without provisions, our position could easily become critical. Our relief party came back suddenly ; it could not go through. The Indians on the Klamath were hostile. Oregon men had shot some Indian dogs down the river, and the young bucks had retaliated by killing a horse. Thus began the so-called Klamath war, that cost the State, and ultimately the nation, a large sum of money. The miners were without delay in council. My party of four had scant rations for four days. At four o'clock we abandoned claims, picks, and shovels and commenced a forced march for the Trinity. I shall not detail the experiences of that hurried tramp on foot over the roughest of mountains. It is enough to say that one day four of us subsisted on a ground squirrel and a woodpecker, and the last day on copious draughts of water when fortunate enough to find it. And when at last we struck the Trinity it was only to be disappointed. The river was deserted ; the miners had gone to winter quarters in the "dry diggings" at Weaverville. Wet, weary, and disgusted, with a dreary prospect for supper, we crawled up the bank and dropped down at a fallen tree to make a fire for the night. The mules were relieved of their packs and left to graze. They were too nearly dead to stray. A smoke was seen a few hundred yards away. I went to reconnoiter. A Mexican pack-train

was encamping. Meeting two muleteers gathering faggots for the fire, I inquired what they had to sell. "*Ninguna cosa*" ("Not a thing") was the answer. Going on to the camp-fire I inquired if they would sell me something to eat. The reply in Spanish was that they only sold by the cargo. Then I observed, sitting by the fire and smoking a cigarette, a Mexican whom I recognized. Stepping up to him I asked in Spanish if he did not know me. He said no.

"But, Don Fernando, do you not remember the man who bought an iron-gray mule of you on the Calaveras last year ? "

"*Ah, si, señor*," and he grasped my hand. I explained the situation in as few words as possible. Instantly, snapping his thumb and finger, he called out to two men :

"*Mira, hombres ! Ven aca ! Dos quintales de harina, carne seca, panoche, y todas cosas por los Americanos ; anda !*" ("Attention, men ! Come here ! Two quintals of flour, dried beef, raw sugar, and everything for the Americans ; travel ! ")

"How much for it all?" I inquired.

"*Ninguno centavo ; gracias á Dios, señor*" ("Not a cent ; thanks to God, sir "), he replied with emphasis, and the *hombres* carried an abundant supply of substantials to our camp. That tall and swarthy Don in brown sugar-loaf hat, his head thrust through a hole in the middle of a blanket that served for a cloak, standing in his spurs, the rowels of which were four inches in diameter, is not a figure to be readily forgotten.

There was an incredible amount of cooking that night. Slapjacks and sugar, ropes of dried beef broiled on the coals, coffee made of an extract—everything was welcome. It was a merry night. I never knew before the intoxication of eating. We cooked, ate, lay back upon the blankets, told stories, returned to the cooking again, and so alternated until sleep overtook us in the warm glow of the fire.

When, in the afternoon, we made our entry into Weaverville, a scattered village of about four hundred miners' cabins, Don Fernando found himself in trouble. He could find but one trader with money in the whole town—and he was a type of the monopolists who have since become the curse of California. He offered the Mexican about half-price for his cargo, and there was no other place to which to carry the goods. It was now our turn. It was suggested that we help Don Fernando out. He had been offered $1200. We told him that we did not want his goods, as we did not know what we were going to do, but we would make the trader pay more for them.

"Tell him we offer you $1500." In a short time we learned that $1600 had been bid.

"Tell him we will give $1800."

Again came a bid of $1900. We offered $2000, and soon were confronted by an angry Missourian, who "was n't goin' to have any durned Yankee git in 'tween him and a greaser in a trade." So he jumped our bid $200. Don Fernando in a whisper said it was *bastante* (enough), and the Missourian was the buyer. We had paid off some of our obligations to Don Fernando and had made a little stir in the new diggings.

The autumn of 1850 was unlike that of 1849. The miners in the dry ravines had thrown up on the banks large quantities of pay-dirt from the beds, and were continuing their work hoping to be able to wash. But little rain fell till the following March. The miners scattered again along the Trinity to pay expenses, and I with others departed for Sacramento.

The early summer of 1851 found me in the mines at Nevada City, in the richest gold-producing section of California, or perhaps of the world. The two mining towns of Nevada and Grass Valley are but four miles apart, and that either of these is more populous than any other town in the Sierra Nevada is evidence of the great wealth of the region. The miners of Nevada County originated or adopted most of the improved methods for facilitating washing and saving gold. The long tom came into use early as the successor of the rocker. It was a trough of boards ten or twelve feet long, two feet wide on the bottom, with sides eight or ten inches high, and was furnished with a perforated sheet-iron plate three feet long, which had the end part curved upward to stop the stones and gravel, while the water, sand, and small gravel dropped through into a riffle-box below, set on an incline to allow the lighter matter to pass off with the water. The long tom was put on an easy grade and supplied with a constant stream of flowing water, enough to drive and wash all the earth thrown into it down upon the perforated screen. Two or more men shoveled the earth into the tom, and one threw out the stones from the screen with a fork or square-pointed shovel, when they were sufficiently washed. As the claim was worked back, the long tom was extended by means of sluice boxes until a dozen or more miners were shoveling dirt into them on both sides. Afterward it was found that by putting riffles into the sluice boxes the long tom could be dispensed with, and miles of sluices of all sizes were seen, some supplied with a few inches of running water, miners' measure, while others bore torrents of the muddy fluid. The sluice requiring a rapid flow of water was set on a grade of say four inches to twelve feet in length. It is plain that in a short distance the pay dirt would have to be lifted higher than the miner's head. A descending bed-rock added to the difficulty,

and sometimes the earth was thrown by one set of miners up on a platform to be shoveled by another set into the sluice. Numerous small boulders were kept in the sluice, around and over which the water boiled and leaped, dissolving the clay. When the gold was fine and difficult to save, quicksilver was poured into the sluices to catch it, the riffles arresting the amalgam as it moved down.

More and more, as experience was gained, water was made to do the labor of men. Instead of carrying the dirt in buckets to the river to be washed, the river was carried to the dirt. Ditches were dug at great expense and water from them was sold at a dollar an inch for ten hours' use, and often it was resold in its muddy state one, two, and three times at decreasing rates. The water belonged to the ditch owner as long as it could be used. The fact may here be noted that one of the first ditches constructed was that from Rock Creek to the hill diggings about Nevada City. It was nine miles long, and cost about ten thousand dollars, and so rich were the diggings and so active the demand for water that the enterprise paid for itself in six weeks.

It was early discovered that the river gorges in which the first mining was done — those deep channels from the high Sierra — cut across ancient river-beds filled with auriferous gravel, the bottoms of which were hundreds of feet above the beds of the modern streams. From these deposits of far-back ages much of the gold found on the later river bars had come, and these ancient storehouses, exposed by the wear and tear of centuries, led to another kind of mining. Great canals from high up the rivers were carried with fine engineering skill and large outlays of labor and money, without the aid of foreign capital but by the pluck, purses, and brawny arms of miners along frightful precipices, across cañons in lofty flumes and through tunnels to the ancient filled river channels. Here the water was carried down the banks in strong iron tubes or hose, and large quantities were compressed through nozzles and thrown with terrific force against the banks of auriferous gravel. Ditches dug in the earth on a moderate grade, or sluices of lumber, caught the muddy debris and separated the gold, leaving it on the bottom. A steady throw of this water against a bank, directed with a miner's judgment, was kept up for days and even months without cessation night or day. This was called hydraulic mining, and it was introduced into California in 1852. To facilitate the work of the monitor or water-cannon that shot the compressed stream, tunnels were run into the banks where they were hard and tons of powder were exploded in them at a single blast, pulverizing the deposit to the extent of acres and often to a depth of more than a hundred feet.

In the great mining region of California, which has given to the world more gold than any other area of like extent on the globe, all this is now over. The fiat of courts has gone forth that no debris of any kind can be allowed to be dumped into any stream or its affluent to the danger of property below or to the impeding of navigable waters. Thus has been destroyed the market value of hundreds of miles of canals, great artificial lakes to store the waters of winter, and vast deposits of auriferous gravel — in a word, a hundred million dollars in mining property. Thousands of miners who have exhausted their energies and the best part of their lives in the mines have, with their families, been reduced to poverty and distress.

The old miner, full of cherished memories of that wonderful past, on revisiting the scenes of his early labors sees no winding line of miners by the river marge, with their rattling rockers or long toms; no smoke from camp-fire or chimney arises from the depths of gorges; cabins are gone; no laughter nor cheery voice comes up from the cañons; no ounce a day is dried by the supper fire. Gone are most of the oaks and pines from the mountain-sides; the beds of the rivers are covered deep with the accumulated debris of years, over which the water, once clear and cold from the melting snows of the Sierra, goes sluggishly, laden with mud, in serpentine windings from bank to bank. On the tableland above, in the chasms made by hydraulic power in the pleiocene drift, the hollow columns of iron that once compressed the water stand rusting away; the monitors lie dismantled like artillery in a captured fortress. All is silence and desolation where once was the roar of water and the noise of busy life.

The same red and brown soil is beneath your feet, the same alternation of ridges and gorges is here, the same skies unflecked by clouds from May to November are overhead; the same pure air is left to breathe in spite of courts and monopolies; a considerable portion of the soil is cultivated; scattered here and there over the mountain slopes are homes surrounded with flowers and fruits — but the early miner sees it all with the sad belief that the glory is gone.

The early miner has never been truly painted. I protest against the flippant style and eccentric rhetoric of those writers who have made him a terror, or who, seizing upon a sporadic case of extreme oddity, some drunken, brawling wretch, have given a caricature to the world as the typical miner. The so-called literature that treats of the golden era is too extravagant in this direction. In all my personal experience in mining-camps from 1849 to 1854 there was not a case of bloodshed, robbery, theft, or actual violence. I doubt if a more orderly society was ever known. How could it be otherwise? The pioneers were young, ardent, uncorrupted, most of them well educated and from the best families in the East. The early miner was ambitious, energetic, and enterprising. No undertaking was too great to daunt him. The pluck and resources exhibited by him in attempting mighty projects with nothing but his courage and his brawny arms to carry them out was phenomenal. His generosity was profuse and his sympathy active, knowing no distinction of race. His sentiment that justice is sacred was never dulled. His services were at command to settle differences peaceably, or with pistol in hand to right a grievous wrong to a stranger. His capacity for self-government never has been surpassed. Of a glorious epoch, he was of a glorious race.

E. G. Waite.

23

Across the Plains in the Donner Party

Virginia Reed Murphy

W. TABER.

"A PIONEER PALACE CAR."

ADAPTED FROM A SKETCH BY A. P. HILL.

ACROSS THE PLAINS IN THE DONNER PARTY (1846).

A PERSONAL NARRATIVE OF THE OVERLAND TRIP TO CALIFORNIA.

I WAS a child when we started to California, yet I remember the journey well and I have cause to remember it, as our little band of emigrants who drove out of Springfield, Illinois, that spring morning of 1846 have since been known in history as the "Ill-fated Donner party" of "Martyr Pioneers." My father, James F. Reed, was the originator of the party, and the Donner brothers, George and Jacob, who lived just a little way out of Springfield, decided to join him.

All the previous winter we were preparing for the journey—and right here let me say that we suffered vastly more from fear of the Indians before starting than we did on the plains; at least this was my case. In the long winter evenings Grandma Keyes used to tell me Indian stories. She had an aunt who had been taken prisoner by the savages in the early settlement of Virginia and Kentucky and had remained a captive in their hands five years before she made her escape. I was fond of these stories and evening after evening would go into grandma's room, sitting with my back close against the wall so that no warrior could slip behind me with a tomahawk. I would coax her to tell me more about her aunt, and would sit listening to the recital of the fearful deeds of the savages, until it seemed to me that everything in the room, from the high old-fashioned bed-posts down even to the shovel and tongs in the chimney corner, was transformed into the dusky tribe in paint and feathers, all ready for the war dance. So when I was told that we were going to California and would have to pass through a region peopled by Indians, you can imagine how I felt.

Our wagons, or the "Reed wagons," as they were called, were all made to order and I can say without fear of contradiction that nothing like our family wagon ever started across the plains. It was what might be called a two-story wagon or "Pioneer palace car," attached to a regular immigrant train. My mother, though a young woman, was not strong and had been in delicate health for many years, yet when sorrows and dangers came upon her she was the bravest of the brave. Grandma Keyes, who was seventy-five years of age, was an invalid, confined to her bed. Her sons in Springfield, Gersham and James W. Keyes, tried to dissuade her from the long and fatiguing journey, but in vain; she would not be parted from my mother, who was her only daughter. So the car in which she was to ride was planned to give comfort. The entrance was on the side, like that of an old-fashioned stage coach, and one stepped into a small room, as it were, in the centre of the wagon. At the right and left were spring seats with comfortable high backs, where one could sit and ride with as much ease as on the seats of a Concord coach. In this little room was placed a tiny sheet-iron stove, whose pipe, running through the top of the wagon, was prevented by a circle of tin from setting fire to the canvas cover. A board about a foot wide extended over the wheels on either side the full length of the wagon, thus forming the foundation for a large and roomy second story in which were placed our beds. Under the spring seats were compartments in which were stored many articles useful for the journey, such as a well filled work basket and a full assortment of medicines, with lint and bandages for dressing wounds. Our clothing was packed—not in Saratoga trunks—but in strong canvas bags plainly marked. Some of mama's young friends

365

added a looking-glass, hung directly opposite the door, in order, as they said, that my mother might not forget to keep her good looks, and strange to say, when we had to leave this wagon, standing like a monument on the Salt Lake desert, the glass was still unbroken. I have often thought how pleased the Indians must have been when they found this mirror which gave them back the picture of their own dusky faces.

ever started across the plains with more provisions or a better outfit for the journey; and yet we reached California almost destitute and nearly out of clothing.

The family wagon was drawn by four yoke of oxen, large Durham steers at the wheel. The other wagons were drawn by three yoke each. We had saddle horses and cows, and last but not least my pony. He was a beauty and his name was Billy. I can scarcely remember

THIRSTY OXEN STAMPEDING FOR WATER.

We had two wagons loaded with provisions. Everything in that line was bought that could be thought of. My father started with supplies enough to last us through the first winter in California, had we made the journey in the usual time of six months. Knowing that books were always scarce in a new country, we also took a good library of standard works. We even took a cooking stove which never had had a fire in it, and was destined never to have, as we cachéd it in the desert. Certainly no family

when I was taught to sit a horse. I only know that when a child of seven I was the proud owner of a pony and used to go riding with papa. That was the chief pleasure to which I looked forward in crossing the plains, to ride my pony every day. But a day came when I had no pony to ride, the poor little fellow gave out. He could not endure the hardships of ceaseless travel. When I was forced to part with him I cried until I was ill, and sat in the back of the wagon watching him be-

CROSSING WATER TO ESCAPE A PRAIRIE FIRE.

come smaller and smaller as we drove on, until I could see him no more.

Never can I forget the morning when we bade farewell to kindred and friends. The Donners were there, having driven in the evening before with their families, so that we might get an early start. Grandma Keyes was carried out of the house and placed in the wagon on a large feather bed, propped up with pillows. Her sons implored her to remain and end her days with them, but she could not be separated from her only daughter. We were surrounded by loved ones, and there stood all my little schoolmates who had come to kiss me good-by. My father with tears in his eyes tried to smile as one friend after another grasped his hand in a last farewell. Mama was overcome with grief. At last we were all in the wagons, the drivers cracked their whips, the oxen moved slowly forward and the long journey had begun.

Could we have looked into the future and have seen the misery before us, these lines would never have been written. But we were full of hope and did not dream of sorrow. I can now see our little caravan of ten or twelve wagons as we drove out of old Springfield, my little black-eyed sister Patty sitting upon the bed, holding up the wagon cover so that Grandma might have a last look at her old home.

That was the 14th day of April, 1846. Our party numbered thirty-one, and consisted chiefly of three families, the other members being young men, some of whom came as drivers.

The Donner family were George and Tamsen Donner and their five children, and Jacob and Elizabeth Donner and their seven children. Our family numbered nine, not counting three drivers — my father and mother, James Frazier and Margaret W. Reed, Grandma Keyes, my little sister Patty (now Mrs. Frank Lewis, of Capitola), and two little brothers, James F. Reed, Jr., and Thomas K. Reed, Eliza Williams and her brother Baylis, and lastly myself. Eliza had been a domestic in our family for many years, and was anxious to see California.

Many friends camped with us the first night out and my uncles traveled on for several days before bidding us a final farewell. It seemed strange to be riding in ox-teams, and we children were afraid of the oxen, thinking they could go wherever they pleased as they had no bridles. Milt Elliott, a knight of the whip, drove our family wagon. He had worked for years in my father's large saw-mill on the Sangamon River. The first bridge we came to, Milt had to stop the wagon and let us out. I remember that I called to him to be sure to make the oxen hit the bridge, and not to forget that grandma was in the wagon. How he laughed at the idea of the oxen missing the bridge! I soon found that Milt, with his "whoa," "haw," and "gee," could make the oxen do just as he pleased.

Nothing of much interest happened until we reached what is now Kansas. The first Indians we met were the Caws, who kept the ferry, and had to take us over the Caw River. I watched them closely, hardly daring to draw my breath, and feeling sure they would sink the boat in the middle of the stream, and was very thankful when I found they were not like grandma's Indians. Every morning, when the wagons were ready to start, papa and I would jump on our horses, and go ahead to pick out a camping-ground. In our party were many who rode on horseback, but mama seldom did;

SCOTT'S BLUFFS (FROM NATURE, 1890).

she preferred the wagon, and did not like to leave grandma, although Patty took upon herself this charge, and could hardly be persuaded to leave grandma's side. Our little home was so comfortable, that mama could sit reading and chatting with the little ones, and almost forget that she was really crossing the plains.

Grandma Keyes improved in health and spirits every day until we came to the Big Blue River, which was so swollen that we could not cross, but had to lie by and make rafts on which to take the wagons over. As soon as we stopped traveling, grandma began to fail, and on the 29th day of May she died. It seemed hard to bury her in the wilderness, and travel on, and we were afraid that the Indians would de-

CHIMNEY ROCK, ON THE NORTH PLATTE (1890).

stroy her grave, but her death here, before our troubles began, was providential, and nowhere on the whole road could we have found so beautiful a resting place. By this time many emigrants had joined our company, and all turned out to assist at the funeral. A coffin was hewn out of a cottonwood tree, and John Denton, a young man from Springfield, found a large gray stone on which he carved with deep letters the name of "Sarah Keyes; born in Virginia," giving age and date of birth. She was buried under the shade of an oak, the slab being placed at the foot of the grave, on which were planted wild flowers growing in the sod. A minister in our party, the Rev. J. A. Cornwall, tried to give words of comfort as we stood about this lonely grave. Strange to say, that grave has never been disturbed; the wilderness blossomed into the city of Manhattan, Kansas, and we have been told that the city cemetery surrounds the grave of Sarah Keyes.

As the river remained high and there was no prospect of fording it, the men went to work cutting down trees, hollowing out logs and making rafts on which to take the wagons over. These logs, about twenty-five feet in length, were united by cross timbers, forming rafts, which were firmly lashed to stakes driven into the bank. Ropes were attached to both ends, by which the rafts were pulled back and forth across the river. The banks of this stream being steep, our heavily laden wagons had to be let down carefully with ropes, so that the wheels might run into the hollowed logs. This was no easy task when you take into consideration that in these wagons were women and children, who could cross the rapid river in no other way. Finally the dangerous work was accomplished and we resumed our journey.

The road at first was rough and led through a timbered country, but after striking the great valley of the Platte the road was good and the country beautiful. Stretching out before us as far as the eye could reach was a valley as green as emerald, dotted here and there with

Traveling up the smooth valley of the Platte, we passed Court House Rock, Chimney Rock and Scott's Bluffs, and made from fifteen to twenty miles a day, shortening or lengthening the distance in order to secure a good camping ground. At night when we drove into camp, our wagons were placed so as to form a circle or corral, into which our cattle were driven, after grazing, to prevent the Indians from stealing them, the camp-fires and tents being on the outside. There were many expert riflemen in the party and we never lacked for game. The plains were alive with buffalo, and herds could be seen every day coming to the Platte

AN EMIGRANT ENCAMPMENT.

flowers of every imaginable color, and through this valley flowed the grand old Platte, a wide, rapid, shallow stream. Our company now numbered about forty wagons, and, for a time, we were commanded by Col. William H. Russell, then by George Donner. Exercise in the open air under bright skies, and freedom from peril combined to make this part of our journey an ideal pleasure trip. How I enjoyed riding my pony, galloping over the plain, gathering wild flowers! At night the young folks would gather about the camp fire chatting merrily, and often a song would be heard, or some clever dancer would give us a barn-door jig on the hind gate of a wagon.

to drink. The meat of the young buffalo is excellent and so is that of the antelope, but the antelope are so fleet of foot it is difficult to get a shot at one. I witnessed many a buffalo hunt and more than once was in the chase close beside my father. A buffalo will not attack one unless wounded. When he sees the hunter he raises his shaggy head, gazes at him for a moment, then turns and runs; but when he is wounded he will face his pursuer. The only danger lay in a stampede, for nothing could withstand the onward rush of these massive creatures, whose tread seemed to shake the prairie.

Antelope and buffalo steaks were the main

OLD TRAIL CROSSING HORSESHOE CREEK, A TRIBUTARY OF THE PLATTE.

article on our bill-of-fare for weeks, and no tonic was needed to give zest for the food; our appetites were a marvel. Eliza soon discovered that cooking over a camp fire was far different from cooking on a stove or range, but all hands assisted her. I remember that she had the cream all ready for the churn as we drove into the South Fork of the Platte, and while we were fording the grand old stream she went on with her work, and made several pounds of butter. We found no trouble in crossing the Platte, the only danger being in quicksand. The stream being wide, we had to stop the wagon now and then to give the oxen a few moments' rest. At Fort Laramie, two hundred miles farther on, we celebrated the fourth of July in fine style. Camp was pitched earlier than usual and we prepared a grand dinner. Some of my father's friends in Springfield had given him a bottle of good old brandy, which he agreed to drink at a certain hour of this day looking to the east, while his friends in Illinois were to drink a toast to his success from a companion bottle with their faces turned west, the difference in time being carefully estimated; and at the hour agreed upon, the health of our friends in Springfield was drunk with great enthusiasm. At Fort Laramie was a party of Sioux, who were on the war path going to fight the Crows or Blackfeet. The Sioux are fine-looking Indians and I was not in the least afraid of them. They fell in love with my pony and set about bargaining to buy him. They brought buffalo robes and beautifully tanned buckskin, pretty beaded moccasins, and ropes made of grass, and placing these articles in a heap alongside several of their ponies, they made my father understand by signs that they would give them all for Billy and his rider. Papa smiled and shook his head; then the number of ponies was increased and, as a last tempting inducement, they brought an old coat, that had been worn by some poor soldier, thinking my father could not withstand the brass buttons!

On the sixth of July we were again on the march. The Sioux were several days in passing our caravan, not on account of the length of our train, but because there were so many Sioux. Owing to the fact that our wagons were strung so far apart, they could have massacred our whole party without much loss to themselves. Some of our company became alarmed, and the rifles were cleaned out and loaded, to let the warriors see that we were prepared to fight; but the Sioux never showed any inclination to disturb us. Their curiosity was annoying, however, and our wagon with its conspicuous stove-pipe and looking-glass attracted their attention. They were continually swarming about trying to get a look at themselves in the mirror, and their desire to possess my pony was so strong that at last I had to ride in the wagon and let one of the drivers take charge of Billy. This I did not like, and in order to see how far back the line of warriors extended, I picked up a large field-glass which hung on a rack, and as I pulled it out with a click, the warriors jumped back, wheeled their ponies and scattered. This pleased me greatly, and I told my mother I could fight the whole Sioux tribe with a spy-glass, and as revenge for forcing me to ride in the wagon, whenever they came near trying to get a peep at their war-paint and feathers, I would raise the glass and laugh to see them dart away in terror.

A new route had just been opened by Lansford W. Hastings, called the " Hastings Cut-off,"[1] which passed along the southern shore of the Great Salt Lake rejoining the old "Fort Hall Emigrant" road on the Humboldt. It was said to shorten the distance three hundred miles. Much time was lost in debating which course to pursue; Bridger and Vasques, who were in charge of the fort, sounded the praises of the new road. My father was so eager to reach California that he was quick to take ad-

1 For an account of Hastings, see THE CENTURY for December 1890, p. 176.— ED.

vantage of any means to shorten the distance, and we were assured by Hastings and his party that the only bad part was the forty-mile drive through the desert by the shore of the lake. None of our party knew then, as we learned afterwards, that these men had an interest in the road, being employed by Hastings. But for the advice of these parties we should have continued on the old Fort Hall road. Our company had increased in numbers all along the line, and was now composed of some of the very best people and some of the worst. The greater portion of our company went by the old road and reached California in safety. Eighty-seven persons took the "Hastings Cut-off," including the Donners, Breens, Reeds, Murphys (not the Murphys of Santa Clara County), C. T. Stanton, John Denton, Wm. McClutchen, Wm. Eddy, Louis Keseburg, and many others too numerous to mention in a short article like this. And these are the unfortunates who have since been known as the "Donner Party."

On the morning of July 31 we parted with our traveling companions, some of whom had become very dear friends, and, without a suspicion of impending disaster, set off in high spirits on the "Hastings Cut-off"; but a few days showed us that the road was not as it had been represented. We were seven days in reaching Weber Cañon, and Hastings, who was guiding a party in advance of our train, left a note by the wayside warning us that the road through Weber Cañon was impassable and advising us to select a road over the mountains, the outline of which he attempted to give on paper. These directions were so vague that C. T. Stanton, William Pike, and my father rode on in advance and overtook Hastings and tried to induce him to return and guide our party. He refused, but came back over a portion of the road, and from a high mountain endeavored to point out the general course. Over this road my father traveled alone, taking notes, and blazing trees, to assist him in retracing his course, and reaching camp after an absence of four days. Learning of the hardships of the advance train, the party decided

to cross towards the lake. Only those who have passed through this country on horseback can appreciate the situation. There was absolutely no road, not even a trail. The cañon wound around among the hills. Heavy underbrush had to be cut away and used for making a road bed. While cutting our way step by step through the "Hastings Cut-off," we were overtaken and joined by the Graves family, consisting of W. F. Graves, his wife and eight children, his son-in-law Jay Fosdick, and a young man by the name of John Snyder. Finally we reached the end of the cañon where it looked as though our wagons would have to be abandoned. It seemed impossible for the oxen to pull them up the steep hill and the bluffs beyond, but we doubled teams and the work was, at last, accomplished, almost every yoke in the train being required to pull up each wagon. While in this cañon Stanton and Pike came into camp; they had suffered greatly on account of the exhaustion of their horses and had come near perishing. Worn with travel and greatly discouraged we reached the shore of the Great Salt Lake. It had taken an entire month, instead of a week, and our cattle were not fit to cross the desert.

We were now encamped in a valley called "Twenty

NATURAL BRIDGE ON LA PRÊLE RIVER.

THE EMIGRANT TRAIL THROUGH THE BAD LANDS, WYOMING.

Wells." The water in these wells was pure and cold, welcome enough after the alkaline pools from which we had been forced to drink. We prepared for the long drive across the desert and laid in, as we supposed, an ample supply of water and grass. This desert had been represented to us as only forty miles wide but we found it nearer eighty. It was a dreary, desolate, alkali waste; not a living thing could be seen; it seemed as though the hand of death had been laid upon the country. We started in the evening, traveled all that night, and the following day and night — two nights and one day of suffering from thirst and heat by day and piercing cold by night. When the third night fell and we saw the barren waste stretching away apparently as boundless as

when we started, my father determined to go ahead in search of water. Before starting he instructed the drivers, if the cattle showed signs of giving out to take them from the wagons and follow him. He had not been gone long before the oxen began to fall to the ground from thirst and exhaustion. They were unhitched at once and driven ahead. My father coming back met the drivers with the cattle within ten miles of water and instructed them to return as soon as the animals had satisfied their thirst. He reached us about daylight. We waited all that day in the desert looking for the return of our drivers, the other wagons going on out of sight. Towards night the situation became desperate and we had only a few drops of water left; another night there meant death. We

GREAT DESERT TO THE WEST OF SALT LAKE.

must set out on foot and try to reach some of the wagons. Can I ever forget that night in the desert, when we walked mile after mile in the darkness, every step seeming to be the very last we could take! Suddenly all fatigue was banished by fear; through the night came a swift rushing sound of one of the young steers crazed

oxen before reaching Bridger's Fort from drinking poisoned water found standing in pools, and had bought at the fort two yoke of young steers, but now all were gone, and my father and his family were left in the desert, eight hundred miles from California, seemingly helpless. We realized that our wagons must be abandoned.

REGISTER ROCK, IDAHO, A LANDMARK OF WESTERN EMIGRATION.

by thirst and apparently bent upon our destruction. My father, holding his youngest child in his arms and keeping us all close behind him, drew his pistol, but finally the maddened beast turned and dashed off into the darkness. Dragging ourselves along about ten miles, we reached the wagon of Jacob Donner. The family were all asleep, so we children lay down on the ground. A bitter wind swept over the desert, chilling us through and through. We crept closer together, and, when we complained of the cold, papa placed all five of our dogs around us, and only for the warmth of these faithful creatures we should doubtless have perished.

At daylight papa was off to learn the fate of his cattle, and was told that all were lost, except one cow and an ox. The stock, scenting the water, had rushed on ahead of the men, and had probably been stolen by the Indians, and driven into the mountains, where all traces of them were lost. A week was spent here on the edge of the desert in a fruitless search. Almost every man in the company turned out, hunting in all directions, but our eighteen head of cattle were never found. We had lost our best yoke of

The company kindly let us have two yoke of oxen, so with our ox and cow yoked together we could bring one wagon, but, alas! not the one which seemed so much like a home to us, and in which grandma had died. Some of the company went back with papa and assisted him in cacheing everything that could not be packed in one wagon. A cache was made by digging a hole in the ground, in which a box or the bed of a wagon was placed. Articles to be buried were packed into this box, covered with boards, and the earth thrown in upon them, and thus they were hidden from sight. Our provisions were divided among the company. Before leaving the desert camp, an inventory of provisions on hand was taken, and it was found that the supply was not sufficient to last us through to California, and as if to render the situation more terrible, a storm came on during the night and the hill-tops became white with snow. Some one must go on to Sutter's Fort after provisions. A call was made for volunteers. C. T. Stanton and Wm. McClutchen bravely offered their services and started on bearing letters from the company to Captain Sutter asking for relief. We resumed our journey and soon reached Gravelly Ford on the Humboldt.

I now come to that part of my narrative which delicacy of feeling for both the dead and the living would induce me to pass over in silence, but which a correct and lucid chronicle of subsequent events of historical importance will not suffer to be omitted. On the 5th day of October, 1846, at Gravelly Ford, a tragedy was enacted which affected the subsequent father a violent blow over the head with his heavy whip-stock. One blow followed another. Father was stunned for a moment and blinded by the blood streaming from the gashes in his head. Another blow was descending when my mother ran in between the men. Father saw the uplifted whip, but had only time to cry: "John, John," when down came the stroke upon mother. Quick as a thought my father's hunting knife was out and Snyder fell, fa-

OLD CALIFORNIA TRAIL TO THE NORTH OF SALT LAKE.

lives and fortunes of more than one member of our company. At this point in our journey we were compelled to double our teams in order to ascend a steep, sandy hill. Milton Elliott, who was driving our wagon, and John Snyder, who was driving one of Mr. Graves's, became involved in a quarrel over the management of their oxen. Snyder was beating his cattle over the head with the butt end of his whip, when my father, returning on horse-back from a hunting trip, arrived and, appreciating the great importance of saving the remainder of the oxen, remonstrated with Snyder, telling him that they were our main dependence, and at the same time offering the assistance of our team. Snyder having taken offense at something Elliott had said declared that his team could pull up alone, and kept on using abusive language. Father tried to quiet the enraged man. Hard words followed. Then my father said: "We can settle this, John, when we get up the hill." "No," replied Snyder with an oath, "we will settle it now," and springing upon the tongue of a wagon, he struck my tally wounded. He was caught in the arms of W. C. Graves, carried up the hill-side, and laid on the ground. My father regretted the act, and dashing the blood from his eyes went quickly to the assistance of the dying man. I can see him now, as he knelt over Snyder, trying to stanch the wound, while the blood from the gashes in his own head, trickling down his face, mingled with that of the dying man. In a few moments Snyder expired. Camp was pitched immediately, our wagon being some distance from the others. My father, anxious to do what he could for the dead, offered the boards of our wagon, from which to make a coffin. Then, coming to me, he said: "Daughter, do you think you can dress these wounds in my head? Your mother is not able, and they must be attended to." I answered by saying: "Yes, if you will tell me what to do." I brought a basin of water and sponge, and we went into the wagon, so that we might not be disturbed. When my work was at last finished, I burst out crying. Papa clasped me in his arms, saying: "I should not have asked so much of you," and talked to me until I controlled my feelings, so that we could go to the tent where mama was lying.

We then learned that trouble was brewing in the camp where Snyder's body lay. At the funeral my father stood sorrowfully by until the last clod was placed upon the grave. He and John Snyder had been good friends, and no one could have regretted the taking of that young life more than my father.

The members of the Donner party then held a council to decide upon the fate of my father, while we anxiously awaited the verdict. They refused to accept the plea of self-defense and decided that my father should be banished from the company and sent into the wilderness alone. It was a cruel sentence. And all this animosity towards my father was caused by Louis Keseburg, a German who had joined our company away back on the plains. Keseburg was married to a young and pretty German girl, and used to abuse her, and was in the habit of beating her till she was black and blue. This aroused all the manhood in my father and he took Keseburg to task — telling him it must be stopped or measures would be

tell. I have thought the subject over for hours but failed to arrive at a conclusion. The feeling against my father at one time was so strong that lynching was proposed. He was no coward and he bared his neck, saying, " Come on, gentlemen," but no one moved. It was thought more humane, perhaps, to send him into the wilderness to die of slow starvation or be murdered by the Indians; but my father did not die. God took care of him and his family, and at Donner Lake we seemed especially favored by the Almighty as not one of our family perished, and we were the only family no one member of which was forced to eat of human flesh to keep body and soul together. When the sentence of banishment was communicated to my father, he refused to go, feeling that he was justified before God and man, as he had only acted in self-defense.

Then came a sacrifice on the part of my mother. Knowing only too well what her life would be without him, yet fearful that if he remained he would meet with violence at the hands of his enemies, she implored him to go, but all to no avail until she urged him to re-

SALT LAKE, LOOKING SOUTH FROM PROMONTORY.

taken to that effect. Keseburg did not dare to strike his wife again, but he hated my father and nursed his wrath until papa was so unfortunate as to have to take the life of a fellow-creature in self-defense. Then Keseburg's hour for revenge had come. But how a man like Keseburg, brutal and overbearing by nature, although highly educated, could have such influence over the company is more than I can

member the destitution of the company, saying that if he remained and escaped violence at their hands, he might nevertheless see his children starving and be helpless to aid them, while if he went on he could return and meet them with food. It was a fearful struggle; at last he consented, but not before he had secured a promise from the company to care for his wife and little ones.

My father was sent out into an unknown country without provisions or arms — even his horse was at first denied him. When we learned of this decision, I followed him through the darkness, taking Elliott with me, and carried him his rifle, pistols, ammunition and some food. I had determined to stay with him, and begged him to let me stay, but he would listen

My mother's despair was pitiful. Patty and I thought we would be bereft of her also. But life and energy were again aroused by the danger that her children would starve. It was apparent that the whole company would soon be put on a short allowance of food, and the snow-capped mountains gave an ominous hint of the fate that really befell us in the Sierra. Our wagon

A DESPERATE SITUATION.   (DRAWN BY CHARLES NAHL.)

to no argument, saying that it was impossible. Finally, unclasping my arms from around him, he placed me in charge of Elliott, who started back to camp with me — and papa was left alone. I had cried until I had hardly strength to walk, but when we reached camp and I saw the distress of my mother, with the little ones clinging around her and no arm to lean upon, it seemed suddenly to make a woman of me. I realized that I must be strong and help mama bear her sorrows.

We traveled on, but all life seemed to have left the party, and the hours dragged slowly along. Every day we would search for some sign of papa, who would leave a letter by the way-side in the top of a bush or in a split stick, and when he succeeded in killing geese or birds would scatter the feathers about so that we might know that he was not suffering for food. When possible, our fire would always be kindled on the spot where his had been. But a time came when we found no letter, and no trace of him. Had he starved by the way-side, or been murdered by the Indians?

was found to be too heavy, and was abandoned with everything we could spare, and the remaining things were packed in part of another wagon. We had two horses left from the wreck, which could hardly drag themselves along, but they managed to carry my two little brothers. The rest of us had to walk, one going beside the horse to hold on my youngest brother who was only two and a half years of age. The Donners were not with us when my father was banished, but were several days in advance of our train. Walter Herron, one of our drivers, who was traveling with the Donners, left the wagons and joined my father.

On the 19th of October, while traveling along the Truckee, our hearts were gladdened by the return of Stanton, with seven mules loaded with provisions. Mr. McClutchen was ill and could not travel, but Captain Sutter had sent two of his Indian vaqueros, Luis and Salvador with Stanton. Hungry as we were, Stanton brought us something better than food — news that my father was alive. Stanton had met him not far from Sutter's Fort; he had been three days without food, and his horse was not able to carry him. Stanton had given him a horse and some provisions and he had gone on. We now packed what little we had left on one mule and started with Stanton. My mother rode on a mule, carrying Tommy in her lap; Patty and Jim rode behind the two Indians, and I behind Mr. Stanton, and in this way we journeyed on through the rain, looking up with fear towards the mountains, where snow was already falling although it was only the last week in October. Winter had set in a month earlier than usual. All trails and roads were covered; and our only guide was the summit which it seemed we would never reach. Despair drove many nearly frantic. Each family tried to cross the mountains but found it impossible. When it was seen that the wagons could not be dragged through the snow, their goods and provisions were packed on oxen and another start was made, men and

might bring yielded to the many, and we camped within three miles of the summit.

That night came the dreaded snow. Around the camp-fires under the trees great feathery flakes came whirling down. The air was so full of them that one could see objects only a few feet away. The Indians knew we were doomed, and one of them wrapped his blanket about him and stood all night under a tree. We children slept soundly on our cold bed of snow with a soft white mantle falling over us so thickly that every few moments my mother would have to shake the shawl — our only covering — to keep us from being buried alive. In the morning the snow lay deep on mountain and valley. With heavy hearts we turned back to a cabin that had been built by the Murphy-Schallenberger party two years before. We built more cabins and prepared as best we could for the winter. That camp, which proved

TRUCKEE CAÑON.

women walking in the snow up to their waists, carrying their children in their arms and trying to drive their cattle. The Indians said they could find no road, so a halt was called, and Stanton went ahead with the guides, and came back and reported that we could get across if we kept right on, but that it would be impossible if snow fell. He was in favor of a forced march until the other side of the summit should be reached, but some of our party were so tired and exhausted with the day's labor that they declared they could not take another step; so the few who knew the danger that the night

the camp of death to many in our company, was made on the shore of a lake, since known as "Donner Lake." The Donners were camped in Alder Creek Valley below the lake, and were, if possible, in a worse condition than ourselves. The snow came on so suddenly that they had no time to build cabins, but hastily put up brush sheds, covering them with pine boughs.

Three double cabins were built at Donner Lake, which were known as the "Breen Cabin," the "Murphy Cabin," and the "Reed-Graves Cabin." The cattle were all killed, and the meat was placed in snow for preservation. My mother had no cattle to kill, but she made arrangements for some, promising to give two for one in California. Stanton and the Indians made their home in my mother's cabin.

Many attempts were made to cross the mountains, but all who tried were driven back by the

ples, some beans, a bit of tripe, and a small piece of bacon. When this hoarded store was brought out, the delight of the little ones knew no bounds. The cooking was watched carefully, and when we sat down to our Christmas dinner mother said, "Children, eat slowly, for

DONNER LAKE, FROM THE OLD SACRAMENTO TRAIL.

pitiless storms. Finally a party was organized, since known as the "Forlorn Hope." They made snow-shoes, and fifteen started, ten men and five women, but only seven lived to reach California; eight men perished. They were over a month on the way, and the horrors endured by that Forlorn Hope no pen can describe nor imagination conceive. The noble Stanton was one of the party, and perished the sixth day out, thus sacrificing his life for strangers. I can find no words in which to express a fitting tribute to the memory of Stanton.

The misery endured during those four months at Donner Lake in our little dark cabins under the snow would fill pages and make the coldest heart ache. Christmas was near, but to the starving its memory gave no comfort. It came and passed without observance, but my mother had determined weeks before that her children should have a treat on this one day. She had laid away a few dried ap-

this one day you can have all you wish." So bitter was the misery relieved by that one bright day, that I have never since sat down to a Christmas dinner without my thoughts going back to Donner Lake.

The storms would often last ten days at a time, and we would have to cut chips from the logs inside which formed our cabins, in order to start a fire. We could scarcely walk, and the men had hardly strength to procure wood. We would drag ourselves through the snow from one cabin to another, and some mornings snow would have to be shoveled out of the fireplace before a fire could be made. Poor little children were crying with hunger, and mothers were crying because they had so little to give their children. We seldom thought of bread, we had been without it so long. Four months of such suffering would fill the bravest hearts with despair.

During the closing days of December, 1846, gold was found in my mother's cabin at Donner Lake by John Denton. I remember the night well. The storm fiends were shrieking in their wild mirth, we were sitting about the fire in our little dark home, busy with our thoughts. Denton with his cane kept knocking pieces off the large rocks used as fire-irons on which to place the wood. Something bright attracted his attention, and picking up pieces of the rock he examined them closely; then turning to my mother he said, " Mrs. Reed, this is gold." My mother replied that she wished it were bread. Denton knocked more chips from the rocks, and he hunted in the ashes for the shining particles until he had gathered about a teaspoonful. This he tied in a small piece of buckskin and placed in his pocket, saying, " If we ever get away from here I am coming back for more." Denton started out with the first relief party but perished on the way, and no one thought of the gold in his pocket. Denton was about thirty years of age; he was born in Sheffield, England, and was a gunsmith and gold-beater by trade. Gold has never been found on the shore of the lake, but a few miles from there in the mountain cañons, from which this rock possibly came, rich mines have been discovered.

Time dragged slowly along till we were no longer on short allowance but were simply starving. My mother determined to make an effort to cross the mountains. She could not see her children die without trying to get them food. It was hard to leave them but she felt that it must be done. She told them she would bring them bread, so they were willing to stay, and with no guide but a compass we started—my mother, Eliza, Milt Elliott and myself. Milt wore snow shoes and we followed in his tracks. We were five days in the mountains; Eliza gave out the first day and had to return, but we kept on and climbed one high mountain after another only to see others higher still ahead. Often I would have to crawl up the mountains, being too tired to walk. The nights were made hideous by the screams of wild beasts heard in the distance. Again, we would be lulled to sleep by the moan of the pine trees, which seemed to sympathize with our loneliness. One morning we awoke to find ourselves in a well of snow. During the night, while in the deep sleep of exhaustion, the heat of the fire had melted the snow and our little camp had gradually sunk many feet below the surface until we were literally buried in a well of snow. The danger was that any attempt to get out might bring an avalanche upon us, but finally steps were carefully made and we reached the surface. My foot was badly frozen, so we were compelled to return, and just in time, for that night a storm came on, the most fearful of the winter, and we should have perished had we not been in the cabins.

We now had nothing to eat but raw hides and they were on the roof of the cabin to keep out the snow; when prepared for cooking and boiled they were simply a pot of glue. When the hides were taken off our cabin and we were left without shelter Mr. Breen gave us a home with his family, and Mrs. Breen prolonged my life by slipping me little bits of meat now and then when she discovered that I could not eat the hide. Death had already claimed many in our party and it seemed as though relief never would reach us. Baylis Williams, who had been in delicate health before we left Springfield, was the first to die; he passed away before starvation had really set in.

I am a Catholic although my parents were not. I often went to the Catholic church before leaving home, but it was at Donner Lake that I made the vow to be a Catholic. The Breens were the only Catholic family in the Donner party and prayers were said aloud regularly in that cabin night and morning. Our only light was from little pine sticks split up like kindling wood and kept constantly on the hearth. I was very fond of kneeling by the side of Mr. Breen and holding these little torches so that he might see to read. One night we had all gone to bed—I was with my mother and the little ones, all huddled together to keep from freezing—but I could not sleep. It was a fearful night and I felt that the hour was not far distant when we would go to sleep—never to wake again in this world. All at once I found myself on my knees with my hands clasped, looking up through the darkness, making a vow that if God would send us relief and let me see my father again I would be a Catholic. That prayer was answered.

On his arrival at Sutter's Fort, my father made known the situation of the emigrants, and Captain Sutter offered at once to do everything possible for their relief. He furnished horses and provisions and my father and Mr. McClutchen started for the mountains, coming as far as possible with horses and then with packs on their backs proceeding on foot; but they were finally compelled to return. Captain Sutter was not surprised at their defeat. He stated that there were no able-bodied men in that vicinity, all having gone down the country with Frémont to fight the Mexicans. He advised my father to go to Yerba Buena, now San Francisco, and make his case known to the naval officer in command. My father was in fact conducting parties there —when the seven members of the Forlorn Hope arrived from across the mountains. Their famished faces told the story. Cattle were killed and men were up all night drying beef and making flour by hand mills, nearly 200 pounds being made in one night, and a party of seven,

ON THE WAY TO THE SUMMIT.

commanded by Captain Reasen P. Tucker, were sent to our relief by Captain Sutter and the alcalde, Mr. Sinclair. On the evening of February 19th, 1847, they reached our cabins, where all were starving. They shouted to attract attention. Mr. Breen, clambered up the icy steps from our cabin, and soon we heard the blessed words, " Relief, thank God, relief! " There was joy at Donner Lake that night, for we did not know the fate of the Forlorn Hope and we were told that relief parties would come and go until all were across the mountains. But with the joy sorrow was strangely blended. There were tears in other eyes than those of children; strong men sat down and wept. For the dead were lying about on the snow, some even unburied, since the living had not had strength to bury their dead. When Milt Elliott died,— our faithful friend, who seemed so like a brother,— my mother and I dragged him up out of the cabin and covered him with snow. Commencing at his feet, I patted the pure white snow down softly until I reached his face. Poor Milt! it was hard to cover that face from sight forever, for with his death our best friend was gone.

On the 22d of February the first relief started with a party of twenty-three — men, women and children. My mother and her family were among the number. It was a bright sunny morning and we felt happy, but we had not gone far when Patty and Tommy gave out. They were not able to stand the fatigue and it was not thought safe to allow them to proceed, so Mr. Glover informed mama that they would have to be sent back to the cabins to await the next expedition. What language can express our feelings? My mother said that she would go back with her children — that we would all go back together. This the relief party would not permit, and Mr. Glover promised mama that as soon as they reached Bear Valley he himself would return for her children. Finally my mother, turning to Mr. Glover said, " Are you a Mason ? " He replied that he was. " Will you promise me on the word of a Mason that if we do not meet their father you will return and save my children ? " He pledged himself that he would. My father was a . member of the Mystic Tie and mama had great faith in the word of a Mason. It was a sad parting — a fearful struggle. The men turned aside, not being able to hide their tears. Patty said, " I want to see papa, but I will take good care of Tommy and I do not want you to come back." Mr. Glover returned with the children and, providing them with food, left them in the care of Mr. Breen.

With sorrowful hearts we traveled on, walking through the snow in single file. The men wearing snow-shoes broke the way and we followed in their tracks. At night we lay down on the snow to sleep, to awake to find our clothing all frozen, even to our shoe-strings. At break of day we were again on the road, owing to the fact that we could make better time over the frozen snow. The sunshine, which it would seem would have been welcome, only added to our misery. The dazzling reflection of the snow was very trying to the eyes, while its heat melted our frozen clothing, making them cling to our bodies. My brother was too small to step in the tracks made by the men, and in order to travel he had to place his knee on the little hill of snow after each step and climb over. Mother coaxed him along, telling him that every step he took he was getting nearer papa and nearer something to eat. He was the youngest child that walked over the Sierra Nevada. On our second day's journey John Denton gave out and declared it would be im-

possible for him to travel, but he begged his companions to continue their journey. A fire was built and he was left lying on a bed of freshly cut pine boughs, peacefully smoking. He looked so comfortable that my little brother wanted to stay with him ; but when the second relief party reached him poor Denton was past waking. His last thoughts seemed to have gone back to his childhood's home, as a little poem was found by his side, the pencil apparently just dropped from his hand.

Captain Tucker's party on their way to the cabins had lightened their packs of a sufficient quantity of provisions to supply the sufferers on their way out. But when we reached the place where the cache had been made by hanging the food on a tree, we were horrified to find that wild animals had destroyed it, and again starvation stared us in the face. But my father was hurrying over the mountains, and met us in our hour of need with his hands full of bread. He had expected to meet us on this day, and had stayed up all night baking bread to give us. He brought with him fourteen men. Some of his party were ahead, and when they saw us coming they called out, " Is Mrs. Reed with you ? If she is, tell her Mr. Reed is here." We heard the call; mother knelt on the snow, while I tried to run to meet papa.

When my father learned that two of his children were still at the cabins, he hurried on, so fearful was he that they might perish before he reached them. He seemed to fly over the snow, and made in two days the distance we had been five in traveling, and was overjoyed to find Patty and Tommy alive. He reached Donner Lake on the first of March, and what a sight met his gaze! The famished little children and the death-like look of all made his heart ache. He filled Patty's apron with biscuits, which she carried around, giving one to each person. He had soup made for the infirm, and rendered every assistance possible to the sufferers. Leaving them with about seven days' provisions, he started out with a party of seventeen, all that were able to travel. Three of his men were left at the cabins to procure wood and assist the helpless. My father's party (the second relief) had not traveled many miles when a storm broke upon them. With the snow came a perfect hurricane. The crying of half-frozen children, the lamenting of the mothers, and the suffering of the whole party was heart-rending ; and above all could be heard the shrieking of the storm King. One who has never witnessed a blizzard in the Sierra can form no idea of the situation. All night my father and his men worked unceasingly through the raging storm, trying to erect shelter for the dying women and children. At times the hurricane would burst forth with such violence that he felt alarmed on account of the tall timber surrounding the camp. The party were destitute of food, all supplies that could be spared having been left with those at the cabins. The relief party had cached provisions on their way over to the cabins, and my father had sent three of the men forward for food before the storm set in; but they could not return. Thus, again, death stared all in the face. At one time the fire was nearly gone; had it been lost, all would have perished. Three days and nights they were exposed to the fury of the elements. Finally my father became snow-blind and could do no more, and he would have died but for the exertions of William McClutchen and Hiram Miller, who worked over him all night. From this time forward, the toil and responsibility rested upon McClutchen and Miller.

The storm at last ceased, and these two determined to set out over the snow and send back relief to those not able to travel. Hiram Miller picked up Tommy and started. Patty thought she could walk, but gradually everything faded from her sight, and she too seemed to be dying. All other sufferings were now forgotten, and everything was done to revive the child. My father found some crumbs in the thumb of his woolen mitten; warming and moistening them between his own lips, he gave them to her and thus saved her life, and afterward she was carried along by different ones in the company. Patty was not alone in her travels. Hidden away in her bosom was a tiny doll, which she had carried day and night through all of our trials. Sitting before a nice, bright fire at Woodworth's Camp, she took dolly out to have a talk, and told her of all her new happiness.

There was untold suffering at that " Starved Camp," as 'the place has since been called. When my father reached Woodworth's Camp, a third relief started in at once and rescued the living. A fourth relief went on to Donner Lake, as many were still there — and many remain there still, including George Donner and wife, Jacob Donner and wife and four of their children. George Donner had met with an accident which rendered him unable to travel; and his wife would not leave him to die alone. It would take pages to tell of the heroic acts and noble deeds of those who lie sleeping about Donner Lake.

Most of the survivors, when brought in from the mountains, were taken by the different relief parties to Sutter's Fort, and the generous hearted captain did everything possible for the sufferers. Out of the eighty-three persons who were snowed in at Donner Lake, forty-two perished, and of the thirty-one emigrants who left Springfield, Illinois, that spring morning, only eighteen lived to reach California. Alcalde Sinclair took my mother and her family to his own home, and we were surrounded with every comfort. Mrs. Sinclair was the dearest of women. Never can I forget their kindness. But our anxiety was not over, for we knew that my father's party had been caught in the storm. I can see my mother now, as she stood leaning against the door for hours at a time, looking towards the mountains. At last my father arrived at Mr. Sinclair's with the little ones, and our family were again united. That day's happiness repaid us for much that we had suffered; and it was spring in California.

Words cannot tell how beautiful the spring appeared to us coming out of the mountains from that long winter at Donner Lake in our little dark cabins under the snow. Before us now lay, in all its beauty, the broad valley of the Sacramento. I remember one day, when traveling down Napa Valley, we stopped at noon to have lunch under the shade of an oak; but I was not hungry; I was too full of the beautiful around me to think of eating. So I wandered off by myself to a lovely little knoll and stood there in a bed of wild flowers, looking up and down the green valley, all dotted with trees. The birds were singing with very joy in the branches over my head, and the blessed sun was smiling down upon all as though in benediction. I drank it in for a moment, and then began kissing my hand and wafting kisses to Heaven in thanksgiving to the Almighty for creating a world so beautiful. I felt so near God at that moment that it seemed to me I could feel His breath warm on my cheek. By and by I heard papa calling, " Daughter, where are you? Come, child, we are ready to start, and you have had no lunch," I ran and caught him by the hand, saying, " Buy this place, please, and let us make our home here." He stood looking around for a moment, and said, " It *is* a lovely spot," and then we passed on.

SAN JOSÉ, CAL.

Virginia Reed Murphy.

24

General Miles's Indian Campaigns

G.W. Baird

GENERAL MILES'S INDIAN CAMPAIGNS.

ENERAL Sherman has called the twenty years of constant Indian warfare following the war of the Rebellion, "The Battle of Civilization." That battle, on this continent, of course, began earlier, but certain facts made that period an epoch by itself. A chief fact to be noted is that the Indians during that time were always well armed, often much better than the troops. At the battle of Bear Paw, for instance, the Indians used magazine rifles of the best pattern, while even now, nearly fourteen years afterward, the army still has to do without them. The field of "The Battle of Civilization" was the vast trans-Missouri region, and civilization did not, during that period, satisfy itself with a gradual advance of its line, as formerly, but became aggressive, pierced the Indian country with three trans-continental railways and so ultimately abolished the frontier. A very large portion of the army (including nearly all of the cavalry and infantry and a small portion of the artillery) was at one time or another occupied with the task and many heroic deeds were done, but the conspicuously successful leaders were few.

General Nelson A. Miles as colonel of the 5th Infantry led his first command against hostile Indians in 1874. In the summer of that year small bands of southern Cheyennes, Kiowas, Arapahoes and Comanches made several raids in the Indian Territory, Texas, southern Kansas and southeastern Colorado, but escaped punishment by flying to their agencies. At last, on the 21st of July, the Department of the Interior gave the Secretary of War authority to punish these Indians wherever found, even to follow them upon their reservations. Under this authority General Miles was ordered into the field. He organized his command at Fort Dodge, Kansas, on the left bank of the Arkansas River. It consisted of eight troops of the 6th Cavalry, four companies of the 5th Infantry, and a section of artillery made up of details from cavalry and infantry. Later in the season four troops of the 8th Cavalry joined this command and some of the 6th Cavalry were withdrawn from the field.

In a summer of exceptional heat and drought even for that region, and through a section eaten bare by the invading army of grasshoppers whose flight was a "pillar of cloud by day" and whose encampment at night was as the devastation of fire, the command pressed rapidly southward from the Arkansas. Even prior to the inception of the movement, the scope of this Indian Territory Expedition, as it was called, differed from some of the notable Indian campaigns in the particular that General Miles waged Indian warfare according to the well-known principles of the art of war, so far as applicable. In too many cases expeditions against Indians had been like dogs fastened by a chain: within the length of the chain irresistible, beyond it powerless. The chain was its wagon train and supplies. A command with thirty days' supplies could inflict a terrible blow if only it could within thirty days come up with the Indians, deliver its blow, and get back to

GENERAL NELSON A. MILES. (FROM A PHOTOGRAPH BY TABER.)

more supplies — otherwise it repeated the historic campaign of "the king of France with forty thousand men." Or if perchance it delivered its blow successfully, it could not, for lack of time, follow up its success and attain the only object of just war, which is peace.

Before leaving Fort Dodge, General Miles applied for supplies such as would be needed should the campaign continue into the winter; an act of foresight which contributed much to his success. As the command moved out the chief of scouts, First-Lieutenant F. D. Baldwin, 5th Infantry, of whom we shall hear more, was detached with scouts and Delaware Indians to move rapidly far from the right flank of the command, to prevent hostile Indians from devastating the settlements in its rear, and with instructions to reach the Canadian River near Adobe Walls, an abandoned trading post where a group of bold buffalo hunters had sustained a siege for several days and inflicted such loss on the besieging Indians that they withdrew. By vigorous and well-timed marches, the main command and its flankers reached the Canadian River about the same time, the scouts putting to flight a

party of hostiles near Adobe Walls, and then sweeping along the right bank of the Canadian and rejoining the command at its crossing-place near Antelope Hills. The results of this advance were two-fold: the General learned that there was no considerable body of hostiles in his rear, and the Indians were made aware that the troops were advancing against them.

On the first day's march south of the Canadian, large camps, recently and hastily abandoned, were found along the Washita River, and a broad trail made by the lodge poles, travois, and ponies led off to the south, crossing the numerous affluents of the great Red River and leading towards the "Llano Estacado," or "Staked Plains," so-called because their ocean-like expanse is so monotonous that stakes were formerly driven along the trails which could not otherwise be identified. As water would be found on the "Yarner" (as the scouts call the Llano) with great difficulty in the extreme drought of summer, the only chance of striking a blow at once was by overtaking the retreating hostiles before they reached that region. The cavalry pushed rapidly forward, and the sturdy infantry, just from garrison, but well seasoned by drills and the gymnastic exercises that General Miles had instituted, marched patiently through heat and dust and " got there " every day. Indians never fight a considerable force while they can fly from it, and none but those who have experienced the hardship of the long pursuit, with its hunger, and thirst, and sleeplessness, can understand the feeling of restfulness and grim satisfaction with which a command sees that the race is over and the fight about to open.

August 30 was the day, and the "breaks" of the Red River, some thirteen miles from its bed, the place where the fight opened. Suddenly, from behind bluff and bush, as if they sprang from the bosom of the earth full armed, the hostiles came tearing down upon Baldwin's scouts and Indians, with the *crack, crack,* of their rifles, and the whoop of their war-cries. But Baldwin was the man for the place and Miles knew it; his sufficient discretion never had a touch of hesitancy or timidity, and he was fitly seconded by brave old " Fall Leaf " of the Delawares. Meantime Colonel Biddle, under the immediate command of General Miles, deployed his battalion of cavalry forward at the run; Colonel Compton, giving rein to his horses, swung his battalion out on the right; Lieutenant Pope's artillery, with infantry support, came rapidly up in the center, and there began a running fight over thirteen miles of sun-baked earth, glowing with a furnace heat, gashed in gullies and deep ravines by the flood-like rains which at times prevail there. Whenever the Indians made a stand the troops were hurled upon them, and the fight, which if it had opened timidly would have been a stoutly contested affair, soon became a rout and a chase. Col. Biddle threw forward Captain Chaffee with his troop as skirmishers, who there made his famous battle-field speech: " Forward! and if any man is killed I 'll make him a corporal! "

Down through the jagged ravines the troops pursued across a half-mile of sand where at times a river flows, up the right bank and into the valley of the Tule, a branch of the Red River, where a burning camp, abandoned utensils, and a trail leading up a precipitous cliff told of the hasty flight of the Indians. The long chase before the fight, the rapid pursuit after through the intolerable heat of sun and earth, and the absence of water made it necessary to call a halt. Men and animals were famishing — some men drank the blood of a buffalo, and all the water found in Red River was a small pool of saturated gypsum and alkali, rendered indescribably vile from having been for a long time a buffalo wallow. With infinite labor the command, after resting, followed the trail over

which Pope, by devoting the night to it, had dragged up his Gatlings, and so climbed out of the valley of the Tule and followed the Indian trail for miles out on the Llano. It became evident that no pursuit could be successful without supplies, and that before a train could be brought through the ravines and breaks of the valley to the table-land on the right bank of the Red River the Indians could get beyond pursuit. Hence a recall was sounded.

The train with escort, commanded by Major W. Lyman of the 5th Infantry, was sent back to Camp Supply to replenish, and, on its return, was attacked near the Washita River by a large force of Comanches and Kiowas who had come up in rear of General Miles's command, fresh from their reservation. Stimulated with the hope of capturing rations and ammunition the Indians for five days laid siege to the train, which was most heroically and successfully defended.

Intent on conquering a peace and not merely beating the Indians in one engagement, General Miles overcame the greatest obstacles in the few weeks of comparative inactivity that ensued. Of these obstacles it must suffice, here, to say they ought never to have existed, yet they would have wrecked the expedition but for the indomitable persistence of its commander. On November 8, a detachment under Lieutenant F. D. Baldwin surprised a large camp of hostiles near the head of McClellan Creek in the early morning, and at once attacked with such vigor as to compel the Indians to abandon the protection of the ravines and retreat to the open country. Time and again they rallied and renewed the defense, but were finally driven by the troops and scattered in utter rout, leaving in their flight two little captive white girls — Adelaide and Julia Germaine — aged five and seven years. Their parents, brother, and one sister were all murdered by the Indians in Kansas, where their two older sisters were captured in the summer previous. The surrender, which crowned the expedition with success, included the older sisters. General Miles became guardian for the four, and upon his recommendation Congress authorized the stoppage from the annuities of the Cheyennes of an amount for their support. In the center of the vast section, including the Pan Handle of Texas and the adjacent portions of the Indian Territory which had been wrested by Miles from the hostiles, was erected a military post named for the gallant Major Elliott of the Seventh Cavalry, who had lost his life November 27, 1868, in Custer's Battle of the Washita.

A CONFLICT WITH SITTING BULL.

THOSE familiar with the frontier twenty or twenty-five years ago will readily recall the estimation in which the numbers and prowess of the Sioux were held; also the prestige that they had after the Fort Phil Kearny massacre in 1866, and the abandonment by the Government, at their dictation, of the Powder River route and of several military posts. More than once, in derogation of laurels won in warfare against other Indians, it was said, "Wait till you meet the Sioux."

Simultaneous with the arrival at Fort Leavenworth, Kansas, of the news of the Custer catastrophe on the Little Big Horn, Montana, came orders to General Miles and the 5th Infantry to proceed to the scene of hostilities to form a subordinate part of the large command already there. In the earlier service of the 7th Cavalry in Kansas most agreeable social relations had existed between many members of the two regiments, and the list of those slain on that fatal 25th of June, 1876, contained many names which were read with a pang of sorrow; and so, though the 5th marched gaily out of Fort Leavenworth, decked with bouquets, to the familiar strains of "The Girl I Left Behind Me," officers and men marched with sad hearts. The long journey up the Missouri and the Yellowstone was accomplished without noteworthy incidents. Summer drew to a close, and the objects of the campaign remained unattained. The two large commands then in the field were ordered to their stations early in the autumn, and General Miles was left on the Yellowstone with his own regiment (the 5th Infantry) and six companies of the 22d Infantry. The task assigned him was to build log huts for his troops and stores, bring forward the winter supplies, by wagon, from the mouth of the Yellowstone, and then the command was expected to hibernate, protecting themselves from attack and holding the ground for a basis of campaign in the following year. Two cantonments were built, one at the mouth of the Tongue River, and the other on the left bank of the Yellowstone, nearly opposite the present city of Glendive, but there was no hibernating, for the disposition of the commander did not favor it, and he was so isolated that action on his own judgment was necessary under the circumstances. Immediately on assuming command General Miles began, as in the Indian Territory Expedition, to plan for a systematic campaign.

The hostiles belonged on the large reservations far to the south and southeast of the Yellowstone, and the General took means of getting the earliest possible information of their absenting themselves therefrom. He became satisfied, early in October, that a very large number of the hostiles were in his vicinity, and this fact, added to a prolonged delay in the expected arrival at the cantonment on Tongue River of a supply train coming up from the cantonment at Glendive, induced him to march out with the 5th Infantry and proceed down on the left bank of the Yellowstone. On the 18th of October he met the train under escort of a battalion of the 22d Infantry commanded by Lieutenant-Colonel E. S. Otis of that regiment. The train had been once obliged to return to Glendive by the strong force of Indians, its teamsters so demoralized that their places were filled by soldiers. When advancing the second time Otis received, October 16, the following note, left on a hilltop by an Indian runner:

YELLOWSTONE.

I want to know what you are doing traveling on this road. You scare all the buffalo away. I want to hunt in this place. I want you to turn back from here. If you don't I will fight you again. I want you to leave what you have got here and turn back from here.

I am your friend, SITTING BULL.

I mean all the rations you have got and some powder. Wish you would write as soon as you can.

Otis sent a firm reply by a scout and proceeded with the train surrounded by the Indians, who, for a considerable time, kept up firing but gradually fell to the rear. When General Miles learned the situation from Colonel Otis he started after Sitting Bull and overtook him near the head of Cedar Creek, a northern affluent of the Yellowstone. Sitting Bull sent a flag of truce to General Miles desiring to communicate, and General Miles met him with Chief Gall and several others between the lines. Sitting Bull shrewdly wished for an "old-fashioned peace" for the winter (when warfare is most difficult), with permission to hunt and trade for ammunition, on which conditions he agreed not to molest the troops. But General Miles's object was permanent peace and the security of the territory then and before dominated by the Sioux, and he told Sitting Bull plainly that peace could come only by absolute submission. When the interview closed the troops were moved with the intention of intercepting the Indians should they try to move northward, and on the 21st of October another similar interview between the lines occurred.

The Indians undoubtedly intended to emulate the act of bad faith by which General Canby lost his life at the hands of the Modocs, April 11, 1873. Several of their younger warriors, with affected carelessness, gradually moved forward in position to surround the party under the flag of truce. General Miles, observing this, moved back a step or two and told Sitting Bull very forcibly that those men were too young for the council, and that the "talk" would end just there unless they returned to their lines. One of them had slipped a carbine up under his buffalo robe. Another muttered to Sitting Bull, "Why don't you talk strong?" and he replied, "When I say that, I am going to shoot him." Meantime the troops were held in readiness to attack, had any act of bad faith been attempted; even the accidental discharge of a firearm would have precipitated an attack in which all between the lines would have fallen. It became evident, at last, that only force could settle the question, and General Miles said to Sitting Bull, " I will either drive you out of this country or you will me. I will take no advantage of you under flag of truce and give you fifteen minutes to get back to your lines; then, if my terms are not accepted, I will open fire." With an angry grunt the old Medicine Man turned and ran back to his lines; the whole country was alive with Indians, not less than a thousand warriors swarmed all about the command, which, in a slender line extended to protect front and flanks and rear, pushed vigorously forward and drove the Indians from the deep valleys at the source of Cedar Creek, compelling them to leave some of their dead on the field, which they never willingly do, and then pursued them so hotly for forty-two miles to the Yellowstone that they abandoned food, lodge poles, camp equipage, and ponies.

On October 27, more than four hundred lodges, about two thousand Indians, surrendered to General Miles, and five chiefs were taken as hostages for the execution by the Indians of their terms of surrender, *i. e.*, to go to their various agencies. Sitting Bull and his immediate following, his family and connections by marriage, broke away from the main body during the pursuit and escaped northward, where he was later joined by Gall and other chiefs with some followers.

The estimated number of warriors in this engagement was one thousand. To General Miles and to the 5th Infantry, three hundred and ninety-eight rifles, is due the honor of this important victory, which had far-reaching consequences. Not since the battle of Little Big Horn had the followers of Sitting Bull been attacked by the troops in offensive battle. This was the first of a series of engagements in which the command of General Miles, or some detachment therefrom, vigorously assumed the offensive, and here began the successful battles and combats which resulted in breaking the power of the dreaded Sioux and bringing security and prosperity to a vast territory which is now penetrated by railways, occupied by hardy and prosperous settlers, dotted over with towns and cities, and already so developed and so permeated by the influences of our civilization that, in the form of new States, or portions thereof, it augments the glory and dignity of the nation.

Returning to the cantonment at Tongue River, General Miles organized a force — four hundred and thirty-four rifles — made up of the 5th and a portion of the 22d Infantry and pushed northward in pursuit of Sitting Bull, but the trail was obliterated by snow near the Big Dry, the broad bed of that which at times becomes a southern affluent of the Missouri. A winter of great severity, even for that region, opened early, and the command suffered intensely but kept the field and scoured the country along the Missouri River above and below old Fort Peck.

On December 7, a detachment of the command,— Companies G, H, and I, 5th Infantry — one hundred officers and men, commanded by First Lieutenant F. D. Baldwin, 5th Infantry, overtook Sitting Bull's camp, one hundred and ninety lodges, and drove it across the Missouri, and on the 18th the same force surprised the camp near the head of Redwater, a southern affluent of the Missouri, and captured camp and contents with sixty animals, the Indians scattering out south of the Yellowstone.

As Sitting Bull did not for a considerable time thereafter enter as a factor into the campaign, it will be permitted to anticipate for a little and describe his subsequent movements. With a small following he shortly after moved northward and camped on the left bank of the Missouri; thence, near the end of the winter, poor and with scarcely any ammunition, he and his scanty following sought refuge north of the international boundary. As a war was raging of which he was an important factor — not so much from military prowess as from his position as a " Medicine Man " and an extreme and inveterate savage Indian, which made him the nucleus of all the disaffected and hostile Sioux — his band ought to have been either disarmed at the boundary or interned. General Miles made repeated and urgent appeals to the higher authorities that action to that end be taken, but unfortunately it was not taken.

Sitting Bull's position and character, as before indicated, and the freedom for a considerable time accorded him and his followers, north of the line, induced a large number of the hostile and disaffected to steal away to him, and so the Northwest Territory of the Dominion became the rendezvous and supply camp of a threatening force. But for the time Sitting Bull was eliminated from the problem of conquering a peace, and the closing months of 1876 saw the beginning of the end of the great Sioux war. The intense cold of a Montana winter did not chill the ardor nor lessen the activity of Miles and his indomitable infantry, and the winter was to witness, on their part, almost incessant and markedly successful campaigning.

CRAZY HORSE BROUGHT TO TERMS.

A MONTANA winter, and so severe a one as that of 1876-77, might well be accounted a sufficient reason for the suspension of active operations. With thermometers rarely above zero, usually far below, and quite often so far that the mercury was solid and only spirit thermometers registered; with snow piled so deep in all the valleys that movement was laborious and tedious in the extreme, and with blizzards sweeping over the country, the thought of seriously attempting protracted expeditions would have entered most minds, if at all, only to be rejected. But General Miles took account of the fact that the difficulties for the troops, as briefly indicated, would be even greater for the Indians who do not voluntarily venture far from their camp in some sheltered valley in severe weather, and believed that if clothing, equipment, and transportation could be so increased as to meet the conditions presented there was promise of unusual successes.

Those who have seen only holiday soldiers or even troops on ordinary field service, would scarcely have recognized the four hundred and thirty-six officers and enlisted men of the 5th and 22d Infantry regiments who started up the valley of Tongue River, Montana, on the 29th of December, 1876. They might have been excused — these supposed spectators — had they concluded that a sportive band of buffaloes were trying to " evolute " into bipeds. Over the heavy woolen clothing supplied to the army for winter wear, the men were, many of them, furclad from head to foot; in lieu of a face there was presented to the observer a frost-covered woolen muffler frozen solidly upon an ice-clad beard, " trimmed with the same " in form of icicles, so that a long thaw had to precede disrobing. Enormous overshoes of rubber or of buffalo skin flesh side out, drawn on over German socks, gave warmth to the feet that they robbed of all nimbleness. Efficiency was the object aimed at, and to this end the army belts and cartridge boxes had given place to canvas belts made by the soldiers, looped with the same to hold a row or two rows of metallic cartridges. (The " prairie belt " since adopted for the army embodies the same principle.) General Miles, by stimulating emulation among the men, encouraged them to devise these improvements, and the men were intelligent and knew well by experience that " one more cartridge " for the modern soldier was like the " one step nearer " for the ancient who had a short sword — it might mean all the difference between success and failure.

The incidents of camp and march illustrative of the effects of the intense cold are capable of most interesting elaboration and illustration : here a soldier hastily removes shoe and stocking and rubs with snow his rapidly freezing feet; there *seems* to be Mark Twain's lightning-rod man replenishing the fire with his wares, but really *is* a scout thawing a rigid rawhide lariat so that he can coil it, and now a teamster with a well-grounded doubt as to his future expresses the hope that St. Peter, when he learns that a man " was one of Miles's teamsters," will give him friendly welcome as one who " has suffered enough."

Already in the expedition northward to the Missouri — as before related — many of the difficulties of a winter campaign had been studied and overcome, and the later days of December, 1876, saw the command at the cantonment on Tongue River equipping itself for a blow at Crazy Horse. This Sioux chief was at the head of the Ogallalas, and had borne a prominent part, if indeed he was not the most prominent, in the repulse administered by the Indians, June 17, 1876, to Crook's command advancing from the department of the Platte toward the Yellowstone; he had also been one of the important chiefs in the battle of the Little Big Horn, where also were Sitting Bull's following, the Uncapapas, and many others.

Crazy Horse, with a large force of Sioux and Northern Cheyennes, was camped along Tongue River and other southern affluents of the Yellowstone, and it soon became evident that the Indians would dispute the passage of the Tongue. Sharp skirmishes took place on the 1st and 3d of January (1877), and on the 7th the advance made a capture of eight Indians, mostly women and children, but of importance, as was found later, because of their relationship to leading men. The Indians made a determined effort to rescue the captives. The scouts in the lead made a bold charge upon them at dark on the 7th and were surrounded. Lieutenant Casey of the 22d Infantry, in command of a detachment of mounted infantry, with great intrepidity dashed in to the rescue with a scanty half-score of brave followers and beat off the Indian rear guard. It was now evident that the contest was at hand and the Indians chose well their field. Near the southern boundary of Montana, where Tongue River breaks through Wolf Mountains and flows in a deep cañon, whose steep walls were then mantled with deep snow or glazed with ice, the Indians sought (January 8) not only to check the advancing troops but to hold them helpless at their mercy while, from the crests above, they should deliberately shoot them down and overwhelm them. Whooping and yelling, as is their custom in battle, they shouted to the troops "You've had your last breakfast." Here again the quick discernment, rapid movements, and bold attack of General Miles changed the nature of the battle and snatched a victory from conditions that were more favorable to defeat. Instead of permitting himself to be cooped up within the narrow valley he determined at once to deploy boldly out, occupying the widely separated hilltops along a broad front with a thin line, and put every man and every rifle at once into the fight. Every man must be a hero, for there is no touch of elbow and no rear rank; every captain must be a capable commander, for the line to right and left is gashed by deep valleys between his and the adjacent companies. No one who has not participated in such an engagement, under like circumstances, can realize how short a line a score or two of men make, springing boldly out in single rank, flanks in air and no support. More than three hundred miles of wintry wilderness were at their backs, there was no reserve, retreat meant disaster, surrender was impossible; victory or death by torture were the alternatives.

Already the Indians held the sharp crests of the steep hills, and were delivering a plunging fire into the troops. Burdened with their heavy clothing, which the polar cold made necessary, stumbling and falling in the deep snow or slipping on the icy acclivities, the troops pressed forward and gained the crests where they could meet the enemy face to face. But now a new danger threatened. As the Indians largely outnumbered the troops, they could maintain the fight in front, while they seized heights which commanded the left flank and rear, and so get the troops into a circle of death-dealing rifles. The heights to the left must be wrested from them, and that speedily. Troops were designated, under command of Captains Butler and McDonald, for that duty, and Pope served his three-inch gun judiciously to aid them—Gunner McHugh of the 5th Infantry especially distinguishing himself. Every minute the crowd of Indians on that hill-top increased, and they could take in reverse the whole left flank. The General, keenly alive to every detail of the situation, decided on the instant to send a reinforcement. Sitting on his horse near the General was Lieutenant F. D. Baldwin, 5th Infantry, then on staff duty. Turning to him and pointing to the left, the General said: "Tell them to take that hill without failure and drive the Indians away." This was the reinforcement, and it was enough. Putting spurs to old "Red Water," Baldwin forced him at the run up the glassy hillside, and then, hat in hand, and with a ringing shout, he newly inspired the weary men, and, with the momentum of his own brave onset, carried them to the coveted crests. The battle was by no means over yet; for hours it raged. Old Winter himself at last took a part and contributed a furious, blinding snow-storm. Disheartened by the death of a prominent medicine man, whom they thought invulnerable, the Indians were at last driven through Wolf Mountains and towards the Big Horn range. They were pursued until it became evident that they could not be overtaken by the command without replenishing its supplies. Polar cold makes extensive demands on the vitality of men and animals; it not only occasions exhaustion, but also impairs the will power. Campaigning on short rations where it prevails would be both cruel and hazardous. The weary, frost-bitten troops welcomed the shelter of the rude log huts and returned to the cantonment which their own labor had built, and while they were resting and recuperating their commander took means to reap the fruits of the important victory he and they had won, not only from armed enemies, but even from the very elements themselves.

Recognizing the ill effects upon the spirits and health of the command of the monotony and confinement at that remote point, to which the mail could be brought only rarely and by sending a strong detachment to Fort Buford, nearly two hundred miles away, General Miles had constructed a large canvas-covered building in which the band of the 5th Infantry furnished choice musical entertainments, interspersed with the well-intentioned efforts of the barn-storming dramatic talent of the command. It was the paradise of the stage-struck soldier, whose most gray-bearded pun or castaneous joke was sure of an encore from an always crowded house.

But work was the occupation of the commander and of those most closely associated with him. Serving as scout and interpreter with the command was John Bruguier, the son of a French trader and an Indian mother, a man whose fidelity and courage were unquestioned and whose knowledge of the customs and language of the Sioux was of great value. The General decided to make use of this man and of a portion of the Indians captured January 7 to communicate with Crazy Horse. Bruguier, although he believed that he would be killed by the Indians as a deserter, started February 1 with two of the captives. Taking up the trail beyond the scene of the battle of January 8, he found the camp on a tributary of the Little Big Horn and got into communication with Crazy Horse without the molestation from the subordinates which he had anticipated. He delivered the message of General Miles, which was: "Surrender at the cantonment on Tongue River, or at your agency, or I will attack you again." The experience of the winter had taught Crazy Horse that this was no idle threat, and a delegation of chiefs came back with Bruguier to satisfy themselves that what he said was true. They arrived February 19. In councils repeated on many days the Indians put forward their orators and diplomats and sought to obtain a modification of the terms. There was probably a mutual fear of treachery in the councils. Officers had no arms in sight but wore their revolvers beneath their coats, and Indians drew their blankets close about their scowling faces, with Winchesters grasped within, their bright, beady eyes intent upon the officers. At one time it seemed that the theater might be the scene of a veritable tragedy, when Little Chief was understood, in his impassioned speech, to advise " the young men to put something in their guns." There was an involuntary start but no other demonstration. The Indian is human and respects the man who can overcome him. At last this delegation recognized that the conditions presented ("Surrender here, or surrender if you prefer at your agencies at the south, or fight") were an ultimatum and they returned to their camp, which was brought near to the forks of Powder River, and a much larger delegation of chiefs came in, March 18, still intent on securing better terms. The experiences of a month before were repeated and with like result. Of the larger delegation was Little Hawk, an uncle of Crazy Horse. He with others accepted the terms and submitted to the retention by General Miles of nine prominent leaders, Sioux and Northern Cheyennes, as hostages that the whole hostile camp would surrender in thirty days. Crazy Horse and Little Hawk led the bulk of the hostiles, more than two thousand, to the Red Cloud and Spotted Tail agencies, in the department of the Platte, where they surrendered. Three hundred, chiefly Cheyennes, led by White Bull, Two Moons, and Hump surrendered at the cantonment.

In six months, including a winter of polar cold, General Miles with his force of sixteen companies of hardy and well-commanded infantry, leaving at all times two garrisons to protect the cantonments, had subdued two powerful forces of Indians, wrested from their control a vast territory, opened the way for the advance of the Northern Pacific Railroad, which had long halted at Bismarck on the left bank of the Missouri, and so inaugurated all that has since become history in that region.

The surrender of the Sioux under their agreement with General Miles took out of the field not only the thousand who followed Crazy Horse, but that brave war chief also, and in a community so little organized as are the Indian tribes the hostility, or the reverse, of a few great leaders has vastly more weight than in a highly organized state in which there is no essential man. Anticipating a little we may give the few additional facts of importance in Crazy Horse's career. After his surrender, he and his people were placed on the reservation near Camp Robinson in Northern Nebraska. For a time he was quiet but later was believed to be planning to lead away his people on the warpath again. It was thought best by the officers in authority there to arrest him, which was done, but while being conducted to the guardhouse he made a desperate break for liberty and attempted to cut down with a knife all who opposed him. He was mortally wounded in the struggle, and died September 7, 1877.

THE SUBJUGATION OF LAME DEER'S BAND.

THE intention of the Government to assemble troops in the spring of 1877, to renew the contest, took shape in orders which brought to General Miles's command four troops of the 2d Cavalry from Fort Ellis, near Bozeman (in the Gallatin valley near the base of the Rockies) eleven troops of the 7th Cavalry and four companies of the 1st Infantry from posts along the Missouri in Dakota. The marked successes of the winter campaign had effected the greater part of the object for which this large command was assembled, but its presence during the summer, and the movements of its various detachments over all parts of the immense territory watered by the Yellowstone and its affluents, confirmed the conquest already achieved and assured the Indians that their sway therein was gone forever. By a singular conjunction of circumstances an important force of Indians was, in the late summer and autumn, imported into that region from the far Pacific slope and by its pursuit beyond the Missouri, and capture near the boundary line, added another hardly contested fight and conspicuous success to Miles's record; but of that later. The first of the reinforcements to arrive were the four troops of the 2d Cavalry, and General Miles speedily equipped a command of this battalion — whose readiness for any service well illustrated its regimental motto, " *Toujours prêt*," — and of six companies of his infantry, two of the 5th, four of the 22d, and marched out, May 1, against a band of Sioux, mostly Minneconjous, under Lame Deer, who had broken away from the main body and refused to surrender.

Having confidence in the sincerity of the Cheyennes and Sioux who had but just surrendered to him, General Miles selected from them a small party headed by White Bull, and took them as scouts. Neither on that occasion nor afterward did these Indians waver in their fidelity. The route of the command was for more than sixty miles up the valley of the Tongue, but springing grass and a stream of limpid water had taken the place of the snowy hillsides and ice-bound river bed which had frowned on the January expedition. Leaving the train at this point to follow with the infantry commanded by Major Dickey of the 22d, the mounted force, chiefly 2d Cavalry but augmented by a detachment of mounted infantry, pushed rapidly out in search of the hostile camp. The minute knowledge of the country possessed by the Indian scouts enabled the command to march by night as well as by day, and so, up through the broken country along the Rosebud, following the same general approach as that pursued by General Custer in the preceding June, the force pressed on with scarcely a pause during two nights and one day, the patient pack-mules jogging along the trail in rear. The stealthy, keen-sighted Indians at last "located the camp," in frontier phrase, and then, giving a few hours for rest, the command was stripped for the fight. Everything not demanded for the rapid march and the vigorous fight was placed on the pack mules; canteens, arms and equipments carefully arranged to avoid noise. The weird half-light of the night, the commands in suppressed tones and the consciousness in all minds that this "meant business" all contributed to that tense frame of mind with which men face a danger that is certain, imminent, and of unknown dimensions. The hostile camp was on an affluent of the Rosebud, then called The Muddy, but since then Lame Deer Creek. Without loud command the force was urged rapidly down through the breaks on the left of the Rosebud, across the bed of that steep-banked stream. Just as the birds were twittering in the trees and the night began to yield to day (May 7), the head of the column turned into the valley of The Muddy. The tenseness of mind before mentioned increases its sensitiveness to small and indifferent objects. The twittering of birds in the trees, the wealth of grass which the Chinook winds spread soft over the sheltered valleys, in contrast with wasting snow-drifts still clinging to the northern sides of the hillcrests, and the Big Horn range, still thick-blanketed in its winter covering, to which haze gave an ecru tinge, all of these irrelevant things the words Lame Deer suggest and evoke from memory.

The Indian scouts reached the wooded hills above the camp at earliest dawn, and watched the unsuspecting hostiles as they untethered their ponies from among the lodges and turned them out to graze. And so, all unannounced, the little force burst upon them. Lieutenant Edward Casey, of the 22d, commanding the mounted infantry and the scouts, charged through the village, sweeping away the ponies and cutting off the hostiles from their herd.

Close in rear of him rode General Miles and staff, leading the cavalry, which was commanded by Captain Ball. It was the General's desire to secure the surrender of the Indians without a fight, and to this end he had instructed White Bull to call to them and explain to them that they could surrender and would be unharmed.

This overture was responded to by a rifle-ball which passed between the arm and the body of the plucky old chief, but the offer was still repeated, and Lame Deer and his head warrior, Iron Star, seemed disposed to accept, even shaking hands with the General and one of his staff, the latter dismounting for the purpose, while another staff officer dismounted to take the Indians' arms. Whether they intended treachery or feared it can never be known, for, hastily withdrawing a few yards, they sought cover behind a bank and opened fire. Parleying and peacemaking were plainly out of place thereafter. General Miles's orderly, just behind him, was killed by a shot plainly aimed at the General, and the troops, for a few moments held in check while the hand-shaking was going on, were now sent vigorously against the Indians. Lame Deer and Iron Star were among the first to fall; their following scattered on foot into the broken, pine-covered hills close to their camp, and were pursued, in small, scattered bands, for some eight miles, leaving their dead in the hands of the troops. The entire camp and its supplies were captured; also four hundred and fifty ponies and horses. These, with the animals of the surrendered Cheyennes, formed the nucleus of the mount of the "11th Cavalry,"[1] as the 5th Infantry, mounted on captured ponies, was called. And so this successful encounter contributed in itself and in that which it supplied very materially to the thorough subjection of the hostiles.

Major Dickey, in command of the infantry, received the merited commendation of the General for the "zeal and energy" with which he urged forward his command, and the sturdy pluck with which he disregarded a rumor of a great disaster which grew out of the fact that one or two pack-mules with their escort, getting separated from the command in the rapid night march, were cut off by the Indians. The change of aspect, from the disaster which he had been led to expect to the victory which he found to have taken place, roused his enthusiasm, and he called for "three cheers," to which his weary but enthusiastic command responded with a will.

Leaving the cavalry to occupy that section the remainder of the command, with captured

[1] The regular cavalry establishment of the army has ten regiments.—G. W. B.

ponies, returned to the cantonment. All active operations, nearly all movements, were interrupted by rain and flood such as have not since visited that region. Supply wagons sank to the hub and were immovable. Dry gullies became great streams and rivers overflowed their banks. Troops in mud-roofed huts found that the roofs were storage reservoirs. It became a serious question for the time whether supplies could be sent to the 2d Cavalry battalion, so many new and rapid rivers filled the ravines and gulches.

Utilizing this period of enforced quiet the General began the organization of the " 11th Cavalry." Companies B, F, G and I, 5th Infantry, formed the first battalion of that most efficient corps, and under command of Captain Simon Snyder of the 5th it became a potent factor in the remainder of the campaign. By subsequent captures ponies to mount the remainder of the regiment were obtained, and the gallant 11th was not dismounted till after the need of its efficient service had passed and General Miles had, by promotion, been transferred to another field of duty.

The Indian pony lends himself to the niceties of drill and parade with even greater reluctance than his master adopts " the white man's road." In vain the irate sergeant ordered his rider to " dress up there on the left," with that vigor of speech which characterized " our army in Flanders "; if the storm came into his face he solemnly turned his haunches towards it and his attitude announced more graphically than even the French tongue could "*J'y suis, j'y reste*"; but no rattle of musketry could disturb the equanimity with which he seized the moment of the hottest fight to clip the scanty herbage while his rider, dismounted, was fighting a little in front of him; he was accustomed to long journeys and short rations, and, to adopt the slang of the region, " rest made him tired." He contributed very materially to subdue his former master, and, with the elk, the buffalo, the antelope, the free unconventional life of the plains and, alas, probably with his old master too, he will soon become only a picturesque reminiscence.

The long rain storm and the floods at last passed away. The remainder of the reinforcements before mentioned reported for duty, also a force of friendly Crow Indians led by First-Lieutenant G. C. Doane, 2d Cavalry. The scattered fragments of Lame Deer's band were so hotly pursued by different detachments of the command that they were forced to seek rest and sue for peace at the Red Cloud and Spotted Tail agencies. Before the close of summer peace and security reigned throughout Dakota and Montana. A large fleet of steamboats plied unmolested between Bismarck, then the Northern

Pacific terminus, and the upper Yellowstone, transporting supplies for the command and building material for the two new posts, Forts Keogh and Custer; the one near the mouth of the Tongue, the other at the junction of Little Big Horn with the Big Horn, in sight of the fatal hill which, like the Alamo, had no messenger to tell of the heroic deeds it had witnessed. These posts and a force at Fort Peck on the Missouri, an outpost towards Sitting Bull's camp in Canada, and the large territory over which they kept watch and ward became the garrisons and the territorial command known as the " District of the Yellowstone," under General Miles's command.

CHIEF JOSEPH AND THE NEZ PERCÉS.

THE summer of 1877 was an unusually attractive one in Montana, the spring rains having thickly carpeted hill and valley with verdure. General Sherman came to the cantonment on his river and wagon journey through to the Pacific, and General Miles took advantage of the visit to request him to present to the soldiers who had performed conspicuous acts of gallantry in the preceding campaigns the medals of honor which had been bestowed upon them by Congress. At a parade of all the troops present, each bronzed and hardy soldier thus honored stepped out as his name was called, and received at the hands of the general-in-chief the token which thereby had for him an added distinction.

The successes before recorded and the arrival of other troops made it possible, in the early summer, to relieve the six companies of the 22d Infantry, and return them to their stations along the great lakes. After a rough march of more than three hundred miles to Bismarck, they shipped their effects, including dress uniforms, to their stations and were just starting for Duluth when a telegraphic order called them to Chicago, then threatened with a riot. The quite unwonted sight of weather-beaten soldiers in campaign suits most essentially patched with bits of sacks that warranted the wearer to be " Best Family Flour," had a wholesome effect. And when in reply to a question from one of the crowd, " You would not fire on us, would you?" the prompt reply came, " Not unless the captain ordered it," the purport was unmistakable. The presence of this disciplined command obviated the need of its employment.

But the season was not destined to pass without another battle and important victory. Away beyond the Rockies dwelt the Nez Percés, a tribe quite advanced in civilization. As the occasion of their outbreak at this time, and the earlier acts of war on the part of both the troops and these Indians, had no relation to the com-

A RECONNAISSANCE.

mand of General Miles, no account of them need appear here. When hostilities had begun their really great and remarkable chief, Joseph, conceived the bold scheme of transporting his whole band, women, children and all, across the Rockies through leagues of rough forest and broken ravines, across deep and broad rivers to Dominion territory, pursued and harassed though he was by several commands. While these Indians were yet in Idaho and before it seemed probable that they could penetrate Montana, General Miles was gathering from every available source information as to their probable route and objective and discussing

and forming plans to capture them. On the 3d of August, six days before the battle of Big Hole in which General Gibbon's command inflicted and suffered much loss, General Miles instructed Lieutenant Doane to "intercept, capture, or destroy" this band. Lieutenant Doane, 2d Cavalry, was then en route to Judith Basin near the Upper Missouri, then abounding in game and believed to be the objective of Joseph.

On the 11th of August, but two days after the battle of Big Hole and while Joseph was yet among the Rockies, the General sent six troops of the 7th Cavalry under command of

ON THE MARCH—THE ADVANCE GUARD.

its colonel, General Sturgis, towards the Upper Yellowstone with orders to "intercept, or pursue and capture or destroy" this band. Lieutenant Doane's command, which included a troop of the 7th Cavalry and a large body of Crow allies, was also placed under General Sturgis's orders for this duty. The action above indicated anticipated instructions received August 21 to the same end. General Sturgis and Lieutenant Doane were instructed to keep General Miles fully informed of all important movements and events. At evening September 17, the General learned at the cantonment, Tongue River, Montana, that the Indians had outstripped their pursuers, evaded and passed General Sturgis's forces, had had an engagement with them in the valley of the Yellowstone near the present site of Billings, and had thus a practically unobstructed route to the boundary—more than two hundred miles. Hastily organizing, from that which was left of his command, its available force, he began to move at once. All through the night the ferryboat was plying, transferring to the left bank of the Yellowstone troops, transportation, and supplies, and the early morning of the 18th saw the force striking rapidly out for the northwest, intending by a march along the hypothenuse of a triangle, to intercept a rapidly marching force which was following the perpendicular and had had five days the start. By small detachments and scouts the General kept himself informed of everything far out to the left and, thus marching, reached the Missouri, at the mouth of the Musselshell, September 23, with the main command, some of the detachments being farther up stream. Major Guido Ilges, from Fort Benton, had with a scanty detachment boldly followed up the Indians for a short distance from their place of crossing the Missouri but had not force enough to effect a decisive result. On the 25th, General Miles learned through Ilges that the Nez Percés had crossed on the 23d; he ferried his command across the Missouri and pushed out with his mounted force,—three troops of the 2d Cavalry commanded by Captain Tyler, three of the 7th Cavalry commanded by Captain Hale, and four companies of the 5th Infantry commanded by Captain Snyder,— leaving his train to follow, and carrying upon pack-mules supplies with which his command could eat sparingly and fight liberally. From early dawn to dark for four days along the grassy plains which border the Little Rockies, the troops were urged on, past tempting herds of buffaloes and flocks of inquisitive antelopes, and, on the 29th, in a snow-swept camp in the gap between the Little Rocky and the Bear Paw Mountains, tidings of the discovery of the trail came from the scouts at the left; Lieutenant Maus' 1st Infantry, commanding the scouts, had used his sleepless vigilance to good purpose. The earliest dawn of the 30th saw the command again crowding forward. Soon the small body of surrendered Cheyennes and Sioux accompanying the command roused from their usual immobility and stripped for a fray: saddles, blankets, and bridles were snatched from their ponies; now and again softly patting their hands together and pointing far down a foggy valley, they threw off blankets, beaded shirts, and leggings and, clad in a waist-cloth and a grim smile, they sprang on their ponies (guided by a lariat about neck and nose) and, rifle in hand, dashed away for the fog-obscured valley where the battle of Bear Paw was about to open. "Camp three miles away!" was shouted from mouth to mouth. General and staff, Tyler, Hale, and Snyder, with their battalions well in hand, started on the trail of the Indian scouts over the rolling hills and smooth grassy valleys which skirt the northern base of the Bear Paw. The three miles proved to be eight and the trot became a gallop. "Let Tyler sweep around to the left and cut off the camp from the herd," was the command communicated by a staff officer who led the 2d Cavalry to its position. This brought the 7th to the front of the charging column, and Hale, sitting his horse with his accustomed grace, his face lighted up with the debonair smile which his friends so well remember, dashed bravely forward to the heroic death that was awaiting him. The two battalions, 7th and 5th, under General Miles's lead charged direct upon the camp. The surprise was complete, Joseph had watched his own trail but had not scouted to his flank. But he was a soldier and a commander. His camp was a stronghold within the curve of a crescent-shaped bank, the bank itself cut by ravines heading in the open country.

The work of the scouts and Tyler's battalion was promptly done, and the Indians, seeing themselves cut off from their animals, turned at bay and met the onset of Hale and Snyder like the brave men they were. The 7th and 5th dismounted and vigorously pressed the attack, holding the Indians in a close-drawn circle; so close were the contestants that faces seen then were afterwards recognized. The Indians fired from cover and their number could not be estimated. The commanding officer, desiring to change the position of the 7th, sent one of his staff to convey the order. He rode to the position of Hale's battalion, all of whom, seeking such slight cover as inequalities of surface afforded, were hotly engaged, gave the customary salute to its commander, who was lying among his men, and began the familiar formula— "The General's compliments and he directs" —when observing that no response was given

LONG-TOM RIFLES ON THE SKIRMISH LINE.

he looked more intently and saw that he was saluting the dead. Near Hale lay his adjutant, Lieutenant J. W. Biddle, 7th Cavalry, worthy son of a brave sire who had given his life in the War for the Union.

Meantime with courage and good judgment Lieutenant McClernand, commanding a troop of the 2d Cavalry, had gathered in the herd of 800 ponies which the Indians who escaped at the first charge tried to rescue. The hot fire and the short range had wrought terrible havoc. Within the first half hour twenty per cent. of the attacking force was laid low, and an unusual percentage was killed outright, but neither party would yield. The Indians dug cellar-like pits which protected them from direct fire. Another charge was ordered and, led by Captain Carter of the 5th Infantry, a portion of that regiment sprang boldly forward, penetrated the village, and inflicted a severe loss, but thirty-five per cent. of the attacking party fell in less time than is required to describe its heroic action. It was evident that success at such a price would be too costly. The courageous and skilful defense and the excellent arms of the Indians, many of whom had magazine guns and

some of whom used explosive bullets, rendered it necessary to adopt the methods of a siege in subduing them. The skilful and brave conduct of Sergeant John McHugh, 5th Infantry, who commanded the artillery detachment and who had distinguished himself at Wolf Mountain, January 8, '77, deserves especial attention. The command was virtually a heavy skirmish line without reserves, and McHugh, regardless of personal exposure, crowded his artillery, one small Hotchkiss breech-loader and a 12-pounder, close upon the line, and deliberately loaded and fired. The exigencies of transportation permitted but few 12-pounder shells. Those few were so skilfully planted that every one of them told. On the 1st of October, the second day of the battle, some willingness to surrender appeared, but not till the 5th of October did the surrender occur. Joseph handed his rifle to General Miles and, with the dignity that well became his handsome figure and noble mien, pointed impressively to the sun and said: " From where the sun now stands I fight no more against the white man." [1]

Four hundred and eighteen Indians surrendered ; 57 were killed or wounded during the

[1] During the battle the besieged and besiegers alike looked, but with very different emotions, towards the northern horizon, and the solicitude of the commander hampered with a large number of wounded and the forebodings of those who were helpless from wounds may perhaps be faintly imagined as time and again large

forces of Indians were reported approaching, indeed apparently were close at hand, and the thick-falling snow driven by a howling wind made it impossible to determine, till the on-coming host had crowned the hills about the battle-field, that they were only a herd of buffaloes.— G. W. B.

fight and siege; 105 including Joseph's daughter escaped when the troops charged, and reached Dominion territory. The captives were taken first to Kansas and then to Indian territory. Nearly seven years later, when General Miles had received promotion and was commanding the department of Columbia, he at last succeeded in having Joseph and the remnant of his band returned to the vicinity of their old home.

The troops killed at the battle of Bear Paw lie side by side in the ceaseless comradeship of a soldier's grave on the field where they fought shoulder to shoulder; like so many other brave men who fell in the "Battle of Civilization," they are unknown or forgotten by those who profited by their victories. In his annual report for 1877, General Miles summarized thus the operations of his troops for the year ending with October: " Distance marched, over 4000 miles. Besides much property captured and destroyed, 1600 animals were taken. Upwards of 7000 Indians were killed, captured, forced to surrender, or driven out of the country."

DRIVING THE SIOUX UNDER THE YOKE.

HAVING been sent by General Miles on a peaceful mission to Dominion territory, in the spring of 1878, I heard that Sitting Bull, so far from coming to the rescue of the besieged Nez Percés, was so terrified by the proximity of the command of "Bear Coat," as the Indians called General Miles, because of a fur-trimmed coat that he wore, that he pulled up stakes and fled incontinently northward. In February, 1878, his following moved south of the boundary, and General Miles made preparations to attack him; he had already sent out his supply train with escort, when a telegram from Washington ordered him back. One of the conditions of the successes of 1876–1877 was the absence of speedy communication. That helpful lack had now been hurtfully supplied and the method adopted of conducting campaigns from a point so remote that prompt and intelligent use of the varying conditions at the scene of hostilities could not be made. But though the expedition north of the Missouri was suspended the entire section south of that river was tranquil and safe. As indicating this I may relate that on my return from the Dominion, in the summer of 1878, accompanied only by one scout, I journeyed across country from Fort Peck to Fort Keogh without seeing an Indian, and was assured of their absence by the quiet grazing of tens of thousands of buffalo among which we rode by day and camped at night. Taking advantage of this period of quiet General Miles started out with a party to visit Yellowstone Park, in

August, 1878, but, while on the way learned that another band of Indians from beyond the mountains was coming into his district, over the route followed by Joseph the year before.

These were the Bannocks from southern Idaho. Sending the ladies and guests of the pleasure party forward on their journey, he took twenty men of the 5th Infantry, and fifteen Crow scouts, and started up Clark's Fork to intercept the invaders. On September 4 he surprised the camp, and in the brief fight 11 Indians were killed and the remainder of the band captured, also their animals, numbering 250. The loss of the attacking party was small in numbers, but among the killed was Captain Andrew S. Bennett, 5th Infantry, a most meritorious officer.

The winter of 1878–9 passed without any general movement of the command, but, as was said of a President of the United States whose term of office covered a period of great excitement, it might be said of Sitting Bull on our northern border that " He sat there like a poultice, drawing all the bad humors to a head." The recalling of the expedition of February, 1878, was practically an abandonment to the hostiles of the valleys of Milk River and other northern affluents of the Missouri in Montana, and they became Sitting Bull's domain, with friendly territory to the north, and there were assembled not only the United States Indians who were hostile, but also Indians and

A WOUNDED WAR-PONY.

half-breeds from north of the line, making a total of some five thousand, with thousands of ponies. The half-breeds became a supply train of ammunition. It was evident at last, even at the seat of government thousands of miles away, that some stop must be put to the progress of affairs in that direction, and in June, 1879, the order came. In the spring the Indian's fancy lightly turns to thoughts of war. The buffaloes, in that olden time, roamed in great herds, " beef on the hoof " without limit, and the grass made the ponies fat, while the broad rivers were booming with the melting

COURIERS.

snows of the mountains, delaying the movement of troops and trains, whereas in the winter the frozen streams afforded smooth and easy roadway to troops and supplies, and the improvident enemy and their starved ponies were least prepared for activity. General Miles's force when assembled at Fort Peck consisted of seven companies of the 5th Infantry mounted on the ponies captured in earlier expeditions, seven troops of the 2d Cavalry, two companies of the 6th Infantry and an artillery detachment, besides surrendered Indian and white scouts, a total of about eight hundred, much the largest command that he ever led against Indians.

On July 17 the advance guard, two companies and Indian scouts, commanded by First-Lieutenant W. P. Clark (" Philo ") 2d Cavalry, attacked a band of more than three hundred Indians near Frenchman's Creek, and after a sharp fight drove them back for twelve miles upon their main body which, issuing out, surrounded the advance. It is doubtful whether " Philo " ever felt a qualm of fear ; he could not have been blamed if he had on this occasion experienced it, for the immense host was encircling him, and, but for the rapid advance of Miles and the main command he would probably not have survived to give his graphic account of the charge that came thundering to his rescue.

The charge was a splendid spectacle and a most efficient one ; the hostiles abandoning their property fled precipitately from the field.

But the 49th parallel, which interposed no obstacle to the hostiles, whether advancing to depredate or retreating before the troops, was an insuperable barrier to those troops and prevented such pursuit as alone could result in success. The half-breeds, with their supply train of unique and indigenous carts, quaintly fashioned of wood and rawhide, without a scrap of iron, received the next attention, and more than eight hundred were arrested and a check put to their traffic.

While, for reasons already stated, this expedition could not achieve an immediate success, it yet so impressed the hostiles with the efficiency and ubiquity of the command that it largely contributed to produce the result desired. The succeeding months witnessed no general hostile movement; occasional raiding parties of Indians appeared and were hotly pursued, killed, captured, or dispersed by the troops that were kept ever alert and ready to start out in any direction at any time of day or night. In the summer and autumn of 1880 large and important surrenders to General Miles were made, the Indians breaking off from Sitting Bull's camp and coming under their own chiefs to Fort Keogh. In this way Spotted Eagle and Broad Trail or Big Road, Rain-in-the-Face, Kicking Bear, Short Bull, etc., and their followers came in and many others, but perhaps the most widely known of the Indians who thus surrendered was Rain-in-the-Face, whose name Longfellow's poem first made familiar and whose story Mrs. Custer's graphic book "Boots and Saddle" relates somewhat at length. Whether from modesty, caution, or a passion for exact statement, is uncertain, but he did not, after his surrender, claim for himself so conspicuous and so ghastly a part in the battle of Little Big Horn as the poem assigns him. Fierce savage though he doubtless was he exhibited marked susceptibilities to the softer vanities of life, took especial pleasure in arraying himself in gaudy attire, and with face highly colored, and having on it a row of simulated raindrops, would "preserve that expression" and "look pleasant" over and over while the photographer "took" him. These Indians numbering some fifteen hundred, also a considerable part of those who had surrendered earlier, were sent in 1881 by a fleet of steamboats to their agencies on the Missouri in Dakota. General Miles had exhibited towards them those qualities which secured their loyalty and confidence. He had conquered them in battle, kept inviolate faith with them in council, treated them justly, trusted and protected them as captives, and during the months of '79 and '80, while keeping every trail hot with detachments in pursuit of the hostiles, had inaugurated a régime of peace and goodwill among those who were camped about Fort Keogh.

Dropping the implements of warfare they took hold of plow, hoe and shovel, made roads, broke the soil, and planted and so made a hopeful start on "the white man's road." When the order for their removal came they clustered about Captain E. P. Ewers, 5th Infantry, who had had immediate charge of them from the first and had ably seconded and executed General Miles's plans for their welfare, and, with tears streaming down their cheeks, besought him to take everything they owned and allow them to remain. Every member of the old campaigning force felt a keen and kindly interest in them. There was not alone the feeling of humanity but of comradeship; for many of them, as enlisted scouts, had marched and fought with the troops and some of them bear the scars of wounds received while fighting for the United States.

The surrender of those who had flocked to Sitting Bull's standard at last took from him the power to assert himself as a great chief. While proof cannot in the nature of the case be adduced, there is little room for doubt that the long tarry of those Indians north of the boundary was brought about by a corrupt alliance of one official with the traders in the Northwest Territory who profited greatly by trading with them. At last, deserted by all but his immediate family following, too weak and ill-supplied to maintain a hostile attitude, too poor by the sale or robbery of his effects to tempt the cupidity of those who graphically describe themselves as "not on the frontier for their health," Sitting Bull surrendered at Fort Buford, at the mouth of the Yellowstone, July 20, 1881. The combination in his mien of the grandeur of the great prince in misfortune and the thriftiness of the showman was irresistibly funny. Holding himself in sorrowful reserve within his tepee, he stationed one of his young men at the entrance to collect a quarter of a dollar from each one of the throng of eager visitors.

General Miles was promoted in December, 1880, which severed his connection with the 5th Infantry. Of that relation, which existed for eleven and a half years, it falls quite within the truth to say, no command was ever more ably led; no commander was ever more loyally and bravely followed.

THE CAPTURE OF GERONIMO'S APACHES.

GENERAL MILES was now assigned to the command of the Department of the Columbia, including Alaska, Washington, and Oregon, and nearly all of Idaho. Before assuming it he was employed on a commission to the Indian Territory, and on other duty in the east. He went to his new headquarters, Vancouver Barracks, in the summer of 1881. He secured the return to their former home of Joseph's band of Nez Percés, who were unhappy in the Indian Territory. In the summer of 1885 there were indications of serious trouble in the Indian Territory, growing out of the conflict between the interests of the owners of immense herds of cattle grazing in that territory and of the Indians whose reservations were thus made a grazing ground, and the President summoned General Miles from the extreme northwest to the Department of the Missouri, with headquarters at Fort Leavenworth, Kansas, in which department the Indian Territory is situated. One-fourth of the army was assembled under his orders and, by its disposition in posts and camps near the scene of the difficulty, peace was maintained, and there opened before the General the prospect of a quiet residence at that most attractive post, Fort Leavenworth, which had been his army home for several years while he was colonel of the 5th Infantry. But, on April 2, 1886, he was sent to command the Department of Arizona to relieve General Crook. And so, a second time within nine months, the President had through the War Department assigned to him a new and most difficult task. The conditions of success were wholly unlike those which obtained in the Sioux war. In the northwest the great numbers of the enemy and the intensity of the cold were

A TYPICAL TROOPER.

these lithe and active savages, who moved so rapidly and stealthily that the fancied security growing out of a period of tranquillity was often the precursor of destruction, robbery, and death. This insecurity and alarm had terrorized the citizens of the territories and caused, on the part of many, an abandonment of their ordinary industrial pursuits. Two tasks confronted him; to capture or destroy the Indians who were actively hostile led by Geronimo and Natchez, and to repress and control those who, through sympathy and relationship with the hostiles, and through instinct and experience, were ready to take the war path and swell the tide of devastation. The mountains and the sun — the first the strongholds of the savages and almost impassable obstacles to the troops, the latter the cause of the desert-like dryness and the intolerable heat which augmented the difficulties of campaigning almost to the point of impossibility — were made his allies, the eyes of his command, and the carriers of swift messages. By a system of heliograph signals, communications were sent with almost incredible swiftness; in one instance a message traveled seven hundred miles in four hours. The messages, flashed by mirrors from peak to peak of the mountains, disheartened the Indians as they crept stealthily or rode swiftly through the valleys, assuring them that all their arts and craft had not availed to conceal their trails, that troops were pursuing them and others awaiting them. The telescopes of the vigilant members of the Signal Corps, who garrisoned the rudely built but impregnable works on the mountains, permitted no movement by day, no cloud of dust even in the valleys below, to escape attention. Little wonder that the Indians thought that the powers of the unseen world were confederated against them.

Fortunately there was a treaty which permitted our troops to pursue the Indians into Mexico, and so the international boundary did

the two chief obstacles to be overcome, whereas in the southwest the hostile force was small and so easily eluded pursuers, and the temperature was torrid. Heat, barrenness, jagged mountain cliffs, steep walled cañons, scant water, or the utter absence of it, these multiplied a hundred fold the prowess of the wily Apaches who had been accustomed for generations to defy these obstacles, to sustain life under these hard conditions, and for years to prey upon the peaceful inhabitants who lived a pastoral or agricultural life on the open plains or along the rivers, or mined the rich ores of the mountains.

Devastating impartially on both sides of the boundary, Arizona, New Mexico, and Northern Mexico were laid under rude tribute by

not, as in the Northwest, interpose to protect them until they had refitted and recuperated. General Miles organized a special force of picked cavalry and infantry, scouts and guides, under Captain H. W. Lawton, 4th Cavalry, to pursue the hostiles whenever they should take to Mexican territory.

Geronimo did not permit this well-devised machine to rust from disuse. In truth, before it was fully in order, he put it to the test, making a blood-red trail from a point 150 miles within the Mexican Territory and invading ours on the 27th of April, just fifteen days after General Miles had taken command. The trail was taken up in succession, by twenty-five different commands or detachments, representing four regiments, each detachment inspired by the energy expressed in a paragraph of General Miles's order in which he said: "Commanding officers are expected to continue a pursuit until capture or until they are assured a fresh command is on the trail." This vigorous pursuit and the five encounters with different commands convinced the Indians that Arizona afforded them no place of security, and they hurried from its borders to the supposed inaccessible fastnesses of the Sierra Madre in Mexico. Though the contests of forces so small may not merit the name of battle, yet in no battle have the participants incurred greater risks or evinced a higher degree of heroism. Captain Lebo of the 10th Cavalry, after a hot pursuit of 200 miles, brought the Indians to bay and there ensued a spirited contest just within the Mexican Territory, in which Lieutenant Powhatan H. Clarke of the 10th Cavalry, then recently from the class-rooms and the drill ground of West Point, distinguished himself by rushing forward at the risk of his life and bearing to a place of safety a wounded veteran soldier who lay helpless under a sharp fire of the enemy. A like act of heroism was a few days later exhibited under similar circumstances by First-Sergeant Samuel Adams of the 4th Cavalry, of the command of Captain Hatfield of that regiment.

Lawton's command (with its sixty days' supplies on pack mules) now took up the trail. The rough nature of the country and the absence of grass and water made it impossible to employ cavalry in a long continued pursuit. Assistant-Surgeon Leonard Wood, who for a part of the time added to his professional duties the command of the infantry of Lawton's force, gives a graphic description of the country and of the chase. He writes:

Sonora, taken as a whole, is a continuous mass of mountains of the most rugged and broken character. Range follows range with hardly an excuse for a valley. It produces nothing save a few wild fruits, cactus, and more or less of game. Troops operating in these sections are dependent for all supplies on pack trains. Such is the roughness of the country in some portions that even these cannot pass through. Water is scanty and often of poor quality. Grass almost wanting during the dry season. The heat is intense, often reaching 120 degrees Fahrenheit.

Of the Apaches of Geronimo's band he says:

Mountaineers from infancy, they found little difficulty in passing through the roughest country. The cactus and various roots furnished food; water or its equivalent was also furnished by the former plant; rats, mice, rabbits, and deer contributing the meat ration, also the horse when forced as far as he could carry his rider. During the latter part of June and July it was my good fortune to command the infantry. In the detachment of Companies D and K, 8th Infantry, were men who had served in India and South Africa, and, in their opinion, this was by far the hardest and roughest service they had ever seen. . . . Infantry on this expedition marched in drawers and undershirts. . . . I do not remember seeing a pair of blue trousers put on after once wearing the lighter articles mentioned above.

Through such a region and with such drafts upon the strength and fortitude of the men this force kept up the pursuit during the intolerable heat of that summer of '86, and with such steadfastness and skill that no craft or device of the savages could throw them off the trail or secure to the pursued an hour's respite. The extreme southern point of pursuit was three hundred miles south of the international boundary and its tortuous windings spread a network of intersecting trails over the mountains and cañons of Sonora. At last (September 4) the Indians, worn out, surrendered. This band was sent ultimately to Alabama. The conduct of Lieutenant C. B. Gatewood, 6th Cavalry, in going unattended by troops into the camp of the hostiles and demanding their surrender, must be recorded as a conspicuous instance of the fortitude which at the call of duty defies danger.

Simultaneously with the winding up of the Geronimo and Natchez campaign and the deporting of them and their followers, the four hundred Warm Spring and Chiricahua Indians at Fort Apache, who were thought to be ready for an outbreak, were also hurried from the territory which they had harried and devasted for years. The citizens of Arizona indicated their appreciation of General Miles's services by presenting to him a richly ornamented sword. For the first time in our history our temple of Janus had closed doors.

THE MESSIAH DISTURBANCE.

WHEN the foregoing was written, more than a year ago, the "Messiah Craze" was beginning to attract the attention of those who were intently observing Indian affairs. It was asserted that Mormon influence was active in stirring up dissatisfaction. The craze took shape from what was, unfortunately, an always present feeling with the Indians — hunger. The Messiah was not only to annihilate the invading whites, but to bring back the boundless herds of buffalo which, but a decade ago, were the Indians' preferred food. The non-progressive, inveterately wild Indians, of whom Sitting Bull was the best known, saw in the disaffection and hallucination an opportunity to recover their fast-waning power; and the boys and young men, who had grown up in a period of peace and had listened to the recital of the deeds of their sires under the old régime, burned with zeal to emulate them.

At that time General Miles was in command of the military division which included our entire Pacific coast. Before the Indian trouble culminated, changes of command fortunately brought him from the West to the Interior, and placed him in command of the Division of the Missouri, in which are all of the Sioux, thousands of whom had surrendered to him during his campaigns of 1876-80, and among whom the craze was the most menacing. With his customary foresight, General Miles formed plans and issued orders, whose careful execution would have illustrated the beneficent work of a disciplined force, not only in preventing violence, but also in protecting non-combatants and their property. Even a partial execution of his plans afforded this protection; during the trouble, from November 15, 1890 to January 25, 1891, not a person was killed by Indians outside the boundaries of an Indian reservation, and the homes and property of adjacent settlers were unmolested.

Doubtless one of Sitting Bull's own race would call him an unbending patriot. "The Great Spirit made me an Indian and did not make me an Agency Indian," he proudly asserted to General Miles under a flag of truce, in the fall of 1876, when backed up by a thousand braves. There are, however, but two goals for the Indians — civilization or annihilation; Sitting Bull has the latter, as doubtless he would have preferred. He was killed December 15,

1890 by men of his own race who were enforcing against him the orders of the whites, whom he hated. Captain Fechet, of the 8th Cavalry, who brought a force to the support of the Agency police, took charge of the body, which was not mutilated nor scalped; he had it carried to Fort Yates, North Dakota, where it was decently buried in a coffin. Whatever the opinion entertained as to Sitting Bull and his taking off, inasmuch as his influence tended always to embroil his following with the dominant race his death will doubtless result in benefit to his own people.

For every Indian war there is a cause; too often that cause has been bad policy, bad faith, bad conduct, or blundering on the part of the whites. This sketch has simply recognized the fact of war and sought to give a true though necessarily an inadequate statement as to the means used by one commander to conduct his Indian campaigns to their uniformly successful issue. Given the fact of war, whatever the cause, the soldier must secure peace, even if he fights to win it. For the savage of to-day, as for civilized man not so many centuries ago, an enemy and his wife and children have no rights. The recognition of this fact would prevent much misconception as to the character of Indians. If I have not, in these sketches, indicated sufficiently the friendly feeling which, in common with nearly all army men, I feel for the Indians, not only friendly feeling but admiration for many of their qualities, I cannot hope to do so in a brief paragraph. The American people, those who really wish and hope to save the Indians from extinction or degradation, must be prepared to use great patience and summon all their wisdom. Indians (the men) naturally look upon the arts of peace very much as the knights of the past ages did. War is their pastime; by it come glory, honor, leadership. It is unlikely that the place of the Indians as peaceful citizens will approach their place as warriors. "Justice and judgment," the one to protect, the other justly to punish them, have been too greatly lacking. It remains yet to be seen whether the future will be better than the past.

G. W. Baird,
Major, U. S. A.

25

Besieged by the Utes

E.V. Sumner

BESIEGED BY THE UTES.

THE MASSACRE OF 1879.

ON THE DEFENSIVE — THE CARTRIDGE BAG.

IN the summer of 1879 trouble occurred between the White River Utes and their agent, N. C. Meeker. The cause is not important, but the trouble finally became serious enough to warrant the call upon the Secretary of War for the support of troops to repress turbulence and disorder amongst the Indians of that nation. In September an expedition was organized in the Department of the Platte, and the following troops were ordered out: one company of the 4th Infantry under Lieutenant Butler D. Price; Troop E, 3d Cavalry, Captain Lawson commanding; and two troops, D (Lt. J. V. S. Paddock) and F (Captain J. S. Payne), of the 5th Cavalry. Major T. T. Thornburgh, 4th Infantry, commanded the whole, and Acting Assistant-Surgeon Grimes was the medical officer.

This command was concentrated at Fort Steele, Wyoming, on the Union Pacific Railroad, and marched south from that point towards White River Agency about the 21st of September. Nothing of an unusual character occurred during the first few days of the march, nor was it supposed that anything of a serious

nature would happen. The agent had asked for one hundred soldiers and more than double that number were in this column. The troops were *en route* to a certain point to preserve order, not expecting to make war. The Utes understood that, and the very evening preceding their attack upon the troops, the chiefs entered the soldiers' camp, partook of their hospitality, and assured them of their friendship. The report of General Crook says, "The last message Meeker ever sent to Thornburgh was to the effect that the Indians were friendly and were flying the United States flag. Yet, in the face of all this, the very next morning these Indians, without provocation, treacherously lay in ambuscade and attacked the troops with the result already known." This, General Crook says, is not war, it is murder; and the General, as usual, is correct. But is it not strange that, with all the horrible examples furnished us in past years, we have never been in the habit of preparing for murder as well as war? It seems at least unfortunate that all our Indian wars must of necessity be inaugurated with the massacre or defeat of the first detachment. It may be interesting, if not instructive, to give a few examples.

The Modoc War of 1872, in which so many valuable lives were lost, was begun by the advance of half a troop of the 1st Cavalry. This force rode up to the Indian camp, dismounted, and were standing to horse, with probably no thought of being murdered or of any serious trouble. It is reported that while the officer in command was talking to the chief a rifle was discharged by an Indian, either accidentally or as a signal, and that instantly thereafter firing on the troops took place and a number were killed and wounded. The Indians, about sixty in number, taking advantage of the confusion among the troops, retired to their stronghold in the lava beds, murdering every white man *en route*. In this stronghold they defied the Government, massacred a commission composed of prominent men sent to them in peace, and withstood the attacks of 1300 soldiers for months, and until both food and water gave out.

ON OUTPOST DUTY.

The Nez Percés War in 1877 commenced in about the same way. Two small troops of cavalry, marching down a deep and long cañon, presented themselves before the camp of Chief Joseph, as if a display of this nature was all that was necessary to capture a force of two hundred and fifty warriors. The Indian, always quick to see an advantage and to profit by it, was not slow in this instance, and the first few shots from the enemy on the left and rear of the line caused a hasty retreat of the soldiers, who no doubt up to that time thought there was to be *nothing serious.*

The Little Big Horn fight in 1876, where General Custer and most of his command were massacred, was surely the result of overestimating one's strength and underrating that of the enemy.

Other examples could be furnished, but are not these, with their attendant losses and failures, sufficient to prove that with the Indian as a foe we must always be prepared, and especially careful when he seems most friendly and still holds on to his rifle? On the other hand, many instances are known where troops have met and overcome at the start more serious obstacles than those mentioned above, and without a shot being fired. A column on the march, prepared to fight if necessary, is not likely to be disturbed, and it is almost

certain that no Indians will be seen or heard from unless they have all the advantages, and unless certainty of success follows their first efforts.

This Ute campaign was a repetition of all the other sad occurrences in Indian warfare. Major Thornburgh, the commander, as noble and brave a man as ever marched with troops, fell as others had, having ignored an enemy in the morning who had the power to defeat him before noon. The march through these mountains and into the valley of Milk River, as described, was made as any march would be conducted on a turnpike through a civilized country and among friends. No danger had threatened; on the contrary, the Indians appeared friendly, and assuring messages had been received from the agent.

Thornburgh, not having had experience with Indians and trusting to appearances, anticipated no trouble, and consequently was wholly unprepared when the attack was made. We can in a measure account for such action on the part of a commander when it is remembered that with some men the desire to appear before their troops free from undue anxiety is greater than their sense of caution. Considering the number of troops in this command, and the fact that not half that number of Indians were opposed to them, it is fair to presume that with proper precaution the command might have gone through to the agency without losing a life, or even hearing a shot; but the officers and men following Thornburgh doubtless like him had no thought of danger to such a column; and had the colonel made sufficient preparation to secure his command, and reached his destination safely on that account, he would have been pronounced an "old granny" for having unduly harassed his troops when no enemy appeared.

The employment of the chiefs, ostensibly as guides, but really detaining them as hostages, would have insured the peace as well as the safety of the command beyond a doubt.

But to go more into details: Thornburgh, after leaving his infantry company at a supply camp, pushed on with his three troops of cavalry, and while on the march on the 29th of September, at 10 A. M., at the crossing of Milk River, the Indians opened fire on the column from all directions, and from what followed where Lieutenant Paddock, in command of D Troop, 5th Cavalry, and the wagon train, had corraled his train, formed his troop, and was prepared to receive and shelter his comrades.

It is not known what orders Lieutenant Paddock had from his commanding officer as to his duties with the rear guard and wagon train, but it is supposed that as no precautions were being taken in front, none were ordered in rear, so that the prompt action of this young officer in arranging his wagon train and troops for a stand, and holding every man to his duty there, was praiseworthy, and was the means of saving many lives. This afforded shelter and a rallying place for the scattered troopers, then being outflanked and driven back by the enemy; indeed, Paddock's command was even receiving attention from the Indians in the way of rifle-balls, for the Indians knew if they could get the train, they could capture or kill the rest of the command before it could escape from the valley. Here there was a halting place, and the

BEHIND THE BREASTWORK.

it would appear that the command was completely surprised, or sufficiently so to make some confusion among the troops. F Troop, 5th Cavalry, and E Troop, 3d Cavalry, were quickly brought into line, and for some time fought well and bravely, but the superior tactics of the Indian, in his usual rôle of turning the flanks, and the loss of many brave men including the commander, soon caused a retreat, and these two troops fell back perhaps half a mile to a point whole command was concentrated behind and about the wagons. The Indians then surrounded the soldiers, fired upon them from all directions, and, setting fire to the grass, advanced to within a short distance of the wagons, being screened by the thick smoke from the fire of the troops.

In this situation the battle was carried on for the rest of that day, the troops being strictly on the defensive, and keeping behind the wagons, while the Indians, lying close to the

THE RIDE OF PRIVATE MURPHY.

to the savage enemy, and all bemoaned the fate of their noble commander, also left on the field. He had proudly led them forward, and when the unlooked-for attack fell upon them still kept at the front; perhaps, having recognized too late the error of over-confidence, he determined to repair the fault even at the sacrifice of his life.

Thornburgh was a noble man, and beloved by all. The troops following him were as good as any in the army, and would have proved more than a match for the enemy if they could have gone into the fight on anything like equal terms.

After dark on this first night a volunteer was called for to take one of the horses yet left alive and if possible steal his way through the enemy's line to the nearest telegraph station. From several volunteers Private Murphy of D Troop, 5th Cavalry, was selected to take this desperate ride, and he accomplished the distance of 170 miles to the railroad in less than 24 hours.

The place selected or rather forced upon Captain Payne, 5th Cavalry, now the senior officer, for the defense of his command, was near the battle-field, and fortunately within reach of the stream called Milk River. It was in a small round valley or opening in the mountains, and within easy rifle range of the tops of the nearest hills surrounding it. On these hills the Indians took position, and while being concealed and well protected themselves, the Indians were able to pick off any soldier showing himself above the breastwork, or while moving about inside of it. The soldiers returned the fire occasionally, but it is not known that an Indian was injured during the siege. The enemy, however, was kept down close behind the ridge, and no advance or open attack on the intrenchment was at any time attempted. The position taken was on a rise or table, and was about two hundred yards from the stream. No water could be obtained during the day, but after dark a party started out to fill their buckets and canteens. They were almost immediately fired upon by the enemy, who, anticipating their necessities, had found concealment on the further side of the river in the thick underbrush. As some of the party were wounded, they returned to the breastwork unsuccessful. Water being an absolute neces-

ground and concealed as much as possible, were able to kill most of the animals and occasionally to pick off a soldier or teamster.

The loss of the animals and the number of wounded men to be cared for and protected made any movement from this spot out of the question. There was nothing to do then but fight it out and hold on until reinforcements could reach them. However, the longest day must have an end, and the sun aided these harassed soldiers by disappearing behind the hills and affording them, under cover of darkness, an opportunity to prepare for the morrow. This first night was employed by the troops in building a breastwork near the water, and in caring for the wounded.

There being no timber within reach, shelter had to be constructed from such material as was at hand. The wagons were unloaded and spare parts used, bundles of bedding, sacks of grain, cracker-boxes and bacon sides were piled up, but this not being sufficient, the bodies of dead horses and mules were dragged to the line and made use of for defense. A pit was sunk in the center of the square, and in this hole in the ground the surgeon placed his wounded, himself being one of the unfortunates. This, then, was the situation of a command of able-bodied, well-equipped soldiers, strong men every one, which, a few hours previously, had struck its camp and marched in all confidence into this valley of death. Where were now the flaunting guidons and the rude jokes about cowardly redskins? Instead thereof, many were mourning the sudden taking away of beloved comrades, whose bodies were left on the plain

sity, even if it cost life, another party was sent out, this time under escort of armed men. As soon as the party was fired upon, the escort discharged their guns, and although firing in the dark and at random, it is supposed that one or more of the enemy were wounded; at any rate the Indians fled, and the troops were not prevented after that from getting water at night sufficient for the next day.

With the dawn of the second day commenced the firing upon the troops from the hill-tops. Not an Indian could be seen on whom to return the fire; only a puff of white smoke indicated from time to time

part of the breastwork, and were used to protect the living.

Exciting accounts have been published of the situation of a party of our countrymen held fast by the ice of the frozen north. It may be said that they had rations, were comparatively comfortable, and had only to wait for a return

UTES WATCHING FOR THE RELIEF COLUMN.

where the bullet came from; and as there was little chance of finding the Indian at the spot from which he had fired, there seemed to be no use wasting ammunition on space, and firing by the troops was kept up only to prevent open attack. On this day nearly all the animals remaining alive were easily disposed of by the enemy, and some men were killed and wounded. Among the latter were Lieutenant Paddock and Surgeon Grimes. The long weary hours of this day must have been trying indeed to the besieged. The suffering and groans of the wounded seemed more terrible than the sight of the bodies of the dead, which could not be removed except at the expense of other lives. It is said that after night these bodies became

of the sun to thaw their prison doors and set them free. But these soldiers, although nearer home, were brought to a stand where a life was called for at every crack of the rifle, and where to them the light of day was the season of distress. From the number of lives already lost in this short time, and the number of wounded requiring care and increasing the anxiety, and considering the time that must elapse before help could possibly reach them, an hour here contained more real suffering than could be felt in many days of waiting only for the sun to shine.

Aside from being constantly harassed by the enemy from the outside, an incident occurred on the inside of the works this day that came near finishing the lives of some of the wounded. One of the horses was shot in such a manner as to make him frantic and unmanageable. He charged about the inclosure in a furious way until exhausted, and then fell into the pit among the wounded. Fortunately no one was injured, but some of the men said that in their nervous

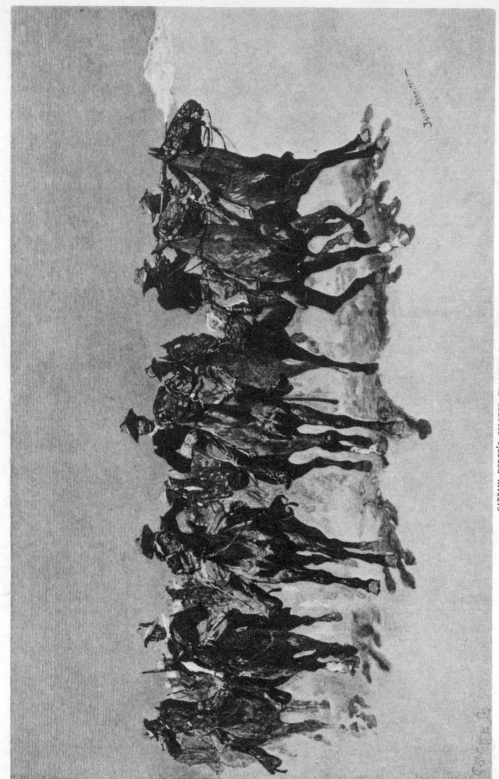

CAPTAIN DODGE'S COLORED TROOPERS TO THE RESCUE.

condition they thought the whole Ute nation had jumped from the tops of the hills to the bottom of the pit.

At an early hour on the morning of October 2d, the sentinel heard the approach of a column of horsemen, and the besieged soon welcomed Captain Dodge, 9th Cavalry, at the head of his troop. The captain, having heard of the situation, came at once to the assistance of his comrades, and managed to get through to the intrenchment without losing any of his men. This reinforcement of two officers and fifty enlisted men added materially to the fighting strength of the command, and they brought with them also the cheering news that the courier had passed through safely. The horses upon which this party rode were soon disposed of by the enemy, and Dodge and his troop became as much of a fixture as any of the besieged. The gallant dash made by these colored troopers brought them into high favor with the rest of the command, and nothing was considered too good for the " Buffalo " soldiers after that. Captain Dodge almost immediately received well-merited promotion, and was the hero of the campaign.

Leaving the besieged to worry through the days and nights that are to pass before relief can reach them, we will go with the swiftly riding courier, and see what follows his arrival at the railroad.

On the morning of October 1st, our quiet garrison at Fort D. A. Russell, near Cheyenne, Wyoming, was aroused by the information received from Department Headquarters, that Thornburgh and most of his command had been massacred by the Ute Indians, and that the few officers and men remaining were intrenched, protecting the wounded and fighting for their lives. The commanding officer, General Wesley Merritt, fortunately possessing all the characteristics of a true cavalryman, always had his command well in hand. At this time he had four troops of the 5th Cavalry and one company of the 4th Infantry, and when this sudden call reached him all that was necessary was to sound " boots and saddles " and go.

The order to take the field reached us about 8 A. M., and at 11 A. M. we had saddled up,

TIDINGS OF THE RELIEF COLUMN—LISTENING TO OFFICERS' CALL.

had marched two miles, and were loaded on the cars,—horses, equipments, pack-mules, rations and all,—and were under way. We reached Rawlins Station, our stopping place, about 1 A. M. next morning, and met there four companies of the 4th Infantry, also ordered for field service under General Merritt. The rest of that night was spent in preparing for the march. The infantry, in wagons, were on the road by 10 A. M.; the cavalry marched a little later, but overtook the infantry about twenty-five miles out at 5 P. M. Then all pushed on together until 11 P. M., when it became necessary to halt and rest the animals. At 7 A. M. we were on the road again, and continued marching until 11 P. M., at that time reaching the camp of the infantry company left behind by Major Thornburgh. Here a short rest was taken, and at dawn of day we resumed the march, reaching the entrance to Big Bear Cañon about 4 P. M. This was a rough, ugly looking place to enter with a command at night, especially with the knowledge of disaster in front and not far off. But the situation called for the greatest exertion, as well as the taking of all the chances, and although we had already made an unheard-of march that day, and on previous days, every man was anxious to go on, and even the animals seemed to be under the influence of the hour. While they were being rubbed down and fed, the men had their coffee and hardtack, and just at dusk we started off for the last march, hoping soon to reach those we knew to be in distress, and who could only be saved by our coming. Getting through that cañon at night was a desperate undertaking, leaving the Indians entirely out of the question, and on looking at the breakneck places afterwards by daylight, over which we had passed, it seemed a miracle that we succeeded in getting through without losing all the wagons carrying the infantry, and some of the horsemen as well. The cavalry was in the lead, but the "charioteers," as the infantry were called, followed close behind, and on the down grade occasionally ran into the rear of the cavalry column. On the ascent the infantrymen

General Merritt at this time was some distance ahead with the cavalry, and crossing the last hill he entered the valley just at dawn of day. It was yet too dark to see the intrenchment, but the column, while pressing on, was soon brought to a halt by a challenge from the besieged. A trumpeter was then summoned and officers' call sounded. This brought all hands to the top of the breastwork, and a lively cheer answered the last note on the trumpet. A wild scene followed this coming together of old comrades, and while it was going on, the enemy, although at their posts within easy range, did not fire a shot. Nor did they seem to be alarmed by the arrival of this overpower-

FREDERIC REMINGTON

THE RELIEF COLUMN.—I.

jumped from their wagons and pushed horses, wagons and all up the grades. On reaching the summit each party boarded its wagon, and, with a cheer, away they went down the grade on the run. All were under so much of a strain that fatigue or sleep was not thought of. Thus it was, up one hill and down another all night, and no light-artillerymen were ever more expert at mounting their limbers, than these infantrymen in getting out of and into those wagons on the run. Between 4 and 5 A. M. we reached a point about four miles from the intrenchment, and at that hour saw a sight that made the blood run cold. A citizen wagon train, hauling supplies to the agency, had been captured by the Indians, and every man belonging to it had been murdered, stripped, and partly burned. As we had had no news from the front since leaving the railroad, this was something of a surprise, and as may be imagined, at that hour in the morning, not a pleasant opening for the day. The wagon train, for the last few miles, had been stretching out a little, but on reaching this spot it was observed that all intervals were rapidly closed up and kept closed. But notwithstanding this depressing sight, some rude jokes were made, as usual, by the old soldiers in passing, and recruits were made to fear that before another sun should rise they would be broiled in like manner.

ing force, but were for the time being quiet spectators of this grand reunion, their portion of the fun probably being in the supposition of " more horses, more shoot him."

The General, having the responsibility, was probably the only one of the party in accord with the Indian idea, and consequently, not wasting much time on congratulations, he immediately set to work to prevent the loss of more men or horses.

The rear was safe in the hands of the infantry, and the cavalry was ordered to take the nearest hills on the flanks. This accomplished, the General moved out a short distance to the front, having a troop of cavalry as escort, but did not advance half a mile before being fired upon. We, however, recovered the body of Major Thornburgh, which up to that time had lain upon the battle-field of the first day. Under existing circumstances, a civilized enemy, or such an one as we are taught to fight in text-books and in field manoeuvers, would have made a hasty retreat over the mountains, and any strategist in command could have made certain calculations, but these Ute Indians, instinctively brave and not at all instructed, had the utmost confidence in their power to resist any number of soldiers attacking them in their mountain homes.

The Sioux Indian, on the open plains, likes

to show himself as much as possible, thinks to intimidate his foe by such display, and by showing himself at different points in a short space of time, to make several Sioux out of one. On the contrary, the whereabouts of the Ute Indian amongst the rocks of the mountain side, nearly his own color, can not easily be discovered; he is not known until the crack of his rifle is heard and his enemy falls, and even then the smoke covers a change of position. It is therefore impossible ever to get a Sioux into the mountains to fight, or to get a Ute out on the plains for the same purpose.

General Merritt, on seeing that the Indians were still determined and prepared to dispute

bearer of the flag was allowed to cross the valley and enter our lines. He proved to be an employé of the Indian Department, and had been sent up from the Uncumpahgre Agency to stop the war, the White River Utes, with whom we were fighting, being in a way under the control of Colorow, the chief of the Uncumpahgres. It is supposed the Indians were ready to stop anyhow, seeing the amount of force now on the ground and prepared to punish them.

This virtually raised the siege and ended the war. Leaving a light picket line to watch the enemy, the rest of the troops were withdrawn and marched back to the intrenchment,

THE RELIEF COLUMN.— II.

any advance on the part of the soldiers, ordered three troops of cavalry and all the infantry deployed to the front at once. Notwithstanding the fatigue of the long march and no breakfast, the men sprang to their feet and moved forward as if for the first time that day. Quite an exciting skirmish resulted from this advance, and the enemy went dancing round on the hilltops like monkeys, under the short-range fire of the cavalry carbines; but when the infantry battalion, which had deployed behind the crest, came up to the top and opened fire, a change of scene was at once perceptible. The first volley from the infantry rifles made a rolling sound through the mountains like artillery; the Utes ceased the ballet performance and disappeared behind the hill, but still kept up their fire on both infantry and cavalry. The troops, however, adopting the Ute tactics, kept quite as well sheltered, and as it was not the intention to advance further that day, everybody being worn out, the tired soldiers actually went to sleep on the line of battle, a few men being on the lookout and firing occasionally.

About noon there seemed to be some excitement going on among the Indians, and a large white flag was displayed to view. Fieldglasses were at once brought to bear, and it was discovered that a white man was waving the flag. Firing on both sides ceased, and the

where a jollification was now in order. The wounded were taken out of the loathsome place where they had suffered so many days, and made comfortable. Those who had not been able to wash since the first day's fight now made themselves more presentable and showed their true faces.

The fearful stench from the intrenchment, owing to the material used in its construction, was such as to necessitate a change of camp, and the whole command, accompanied now by the rescued party, moved back on the road about one mile, to clean ground and plenty of pure water.

An unconquerable desire to sleep and rest then overtook these worn-out soldiers. All forms and ceremonies for the rest of that day were dispensed with, and the valley, lately ringing with the sound of men in combat, was now as quiet and still as was its wont.

In this short campaign there were 13 men killed and 48 wounded, out of a command 150 strong.[1] The papers throughout the country mentioned it for a day or two as "the Ute affair," and there it rests, being one of several instances where the percentage of loss is greater than that experienced in battles of which monuments are being erected and elaborate me-

1 Killed 8 ⅔ per cent., and 32 per cent. wounded.

INFANTRY COVERING THE WITHDRAWAL OF CAVALRY.

morials published to commemorate deeds of bravery.

AFTER the command brought down by General Merritt had been well rested and was ready for another advance, it proceeded through the mountains to White River and the agency. It was a beautiful bright morning in October when we bade good-by to the rescued command under Captain Payne, whose faces were turned towards home, while we marched south to rescue the employés at the agency. The infantry and wagon train marched on the road, while the cavalry were well out on the flanks and in advance. The white horses of B Troop, 5th Cavalry, could be seen now and then winding along the crests of the hills on one side, while the blacks of A Troop kept pace with them on the other. No attack could have been made on that column without due warning, and the result was we crossed the high hills and wound through cañon after cañon, reaching the valley of White River and the agency without hearing a shot or, to my knowledge, seeing an Indian.

At the agency a horrible sight presented itself. Every building had been burned, the bodies of all the male employés were stretched upon the ground where they had been murdered a few days before, and the women had been carried off into a captivity worse than death. After the dead had been buried, the command went into camp on White River.

The Indians had taken to the mountains, and in order to follow them it was necessary to abandon wagon transportation and fit up pack trains. While these preparations were going on, we had still another sad experience, and a reminder that the Utes were still near us and relentless enough to take any advantage presenting itself.

A party under Lieutenant Hall, regimental quartermaster, was sent out to reconnoiter and look for a trail across the mountains from White River to Grand River. With this party was Lieutenant William Bayard Weir, of the Ordnance Department, and his sergeant, Humme. Weir went out as a volunteer to accompany Hall, and to hunt. As the party were riding along on the trail, a small herd of deer was discovered off to the left in a ravine. Weir and Humme went after them, while Hall kept on to the front. He had not gone far, however, before he saw fresh Indian signs, and soon afterwards heard sharp firing to his left and rear. On turning back to ascertain the cause and to help Weir if he should be in trouble, he was fired upon himself, and discovered that he was surrounded by Indians. He covered his party as quickly as possible in the dry bed of a stream near at hand, and kept the Indians off until after dark. Then riding into camp he first discovered that Weir had not come in, and reported that he was probably killed. The battalion of the 5th Cavalry was turned out at once, and, as it was 10 P. M., we had an all-night march ahead of us. Just at dawn we reached the place where Weir had left Hall, and we took his trail and followed it up until we found his dead body lying cold and stiff on the mountain side. This seemed indeed an unnecessary sacrifice. Weir was a noble fellow, beloved by all, and the gathering of that sorrowing crowd of soldiers about his body was a sad experience even to the oldest of them. His face still bore the familiar and kindly expression we knew so well. An overcoat was wrapped around the body, and it was then strapped on a cavalry horse. We returned to camp as sad a funeral procession as one could well imagine.

The country through which we were then operating was a howling wilderness; it is now traversed by railroads and covered with villages and farms. Children at play unwittingly trample the grass over the graves of soldiers who gave their lives that they might live and thrive, and communities throughout the West generally send representatives to Congress, some of whom, in the peace and plenty of their comfortable homes, fail to recognize, in Washington, the hardships, privations, and sacrifice of life suffered by the army, before their prosperity could be possible or the lives of their constituents assured.

In this the simple duty of soldiers was performed, and no credit is claimed, but should not the record of past deeds such as these, accompanied by the prosperity that has followed, at least guarantee a more generous feeling for the army by all citizens, more especially by those who are called upon to support it?

E. V. Sumner,
Lt.-Colonel 5th Cavalry, U. S. A.

26

The First Emigrant Train to California

John Bidwell

A PERIL OF THE PLAINS.

THE FIRST EMIGRANT TRAIN TO CALIFORNIA.

BY JOHN BIDWELL (PIONEER OF '41).

IN the spring of 1839, — living at the time in the western part of Ohio, — being then in my twentieth year, I conceived a desire to see the great prairies of the West, especially those most frequently spoken of, in Illinois, Iowa, and Missouri. Emigration from the East was tending westward, and settlers had already begun to invade those rich fields.

Starting on foot to Cincinnati, ninety miles distant, I fortunately got a chance to ride most of the way on a wagon loaded with farm produce. My outfit consisted of about $75, the clothes I wore, and a few others in a knapsack which I carried in the usual way strapped upon my shoulders, for in those days travelers did not have valises or trunks. Though traveling was considered dangerous, I had no weapon more formidable than a pocket-knife. From Cincinnati I went down the Ohio River by steamboat to the Mississippi, up the Mississippi to St. Louis, and thence to Burlington,

in what was then the Territory of Iowa. Those were bustling days on the western rivers, which were then the chief highways of travel. The scenes at the wood landings I recall as particularly lively and picturesque. Many passengers would save a little by helping to "wood the boat," *i. e.*, by carrying wood down the bank and throwing it on the boat, a special ticket being issued on that condition. It was very interesting to see the long lines of passengers coming up the gang-plank, each with two or three sticks of wood on his shoulders. An anecdote is told of an Irishman who boarded a western steamer and wanted to know the fare to St. Louis, and, being told, asked, "What do you charge for 150 pounds of freight?" Upon learning the price, a small amount, he announced that he would go as freight. "All right," said the captain; "put him down in the hold and lay some flour barrels on him to keep him down."

In 1839 Burlington had perhaps not over two hundred inhabitants, though it was the capital of Iowa Territory. After consultation with the governor, Robert Lucas of Ohio, I concluded to go into the interior and select a tract of land on the Iowa River. In those days one was permitted to take up 160 acres, and where practicable it was usual to take part timber and part prairie. After working awhile at putting up a log house — until all the people in the neighborhood became ill with fever and ague — I concluded to move on and strike out to the south and southwest into Missouri. I traveled across country, sometimes by the sun, without road or trail. There were houses and settlements, but they were scattered; sometimes one would have to go twenty miles to find a place to stay at night. The principal game seen was the prairie hen (*Tetraonidæ cupido*); the prairie wolf (*Canis latrans*) also abounded. Continuing southwest and passing through Huntsville I struck the Missouri River near Keytesville in Chariton County. Thence I continued up the north side of the river till the westernmost settlement in Missouri was reached ; this was in Platte County. The Platte Purchase, as it was called, had been recently bought from the Indians, and was newly but thickly settled, on account of its proximity to navigation, its fine timber, good water, and unsurpassed fertility.

On the route I traveled I cannot recall seeing an emigrant wagon in Missouri. The western movement, which subsequently filled Missouri and other Western States and overflowed into the adjoining Territories, had then hardly begun, except as to Platte County. The contest in Congress over the Platte Purchase, which by increasing the area of Missouri gave more territory to slavery, called wide attention to that charming region. The antislavery sentiment even at that date ran quite high. This was, I believe, the first addition to slave territory after the Missouri Compromise. But slavery won. The rush that followed in the space of one or two years filled the most desirable part of the purchase to overflowing. The imagination could not conceive a finer country — lovely, rolling, fertile, wonderfully productive, beautifully arranged for settlement, part prairie and part timber. The land was unsurveyed. Every settler had aimed to locate a half-mile from his neighbor, and there was as yet no conflict. Peace and contentment reigned. Nearly every place seemed to have a beautiful spring of clear cold water. The hills and prairies and the level places were alike

covered with a black and fertile soil. I cannot recall seeing an acre of poor land in Platte County. Of course there was intense longing on the part of the people of Missouri to have the Indians removed, and a corresponding desire, as soon as the purchase was consummated, to get possession of the beautiful land. It was in some sense perhaps a kind of Oklahoma movement. Another feature was the abundance of wild honeybees. Every tree that had a hollow in it seemed to be a bee-tree, and every hollow was full of rich golden honey. A singular fact which I learned from old hunters was that the honey-bee was never found more than seventy or eighty miles in advance of the white settlements on the

JOHN BIDWELL.
(FROM A DAGUERREOTYPE TAKEN BY BRADY IN 1850.)

frontier. On this attractive land I set my affections, intending to make it my home.

On my arrival, my money being all spent, I was obliged to accept the first thing that offered, and began teaching school in the country about five miles from the town of Weston, which was located on the north side of the Missouri River and about four miles above Fort Leavenworth in Kansas Territory.

THE MISSOURI RIVER AT WESTON, FROM THE KANSAS SIDE.

SITE OF THE OLD STOCKADE, FORT LEAVENWORTH.

Possibly some may suppose it did not take much education to teach a country school at that period in Missouri. The rapid settlement of that new region had brought together people of all classes and conditions, and had thrown into juxtaposition almost every phase of intelligence as well as of illiteracy. But there was no lack of self-reliance or native shrewdness in any class, and I must say that I learned to have a high esteem for the people, among whom I found warm and lifelong friends.

But even in Missouri there were drawbacks. Rattlesnakes and copperheads were abundant. One man, it was said, found a place to suit him, but on alighting from his horse heard so many snakes that he concluded to go farther. At his second attempt, finding more snakes instead of fewer, he left the country altogether. I taught school there in all about a year. My arrival was in June, 1839, and in the fall of that year the surveyors came on to lay out the country: the lines ran every way, sometimes through a man's house, sometimes through his barn, so that there was much confusion and trouble about boundaries, etc. By the favor of certain men, and by paying a small amount for a little piece of fence here and a small clearing there, I got a claim, and purposed to make it my home, and to have my father remove there from Ohio.

In the following summer, 1840, the weather was very hot, so that during the vacation I could do but little work on my place, and needing some supplies,—books, clothes, etc.,— I concluded to take a trip to St. Louis, which

I did by way of the Missouri River. The distance was six hundred miles by water; the down trip occupied two days, and was one of the most delightful experiences of my life. But returning, the river being low and full of snags, and the steamboat heavily laden,— the boats were generally light going down,— we were continually getting on sand bars, and were delayed nearly a month. This trip proved to be the turning-point in my life, for while I was gone a man had jumped my land. Generally in such cases public sentiment was against the jumper, and it was decidedly so in my case. But the scoundrel held on. He was a bully—had killed a man in Callaway County—and everybody seemed afraid of him. Influential friends of mine tried to persuade him to let me have eighty acres, half of the claim. But he was stubborn, and said that all he wanted was just what the law allowed him. Unfortunately for me, he had the legal advantage. I had worked some now and then on the place, but had not actually lived on it. The law required a certain residence, and that the preëmptor should be twenty-one years of age or a man of family. I was neither, and could do nothing. Nearly all I had earned had been spent upon the land, and when that was taken I lost about everything I had. There being no possibility of getting another claim to suit me, I resolved to go elsewhere when spring should open.

In November or December of 1840, while still teaching school in Platte County, I came across a Frenchman named Roubideaux, who said he had been to California. He had been a trader in New Mexico, and had followed the road traveled by traders from the frontier we could ask him was answered favorably. Generally the first question which a Missourian asked about a country was whether there was any fever and ague. I remember his answer distinctly. He said there was but one man in California that had ever had a chill there, and it was a matter of so much wonderment to the people of Monterey that they went eighteen miles into the country to see him shake. Nothing could have been more satisfactory on the

LOW WATER ON THE MISSOURI.

of Missouri to Santa Fe. He had probably gone through what is now New Mexico and Arizona into California by the Gila River trail used by the Mexicans. His description of California was in the superlative degree favorable, so much so that I resolved if possible to see that wonderful land, and with others helped to get up a meeting at Weston and invited him to make a statement before it in regard to the country. At that time when a man moved out West, as soon as he was fairly settled he wanted to move again, and naturally every question imaginable was asked in regard to this wonderful country. Roubideaux described it as one of perennial spring and boundless fertility, and laid stress on the countless thousands of wild horses and cattle. He told about oranges, and hence must have been at Los Angeles, or the mission of San Gabriel, a few miles from it. Every conceivable question that score of health. He said that the Spanish authorities were most friendly, and that the people were the most hospitable on the globe; that you could travel all over California and it would cost you nothing for horses or food. Even the Indians were friendly. His description of the country made it seem like a Paradise.

The result was that we appointed a corresponding secretary, and a committee to report a plan of organization. A pledge was drawn up in which every signer agreed to purchase a suitable outfit, and to rendezvous at Sapling Grove in what is now the State of Kansas, on the 9th of the following May, armed and equipped to cross the Rocky Mountains to California. We called ourselves the Western Emigration Society, and as soon as the pledge was drawn up every one who agreed to come signed his name to it, and it took like wildfire.

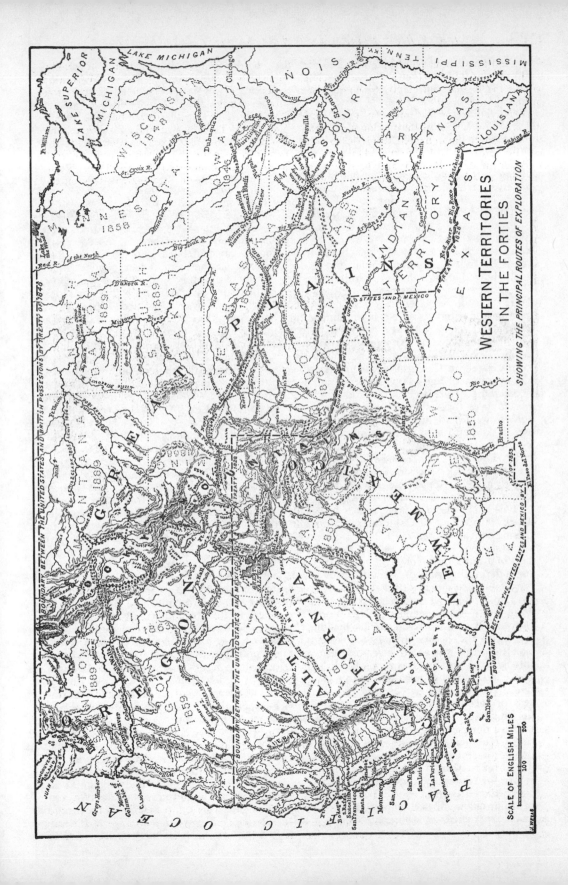

WESTERN TERRITORIES
IN THE FORTIES

SHOWING THE PRINCIPAL ROUTES OF EXPLORATION

SCALE OF ENGLISH MILES
100   200

In a short time, I think within a month, we had about five hundred names; we also had correspondence on the subject with people all over Missouri, and even as far east as Illinois and Kentucky, and as far south as Arkansas. As soon as the movement was announced in the papers we had many letters of inquiry, and we expected people in considerable numbers to join us. About that time we heard of a man living in Jackson County, Missouri, who had received a letter from a person in California named Dr. Marsh, speaking favorably of the country, and a copy of this letter was published.

Our ignorance of the route was complete. We knew that California lay west, and that was the extent of our knowledge. Some of the maps consulted, supposed of course to be correct, showed a lake in the vicinity of where Salt Lake now is; it was represented as a long lake, three or four hundred miles in extent, narrow and with two outlets, both running into the Pacific Ocean, either apparently larger than the Mississippi River. An intelligent man with whom I boarded — Elam Brown, who till recently lived in California, dying when over ninety years of age — possessed a map that showed these rivers to be large, and he advised me to take tools along to make canoes, so that if we found the country so rough that we could not get along with our wagons we could descend one of those rivers to the Pacific. Even Frémont knew nothing about Salt Lake until 1843, when for the first time he explored it and mapped it correctly, his report being first printed, I think, in 1845.

This being the first movement to cross the Rocky Mountains to California, it is not surprising that it suffered reverses before we were fairly started. One of these was the publication of a letter in a New York newspaper giving a depressing view of the country for which we were all so confidently longing. It seems that in 1837 or 1838 a man by the name of Farnham, a lawyer, went from New York City into the Rocky Mountains for his health. He was an invalid, hopelessly gone with consumption it was thought, and as a last resort he went into the mountains, traveled with the trappers, lived in the open air as the trappers lived, eating only meat as they did, and in two or three years he entirely regained his health; but instead of returning east by way of St. Louis, as he had gone, he went down the Columbia River and took a vessel to Monterey and thence to San Blas, making his way through Mexico to New York. Upon his return — in February or March, 1841 — he published the letter mentioned. His bad opinion of California was based wholly on his unfortunate experience in Monterey, which I will recount.

In 1840 there lived in California an old Rocky Mountaineer by the name of Isaac Graham. He was injudicious in his talk, and by boasting that the United States or Texas would some day take California, he excited the hostility and jealousy of the people. In those days Americans were held in disfavor by the native Californians on account of the war made by Americans in Texas to wrest Texas from Mexico. The number of Americans in California at this time was very small. When I went to California in 1841 all the foreigners — and all were foreigners except Indians and Mexicans — did not, I think, exceed one hundred; nor was the character of all of them the most prepossessing. Some had been trappers in the Rocky Mountains who had not seen civilization for a quarter of a century; others were men who had found their way into California, as Roubideaux had done, by way of Mexico; others still had gone down the Columbia River to Oregon and joined trapping parties in the service of the Hudson Bay Company going from Oregon to California — men who would let their beards grow down to their knees, and wear buckskin garments made and fringed like those of the Indians, and who considered it a compliment to be told "I took ye for an Injin." Another class of men from the Rocky Mountains were in the habit of making their way by the Mohave Desert south of the Sierra Nevada into California to steal horses, sometimes driving off four or five hundred at a time. The other Americans, most numerous perhaps, were sailors who had run away from vessels and remained in the country. With few exceptions this was the character of the American population when I came to California, and they were not generally a class calculated to gain much favor with the people. Farnham happened to come into the bay of Monterey when this fellow Graham and his confederates, and all others whom the Californians suspected, were under arrest in irons on board a vessel, ready for transportation to San Blas in Mexico, whither indeed they were taken, and where some of them died in irons. I am not sure that at this time the English had a consul in California; but the United States had none, and there was no one there to take the part of the Americans. Farnham, being a lawyer, doubtless knew that the proceeding was illegal. He went ashore and protested against it, but without effect, as he was only a private individual. Probably he was there on a burning hot day, and saw only the dreary sandhills to the east of the old town of Monterey. On arriving in New York he published the letter referred to, describing how Americans were oppressed by the native Californians, and how dangerous it was for Americans to go there. The merchants of Platte

"I TOOK YE FOR AN INJIN."

County had all along protested against our go-ing, and had tried from the beginning to dis-courage and break up the movement, saying it was the most unheard-of, foolish, wild-goose chase that ever entered into the brain of man for five hundred people to pull up stakes, leave that beautiful country, and go away out to a region that we knew nothing of. But they made lit-tle headway until this letter of Farnham's ap-peared. They republished it in a paper in the town of Liberty in Clay County,— there be-ing no paper published in Platte County,— and sent it broadcast all over the surrounding re-gion. The result was that as the people began to think more seriously about the scheme the membership of the society began dropping off, and so it happened at last that of all the five hundred that signed the pledge I was the only one that got ready ; and even I had hard work

to do so, for I had barely means to buy a wagon, a gun, and provisions. Indeed, the man who was going with me, and who was to furnish the horses, backed out, and there I was with my wagon !

During the winter, to keep the project alive, I had made two or three trips into Jackson County, Missouri, crossing the Missouri River, always dangerous in winter when ice was run-ning, by the ferry at Westport Landing, now Kansas City. Sometimes I had to go ten miles farther down — sixty miles from Weston — to a safer ferry at Independence Landing in order to get into Jackson County, to see men who were talking of going to California, and to get information.

At the last moment before the time to start for the rendezvous at Sapling Grove — it seemed almost providential — along came a man named George Henshaw, an invalid, from Illinois, I think. He was pretty well dressed, was riding a fine black horse, and had ten or fifteen dollars. I persuaded him to let me take his horse and trade him for a yoke of steers to pull the wagon and a sorry-looking, one-eyed mule for him to ride. We went *via* Weston to lay in some supplies. One wagon and four or five persons here joined us. On leaving Weston, where there had been so much opposition, we were six or seven in number, and nearly half the town followed us for a mile, and some for five or six miles, to bid us good-by, showing the deep interest felt in our journey. All expressed good wishes and desired to hear from us. When we reached Sapling Grove, the place of rendezvous, in May, 1841, there was but one wagon ahead of us. For the next few days one or two wagons would come each day, and among the recruits were three families from Arkansas. We organized by electing as captain of the company a man named Bartleson from Jackson County, Missouri. He was not the best man for the position, but we were given to understand that if he was not elected captain he would not go; and as he had seven or eight men with him, and we did not want the party diminished, he was chosen. Every one furnished his own supplies. The party consisted of sixty-nine, including men, women, and children. Our teams were of oxen, mules, and horses. We had no cows, as the later emigrants usually had, and the lack of milk was a great deprivation to the children. It was understood that every one should have not less than a barrel of flour with sugar and so forth to suit; but I laid in one hundred pounds of flour more than

the usual quantity, besides other things. This I did because we were told that when we got into the mountains we probably would get out of bread and have to live on meat alone, which I thought would kill me even if it did not others. My gun was an old flint-lock rifle, but a good one. Old hunters told me to have nothing to do with cap or percussion locks, that they were unreliable, and that if I got my caps or percussion wet I could not shoot, while if I lost my flint I could pick up another on the plains. I doubt whether there was one hundred dollars in money in the whole party, but all were enthusiastic and anxious to go.

In five days after my arrival we were ready to start, but no one knew where to go, not even the captain. Finally a man came up, one of the last to arrive, and announced that a company of Catholic missionaries were on their way from St. Louis to the Flathead nation of Indians with an old Rocky Mountaineer for a guide, and that if we would wait another day they would be up with us. At first we were independent, and thought we could not afford to wait for a slow missionary party. But when we found that no one knew which way to go, we sobered down and waited for them to come up; and it was well we did, for otherwise probably not one of us would ever have reached California, because of our inexperience. Afterwards when we came in contact with Indians our people were so easily excited that if we had not had with us an old mountaineer the result would certainly have been disastrous. The name of the guide was Captain Fitzpatrick; he had been at the head of trapping parties in the Rocky Mountains for many years. He and the missionary party went with

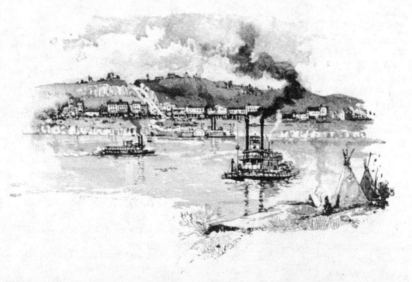

WESTPORT LANDING, KANSAS CITY. (FROM A PRINT OF THE PERIOD.)

FATHER DE SMET.

ness and great affability under all circumstances; nothing seemed to disturb his temper. The Canadians had mules and Red River carts, instead of wagons and horses,—two mules to each cart, five or six of them,—and in case of steep hills they would hitch three or four of the animals to one cart, always working them tandem. Sometimes a cart would go over, breaking everything in it to pieces; and at such times Father De Smet would be just the same — beaming with good humor.

In general our route lay from near Westport, where Kansas City now is, northwesterly over the prairie, crossing several streams, till we struck the Platte River. Then we followed along the south side of the Platte to and a day's journey or so along the South Fork. Here the features of the country became more bold and interesting. Then crossing the South Fork of the Platte, and following up the north side for a day or so, we went over to the North Fork and camped at Ash Hollow; thence up the north side of that fork, passing those noted landmarks known as the Court House Rocks, Chimney Rock, Scott's Bluffs, etc., till we came to Fort Laramie, a trading post of the American Fur Company, near which was Lupton's Fort, belonging, as I understood, to some rival company. Thence after several days we came to another noted landmark called

us as far as Soda Springs, now in Idaho Territory, whence they turned north to the Flathead nation. The party consisted of three Roman Catholic priests — Father De Smet, Father Pont, Father Mengarini — and ten or eleven French Canadians, and accompanying them were an old mountaineer named John Gray and a young Englishman named Romaine, and also a man named Baker. They seemed glad to have us with them, and we certainly were glad to have their company. Father De Smet had been to the Flathead nation before. He had gone out with a trapping party, and on his return had traveled with only a guide by another route, farther to the north and through hostile tribes. He was genial, of fine presence, and one of the saintliest men I have ever known, and I cannot wonder that the Indians were made to believe him divinely protected. He was a man of great kind-

A BIT OF ROUGH ROAD.

ON THE WAY TO THE PLATTE.

Independence Rock, on a branch of the North Platte called the Sweetwater, which we followed up to the head, soon after striking the Little Sandy, and then the Big Sandy, which empties into Green River. Next we crossed Green River to Black Fork, which we followed up till we came to Ham's Fork, at the head of which we crossed the divide between Green and Bear rivers. Then we followed Bear River down to Soda Springs. The waters of Bear Lake discharged through that river, which we continued to follow down on the west side till we came to Salt Lake. Then we went around the north end of the lake and struck out to the west and southwest.

For a time, until we reached the Platte River, one day was much like another. We set forth every morning and camped every night, detailing men to stand guard. Captain Fitzpatrick and the missionary party would generally take the lead and we would follow. Fitzpatrick knew all about the Indian tribes, and when there was any danger we kept in a more compact body, to protect one another. At other times we would be scattered along, sometimes for half a mile or more. We were generally together, because there was often work to be done to avoid delay. We had to make the road, frequently digging down steep banks, filling gulches, removing stones, etc. In such cases everybody would take a spade or do something to help make the road passable. When we camped at night we usually drew the wagons and carts together in a hollow square and picketed our animals inside the corral. The wagons were common ones and of no special pattern, and some of them were

effect, to control and pacify them. Every man started his team into a run, till the oxen, like the mules and horses, were in a full gallop. Captain Fitzpatrick went ahead and directed them to follow, and as fast as they came to the bank of the river he put the wagons in the form of a hollow square and had all the animals securely picketed within. After a while the Indians came in sight. There were only forty of them, but they were well mounted on horses, and were evidently a war party, for they had no women except one, a medicine woman. They came up and camped within a hundred yards of us on the river below. Fitzpatrick told us that they would not have come

A POWWOW WITH CHEYENNES.

covered. The tongue of one would be fastened to the back of another. To lessen the danger from Indians, we usually had no fires at night and did our cooking in the daytime.

The first incident was a scare that we had from a party of Cheyenne Indians just before we reached the Platte River, about two weeks after we set out. One of our men who chanced to be out hunting, some distance from the company and behind us, suddenly appeared without mule, gun, or pistol, and lacking most of his clothes, and in great excitement reported that he had been surrounded by thousands of Indians. The company, too, became excited, and Captain Fitzpatrick tried, but with little

in that way if they were hostile. Our hunter in his excitement said that there were thousands of them, and that they had robbed him of his gun, mule, and pistol. When the Indians had put up their lodges Fitzpatrick and John Gray, the old hunter mentioned, went out to them and by signs were made to understand that the Indians did not intend to hurt the man or to take his mule or gun, but that he was so excited when he saw them that they had to disarm him to keep him from shooting them; they did not know what had become of his pistol or of his clothes, which he said they had torn off. They surrendered the mule and the gun, thus showing that they were friendly. They proved to be Cheyenne Indians.

SPLITTING THE HERD.

Ever afterwards that man went by the name of Cheyenne Dawson.

As soon as we struck the buffalo country we found a new source of interest. Before reaching the Platte we had seen an abundance of antelope and elk, prairie wolves and villages of prairie dogs, but only an occasional buffalo. We now began to kill buffaloes for food, and at the suggestion of John Gray, and following the practice of Rocky Mountain white hunters, our people began to kill them just to get the tongues and the marrow bones, leaving all the rest of the meat on the plains for the wolves to eat. But the Cheyennes, who traveled ahead of us for two or three days, set us a better example. At their camps we noticed that when they killed buffaloes they took all the meat, everything but the bones. Indians were never wasteful of the

buffalo except in winter for the sake of the robes, and then only in order to get the whisky which traders offered them in exchange. There is no better beef in the world than that of the buffalo; it is also very good jerked, *i. e.*, cut into strings and thoroughly dried. It was an easy matter to kill buffaloes after we got to where they were numerous, by keeping out of sight and to the leeward of them. I think I can truly say that I saw in that region in one day more buffaloes than I have seen of cattle in all my life. I have seen the plain black with them for several days' journey as far as the eye could reach. They seemed to be coming northward continually from the distant plains to the Platte to get water, and would plunge in and swim across by thousands — so numerous were they that they changed not only the color of the

A RECRUIT FROM CIVILIZATION.

water, but its taste, until it was unfit to drink; but we had to use it. One night when we were encamped on the South Fork of the Platte they came in such droves that we had to sit up and fire guns and make what fires we could to keep them from running over us and trampling us into the dust. We were obliged to go out some distance from camp to turn them: Captain Fitzpatrick told us that if we did not do this the buffaloes in front could not turn aside for the pressure of those behind. We could hear them thundering all night long; the ground fairly trembled with vast approaching bands; and if they had not been diverted, wagons, animals, and emigrants would have been trodden under their feet. One cannot nowadays describe the rush and wildness of the thing. A strange feature was that when old oxen, tired and foot-sore, got among a buffalo herd, as they sometimes would in the night, they would soon become as wild as the wildest buffalo; and if ever recovered it was because they could not run so fast as the buffaloes or one's horse. The ground over which the herds trampled was left rather barren, but buffalo-grass being short and curling, in traveling over it they did not cut it up as much as they would other kinds.

On the Platte River, on the afternoon of one of the hottest days we experienced on the plains, we had a taste of a cyclone: first came a terrific shower, followed by a fall of hail to the depth of four inches, some of the stones being as large as turkeys' eggs; and the next day a waterspout—an angry, huge, whirling cloud column, which seemed to draw its water from the Platte River—passed within a quarter of a mile behind us. We stopped and braced ourselves against our wagons to keep them from being overturned. Had it struck us it doubtless would have demolished us.

Above the junction of the forks of the Platte we continued to pass notable natural formations—first O'Fallon's Bluffs, then Court House Rocks, a group of fantastic shapes to which some of our party started to go. After they had gone what seemed fifteen or twenty miles the huge pile looked just as far off as when they started, and so they turned and came back—so deceptive are distances in the clear atmosphere of the Rocky Mountains. A noted landmark on the North Fork, which we sighted fifty miles away, was Chimney Rock. It was then nearly square, and I think it must have been fifty feet higher than now, though after we passed it a portion of it fell off. Scott's Bluffs are known to emigrants for their picturesqueness. These formations, like those first mentioned, are composed of indurated yellow clay or soft sand rock; they are washed and broken

O'FALLON'S BLUFFS FROM NEAR THE JUNCTION OF THE FORKS OF THE PLATTE.

into all sorts of fantastic forms by the rains and storms of ages, and have the appearance of an immense city of towers and castles. They are quite difficult to explore, as I learned by experience in an effort to pursue and kill mountain sheep or bighorn. These were seen in great numbers, but we failed to kill any, as they in-

Mountains to whom they might sell it. This was a surprise to many of us, as there had been no drinking on the way. John Gray was sent ahead to see if he could find a trapping party, and he was instructed, if successful, to have them come to a certain place on Green River. He struck a trail, and overtook a party on

FORT LARAMIE IN 1849.

habit places almost inaccessible and are exceedingly wild.

As we ascended the Platte buffaloes became scarcer, and on the Sweetwater none were to be seen. Now appeared in the distance to the north of west, gleaming under its mantle of perpetual snow, that lofty range known as the Wind River Mountains. It was the first time I had seen snow in summer; some of the peaks were very precipitous, and the view was altogether most impressive. Guided by Fitzpatrick, we crossed the Rockies at or near the South Pass, where the mountains were apparently low. Some years before a man named William Subletts, an Indian fur trader, went to the Rocky Mountains with goods in wagons, and those were the only wagons that had ever been there before us; sometimes we came across the tracks, but generally they were obliterated, and thus were of no service. Approaching Green River in the Rocky Mountains, it was found that some of the wagons, including Captain Bartleson's, had alcohol on board, and that the owners wanted to find trappers in the Rocky

their way to the buffalo region to lay in provisions, *i. e.,* buffalo meat, and they returned, and came and camped on Green River very soon after our arrival, buying the greater part, if not all, of the alcohol, it first having been diluted so as to make what they called whisky — three or four gallons of water to a gallon of alcohol. Years afterwards we heard of the fate of that party: they were attacked by Indians the very first night after they left us and several of them killed, including the captain of the trapping party, whose name was Frapp. The whisky was probably the cause.

Several years ago when I was going down Weber Cañon, approaching Salt Lake, swiftly borne along on an observation car amid cliffs and over rushing streams, something said that night at the camp-fire on Green River was forcibly recalled to mind. We had in our party an illiterate fellow named Bill Overton, who in the evening at one of the camp-fires loudly declared that nothing in his life had ever surprised him. Of course that raised a dispute. "Never surprised in your life?" "No, I never was surprised." And, moreover, he swore that nothing ever *could* surprise him. "I should not be surprised," said he, "if I were to see a steamboat come plowing over these mountains this minute." In rattling down the cañon of Weber River it occurred to me that the reality was almost equal to Bill Overton's extravaganza, and I could but wonder what he would have said had he suddenly come upon this modern scene.

As I have said, at Soda Springs — at the northernmost bend of Bear River — our party separated. It was a bright and lovely place. The abundance of soda water, including the intermittent gushing so-called Steamboat Spring; the beautiful fir and cedar covered hills; the huge piles of red or brown sinter, the result of fountains once active but then dry — all these, together with the river, lent a charm to its wild beauty and made the spot a notable one. Here the missionary party were to turn north and go into the Flathead nation. Fort Hall, about forty miles distant on Snake River, lay on their route. There was no road; but something like a trail, doubtless used by the trappers, led in that direction. From Fort Hall there was also a trail down Snake River, by which trapping parties reached the Columbia River and Fort Vancouver, the headquarters of the Hudson Bay Company.

Our party, originally sixty-nine, including women and children, had become lessened to sixty-four in number. One had accidentally shot and killed himself at the forks of the Platte. Another of our party, named Simpson, had left us at Fort Laramie. Three had turned back from Green River, intending to make their way to Fort Bridger and await an opportunity to return home. Their names were Peyton, Rodgers, and Amos E. Frye. Thirty-two of our party, becoming discouraged, decided not to venture without path or guide into the unknown and trackless region towards California, but concluded to go with the missionary party to Fort Hall and thence find their way down Snake and Columbia rivers into Oregon.[1] The rest of us — also thirty-two in number, including Benjamin Kelsey, his wife and little daughter — remained firm, refusing to be diverted from our original purpose of going direct to California. After getting all the information we could from Captain Fitzpatrick, we regretfully bade good-by to our fellow emigrants and to Father De Smet and his party.

We were now thrown entirely upon our own resources. All the country beyond was to us

a veritable *terra incognita*, and we only knew that California lay to the west. Captain Fitzpatrick was not much better informed, but he had heard that parties had penetrated the country to the southwest and west of Salt Lake to trap for beaver; and by his advice four of our men went with the parties to Fort Hall to consult Captain Grant, who was in charge there, and to gain information. Meanwhile our depleted party slowly made its way down the west side of Bear River.

Our separation at Soda Springs recalls an incident. The days were usually very hot, the nights almost freezing. The first day our little company went only about ten miles and camped on Bear River. In company with a man named James John — always called " Jimmy John " — I wandered a mile or two down the river fishing. Seeing snow on a high mountain to the west we longed to reach it, for the heat where we were was intense. So, without losing time to get our guns or coats or to give notice at the camp, we started direct for the snow, with the impression that we could go and return by sundown. But there intervened a range of lower mountains, a certain peak of which seemed almost to touch the snow. Both of us were fleet of foot and made haste, but we only gained the summit of the peak about sundown. The distance must have been twelve or fifteen miles. A valley intervened, and the snow lay on a higher mountain beyond. I proposed to camp. But Jimmy gave me a disdainful look, as much as to say, "You are afraid to go," and quickened his gait into a run down the mountain towards the snow. I called to him to stop, but he would not even look back. A firm resolve seized me — to overtake him, but not again to ask him to return. We crossed the valley in the night, saw many Indian campfires, and gained a sharp ridge leading up to the snow. This was first brushy and then rough and rocky. The brush had no paths except those made by wild animals; the rocks were sharp, and soon cut through our moccasins and made our feet bleed. But up and up we went until long after midnight, and until a cloud covered the mountain. We were above the timber line, excepting a few stunted fir trees, under one of which we crawled to wait for day, for it was too dark to see. Day soon dawned, but we were almost frozen. Our fir-tree nest had been the lair of grizzly bears that had wallowed there and shed quantities of shaggy hair. The

[1] Of the party leaving us at Soda Springs to go into Oregon I can now, after the lapse of forty-nine years, recall by their names only the following: Mr. Williams and wife; Samuel Kelsey, his wife and five children; Josiah Kelsey and wife; C. W. Flugge; Mr. Carroll; Mr. Fowler; a Methodist Episcopal preacher, whose name I think was also Williams; "Cheyenne Dawson"; and another called "Bear Dawson." Subsequently we heard that the party safely arrived in Oregon, and some of them we saw in California. One (C. W. Flugge) was in time to join a party and come from Oregon to California the same year (1841).

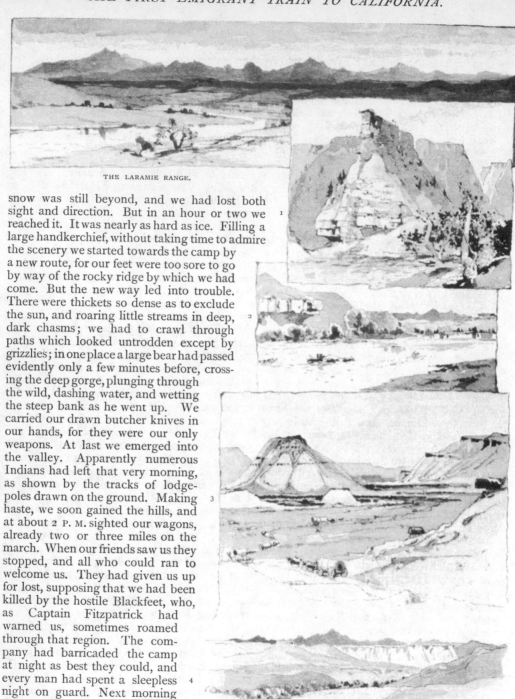

THE LARAMIE RANGE.

snow was still beyond, and we had lost both sight and direction. But in an hour or two we reached it. It was nearly as hard as ice. Filling a large handkerchief, without taking time to admire the scenery we started towards the camp by a new route, for our feet were too sore to go by way of the rocky ridge by which we had come. But the new way led into trouble. There were thickets so dense as to exclude the sun, and roaring little streams in deep, dark chasms; we had to crawl through paths which looked untrodden except by grizzlies; in one place a large bear had passed evidently only a few minutes before, crossing the deep gorge, plunging through the wild, dashing water, and wetting the steep bank as he went up. We carried our drawn butcher knives in our hands, for they were our only weapons. At last we emerged into the valley. Apparently numerous Indians had left that very morning, as shown by the tracks of lodgepoles drawn on the ground. Making haste, we soon gained the hills, and at about 2 P. M. sighted our wagons, already two or three miles on the march. When our friends saw us they stopped, and all who could ran to welcome us. They had given us up for lost, supposing that we had been killed by the hostile Blackfeet, who, as Captain Fitzpatrick had warned us, sometimes roamed through that region. The company had barricaded the camp at night as best they could, and every man had spent a sleepless night on guard. Next morning they passed several hours in scouring the country. Their first questions were: "Where have you been?" "Where have you been?" I was able to answer triumphantly, "*We have been up to the snow!*" and to demonstrate the fact by showing all the

1. THE PLATTE CAÑON.   2. BRIDGER'S FORD.   3. THE BAD LANDS OF THE OLD TRAIL NEAR DOUGLAS (NO VEGETATION).   4. ON THE OLD CALIFORNIA TRAIL OVER THE LA PRÊLE (BRANCH OF THE PLATTE).

THE GRIZZLY (URSUS HORRIBILIS). (FROM AN ORIGINAL PAINTING BY THE LATE CHARLES NAHL.)

snow I had left, which was now reduced to a ball about the size of my fist.

In about ten days our four men returned from Fort Hall, during which time we had advanced something over one hundred miles towards Salt Lake. They brought the information that we must strike out west of Salt Lake, — as it was even then called by the trappers,— being careful not to go too far south, lest we should get into a waterless country without grass. They also said we must be careful not to go too far north, lest we should get into a broken country and steep cañons, and wander about, as trapping parties had been known to do, and become bewildered and perish.

September had come before we reached Salt Lake, which we struck at its northern extremity. Part of the time we had purposely traveled slowly to enable the men from Fort Hall the sooner to overtake us. But unavoidable delays were frequent : daily, often hourly, the road had to be made passable for our wagons by digging down steep banks, filling gulches, etc. Indian fires obscured mountains and valleys in a dense, smoky atmosphere, so that we could not see any considerable distance in order to avoid obstacles. The principal growth, on plain and hill alike, was the interminable sage-brush (*Artemisia*), and often it was difficult, for

miles at a time, to break a road through it, and sometimes a lightly laden wagon would be overturned. Its monotonous dull color and scraggy appearance gave a most dreary aspect to the landscape. But it was not wholly useless : where large enough it made excellent fuel, and it was the home and shelter of the hare — generally known as the "jack rabbit" — and of the sage-hen. Trees were almost a sure sign of water in that region. But the mirage was most deceptive, magnifying stunted sage-brush on diminutive hillocks into trees and groves. Thus misled, we traveled all day without water, and at midnight found ourselves in a plain, level as a floor, incrusted with salt, and as white as snow. Crusts of salt broken up by our wagons, and driven by the chilly night wind like ice on the surface of a frozen pond, was to me a most striking counterfeit of a winter scene. This plain became softer and softer until our poor, almost famished, animals could not pull our wagons. In fact, we were going direct to Salt Lake and did not know it. So, in search of water, we turned from a southerly to an easterly course, and went about ten miles, and soon after daylight arrived at Bear River. So near to Salt Lake were we that the water in the river was too salt for us or our animals to use, but we had to use it; it would not quench thirst, but it did save life. The grass looked most luxuriant, and sparkled as if covered with frost. But it was salt; our hungry, jaded animals refused to eat it, and we had to lie by a whole day to rest them before we could travel.

Leaving this camp and bearing northwest we crossed our tracks on the salt plain, having thus described a triangle of several miles in dimensions. One of the most serious of our troubles was to find water where we could camp at night. So soon came another hot day, and hard travel all day and all night without water! From a westerly course we turned directly north, and, guided by antelope trails, came in a few miles to an abundance of grass and good water. The condition of our animals compelled us to rest here nearly a week. Meanwhile two of the men who had been to Fort Hall went ahead to explore. Provisions were becoming scarce, and we saw that we must avoid unnecessary delay. The two men were gone about five days. Under their lead we set forth, bearing west, then southwest, around Salt Lake, then again west. After two or three fatiguing days,—one day and a night without water,— the first notice we had of approach to any considerable mountain was the sight of crags, dimly seen through the smoke, many hundred feet above our heads. Here was plenty of good grass and water. Nearly all now said, " Let us

saddles used by the trapping party, and had learned a little about how to make them. Packing is an art, and something that only an experienced mountaineer can do well so as to save his animal and keep his pack from falling off. We were unaccustomed to it, and the difficulties we had at first were simply indescribable. It is much more difficult to fasten a pack on an ox than on a mule or a horse. The trouble began the very first day. But we started— most of us on foot, for nearly all the animals, including several of the oxen, had to carry packs. It was but a few minutes before the packs began to turn; horses became scared, mules kicked, oxen jumped and bellowed, and articles were scattered in all directions. We took more pains, fixed things, made a new start, and did better, though packs continued occasionally to fall off and delay us.

Those that had better pack-saddles and had tied their loads securely were ahead, while the others were obliged to lag behind, because they had to repack, and sometimes things would be strewn all along the route. The first night I happened to be among those that kept pretty well back, because the horses out-traveled the oxen. The foremost came to a place and stopped where there was no water or grass, and built a fire so that we could see it and come up to them. We got there about midnight, but some of our oxen that had packs on had not come up, and among

MONUMENT POINT, SALT LAKE.

leave our wagons, otherwise the snows will overtake us before we get to California." So we stopped one day and threw away everything we could not carry, made pack-saddles and packed the oxen, mules, and horses, and started.

On Green River we had seen the style of pack-

them were my two. So I had to return the next morning and find them, Cheyenne Dawson alone volunteering to go with me. One man had brought along about a quart of water, which was carefully doled out before we started, each receiving a little canister-cover full—less

WATER!

than half a gill; but as Dawson and I had to go for the oxen, we were given a double portion. This was all the water I had until the next day. It was a burning hot day. We could not find the trail of the oxen for a long time, and Dawson refused to go any farther, saying that there were plenty of cattle in California; but I had to do it, for the oxen were carrying our provisions and other things. Afterwards I struck the trail, and found that the oxen instead of going west had gone north, and I followed them until nearly sundown. They had got into a grassy country, which showed that they were nearing water. Seeing Indian tracks on their trail following them, I felt there was imminent danger, and at once examined my gun and pistols to see that they were primed and ready. But soon I found my oxen lying down in tall grass by the side of the trail. Seeing no Indians, I hastened to fasten the packs and make my way to overtake the company. They had promised to stop when they came to water and wait for me. I traveled all night, and at early dawn came to where there was plenty of water and where the company had taken their dinner the day before, but they had failed to stop for me according to promise. I was much perplexed, because I had seen many fires in the night, which I took to be Indian fires, so I fastened my oxen to a scraggy willow and began to make circles around to see which way the company had gone. The ground was so hard that the animals had made no impression, which bewildered me. Finally, while making a circle of about three miles away off to the south, I saw two men coming on horseback. In the glare of the mirage, which distorted everything, I could not tell whether they were Indians or white men, but I supposed them to be Indians, feeling sure our party would go west and not south. In a mirage a man on horseback looks as tall as a tree, and I could only tell by the motion that they were mounted. I made a bee-line to my oxen, to make breastworks of them. In doing this I came to a small stream resembling running water, into which I urged my horse, whereupon he went down into a quagmire, over head and ears, out of sight. My gun also went under the mire. I got hold of something on the bank, threw out my gun, which was full of mud and water, and holding to the rope attached to my horse, by dint of hard pulling I succeeded in getting him out — a sorry sight, his ears and eyes full of mud, and his body covered with it. At last, just in time, I was able to move and get behind the oxen. My gun was in no condition to shoot. However, putting dry powder in the pan I determined to do my best in case the supposed Indians should come up; but lo! they were two of our party coming to meet me, bringing water and provisions. It was a great relief. I felt indignant that the party had not stopped for me — not the less so when I learned that Captain Bartleson had said, when they started back to find me, that they "would be in better business to go ahead and look for a road." He had not forgotten certain comments of mine on his qualities as a student of Indian character. An instance of this I will relate.

One morning, just as we were packing up, a party of about ninety Indians, on horseback, a regular war party, were descried coming up. Some of us begged the captain to send men out to prevent them from coming to us while we were in the confusion of packing. But he said, " Boys, you must not show any sign of hostility ; if you go out there with guns the Indians will think us hostile, and may get mad and hurt us." However, five or six of us took our guns and went out, and by signs made them halt. They did not prove to be hostile, but they had carbines, and if we had been careless and had let them come near they might, and probably would, have killed us. At last we got packed up and started, and the Indians traveled along three or four hundred yards one side or the other of us or behind us all day. They appeared anxious to trade, and offered a buckskin, well dressed, worth two or three dollars, for three or four charges of powder and three or four balls. This showed that they were in want of ammunition. The carbines indicated that they had had communication with some trading-post belonging to the Hudson's Bay Company. They had buffalo-robes also, which showed that they were a roving hunting party, as there were no buffaloes within three or four hundred miles. At this time I had spoken my mind pretty freely concerning Captain Bartleson's lack of judgment, as one could scarcely help doing under the circumstances.

We now got into a country where there was no grass nor water, and then we began to catechize the men who had gone to Fort Hall. They repeated, " If you go too far south you will get into a desert country and your animals will perish ; there will be no water nor grass." We were evidently too far south. We could not go west, and the formation of the country was such that we had to turn and go north across a range of mountains. Having struck a small stream we camped upon it all night, and next day continued down its banks, crossing from side to side, most of the time following Indian paths or paths made by antelope and deer. In the afternoon we entered a cañon, the walls of which were precipitous and several hundred feet high. Finally the pleasant bermy banks gave out entirely, and we could travel only in the dry bed of what in the wet season was a raging river. It became a solid mass of stones and huge boulders, and the animals became tender-footed and sore so that they could hardly stand up, and as we continued the way became worse and worse. There was no place for us to lie down and sleep, nor could our animals lie down; the water had given out, and the prospect was indeed gloomy — the cañon had been leading us directly north. All agreed that the animals were too jaded and worn to go back. Then we called the men : " What did they tell you at Fort Hall about the northern region ? " They repeated, " You must not go too far north ; if you do you will get into difficult cañons that lead towards the Columbia River, where you may become bewildered and wander about and perish." This cañon was going nearly north; in fact it seemed a little east of north. We sent some men to see if they could reach the top of the mountain by scaling the precipice somewhere and get a view, and they came back about ten or eleven o'clock, saying the country looked better three or four miles farther ahead. So we were encouraged. Even the animals seemed to take courage, and we got along much better than had been thought possible, and by one o'clock that day came out on what is now known as the Humboldt River. It was not until four years later (1845) that General Frémont first saw this river and named it Humboldt.

Our course was first westward and then southward, following this river for many days, till we came to its Sink, near which we saw a solitary horse, an indication that trappers had sometime been in that vicinity. We tried to catch him but failed ; he had been there long enough to become very wild. We saw many Indians on the Humboldt, especially towards the Sink. There were many tule marshes. The tule is a rush, large, but here not very tall. It was generally completely covered with honeydew, and this in turn was wholly covered with a pediculous-looking insect which fed upon it. The Indians gathered quantities of the honey and pressed it into balls about the size of one's fist, having the appearance of wet bran. At first we greatly relished this Indian food, but when we saw what it was made of—that the insects pressed into the mass were the main ingredient—we lost our appetites and bought no more of it.

From the time we left our wagons many had to walk, and more and more as we advanced. Going down the Humboldt at least half were on foot. Provisions had given out; except a little coarse green grass among the willows along the river the country was dry, bare, and desolate; we saw no game except antelope, and they were scarce and hard to kill; and walking was very fatiguing. Tobacco lovers would surrender their animals for anyone to ride who would furnish them with an ounce or two to chew during the day. One day one of these devotees lost his tobacco and went back for it, but failed to find it. An Indian in a friendly manner overtook us, bringing the piece of tobacco, which he had found on our trail or at our latest camp, and surrendered it. The owner, instead of being thankful, accused the Indian of having stolen it—an impossibility, as we had seen no Indians or Indian signs for some days. Perhaps the Indian did not know what it was, else he might have kept it for smoking. But I think otherwise, for, patting his breast, he said, "Shoshone, Shoshone," which was the Indian way of showing he was friendly. The Shoshones were known as always friendly to the whites, and it is not difficult to see how other and distant tribes might claim to be Shoshones as a passport to favor.

On the Humboldt we had a further division of our ranks. In going down the river we went sometimes on one side and sometimes on the other, but mostly on the north side, till we were nearing what are now known as the Humboldt Mountains. We were getting tired, and some were in favor of leaving the oxen, of which we then had only about seven or eight, and rushing on into California. They said there was plenty of beef in California. But some of us said: "No; our oxen are now our only supply of food. We are doing well,

THE HUMBOLDT PALISADES.— THE HUMBOLDT SINK.

TRUCKEE MEADOWS.

making eighteen or twenty miles a day." One morning when it was my turn at driving the oxen, the captain traveled so fast that I could not keep up, and was left far behind. When night came I had to leave the trail and go over a rocky declivity for a mile and a half into a gloomy, damp bottom, and unpack the oxen and turn them out to eat, sleeping myself without blankets. I got up the next morning, hunted the oxen out of the willow thicket, and repacked them. Not having had supper or breakfast, and having to travel nine miles before I overtook the party, perhaps I was not in the best humor. They were waiting, and for the very good reason that they could have nothing to eat till I came up with the oxen and one could be killed. I felt badly treated, and let the captain know it plainly; but, much to my surprise, he made no reply, and none of his men said a word. We killed an ox, ate our breakfast, and got ready to start about one or two o'clock in the afternoon. When nearly ready to go, the captain and one or two of his mess came to us and said: "Boys, our animals are better than yours, and we always get out of meat before any of the rest of you. Let us have the most of the meat this time, and we will pay you back the next ox we kill." We gladly let them have all they wished. But as soon as they had taken it, and were mounted ready to start, the captain in a loud voice exclaimed: "Now we have been found fault with long enough, and we are going to California. If you can keep up with us, all right; if you cannot, you may go to ——"; and away they started, the captain and eight men. One of the men would not go with the captain; he said, "The captain is wrong, and I will stay with you, boys."

In a short time they were out of sight. We followed their trail for two or three days, but after they had crossed over to the south side of the Humboldt and turned south we came into a sandy waste where the wind had entirely obliterated their tracks. We were then thrown entirely upon our own resources. It was our desire to make as great speed as

possible westward, deviating only when obstacles interposed, and in such case bearing south instead of north, so as to be found in a lower latitude in the event that winter should overtake us in the mountains. But, diverted by following our fugitive captain and party across the Humboldt, we thereby missed the luxuriant Truckee meadows lying but a short distance to the west, a resting-place well and favorably known to later emigrants. So, perforce, we followed down to the Sink of the Humboldt and were obliged to drink its water, which in the fall of the year becomes stagnant and of the color of lye, and not fit to drink or use unless boiled. Here we camped. Leaving the Sink of the Humboldt, we crossed a considerable stream which must have been Carson River, and came to another stream which must have been Walker River, and followed it up to where it came out of the mountains, which proved to be the Sierra Nevada. We did not know the name of the mountains. Neither had these rivers then been named; nor had they been seen by Kit Carson or Joe Walker, for whom they were named, nor were they seen until 1845 by Frémont, who named them.

We were now camped on Walker River, at the very eastern base of the Sierra Nevada, and had only two oxen left. We sent men ahead to see if it would be possible to scale the mountains, while we killed the better of the two oxen and dried the meat in preparation for the ascent. The men returned towards evening and reported that they thought it would be possible to ascend the mountains, though very difficult. We had eaten our supper, and were ready for the climb in the morning. Looking back on the plains we saw something coming, which we decided to be Indians. They traveled very slowly, and it was difficult to understand their movements. To make a long story short, it was the eight men that had left us nine days before. They had gone farther south than we and had come to a lake, probably Carson Lake, and there had found Indians who supplied them plentifully with fish and pine nuts. Fish caught in such water are not fit to eat at any time, much less in the fall of the year. The men had all eaten heartily of fish and pine nuts, and had got something akin to cholera morbus. We were glad to see them although they had deserted us. We ran out to meet them and shook hands, and put

sible to get through down the smaller cañon. I was one of them, Jimmy John the other. Benjamin Kelsey, who had shown himself expert in finding the way, was now, without any election, still recognized as leader, as he had been during the absence of Bartleson. A party

ABANDONED.

our frying-pans on and gave them the best supper we could. Captain Bartleson, who when we started from Missouri was a portly man, was reduced to half his former girth. He said: " Boys, if ever I get back to Missouri I will never leave that country. I would gladly eat out of the troughs with my dogs." He seemed to be heartily sick of his late experience, but that did not prevent him from leaving us twice after that.

We were now in what is at present Nevada, and probably within forty miles of the present boundary of California. We ascended the mountains on the north side of Walker River to the summit, and then struck a stream running west which proved to be the extreme source of the Stanislaus River. We followed it down for several days and finally came to where a branch ran into it, each forming a cañon. The main river flowed in a precipitous gorge in places apparently a mile deep, and the gorge that came into it was but little less formidable. At night we found ourselves on the extreme point of the promontory between the two, very tired, and with neither grass nor water. We had to stay there that night. Early the next morning two men went down to see if it would be pos-

also went back to see how far we should have to go around before we could pass over the tributary cañon. The understanding was, that when we went down the cañon if it was practicable to get through we were to fire a gun so that all could follow; but if not, we were not to fire, even if we saw game. When Jimmy and I got down about three-quarters of a mile I came to the conclusion that it was impossible to get through, and said to him, " Jimmy, we might as well go back; we can't go here." " Yes, we can," said he; and insisting that we could, he pulled out a pistol and fired. It was an old dragoon pistol, and reverberated like a cannon. I hurried back to tell the company not to come down, but before I reached them the captain and his party had started. I explained, and warned them that they could not get down; but they went on as far as they could go, and then were obliged to stay all day and night to rest the animals, and had to go about among the rocks and pick a little grass for them, and go down to the stream through a terrible place in the cañon to bring water up in cups and camp-kettles, and some of the men in their boots, to pour down the animals' throats in order to keep them from perishing. Finally, four of them pulling and four of them pushing a mule, they managed to get them up one by one, and then carried all the things up again on their backs — not an easy job for exhausted men.

In some way, nobody knows how, Jimmy got through that cañon and into the Sacramento Valley. He had a horse with him — an Indian horse that was bought in the Rocky Mountains, and which could come as near climbing a tree as any horse I ever knew. Jimmy was a character. Of all men I have ever known I think he was the most fearless; he had the bravery of a bulldog. He was not seen for two months — until he was found at Sutter's, afterwards known as Sutter's Fort, now Sacramento City.

We went on, traveling west as near as we could. When we killed our last ox we shot and ate crows or anything we could kill, and one man shot a wild-cat. We could eat anything. One day in the morning I went ahead, on foot of course, to see if I could kill something, it being understood that the company would keep on as near west as possible and find a practicable road. I followed an Indian trail down into the cañon, meeting many Indians on the way up. They did not molest me, but I did not quite like their looks. I went about ten miles down the cañon, and then began to think it time to strike north to intersect the trail of the company going west. A most difficult time I had scaling the precipice. Once I threw my gun up ahead of me, being unable to hold it and climb, and then was in despair lest I could not get up where it was, but finally I did barely manage to do so, and made my way north. As the darkness came on I was obliged to look down and feel with my feet lest I should pass over the trail of the party without seeing it. Just at dark I came to an enormous fallen tree and tried to go around the top, but the place was too brushy, so I went around the butt, which seemed to me to be about twenty or twenty-five feet above my head. This I suppose to have been one of the fallen trees in the Calaveras Grove of *Sequoia gigantea* or mammoth trees, as I have since been there, and to my own satisfaction identified the lay of the land and the tree. Hence I concluded that I must have been the first white man who ever saw the *Sequoia gigantea*, of which I told Frémont when he came to California in 1844. Of course sleep was impossible, for I had neither blanket nor coat, and burned or froze alternately as I turned from one side to the other before the small fire which I had built, until morning, when I started eastward to intersect the trail, thinking the company had turned north. But I traveled until noon and found no trail; then striking south, I came to the camp which I had left the previous

morning. The party had gone, but not where they had said they would go; for they had taken the same trail I had followed, into the cañon, and had gone up the south side, which they had found so steep that many of the poor animals could not climb it and had to be left. When I arrived the Indians were there cutting the horses to pieces and carrying off the meat. My situation, alone among strange Indians killing our poor horses, was by no means comfortable. Afterward we found that these Indians were always at war with the Californians. They were known as the Horse Thief Indians, and lived chiefly on horse flesh; they had been in the habit of raiding the ranches even to the very coast, driving away horses by the hundreds into the mountains to eat. That night after dark I overtook the party in camp.

A day or two later we came to a place where there was a great quantity of horse bones, and we did not know what it meant; we thought that an army must have perished there. They were of course horses that the Indians had driven in there and slaughtered. A few nights later, fearing depredations, we concluded to stand guard — all but one man, who would not. So we let his two horses roam where they pleased. In the morning they could not be found. A few miles away we came to a village; the Indians had fled, but we found the horses killed and some of the meat roasting on a fire.

We were now on the edge of the San Joaquin Valley, but we did not even know that we were in California. We could see a range of mountains lying to the west, — the Coast Range, — but we could see no valley. The evening of the day we started down into the valley we were very tired, and when night came our party was strung along for three or four miles, and every man slept right where darkness overtook him. He would take off his saddle for a pillow and turn his horse or mule loose, if he had one. His animal would be too poor to walk away, and in the morning he would find him, usually within fifty feet. The jaded horses nearly perished with hunger and fatigue. When we overtook the foremost of the party the next morning we found they had come to a pond of water, and one of them had killed a fat coyote; when I came up it was all eaten except the lights and the windpipe, on which I made my breakfast. From that camp we saw timber to the north of us, evidently bordering a stream running west. It turned out to be the stream that we had followed down in the mountains — the Stanislaus River. As soon as we came in sight of the bottom land of the stream we saw an abundance of antelopes and sandhill cranes. We killed two of each the first evening.

Wild grapes also abounded. The next day we killed thirteen deer and antelopes, jerked the meat and got ready to go on, all except the captain's mess of seven or eight, who decided to stay there and lay in meat enough to last them into California! We were really almost down to tidewater, but did not know it. Some thought it was five hundred miles yet to California. But all thought we had to cross at least that range of mountains in sight to the west before entering the promised land, and how many more beyond no one could tell. Nearly all thought it best to press on lest the snows might overtake us in the mountains before us, as they had already nearly done on the mountains behind us (the Sierra Nevada). It was now about the first of November. Our party set forth bearing northwest, aiming for a seeming gap north of a high mountain in the chain to the west of us. That mountain we found to be Mount Diablo. At night the Indians attacked the captain's camp and stole all their animals, which were the best in the company, and the next day the men had to overtake us with just what they could carry in their hands.

The next day, judging by the timber we saw, we concluded there was a river to the west. So two men went ahead to see if they could find a trail or a crossing. The timber seen proved to be along what is now known as the San Joaquin River. We sent two men on ahead to spy out the country. At night one of them returned, saying they had come across an Indian on horseback without a saddle who wore a cloth jacket but no other clothing. From what they could understand the Indian knew Dr. Marsh and had offered to guide them to his place. He plainly said "Marsh," and of course we supposed it was the Dr. Marsh before referred to who had written the letter to a friend in Jackson County, Missouri, and so it proved. One man went with the Indian to Marsh's ranch and the other came back to tell us what he had done, with the suggestion that we should go on and cross the river (San Joaquin) at the place to which the trail was leading. In that way we found ourselves two days later at Dr. Marsh's ranch, and there we learned that we were really in California and our journey at an end. After six months we had now arrived at the first settlement in California, November 4, 1841.

The account of our reception, and of my own experiences in California in the pastoral period before the gold discovery, I must reserve for another paper.

John Bidwell.

27

The North American Indian of To-day

George Bird Grinnell

THE NORTH AMERICAN INDIAN OF TO-DAY.

By George Bird Grinnell.

WITHIN the last twenty years the Indian has changed, and it may be doubted whether the change is altogether for the better. He has lost his picturesqueness and has become commonplace; where he was once keen and active he is now slow and inert. We have taken from him his old free life—the life which he loved because it had been his father's and was his own, and because he knew nothing better—and we are trying to make him live our life with all its restraints and limitations. We are trying to force this wild creature, who once was free, into the hard, rigid mold of civilization, and we do not find him plastic. He does not fit the mold; he will not go into it. Why should he? It is asking much to expect that the Indian shall at once become a civilized man, and we should not forget that we are insisting that he shall accomplish in a generation a measure of advancement which it took our own race some thousands of years to attain. We require, too, that his child mind shall at once accept, even though it does not assimilate, our modern ideas.

When the white men first set foot in America, they found it inhabited by a people who were absolutely primitive, and whose development had been slow; for although man had inhabited the continent at least since preglacial time, his culture had progressed no further than that of the Neolithic age, so called. Some tribes practised agriculture, and all gathered the natural fruits of the earth, but they depended for food chiefly on the abundant fish and game which swarmed in the rivers or on the uplands, and which yielded them an easy subsistence. The animals were trapped and snared, and were killed also with arrows

WHITE GRAND CHEYENNE.

JACK BULL BEAR—COMANCHE.

[The interesting collection of Indian portraits here presented has been obtained through the courtesy of Mr. Edward Rosewater, to whom Omaha owes such a debt in connection with the success of the Exposition of 1898.]

449

—tipped with points of stone and bone, for the Indians had no knowledge of metals. While many of the tribes occupied permanent villages, in which the dwellings were made of dirt or grass or poles, yet the conditions of their lives obliged them to make frequent extended journeys far from home; all used movable tents or lodges, consisting of a framework of slender poles covered with skin or bark. These lodges were of similar type over almost the whole continent. The popula-

he came nothing is positively known. Of one thing, however, we are certain. The Indians constitute a well-differentiated race of very great antiquity—as men view time. Throughout the different tribes the physical characters of these people are everywhere the same. These physical likenesses, together with the extraordinary diversity of language found among them, are very suggestive of the great length of time that these people have occupied America. To say nothing of languages which have

OMAHAS.

tion of North America was sparse in these pre-Columbian days, and we may suppose that the people lived a contented life, usually unbroken by wars and devoted chiefly to gaining a subsistence.

The white people had not been here long before they began to speculate on the origin of the Indian; but to this day no one has reached any definite conclusion as to his origin. Some authorities are quite certain that his home must have been Asia, while others, with greater probability, believe that he came from Europe; but of when or how

become extinct without leaving any record, we know of between fifty and sixty distinct linguistic stocks in North America, north of Mexico; groups of languages which appear to be as different from each other as the Semitic is from the Aryan or the Turanian. Within a single linguistic family we may have a number of tribes speaking different languages: as in the Algonquin family, the Ojibways, Blackfoots, Cheyennes and Arapahoes speak four different tongues, each uncomprehended by the others; just as four Europeans of Aryan family might speak

English, Spanish, German and Russian. It must have taken a long time for these different linguistic stocks to become developed.

When the white man had come, it took him but a short time to teach the Indians that he was an enemy, and for four hundred years they learned and acted on this lesson, fighting bravely in their own fashion until overwhelmed by numbers. For a long time the settlement of the country made but little impression on the tribes that lived far from the seaboard, and it is only since the completion of the Union Pacific railroad that the power of the white man has been brought home to the tribes that wandered over the great plains and the mountains of the farther West. For one hundred years before that, the Indians of many tribes had possessed horses and metal knives and sheet-iron arrow-points, and the task of securing food had thus been made easier for them, but beyond this the coming of the white man had worked little change in their ways of life.

When the railroad entered the Indian's country, its whistle sounded the beginning of the end of his old life. This was not so much because the railroad brought the white man into actual contact with the Indian, as because it at once opened a market for the hides and furs of the animals on which he subsisted, and because, to supply the demand for the skins of these animals, white hunters proceeded at once to exterminate them, and thus soon deprived the Indian of his natural food. So within a few years the savage found that the prairie no longer yielded him a living, and that if he would escape starvation he must present himself at the agency to receive his weekly ration of beef.

CROOKED NOSE—CHEYENNE

This, then, was the beginning of the Indian problem as we know it to-day—a problem of assimilation, of civilization, wholly different from the old war problem, which was settled once and for all with the disappearance of the buffalo.

Up to that time, the Indians of the Western plains had followed the buffalo herds from place to place, in the earliest times capturing the game by means of surrounds, or by leading them into traps, in which numbers might be taken at one time. After they ob-

CASIMIOO—SANTA CLARA PUEBLO.

tained horses, they ran the buffalo, the rider forcing his steed close to the animal's side and driving the arrow into it with his powerful

BLACK HORSE—ARAPAHOE.

bow, or thrusting his lance deep into its vitals. The meat of the buffalo was dried in the sun, and served to tide the Indians over those periods when no fresh game could be had.

Perhaps no event has ever happened to a people that worked a greater change in their method of life than did the acquisition of horses for the Indians. Until these strange beasts came to them, all their journeyings had been on foot, for their only domestic animal was the dog, on which they used to pack light loads, and which dragged the primitive Indian vehicle—the travois. Most of their possessions, however, were transported on their own backs, men, women and children alike carrying packs proportionate to their strength; but when the horse came, all this was changed. On a sudden, they had a beast of burden which would transport not only their possessions, but themselves, and which enabled them with slight effort to cover distances that before they had not dreamed of. Here was at once a freedom which they had never known. If they had enemies, they could swiftly ride long distances to attack them, and as swiftly ride away. Therefore, as I have elsewhere said, the possession

of horses stimulated the Indians to war with their neighbors, and wrought a most important change in the character of the people.

In his old wild life the Indian was one of the most active of beings. He was forced to work hard to obtain his desired food from day to day, or if food were abundant, his ambition—a desire for the approval of his fellows—led him to go continually on the warpath. Thus he was lean, sinewy and tough, living a wholesome natural existence, and always in the best of training. Those who reached maturity were literally the fittest of their race, for no weakling child survived the hardship and exposure of the primitive life. When the Indian was obliged to cease his wanderings and to become sedentary, a change took place in his physical condition. He ceased to be a worker, and sat about doing nothing. He no longer had any ambition, but brooded over the past. New conditions of life arose. He began to live in houses, and he and

HENRY WILSON AND WIFE—MOJAVE (APACHES).

his children no longer subsisted on the flesh of the buffalo, but were obliged to accustom themselves to a diet which was largely vegetable. The changed conditions had a marked effect on his health. He became less able to resist disease, and contact with the whites brought to him new maladies a thousand times more fatal than those he had formerly known. In the transition stage between a life passed wholly in tents and one altogether in houses, and between a diet exclusively of fresh meat and one largely vegetable, the race suffered severely, and the death-rate became far heavier than it had been under ordinary conditions in the old time. But when the Indians had become thoroughly habituated to the new mode of life, the death-rate again became lower, so that now some tribes are increasing in numbers.

WHITE BUFFALO—ARAPAHOE.

Among the many Indian tribes which are now cared for by the government, there are different degrees of progress. Some are as untaught to-day as they were twenty years ago; others, who have had their well-being looked after and who have had more intelligent guidance, have made long strides toward self-support. All are wrestling with problems of which they know little or nothing, and are perplexed and discouraged. While marked improvement has taken place in the Indian service of late years, the same old methods, long known to be inefficient, are practised in caring for them. It is not enough to furnish a tribe of Indians subsistence, an agent to look after them, and a few white employees to assist them. Unless they have more than that, no Indian tribe will ever make much progress toward self-support. As Indians are only grown-up children, they must be taught, as children are taught, all the knowledge which is unconsciously absorbed by the white man from

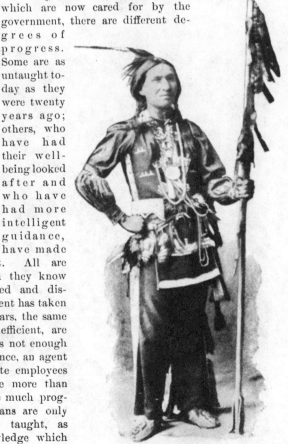

HIDING WOMAN—ARAPAHOE.

SAN CARLOS APACHES.

his early associations and his reading. Until the men employed in the field service of the Indian bureau shall be sufficiently intelligent to understand the mental attitude of the Indian, and sufficiently interested to give special attention to this, his advancement must necessarily be slow. And if it is slow, this is only because we do not see that men are chosen for this service who are competent to teach the Indians how to live in our way, and to convey to the savage man of the stone age the intelligence of the civilized man of the present day.

To-day Indians understand that they must work to live, but in many cases it is demanded of them that they shall make bricks without straw. They are asked to support themselves, but are given no tools to work with. Some tribes have had cattle issued to them, but little has been done to teach them how to care for these cattle, and the work with them which the agency employees are supposed to do is frequently altogether neglected. We blame the Indians

ARAPAHOES.

for not being civilized by this time, but in fact the fault is ours and that of our representatives in Congress, for assenting to a system which places the Indians in charge of men some of whom are unintelligent, inefficient, careless and sometimes criminal.

In many respects conditions are much better now than they used to be. The Indian Bureau struggles hard to improve matters, but is hampered by old methods and traditions, and above all by the manner in which a large number of the Indian agents are chosen. The condition of the Indians will not greatly improve until the agents are

ASSINIBOINS.

selected by reason of actual qualifications for their work, instead of receiving the position as a reward for political services performed.

There is probably not an Indian tribe in the United States which could not, under the direction of the right kind of man, become entirely self-supporting within ten years, but it would be necessary that those tribes which to-day are absolutely without property—as the Northern Cheyennes—should be given a start in some way. Thus these Cheyennes—to take a specific example—who live in a country which is too dry for farming yet is a good stock range, ought to have issued to them as their individual property one thousand five hundred head of cattle, and to be taught how to manage this live stock. The continual agitation by the neighboring white population of the question of this tribe's removal to some other part of the West, ought to be put an end to, and the title to their lands to be confirmed. In the same way the condition of each individual tribe should be studied, and it should be treated according to its needs.

Usually no prejudice exists against the individual Indian when he is brought into contact with white

STANDING ELK—CHEYENNE.

people, but against a body of Indians—as a tribe located on a reservation—there is almost always a very strong antagonism among the adjacent population. As a rule, this prejudice is not felt by such Western people as have had dealings with the Indians, and so know them, but only by those who, though their neighbors, have never been brought in direct contact with them. I believe that this prej-

udice is less strong than it was a few years ago, and that ultimately it will cease to exist. Thus, in the future—provided intelligent effort is expended in teaching the Indian how to think like white men, how to work and how to labor to the best advantage—these people may become a self-supporting and self-respecting part of our population.

When I walked through the Omaha Exposition grounds one hot Sunday last September on my way to the encampment of the Indian Congress, I found it difficult to realize that fifty years ago the ground where Omaha now stands was a camping-

CLEVER WARDEN—ARAPAHOE.

place for Indians, while twenty-five years later Nebraska, only one hundred and fifty miles west of Omaha, was a dangerous country to pass through, because it was the home and the hunting-ground of hostile Indians. All this has been forgotten now, except by those who took part in the old life of those times, and it was well that this past should be recalled, and that the former wild inhabitants of this fertile state should be seen by the

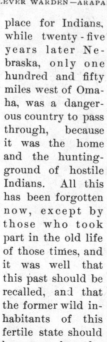

OWL—OMAHA.

CHIEF WOLFROBE—CHEYENNE.

LITTLE CHIEF—ARAPAHOE.

BRAVE PANTHER—ARAPAHOE.

STANDING ELK—OMAHA.

sturdy farmers who till it now.

There were many Indians there, and Indians of all sorts. Some were the pure-blooded people of the old wild days, while others were men of white skin with brown hair and long mustaches and goatees, who could perhaps boast an eighth or a quarter of Indian blood.

The sight-seers at the Omaha Exposition seemed much interested in the Indians, and as I sat there that afternoon in Mountain Chief's skin lodge, many visitors looked in at the door and asked questions which showed how little they knew about the race; and as I listened to these questions, and answered some of them, I hoped that the interest thus manifested might lead some of these visitors to endeavor to learn more about what Indians really are, and what, under proper direction, they might become.

The history of the intercourse between the white race and the red, if studied, will lead the thoughtful American to feel that some consideration is due from us to them. If we can divest ourselves of prejudice—a hard thing to do—we must acknowledge that the Indians ought to be treated honestly, and therefore justly, as they have never yet been treated. Our prejudice against the race is merely that of an enemy. In fighting, in massacres and surprises, in the treatment of the dead who have fallen in battle, we who are civilized have little to boast of over those who are savage. The stories of the Chivington fight, of the Dull Knife outbreak at Fort

Robinson, and of the Baker affair in Montana, where of the one hundred and seventy-six unoffending Piegan Indians killed in the surprised smallpox-stricken camp only eighteen were fighting-men and the rest old men, women and little children, show that there are two sides to the history of Indian warfare.

We may say that all the ill treatment of Indians could not have been avoided, that savagery must yield to civilization, that the fittest will survive and the weakest go to the wall. If all this be true, it is also true that this nation is now old enough to lay aside the prejudices of its childhood and, with the beginning of the new century, commence to treat the Indian intelligently, which only means fairly. A few years of such treatment and a moderate investment to enable the poorest of the tribes to make a start at gaining a livelihood, would soon pay for itself in the re-

RUSTY FOOT AND NEVER AFRAID—OMAHAS.

duction of appropriations for Indian support. From all points of view, we should have a change.

The Indian population of the United States to-day is undoubtedly much less than it was at the time of the last census, in 1890. The total number of Indians in the country then, exclusive of those in Alaska, was reported to be two hundred and forty-nine thousand two hundred and seventy-three. This figure, however, included some thirty-two thousand taxed or taxable Indians, ninety-eight per cent. of whom were not on reservations. The number on reservations or at school was put down as one hundred and thirty-three thousand three hundred and eighty-two.

It is an interesting fact to note that out of the grand total of nearly a quarter of a million only one hundred and eighty-four were incarcerated in state or territorial prisons, showing conclusively that, in the eye of the law at least, all live Indians were not "bad Indians." Of course, those who had been captured in arms against the government were prisoners of war and not included.

Just what progress, accord-

SAN CARLOS APACHES.

ing to official data, the Indian is now making toward becoming civilized and self-supporting, can be determined by the curious by comparing the reports of the next census with that of 1890. The self-supporting Indians then consisted of the five civilized tribes, that is, the Cherokees, the Chickasaws, the Choctaws, the Creeks and the Seminoles, numbering fifty-two thousand and sixty-five.

In New Mexico and South Dakota the Indian population is the largest, numbering about twenty thousand in each. Arizona and California contain about fifteen thousand each. No other state or territory has over ten thousand except Montana. Perhaps there is no better illustration of how rapidly enforced civilization exterminates the Indian race than the case of the tribes in Maine. The once numerous and powerful Penobscots were vigorously civilized and watched over until now there are but a handful of them left, only about a hundred on their river island at Old Town. Other tribes, to be sure, have become absolutely extinct. It is more than likely that the Penobscots, despite the benefits of civilization, the protection of the government and the advantages of peace, will be the next tribe to exist only in memory on the North American continent.

YELLOW SMOKE—OMAHA.

ARAPAHOES.

The annual appropriations by Congress for the Indian service are usually between eight and nine million dollars. This sum is disbursed for current and contingent expenses, treaty obligations, miscellaneous support and gratuities, the support of schools, payments for land, interest on trust funds, and incidental expenses. It costs about two million dollars a year to maintain the Indian schools and about three million dollars to fulfil the treaty obligations. To a careful student these figures furnish considerable food for thought.

At Omaha, while the Exposition was in progress, there were contingents from the various tribes of Sioux, Omahas, Crows, Blackfoots, Winnebagoes, Sacs and Foxes, Piutes, Apaches, Cheyennes, Zunis, Navajoes, Moquis, Cherokees, Creeks, Seminoles, Comanches, Poncas, Delawares, and Digger Umatillas, all encamped on the vast fields back of the Transportation Building. This gathering was not a show; it had no connection with the Midway, some of whose most interested and amused visitors were the red men themselves. The government's Indian Bureau undertook the establishment of the encampment or "Congress," as it was called. The director of the project was Capt. W. A. Mercer, U. S. A., of the Omaha reservation, assisted by Professor James Mooney, of the Bureau of Ethnology.

28

An Arizona Episode

Pearl Heart

PEARL HART READING OVER HER STATEMENT.

AN ARIZONA EPISODE.

THE evolution of the new woman takes many strange phases. A late and unique one is that of her appearance in the character of Dick Turpin. There have been many female stage-robbers in books and stories, but only one in the flesh. Viewed psychologically, the statement of such a woman is curious. Starting with one of the humdrum tragedies that are lived in so many lives, the story of her life is told by herself until it reaches the startling climax with which telegraphic reports have made us familiar. Pearl Hart, the woman who "held up" the Globe stage at Cane Springs cañon, Arizona, on May 30th of this year, in company with a male partner, had lived the hard life of the frontier after a disastrous matrimonial experience beginning when she was but sixteen years old. She claims that she was driven to desperation by news of the dangerous illness of her mother. She had no money. She could get none, although she tried in various ways, until, finally, familiar with the exploits of the Western Dick Turpins, she determined to imitate them. She is a small woman, weighing less than a hundred pounds, with features of the most common type. Donning a set of man's clothes and taking the necessary revolver, and securing a male companion, she appeared on the highway. The leveled revolvers quickly brought the coach and its occupants to a standstill. Then, under the cool eye of this bit of a creature, the passengers handed over some four hundred dollars. The attempt to escape, the chase, and the capture that followed—the whole story furnishes an interesting side-light on life in the Southwest.

"WHEN I was but sixteen years old, and while still at boarding-school, I fell in love with a man I met in the town in which the school was situated. I was easily impressed. I knew nothing of life. Marriage was to me but a name. It did not take him long to get my consent to an elopement. We ran away one night and were married.

"I was happy for a time, but not for long.

463

My husband began to abuse me, and presently he drove me from him. Then I returned to my mother, in the village of Lindsay, Ontario, where I was born.

"Before long, my husband sent for me, and I went back to him. I loved him, and he promised to do better. I had not been with him two weeks before he began to abuse me again, and after bearing up under his blows as long as I could I left him again. This was just as the World's Fair closed in Chicago, in the fall of 1893. Instead of going home to my mother again, as I should have done, I took the train for Trinidad, Colorado. I was only twenty-two years old. I was good-looking, desperate, discouraged, and ready for anything that might come.

"I do not care to dwell on this period of my life. It is sufficient to say that I went from one city to another until some time later I arrived in Phœnix. I came face to face with my husband on the street one afternoon. I was not then the innocent school-girl he had enticed from home, father, mother, family and friends—far from it. I had been inured to the hardships of the world and knew much of its wickedness. Still, the old infatuation came back. I struggled against it. I knew if I went back to him I should be more unhappy than I was, but I lost the battle. I did go back. We lived together for three years, and I was happy and good, for I dearly loved the man whose name I bore. During the first year of my married life a boy was born to us, and a girl while we were together at Phœnix.

"He was not content. He began to abuse me as of old, and I left him for the third time, vowing never to speak to him again. I sent my children home to my dear old mother and went East, where I supported myself by working as a servant. I heard of my husband occasionally. I tried to forget him, but could not. He was the father of my children and I loved him, in spite of all the abuse he had heaped on me.

"Two years after I had left him the third time, he found out where I was. He came to me and begged me to go back to the West with him, making me all kinds of smooth promises. I went back. I followed him to Tucson. After the money I

had saved had been spent, he began beating me, and I lived in hell for months. Finally, he joined McCord's regiment and went to the war. And as for me—why, I went back to Phœnix and got along as best I could.

"I was tired of life. I wanted to die, and tried to kill myself three or four times. I was restrained each time, and finally I got employment cooking for some miners at Mammoth. I lived there for a while, living in a tent pitched on the banks of the Gila river. The work was too hard, and I packed my goods in a wagon and started to go to Globe. I had to return to my old camp because the horses were unable to pull us through. A man named Joe Boot wanted to go to Globe, too, and we made an arrangement with two Mormon boys to freight the whole outfit to Globe for eight dollars. We camped out three miles from Globe, and next day moved in, and I went to work again in a miners' boarding-house. Then one of the big mines shut down and that left me with nothing to do.

"I had saved a little money. One of my brothers found my address and wrote me for some money to help him out of a scrape. I sent him all I had, and was just about to move on to some other town when my husband appeared again. He had been mustered out of his regiment and had followed me to Globe. He was too lazy to work and wanted me to support him. We had another quarrel and parted. I haven't seen him since and I hope I never shall see him again.

"On top of all my other troubles, I got a letter just at this time saying my mother was dying and asking me to come home if I wanted to see her alive again. That letter drove me crazy. No matter what I had been, my mother had been my dearest, truest friend, and I longed to see her again before she died. I had no money. I could get no money. From what I know now, I believe I became temporarily insane.

"Joe Boot, the man who freighted his goods over to Globe with me, told me he had a mining-claim and offered to go out with me and try to dig up enough metal to get a passage home to Canada. We went out to the claim and both worked night and day. It was useless. The claim was no good. I handled pick and shovel like a man, and began wearing man's clothes while I was mining there. I have never worked so hard in my life, and I have had some pretty hard experiences, too.

"When we found there wasn't a sign of color in the claim, I was frantic. I wanted to see my mother. It was the only wish I had. Boot sympathized with me, but he had no money and could not get any. He proposed that we rob the Globe stage. I protested. He said it was the only way to get money. Then I weakened so far as the moral part of it was concerned, but said I was afraid to rob a stage. It seemed a desperate undertaking for a woman of my size. Joe finally said it was easy enough and no one would get hurt. 'A bold front,' he said, 'is all that is necessary to rob any stage.'

" 'Joe,' I said, 'if you will promise me that no one will be hurt, I will go with you.'

"He promised, and we made our plans.

"On the afternoon of the robbery we took our horses and rode over the mountains and through the cañons, and at last hit the Globe road. We rode along slowly until we came to a bend in the road, which was a most favorable spot for our undertaking. We halted and listened till we heard the stage. Then we went forward on a slow walk, till we saw the stage coming around the bend. We then pulled to one side of the road. Joe drew a 'forty-five,' and said, 'Throw up your hands!' I drew my little 'thirty-eight' and likewise covered

THE FEMALE BANDIT AND HER PET WILDCAT.

the occupants of the stage. Joe said to me, 'Get off your horse.' I did so, while he kept the people covered. He ordered them out of the stage. They were a badly scared outfit. I learned how easily a job of this kind could be done.

"Joe told me to search the passengers for arms. I carefully went through them all. They had no pistols. Joe motioned toward the stage. I advanced and searched it, and found the brave passengers had left two of their guns behind

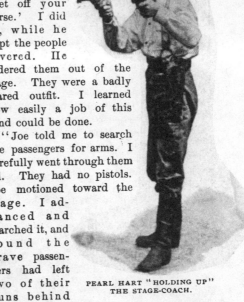

PEARL HART "HOLDING UP" THE STAGE-COACH.

them when ordered out of the stage. Really, I can't see why men carry revolvers, because they almost invariably give them up at the very time they were made to be used. They certainly don't want revolvers for playthings. I gave Joe a 'forty-four,' and kept the 'forty-five' for myself. Joe told me to search the passengers for money. I did so, and found on the fellow who was shaking the worst three hundred and ninety dollars. This fellow was trembling so I could hardly get my hand in his pockets. The other fellow, a sort of a dude, with his hair parted in the middle, tried to tell me how much he needed the money, but he yielded thirty-six dollars, a dime and two nickels. Then I searched the remaining passenger, a Chinaman. He was nearer my size and I just scared him to death. His clothes enabled me to go through him quickly. I only got five dollars, however.

"The stage-driver had a few dollars, but after a council of war we decided not to rob him. Then we gave each of the others a charitable contribution of a dollar apiece and ordered them to move on, Joe warning them all not to look back as they valued their lives.

"Joe and I rode slowly up the road for a few miles, planning our future movements. We turned off the well-traveled road to the right. We sought the roughest and most inaccessible region that we could find. We passed at right angles over cañons, and repassed those same cañons the same day, to cover a trail that we knew would be a hot one before many hours. This undertaking, to throw the officers off the track, was most hazardous, and as I look back upon that wild ride, that effort to escape from the consequences of our bloodless crime, I marvel that we did not lose our lives. As it was, we had many very close escapes. Our horses were likewise in perilous positions several times. It seems to me now that nothing but the excitement of the hour could have carried me through this awful ride, over the perilous trails and the precipitous cañons. To-day I cannot tell how we ever got through the ride that day. Many noises in the great mountains and cañons led us to believe that our pursuers were at hand, but these turned out to be the workings of our guilty consciences.

"Just at dark that night we came out on the road near Cane Springs. Here Joe left me to take care of the two horses, and went to see if the road ahead was clear. He reported things all right. We then rode toward Riverside, passing that place in the dark about ten o'clock. We continued on for six miles, then crossed the river and camped for the rest of the night and the next day, hobbling our horses as soon as it became dark. We started for the railroad. Our horses were much worn, but in the night we came to a big haystack and got a small feed for each of them, then pushed to within six miles of Mammoth. We were well known there

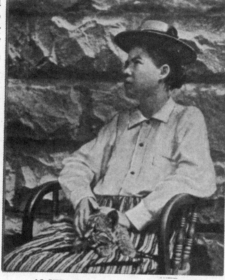

AS SHE APPEARS IN THE JAIL-YARD.

and had to be very careful. We first lay down in the bushes, but we heard wagons pass, and, afterward, men on horseback, which made us very uneasy. We kept quiet until the sounds ceased, then crawled and walked up the side of a big sandstone hill where there were many small caves, or holes, of a circular shape, not much larger than a man's body.

"Upon reaching this spot of safety we found it to be the home of wild or musk hogs, which abound in this locality. These hogs will fight if they have to. However, our peril was so great that we could not hesitate about other chances, and we selected a hole into which we could crawl. Joe started in and I followed. Of course, we had to look out for rattlesnakes, too, which made our entrance very slow. After we had crawled about twenty feet, Joe stopped, saying he could see two shining eyes ahead and was going to take a shot.

"I confess I felt very creepy, but we were between the devil and the deep sea and I listened to hear Joe, from his point ahead of me, tell of his success. The animal was shot and killed, and proved to be a big musk-hog. We soon found the powder-smoke annoying, and as we could not turn around we backed to near the entrance for fresh air. We stayed there all day, and what a long day it was!

"When it got dark we saddled our horses. Joe stole into Mammoth for food and tobacco, and got back without arousing suspicion. After passing Mammoth, we crossed the river and went as far as the school-house, where we hid ourselves and the horses in the bushes at the farther end of a big field. We secured feed for our animals here, and filled a cotton bag with straw to carry. Tired out, we forgot our troubles and slept soundly. At daylight

Joe got some food, and we started on; but after going ten miles our horses showed signs of distress, and I realized how much depended on our animals and would have done anything to secure rest and food for them. I remonstrated with my partner about the condition of things, proposing to put our horses in a field and capture others; also to abandon the horses and walk, or to separate for our own safety. His answer was a peremptory No and we pushed on, passing a Mexican squatter's settlement and coming to a wide ditch. My horse jumped across, but Joe's horse fell in, and for a while I thought they would both be drowned. They finally got out. I sat in my saddle perfectly helpless during the struggle.

"This day, which proved to be our last day of freedom, at least for a while, we spent sleeping and cooking. The rain fell in torrents and we were very uncomfortable. At night we again started, and rode until five o'clock in the morning. Just after daylight we came across a mountain lion and gave chase for two miles, but could not get a shot. After this we lay down, but were destined not to sleep long. About three hours after lying down we were awakened by yelling and shooting. We sprang up and grabbed our guns, but found we were looking straight into the mouths of two gaping Winchesters in the hands of the sheriff's posse. Resistance was worse than useless, and we put up hands. At the time of our capture we were within twenty miles of

GUARDING CAMP.

Benson, the railroad station we were making for. Had we reached Benson, I believe we should have escaped.

"We were taken as prisoners first to Benson, thence through Tucson to Casa Grande by rail, and then to Florence. We were kindly treated. The worst thing we suffered was from the curious who came to look at and make fun of us. It would have given me pleasure to meet some of these curious fellows as we met the men in the stage, just to see what they were made of.

"On the 20th, I was transferred to the Tucson jail, as the accommodations here were better adapted to a woman, but I did hate to leave Joe, who had been so considerate of me during all the ups and downs of the wild chase we had been through. His entire trouble was brought on by trying to get money for me to reach mother. We took an oath at parting never to serve out a term in the penitentiary, but rather to find that rest a tired soul seeks. It is, of course, public that I tried to kill myself the day they separated me from Joe at Florence, and to-day I am sorry I didn't succeed."

PEARL HART IN WOMAN'S ORDINARY ATTIRE.

29

A Mountain of Gold

C.S. Pelham-Clinton

A Mountain of Gold.

By C. S. Pelham-Clinton.

"IT'S a mountain of gold," said Mr. Samuel Newhouse as we came in sight of Seaton Mountain, "and I've the key to the treasure!"

Having been in America a good deal, I was somewhat sceptical with regard to the value of this mass of dark grey stone that was the most prominent feature of the landscape for miles; and also to the "open sesame" he spoke of as well; but that we were in a golden region was very plain to anyone, even if I had not known before that Central City, the point for which we were making, was the principal town of the "Little Kingdom of Gilpin," and for years had been an established gold camp.

As the train slowly wound its way up the grade which seemed far too steep for safety, along the banks of the very muddy creek that a boy could jump with ease, at every turn we saw signs of the precious metal.

While the stream itself, at the time of our visit, was not more than a few feet wide, the width of its course in flood-times was very clearly defined, and the bed of the now almost dry creek was now the scene of great activity—hundreds of men of every nationality being busily engaged in washing for gold. It was a "no man's land," the only notice of ejectment from which was a flood, and when that had subsided the results were that fresh gold had been brought down from the mountain sides above by the torrents, and been deposited in the bed of the creek to await discovery at the hands of the diligent crowd of men who, with no capital but their thews and sinews, and with the rudest of implements, were working so busily as we passed by.

Along the banks of the stream higher up were the crushers, where the gold-bearing quartz brought from the mines is ground to powder and the gold extracted. A considerable amount is lost, however, even in the best processes; this is carried down in minute particles by the stream, is deposited in its bed, and eventually becomes the spoil of the herd of toilers down below.

At every turn we came in sight of fresh crushing plants and fresh mines perched on the hill-side in apparently inaccessible places. "Clear Creek," as it is called, had become even more than before the opposite to its name, and had also dwindled down to almost an apology for a stream, and its banks had narrowed considerably, showing we were close to Central City, which stands at the head of the gulch.

Central City is rich in gold, but however alluring that metal may be, the city is by no means attractive itself. However, it has a history, which is a good deal more than many American cities can boast of. In 1859 a prospector of the name of John H. Gregory discovered the Gregory lode, and a mining authority gave me the following information, which shows this part of Colorado — whatever other gold-fields in America may be doing—is more than holding her own :—

"From the first pan of dirt $4 in gold were obtained; the following day, Mr. Gregory and his partner washed over $40 from forty pans of dirt. This was the beginning of the great Pike's Peak craze, which has endured under different forms in various districts of

SEATON MOUNTAIN—THE MOUNTAIN OF GOLD. [Photograph.

From a]   CENTRAL CITY.   [*Photograph.*

the State to the present day. Many thousand people rushed to Central City, Black Hawk, and Nevadaville, a continuous city under three corporations, and along whose gulches have been discovered, and are still being discovered, the greatest mines in the West. Among these are the Bates, Bobtail, Hunter, Gunnel, Clay County, Fisk, and Mammoth. In 1867 the Boston and Colorado Smelting Works were established in Black Hawk by Professor N. P. Hill, and successfully treated ore that could not be treated in a stamp-mill. Central City and its environs remained a typical early mining camp until 1878, the year of the advent of the Colorado Central Railroad, which was extended to Central City from Black Hawk by means of switch-backs, requiring four miles of road to go one mile in distance. Since that date the " Little Kingdom of Gilpin " has been transformed into a modern mining metropolis with tramway systems, electric and hoisting appointments, and all other conveniences of a well-equipped mining centre. The Gilpin Tramway Company commenced hauling ore in 1888 on a two-foot gauge railroad from the principal mines to Black Hawk ; it then had one locomotive. They now have three locomotives and over 125 cars, and nearly twenty miles of track, the line running up Clear Creek, Chase Gulch, over Winnebago, Gunnel and Quartz Hills, to Russell and Willis Gulches. In estimating the value of the product of Gilpin County mines up to January 1st, 1879, two systems have been used by statisticians, illustrating the difference between the value in coin and the depreciated currency in circulation during most of the time in which the

record was made. The total product to that date is thus given : Coin value of product, $28,077,000 ; currency value, $35,000,000. Computed at its coin value, this product is thus classified : Gold, $26,917,000 ; silver, $690,000 ; copper and lead, $470,000 ; total to January 1st, 1879, $28,077,000. During the year 1872 the mines of Gilpin County yielded in value to the amount of $2,431,291, exceeding the output of any previous year. The output for 1889 was $3,334,300 ; that of 1890 was $2,624,925. The total output since January 1st, 1879, aggregates over $30,000,000, so that the coin value of the yield of Gilpin County mines from the year 1859 to 1891 very nearly reaches the enormous sum of $60,000,000, and this has largely increased during the past three years."

To show the great value of these Colorado mines, I quote from what appeared in the financial columns of a leading London paper :—

" Messrs. Eives and Allen have sent us the Annual Report of Mr. John J. Valentine, the president of Wells, Fargo, and Co., bank and express agency, on the precious metals product of the United States and Mexico in the year 1894. From this it appears that the total production of gold in states and territories west of the Missouri River, including British Columbia, was, roundly, £9,180,000, and of silver £5,740,000. This latter value is arrived at by taking silver at 31½d. per ounce, which is rather high. The largest output of gold was in Colorado, which gave £2,435,000. Next came California with £2,140,000, and then Montana with £1,030,000. Colorado was also the largest producer of silver. Including copper and lead, the total output of the United States, British Columbia, and the West Coast of Mexico, due to mining for the precious metals, is valued at £21,023,000 for the year 1894. Looking back over past years, the production of gold is found to have been much increased, and that of silver to be much reduced, compared with the average of any series of years since 1874. The highest production of silver in the States was in the year 1889, when the total was valued at almost £13,000,000 ; but, of course, prices were much higher then and in previous years than now. Last year's output of gold was the highest since 1870, beyond which date Mr. Valentine's tables do not go. The year which came nearest to it was 1877, when the total was returned at £8,976,000. These figures are only put forth as approximately correct, but they are the best obtainable."

So much for statistics ; these were necessary but dry, so we took the two-horse buggy that had been "hitched up" and made a start for Idaho Springs, passing over the top of Seaton Mountain.

It was a glorious day, and at the height we were at, over 8,000ft., the air was perfection. Slowly we wound our way up the side of the hill, passing dozens of miners hard at work, bringing out the gold-bearing rock, until Central City seemed a tiny village in the gorge below us. We were over 10,000ft. above sea-level, and had a gorgeous distant panorama around us, though the actual scenery of Seaton Mountain is tame, and not improved by the hundreds of rough buildings that dot the landscape on all sides.

Still, we had come to see the golden mountain, and here we were at its summit. Slowly Mr. Newhouse explained the situation and his project, and a map could not have explained as fully in a week as a glance did here. There were the mines, the occupants doing their best to wrest the golden treasure from the mountain under difficulties that are hardly credible, for without seeing the country one could hardly appreciate these difficulties. To begin with, the roads to the various mines are simply tracks worn by the waggon-wheels into some semblance of a road ; down these come the waggons with four horses bearing the blocks of quartz. Once on the main road their task is

MR. SAMUEL NEWHOUSE.
From a Photo. by Nast, Denver.

more simple, but the return journey is very different. The main difficulty the miners have to contend with is water, and the deeper they go the worse this trouble seems to be. In fact, they say that in one instance, for every ton of ore taken out, forty tons of water had to be pumped. To pump you must have steam, and steam requires coal, every pound of which has to be hauled up to the mine-mouth. When I say a waggon can bring down six tons of ore and not take up half a ton of coal, the difficulties of making the two ends meet will partly be appreciated. Besides the pumping, hauling gear has to be kept in order, horse-flesh replaced, every bit of fodder being hauled up these inclines ; wages are high, and unless the ore is high grade it does not pay to work the mine. Low-grade ores are valueless now, but when the Newhouse tunnel taps the seams, the low-grade seams will be worked as much as the high-grade.

To begin with, the seams, which are numberless, and commence about a mile from Idaho Springs and continue to Central City, are vertical : this is the key to Mr. Newhouse's scheme, and makes it of such value. It has been proved that the lower the seams go the better the ore becomes, but the cost of working is so increased that it does not pay. The question was : how deep did the veins go ? Geology can tell us a lot, but it cannot, for certain, tell us what there is 5,000ft. below, in the midst of a mass of granite ; but that the seams went down deep had been proved by one of the mines going down over 2,000ft. before the water became too strong.

Mr. Samuel Newhouse knew this part of the country well ; he had been over every foot of it when the boom of about twenty years back had brought such crowds to this part of the world. The expenses of mining and the difficulties were a puzzle that he set himself to overcome.

Taking elevations, he found that the

seat. The builder of that buggy believed no man was more than 5ft. 6in., or else he meant to build it bigger and ran short of material. I have seldom enjoyed a ride more — my head against the roof, my knees wedged against the seat in front, my backbone rubbing the seat behind: we tore down that hill at a rate that in a good road would have been terrific, but on this hundredth cousin to a macadam road was diabolical. A recent flood had brought out a new vintage of rocks, and carried off the little earth that ever had made that causeway believe itself a road. "Pet," I think that was the name of one of the horses, was almost down once or twice, but the pace saved him. Newhouse lost his spectacles, the driver his voice, the horses their wind, and I a good deal of skin, before, after a wild tear of at least three miles, we swung into Idaho Springs. Truly, if the material of that buggy was scanty it was good, or a handful of remnants on the sides of Seaton Mountain would have been all that was left of us. Peace be to that driver, and may he one day take a party of my

difference between Idaho Springs and Central City was about 3,000ft., and he also saw that the veins, which run very regularly, were at right angles to a line drawn between these two places. The idea of a tunnel then occurred to him, and he mooted the project to some friends, who, while appreciating the idea, laughed at it, as the expenses would be so enormous as to preclude any chance of building it. Not to be deterred, however, Mr. Newhouse quietly bought a piece of land a little distance below Idaho Springs, and started without any flourish of trumpets what is now the talk of every gold-miner in the United States.

Sitting as we were on the top of Seaton Mountain, to get to Idaho Springs to see the tunnel required an adjournment to the "top buggy," as the instrument of torture that was awaiting us is called.

I forget the name of the horses, though the driver kept apostrophizing them by name all the way down the hill "to get up and paddle!" The road was narrow, it was steep, it was also rocky. The buggy had a top and, being a two-seated affair, Mr. Newhouse sat beside the driver while I occupied the back

dearest enemies down that descent after a flood.

However our angles had suffered, our appetites were not the worse, and Tom Henahen's, the manager's, excellent luncheon was inward oil and wine to our bruised anatomies; then, after smoking the pipe of peace, a short walk brought us to the tunnel.

The entrance shows but little of the great scheme, and might be anything of a very ordinary nature, and it is only when the ore begins to come out that it will make a big showing.

From a]   THE DRILL.   [Photograph.

The tunnel will, when finished, be four miles long, and its furthest extremity will be almost directly under Central City, but about 2,000ft. below it. It is about 14ft. wide and about 10ft. high. In the centre, between the two lines of railroad, is a waterway cut in the solid rock, about 3ft. wide and 2ft. deep, which carries off all the superfluous water that has in mines to be pumped out, for the rise in the grade of the tunnel is enough to carry out the water, and also facilitates by gravity the exit of the cars laden with ore, while it is not great enough to render much force necessary to push the empty cars into the mine. Thus at only the expense of cutting the watercourse the whole question of water is disposed of. When a vein of ore is reached in the tunnel, cross-cuts will be made and the vein followed until a sufficient distance for proper development is attained. No roofing is required, the rock on either side being of the hardest granite; and, indeed, its hardness, while of benefit in this respect, is such that the boring is of necessity a slow process. It will readily be seen that so cheap a method of mining will, when once the tunnel is made, enable the low-grade ores to be as readily mined as those of better quality, and as each vein is cut, it will be driven on, the ore

From a]   THE MOUTH OF THE TUNNEL.   [Photograph.

AT WORK WITH THE DRILL 1,800FT. FROM THE MOUTH.

drills for eight hours apiece, and are making a progress of over 10ft. a day, the work being continuous day and night, with only a few pauses to blast and clear away the débris, which is carried out in cars to the "dump" at the entrance to the tunnel.

Two hydraulic plants are ready, so, in case anything should happen to the one, the other is at hand, and the progress being made is very rapid for the nature of the work. The rich ore-bed will be reached in about a year's time, and the harvest commenced. The tunnel will take about four years to complete, and experts declare that when finished the vast sum of three hundred millions of dollars worth of gold, or sixty million sterling, will be accessible, so Mr. Newhouse's remark about having the key to the treasure was the truth after all, and that the mountain is one of gold, statistics, geology, and experiment very clearly demonstrate.

being brought out through the tunnel, and thus the whole mining business of this large district will be centred under one administration. The company owns a large number of the veins, which it will work for its own benefit, those belonging to others being operated on a royalty basis.

The company will on the land at the mouth of the tunnel have huge smelters and stamp-mills, and be able to treat every pound of ore that comes out. If the tunnel proves too narrow, Mr. Newhouse says he can enlarge it. There will be ample room inside in the transverse cuttings for sidings for cars, and the tunnel in its present size is capable of handling thousands of tons of ore a day. At the present moment, the tunnel is about three-quarters of a mile into the mountain, and three shifts of five men each are at work with two Leyner

IN THE HEART OF THE MOUNTAIN OF GOLD.